American Issues

Issues

A DOCUMENTARY READER

EDITED BY

Charles M. Dollar
University of British Columbia

Gary W. Reichard
California State University, Long Beach

**Glencoe
McGraw-Hill**

New York, New York   Columbus, Ohio   Woodland Hills, California   Peoria, Illinois

Glencoe/McGraw-Hill

A Division of The **McGraw·Hill** *Companies*

Send all inquiries to:
 Glencoe/McGraw-Hill
 8787 Orion Place
 Columbus, OH 43240

ISBN: 0-07-825814-6 (Student Edition)
ISBN : 0-07-825815-4 (Teacher's Guide)

 7 8 9 10 100 08 07 06 05

ABOUT THE AUTHORS

Charles M. Dollar is Professor Emeritus of the University of British Columbia and Senior Consultant at Cohasset Associates. He formerly was a member of the staff of the National Archives and Records Administration and Associate Professor of History at Oklahoma State University. Dollar is General Editor of *America: Changing Times,* a college-level textbook, and has previously published in the areas of quantitative history, the history of the South, and archival administration.

Gary W. Reichard is Professor of History and Associate Vice President for Academic Affairs at California State University, Long Beach. He previously taught at the College of Wooster, The Ohio State University, the University of Delaware, the University of Maryland at College Park, and Florida Atlantic University. He has published a number of books and articles in the field of recent American political history and was coauthor of *America: Changing Times.* For more than a decade, he has served as a reader of Advanced Placement examinations in United States History.

Reviewers

Helen Longley
Louisville Collegiate School
Louisville, Kentucky

Fred Dorsett
Northeast High School
St. Petersburg, Florida

Howard Shorr
Downtown Business Magnet
  High School
Los Angeles, California

William J. Fetsko
Liverpool Central School District
Liverpool, New York

Mike Kinney
Central Hardin High School
Cecilia, Kentucky

Denny Schillings
President, National Council
  for the Social Studies

Chapter **6**

A Republic Takes Shape   **87**

Chapter **7**

The Invention of Political Parties   **103**

Chapter 8

Westward Movement: People and the Land   120

PART THREE   *Problems of Union, 1820–1860*   139

Chapter 9

Dimensions of American Nationalism: The Age of Jackson   139

Chapter 10

The Imperatives of Expansion 154

Chapter 11

Reform Ferment: Utopianism, Abolitionism, and Feminism 170

Chapter 12

PART FOUR — *The Civil War and After, 1860–1877*   205

Chapter 13

PART FIVE

Industrialization and Modernization, 1877–1920   275

Chapter 17

Industrialization and Reorganization of the American Economy, 1875–1900   275

Chapter 18

A Nation of Immigrants   295

Chapter 19

Chapter 20

PART SIX

Prosperity, Depression, and War, 1920–1945   341

Chapter 21

Cultural Tensions in the New Era: The 1920s   341

Chapter 22

Depression and New Deal   358

Chapter 27

Chapter 28

Chapter 29

Chapter 30

AMERICAN ISSUES:
A Documentary Reader

Introduction

T his book, designed to supplement American history high school text-books, contains a selection of excerpts from more than two hundred original sources. Included among these sources are documents, commentary and interpretations of critical events or processes in American history, and visual material. This selection does not attempt to cover all the critical events in America's past. Rather, the various readings and images focus upon important themes of America's past and present, viewed from the perspective of the early 21st century. Among the themes considered here are the evolution of democratic institutions and processes; the development of presidential leadership; the role of the Constitution; the effects of slavery, industrialization, urbanization, and technology; relations between different racial and ethnic groups; male and female roles in American society; and the rise of the United States to world power. Students will find that a careful reading of the various selections and examination of the visual material will help them appreciate the richness of American history and understand the continuity between past and present.

American Issues is divided into seven parts that follow a chronological order—from the exploration and settlement of North America to America since 1945. Each part is divided into chapters that focus on major themes. The selected readings and visual material of the chapters address a number of related issues. Each chapter begins with an introduction that discusses the theme and provides a broad historical context for the readings that follow. The purpose of the introduction is not to cover a topic or time period in depth, but to introduce topics,

1

issues, and questions that the readings address. Following the introduction is a chronology identifying important dates, people, events, and developments in the period under study. The chronology provides a time frame for the selections in the chapter. A list of the chapter's readings and visual material comes at the end of the introduction.

Another objective of this book of readings is to help students understand how historians work and to show what is involved in developing a plausible description and explanation of past events. Historians generally use a method known as historical analysis. This involves three steps: selecting evidence, analyzing this evidence, and framing the results into a written narrative. In selecting evidence, historians are usually guided by preliminary questions and tentative ideas or conclusions. These questions and tentative conclusions typically reflect the historian's implicit or explicit assumptions about the relationship between individuals and institutions in a given society.

Most of the evidence that historians use falls into three categories: primary sources, secondary sources, and visual sources. Primary sources include information recorded by participants involved in the subject under study. In many instances, the identity of the author or artist is known, but in other cases—a law or treaty, for example—the source material may not have a specific author. Primary sources (where they exist) constitute the building blocks of evidence that historians use in showing what people thought, how they acted, and what they accomplished.

Primary sources are only as good as the people who produced them, however. Historians must establish the accuracy and reliability of their primary sources through external and internal criticism. External criticism involves comparison with other primary sources in order to uncover errors and forgeries. Internal criticism focuses on the document itself and consists of identifying the writer's motives, inconsistencies, assumptions, and use of language. An example of a primary source might be an entry in a diary or a letter written by a participant in a particular event. Most primary sources reprinted here appear in their original versions, and archaic forms of spelling and grammar in some of the older documents have not been changed.

Most secondary sources are written by scholars long after the occurrence of the event under study. Usually, they are interpretations derived from an analysis of primary sources and a review of other secondary sources. Inevitably, these interpretations reflect certain interests, values, and viewpoints—especially of the time period in which they are written. In some respects, secondary sources are a historical barometer, measuring and reflecting changing cultural values and societal interests. For example, the growing interest of historians in the role of women in American history clearly parallels the rise of feminism. It should come as no surprise, therefore, that historical emphasis and interpretations of various subjects change over time. After all, historians, like everyone else, view the past from the perspective of the present.

The different interests, values, and viewpoints that historians hold inevitably lead to important differences among them about how to understand the significance of historical events and developments. For this reason, secondary sources must be read with a critical eye and used judiciously. You need to consider carefully the reliability and accuracy of the evidence the writer uses and be alert to the biases underlying a particular interpretation. It is also important to examine the logic of the writer's argument, giving special attention to assumptions that must be made in order to accept the argument. Finally, you should weigh the interpretation against counterevidence and counterarguments and then decide how well the writer's explanation and interpretation stand up against other explanations and interpretations.

Visual sources are illustrative sources of what people thought and did in the past. They include works of art, cartoons, illustrations, sculptures, buildings, and photographs. Visual sources can provide valuable insights into a particular event or historical development, and they can make a point succinctly. For these reasons, visual sources are indeed sometimes worth a thousand words. Visual sources created in the time period under consideration may be treated as primary sources, though of course historians sometimes disagree about how these sources should be interpreted.

Maps constitute a special type of visual source. Maps can either be primary sources in themselves or they may incorporate primary source elements and secondary sources. A basic function of maps is to summarize multidimensional relationships, such as the correlation between the increase in the slave population and the increase in cotton production in the South during the 1840s and 1850s.

The order in which the selections are presented in this book reflects the editors' view of the sequence in which they should be read or seen. For example, the first document in Chapter 1 is a secondary source that deals with the cultural differences between the first Americans and European explorers around 1500. This is followed by a visual source, a map showing Indian language groups in North America. The next document is a primary source, an excerpt from a letter that Christopher Columbus wrote in 1493. Examining these documents in sequence should help you gain a greater understanding of this early period in American history.

Preceding each document is a short introductory note that explains the nature of the source, places the source in its historical context, and raises a number of relevant issues. In some cases, this note will call attention to other selections that address the issue under consideration, especially those concerned with another time period. Also included in this introductory note are several broad questions that focus on major themes in the document as well as in other documents in the chapter (or preceding chapters).

part one

EXPLORATION AND SETTLEMENT OF NORTH AMERICA TO 1763

Chapter 1

European Exploration and Settlement in North America to 1620

The popular view that Columbus discovered America is both incorrect and historically irrelevant. The inhabitants of this continent had preceded Columbus by thousands of years and developed very complex civilizations. They were neither newcomers nor savages. Furthermore, Norse expeditions—probably led by Leif Ericsson—had reached North America almost five centuries earlier. The significance of Columbus's voyage and those of other European explorers is that they represented the first wave of an expansion of Europe that eventually conquered and displaced the earliest inhabitants of America, the people whom the Europeans called "Indians."

The timing of European expansion was not accidental. Innovations in navigational technology, together with economic, political, and religious developments in Europe, created the impetus necessary for undertaking colonizing efforts.

The initial entry of Spanish explorers into North and South America was followed by French, English, Dutch, and Portuguese exploration and settlements in the sixteenth century. By 1620 Spain, France, and England were the most important European powers in the hemisphere. In their competition to conquer and exploit the continent, these nations followed separate paths and the exploration and settlements of each took on a distinctive character. And, of course, the way of life of the "first Americans"—the Indians—was changed dramatically.

This chapter focuses upon the broad theme of the exploration and settlement in the Americas as a westward expansion of Europe. Two topics are considered: European exploration efforts in North America and European perceptions of American Indians. Several selections address issues relating to exploration efforts, including the impact of geography, different exploration and settlement strategies, and the promotion of economic nationalism. The other selections reflect European impressions and expectations of American Indians.

Chronology

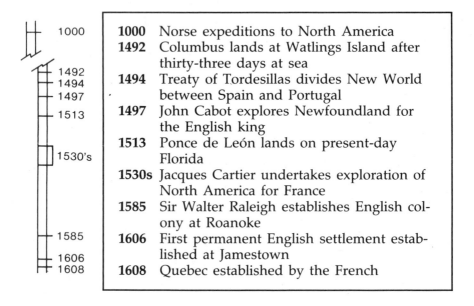

1000	Norse expeditions to North America
1492	Columbus lands at Watlings Island after thirty-three days at sea
1494	Treaty of Tordesillas divides New World between Spain and Portugal
1497	John Cabot explores Newfoundland for the English king
1513	Ponce de León lands on present-day Florida
1530s	Jacques Cartier undertakes exploration of North America for France
1585	Sir Walter Raleigh establishes English colony at Roanoke
1606	First permanent English settlement established at Jamestown
1608	Quebec established by the French

Documents

1.1   The First Americans

L. S. Stavrianos

In this selection from his book, *Man's Past and Present*, historian L. S. Stavrianos describes the conflict between the Indians and the first European settlers as an "unequal contest" that resulted in a speedy European victory. In contrast to many historians, Stavrianos attempts to view the European conquest of the Americas within the context of Indian social, technological, and organizational practices. He identifies both European and Indian strengths and weaknesses, which he believes help explain the very rapid European conquest of the Americas. Among the most significant of the Indian weaknesses, according to Stavrianos, was their susceptibility to diseases such as measles and smallpox, which Europeans brought with them.

Consider:

1. Whether Stavrianos reflects a cultural bias—a kind of historical determinism—in which no other outcome was possible, given the circumstances at the time;
2. Whether he overlooks or ignores other evidence in forming his conclusions.

Until recently it was believed that the Indians first began crossing over from Siberia to the Americas about 10,000 years ago. New archaeological findings, together with the use of carbon-14 dating, have forced drastic revision of this estimate. It is now generally agreed that man certainly was in the New World 20,000 years ago, and probably 20,000 years or more before that. The last major migration of Indians took place about 3,000 years ago. The actual crossing to the New World presented little difficulty to these early newcomers. The last of the Ice Ages had locked up vast quantities of sea water, lowering the ocean level by 160 feet and thus exposing a 1,300-mile-wide land bridge connecting Siberia and Alaska. A "bridge" of such proportions was, in effect, a vast new subcontinent, that allowed ample scope for the vast diffusion of plants and animals that now took place. Even after rising temperatures lifted the sea level and submerged the connecting lands, the resulting narrow straits easily could have been crossed in crude boats without even losing sight of shore.

Most of those who crossed to Alaska moved on into the heart of North America through a gap in the ice sheet in the central Yukon plateau. They were impelled to press forward by the same forces that led them to migrate to America—the search for new hunting grounds and the continual pressure of tribes from the rear. In this manner both

SOURCE: *L. S. Stavrianos, Man's Past and Present: A Global History, 2/e, ©1975, pp. 213–14, 217–18. Reprinted by permission of Prentice-Hall, Inc., Englewood Cliffs, New Jersey.*

the continents were soon peopled by scattered tribes of hunters. Definite evidence has been found that indicates that the migrants from Asia reached the southern tip of South America by 11,000 years ago. . . .

The migrants to the New World brought little cultural baggage with them since they came from northeast Siberia, one of the least advanced regions of Eurasia. They were, of course, all hunters, organized in small bands, possessing only crude stone tools, no pottery, and no domesticated animals, except perhaps the dog. Since they were entering an uninhabited continent they were completely free to evolve their own institutions without the influences from native populations that the Aryans had been subject to when they migrated to the Indus Valley, or the Achaeans and Dorians when they reached Greece.

During the ensuing millennia the American Indians did develop an extraordinarily rich variety of cultures, adapted to one another as well as to the wide range of physical environments they encountered. Some remained at the hunting-band stage while others developed kingdoms and empires. Their religions encompassed all known categories, including monotheism. They spoke some 2,000 distinct languages, some as different from one another as Chinese and English. This represents as much variation in speech as in the entire Old World, where about 3,000 languages are known to have existed in A.D. 1500. Nor were these languages primitive, either in vocabulary or in any other respect. Whereas Shakespeare used about 24,000 words, and the King James Bible about 7,000, the Nahuatl of Mexico used 27,000 words, while the Yahgans of Tierra del Fuego, considered to be one of the world's most retarded peoples, possess a vocabulary of at least 30,000 words.

Taking all types of institutions and practices into account, anthropologists have defined some twenty-two culture areas in the New World—the Great Plains area, the Eastern Woodlands, the Northwest Coast area, and so forth. A simpler classification, on the basis of how food was obtained, involves three categories: hunting, gathering, and fishing cultures; intermediate farming cultures; and advanced farming cultures. This scheme is not only simpler but it is also meaningful from the viewpoint of world history, for it helps to explain the varied responses of the Indians to the European intrusion.

The advanced farming cultures were located in Mesoamerica (central and southern Mexico, Guatemala, and Honduras) and the Andean highland area (Ecuador, Peru, Bolivia, and northern Chile). The intermediate farming cultures were generally in the adjacent regions, while the food-gathering cultures were in the more remote regions— the southern part of South America, and the western and northern part of North America. . . .

. . . In agriculture, the Indians were brilliantly successful in domesticating plants but much less effective in actual production. Their cultivation techniques never advanced beyond the bare minimum necessary for feeding populations that rarely reached the density of those of the Old World. Their tools were made only of stone, wood, or bone. They were incapable of smelting ores, and though they did work with metal, it was almost exclusively for ornamental purposes. The only ships they constructed were canoes and seagoing rafts. For land transportation they made no use of the wheel, which they knew but used only as a toy. Only the human back was available for transportation, with the exception of the llama and the alpaca, which were used in the Andes but which could not carry heavy loads.

The immediate significance of this technological lag should not be exaggerated. The Indians obviously were at a grave disadvantage with their spears and arrows against the Spaniards' horses and guns. But after the initial shock, the Indians became accustomed to firearms and cavalry. Furthermore, the Spaniards soon discovered that the Indian weapons were sharp and durable, and they came to prefer the Indian armor of quilted cotton to their own.

This suggests that factors in addition to technological disparity lay behind the Spanish victories. One was the lack of unity amongst the Indian peoples. In both Mexico and Peru the Spaniards were able to use disaffected subject tribes that had been alienated by the oppressive rule of Cuzco and Tenochtitlán. The Indians were also weakened by over-regimentation. They had been so indoctrinated and accustomed to carrying out orders without question that when their leaders were overthrown they were incapable of organizing resistance on their own. . . .

If the great civilizations of the New World lacked the power and the cohesion to resist the Europeans, this was even more true of the less developed food gathering and intermediate farming culture areas. Precisely because they were less developed, they also had smaller populations, so that when the Europeans appeared they simply lacked the numbers to hold their ground. Their weakness in this respect was accentuated by the diseases that the first explorers brought with them. The Indians, lacking immunity, were decimated by the epidemics, so that the early colonists often found abandoned fields and deserted village sites that they could take over.

Later, when the full flood of immigration from Europe got under way, the Indians were hopelessly overwhelmed. First came the traders who penetrated throughout the Americas with little competition or resistance, for the Americas, unlike Africa, had no rival native merchant class. Then appeared the settlers who, attracted by the combination of salubrious climate and fertile land, came in ever-increasing numbers and inundated the hapless Indians. When the latter occasionally took up arms in desperation, they were foredoomed to failure because they lacked both unity and the basic human and material resources. Thus, the unequal contest ended relatively quickly with the victorious white man in possession of the choice lands and the Indians relegated to reservations or to the less desirable regions that did not interest the new masters. . . .

1.2   Indian Language Groups in 1500

Just as the landscape of the American continent varied widely, so did the "first Americans." Although American Indians shared a common ancestry dating back to 25,000 B.C., anthropologists have concluded that major cultural and institutional differences set these tribes apart from one another. One such difference is evident in the existence and geographic distribution of diverse language groups. The following map of North America shows Indian language groups around the beginning of the sixteenth century, noting about thirty different groups among some three hundred tribes.

Consider:

1. *How these different language groups affect the idea of a monolithic American Indian culture;*
2. *Whether the existence of these language groups supports the arguments Stavrianos makes in Document 1.1.*

INDIAN LANGUAGE GROUPS, 1500

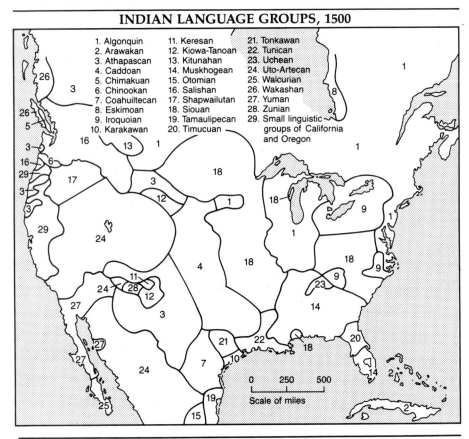

1. Algonquin
2. Arawakan
3. Athapascan
4. Caddoan
5. Chimakuan
6. Chinookan
7. Coahuiltecan
8. Eskimoan
9. Iroquoian
10. Karakawan
11. Keresan
12. Kiowa-Tanoan
13. Kitunahan
14. Muskhogean
15. Otomian
16. Salishan
17. Shapwailutan
18. Siouan
19. Tamaulipecan
20. Timucuan
21. Tonkawan
22. Tunican
23. Uchean
24. Uto-Artecan
25. Waicurian
26. Wakashan
27. Yuman
28. Zunian
29. Small linguistic groups of California and Oregon

Scale of miles 0   250   500

SOURCE: *Charles O. Paullin,* Atlas of the Historical Geography of the United States *(Washington, D.C.: Carnegie Institute, 1932).*

1.3   Letter of Columbus to Luis de Santangel, 1493

Christopher Columbus

On Friday, October 12, 1492, after having been at sea for more than a month, Christopher Columbus and several officers and crew members from his fleet landed on an island in what is now the Bahamas. He called the island San Salvador and took possession of it for King Ferdinand and Queen Isabella of Spain. Over the next four months, Columbus explored the area southwest of this island, including present-day Cuba, Haiti, and the Dominican Republic. During his return voyage to Spain in February 1493, he wrote a summary report of his voyage, which he later sent to Luis de Santangel, Comptroller of the Treasury of Ferdinand and Isabella. In the report Columbus discussed the nature of the inhabitants and how they received him and his men.

Consider:

1. *To what extent Columbus's description of the natives reflects European cultural biases;*
2. *Whether his account suggests that the natives lived more or less in an idyllic state of innocence and docility;*
3. *The divergence between Columbus's description of the Indians and the hostility of the Indians toward Europeans in later years.*

. . . The people of this island, and of all the others which I have become acquainted with, go naked as they were born, although some of the women wear at the loins a leaf, or bit of cotton cloth which they prepare for that purpose. They do not possess iron, steel, or weapons, and seem to have no inclination for the latter, being timorous to the last degree. They have an instrument consisting of a cane, taken while in seed, and headed with a sharp stick, but they never venture to use it. Many times I have sent two or three men to one of their villages, when whole multitudes have taken to flight at the sight of them, and this was not by reason of any injury we ever wrought them, for at every place where I have made any stay, and obtained communication with them, I have made them presents of cloth and such other things as I possessed, without demanding anything in return. After they have shaken off their fear of us, they display a frankness and liberality in their behaviour which no one would believe without witnessing it. No request of anything from them is ever refused, but they rather invite acceptance of what they possess, and manifest such

---

SOURCE: *Christopher Columbus,* Journal of First Voyage to America, *ed. Van Wyck Brooks.* (New York: Albert & Charles Boni, 1924), 225–27.

a generosity that they would give away their own hearts. Let the article be of great or small value, they offer it readily, and receive anything which is tendered in return with perfect content. I forbade my men to purchase their goods with such worthless things as bits of platters and broken glass, or thongs of leather, although when they got possession of one of these, they estimated it as highly as the greatest jewel in the world. The sailors would buy of them for a scrap of leather, pieces of gold, weighing two *castellanos* and a half, and even more of this metal for something still less in value. The whole of an Indian's property might be purchased of him for a few *blancas*, this would amount to two or three *castellanos'* value of gold, or the same of cotton thread. Even the pieces of broken hoops from the casks they would receive in barter for their articles, with the greatest simplicity. I thought such traffic unjust, and therefore forbade it. I presented them with a variety of things, in order to secure their affection, and that they may become Christians, and enter into the service of their Highnesses and the Castilian nation, and also aid us in procuring such things as they possess, and we stand in need of. They are not idolators, nor have they any sort of religion, except believing that power and goodness are in heaven, from which place they entertained a firm persuasion that I had come with my ships and men. On this account, wherever we met them, they showed us the greatest reverence after they had overcome their fear. Such conduct cannot be ascribed to their want of understanding, for they are a people of much ingenuity, and navigate all those seas, giving a remarkably good account of every part, but do not state that they have met with people in clothes, or ships like ours. On my arrival at the Indies I took by force from the first island I came to a few of the inhabitants, in order that they might learn our language and assist us, in our discoveries. We succeeded ere long in understanding one another, by signs and words, and I have them now with me, still thinking we have come from heaven, as I learn by much conversation which I have had with them. This, they were the first to proclaim wherever we went, and the other natives would run from house to house, and from village to village, crying out *"come and see the men from heaven,"* so that all the inhabitants, both men and women, having gathered confidence, hastened towards us, bringing victuals and drink, which they presented to us with a surprising good will. . . .

1.4   Papal Bull, *Inter Caetera*, May 4, 1493

Spain and Portugal led the way in a search for new routes to the East, with Portuguese ships the first to make their way around Africa to India. Sailing for Queen Isabella of Spain, Columbus had discovered, in the western Atlantic, some islands and a continent previously unknown to Europeans. These he called the Indies. In 1493 the Spanish rulers sought a ruling from the Pope in Rome that would protect the lands Columbus had claimed for Spain. As the spiritual head of Christianity, Pope Alexander VI had the authority to decide the sovereignty of heathen lands not already controlled by a Christian ruler. On May 4, 1493, the Pope issued a formal document, or bull, called *Inter Caetera*, which established a demarcation line, awarding the land west of the line to Spain and the land east of the line to Portugal. A year later, in the Treaty of Tordesillas, Spain agreed to another demarcation line farther west. In this agreement, Spain and Portugal in effect divided the world between themselves.

Consider:

1. *The assumptions this document makes about the world and about political sovereignty;*
2. *Whether this European view of political sovereignty supports any of Stavrianos's conclusions in Document 1.1;*
3. *Whether this papal bull is primarily a religious declaration or a political declaration.*

. . . We have indeed learned that you, who for a long time had intended to seek out and discover certain islands and mainlands remote and unknown and not hitherto discovered by others, to the end that you might bring to the worship of our Redeemer and the profession of the Catholic faith their residents and inhabitants . . . chose our beloved son, Christopher Columbus, a man assuredly worthy and of the highest recommendations and fitted for so great an undertaking, whom you furnished with ships and men equipped for like designs, not without the greatest hardships, dangers, and expenses, to make diligent quest for these remote and unknown mainlands and islands through the sea, where hitherto no one had sailed; and they at length, with divine aid and with the utmost diligence sailing in the ocean sea, discovered certain very remote islands and even mainlands that hitherto had not been discovered by others. . . . Wherefore, as becomes Catholic kings and princes, after earnest consideration of all matters, especially of the rise and spread of the Catholic faith, as was the fashion of your ancestors, kings of renowned memory, you have purposed with the favor of divine clemency to bring under your sway the said mainlands

SOURCE: *Francis Gardner Davenport, ed.,* European Treaties bearing on the History of the United States and its Dependencies to 1648 *(Washington, D.C.: Carnegie Institution, 1917),* 76–78.

and islands with their residents and inhabitants and to bring them to the Catholic faith. . . . And, in order that you may enter upon so great an undertaking with greater readiness and heartiness endowed with the benefit of our apostolic favor, we, of our own accord, not at your instance nor the request of anyone else in your regard, but of our own sole largess and certain knowledge and out of the fullness of our apostolic power, by the authority of Almighty God conferred upon us in blessed Peter and of the vicarship of Jesus Christ, which we hold on earth, do by tenor of these presents, should any of said islands have been found by your envoys and captains, give, grant, and assign to you and your heirs and successors, kings of Castile and Leon, forever, together with all their dominions, cities, camps, places, and villages, and all rights, jurisdictions, and appurtenances, all islands and mainlands found and to be found, discovered and to be discovered towards the west and south, by drawing and establishing a line from the Arctic pole, namely the north, to the Antarctic pole, namely the south, no matter whether the said mainlands and islands are found and to be found in the direction of India or towards any other quarter, the said line to be distant one hundred leagues towards the west and south from any of the islands commonly known as the Azores and Cape Verde. With this proviso however that none of the islands and mainlands, found and to be found, discovered and to be discovered, beyond that said line towards the west and south, be in the actual possession of any Christian king or prince up to the birthday of our Lord Jesus Christ just past from which the present year one thousand four hundred and ninety-three begins. . . . Moreover we command you in virtue of holy obedience that, employing all due diligence in the premises, as you also promise—nor do we doubt your compliance therein in accordance with your loyalty and royal greatness of spirit— you should appoint to the aforesaid mainlands and islands worthy, God-fearing, learned, skilled, and experienced men, in order to instruct the aforesaid inhabitants and residents in the Catholic faith and train them in good morals. Furthermore, under penalty of excommunication *late sententie* to be incurred *ipso facto*, should anyone thus contravene, we strictly forbid all persons of whatsoever rank, even imperial and royal, or of whatsoever estate, degree, order, or condition, to dare, without your special permit or that of your aforesaid heirs and successors, to go for the purpose of trade or any other reason to the islands or mainlands, found and to be found, discovered and to be discovered, towards the west and south, by drawing and establishing a line from the Arctic pole to the Antarctic pole, no matter whether the mainlands and islands, found and to be found, lie in the direction of India or toward any other quarter whatsoever, the said line to be distant one hundred leagues towards the west and south, as is aforesaid, from any of the islands commonly known as the Azores and Cape Verde . . .

1.5 "First Americans" at Work

John White

Many of the first impressions that Europeans had of North America were influenced by the work of artist John White. Between 1585 and 1587, White made two trips to Roanoke Island, the first English settlement in America. His primary assignment on these trips was to sketch everything that might be of value in obtaining an overall picture of the country, to survey the area, and to make a map. Although the exact number of sketches and drawings he produced is unknown, seventy-five of his original watercolors are in the British Museum in London. The reproduction here, called "The Manner of Their Fishing," probably was done at Roanoke Island. The scene depicted is not supposed to be a realistic portrayal, but a composite drawn from a number of different sketches.

Consider:

1. *The message White is trying to convey about the "First Americans";*
2. *How this scene compares with the views of Stavrianos in Document 1.1;*
3. *The type of Indian culture White is depicting, and why no women appear in the scene.*

SOURCE: *Reproduced by courtesy of the Trustees of the British Museum.*

1.6   Europe's First Frontier

Ray Allen Billington

In this selection, historian Ray Allen Billington describes how Spain, after the failure of several expeditions and settlement efforts, embarked upon a new form of colonization. Roman Catholic missionaries began to establish mission stations in the wilderness, build small chapels, and convert the Indians to Christianity. In contrast to others, such as Hernando de Soto, these Franciscan missionaries were a smashing success.

Consider:

1. *Whether this religious colonization effort suggests a willingness to incorporate Indians into Spanish colonial life rather than to displace them;*
2. *Whether this approach contains elements that in the long run might make it difficult for the Spanish to maintain control of their territory;*
3. *How this colonization effort differs from that of the English in Virginia.*

De Soto's disastrous failure, by ending hope of rich finds in the interior of eastern North America, ushered in a phase of the Spanish conquest in which colonization rather than exploitation became the ambition of the nation's rulers. . . .

. . . In Central and South America the labor of large numbers of relatively advanced and frequently docile Indians could be utilized for work in mines and fields, so that comparatively few Spaniards could control large areas. North of the Gulf of Mexico, however, the country was poor and the native population wild and thinly scattered. . . . these uncivilized red men could not be forced to work, while the colonists, accustomed to living on the labor of submissive natives, were usually unwilling to perform the back-breaking tasks themselves. Nor could the mother country send out enough white settlers to hold the northern coast . . .

Under these circumstances Spain was forced to devise a new frontier technique suitable to the peculiar conditions of North America. Her answer was the mission station. Earnest friars, clad in fibre sandals and sackcloth gowns worn scant and thin, painfully learning the native tongues when they found to their mild amazement that "the Indians did not understand Latin," succeeded where the armed might of Spain failed. They established their tiny chapels in the forbidding wilderness, gathered about them groups of Indians who were taught agriculture as well as Christianity, and gradually extended their influence through conversions until all northern Florida was pacified. Thus the holy

SOURCE: *Ray Allen Billington*, Westward Expansion, A History of the American Frontier, *(New York: Macmillan, 1960), 22, 25–26, 28, Second Edition © copyright, The Macmillan Publishing Co. 1960.*

fathers built up a loyal population, ready to defend for crown and church a great domain that might otherwise have fallen sooner into alien hands. . . .

The mission stations won southeastern North America for Spain. Zealous friars, willing to live with their savage wards, follow them through the forests in search of acorns during the starving times, and tremble before their treachery in periodic revolts, secured the empire that the *conquistadors* had failed to win. Their loyal native converts were ready to drive out any intruders, be they hostile tribesmen from the north or heretic Europeans from overseas. The Franciscans gave their church and king a monopoly in the Florida country which late-comers would have to break. . . .

1.7   Jamestown in 1607 and 1614

These two representations of Jamestown offer an idea of the changes that must have taken place in Jamestown between 1607 and 1614. The first is an artist's reconstruction of Jamestown as a fortified settlement in 1607, based largely on archaeological evidence. The second is an artist's impression of Jamestown seven years later.

Consider:

1. *The major differences in the two Jamestowns;*
2. *How these differences might have been reflected in day-to-day activity;*
3. *Which Jamestown you would have preferred to live in.*

SOURCE: *Above, 1607, Colonial Williamsburg Foundation; top of page 18, Sidney King painting of Jamestown in 1614, courtesy of Colonial National Historical Park, Yorktown, Virginia.*

CHAPTER QUESTIONS

1. *In what ways did the Spanish and English exploration and settlement of North America up to 1620 differ? What were some of the characteristics of successful exploration and settlement?*
2. *Within a century of its issuance, the Papal Bull of 1493 no longer provided the model for settling territorial boundary questions. What developments in Europe and North America undermined its force?*

Chapter 2

The Search for Freedom and Fortune: Colonizing British America

Between 1620 and 1763 thousands of Europeans, many of them from England, left familiar surroundings and moved permanently to British North America. Many of the first settlers experienced great hardships—inadequate food, disease, conflict with Indians, and early death. Despite these difficulties, the population numbered almost 1,500,000 by 1760. Most of these settlers had come from England to escape religious persecution or economic hardship. In general, it was not the desperately poor at the very bottom of the economic ladder who emigrated to North America but rather young displaced farmers and skilled workers in search of land. Most of the young women who emigrated came as indentured servants, or as wives, or with the prospect of marriage.

Why were these young women and men so desperate that they were willing to undergo the risks of crossing the Atlantic and living in a strange and dangerous environment? Who paid for the expensive trip across the sea? What happened to these early settlers? How successful were they? And what about those black "immigrants" who were forcibly brought to North America from Africa as slaves?

The search of white Europeans for freedom and fortune put them on a collision course with the first Americans, who had lived on the continent for thousands of years. How did these European settlers justify this encroachment? In the southern colonies, where slavery predominated, how did the white settlers justify its existence?

This chapter takes as its theme this search for freedom and fortune in North America. The reading selections focus on the promotion of settlement in the colonies as a British national policy, the quest by individuals for religious freedom and economic gain, the plight of indentured servants, and issues relating to Indian-white relations and black slavery. Although the selections deal with these issues in the context of the seventeenth and eighteenth centuries, most of them reappear again in the nineteenth and twentieth centuries, albeit in a different form and focus.

Chronology

1619	**1619**	First blacks arrive in British North America
1620	**1620**	Separatist Pilgrims settle Plymouth colony
1629		
1634	**1629**	Puritans emigrate to Massachusetts Bay
1642-1649	**1634**	Settlement of Maryland
	1642–49	Civil war in England
1688	**1688**	William and Mary assume throne of England
1705	**1705**	Virginia unifies laws on slavery
1734	**1734**	Settlement of Georgia

Documents

2.1   A Vision of Utopia, Sir Thomas More (primary source)
2.2   Reasons for Colonization, Richard Hakluyt the Elder (primary source)
2.3   Plymouth Plantation, William Bradford (primary source)
2.4   Advice to Prospective Settlers in Jamestown, Virginia, 1622 (visual source)
2.5   An Indentured Servant Writes Home, Richard Frethorne (primary source)
2.6   Indentured Servitude, Richard B. Hofstadter (secondary source)
2.7   Virginia Laws for Blacks (primary source)
2.8   Indian Warfare in New England, Increase Mather (primary source)

2.1   A Vision of Utopia

Sir Thomas More

In 1516, Thomas More, a member of the British Parliament and speaker of the House of Commons, wrote a two-volume study entitled *Utopia*. The first volume describes English life at the beginning of the sixteenth century, while the second portrays an ideal society on an imaginary island called Utopia. Translated from Latin into English in 1551, *Utopia* helped reinforce the popular perception that America was a place where a perfect society could be created. This selection is taken from the second volume.

Consider:

1. *What values underlie the type of perfection More describes in Utopia;*
2. *More's view of the rights of natives to the land they occupy;*
3. *The relation between More's view and the view settlers generally had of Indian rights to land.*

The city is compassed about with a high and thick stone wall full of turrets and bulwarks. . . . The houses be of fair and gorgeous building, and on the street side they stand joined together in a long row through the whole street without any partition or separation. The streets be twenty foot broad. On the back side of the houses, through the whole length of the street, lie large gardens enclosed round about with the back part of the streets. Every house hath two doors, one into the street, and a postern door on the back side into the garden. . . . Whoso will may go in, for there is nothing within the houses that is private or any man's own. . . .

They set great store by their gardens. In them they have vineyards, all manner of fruit, herbs, and flowers, so pleasant, so well furnished, and so finely kept, that I never saw thing more fruitful nor better trimmed in any place. . . . But if the multitude throughout the whole island pass and exceed the due number, then they choose out of every city certain citizens, and build up a town under their own laws in the next land where the inhabitants have much waste and unoccupied ground, receiving also of the same country people to them, if they will join and dwell with them. They thus joining and dwelling together do easily agree in one fashion of living, and that to the great wealth of both the peoples. For they so bring the matter about by their laws, that the ground which before was neither good nor profitable for the one nor for the other is now sufficient and fruitful enough for them

SOURCE: *Sir Thomas More, Utopia (1516),* in Everyman's Library (1910), 60–61, 70, 72, 117–20.

both. But if the inhabitants of that land will not dwell with them to be ordered by their laws, then they drive them out of those bounds which they have limited and appointed out for themselves. And if they resist and rebel, then they make war against them. For they count this the most just cause of war, when any people holdeth a piece of ground void and vacant to no good nor profitable use, keeping others from the use and possession of it which notwithstanding by the law of nature ought thereof to be nourished and relieved. . . .

OF THE RELIGIONS IN UTOPIA

There be divers kinds of religion not only in sundry parts of the island, but also in divers places of every city. . . .

They also which do not agree to Christ's religion fear no man from it nor speak against any man that hath received it, . . . For this is one of the ancientest laws among them, that no man shall be blamed for reasoning in the maintenance of his own religion. . . .

This law did King Utopus make, not only for the maintenance of peace, which he saw through continual contention and mortal hatred utterly extinguished, but also because he thought this decree should make for the furtherance of religion. . . . But if contention and debate in that behalf should continually be used, as the worst men be most obstinate and stubborn and in their evil opinion most constant, he perceived that then the best and holiest religion would be trodden underfoot and destroyed by most vain superstitions, . . . Therefore . . . he gave to every man free liberty and choice to believe what he would; saving that he earnestly and straitly charged them that no man should conceive so vile and base an opinion of the dignity of man's nature as to think that the souls do die and perish with the body, or that the world runneth at all aventures, governed by no divine providence.

2.2 Reasons for Colonization

Richard Hakluyt the Elder

Richard Hakluyt the Elder and his cousin Richard Hakluyt the Younger were successful sixteenth-century promoters of English settlement in America. The elder Hakluyt, in particular, offered specific proposals on the profitable use of land in America. His theory on the economic advantage to be gained from settlements in America foreshadowed the policies that came to be known as mercantilism. The following selection offers more than thirty reasons why English settlements should be established in North America.

Consider:

1. *What Hakluyt believes to be the single most important reason for colonization;*
2. *The economic role Hakluyt outlines for the English settlements in America;*
3. *The long-term effects this economic role for the colonies could have on their relations with England.*

The glory of God by planting of religion among those infidels.

The increase of the force of the Christians.

The possibility of the enlarging of the dominions of the Queen's Most Excellent Majesty, and consequently of her honour, revenues, and of her power by this enterprise.

An ample vent in time to come of the woollen cloths of England, especially those of the coarsest sorts, to the maintenance of our poor, that else starve or become burdensome to the realm; and vent also of sundry our commodities upon the tract of that firm land, and possibly in other regions from the northern side of that main. . . .

By return thence, this realm shall receive . . . most or all the commodities that we receive from the best parts of Europe, and we shall receive the same better cheap than now we receive them, as we may use the matter.

Receiving the same thence, the navy, the human strength of this realm, our merchants and their goods, shall not be subject to arrest of ancient enemies and doubtful friends as of late years they have been.

If our nation do not make any conquest there but only use traffic and change of commodities, yet, by means the country is not very mighty but divided into petty kingdoms, they shall not dare to offer us any great annoy but such as we may easily revenge with sufficient chastisement to the unarmed people there. . . .

The great plenty of buff hides and of many other sundry kinds of hides there now presently to be had, the trade of whale and seal fishing and of divers other fishings in the great rivers, great bays, and seas there, shall presently defray the charge in good part or in all of the first enterprise. . . .

The great broad rivers of that main that we are to enter into, so many leagues navigable or portable into the mainland, lying so long a tract with so excellent and so fertile a soil on both sides, do seem to promise all things that the life of man doth require and whatsoever men may wish that are to plant upon the same or to traffic in the same. . . .

SOURCE: *Elizabeth Taylor, ed.,* Original Writings of the Two Richard Hakluyts *(1585), II, 327–38.*

If we find the country populous and desirous to expel us and injuriously to offend us, that seek but just and lawful traffic, then, by reason that we are lords of navigation and they not so, we are the better able to defend ourselves by reason of those great rivers and to annoy them in many places. . . .

The known abundance of fresh fish in the rivers, and the known plenty of fish on the sea-coast there, may assure us of sufficient victual in spite of the people, if we will use salt and industry.

The known plenty and variety of flesh of divers kinds of beasts at land there may seem to say to us that we may cheaply victual our navies to England for our returns. . . .

The navigating of the seas in the voyage, and of the great rivers there, will breed many mariners for service and maintain much navigation. . . .

Since great waste woods be there of oak, cedar, pine, walnuts, and sundry other sorts, many of our waste people may be employed in making of ships, hoys, busses, and boats, and in making of rosin, pitch, and tar. . . .

If mines of white or grey marble, jet, or other rich stone be found there, our idle people may be employed in the mines of the same and in preparing the same to shape, and, so shaped, they may be carried into this realm as good ballast for our ships and after serve for noble buildings. . . .

. . . Moreover, we shall not only receive many precious commodities besides from thence, but also shall in time find ample vent of the labour of our poor people at home, by sale of hats, bonnets, knives, fish-hooks, copper kettles, beads, looking-glasses, bugles, and a thousand kinds of other wrought wares that in short time may be brought in use among the people of that country, to the great relief of the multitude of our poor people and to the wonderful enriching of this realm. And in time, such league and intercourse may arise between our stapling seats there, and other ports of our Northern America, and of the islands of the same, that incredible things, and by few as yet dreamed of, may speedily follow, tending to the impeachment of our mighty enemies and to the common good of this noble government.

2.3   Plymouth Plantation

William Bradford

The most celebrated settlement in American history started with a congregation of thirty-five English Separatists, who landed at Plymouth Bay in December of 1620. They sailed from Holland, where they had moved some ten years earlier so they could hold religious services without interference from the English government. Their subsequent move to America involved both the desire to worship freely and to gain economic independence. The following selection is taken from a history of Plymouth Plantation written by William Bradford, the colony's leader in America. Bradford explains why the congregation decided to make its move.

Consider:

1. *Why these English Separatists, who had been free to practice their religious beliefs in Holland, decided to emigrate to America;*
2. *How these Separatists viewed the Indians and what sort of relationship with them they had in mind.*

. . . In the agitation of their thoughts, and much discourse of things hereabout, at length they began to incline to this conclusion: of removal to some other place. Not out of any newfangledness or other such like giddy humor by which men are oftentimes transported to their great hurt and danger, but for sundry weighty and solid reasons, some of the chief of which I will here briefly touch. . . .

. . . For many that came to them, and many more that desired to be with them, could not endure that great labour and hard fare, with other inconveniences. . . . Yea, their pastor would often say that many of those who both wrote and preached now against them, if they were in a place where they might have liberty and live comfortably, they would then practice as they did.

. . . And therefore according to the divine proverb, that a wise man seeth the plague when it cometh, and hideth himself, Proverbs xxii.3, so they like skillful and beaten soldiers were fearful either to be entrapped or surrounded by their enemies so as they should neither be able to fight nor fly. And therefore thought it better to dislodge betimes to some place of better advantage and less danger, if any such could be found.

. . . For many of their children that were of best dispositions and gracious inclinations, having learned to bear the yoke in their youth and . . . the vigour of nature being consumed in the very bud as it were. . . . Some became soldiers, others took upon them far voyages by sea, and others some worse courses tending to dissoluteness and the danger of their souls, to the great grief of their parents and dishonour of God. . . .

. . . the which they afterward prosecuted with so great difficulties, as by the sequel will appear.

. . . This proposition being made public and coming to the scanning of all, it raised many variable opinions amongst men and caused many fears and doubts amongst themselves. Some, from their reasons and

SOURCE: *William Bradford, Of Plymouth Plantation 1620–1647, ed. Samuel Eliot Morison (New York: Knopf, 1966), 23–27.*

hopes conceived, laboured to stir up and encourage the rest to undertake and prosecute the same; others again, out of their fears, objected against it and sought to divert from it; alleging many things, and those neither unreasonable nor unprobable; . . . The change of air, diet and drinking of water would infect their bodies with sore sicknesses and grievous diseases. . . .

And surely it could not be thought but the very hearing of these things could not but move the very bowels of men to grate within them and make the weak to quake and tremble. . . . Also many precedents of ill success and lamentable miseries befallen others in the like designs were easy to be found, and not forgotten to be alleged; besides their own experience, in their former troubles and hardships in their removal into Holland, and how hard a thing it was for them to live in that strange place, though it was a neighbour country and a civil and rich commonwealth.

. . . True it was that such attempts were not to be made and undertaken without good ground and reason, not rashly or lightly as many have done for curiosity or hope of gain, etc. But their condition was not ordinary, their ends were good and honourable, their calling lawful and urgent; and therefore they might expect the blessing of God in their proceeding. Yea, though they should lose their lives in this action, yet might they have comfort in the same and their endeavours would be honourable. They lived here but as men in exile and in a poor condition, and as great miseries might possibly befall them in this place; for the twelve years of truce were now out and there was nothing but beating of drums and preparing for war, the events whereof are always uncertain. The Spaniard might prove as cruel as the savages of America, and the famine and pestilence as sore here as there, and their liberty less to look out for remedy.

2.4   Advice to Prospective Settlers in Jamestown, Virginia, 1622

In 1606 a joint-stock company in London received a charter from James I to establish a colony in Virginia. The Virginia Company of London, as it was officially called, was a profit-making enterprise with the aim of finding gold or other treasurers. The owners of the Virginia Company worked hard to build up the colony, offering a number of inducements to those willing to emigrate. In this poster of 1622, the Virginia Company estimated that the cost of food, clothing, weapons, and tools for one year, along with passage, was £20. At the time, the average agricultural worker in England earned less than £3 a year.

Consider:

1. The type of individual the Virginia Company expected to recruit, judging from this list of supplies and equipment;
2. The assumptions about living and working conditions in Jamestown that are implicit in this poster;
3. The inducements offered by the Virginia Company to those willing to move to Jamestown.

THE INCONVENIENCIES
THAT HAVE HAPPENED TO SOME PER-
SONS WHICH HAVE TRANSPORTED THEMSELVES

from *England* to *Virginia*, vvithout prouifions neceffary to fuftaine themfelues, hath greatly hindred the *Progreffe* of that noble *Plantation*: For preuention of the like diforders heereafter, that no man fuffer, either through ignorance or mifinformation; it is thought requifite to publifh this fhort declaration: wherein is contained a particular of fuch neceffaries, as either priuate families or fingle perfons fhall haue caufe to furnifh themfelues with, for their better fupport at their firft landing in Virginia; whereby alfo greater numbers may receiue in part, directions how to prouide themfelues.

Apparrell.

	li.	s.	d.
One Monmouth Cap	oo	o1	10
Three falling bands	—	o1	o3
Three fhirts	—	o7	o6
One wafte-coate	—	o2	o2
One fuite of Canuafe	—	o7	o6
One fuite of Frize	—	10	oo
One fuite of Cloth	—	15	oo
Three paire of Irifh ftockins	—	o4	—
Foure paire of fhooes	—	c8	o8
One paire of garters	—	oo	10
One doozen of points	—	oo	o3
One paire of Canuafe fheets	—	c8	oo
Seuen ells of Canuafe, to make a bed and boulfter, to be filled in *Virginia* 8.s.			
One Rug for a bed 8. s. which with the bed feruing for two men, halfe is	c8	oo	
Fiue ells coorfe Canuafe, to make a bed at Sea for two men, to be filled with ftraw, iiij.s.			
One coorfe Rug at Sea for two men, will coft vj.s. is for one	o5	oo	
	o4	oo	oo

Apparrell for one man, and fo after the rate for more.

For a family of 6. perfons and fo after the rate for more.

Victuall.

	li.	s.	d.
Eight bufhels of Meale	o2	oo	oo
Two bufhels of peafe at 3.s.	—	o6	oo
Two bufhels of Oatemeale 4.s. 6.d.	—	o9	oo
One gallon of *Aquauitæ*	—	o2	o6
One gallon of Oyle	—	o3	o6
Two gallons of Vineger 1.s.	—	o2	oo
	o3	o3	oo

For a whole yeere for one man, and fo for more after the rate.

Armes.

	li.	s.	d.
One Armour compleat, light	—	17	oo
One long Peece, fiue foot or fiue and a halfe, neere Musket bore	o1	o2	—
One fword	—	o5	—
One belt	—	o1	—
One bandaleere	—	o1	o6
Twenty pound of powder	—	18	oo
Sixty pound of fhot or lead, Piftoll and Goofe fhot	—	o5	oo
	o3	o9	o6

For one man, but if halfe of your men haue armour it is fufficient fo that all haue Peeces and fwords.

Tooles.

	li.	s.	d.
Fiue broad howes at 2.s. a piece	—	10	—
Fiue narrow howes at 16.d. a piece	—	o6	c8
Two broad Axes at 3.s. 8.d. a piece	—	o7	c4
Fiue felling Axes at 18.d. a piece	—	o7	o6
Two fteele hand fawes at 16.d. a piece	—	o2	c8
Two two-hand-fawes at 5. s. a piece	—	10	—
One whip-faw, fet and filed with box, file, and wreft	—	10	—
Two hammers 12.d. a piece	—	o2	oo
Three fhouels 18.d. a piece	—	o4	o6
Two fpades at 18.d. a piece	—	o3	—
Two augers 6.d. a piece	—	o1	oo
Sixe chiffels 6.d. a piece	—	o3	oo
Two percers ftocked 4.d. a piece	—	oo	c8
Three gimlets 2.d. a piece	—	oo	o6
Two hatchets 21.d. a piece	—	o3	o6
Two froues to cleaue pale 18.d.	—	o3	oo
Two hand bills 20. a piece	—	o3	o4
One grindleftone 4 s.	—	o4	oo
Nailes of all forts to the value of	o2	oo	—
Two Pickaxes	—	o3	—
	o6	o2	o8

For a family of 6. perfons, and fo for more or leffe after the rate.

Houfhold Implements.

	li.	s.	d.
One Iron Pot	—	o7	—
One kettle	—	o6	—
One large frying-pan	—	o2	o6
One gridiron	—	o1	o6
Two skillets	—	o5	—
One fpit	—	o2	—
Platters, difhes, fpoones of wood	—	o4	—
	o1	o8	oo

For a family of 6. perfons, and fo for more or leffe after the rate.

	li.	s.	d.
For Suger, Spice, and fruit, and at Sea for 6.men	oo	12	o6

So the full charge of Apparrell, Victuall, Armes, Tooles, and houfhold ftuffe, and after this rate for each perfon, will amount vnto about the fumme of — 12 | 10 | —
The paffage of each man is — o6 | oo | —
The fraight of thefe prouifions for a man, will bee about halfe a Tun, which is — o1 | 10 | —

So the whole charge will amount to about — 20 | oo | oo

Nets, hookes, lines, and a tent muft be added, if the number of people be greater, as alfo fome kine.

And this is the vfuall proportion that the Virginia Company doe beftow vpon their Tenants which they fend.

Whofoeuer tranfports himfelfe or any other at his owne charge vnto *Virginia*, fhall for each perfon fo tranfported before Midfummer 1625. haue to him and his heires for euer fifty Acres of Land vpon a firft, and fifty Acres vpon a fecond diuifion.

FELIX KYNGSTON. 1622.

SOURCE: *Courtesy of the John Carter Brown Library at Brown University.*

2.5   An Indentured Servant Writes Home
Richard Frethorne

Despite their great expectations for a new life in Virginia, most settlers who moved to Jamestown between 1619 and 1623 encountered hunger, disease, and eventual death. The mortality rate during those years was between 75 and 80 percent. This letter written in 1623 by an indentured servant, Richard Frethorne, graphically portrays what life must have been like. Nothing else is known about Frethorne; the odds are that he, too, died in Virginia in 1623.

Consider:

1. *Why the colonists suffered from starvation in Virginia, though the Indians had survived there for many years;*
2. *To what extent the location of Jamestown could explain diseases "which maketh the body very poor and weak."*

Loveing and kind father and mother my most humble duty remembred to you hopeing in God of yor good health, as I my selfe am . . . at the makeing hereof, this is to let you vnderstand that I yor Child am in a most heavie Case by reason of the nature of the Country . . . is such that it Causeth much sicknes, as the scurvie and the bloody flix, and divers other diseases, wch maketh the bodie very poore, and Weake, and when wee are sicke there is nothing to Comfort vs; for since I came out of the ship, I never at [ate] anie thing but pease, and loblollie (that is water gruell) as for deare or venison I never saw anie since I came into this land, ther is indeed some foule, but Wee are not allowed to goe, and get yt, but must Worke hard both earelie, and late for a messe of water gruell, and a mouthfull of bread, and beife, a mouthfull of bread for a pennie loafe must serve for 4 men wch is most pitifull . . . people crie out day, and night, Oh that they were in England without their lymbes and would not care to loose anie lymbe to bee in England againe, yea though they beg from doore to doore, for wee live in feare of the Enimy eu'ie hower [every hour], yet wee haue had a Combate with them on the Sunday before Shrovetyde, and wee tooke two alive, and make slaves of them, but it was by pollicie, for wee are in great danger, for o^r Plantačon is very weake, by reason of the dearth, and sicknes, of o^r Companie, for wee came but Twentie for the marchaunte [merchants], and they are halfe dead Just; and wee looke everie hower When two more should goe, yet there came some for other men yet to Jyve with vs, of which ther is but one alive, and our Leiften^ant is dead, and his ffather, and his

SOURCE: *Richard Frethorne, Letter to his father and mother, March 20, April 2 and 3, 1623, in* The Records of the Virginia Company of London, *ed. Susan M. Kingsbury, IV (Washington, D.C.: U.S. Government Printing Office, 1935), 58–62.*

brother, I haue nothing to Comfort me, nor ther is nothing to be gotten here but sicknes, and death, except that one had money to lay out in some thinges for profit; But I haue nothing at all, no not a shirt to my backe, but two Ragges [2] nor no Clothes, but one poore suite, nor but one paire of shooes, but one paire of stockins, but one Capp, but two bande, my Cloke is stollen by one of my owne fellowes, and to his dying hower would not tell mee what he did with it but some of my fellows saw him have butter and beife out of a ship, wch my Cloke I doubt paid for, so that I have not a penny, nor a a penny Worth to helpe me to either spice, or sugar, or strong Waters, without the wch one cannot lyue here, for as strong beare in England doth fatten and strengthen them so water here doth wash and weaken theis here, onelie keepe life and soule togeather. but I am not halfe a quarter so strong as I was in England, and all is for want of victualls, for I doe protest vnto you, that I haue eaten more in day at home then I haue allowed me here for a Weeke. you haue given more then my dayes allowance to a beggar at the doore; and if Mr Jackson had not releived me, I should bee in a poore Case, but he like a ffather and shee like a loveing mother doth still helpe me, for when wee goe vp to James Towne that is 10 myles of vs, there lie all the ships that Come to the land, and there they must deliver their goode, and when wee went vp to Towne as it may bee on Moonedaye, at noone, and come there by night, then load the next day by noone, and goe home in the afternoone, and vnload, and then away againe in the night, and bee vp about midnight, then if it rayned, or blowed never so hard wee must lye in the boate on the water, and haue nothing but alitle bread, for when wee go into the boate wee haue a loafe allowed to two men, and it is all if we staid there 2 dayes, wch is hard, and must lye all that while in the boate, but that Goodman Jackson pityed me & made me a Cabbin to lye in alwayes when I come vp, and he would giue me some poore Jacke home with me wch Comforted mee more then pease, or water gruell. Oh they bee verie godlie folkes, and loue me verie well, and will doe anie thing for me, and he much marvailed that you would send me a servaunt to the Companie, he saith I had beene better knockd on the head, and Indeede so I fynd it now to my greate greife and miserie, and saith, that if you love me you will redeeme me suddenlie, good ffather doe not forget me, but haue m^{9}cie [mercy] and pittye my miserable Case. I know if you did but see me you would weepe to see me, for I haue but one suite, but it is a strange one, it is very well guarded, wherefore for Gode sake pittie me, I pray you to remember my loue my love to all my ffreinde, and kindred, I hope all my Brothers and Sisters are in good health, and as for my part I have set downe my resolucon that certainelie Wilbe, that is, that the Answeare of this letter wilbee life or death to me, therefore good ffather send as soone as you can.

Richard Ffrethorne
Martyns Hundred.

2.6   Indentured Servitude

Richard B. Hofstadter

The notion of people selling four to seven years of their lives to pay their way to America seems alien to us today. Because the cost of passage was so high (from two to four times more than an agricultural worker earned in one year), only the very well off could afford to make the trip, to say nothing of paying other necessary expenses. Thus indentured servitude seemed attractive to poor or unemployed young men and women who wished to move to America. At the same time, indentured servitude comprised a relatively inexpensive source of labor in the new land. In this selection, historian Richard Hofstadter describes the way in which indentured servitude worked and the economic circumstances of those who completed their service.

Consider:

1. *The advantages and disadvantages of becoming an indentured servant;*
2. *Whether indentured servitude was simply another name for slavery;*
3. *Whether indentured servants were better off than slaves.*

Indentured servitude had its roots in the widespread poverty and human dislocation of seventeenth-century England. Still a largely backward economy with a great part of its population permanently unemployed, England was moving toward more modern methods in industry and agriculture; yet in the short run some of the improvements greatly added to the unemployed. Drifting men and women gathered in the cities, notably London, where they constituted a large mass of casual workers, lumpenproletarians, and criminals. The mass of the poverty-stricken was so large that Gregory King, the pioneer statistician, estimated in 1696 that more than half the population—cottagers and paupers, laborers and outservants—were earning less than they spent. They diminished the wealth of the realm, he argued, since their annual expenses exceeded income and had to be made up by the poor rates, which ate up one-half of the revenue of the Crown. In the early eighteenth century, this situation made people believe the country was overpopulated and emigration to the colonies was welcomed; but in the latter part of the century, and in the next, the overpopulation theory gave way to the desire to hoard a satisfactory labor surplus. Yet the strong outflow of population did not by any means cease. From the large body of poor drifters, many of them diseased, feckless, or given to crime, came a great part of the labor supply of the rich

SOURCE: *Richard B. Hofstadter,* America at 1750: A Social Portrait *(New York: Alfred A. Knopf, Inc., 1971), 34–35, 50–51, 59–62.*

sugar islands and the American mainland. From the London of Pepys and then of Hogarth, as well as from many lesser ports and inland towns, the English poor, lured, seduced, or forced into the emigrant stream, kept coming to America for the better part of two centuries. It is safe to guess that few of them, and indeed few persons from the other sources of emigration, knew very much about what they were doing when they committed themselves to life in America. . . .

The system of indenture was an adaptation, with some distinctively harsh features, of the old institution of apprenticeship. In fact, a few native-born colonials, usually to discharge a debt or answer for a crime but sometimes to learn a trade, entered into indentures not altogether unlike those undertaken by immigrants. In law an indenture was a contract in which the servant promised faithful service for a specified period of time in return for his housing and keep and, at the end of his term of work, that small sum of things, known as "freedom dues," which his master promised him upon their parting. The typical term was four or five years, although it might run anywhere from one or two years to seven. Longer terms were commonly specified for children, and were calculated to bring them to freedom at or just past the time they reached majority. Most indentures followed a standard pattern: as early as 1636 printed forms were available, needing only a few details to be filled out by the contracting parties. Often an emigrant's original indenture was made out to a merchant or a ship's captain and was sold with its holder to an employer on arrival. Indentures became negotiable instruments in the colonies, servants bound under their terms being used to settle debts, even gambling debts. In theory the contract protected the servant from indefinite exploitation, but in practice it had quite limited powers. It was a document vulnerable to loss, theft, or destruction, and when one considers both the fecklessness and inexperience of most indentured servants and the lack of privacy under which they lived, it is little wonder that their contracts often disappeared.

During the eighteenth century, however, circumstances began to alter the prevailing system of indentures and to lessen its severities, particularly when a special class of bonded servants, the redemptioners, became numerous. The redemptioner appeared at the beginning of the century, coming largely from the Continent, often emigrating with a family and with a supply of tools and furnishings. . . . Indentured servants were simply a part of a ship's cargo, but redemptioners were low-grade, partially paid-up passengers. The redemptioner embarked without an indenture, sometimes having paid part of the money for his own and his family's passage, and arranged with the shipping merchant to complete payment within a short time after landing. Once here, he might try to find relatives or friends to make up his deficit; failure to pay in full meant that he would be sold to the highest bidder to redeem whatever part of his fare was unpaid. The length of his servitude would depend upon the amount to be redeemed. It could be as short as one or two years, although four years seems to have been much more common. Redemptioners would try to go into service as a whole family group. Although redemptioners were often swindled because of their lack of English and were overcharged for interest, insurance, and the transportation of their baggage, it was less profitable to carry them than indentured servants. Still, merchants were eager to fill their ships as full as possible with a ballast of redemptioners. . . .

What was the economic situation of the servant after completing his servitude? It varied, no doubt, from colony to colony, and with the availability of lands. In the mainland colonies, it appears to have been assumed that an ex-servant was to be equipped for work as a free hired man with enough clothes and tools or money to give him a small start. It was assumed that wages for a freeman were high enough to enable him to earn an adequate competence or to provide himself with a plot of land within a fairly short time. Some ex-servants no doubt went westward and took up new lands. "The inhabitants of our frontiers," wrote Governor Alexander Spotswood of Virginia in 1717, "are composed generally of such as have been transported hither as servants, and being out of their time, settle themselves where land is to be taken up that will produce the necessaries of life with little labour." But it is quite likely that Spotswood erred considerably on the side of optimism. For example, in Maryland, where a freed servant in the seventeenth century was entitled to 50 acres of land upon showing his certificate of freedom at the office of the land office secretary, the records show that relatively few became farmers, though many assumed their land rights and sold them for cash. Abbott E. Smith, in one of the most authoritative studies of colonial servitude, estimates that only one out of ten indentured servants (not including redemptioners) became a substantial farmer and another became an artisan or an overseer in reasonably comfortable circumstances. The other eight, he suggests, either died during servitude, returned to England when it was over, or drifted off to become the "poor whites" of the villages and rural areas. There is reason to think that in most places servants who had completed a term of bondage and had a history of local residence met the prevailing parochial, almost tribal qualifications for poor relief, and were accepted as public charges. Redemptioners, Smith remarks, did a good deal better, but the scrappy evidence that has thus far been found does not yet allow much precision. . . .

As for the indentured servants, the dismal estimate that only two out of ten may have reached positions of moderate comfort is an attempt to generalize the whole two centuries of the experience of English servitude, taking the seventeenth century when the system was brutal and opportunities were few with the eighteenth, when it became less severe. In the early years more servants returned to England, and mortality was also higher. But it will not do simply to assume that freed servants, especially those from the tobacco fields, were in any mental or physical condition to start vigorous new lives, or that long and ripe years of productivity lay ahead for them. If we consider the whole span of time over which English indentured servitude prevailed, its heavy toll in work and death is the reality that stands out.

The Horatio Alger mythology has long since been torn to bits by students of American social mobility, and it will surprise no one to learn that the chance of emergence from indentured servitude to a position of wealth or renown was statistically negligible. . . .

2.7 Virginia Laws for Blacks

Blacks were first introduced to British North America in 1619 when settlers in Jamestown bought twenty laborers from a Dutch sea captain. Thirty years later, there were about three hundred blacks in Virginia; most were legally categorized as indentured servants. However, unlike white indentured servants, blacks had to contend with an inferior and discriminatory status that the English imposed on them. As tobacco production developed and became Virginia's major cash crop, indentured servitude proved an unreliable source of cheap labor. Economic necessity, therefore, aided by white attitudes of black inferiority, gradually gave rise to the legal institutionalization of slavery in Virginia. This evolution is evident in legislation that the Virginia House of Burgesses enacted between 1630 and 1705, portions of which are excerpted in the document here.

Consider:

1. *The underlying attitudes toward blacks that these statutes reveal;*
2. *What these statutes suggest were of greatest concern to Virginia lawmakers;*
3. *How white settlers in Virginia could reconcile black slavery with their religious faith.*

"September 17th, 1630. Hugh Davis to be soundly whipped, before an assembly of Negroes and others for abusing himself to the dishonor of God and shame of Christians, by defiling his body in lying with a negro; which fault he is to acknowledge next Sabbath day." . . . 1640. . . .

Robert Sweet to do penance in church according to laws of England, for getting a negroe woman with child and the woman whipt. . . .

SOURCE: *William Waller Hening,* Laws of Virginia, 1619–1792 *(1823), I–III.*

1662

ACT XII.

Negro womens children to serve according to the condition of the mother. (a)

WHEREAS some doubts have arrisen whether children got by any Englishman upon a negro woman should be slave or ffree, *Be it therefore enacted and declared by this present grand assembly,* that all children borne in this country shalbe held bond or free only according to the condition of the mother, *And* that if any christian shall committ ffornication with a negro man or woman, hee or shee soe offending shall pay double the ffines imposed by the former act. . . .

1680

ACT X.

An act for preventing Negroes Insurrections.

WHEREAS the frequent meeting of considerable numbers of negroe slaves under pretence of feasts and burialls is judged of dangerous consequence; for prevention whereof for the future, *Bee it enacted by the kings most excellent majestie by and with the consent of the generall assembly, and it is hereby enacted by the authority aforesaid,* that from and after the publication of this law, it shall not be lawfull for any negroe or other slave to carry or arme himselfe with any club, staffe, gunn, sword or any other weapon of defence or offence, nor to goe or depart from of his masters ground without a certificate from his master, mistris or overseer, and such permission not to be granted but upon perticuler and necessary occasions; and every negroe or slave soe offending not haveing a certificate as aforesaid shalbe sent to the next constable, who is hereby enjoyned and required to give the said negroe twenty lashes on his bare back well layd on, and soe sent home to his said master, mistris or overseer. *And it is further enacted by the authority aforesaid* that if any negroe or other slave shall presume to lift up his hand in opposition against any christian, shall for every such offence, upon due proofe made thereof by the oath of the party before a magistrate, have and receive thirty lashes on his bare back well laid on. . . .

1705

CHAP. XLIX.

. . . IV. *And also be it enacted, by the authority aforesaid, and it is hereby enacted,* That all servants imported and brought into this country, by sea or land, who were not christians in their native country, (except Turks and Moors in amity with her majesty, and others that can make due proof of their being free in England, or any other christian country, before they were shipped, in order to transportation hither) shall be accounted and be slaves, and as such be here bought and sold notwithstanding a conversion to christianity afterwards. . . .

XIX. And for a further prevention of that abominable mixture and spurious issue, which hereafter may increase in this her majesty's colony and dominion, as well by English, and other white men and women intermarrying with negros or mulattos, as by their unlawful coition with them, *Be it enacted, by the authority aforesaid, and it is hereby enacted,* That whatsoever English, or other white man or woman, being free, shall intermarry with a negro or mulatto man or woman, bond or free, shall, by judgment of the county court, be committed to prison, and there remain, during the space of six months, without bail or mainprize; and shall forfeit and pay ten pounds current money of Virginia, to the use of the parish, as aforesaid. . . .

XXXIV. And if any slave resist his master, or owner, or other person, by his or her order, correcting such slave, and shall happen to be killed in such correction, it shall not be accounted felony; but the master, owner, and every such other person so giving correction, shall be free and acquit of all punishment and accusation for the same, as if such accident had never happened: And also, if any negro, mulatto, or Indian, bond or free, shall at any time, lift his or her hand, in opposition against any christian, not being negro, mulatto, or Indian, he or she so offending, shall, for every such offence, proved by the oath of the party, receive on his or her bare back, thirty lashes, well laid on; cognizable by a justice of the peace for that county wherein such offence shall be committed.

XXXV. *And also be it enacted, by the authority aforesaid, and it is hereby enacted,* That no slave go armed with gun, sword, club, staff, or other weapon, nor go from off the plantation and seat of land where such slave shall be appointed to live, without a certificate of leave in writing, for so doing, from his or her master, mistress, or overseer: And if any slave shall be found offending herein, it shall be lawful for any person or persons to apprehend and deliver such slave to the next constable or head-borough, who is hereby enjoined and required, without further order or warrant, to give such slave twenty lashes on his or her bare back, well laid on, and so send him or her home: And all horses, cattle, and hogs, now belonging, or that hereafter shall belong to any slave, or of any slaves mark in this her majesty's colony and dominion, shall be seised and sold by the church-wardens of the parish, wherein such horses, cattle, or hogs shall be, and the profit thereof applied to the use of the poor of the said parish. . . .

XXXVI. *And also it is hereby enacted and declared,* That baptism of slaves doth not exempt them from bondage; and that all children shall be bond or free, according to the condition of their mothers, and the particular directions of this act. . . .

2.8   Indian Warfare in New England

Increase Mather

The first major Indian-white conflict occurred in Massachusetts in 1675. An Indian chief, King Philip, opened warfare against whites in retaliation for the execution of three Indians who had been found guilty of murdering another Indian. Together with other Indian tribes, King Philip and his forces ravaged many New England towns until he was killed in August 1676. Increase Mather, a noted Puritan minister and president of Harvard College, followed the war closely and wrote a book entitled *A History of King Philip's War*. The excerpt here describes the circumstances of King Philip's death. It provides an interesting complement to Columbus's description of American Indians (see Document 1.3).

Consider:

1. *The values that underlie Mather's characterization of King Philip and the war;*
2. *The assumptions that Mather makes about the Indians and the English;*
3. *Why Mather's attitude toward Indians is so different from that of Christopher Columbus (Document 1.3).*

August 12. This is the memorable day wherein *Philip*, the perfidious and bloudy Author of the War and wofull miseryes that have thence ensued, was taken and slain. And God brought it to pass, chiefly by *Indians* themselves. For one of *Philips* men (being disgusted at him, for killing an *Indian* who had propounded an expedient for peace with the *English*) ran away from him, and coming to Road-Island, informed that *Philip* was now returned again to *Mount-Hope*, and undertook to bring them to the swamp where he hid himself. Divine Providence so disposed, as that Capt. *Church of Plymouth* was then in Road-Island, in order to recruiting his Souldiers, who had been wearied with a tedious march that week. But immediately upon this Intelligence, he set forth again, with a small company of *English* and *Indians*. It seemeth that night *Philip* (like the man, in the Host of *Midian*) dreamed that he was fallen into the hands of the *English*, and just as he was saying to those that were with him, that they must fly for their lives that day, lest the *Indian* that was gone from him should recover where he was. Our Souldiers came upon him and surrounded the *Swamp* (where he with seven of his men absconded). Thereupon he betook himself to flight; but as he was coming out of the Swamp, an *English-man* and

SOURCE: *Increase Mather*, A History of King Philip's War *(1862), 193–95.*

an *Indian* endeavoured to fire at him, the *English-man* missed of his aime, but the *Indian* shot him through the heart, so as that he fell down dead. The *Indian* who thus killed *Philip* did formerly belong to Squaw-Sachim of *Pocasset*, being known by the name of *Alderman*. In the beginning of the war, he came to the Governour of *Plymouth*, manifesting his desire to be at peace with the *English*, and immediately withdrew to an Island not having engaged against the *English* nor for them, before this time. Thus when *Philip* had made an end to deal treacherously, his own Subjects dealt treacherously with him. This Wo was brought upon him that spoyled when he was not spoyled. And in that very place where he first contrived and began his mischief, was he taken and destroyed, and there was he (like as Agag was hewed in pieces before the Lord) cut into four quarters, and is now hanged up as a monument of revenging Justice, his head being cut off and carried away to *Plymouth*, his Hands were brought to *Boston*. *So let all thine Enemies perish, O Lord!*

CHAPTER QUESTIONS

1. *In 1620, England had two small settlements in North America. Less than a century and a half later, those few struggling Englishmen had developed into a vigorous society with a population of nearly two million. How do you account for this spectacular success?*
2. *Compare the northern and southern colonies of British North America in terms of the type of settlers, economic activity, religion, land distribution, and political institutions in Massachusetts and Virginia. Do you see any clues to future sectional conflicts in this comparison?*
3. *How did white settlers in British North America view Indians and blacks? Do these views suggest any long-term problems?*

Chapter 3

The Colonial Relationship Defined, 1620–1763

O ne interesting aspect of early American history is the way the relationship between the colonies and England changed in the seventeenth and eighteenth centuries. The colonies started off as entities subordinate to and dependent on the power of England, but as time went by, they came to manage more and more of their own affairs. Although Parliament made some efforts in the seventeenth century to establish an overall colonial policy—notably through the Navigation Act of 1660—it was not until the following century that a definite program began to emerge. By then settlement had been completed and the colonies were firmly established.

In the early 1700s, Parliament and the king began to use the strength and power of the colonies to promote England's national interest and security. Gradually, a British colonial policy began to take shape. Its main points concerned limiting the self-government that had developed in the colonies and restricting the expanding colonial economy for the benefit of England. The colonies resisted this policy through a variety of means. By the time the Seven Years' War had ended in 1763, the scene was set for a major confrontation between the colonial legislatures and the king and Parliament over the proper place and role of the colonies. Parliament controlled trade, while colonial assemblies controlled taxation, appointed lower officials, and raised troops.

Historians have offered conflicting interpretations of this evolving relationship between the colonies and England, tracing economic, constitutional, and political trends. Any discussion of how the two sides attempted to define their relationship must take into account a multiplicity of facts and issues. The documents in this chapter present some of these facts and issues from the viewpoint of England as well as the colonies. The purpose is not to establish causes or to fix responsibility on individuals or groups. Rather, the goal is to illustrate the evolution of British policy toward the colonies and the responses that policy produced.

Chronology

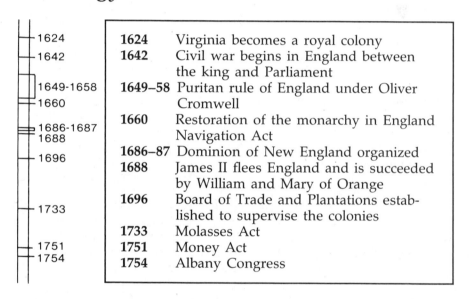

1624	Virginia becomes a royal colony
1642	Civil war begins in England between the king and Parliament
1649–58	Puritan rule of England under Oliver Cromwell
1660	Restoration of the monarchy in England Navigation Act
1686–87	Dominion of New England organized
1688	James II flees England and is succeeded by William and Mary of Orange
1696	Board of Trade and Plantations established to supervise the colonies
1733	Molasses Act
1751	Money Act
1754	Albany Congress

Documents

3.1 First Representative Assembly in Virginia, 1619 (primary source)
3.2 The Plymouth Compact, William Bradford (primary source)
3.3 Mercantilism, Gerald N. Grob and George A. Billias (secondary source)
3.4 Navigation Act of 1660 (primary source)
3.5 Memorial of Governor Shute to the King, 1723 (primary source)
3.6 The Role of the Lower Houses of Assembly, Jack P. Greene (secondary source)
3.7 Colonial Stirrings: "Join or Die" (visual source)

3.1   First Representative Assembly in Virginia, 1619

In 1606, King James I issued to a group of investors a charter establishing the Virginia Company of London. The charter provided for a council appointed by the king to direct affairs from England and another council located in the colony to manage day-to-day activities. In 1618, the London Council authorized the Virginia governor to call for the election of two representatives, or burgesses, from each of eleven settlements (plantations). They would meet with him and the council and suggest solutions to various problems. This group of representatives convened on July 30, 1619, in what is called the first representative assembly in America. The records of that first meeting, excerpted here, reveal the issues and concerns of the burgesses.

Consider:

1. *The reasons given for the meeting of the assembly;*
2. *The kinds of issues the burgesses regarded as most important in their enactment of laws;*
3. *Whether the participants recognized that the meeting of the assembly was a historic event.*

. . . the Speaker . . . read unto them the commission for establishing the Counsell of Estate and the general Assembly, wherein their duties were described to the life.

Having thus prepared them, he read over unto them the greate Charter, or commission of priviledges, orders and lawes, sent by Sir George Yeardly out of Englande. . . . so they were referred to the perusall of twoe Comitties, wth did reciprocally consider of either and accordingly brought in their opinions. But some men may here objecte to what ende we should presume to referre that to the examination of the Comitties wch the Counsell and Company in England had already resolved to be perfect, and did expecte nothing but our assente thereunto? To this we answere that we did it not to the ende to correcte or controll anything therein contained, but onely in case we should finde ought not perfectly squaring wth the state of this Colony or any lawe wch did presse or binde too harde, that we might by waye of humble petition, seeke to have it redressed. . . .

The nexte daye, therefore, out of the opinions of the said Comitties, it was agreed, these Petitions ensuing should be framed, to be presented to the Treasurer, Counsel & Company in England. . . .

SOURCE: *Albert B. Hart, ed.,* American History Told by Contemporaries *(New York: Macmillan, 1931), I, 219–24.*

At the same time, there remaining no farther scruple in the mindes of the Assembly, touching the said great Charter of lawes, orders and priviledges, the Speaker putt the same to the question, and so it had both the general assent and the applause of the whole assembly. . . .

By this present Generall Assembly be it enacted, that no injury or oppression be wrought by the Englishe against the Indians whereby the present peace might be disturbed and antient quarrells might be revived. And farther be it ordained that the Chicohomini are not to be excepted out of this lawe; untill either that suche order come out of Englande, or that they doe provoke us by some newe injury.

Against Idleness, Gaming, durunkenes & excesse in apparell the Assembly hath enacted as followeth:

First, in detestation of Idlenes be it enacted, that if any men be founde to live as an Idler or renagate, though a freedman, it shalbe lawfull for that Incorporation or Plantation to wch he belongeth to appoint him a M^r to serve for wages, till he shewe apparant signes of amendment.

Against gaming at dice & Cardes be it ordained by this present assembly that the winner or winners shall lose all his or their winninges and both winners and loosers shall forfaicte ten shillings. . . .

Against drunkenness be it also decreed that if any private person be found culpable thereof, for the first time he is to be reprooved privately by the Minister, the second time publiquely, the thirde time to lye in boltes 12 howers in the house of the Provost Marshall & to paye his fee, and if he still continue in that vice, to undergo suche severe punishment as the Governo^r and Counsell of Estate shall thinke fitt to be inflicted on him. . . .

Be it enacted by this present assembly that for laying a surer foundation of the conversion of the Indians to Christian Religion, eache towne, citty, Borrough, and particular plantation do obtaine unto themselves by just means a certaine number of the natives' children to be educated by them in the true religion and civile course of life—of wch children the most towardly boyes in witt & graces of nature to be brought up by them in the first elements of litterature, so to be fitted for the Colledge intended for them that from thence they may be sente to that worke of conversion. . . .

Be it further ordained by this General Assembly, and we doe by these presents enacte, that all contractes made in England between the owners of lande and their Tenants and Servantes wch they shall sende hither, may be caused to be duely performed, and that the offenders be punished as the Governour and Counsell of Estate shall thinke just and convenient.

Be it established also by this present Assembly that no crafty or advantagious means be suffered to putt in practise for the inticing awaye the Tenants or Servants of any particular plantation from the place where they are seatted.

3.2 The Plymouth Compact, 1620

William Bradford

In September 1620, thirty-five "Pilgrims" along with sixty-six other emigrants sailed for North America on the *Mayflower*. They were heading for Virginia, where they had a charter permitting settlement, but they were forced by contrary winds to sail farther north than planned and landed in New England. Unable to work their way south during winter, the leaders decided to settle on Cape Cod.

The Pilgrim settlers faced two major problems: their charter from the Virginia Company was not valid in New England, and some of the "strangers" (i.e., nonbelievers) refused to live under the jurisdiction of the company. To deal with this issue of liberty versus order, the Pilgrims drew up a covenant, or religious agreement, that extended the church jurisdiction to civil conditions. Before going ashore, forty-one adults (including six of the nonbelievers) signed the covenant, agreeing to work together for the general good of the colony. This selection from William Bradford's *Of Plymouth Plantation* includes the text of the agreement, generally known as the Mayflower Compact.

Consider:

1. What nonreligious objectives were set forth in the compact;
2. Whether the compact establishes majority rule;
3. Whether a conflict exists between the "common good" and a democracy.

I shall a little return back, and begin with a combination made by them before they came ashore; being the first foundation of their government in this place. Occasioned partly by the discontented and mutinous speeches that some of the strangers amongst them had let fall from them in the ship: That when they came ashore they would use their own liberty, for none had power to command them, the patent they had being for Virginia and not for New England, which belonged to another government, with which the Virginia Company had nothing to do. And partly that such an act by them done, this their condition considered, might be as firm as any patent, and in some respects more sure.

The form was as followeth:

IN THE NAME OF GOD, AMEN.

We whose names are underwritten, the loyal subjects of our dread Sovereign Lord King James, by the Grace of God of Great Britain, France, and Ireland King, Defender of the Faith, etc.

SOURCE: *William Bradford,* Of Plymouth Plantation, *ed. Samuel Eliot Morison (New York: Knopf, 1952), 75–76.*

Having undertaken, for the Glory of God and advancement of the Christian Faith and Honour of our King and Country, a Voyage to plant the First Colony in the Northern Parts of Virginia, do by these presents solemnly and mutually in the presence of God and one of another, Covenant and Combine ourselves together into a Civil Body Politic, for our better ordering and preservation and furtherance of the ends aforesaid; and by virtue hereof to enact, constitute and frame such just and equal Laws, Ordinances, Acts, Constitutions and Offices, from time to time, as shall be thought most meet and convenient for the general good of the Colony, unto which we promise all due submission and obedience. In witness whereof we have hereunder subscribed our names at Cape Cod, the 11th of November, in the year of the reign of our Sovereign Lord King James, of England, France and Ireland the eighteenth, and of Scotland the fifty-fourth. Anno Domini 1620.

3.3   Mercantilism

Gerald N. Grob and George A. Billias

In the sixteenth and seventeenth centuries, every major European power involved in exploration and settlement practiced some form of mercantilism. Mercantilism, as such, was not so much a set of economic theories as some basic assumptions about national security and economic interest that colonial policy was designed to promote. For this reason, the concept of mercantilism is a key element in understanding the relationship that evolved between the colonies and England. The following selection from the work of historians Gerald N. Grob and George A. Billias summarizes the main features of mercantilism.

Consider:

1. *Whether a colonial policy based upon mercantilism would have adversely affected the economic well-being of the colonies;*
2. *How the primary economic activity of a colony might affect the way colonists viewed mercantilism.*

. . . At the time that the first colonies were being founded, the basic assumption of English mercantilist thinkers was that nation-states should regulate their economic life in such a way as to strengthen themselves for competition with other nation-states. As far back as

SOURCE: *Reprinted with permission of The Free Press, a Division of Macmillan, Inc., from* Interpretations of American History: Patterns and Perspectives, *Volume 1 to 1877, Second Edition, by Gerald N. Grob and George A. Billias, 128–30. Copyright © 1967, 1972 by The Free Press.*

the fifteenth century, the English government had adopted policies on a nation-wide basis regulating the buying and selling of goods so as to encourage trade which was good for England and to discourage that which was bad. England was not alone in adopting the concept of mercantilism; the same economic philosophy was being practiced by all the major countries of western Europe. Each nation, however, decided to stress those distinctive features of mercantilism which would produce for it the greatest prosperity and national strength. Spain, for example, stressed the amassing of precious metals, Holland the control of external trade, and France the regulation of internal trade.

England, on the other hand, emphasized four major aims in her mercantilism: (1) to encourage the growth of a native merchant marine fleet so that England might control the shipping of her own goods: (2) to provide protection for England's manufactures; (3) to protect England's agriculture, especially her grain farmers; and (4) to accumulate as much hard money as possible. The ultimate objective of these mercantilist measures was always the same—to make England self-sufficient, rich, and strong as a military power.

Beginning in the seventeenth century, the British government sought to extend these mercantilist principles to its colonies. Mercantilist thinkers emphasized that no nation could achieve greatness without colonies and Britain rather belatedly embarked upon a career as a colonizing power. Colonies were expected to supplement the economy of the mother country in three ways: by supplying the mother country with raw materials, serving as markets for English manufactures, and conducting their trade in such a way as to benefit Britain. In order that various segments of the British empire might fit into this mercantilist framework, Parliament passed laws which regulated, in part, the economic life of all her colonies.

Parliament's program for the American colonies in this regard during the century between the 1650's and 1750's was called the Old Colonial System. . . . One of the main features of this system was a series of Navigation Acts designed to channel colonial commerce into paths profitable for the mother country. To assure the dominance of the British merchant marine fleet over the lucrative carrying trade between England and America, Parliament passed the Navigation Act of 1651. This act required all goods traded within the empire to be carried in British or American ships, or in the ships of the country of manufacture. To make certain that the mother country would receive the benefit of valuable raw materials produced in the colonies, the Enumerated Commodities Act of 1660 was passed. This law specified that certain colonial products such as tobacco, sugar, and indigo could be shipped only to England or to other English colonies. The mother country exercised control over colonial imports as well as exports. Under the Staples Act of 1663, Parliament ruled that some goods shipped from Europe to the American colonies had to pass through English ports first. Thus, duties could be placed on European goods before they were shipped to America, thereby protecting British merchants from foreign competition in the colonial market.

A second aim of the Old Colonial System was to make it possible for England to continue to accumulate hard money. There was an unfavorable balance of trade between Britain and the American colonies, and, whenever possible, the mother country insisted upon being paid in specie. Consequently, whatever hard money the colonies obtained in their trade with the West Indies or other parts of the world was drained off to England. English merchants refused for the most part to accept colonial paper money in payment for debts and Parliament backed them by ruling that colonial notes were not legal tender for such transactions. British merchants made it a rule never to send bullion or gold or silver coins to America and eventually Parliament passed a law to that effect. Statutes regulating the flow of hard money, then, were designed to protect the mother country.

Certain American industries were also subjected to regulation under the system to prevent them from competing with Britain. The woolen industry was restricted to some degree by the Woolens Act of 1699 which prohibited the export of wool, yarn, or woolen cloth in foreign or intercolonial trade. In 1732, the Hat Act prohibited the sale of hats abroad or to any other colonies. Under the Iron Act of 1750, steps were taken to prohibit the making of many finished iron products. American attempts at manufacturing were also discouraged to some degree by British laws which made it a crime to lure skilled workers or import textile machinery from England. . . .

3.4   Navigation Act of 1660

The goal of mercantilism was economic self-sufficiency. This was to be achieved by the colonies providing raw material to the mother country and the mother country providing manufactured goods in return. In the Navigation Act of 1660, excerpted here, Parliament incorporated the principal elements of mercantilism. The act imposed very specific trade requirements on the colonies.

Consider:

1. *The number of specific regulations on colonial trade included in this act;*
2. *Why Parliament enacted this bill;*
3. *The economic impact of the Navigation Act on different colonies.*

SOURCE: *Merrill Jensen, ed.,* English Historical Documents, American Colonial Documents to 1776 *(New York: Oxford University Press, 1955), 354–56.*

For the increase of shipping and encouragement of the navigation of this nation wherein, under the good providence and protection of God, the wealth, safety, and strength of this kingdom is so much concerned; be it enacted by the king's most excellent Majesty, and by the Lords and Commons in this present Parliament assembled, and by the authority thereof, that from and after the first day of December, one thousand six hundred and sixty, and from thence forward, no goods or commodities whatsoever shall be imported into or exported out of any lands, islands, plantations, or territories to his Majesty belonging or in his possession, or which may hereafter belong unto or be in the possession of his Majesty, his heirs, and successors, in Asia, Africa, or America, in any other ship or ships, vessel or vessels whatsoever, but in such ships or vessels as do truly and without fraud belong only to the people of England or Ireland, dominion of Wales or town of Berwick upon Tweed, or are of the built of and belonging to any the said lands, islands, plantations, or territories, as the proprietors and right owners thereof, and whereof the master and three fourths of the mariners at least are English; . . .

II. And be it enacted, that no alien or person not born within the allegiance of our sovereign lord the king, his heirs and successors, or naturalized, or made a free denizen, shall from and after the first day of February, which will be in the year of our Lord one thousand six hundred sixty-one, exercise the trade or occupation of a merchant or factor in any the said places; . . .

III. And it is further enacted by the authority aforesaid, that no goods or commodities whatsoever, of the growth, production or manufacture of Africa, Asia, or America, or of any part thereof, or which are described or laid down in the usual maps or cards of those places, be imported into England, Ireland, or Wales, islands of Guernsey and Jersey, or town of Berwick upon Tweed, in any other ship or ships, vessel or vessels whatsoever, but in such as do truly and without fraud belong only to the people of England or Ireland, dominion of Wales, or town of Berwick upon Tweed, or of the lands, islands, plantations or territories in Asia, Africa, or America, to his Majesty belonging, as the proprietors and right owners thereof, and whereof the master, and three fourths at least of the mariners are English; . . .

XVIII. And it is further enacted by the authority aforesaid, that from and after the first day of April, which shall be in the year of our Lord one thousand six hundred sixty-one, no sugars, tobacco, cotton-wool, indigoes, ginger, fustic, or other dyeing wood, of the growth, production, or manufacture of any English plantations in America, Asia, or Africa, shall be shipped, carried, conveyed, or transported from any of the said English plantations to any land, island, territory, dominion, port, or place whatsoever, other than to such other English plantations as do belong to his Majesty, his heirs and successors, or to the kingdom of England or Ireland, or principality of Wales, or town of Berwick upon Tweed, there to be laid on shore; . . .

XIX. And be it further enacted by the authority aforesaid, that for every ship or vessel, which from and after the five and twentieth day of December in the year of our Lord one thousand six hundred and sixty shall set sail out of or from England, Ireland, Wales, or town of Berwick upon Tweed, for any English plantation in America, Asia, or Africa, sufficient bond shall be given with one surety to the chief officers of the custom-house of such port or place from whence the said ship shall set sail, to the value of one thousand pounds, if the ship be of less burden than one hundred tons; and of the sum of two thousand pounds, if the ship shall be of greater burden; that in case the said ship or vessel shall load any of the said commodities at any of the said English plantations, that the same commodities shall be by the said ship brought to some port of England, Ireland, Wales, or to the port or town of Berwick upon Tweed, and shall there unload and put on shore the same, the danger of the seas only excepted; . . .

3.5 Memorial of Governor Shute to the King, 1723

A key factor in the evolving relationship between the colonies and England was the rise of the assembly, an elected body of representatives that generally attempted to limit the power and authority of the governor (see Document 3.1). By the early eighteenth century, the General Assembly in Massachusetts had become very independent, regularly ignoring the wishes of the royally appointed governor. This selection is part of a memorial to the king from Samuel Shute, governor of Massachusetts from 1716 to 1723. In it he complains of the ways the General Assembly was usurping the king's authority, and he advances the view that such actions required the intervention of Parliament. That body, of course, did not intervene decisively for almost four decades.

Consider:

1. *The assumptions that Shute makes on the proper role of the General Assembly; and also Shute's expectations;*
2. *Whether the actions of the General Assembly were intended as a direct challenge to king and Parliament;*
3. *What would happen if these actions of the General Assembly were left unchecked over a period of years.*

. . . I soon called the General Assembly together. I found the House of Representatives, who are chosen annually, possessed of all the same powers of the House of Commons, and of much greater, they having the power of nominating once a year the persons that constitute your

SOURCE: *Merrill Jensen, ed., English Historical Documents, American Colonial Documents to 1776 (New York: Oxford University Press, 1955), 260–64.*

Majesty's Council, etc., and giving the salary of the governor and lieutenant-governor but from six months to six months; . . . The said House likewise appoint the salary of the treasurer every year whereby they have in effect the sole authority over that important office, which they often use in order to intimidate the treasurer from obeying the proper orders for issuing money, if such orders are not agreeable to their views and inclinations. By all which means the House of Representatives are in a manner the whole legislative, and in a good measure the executive power of the province. . . . The House of Representatives . . . have for some years last past been making attempts upon the few prerogatives that have been reserved to the Crown; which for that reason, as well as from the obligation of my oath and the trust reposed in me by your Majesty, I have endeavoured to my utmost to maintain against all invasions whatsoever.

I would humbly beg leave to lay before your Majesty some instances in which they have endeavoured to wrest those prerogatives out of your royal hands. (1) The House of Representatives have denied your Majesty's right to the woods in the province of Maine, contrary to the reservations in their charter, to an act of Parliament of Great Britain, and the instructions I received from your Majesty, etc. . . . (2) The House of Representatives would have refused me the power of a negative on the choice of their Speaker, which I thought it necessary to make use of against Mr. Cooke when he was chosen to that office, he having publicly opposed your Majesty's known rights to those woods. And the said House, insisting on their choice notwithstanding the negative I had given it, I dissolved that Assembly and then made a representation of the whole matter to the right honourable, the Lords of Trade, who sent me the opinion of your Majesty's Attorney-General, that the power was vested in your Majesty's governor for the time being. And when they acquainted me at the next meeting of the House of Representatives by a message, that they had chosen Mr. Clarke for their Speaker, and I had returned them for answer that I approved their said choice, the House of Representatives sent me this message, viz., "that they did not send up the foregoing message for my approbation, but for my information only", and since that time, whenever the Speaker has been absent by sickness, or otherwise, they have never failed to choose the said Mr. Cooke Speaker *pro tempore*. (3) The House of Representatives voted a public fast throughout your Majesty's said province, a thing never attempted by any of their predecessors; it being very well known that that power was always vested in and exercised by your Majesty's governor in that and all other colonies in America. (4) Though the royal charter has vested in the governor only the power of proroguing the General Assembly, yet the House of Representatives sent up a vote to the Council adjourning the General Assembly to the town of Cambridge; to which I refused to give my assent, and yet after this they adjourned themselves for several days without my consent or privity, and did not meet me on the day to which I had adjourned the General Assembly. . . . (7) The House of Representatives ordered a committee to command the officers at the eastern and western parts of the province to draw out their forces and muster them only under colour of an order signed by their Speaker. . . . upon my arrival I had good reason given to me to expect that they would allow me for my salary, £1,500 per annum of the money current there. But they gave me no more the first year than £1,200 of that money. . . . though provisions have been much dearer since, they have given me no more than £1,000 per annum of that money, which is now so much reduced in its value that £260 is but equal to £100 sterling, and therefore is now above a third less in value than when I first arrived there, . . . They vote me that sum by moieties at each session of their Assembly, which is once in six months, but even that they don't give me till I have passed the bills in the respective sessions, thereby to constrain me as far as they can to consent to any bills they lay before me. In the last sessions of the Assembly they have voted me no salary at all, so that I have been, and must be, without any support from them for some time. . . .

3.6   The Role of the Lower Houses of Assembly

Jack P. Greene

The lower houses of the colonial legislatures, sometimes called assemblies, tended to be made up of an emerging colonial elite. The assemblies continually sought greater political authority, even when it meant rejecting acts of Parliament and the instructions of the king. Colonials argued that the assemblies were lawmaking institutions that were not subordinate to Parliament or the crown. The English, on the other hand, tended to view the colonies as subordinate to both. By the middle of the eighteenth century, these divergent views were coming into clear focus. In this selection, historian Jack P. Greene examines the successful quest of the colonial assemblies for power.

Consider:

1. The similarities between Greene's description of the colonial assemblies' quest for authority and the complaints of Governor Shute (Document 3.5);
2. The validity of Greene's conclusion that the successful quest of the assemblies for political authority formed the basis for "the theory of colonial equality with the mother country";
3. Whether the growing controversy over the relationship of the colonies to England was simply a matter of honest disagreement between men of good will, and whether these disagreements were reconcilable.

The rise of the representative assemblies was perhaps the most significant political and constitutional development in the history of Britain's overseas empire before the American Revolution. Crown and proprietary authorities had obviously intended the governor to be the focal point of colonial government with the assemblies merely subordinate bodies called together when necessary to levy taxes and ratify local ordinances proposed by the executive. Consequently, except in the New England charter colonies, where the representative bodies early assumed a leading role, they were dominated by the governors and councils for most of the period down to 1689. But beginning with the Restoration and intensifying their efforts during the years following the Glorious Revolution, the lower houses engaged in a successful quest for power as they set about to restrict the authority of the executive, undermine the system of colonial administration laid down by imperial and proprietary authorities, and make themselves paramount in the affairs of their respective colonies. . . .

Before the Seven Years' War the quest was characterized by a considerable degree of spontaneity, by a lack of awareness that activities of the moment were part of any broad struggle for power. Rather than consciously working out the details of some master plan designed to bring them liberty or self-government, the lower houses moved along from issue to issue and from situation to situation, primarily concerning themselves with the problems at hand and displaying a remarkable capacity for spontaneous action, for seizing any and every opportunity to enlarge their own influence at the executive's expense and for holding tenaciously to powers they had already secured. . . .

Fundamentally, the quest for power in both the royal and the proprietary colonies was a struggle for political identity, the manifestation of the political ambitions of the leaders of emerging societies within each colony. . . . In the eighteenth century a group of planters, merchants, and professional men had attained or were rapidly acquiring within the colonies wealth and social position. The lower houses' aggressive drive for power reflects the determination of this new elite to attain through the representative assemblies political influence as well. . . .

But the quest for power involved more than the extension of the authority of the lower houses within the colonies at the expense of the colonial executives. After their initial stage of evolution, the lower houses learned that their real antagonists were not the governors but the proprietors or Crown officials in London. . . .

Behind the struggle between colonial lower houses and the imperial authorities were two divergent, though on the colonial side not wholly

SOURCE: Jack P. Greene, "The Role of the Lower Houses of Assembly in Eighteenth-Century Politics," Journal of Southern History 27 (1961): 451–53, 455–59, 460. Copyright © 1961 by the Southern Historical Association. Reprinted by permission of the Managing Editor.

articulated, concepts of the constitutions of the colonies and in particular of the status of the lower houses. To the very end of the colonial period, imperial authorities persisted in the views that colonial constitutions were static and that the lower houses were subordinate governmental agencies with only temporary and limited lawmaking powers . . . In working out a political system for the colonies in the later seventeenth century, imperial officials had institutionalized these views in the royal commissions and instructions. Despite the fact that the lower houses were yearly making important changes in their respective constitutions, the Crown never altered either the commissions or instructions to conform with the realities of the colonial political situation and continued to maintain throughout the eighteenth century that they were the most vital part of the constitutional structure of the royal colonies. . . .

. . . the lower houses . . . found it necessary to develop a body of theory with which to oppose unpopular instructions from Britain and to support their claims to greater political power. . . .

One of the most important of these rights was the privilege of representation. . . . an elected assembly was a fundamental right of a colony arising out of an Englishman's privilege to be represented and that they did not owe their existence merely to the King's pleasure. . . . The logical corollary to this argument was that the lower houses were equivalents of the House of Commons and must perforce in their limited spheres be entitled to all the privileges possessed by that body in Great Britain. . . .

. . . With the rapid economic and territorial expansion of the colonies in the years before 1763 had come a corresponding rise in the responsibilities and prestige of the lower houses and a growing awareness among colonial representatives of their own importance, which had served to strengthen their long-standing, if still imperfectly defined, impression that colonial lower houses were the American counterparts of the British House of Commons. Under the proper stimuli, they would carry this impression to its logical conclusion: that the lower houses enjoyed an equal status under the Crown with Parliament. Here, then, well beyond the embryonic stage, was the theory of colonial equality with the mother country, one of the basic constitutional principles of the American Revolution, waiting to be nourished by the series of crises that beset imperial-colonial relations between 1763 and 1776.

3.7   Colonial Stirrings: "Join or Die"

In 1754, in response to instructions from the Board of Trade in England, commissioners from the different colonies met in Albany, New York, to confer with Indian chiefs from the Iroquois Confederation about joint defense against the French and their Indian allies. Benjamin Franklin, who was a commissioner from Pennsylvania at the time, drew up a plan for uniting the colonies under one government for common defense against the French and Indians. The Congress adopted the Albany Plan of Union that Franklin had proposed. In an effort to promote adoption of the plan by colonial assemblies, Franklin printed the following sketch in his newspaper. This engraving, which was reproduced widely in other newspapers, has been called the first political cartoon in American history.

Consider:

1. *The message that Franklin was trying to convey to his readers;*
2. *Whether the image of a snake had a particular significance;*
3. *What each piece of the snake represented, and why there were only eight pieces.*

SOURCE: *Courtesy of the Library of Congress.*

CHAPTER QUESTIONS

1. *What might the king and Parliament have done to retain control of colonial affairs and minimize the trend toward independence? Could such policies have succeeded?*
2. *Over the years historians have offered three broad explanations—political, constitutional, and economic—for the growth of colonial conflict with England. Of these three explanations, which one do you think best fits the available evidence?*

Chapter 4

Societal Patterns in British North America

Between 1620 and 1763, the population of British North America increased from about 2,000 to more than 2,000,000, and the two initial settlements—Jamestown and Plymouth Plantation—expanded to thirteen colonies. Although most of the population was English, there were also many immigrants from other European countries who brought with them different social values, religious beliefs, languages, and customs. And even among the English there were major differences that showed up in regional societal patterns.

In the New England colonies, religious uniformity provided the basis for a cohesiveness and order in society that persisted well into the eighteenth century, long after the pressure for religious conformity had declined. In the Southern colonies, the expansion of slavery made the issue of race an increasingly important dimension of life. Finally, the Middle colonies, which were peopled by diverse ethnic groups, developed the cultural pluralism that has become a distinctive characteristic of American society. A key aspect of this cultural pluralism was religious toleration.

Over the years, Americans have deemphasized this diversity in colonial life, focusing instead on the building of the "democratic" foundation in the seventeenth and eighteenth centuries. This foundation included religious freedom, the town meeting as an expression of democracy, and the absence of class and status issues.

The documents in this chapter focus on these and other prominent societal patterns in the colonies. These patterns, along with the political developments discussed in the previous chapter, helped set the stage for severing the colonial ties with Britain in 1776.

Chronology

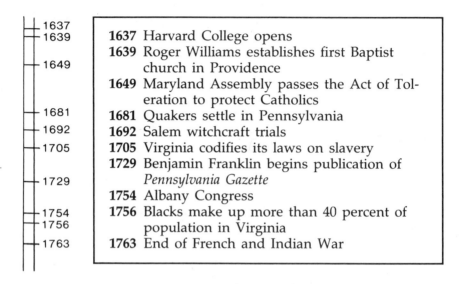

1637	**1637** Harvard College opens
1639	**1639** Roger Williams establishes first Baptist church in Providence
1649	**1649** Maryland Assembly passes the Act of Toleration to protect Catholics
1681	**1681** Quakers settle in Pennsylvania
1692	**1692** Salem witchcraft trials
1705	**1705** Virginia codifies its laws on slavery
1729	**1729** Benjamin Franklin begins publication of *Pennsylvania Gazette*
1754	**1754** Albany Congress
1756	**1756** Blacks make up more than 40 percent of population in Virginia
1763	**1763** End of French and Indian War

Documents

4.1 Religious Freedom

Roger Williams   Nathaniel Ward

In the first half of the seventeenth century, religious toleration was the exception rather than the rule in colonial America. By 1650, only two colonies—Maryland and Rhode Island—permitted religious toleration. Roger Williams, a Puritan minister and the founder of Rhode Island, was a leading exponent of religious toleration who believed that church and state should be separated. True religion, he argued, could flourish only if the government did not coerce uniformity in religious practice. In his book *The Bloody Tenent of Persecution for the Cause of Conscience*, 1644, Williams spelled out his views. Three years later, Nathaniel Ward, a Puritan minister in the Massachusetts Bay Colony, published a tract called *The Simple Cobbler of Aggawam*, which attacked religious toleration. The selection here consists of two excerpts, one from each of these two works.

Consider:

1. *What assumptions Williams and Ward each make about the nature and governance of colonial American society;*
2. *Whether religious toleration is simply indifference, as Ward suggests;*
3. *How a pluralistic society can perpetuate religious values and beliefs without governmental coercion.*

ROGER WILLIAMS, "THE BLOODY TENET OF PERSECUTION"

First, That the blood of so many hundred thousand soules of *Protestants* and *Papists*, split in the *Wars* of *present* and *former Ages*, . . . is not *required* nor *accepted* by *Jesus Christ* the *Prince* of *Peace*.

Secondly, Pregnant *Scripturs* and *Arguments* are throughout the Worke proposed against the *Doctrine* of *persecution* for *cause* of *Conscience*.

Thirdly, Satisfactorie Answers are given to *Scriptures*, and objections produced by Mr. *Calvin*, *Beza*, Mr. *Cotton*, and the Ministers of the New English Churches and others former and later, tending to prove the *Doctrine of persecution* for cause of *Conscience*.

Fourthly, The *Doctrine of persecution* for cause of *Conscience*, is proved guilty of all the *blood* of the *Soules* crying for *vengeance* under the *Altar*.

Fifthly, All *Civill States* with their *Officers* of *justice* in their respective *constitutions* and *administrations* are proved *essentially Civill*, and therefore not *Judges*, *Governours* or *Defendours* of the *Spirituall* or *Christian state* and *Worship*.

Sixthly, It is the will and command of *God*, that (since the coming of his *Sonne* the *Lord Jesus*) a *permission* of the most *Paganist*, *Jewish*, *Turkish*, or *Antichristian consciences* and *worships*, bee granted to *all* men in all *Nations* and *Countries*: and they are onely to bee *fought* against with that *Sword* which is only (in *Soule matters*) *able* to *conquer*, to wit, the *Sword of Gods Spirit*, the *Word of God*.

Seventhly, The *state* of the Land of *Israel*, the *Kings* and *people* thereof in *Peace & War*, is proved *figurative* and *ceremoniall*, and no *patterne* nor *president* for any *Kingdome* or *civill state* in the *world* to follow.

Eightly, God requireth not an *uniformity* of *Religion* to be *inacted* and *inforced* in any *civill state;* which inforced *uniformity* (sooner or later) is the greatest occasion of *civill Warre* . . .

SOURCE: *Roger Williams, The Bloody Tenent of Persecution (1644), 3–4; Nathaniel Ward, The Simple Cobbler of Aggawam in America (1647), 9–12.*

Ninthly, In holding an inforced *uniformity* of *Religion* in a *civill state*, wee must necessarily *disclaime* our desires and hopes of the *Iewes* [Jews'] *conversion to Christ*.

Tenthly, An inforced *uniformity* of *Religion* throughout a *Nation* or *civill state*, confounds the *Civill* and *Religious*, denies the principles of Christianity and civility, and that *Jesus Christ* is come in the Flesh.

Eleventhly, The permission of other *consciences* and *worships* than a state professeth, only can (according to God) procure a firme and lasting *peace*, (good *assurance* being taken according to the *wisdome* of the *civill state* for *uniformity* of *civill obedience* from all sorts).

Twelfthly, lastly, true *civility* and *Christianity* may both flourish in a *state* or *Kingdome*, notwithstanding the *permission* of divers and contrary *consciences*, either of *Iew* or *Gentile*.

NATHANIEL WARD, "THE SIMPLE COBBLER OF AGGAWAM"

He that is willing to tolerate any religion, or discrepant way of religion, besides his own, unless it be in matters merely indifferent, either doubts of his own or is not sincere in it.

He that is willing to tolerate any unsound opinion, that his own may also be tolerated, though never so sound, will for a need hang God's Bible at the devil's girdle.

Every toleration of false religions, or opinions, hath as many errors and sins in it as all the false religions and opinions it tolerates, and one sound one more.

That state that will give liberty of conscience in matters of religion, must give liberty of conscience and conversation in their moral laws, or else the fiddle will be out of tune and some of the strings crack.

He that will rather make an irreligious quarrel with other religions than try the truth of his own by valuable arguments, and peaceable sufferings, either his religion, or himself, is irreligious. . . .

That there is no rule given by God for any state to give an affirmative toleration to any false religion or opinion whatsoever; . . .

The Scripture saith there is nothing makes free but truth, and truth saith there is no truth but one. If the states of the world would make it their . . . care to preserve this one truth in its purity and authority it would ease them of all other political cares. I am sure Satan makes it his grand, if not only task, to adulterate truth . . .

There is talk of an universal toleration. I would talk what I could against it did I know what more apt and reasonable sacrifice England could offer to God for his late performing all his heavenly truths than an universal toleration of all hellish errors, or how they shall make an universal reformation but by making Christ's academy the devil's university, where any man may commence heretique *per saltum;* where he that is *filius Diabolicus*, or *simpliciter pessimus*, may have his grace to go to hell *cum Publico Privilegio;* and carry as many after him as he can.

4.2 Democracy in Massachusetts
Michael Zuckerman

Traditionally, the New England town meeting has been considered one of the foundation stones of American democracy. According to this view, the relatively egalitarian nature of New England colonial society was reflected in the town meeting, where issues of common concern were discussed by the community and a course of action was decided. This was "grass-roots" democracy in which the people were full participants. In the selection here, historian Michael Zuckerman challenges this view, arguing that consensus rather than majority rule governed the political process in local Massachusetts communities.

Consider:

1. *The connection between Puritanism and the emphasis on consensus and unanimity in New England town meetings;*
2. *The arguments that can be raised against Zuckerman's interpretation;*
3. *What connection there is between town meetings and twentieth-century democracy in the United States.*

. . . Committed to a conception of the social order that precluded pluralism, the townsmen of Massachusetts never made a place for those who were not of their own kind. The community they desired was an enclave of common believers, and to the best of their ability they secured such a society, rooted not only in ethnic and cultural homogeneity but also in common moral and economic ideas and practices. Thus, the character of the community became a critical—and non-democratic—condition of provincial democracy; for a wide franchise could be ventured only after a society that sought harmony had been made safe for such democracy. In that society it was possible to let men vote precisely because so many men were not allowed entry in the first place.

Thus we can maintain the appearance of democracy only so long as we dwell on elections and elections alone, instead of the entire electoral process. As soon as we depart from that focus, the town meetings of Massachusetts fall short of any decent democratic standard. Wide participation did obtain, but it was premised on stringently controlled access to eligibility, so that open elections presupposed anterior constriction of the electorate. Similarly, most men could vote, but their voting was not designed to contribute to a decision among meaningful alternatives. The town meeting had one prime purpose, and it was

SOURCE: *Michael Zuckerman, "The Social Context of Democracy in Massachusetts,"* William and Mary Quarterly 25 (1968): 538–40, 544.

not the provision of a neutral battleground for the clash of contending parties or interest groups. In fact, nothing could have been more remote from the minds of men who repeatedly affirmed, to the very end of the provincial period, that "harmony and unanimity" were what "they most heartily wish to enjoy in all their public concerns." Conflict occurred only rarely in these communities . . . When it did appear it was seen as an unnatural and undesirable deviation from the norm. . . . and in the absence of any socially sanctioned role for dissent, contention was generally surreptitious and scarcely ever sustained for long. The town meeting accordingly aimed at unanimity. Its function was the arrangement of agreement or, more often, the endorsement of agreements already arranged, and it existed for accommodation, not disputation.

Yet democracy devoid of legitimate difference, dissent, and conflict is something less than democracy; and men who are finally to vote only as their neighbors vote have something less than the full range of democratic options. Government by mutual consent may have been a step in the direction of a deeper-going democracy, but it should not be confused with the real article. Democratic consent is predicated upon legitimate choice, while the town meetings of Massachusetts in the provincial era, called as they were to reach and register accords, were still in transition from assent to such consent. . . .

This demand for unanimity found its ultimate expression in rather frequent denials of one of the most elementary axioms of democratic theory, the principle of majority rule. A mere majority often commanded scant authority at the local level and scarcely even certified decisions as legitimate. In communities which provided no regular place for minorities a simple majority was not necessarily sufficient to dictate social policy. . . .

. . . Most men may have been able to vote in the eighteenth-century town, but the town's true politics were not transacted at the ballot box so much as at the tavern and all the other places, including the meeting itself, where men met and negotiated so that the vote might be a mere ratification, rather than a decision among significant alternatives. Alternatives were antithetical to the safe conduct of the community as it was conceived at the Bay, and so to cast a vote was only to participate in the consolidation of the community, not to make a choice among competing interests or ideals.

4.3   Salem Witchcraft Trials

In 1692, the community of Salem, Massachusetts, became caught up in hysteria over the alleged practice of witchcraft. The strange behavior of several children and the mysterious actions of two West Indian slaves, who purportedly practiced voodoo, led to widespread accusations of witchcraft. Eventually, nineteen residents of Salem were put to death. The picture here depicts the trial of George Jacobs (kneeling at right), who was charged by Salem girls (left foreground) with practicing witchcraft. The court found Jacobs guilty and ordered him hanged on August 19, 1692.

Consider:

1. *The basic message the artist is trying to convey in this picture;*
2. *Why the girl in the left foreground is stretched out and being attended to by several adults;*
3. *Why witchcraft trials occurred only in New England.*

SOURCE: *Courtesy of the Essex Institute, Salem, Massachusetts.*

4.4   Colonial Class Status
Arthur M. Schlesinger, Sr.

Among the more common ideas that Americans have of themselves and their past is the notion of a democracy of the middle class. This applies, in particular, to the seventeenth and eighteenth centuries in British North America, when a titled nobility failed to take root. Nonetheless, a governing class or informal power structure did exist, one that was open only to free, successful white adult males. Historians have noted that colonial society accorded members of this governing class the "deference" due to social superiors. In the following selection, historian Arthur M. Schlesinger, Sr., although not specifically using the term "deference," describes the stratified society in colonial America and tells how it worked.

Consider:

1. *How deference to members of the governing class in colonial society can be reconciled with the concept of democracy and the revolt against British authority;*
2. *Whether class and status are inherent in society, regardless of the political structure.*

The colonists unhesitatingly took for granted the concept of a graded society. It was the only kind they had known in Europe, and they had no thought of foregoing it in their new home. Indeed, they possessed a self-interested reason for retaining it. In this outpost of civilization it was man alone, not his ancestors, who counted. Even the humblest folk could hope to better their condition, for the equality of opportunity which they now had attained meant, as well, the opportunity to be unequal. The indentured servant, the apprentice, the common laborer, everyone in fact but the Negro bondsman, could expect to stand on his own feet and get on and up in the world. . . .

For the settlers to build a structured society on their own initiative and in their own interest was, however, quite another matter. This they proceeded to do in colony after colony as rapidly as time and circumstances permitted. In the case of Massachusetts, though, they did not have to wait. Not only did the founders themselves belong to Britain's rural and urban gentry but, as good Puritans, they considered their superior station divinely ordained. In the words of their first governor, John Winthrop, "God Almightie in his most holy and wise providence hath soe disposed of the Condicion of mankinde, as in all

SOURCE: *Arthur M. Schlesinger, Sr., "The Aristocracy in Colonial America,"* Proceedings of the Massachusetts Historical Society *74 (1962): 3–21. Courtesy Massachusetts Historical Society.*

times some must be rich some poore, some highe and emminent in power and dignitie; others mean and in subieceion." Accordingly, the men so favored immediately assumed the key positions in government and society, sharing the honors with the foremost clergymen. . . .

But the Southern aristocracy attained the closest resemblance to the English landed gentry. There, in a predominantly rural economy, men on the make enjoyed the decisive advantage of an extensive servile class as well as of broad acres. . . .

The Southern gentry, however, possessed an energy and resourcefulness uncharacteristic of its Old World prototype. To maintain its position the members had to be men of affairs—tireless and responsible directors of a system of agricultural labor alien to the homeland, which, moreover, was used for the raising of staple crops uncultivated there and grown on great and often scattered plantations. They could not, however much they wished, constitute in the same sense a leisure class. . . .

The continuous recruitment of the top stratum of the community from beneath reveals sharply the basic aspect of colonial society: its fluidity, the incessant movement of people upward. The American aristocracy, however undemocratic when once it took form, was undeniably democratic in the method of its forming. The only class struggle in that far day was the struggle to climb out of a lower class into a higher one, for, as Nathaniel Ames put it in one of his almanacs,

> *All Men are by Nature equal,*
> *But differ greatly in the sequel.*

The self-made man thus began his career in America, to become in time a national folk hero. In the absence of England's officially prescribed ranks it was, above all, the acquisition of wealth which elevated a family to the social heights. Extensive land grants and other perquisites from the government, obtained perhaps through favoritism or fraud, might expedite the process. Further help could, and often did come, from lucrative marriages. . . . But, for the most part, it was industry and ability applied imaginatively to beckoning opportunities that ensured the outcome. . . .

By 1776 the colonial aristocracy had endured for more than a century and a half in the oldest regions, for over a century in others, and had sunk deep roots elsewhere. With the passage of time it had consolidated its position and constantly replenished its vitality with transfusions of new blood. Its members had not, moreover, used their station exclusively for self-aggrandizement and outward show but, as a class, had considered themselves trustees for the common good, identifying their welfare with that of the community at large. In the case of the Southern gentry the need to superintend the lives of hosts of slaves served to heighten this sense of stewardship, making them feel as fit to rule as were the guardians to whom Plato had entrusted his republic.

In all the colonies men of quality occupied responsible posts in every sphere of official activity: the executive department, the provincial and local lawmaking branches, the armed forces, the judiciary. True, the alternative would have been to allow ill-prepared and possibly rash underlings to seize the reins, but the deeper reason lay in the conviction that only the rich and wellborn possessed the required wisdom and capacity. In no less degree they provided the cultural leadership. They not only exemplified for all to see the refinements of living, but they set standards of tasteful architecture and well-kept grounds and through their patronage enabled portrait painters to pursue their calling. In like fashion they assembled the best private libraries and afforded their sons superior intellectual advantages. And from their largess came the principal benefactions to religion and education, to charity and projects of community improvement.

Nor did their role in any of these respects excite resentment among the mass of the population. Men in every walk of life not only accepted the concept of a layered society, but believed in its rightness. The clergy preached it; all classes practiced it. Whatever might be the shortcomings of the English aristocracy—and colonial editors repeated from the London press lurid accounts of its immoralities and profligacy—the American variety was no privileged group living off the unearned increment of ancestral reputations. They, by and large, had mounted the heights through shrewdness and ability and had stayed there by the continued exercise of those faculties. The ordinary citizen deemed it only proper to accord them deference. . . .

4.5 Distribution of Wealth in Boston, 1687 and 1771

One way of evaluating the extent of hierarchy in American colonial society is by the distribution of wealth. The more evenly wealth is distributed, the more open and fluid the social structure. In the following graph, historian James Henretta summarizes statistical data derived from the tax records of Boston. The data show that between 1687 and 1771, the number of people who controlled the bulk of taxable wealth in Boston declined, while the number of adult males having no property increased.

Henretta uses a statistical device called the Lorenz Curve to show this unequal distribution of wealth. The solid straight diagonal line moving from right to left represents a perfectly equal distribution of wealth. In a Lorenz Curve, the more unequal the distribution, the further the curve lies from the line of equality. In this graph, the solid curved line represents the distribution of wealth in 1687, while the broken line represents the distribution of wealth in 1771. The graph shows clearly that a significant shift took place between 1687 and 1771, with more taxable wealth being controlled by fewer people.

Consider:

1. *Whether the growing inequality in the distribution of taxable wealth indicates that society was becoming more rigid and stratified;*
2. *The impact geographic mobility (that is, the poor and the unsuccessful leaving Boston to try their luck elsewhere) would have on the actual "openness" of society;*
3. *Assuming that Henretta is correct about the unequal distribution of wealth, why a class-conscious urban proletariat failed to emerge to demand a more equal distribution of the wealth.*

DISTRIBUTION OF WEALTH IN BOSTON IN 1687 AND 1771

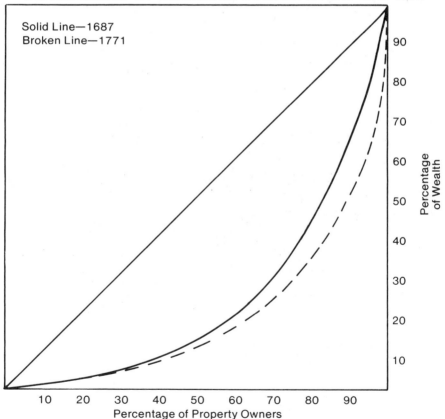

SOURCE: *James A. Henretta, "Economic Development and Social Development in Colonial Boston,"* William and Mary Quarterly *22 (1965): 92.*

4.6   Distribution of Slavery

Generally speaking, both the distribution and the growth of slavery in British North America in the seventeenth and eighteenth centuries were functions of the economy. For example, agricultural slavery was profitable only where a significant cash crop, such as tobacco or indigo, could be produced. Although the map here is based on statistics in 1775, the distribution of slavery reflects the overall picture in the eighteenth century.

Consider:

1. *Whether the density of the slave population affected the form slavery took in different places;*
2. *The effect the density of slave population might have had on the way slaves viewed themselves and their culture.*

SLAVERY IN THE COLONIES

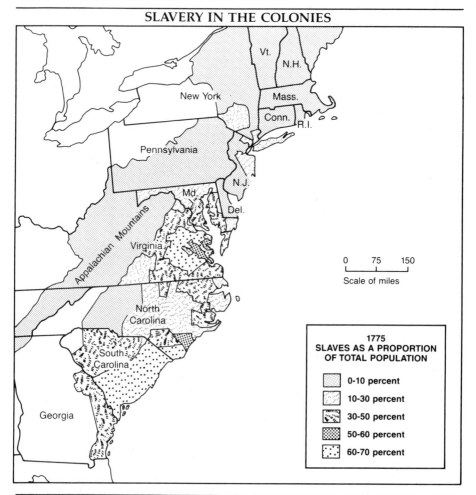

SOURCE: *James A. Henretta et al.,* America's History *(Chicago: Dorsey Press, 1987), I, 103.*

4.7   Cultural Pluralism in the Middle Colonies

Frederick B. Tolles

Between New England and the South lay the four Middle Colonies—New York, New Jersey, Delaware, and Pennsylvania. Unlike the colonies of New England and the South, the Middle Colonies had no established religions and their inhabitants represented a diverse mixture of Europeans, many of whom settled in enclaves and retained their own ethnic identities. In the following excerpt from an article entitled "The Culture of Early Pennsylvania," historian Frederick B. Tolles argues that ethnic diversity in Pennsylvania both permitted and required disparate elements to mingle and compete, resulting in cultural pluralism.

Consider:

1. *The basic elements of the cultural pluralism that Tolles describes;*
2. *The extent to which cultural pluralism accounts for differences between life in the Middle Colonies and life in the colonies of New England and the South;*
3. *Whether cultural pluralism is inevitably the constructive force that Tolles suggests it to be.*

A cultural map of the settled portion of Pennsylvania in 1740 would show a band of Quaker country roughly parallel with the Delaware River and extending back twenty-five or thirty miles, its western outposts near Coatesville, Pottstown, and Quakertown. Behind it would be a broad belt of Pennsylvania Dutch country, anchored at Bethlehem to the northeast and at Lancaster to the southwest. Still farther west in the Susquehanna Valley would be a sparse strip of Scotch-Irish settlement, overlapping on its eastern side with the Pennsylvania Dutch country and swinging eastward in upper Bucks County, near where Neshaminy Creek joins the Delaware. There were a hundred thousand people in all, perhaps more. Scattered over these broad culture areas would be small pockets of people with different backgrounds—English and Welsh Baptists in the Quaker country, a handful of Roman Catholic and Jewish families in Philadelphia, four or five thousand Negroes, slaves and freedmen, and, here and there, some remnants of the ancient inhabitants of Pennsylvania—the Lenni Lenape or Delaware Indians.

Two of these "pocket groups" demand special mention. Along the Delaware south of Philadelphia lived several hundred descendants of the "old colonists"—the Swedes, Finns, and Dutch who had brought

SOURCE: *Frederick B. Tolles, "The Culture of Early Pennsylvania," Pennsylvania Magazine of History and Biography 81 (1957): 119–37. Reprinted with permission.*

the white man's culture to the Delaware Valley long before William Penn. By the end of a century, however, they had lost most of their distinguishing characteristics and had merged with the English culture around them. In Philadelphia there was a strong and growing Anglican community, which worshiped in style in the Palladian elegance of Christ Church. . . .

It was this region primarily that Hector St. John de Crèvecoeur had in mind when he asked his famous question, "What then is the American, this new man?" . . . Here, says Crèvecoeur, "individuals of all nations are melted into a new race of men, whose labors and posterity will one day cause great changes in the world." . . .

The familiar image of the melting pot seems to imply "a giant caldron in which foreigners are boiled down into a colorless mass— as insipid as any stew." Clearly that is not an accurate image of early Pennsylvania. To be sure, some groups melted. The Welsh apparently did. So did the Dutch in Germantown and the Swedes along the Delaware. But the Germans, by and large, did not. Indeed they seem to have become self-consciously German for the first time in Pennsylvania. . . . Some Philadelphia Quakers become Episcopalians, but the great majority did not; and there was never any *rapprochement* between the Quakers of the east and the Scotch-Irish Presbyterians of the west. . . .

. . . from about 1740 to the end of the eighteenth century Philadelphia was the intellectual and cultural capital of North America. In science, in medicine, in humanitarianism, in music and the drama and *belles lettres* its pre-eminence was unquestioned. How shall we explain this remarkable quick maturing in the youngest of the colonial towns? . . . the source of colonial Philadelphia's flowering . . . in the creative interaction of the elements in its cultural hinterland. . . .

. . . By opening the doors of Pennsylvania to people of every nation and every religion, he [William Penn] established a situation of cultural pluralism and thereby created the conditions for cultural growth. And the atmosphere was freedom.

CHAPTER QUESTIONS

1. *What were the main societal patterns in existence in the colonies by 1763?*
2. *What basic ideas and attitudes underlay the colonial societal patterns that developed between 1620 and 1763?*

part two

THE NEW NATION TAKES SHAPE, 1763–1820

Chapter 5

Choosing Sides in the Revolution

The decision for revolution did not come quickly or easily to the colonies. The causes were many and complex, and the steps leading up to final rupture were hesitant and marked by doubts. Throughout the critical decade between the Stamp Act and the outbreak of hostilities at Lexington and Concord, both radicals and moderates tried to gain control of the colonies' response to British authority. By the time revolution broke out in 1776, the radicals had gained control. Many of the moderates joined them enthusiastically in the cause of revolution. But there were others who were not convinced that it was better to fight England than to stay within the British Empire. These "Loyalists" chose to side with the British in the American Revolution.

Because history is usually written from the point of view of the winners, the Loyalist cause in the Revolution generally receives unflattering treatment. It must be remembered, however, that in the 1760s and 1770s the choice might not have been so clear for the colonists. Exposed to emotional and logical arguments on both sides of the question, and driven by pressures of community and family, individuals had to balance abstract principles with very practical concerns in reaching their decisions. Many did not decide until fighting had broken out; some probably never made a choice at all.

It is tempting, in retrospect, to conclude that at some point the American Revolution became inevitable. But inevitability in history is rare, and, besides, the inevitable is not always easy to recognize at the time. Those choosing sides in the 1770s had no idea how things would turn out. As in all revolutions, there was no "safe" choice.

This chapter focuses on the events and forces that led Americans to take one side or the other in the Revolution. The selections include the views of radicals and moderates and loyalists. Also included here are excerpts from the works of historians who have focused on the social context in which the American Revolution developed.

Chronology

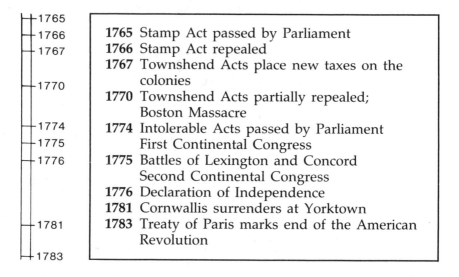

1765	Stamp Act passed by Parliament
1766	Stamp Act repealed
1767	Townshend Acts place new taxes on the colonies
1770	Townshend Acts partially repealed; Boston Massacre
1774	Intolerable Acts passed by Parliament First Continental Congress
1775	Battles of Lexington and Concord Second Continental Congress
1776	Declaration of Independence
1781	Cornwallis surrenders at Yorktown
1783	Treaty of Paris marks end of the American Revolution

Documents

5.1 Objections to Parliamentary Taxation, John Dickinson (primary source)

5.2 The Boston Massacre (visual source)

5.3 Women and the Revolutionary Cause, Mary Beth Norton (secondary source)

5.4 Justifying Rebellion (primary source)

5.5 A Loyalist Viewpoint, 1776, Charles Inglis (primary source)

5.6 A Call for Patriotic Resolve, Thomas Paine (primary source)

5.7 Forces for Conformity, Michael Zuckerman (secondary source)

5.8 Dealing with the Problem of Loyalists, Robert M. Calhoon (secondary source)

5.9 A Cartoon View of the Revolution (visual source)

5.1   Objections to Parliamentary Taxation

John Dickinson

Colonial opposition to the Stamp Act of 1765 led to its repeal. Parliament, however, continued to insist on its right to enact laws for the colonies in "all cases whatsoever." In 1767, it passed the Townshend Acts, which set duties on several basic goods from England. A particularly effective response from the colonies was written by John Dickinson. His *Letters from a Farmer in Pennsylvania* captured what appeared to be the prevailing sentiment in America: that there were limits to the authority of Parliament. However, the fine distinctions drawn by Dickinson in this selection were bypassed in the course of events, as the conflict between England and the colonies escalated sharply.

Consider:

1. *The distinctions Dickinson makes between the rights of the colonies and the authority of Parliament;*
2. *Whether his arguments were too narrow to succeed, or whether, under other circumstances, they might have provided a basis for settlement of the dispute.*

My dear Countrymen,

There is another late act of parliament, which appears to me to be unconstitutional, and as destructive to the liberty of these colonies, as that mentioned in my last letter; that is, the act for granting the duties on paper, glass, etc.

The parliament unquestionably possesses a legal authority to *regulate* the trade of *Great Britain*, and all her colonies. Such an authority is essential to the relation between a mother country and her colonies; and necessary for the common good of all. He who considers these provinces as states distinct from the *British Empire*, has very slender notions of *justice*, or of their *interests*. We are but parts of a *whole*; and therefore there must exist a power somewhere, to preside, and preserve the connection in due order. This power is lodged in the parliament; and we are as much dependent on *Great Britain*, as a perfectly free people can be on another.

I have looked over *every statute* relating to these colonies, from their first settlement to this time; and I find every one of them founded on this principle, till the *Stamp Act* administration. *All before*, are calculated

SOURCE: *John Dickinson*, Letters from a Farmer in Pennsylvania *(1767–68)*, in Empire and Nation, *ed. Forrest McDonald (Englewood Cliffs, N.J.: Prentice-Hall, Inc., 1962), 7–15.*

to regulate trade, and preserve or promote a mutually beneficial intercourse between the several constituent parts of the empire; and though many of them imposed duties on trade, yet those duties were always imposed *with design* to restrain the commerce of one part, that was injurious to another, and thus to promote the general welfare. The raising of a revenue thereby was never intended. Thus the King, by his judges in his courts of justice, imposes fines, which all together amount to a very considerable sum, and contribute to the support of government: But this is merely a consequence arising from restrictions that only meant to keep peace and prevent confusion; . . . Never did the *British* parliament, till the period above mentioned, think of imposing duties in *America* FOR THE PURPOSE OF RAISING A REVENUE. . . .

The [Townshend Act], granting duties upon paper, etc. carefully pursues these modern precedents. The preamble is, "Whereas it is expedient THAT A REVENUE SHOULD BE RAISED IN YOUR MAJESTY'S DOMINIONS IN AMERICA, *for making a more certain and adequate provision for defraying the charge of the administration of justice, and the support of civil government in such provinces, where it shall be found necessary; and towards further defraying the expences of defending, protecting and securing the said dominions, we your Majesty's most dutiful and loyal subjects, the* COMMONS OF GREAT BRITAIN, etc. GIVE and GRANT," etc. as before.

Here we may observe an authority *expressly* claimed and exerted to impose duties on these colonies; not for the regulation of trade; not for the preservation or promotion of a mutually beneficial intercourse between the several constituent parts of the empire, heretofore the *sole objects* of parliamentary institutions; *but for the single purpose of levying money upon us.*

This I call an innovation; and a most dangerous innovation. It may perhaps be objected, that *Great Britain* has a right to lay what duties she pleases upon her exports, and it makes no difference to us, whether they are paid here or there.

To this I answer. These colonies require many things for their use, which the laws of *Great Britain* prohibit them from getting any where but from her. Such are paper and glass.

That we may legally be bound to pay any *general* duties on these commodities, relative to the regulation of trade, is granted; but we being *obliged by her laws* to take them from *Great Britain*, any *special* duties imposed on their exportation *to us only, with intention to raise a revenue from us only*, are as much *taxes* upon us, as those imposed by the *Stamp Act*. . . .

Some persons perhaps may say that this act lays us under no necessity to pay the duties imposed because we may ourselves manufacture the articles on which they are laid; whereas by the *Stamp Act* no instrument of writing could be good unless made on *British* paper, and that too stamped. . . .

. . . But is no injury a violation of right but the *greatest* injury? If the eluding the payment of the taxes imposed by the *Stamp Act*, would have subjected us to a more dreadful inconvenience than the eluding of the payment of those imposed by the late act; does it therefore follow, that the last is *no violation* of our rights, tho' it is calculated for the same purpose the other was, that is, *to raise money upon us,* WITHOUT OUR CONSENT?

This would be making *right* to consist, not in an exemption from *injury,* but from a certain *degree of injury.*

. . . my dear countrymen, ROUSE yourselves, and behold the ruin hanging over your heads. If you ONCE admit, that *Great Britain* may lay duties upon her exportations to us, *for the purpose of levying money on us only,* she then will have nothing to do, but to lay those duties on the articles which she prohibits us to manufacture—and the tragedy of *American* liberty is finished. We have been prohibited from procuring manufactures, in all cases, any where but from *Great Britain.* . . . We have been prohibited, in some cases, from manufacturing for ourselves; and may be prohibited in others. . . . If *Great Britain* can order us to come to her for necessaries we want, and can order us to pay what taxes she pleases before we take them away, or when we land them here, we are as abject slaves as *France* and *Poland* can show in wooden shoes and with uncombed hair. . . .

. . . I think this uncontrovertible conclusion may be deduced, that when a ruling state obliges a dependent state to take certain commodities from her alone, it is implied in the nature of that obligation; . . . *that those commodities should never be loaded with duties,* FOR THE SOLE PURPOSE OF LEVYING MONEY ON THE DEPENDENT STATE.

Upon the whole, the single question is, whether the parliament can legally impose duties to be paid *by the people of these colonies only,* FOR THE SOLE PURPOSE OF RAISING A REVENUE, *on commodities which she obliges us to take from her alone,* or, in other words, whether the parliament can legally take money out of our pockets, without our consent. If they can, our boasted liberty is but

> *Vox et praeterea nihil.*
> A sound and nothing else.

5.2 The Boston Massacre: A Rallying Point for Rebellion

On March 5, 1770, rioting broke out in Boston, which had become a trouble spot for the British. A small group of townspeople set upon a British sentry near the custom house. A crowd gathered, British soldiers were summoned, and in the ensuing clash, five Bostonians were killed by gunfire from British troops. The "Boston Massacre," as the Americans called it, instantly became a symbol of British oppression. The engraving shown here was being circulated by Paul Revere within a day of the "massacre" in an effort to drum up public support for resistance.

Consider:

1. *What story the engraving tells about the event, and how this version of the event compares to the way it actually happened;*
2. *Whether "visual" propaganda is as effective as written and/or spoken propaganda.*

The BLOODY MASSACRE perpetrated in King—⊥—Street BOSTON on March 5th 1770 by a party of the 29th REGT.

Unhappy BOSTON! see thy Sons deplore,
Thy hallow'd Walks besmear'd with guiltless Gore.
While faithless P—n and his savage Bands,
With murd'rous Rancour stretch their bloody Hands;
Like fierce Barbarians grinning o'er their Prey,
Approve the Carnage, and enjoy the Day.

If scalding drops from Rage from Anguish Wrung,
If speechless Sorrows lab'ring for a Tongue,
Or if a weeping World can ought appease
The plaintive Ghosts of Victims such as these;
The Patriot's copious Tears for each are shed,
A glorious Tribute which embalms the Dead.

But know, Fate summons to that awful Goal,
Where JUSTICE strips the Murd'rer of his Soul:
Should venal C—ts the scandal of the Land,
Snatch the relentless Villain from her Hand,
Keen Execrations on this Plate inscrib'd,
Shall reach a JUDGE who never can be brib'd.

Engrav'd Printed & Sold by PAUL REVERE BOSTON

The unhappy Sufferers were Mess.rs SAM.L GRAY, SAM.L MAVERICK, JAM.S CALDWELL, CRISPUS ATTUCKS & PAT.K CARR
Killed. Six wounded two of them (CHRIST.R MONK & JOHN CLARK) Mortally

---

SOURCE: *Yale University Art Gallery, The John Morgan Hill Collection.*

5.3   Women and the Revolutionary Cause: The Daughters of Liberty

Mary Beth Norton

Whether to join in the escalating protest against British taxes and controls was a decision faced by women in the colonies, as well as by men. In the late 1760s, some women made effective contributions to the boycott of British goods and to the movement to stimulate "home industry" to promote greater economic independence for America. The spinning bees of the Daughters of Liberty were a part of the latter effort. As described in this selection by historian Mary Beth Norton, the bees suggested a changing role for American women, but at the same time they reinforced existing cultural stereotypes.

Consider:

1. *The sorts of women who would have been likely to participate in spinning bees;*
2. *The motives, besides the commitment to the cause of resistance, that might have fostered the Daughters of Liberty movement;*
3. *What kind of contribution women could make to the cause of resistance against the British.*

Women could hardly have remained aloof from the events of the 1760s and early 1770s even had they so desired, for, like male Americans, they witnessed the escalating violence of the prerevolutionary decade. . . .

. . . The male leaders of the boycott movement needed feminine cooperation, but they wanted to set the limits of women's activism. They did not expect, or approve, signs of feminine autonomy.

. . . [and they] failed to come to terms with the implications of the issues raised by the growing interest in politics among colonial women.

American men's inability to perceive the alterations that were occurring in their womenfolk's self-conceptions was undoubtedly heightened by the superficially conventional character of feminine contributions to the protest movement. Women participating in the boycott simply made different decisions about what items to purchase and consume; they did not move beyond the boundaries of the feminine sphere. Likewise, when colonial leaders began to emphasize the importance of producing homespun as a substitute for English cloth, they did not ask women to take on an "unfeminine" task: quite the contrary, for spinning was the very role symbolic of femininity itself. . . .

SOURCE: *Mary Beth Norton*, Liberty's Daughters: The Revolutionary Experience of American Women, 1750–1800 *(Boston: Little Brown and Co., 1980), 156, 163, 166–68. Copyright © 1980 Mary Beth Norton.*

Initially, the authors of newspaper articles recommending an expansion of home manufactures did not single out women for special attention. . . .

But this neglect did not continue beyond the end of 1768, for, as a writer in the *Providence Gazette* had noted late the previous year, "[W]e must after all our efforts depend greatly upon the female sex for the introduction of economy among us." The first months of 1769 brought an explosion in the newspaper coverage of women's activities, especially in New England. Stories about spinning bees . . . became numerous and prominently featured. . . .

It is impossible to know whether the increased coverage of spinning bees in 1769 indicated that women's activities expanded at precisely that time, or whether the more lengthy, detailed, and numerous stories merely represented the printers' new interest in such efforts. But one fact is unquestionable: the ritualized gatherings attended by women often termed Daughters of Liberty carried vital symbolic meaning both to the participants and to the editors . . .

The meetings, or at least the descriptions of them, fell into a uniform pattern. Early in the morning, a group of eminently respectable young ladies (sometimes as many as one hundred, but normally twenty to forty), all of them dressed in homespun, would meet at the home of the local minister. There they would spend the day at their wheels, all the while engaging in enlightening conversation. . . . At nightfall, they would present their output to the clergyman, who might then deliver a sermon on an appropriate theme. For example, . . . the Reverend John Cleaveland of Ipswich told the seventy-seven spinners gathered at his house, "[T]he women might recover to this country the full and free enjoyment of all our rights, properties and privileges (which is more than the men have been able to do)" by consuming only American produce and manufacturing their own clothes.

The entire community became involved in the women's activities. . . .

The formal spinning groups had a value more symbolic than real. They do not seem to have met regularly, and in most cases their output appears to have been donated to the clergyman for his personal use. The women might not even have consistently called themselves Daughters of Liberty, for many newspaper accounts did not employ that phrase at all. But if the actual production of homespun did not motivate the meetings, they were nonetheless purposeful. The public attention focused on organized spinning bees helped to dramatize the pleas for industry and frugality in colonial households, making a political statement comparable to men's ostentatious wearing of homespun on public occasions during the same years. The spinning bees were ideological showcases: they were intended to convince American women that they could render essential contributions to the struggle against Britain, . . .

5.4   Justifying Rebellion: "Declaration of the Causes and Necessity of Taking Up Arms," 1775

Less than a month after the skirmishes at Lexington and Concord, the Second Continental Congress convened in Philadelphia to work out plans for the emerging rebellion. Both radicals and moderates tried to impose their views. On July 5, 1775, Congress adopted a conciliatory "Olive Branch Petition" that held out the hope of reconciliation with the king. Then on July 6, Congress adopted a "Declaration of the Causes and Necessity of Taking Up Arms." Drafted largely by Thomas Jefferson and John Dickinson, the language of the declaration, excerpted below, was both rousing and cautious. It reflected a delicate balance between the opposing views of the delegates to the Congress.

Consider:

1. *The audience to which this statement is addressed, and whether it is really an appeal to the people to support the cause of liberty or a message to the king;*
2. *How radical a statement this was in the context of events in July 1775;*
3. *How persuasive the arguments presented are.*

Our forefathers, inhabitants of the island of Great-Britain, left their native land, to seek on these shores a residence for civil and religious freedom. At the expense of their blood, at the hazard of their fortunes, without the least charge to the country from which they removed, by unceasing labour, and an unconquerable spirit, they effected settlements in the distant and inhospitable wilds of America, then filled with numerous and warlike nations of barbarians.—Societies or governments, vested with perfect legislatures, were formed under charters from the crown, and an harmonious intercourse was established between the colonies and the kingdom from which they derived their origin. . . . It is universally confessed, that the amazing increase of the wealth, strength, and navigation of the realm, arose from this source; and the minister, who so wisely and successfully directed the measures of Great-Britain in the late war, publicly declared, that these colonies enabled her to triumph over her enemies.—Towards the conclusion of that war, it pleased our sovereign to make a change in his counsels.— From that fatal moment, the affairs of the British empire began to fall into confusion. . . . Parliament was influenced to adopt the pernicious

SOURCE: Documents Illustrative of the Formation of the Union of the American States *(Washington, D.C.: Government Printing Office, 1927), 10–13, 15–16.*

project, and assuming a new power over [the colonies], have in the course of eleven years, given such decisive specimens of the spirit and consequences attending this power, as to leave no doubt concerning the effects of acquiescence under it. They have undertaken to give and grant our money without our consent; . . . statutes have been passed for extending the jurisdiction of courts of admiralty and vice-admiralty beyond their ancient limits; . . . for suspending the legislature of one of the colonies; for interdicting all commerce to the capital of another; and for altering fundamentally the form of government established by charter. . . .

But why should we enumerate our injuries in detail? By one statute it is declared, that parliament can "of right make laws to bind us in all cases whatsoever." What is to defend us against so enormous, so unlimited a power? Not a single man of those who assume it, is chosen by us; or is subject to our control or influence; . . . We for ten years incessantly and ineffectually besieged the throne as supplicants; we reasoned, we remonstrated with parliament, in the most mild and decent language. . . .

. . . A Congress of delegates from the United Colonies was assembled at Philadelphia, on the fifth day of last September. We resolved again to offer an humble and dutiful petition to the King, and also addressed our fellow-subjects of Great-Britain. We have pursued every temperate, every respectful measure. . . . but subsequent events have shown, how vain was this hope of finding moderation in our enemies. . . .

. . . We are reduced to the alternative of choosing an unconditional submission to the tyranny of irritated ministers, or resistance by force.— The latter is our choice.—We have counted the cost of this contest, and find nothing so dreadful as voluntary slavery.—Honour, justice, and humanity, forbid us tamely to surrender that freedom which we received from our gallant ancestors, and which our innocent posterity have a right to receive from us. We cannot endure the infamy and guilt of resigning succeeding generations to that wretchedness which . . . awaits them, if we basely entail hereditary bondage upon them.

Our cause is just. Our union is perfect. Our internal resources are great, and, if necessary, foreign assistance is undoubtedly attainable.— We gratefully acknowledge, as signal instances of the Divine favour towards us, that his Providence would not permit us to be called into this severe controversy, until we were grown up to our present strength, had been previously exercised in warlike operation, and possessed of the means of defending ourselves. . . .

Lest this declaration should disquiet the minds of our friends and fellow-subjects in any part of the empire, we assure them that we mean not to dissolve that union which has so long and so happily subsisted between us, and which we sincerely wish to see restored. . . . We exhibit to mankind the remarkable spectacle of a people attacked by unprovoked enemies, without any imputation or even suspicion of offence. . . .

In our own native land, in defence of the freedom that is our birthright, and which we ever enjoyed till the late violation of it—for the protection of our property, acquired solely by the honest industry of our fore-fathers and ourselves, against violence actually offered, we have taken up arms.

5.5 A Loyalist Viewpoint, 1776

Charles Inglis

Thomas Paine's eloquent and inflammatory pamphlet *Common Sense*, published in January 1776, became an overnight best-seller. It sold 20,000 copies within a few months and raised the level of political rhetoric to new heights. But the Loyalist cause, too, had effective pamphleteers, and, like the advocates of rebellion, Loyalist writers employed both logic and emotionalism in their arguments. In this tract, written in direct response to *Common Sense*, an Anglican clergyman named Charles Inglis set forth the advantages of a quick reconciliation between the colonies and Great Britain.

Consider:

1. *To what degree Inglis used logic and emotionalism in his arguments;*
2. *Whether Inglis based his appeal on humanitarian grounds, and whether humanitarian appeals are an effective way to win converts to a cause;*
3. *The kinds of arguments that could be developed to counter Inglis's position.*

CHARLES INGLIS:

The True Interest of America

I THINK IT NO DIFFICULT MATTER to point out many advantages which will certainly attend our reconciliation and connection with Great Britain. . . .

By a reconciliation with Britain, a period would be put to the present calamitous war, by which so many lives have been lost, and so many more must be lost if it continues. . . .

By a reconciliation with Great Britain, peace—that fairest offspring and gift of heaven—will be restored. In one respect peace is like health— we do not sufficiently know its value but by its absence. . . .

Agriculture, commerce, and industry would resume their wonted vigor. . . .

SOURCE: *Charles Inglis, "The True Interest of America," in* The Annals of America, II: 1755– 1783, Resistance and Revolution (*Chicago: Encyclopaedia Britannica, Inc., 1968*), 403–04, 406, 409.

By a connection with Great Britain, our trade would still have the protection of the greatest naval power in the world. . . . Past experience shows that Britain is able to defend our commerce and our coasts; and we have no reason to doubt of her being able to do so for the future.

The protection of our trade, while connected with Britain, will not cost us a *fiftieth* part of what it must cost were we ourselves to raise a naval force sufficient for the purpose.

While connected with Great Britain, we have a bounty on almost every article of exportation; and we may be better supplied with goods by her than we could elsewhere. . . . The manufactures of Great Britain confessedly surpass any in the world, particularly those in every kind of metal, which we want most; and no country can afford linens and woolens of equal quality cheaper. . . .

These advantages are not imaginary but real. . . .

The Americans are properly Britons. They have the manners, habits, and ideas of Britons; and have been accustomed to a similar form of government. But Britons never could bear the extremes, either of monarchy or republicanism. Some of their kings have aimed at despotism, but always failed. Repeated efforts have been made toward democracy, and they equally failed. Once, indeed, republicanism triumphed over the constitution; the despotism of one person ensued; both were finally expelled. The inhabitants of Great Britain were quite anxious for the restoration of royalty in 1660, as they were for its expulsion in 1642, and for some succeeding years. If we may judge of future events by past transactions, in similar circumstances, this would most probably be the case of America were a republican form of government adopted in our present ferment. . . .

However distant humanity may wish the period, yet, in the rotation of human affairs, a period may arrive when (both countries being prepared for it) some terrible disaster, some dreadful convulsion in Great Britain may transfer the seat of empire to this Western Hemisphere—where the British constitution, like the Phoenix from its parent's ashes, shall rise with youthful vigor and shine with redoubled splendor.

But if America should now mistake her real interest . . . they will infallibly destroy this smiling prospect. They will dismember this happy country, make it a scene of blood and slaughter, and entail wretchedness and misery on millions yet unborn.

5.6   A Call for Patriotic Resolve, 1776

Thomas Paine

After publishing *Common Sense* in early 1776, Thomas Paine joined the Continental Army. Later that year, he began publication of a series of pamphlets, collectively entitled *The Crisis*, that were designed to keep patriotic resolve at full strength. In the first pamphlet of *The Crisis*, excerpted here, Paine has a particularly interesting discussion of the Loyalists, or "Tories," and their motives.

Consider:

1. *The audience to which Paine directs his arguments;*
2. *How Paine attempts to appeal to those who may be sympathetic to Loyalists and Loyalist arguments;*
3. *The logic of Paine's suggestion that Loyalists, if unwilling to fight, should abandon their support for the British cause.*

THE CRISIS.

NUMBER I.

THESE are the times that try men's souls. The summer soldier and the sunshine patriot will, in this crisis, shrink from the service of his country; . . . Tyranny, like hell, is not easily conquered; yet . . . the harder the conflict, the more glorious the triumph. What we obtain too cheap, we esteem too lightly. . . .

. . . God Almighty will not give up a people to military destruction, or leave them unsupportedly to perish, who have so earnestly and so repeatedly sought to avoid the calamities of war, by every decent method which wisdom could invent. . . . I cannot see on what grounds the king of Britain can look up to heaven for help against us: a common murderer, a highwayman, or a house-breaker, has as good a pretence as he. . . .

I shall conclude this paper with some miscellaneous remarks. . . . Why is it that the enemy have left the New England provinces, and made these middle ones the seat of war? The answer is easy: New England is not infested with tories, and we are. . . . And what is a tory? Good God! what is he? I should not be afraid to go with a hundred whigs against a thousand tories, were they to attempt to get into arms. Every tory is a coward; for servile, slavish, self-interested fear is the foundation of toryism; and a man under such influence, though he may be cruel, never can be brave. . . .

. . . let us reason the matter together: your conduct is an invitation to the enemy, yet not one in a thousand of you has heart enough to join him. [British General] Howe is as much deceived by you as the American cause is injured by you. He expects you will all take up arms, and flock to his standard, with muskets on your shoulders. Your

SOURCE: *Thomas Paine,* The Crisis, *No. 1 (December 23, 1776), in* The Complete Political Works of Thomas Paine *(New York: The Freethought Press Association, 1954), II, 69–70, 73–78.*

opinions are of no use to him, unless you support him personally, for 'tis soldiers, and not tories, that he wants.

I once felt all that kind of anger, which a man ought to feel, against the mean principles that are held by the tories: a noted one, who kept a tavern at Amboy, was standing at his door, with as pretty a child in his hand, about eight or nine years old, as I ever saw, and after speaking his mind as freely as he thought was prudent, finished with this unfatherly expression, *"Well! give me peace in my day."* Not a man lives on the continent but fully believes that a separation must some time or other finally take place, and a generous parent should have said, *"If there must be trouble, let it be in my day, that my child may have peace;"* and this single reflection, well applied, is sufficient to awaken every man to duty. Not a place upon earth might be so happy as America. Her situation is remote from all the wangling world, and she has nothing to do but to trade with them. A man can easily distinguish in himself between temper and principle, and I am as confident, as I am that God governs the world, that America will never be happy till she gets clear of foreign dominion. Wars, without ceasing, will break out till that period arrives, and the continent must in the end be conqueror; for though the flame of liberty may sometimes cease to shine, the coal can never expire. . . .

Quitting this class of men, I turn with the warm ardor of a friend to those who have nobly stood, and are yet determined to stand the matter out: I call not upon a few, but upon all: not on *this* state or *that* state, but on *every* state; . . . Let it be told to the future world, that in the depth of winter, when nothing but hope and virtue could survive, that the city and the country, alarmed at one common danger, came forth to meet and to repulse it. . . . Not all the treasures of the world, so far as I believe, could have induced me to support an offensive war, for I think it murder; but if a thief breaks into my house, burns and destroys my property, and kills or threatens to kill me, or those that are in it, and to *"bind me in all cases whatsoever,"* to his absolute will, am I to suffer it? What signifies it to me, whether he who does it is a king or a common man; . . . Let them call me rebel, and welcome, I feel no concern from it; but I should suffer the misery of devils, were I to make a whore of my soul by swearing allegiance to one whose character is that of a sottish, stupid, stubborn, worthless, brutish man. . . .

There are cases which cannot be overdone by language, and this is one. . . . It is the madness of folly, to expect mercy from those who have refused to do justice; . . .

I thank God that I fear not. I see no real cause for fear. I know our situation well, and can see the way out of it. . . . Once more we are again collected and collecting, our new army at both ends of the continent is recruiting fast, and we shall be able to open the next campaign with sixty thousand men, well armed and clothed. . . . By perseverance and fortitude we have the prospect of a glorious issue. . . .

5.7   Forces for Conformity

Michael Zuckerman

Social pressures often played a major role in the decision individuals made about which side to support in the Revolution. This was especially true in areas such as New England, where the bonds of local community were very strong. At the least, such pressures could cause those favoring the British side to remain silent, even if they did not change their views.
The selection here, taken from Michael Zuckerman's book on eighteenth-century New England town life, describes the ways in which these community pressures were brought to bear on individual residents.

Consider:

1. The influence of religion on the nature of the "committees of inspection";
2. How the sense of "community" described here compares to the more general conditions of New England "democracy" discussed by Zuckerman in Document 4.2;
3. Whether the activities of the committees, and the existence of such strong social pressures for conformity, are inconsistent with political democracy.

. . . men behaved in the era of the Revolution much as they had grown accustomed to behave before. Public opinion was still their essential engine of control, and they still assumed the canons of consensus because they lived in communities of consensus and knew no other norms. What they had done for almost a century, they continued to do for the few years of the Revolution.

Long before battle itself broke out, massive majorities were binding themselves to a common course while exerting no sanctions against the few who failed to comply but the sanctions of exposure. In the nonimportation agreements of 1770, for instance, towns such as Newburyport resolved not to use or buy foreign tea, and, according to a town historian, "public opinion was the principal means of enforcement [of their resolution] by the threat of publishing the names of unrepentant offenders as 'pests of Society & Enemies of ye Country.'" Newburyport did appoint a committee of inspection to give effect to the agreement, but even its efforts were essentially appeals to publicity, being basically the circulation of "a pledge to be signed by all the inhabitants determined not to buy, sell, or use India tea,"with those who refused to sign "to be reported to the next town meeting.". . . Similar sanctions applied in other towns, and they continued to apply until the very eve of armed rebellion. . . .

SOURCE: *Michael Zuckerman,* Peaceable Kingdoms: New England Towns in the Eighteenth Century, *240–47. Copyright © 1970 by Michael Zuckerman. Reprinted by permission of Alfred A. Knopf, Inc.*

Of course exposure was no empty threat—moral isolation was not easy to maintain in a town of two or three hundred families—but the essential point is that exposure was often the only threat. The committees of inspection in such cases were given no police powers, only the powers of publicity; and even the few who refused compliance were at first urged only to reconsider their recalcitrance. The truth was that town discipline in the Revolution resembled nothing so much as church discipline throughout the provincial era. Reform rather than retribution was its primary purpose, because punishment could, at best, purge the community, whereas repentance restored its moral integration. . . .

Formal censure was the simplest expression of that pressure, and its power carried far beyond its ostensible objects because, like every other exemplary punishment, it threatened everyone. For every man explicitly disciplined, there were a hundred others on whom the lesson was not lost, a hundred others who were also reminded to consider the consequences of defiance. But formal censure was certainly not the only instrument of intimidation nor the only technique to dispel dissent. In other towns accusation served, and in still others, interrogation and scrutiny or the drafting of statements to be subscribed by all inhabitants deemed dubious in their loyalty.

The essential point is that in every case it was publicity which was the purpose, and even when men went beyond moral suasion to physical coercion, exposure was still their ultimate intention. . . . Tarring-and-feathering too lacked any basic intention to inflict bodily injury for its own sake. The crucial part of the penalty occurred *after* the application of tar and feathers, when the culprit was carted about the town so that his disgrace might serve "as an object lesson to others as well as himself," for "the shame and ridicule of carting acted as a more effective deterrent . . . than either imprisonment or stripes." Physical force simply could not compare with social sanctions. The same didactic design also guided the hanging-in-effigy, a sanction even more obviously exemplary in its intention than the tar brush. . . .

. . . In this sense it did not matter that some towns tarred and feathered and others hung in effigy, that some accused and others inquisitioned or insisted upon sworn statements. These were only vagaries of town taste in tactics, not indications of deeper-lying differences in strategy. Dissent was conceived as a danger in every town, and everywhere men were discontent with a simple majority. Dissident minorities were to be eliminated rather than merely outvoted, for no town aimed at anything less than perfect unity.

Thus the unanimous votes that characterized the years of revolutionary crisis were consciously created. . . .

An important instrument of agreement was the town committee. The fundamental function of a committee, ordinarily, was the formal arrangement of its community's internal accord. . . . if the community was in fact divided, committees could also be established in many places, to create common feelings where none existed before. In those cases they were composed of representatives of the contending factions, and they were set apart so that their differences could be composed and a common ground discovered. . . .

If the gentle methods of committees and publicity failed, then more rigorous ones were used. Sometimes they entailed only an attack on the appearance of protest, as when town records were adjusted or falsified. But on other occasions they aimed at the protest itself, and even at the protestants. In Stockbridge, for example, a man had to flee for the mountains, "where his family fed him until the worst of the excitement died down," after he cast the town's lone dissenting vote against national independence. In other places other disabilities and dangers confronted dissenters, particularly those who professed loyalism. They and their families were isolated within the community—the very term "Tory" was one of obvious opprobrium, its effect not much different than a hanging in effigy—and then, often, they were driven from it, by demands for a conformity beyond their capacity. The demands were rather commonly enforced by an impetuous populace suddenly mounted as a mob, and mobs sprang up all over the province. . . .

Of course, it was not every dissident who was menaced by a mob—although many were—nor every loyalist who lost all his local property in confiscation proceedings—although many more did. But it was the case, quite commonly, that the cost of safety was silence. It was a fact that open opposition to the communal course was apt to irritate or even enrage a band of men bent on an appearance of absolute agreement, and it was a fact that, inexorably, dissenting impulses were extinguished, in high places and in low. . . .

This was the way in which the broad social imperatives of consensus impinged on particular men in particular places and drove dissent from the community. This was the coercive power of common attitudes and expectations.

5.8   Dealing with the Problem of Loyalists
Robert McCluer Calhoon

The question of how to treat Americans who sympathized with the British posed complex problems. The Revolution had, of course, grown out of dissent. It was difficult, then, for the rebels to deny the right of dissent. On the other hand, this was war; opposition to the revolutionary cause could be justifiably viewed as treason. But was the Revolution in effect a *civil* war? If so, how should the revolutionary governments deal with men and women who, following their consciences, chose not to rebel? This selection describes the treatment of Loyalists in Pennsylvania, traditionally a haven of tolerance within America.

Consider:

1. *Whether the definitions and prescribed punishments for treason in the 1777 Pennsylvania law seem consistent with the principles underlying the Revolution;*
2. *Whether the American Revolution should be considered essentially a civil war;*
3. *Whether treason should be defined and/or punished differently in a civil war than in a war against a foreign nation.*

. . . In response to Congress's recommendation in June 1776 that states make treason a crime, the Pennsylvania Constitutional Convention on September 5, 1776, assuming legislative authority, enacted a rather conventional statute defining treason as the levying of war against Pennsylvania, the adherence to the King, or the aiding and comforting of the British by any inhabitant or voluntary resident of the state. . . . concealing knowledge of traitorous actions or aiding persons involved in them was the lesser crime of "misprision of treason." The lack of a court system at this early stage in the state's independence, however, prevented this moderate law from ever being enforced. A less-restrained ordinance against "seditious utterances" allowed justices of the peace to jail without jury trial or bail persons who spoke or wrote in opposition to the work of Congress and were deemed to possess dangerous influence. . . .

Goaded by their inability to command broad public support, the radical Whigs looked for scapegoats. In November 1776 a group of partisans launched a vigilante campaign, breaking into homes and seizing and jailing suspected loyalists. . . . The house searches had turned up no documentary evidence, and the only evidence presented at the hearing was testimony that the suspects had been overheard singing "God Save the King" at private social gatherings. Support for the drive against suspected loyalists dissipated, and by the middle of September 1777 the Council of Safety had paroled all but one of the victims of the November raids. Even this rather weak drive against British sympathizers, however, altered the precarious balance in Pennsylvania between tendencies of toleration and vengeance; . . . "The significant result of this flare-up," Henry J. Young writes, "was that some of the ablest men in the state were alienated" from the new government by the actions of "an irresponsible minority." . . .

The moderates reasserted themselves when the legislature created a legal system for the state in January and February 1777. It declared English common law binding in Pennsylvania so far as it did not conflict with the creation of republican government and the defense of independence, and it replaced the treason ordinance of 1776 with

SOURCE: *Robert M. Calhoon,* The Loyalists in Revolutionary America, 1760–1781. *Copyright © 1965, 1969, 1973 by Robert M. Calhoon. Reprinted by permission of Harcourt Brace Jovanovich, Inc.*

a new statute . . . the act designated seven offenses as high treason, punishable by death, forfeiture of all property, and disinheritance of the traitor's family: accepting a commission from the British, levying war, enlisting in the King's service, recruiting others to enlist, furnishing arms or supplies to the enemy, corresponding with British officials, or giving them intelligence. . . . the new treason law defined the lesser offense of misprision of treason as speaking or writing against military preparedness, attempting to send intelligence to the British, attempting to incite others to submit to British authority, discouraging men from enlisting in the American forces, "stirring up tumults or disposing people to favor the enemy, opposing or endeavoring to prevent . . . revolutionary measures." . . .

. . . the legislature created, in March 1778, a more drastic weapon— a confiscation act providing for bills of attainder. This legislation named particular loyalists who had joined the British and gave them until April 21, 1778, to surrender themselves and stand trial for treason. . . . eight separate proclamations between 1778 and 1781 invoked the penalties on nearly 500 persons. . . . The sheer volume of treason convictions under the Act of Attainder meant that some innocent people lost their estates on flimsy and unsubstantiated evidence, although 386 of the 500 persons named failed to appear within the time limits set by the attainder proclamations because they had fled to the protection of the British. Of the 113 who did surrender, less than twenty ever came to trial, because there was insufficient evidence to warrant prosecution. . . .

. . . The most dangerous figures were not men who had fled to the British and could be handled by attainder prosecutions that confiscated their property; on the contrary, they were gangs of outlaws who aided the British and also enriched themselves in the process. . . . it was easier to convict loyalists of robbery and counterfeiting than of actual treason, and to impose the death penalty for the lesser offense. . . . Forty-eight men were hanged in Pennsylvania during the War for Independence for offenses other than treason. Of twenty-two men tried for counterfeiting in Pennsylvania between 1779 and 1782, eleven were convicted and five hanged.

5.9   A Cartoon View of the Revolution

At the time of the Revolution, political cartoons were not common in the colonies, but British cartoons were available. The cartoon here, published in England in 1779, attempted to portray a complex situation through a simple drawing with no text. In many English cartoons of the time, America is portrayed by an Indian, usually a female. In this drawing, the horse represents the colonies and King George III is the rider; the figure in the background is a Frenchman.

Consider:

1. *What the lash held by the rider conveys about the artist's opinion of the American Revolution;*
2. *The implications of portraying America as an Indian, and whether America as a horse portraying in this drawing had different implications;*
3. *The possible significance of the presence of a Frenchman in the background of this drawing.*

THE HORSE AMERICA, *throwing his Master.*

Pub.d as the Act directs Aug.t 1.st 1779. by W.m White, Angel Court, Westminster.

SOURCE: *"The Horse America, Throwing His Master"* (August 1779, William White), in The American Revolution in Drawings and Print, *ed. Donald H. Cresswell (Washington, D.C.: Library of Congress, 1975), plate 749.*

CHAPTER QUESTIONS

1. *Did the political principles of the American revolutionaries make them inclined to tolerate dissent from their cause? To what extent is it possible for a people at war to tolerate dissent?*
2. *Why did the colonists take pains at first to direct their complaints against Parliament rather than against the king? Do you think this distinction may have helped broaden the base of support for the Revolution?*
3. *Did it require more courage for a colonist to support the Revolution or to remain loyal to the British crown?*

Chapter 6

A Republic Takes Shape

A s the conflict between the colonists and Britain developed, Americans relied increasingly on ideas of representative democracy, or "republicanism," to make their case for independence. It was to be expected, then, that once freed of imperial control, they would try to establish a republican form of government.

In developing their arguments, the Americans felt they were upholding, rather than challenging, English political thought and practice. Citing philosophers such as John Locke and Montesquieu, the disgruntled colonists emphasized the social contract as the basis for legitimate government and the need for powers to be separated and "balanced" to avoid tyranny.

Many of the views expressed by colonial leaders differed sharply from accepted principles of English politics. American ideas about sovereignty, representation, and equality were all novelties; as a basis for a national government, they had no precedent. In this sense, Americans were shaping an entirely new kind of political system even though they drew—consciously and with pride—from British experience.

It soon became clear that it would be no simple matter to balance the egalitarian spirit of the Declaration of Independence with requirements for social order, morality, and the defense of property. These last three points were considered essential by those who were building the new republic. If sovereignty lay with the people, it was nonetheless thought necessary to guard against the kinds of excesses that, historically, had plagued democracies. And, though all men were conceded to have "unalienable" rights, it was felt that some men were more fit to govern than others. In this setting, the forces supporting democratic idealism contended with those favoring elitist conservatism. In the end, these conflicting views led to the document that provided the framework for the new republic—the United States Constitution.

This chapter focuses on both the idealism and the underlying skepticism and practicality that influenced the way the republic developed. The selections that follow reveal the optimism that Americans felt about republicanism, and show how the new republic created a mythology to help sustain itself.

Chronology

┤1776 ┤1777 ┤1781 ┤1783 ┤1786 ┤1787 ┤1788 ┤1789	**1776** Declaration of Independence **1777** Articles of Confederation written **1781** Articles of Confederation ratified **1783** Treaty of Paris marks end of American Revolution **1786** Shays's Rebellion **1787** Northwest Ordinance 　　　Constitutional Convention 　　　*The Federalist* written by Hamilton, Jay, and Madison (October 1787–April 1788) **1788** The Constitution ratified June 21 **1789** George Washington inaugurated as first President April 30

Documents

6.1   High Hopes for the Republic, Gordon S. Wood (secondary source)

6.2   The Decline of Political Deference, William J. Cooper, Jr. (secondary source)

6.3   A Government of Laws, Timothy Stone (primary source)

6.4   Washington: Hero of the Republic, John Trumbull (visual source)

6.5   Controlling Factions in the Republic, James Madison (primary source)

6.6   Minority Rights in the Republic, Timothy Ford (primary source)

6.7   Justifying Slavery in the Republic, David Brion Davis (secondary source)

6.8   Woman's Place in the Republic, Linda Kerber (secondary source)

6.9   The Republic in Art, Abijah Canfield (visual source)

6.1   High Hopes for the Republic

Gordon S. Wood

In breaking away from England in 1776, the colonies did not necessarily intend to abandon the English type of government. British principles of mixed government and republicanism were taken over by the revolutionaries and adapted in a new, uniquely American type of government. This selection, from Gordon Wood's book on the political principles underlying the Constitution, describes the high hopes Americans had that a republican government could "regenerate" the people. The selection also tells of the colonists' sense of the great risks of their venture.

Consider:

1. *What aspects of republicanism, as the revolutionaries understood it, made Americans so optimistic;*
2. *To what extent republicanism exerts a force for "reestablishing and preserving . . . virtue and equality" in society.*

The Americans' confidence in their republican future, bred from the evils and anxieties of the past, was not as illusory and as unjustified as it might on the face of it seem. Their new republican governments were to be more than beacons to the oppressed of the world, more than the consequences of revolution. They were themselves to be the agencies of revolution. There was, the eighteenth century believed, a reciprocating relationship between the structure of the government and the spirit of its people. . . . On one hand, there was no doubt that the nature of the government must be adapted to the customs and habits of the people. . . . Yet, on the other hand, politics was not regarded simply as a matter of social determinism; the form of government was not merely a passive expression of what the spirit of the people dictated. . . . Republicanism was therefore not only a response to the character of the American people but as well an instrument of reform. "If there is a form of government, then," John Adams asked of his countrymen in 1776, "whose principle and foundation is virtue, will not every sober man acknowledge it better calculated to promote the general happiness than any other form?" A republican constitution "introduces knowledge among the people, and inspires them with a conscious dignity becoming freemen; a general emulation takes place, which causes good humor, sociability, good manners, and good morals to be general. That elevation of sentiment inspired by such a government,

SOURCE: *Gordon S. Wood, The Creation of the American Republic, 1776–1787, 118–21, 123–24. Copyright © 1969 The University of North Carolina Press. Reprinted by permission of the publisher and author.*

makes the common people brave and enterprising. That ambition which is inspired by it makes them sober, industrious, and frugal.". . .

. . . By the repeated exertion of reason, by "recalling the lost images of virtue: contemplating them, and using them as motives of action, till they overcome those of vice again and again until after repeated struggles, and many foils they at length acquire the habitual superiority," by such exertions it seemed possible for man to recover his lost innocence and form a society of "habitual virtue." From these premises flowed much of the Americans' republican iconography—the "Pomp and Parade," as John Adams called it. . . .

Only this faith in the regenerative effects of republican government itself on the character of the people can explain the idealistic fervor of the Revolutionary leaders in 1776. Concentrating on the nicely reasoned constitutional arguments of John Adams or Jefferson in order to prove the moderation of the Revolution not only overlooks the more inflamed expressions of other Whigs but also misses the enthusiastic and visionary extravagance in the thinking of Adams and Jefferson themselves. . . . For Jefferson, faith in the future was always easier than for Adams, and he of all the Revolutionary leaders never seemed to lose heart. . . . In Jefferson's mind the Revolution was just beginning in 1776. . . .

Yet even as the clergy and Revolutionary leaders were filling the air with their visionary and passionate anticipations in 1776, the underlying anxiety was never lost. . . . Their image of themselves was truly ambivalent. With their eyes and ears turned toward Europe they marveled at their republican mediocrity and simplicity. Yet when they searched inward they saw all the evils the Enlightenment had told them they lacked. Their society seemed strangely both equal and unequal, virtuous and vicious. The erecting of republican governments, therefore, was not only a natural political adjustment to the social reality of the New World, but also (and hopefully) the instrument for reestablishing and preserving the virtue and equality Americans thought they had been losing prior to the Revolution. . . .

It was a grandiose and dangerous experiment, and because it has succeeded so well (although not as the Revolutionaries anticipated), it is difficult to appreciate their sense of the precariousness of what they were attempting. They realized fully the delicacy of the republican polity and the difficulties involved in sustaining it. . . .

Indeed, it is only in the context of this sense of uncertainty and risk that the Americans' obsessive concern in 1776 with their social character can be properly comprehended. They knew only too well where the real source of danger lay. "We shall succeed if we are virtuous," Samuel Adams told John Langdon in the summer of 1777. "I am infinitely more apprehensive of the Contagion of Vice than the Power of all other Enemies."

6.2   The Decline of Political Deference
William J. Cooper, Jr.

Throughout the seventeenth and much of the eighteenth centuries, patterns of political deference prevailed in colonial society, especially in the South (see Document 4.4). Political deference refers to the attitude of respect colonists accorded members of the governing class. As this selection suggests, the Revolution loosened the hold of these patterns of behavior, which were not easy to reconcile with the egalitarian tone of the Declaration of Independence. The Constitution, however, had a very different tone. Many of those who participated in drafting the Constitution regarded themselves as the "natural leaders" of the new nation, and their attitude was reflected in the document. Indeed, *The Federalist* writers argued that political deference was fundamental to republican government's success.

Consider:

1. *The nature of the conflict between Thompson and Rutledge;*
2. *Whether the rise to prominence of men like Elijah Clarke suggests that, despite the decline of deference, one established leadership was being replaced by another.*

Because of the Revolution white southerners of the lower social orders began to question the deference they had previously shown to their social betters. When dealing with such broad societal attitudes, the focus has to be on trends, not on absolutes. In the colonial period there had surely been lower-class southerners who refused to fit neatly into their expected role; just as surely after the Revolution many of them continued to feel comfortable with the old deferential ways. But the Revolution did spawn a general shift away from deference, a shift illustrated by an episode that occurred in South Carolina in 1784.

In that year the South Carolina assembly threatened to banish from the state one William Thompson, a tavern keeper, for insulting John Rutledge, a former governor and dominant figure in the ruling group. In a public address defending himself Thompson stood deference on its head. Admitting that Rutledge "conceived me his inferior," Thompson announced that he could not understand Rutledge's attitude. As a former officer in the revolutionary army, Thompson said he only requested the respect he deserved. Calling himself "a *wretch* of no higher rank in the Commonwealth than that of Common-Citizen" and identifying himself with "those who more especially, who go at this day, under the opprobrious appelation of, the *Lower Orders of Men*," Thompson

SOURCE: *William J. Cooper, Jr.,* Liberty and Slavery: Southern Politics to 1860 *(New York: Alfred A. Knopf, Inc., 1983), 43–44.*

pitched into "*John Rutledge*, or any of the NABOB *tribe*," who claim "to compose the grand hierarchy of the State. . . ." Thompson argued that leadership of an independent people, of a republic required of men "being *good, able, useful* and *friends to social equality*," and nothing more. Not only did Thompson fail to act deferentially, he also assaulted the citadel of deferential government.

More and more men who shared William Thompson's view of the requirements for republican rulers began populating assemblies, or legislatures as they came to be called, and taking a more active role in government. In Virginia the number of wealthy men in the legislature declined by half after the war. Similarly in Maryland and South Carolina more ordinary citizens sought and won election to the legislature. Military leadership brought such rough-hewn, untutored men as Elijah Clarke of Georgia to prominence. A back-country guerrilla leader, Clarke used his wartime reputation to embark on a notable postwar career in his state. Individuals such as Clarke would probably not have become important figures before 1775. The war breached forever old walls of political leadership as a sanctuary of the privileged.

The disestablishment of the Anglican church also contributed to the weakening of deference. Everywhere in the 1780s legislatures dismantled the legal framework that had given Anglicanism special privileges. This elimination of an established church removed an important prop that had helped support the special station of the gentry, most of whom were Anglican. While the Anglican church lost its status as the established church, the evangelical Protestant denominations surged across the South. Led by the Baptists and the Methodists, these churches brought increasingly large numbers of southerners into their fold. Emphasizing individualism and shunning any trappings of rank or privilege, the evangelicals offered only meager assistance to a concept of deference already beleaguered by secular forces. Although the bulk of the political leadership still retained its Anglican ties, the increasing political influence of the evangelicals testified to the impact of their rapidly growing denominations. . . .

6.3   A Government of Laws

Timothy Stone

The Constitution—particularly with the addition of the Bill of Rights—was intended as a safeguard against potentially unjust laws. Yet a basic tenet of republicanism was that the citizens should pass laws to govern themselves, and the new republic was to be a government of laws, rather than of men. This selection, taken from a 1792 sermon by a Congregationalist minister, argues strongly that just laws, conscientiously enforced and equally binding upon all citizens, are the ultimate guarantee of civil liberty.

Consider:

1. *How Stone's definition of "civil liberty" compares with the common understanding of the term today, and whether his definition makes sense;*
2. *Whether Stone's position can be reconciled with the practice of political deference;*
3. *How Stone's argument about the faithful execution of all laws compares with the colonists' reaction to British laws they considered unjust.*

Civil liberty is one of the most important blessings which men possess of a temporal nature, the most valuable inheritance on this side of heaven. That constitution may therefore be esteemed the best, which doth most effectually secure this treasure to a community. . . . Civil liberty, consists in the being and administration of such a system of laws, as doth bind all classes of men, rulers and subjects, to unite their exertions for the promotion of virtue and public happiness. . . . A state of society necessarily implies reciprocal dependence in all its members; and rational government, is designed to realize and strengthen this dependance, and to render it, in such sense equal in all ranks, from the supreme magistrate, to the meanest peasant, that each one may feel himself bound to seek the good of the whole. . . . The laws of a state, should equally bind every member, whether his station be the most conspicuous, or, the most obscure. Rulers in a righteous government, are as really under the control of laws, as the meanest subject: and the one equally with the other, should be subjected to punishment, when ever he becomes criminal, by a violation of the law. Rewards and punishments, should be equally distributed. . . .

Enacting salutary laws, discovers the wisdom and good design of legislators: but the liberty and happiness of the community, essentially depend upon their regular execution. The best code of laws can answer no good purposes, any further than it is executed. Every member in society is bound, in duty to the community, himself, and posterity, to use his endeavours that the laws of the state be carried into execution. . . .

. . . Laws while they remain such, ought to be executed, when found to be useless or hurtful, they may be repealed: to have laws in force and not executed, or to obstruct the natural course of law in a free state, must be dangerous; will have many hurtful tendencies, will greatly weaken government, and render all the interests of the community insecure. Liberty, property and life, are all precarious, in a state where laws cease in their execution. . . . it must be the wisdom, the indispensible duty of all characters in society, to unite their exertions, for the support of righteous laws, in their regular administration. . . .

SOURCE: *Timothy Stone, "Election Sermon" (Hartford, Connecticut, 1792), in* American Political Writing During the Founding Era, 1760–1805, *eds. Charles S. Hyneman and Donald S. Lutz (Indianapolis: Liberty Press, 1983), II, 842–44.*

6.4   Washington: Hero of the Republic
John Trumbull

The concept of the equality of all men was one of the basic assumptions underlying the new republic, and it was expressed explicitly in the Declaration of Independence. The government of laws was to affect all people equally. Yet many historians have contended that George Washington, had he so desired, might have become monarch—or at least President for life—of the new nation. This painting by John Trumbull (1756–1843), completed in the early years of Washington's presidency, depicts Washington's victory at Trenton in 1776 in a heroic fashion. Often called "the painter of the Revolution," Trumbull captures here the reverential attitude of the public toward the nation's first President.

Consider:

1. *The elements in Trumbull's composition that suggest an "unrepublican" attitude toward Washington;*
2. *How this painting compares to the other example of "republican art" included in this chapter (Document 6.9).*

SOURCE: *John Trumbull, "Capture of the Hessians at Trenton" (1789). Copyright Yale University Art Gallery.*

6.5   Controlling Factions in the Republic

James Madison

The Constitution produced in 1787 by the convention at Philadelphia was by no means uncontroversial. It had to be "sold" to the people as a document that carried forward the principles of the Declaration of Independence and would also reflect accepted attitudes about political and social relations. One important issue, for example, was how "interests," or "factions"—especially those based on property and economic considerations—might fit into the new form of government. In *The Federalist, No. 10*, James Madison (1751–1836) addresses this issue. Writing under the pseudonym "Publius," he presents a tightly reasoned argument that the republican government described in the Constitution afforded the best possible protection against the dangers of "faction."

Consider:

1. *On the basis of this essay, how Madison felt about "deference" in politics;*
2. *How the tone and spirit of* The Federalist, No. 10, *compares with the optimism about republicanism described in the first selection in this chapter (Document 6.1);*
3. *Madison's views on minority rights as reflected in this selection.*

Among the numerous advantages promised by a well-constructed Union, none deserves to be more accurately developed than its tendency to break and control the violence of faction. . . .

By a faction, I understand a number of citizens, whether amounting to a majority or minority of the whole, who are united and actuated by some common impulse of passion, or of interest, adverse to the rights of other citizens, or to the permanent and aggregate interests of the community. . . .

The latent causes of faction are thus sown in the nature of man . . . A zeal for different opinions concerning religion, concerning government, and many other points, as well of speculation as of practice; an attachment to different leaders ambitiously contending for preeminence and power; or to persons of other descriptions whose fortunes have been interesting to the human passions, have, in turn, divided mankind into parties, inflamed them with mutual animosity, and rendered them much more disposed to vex and oppress each other than

---

SOURCE: *James Madison*, The Federalist, No. 10 *(November 23, 1787), in* The Federalist, or the New Constitution: Papers by Alexander Hamilton, James Madison, John Jay, *with an Introduction by Carl Van Doren (New York: The Heritage Press, 1945), 54–62.*

to co-operate for their common good. . . . But the most common and durable source of factions has been the various and unequal distribution of property. . . .

. . . the *causes* of faction cannot be removed, and relief is only to be sought in the means of controlling its *effects*.

If a faction consists of less than a majority, relief is supplied by the republican principle, which enables the majority to defeat its sinister views by regular vote. . . . When a majority is included in a faction, the form of popular government, on the other hand, enables it to sacrifice to its ruling passion or interest both the public good and the rights of other citizens. To secure the public good and private rights against the danger of such a faction, and at the same time to preserve the spirit and the form of popular government, is then the great object to which our inquiries are directed. . . .

By what means is this object attainable? Evidently by one of two only. Either the existence of the same passion of interest in a majority at the same time must be prevented, or the majority, having such coexistent passion or interest, must be rendered, by their number and local situation, unable to concert and carry into effect schemes of oppression. . . .

. . . a pure democracy, by which I mean a society consisting of a small number of citizens, who assemble and administer the government in person, can admit of no cure for the mischiefs of faction. A common passion or interest will, in almost every case, be felt by a majority of the whole . . . and there is nothing to check the inducements to sacrifice the weaker party or an obnoxious individual. Hence it is that such democracies have ever been spectacles of turbulence and contention . . .

A republic, by which I mean a government in which the scheme of representation takes place, opens a different prospect, and promises the cure for which we are seeking. . . .

The two great points of difference between a democracy and a republic are: first, the delegation of the government, in the latter, to a small number of citizens elected by the rest; secondly, the greater number of citizens, and greater sphere of country, over which the latter may be extended.

The effect of the first difference is, on the one hand, to refine and enlarge the public views, by passing them through the medium of a chosen body of citizens, whose wisdom may best discern the true interest of their country, and whose patriotism and love of justice will be least likely to sacrifice it to temporary or partial considerations. . . .

. . . it is to be remarked that, however small the republic may be, the representatives must be raised to a certain number, in order to guard against the cabals of a few; and that, however large it may be, they must be limited to a certain number, in order to guard against the confusion of a multitude. . . . it follows that, if the proportion of fit characters be not less in the large than in the small republic, the former will present a greater option, and consequently a greater probability of a fit choice.

In the next place, as each representative will be chosen by a greater number of citizens in the large than in the small republic, it will be more difficult for unworthy candidates to practise with success the vicious arts by which elections are too often carried . . .

The other point of difference is, the greater number of citizens and extent of territory which may be brought within the compass of republican than of democratic government; . . .

The influence of factious leaders may kindle a flame within their particular States, but will be unable to spread a general conflagration through the other States. . . .

In the extent and proper structure of the Union, therefore, we behold a republican remedy for the diseases most incident to republican government.

6.6   Minority Rights in the Republic
Timothy Ford

For those who had brought about a revolution and now faced the task of setting up a republican government, one fundamental issue was how to deal with the rights of the minority. There were some who were troubled by the prospects of unqualified majority rule, and their arguments were to be revived again and again as the conflict over slavery deepened during the first half of the nineteenth century. This selection, written in 1794 to protest the projected reapportionment of the South Carolina legislature, argues for the protection of minority rights. The "compact" theory of government it supports foreshadows the position taken by John C. Calhoun and others in the next century.

Consider:

1. *When, according to the author, a majority "infringes" the social contract;*
2. *The results of such an "infringement";*
3. *How a republic can ensure the rights of a minority.*

SOURCE: *Americanus* [Timothy Ford], *"The Constitutionalist: Or, An Inquiry How Far It Is Expedient and Proper to Alter the Constitution of South Carolina,"* Charleston City Gazette and Daily Advertiser *(1794), in* American Political Writing During the Founding Era, 1760–1805, *eds. Charles S. Hyneman and Donald S. Lutz (Indianapolis: Liberty Press, 1983), II, 909–11.*

. . . The common notions of a contract utterly exclude the idea of a right residing in one party to alter or rescind it—*mutual obligation* forms its very essence. To bind one party, and leave the other at large, is to impose a law upon a conquered people, instead of forming a contract between free and equal parties.

Mere power can never constitute a legitimate right, and yet by what other claim can one party presume, of their own accord, to change the compact? It is said indeed, that the majority ought to govern. This principle is true under modifications, but it is not indefinitely so. It is a principle very capable of being perverted, and likely always to be enlisted on the side of those who have or hope to have a majority, let their views or principles be what they may.

But I contend, 1st. That the majority of an associated people have no right to infringe the social compact. If they have, then it follows that the compact has no existence longer than while the contracting interests are equal in point of number or power. It would derive its sanctions not from mutual assent, nor from moral obligation, but from physical force. It would be no breach of civil duty to attempt a subversion of the government at any time, provided the enterprizing leader had a tolerable prospect of gaining a successful majority; for it never can be unlawful to attempt that which would be lawful if attended with success; . . .

The weaker party in society would literally have *no right whatever*: neither life, liberty or property would be guaranteed to *them* by the social compact, seeing the majority are not bound by it, but might destroy the whole, and by the same rule any part of it at pleasure. . . . Virtue and vice would lose their distinction; the most vicious views would be sanctified, if pursued by the greater number, and the most virtuous resistance punishable in the less. 2d. If the principles of justice are derived from a higher source than human institutions, (and who will deny it?) I contend that the majority have no right to infringe them. Society is made up of different descriptions of men; between each description a common interest creates a common sympathy. The merchants, the farmers, the planters and the manufacturers, each have their common interests; each of these interests have their respective rights annexed to them, independently of the great natural rights which are common to all. . . .

. . . The truth is, that the term majority is a *relative term*, and supposes a compact already made; by which compact it is stipulated or implied, that the general will *in the functions of government* shall be taken to be that which a majority declares. But take away the idea of a compact or association, and to what does this term then relate? It relates to nothing; or, which is the same thing, to an indefinite number of un-associated men, none of whom have any power or controul over the others. If then the rights of the majority (be they what they may) derive themselves from a previous compact, the compact is the *principal*, and those rights the *accessory* dependant upon it; and whenever the . . . latter attempt to destroy the former, it in the same instant destroys itself. And what sort of right must that be, the exercise of which necessarily works its own destruction?

6.7   Justifying Slavery in the Republic
David Brion Davis

Slavery, legal in most of the states when the Constitution was ratified, posed a major dilemma in the new republic. Those who had fought a revolution for "liberty" had to reconcile those aspirations somehow with an institution that denied liberty totally to most blacks in America. This tension between slavery and liberty has been the subject of much historical writing on the origins of American government. In this selection, David Brion Davis echoes the arguments of another leading historian, Edmund Morgan, that the existence of slavery in the early republic actually served to define and reinforce the concepts of liberty that underlay the new government.

Consider:

1. *Why Americans might have objected to "unearned" emancipation, and whether this attitude was consistent with the principles of the Declaration of Independence;*
2. *How the existence of slavery could be reconciled with a "social contract" theory of republican government;*
3. *Whether, in a democratic society, the notion of a "stake in society" justifies the denial of rights to any group.*

. . . The Revolution could not have opened avenues toward general emancipation unless the slaves themselves had become involved as a significant military force. Historians have too often underestimated the economic strength of slavery during the Revolutionary period, exaggerated the force of antislavery sentiment in the Upper South, and minimized the obstacles that abolitionists faced even in the northern states. The American colonists were fighting, after all, for self-determination. And it is now clear that slavery was of central importance to both the southern and national economies, and thus to the viability of the "American system.". . .

. . . Since the Revolution tended to define liberty as the reward for righteous struggle, it was difficult to think of freedom as something that could be granted to supposedly passive slaves. As a reform movement, anti-slavery probed and helped to define the boundaries of an

SOURCE: *Reprinted from David Brion Davis,* The Problem of Slavery in the Age of Revolution, *1770-1823 (Ithaca, New York: Cornell University Press, 1975), 256-57, 259, 261-62. Used py permission of the publisher, Cornell University Press.*

emerging republican ideology. It embodied some of the central tensions of eighteenth-century thought, and also revealed the limits of change which a given society could envision or assimilate. . . .

A free society . . . was by no means incompatible with dependent classes of workers. Its central prerequisite was a large class of freeholders, unencumbered by feudal, military, or political obligations. Liberty required independence, and independence required freehold property. . . . any scheme of emancipation ran the risk of undermining property, of increasing the powers of government, and thus of endangering the very foundations of liberty.

If demands for freedom weakened the traditional justifications for slavery, demands for self-determination raised new obstacles to emancipation. . . .

. . . like their English contemporaries, the American colonists equated social responsibility with independence, and independence with land ownership. They feared and mistrusted men, regardless of race, who lacked any tangible stake in society. . . . eighteenth-century southern leaders could promote the ideal of a free white yeomanry and profess allegiance to the rights of all Englishmen precisely because black slaves had taken the place of a lower caste of whites. . . .

The American colonists were not trapped in an accidental contradiction between slavery and freedom. Their unique social order had arisen from many choices. They had resolved some of mankind's deepest social dilemmas, but at a heavy price. Their rhetoric of freedom was functionally related to the existence—and in many areas to the continuation—of Negro slavery. In a sense, then, demands for consistency between principles and practice, no matter how sincere, were rather beside the point. Practice was what made the principles possible.

6.8   Woman's Place in the Republic
Linda Kerber

The active support given to the Revolution by many educated American women (called "bluestockings") presented a dilemma in a male-dominated society that embraced republican—and to a degree, egalitarian—principles. This selection describes the ways in which the leaders of the young republic attempted to resolve the dilemma. In relations between men and women, as in those between whites and blacks, practical considerations often had to be balanced with ideals.

Consider:

1. *The contradictions between the "place" assigned to women in the new republic and the qualities that were ascribed to women;*
2. *The exercise of influence within the home as a form of political power;*

3. *Whether the "place" assigned to women in the new republic can be reconciled with the principles of republicanism discussed in other selections in this chapter.*

Rarely, in the literature of the early Republic, do we find any objection to the notion that women belong in the home; what emerges is the argument that the Revolution had enlarged the significance of what women did in their homes. . . . By their household management, by their refusal to countenance vice, crime, or cruelty in their suitors and husbands, women had the power to direct the moral development of the male citizens of the republic. The influence women had on children, especially on their sons, gave them ultimate responsibility for the future of the new nation. . . .

Defined this way, the educated woman ceased to threaten the sanctity of marriage; the bluestocking need not be masculine. In this awkward—and in the 1790s still only vaguely expressed—fashion, the traditional womanly virtues were endowed with political purpose. A pivotal political role was assigned to the least political inhabitants of the Republic. Ironically, the same women who were denied political identity were counted on to maintain the republican quality of the new nation. "Let the ladies of a country be educated properly," [Benjamin] Rush said, "and they will not only make and administer its laws, but form its manners and character."

When Americans addressed themselves to the matter of the role of women, they found that those who admired bluestockings and those who feared them could agree on one thing: in a world where moral influences were fast dissipating, women as a group seemed to represent moral stability. Few in the early republic demanded, in a sustained way, substantial revisions in women's political or legal status; few spoke to the nascent class of unskilled women workers. But many took pride in the assertion that properly educated republican women would stay in the home and, from that vantage point, would shape the characters of their sons and husbands in the direction of benevolence self-restraint, and responsible independence. They refuted charges of free love and masculinization; in doing so they created a justification for woman as household goddess so deeply felt that one must be permitted to suspect that many women of their generation were *refusing* to be household goddesses. They began to make the argument for intelligent household management that Catharine Beecher, a generation later, would enshrine in her *Treatise on Domestic Economy* as woman's highest goal. The Daughters of Columbia became, in effect, the Mothers of the Victorians.

SOURCE: *Linda Kerber, "Daughters of Columbia: Educating Women for the Republic, 1787–1805,"* in The Hofstadter Aegis: A Memorial, *eds. Stanley Elkins and Eric McKitrick (New York: Alfred A. Knopf, Inc., 1974), 56–59.*

6.9   The Republic in Art
Abijah Canfield

Efforts to glorify the new republic were evident in American arts and letters in the first decades after independence. This painting, which dates from about 1800, includes a number of republican symbols that were already familiar to Americans. The eagle, for example, had been included by Congress as a part of the Great Seal of the United States in 1782.

Consider:

1. *The symbols of republicanism in this painting, and their significance;*
2. *The role artists and their art can play in politics and in shaping "national character."*

SOURCE: *Courtesy of the Library of Congress.*

CHAPTER QUESTIONS

1. *What elements in the Constitution were "undemocratic"? If the Constitutional Convention had favored a more purely democratic instrument of government, could it have been "sold" to the public? Why or why not?*
2. *How great a concern did the framers of the Constitution have for the rights of minorities? Do you think the rights of minorities might have been better protected? Give examples.*

Chapter 7

The Invention of Political Parties

I n establishing the new government, American leaders made no provision for political parties. Believing political parties to be tools of special interests that by their very nature conflicted with the "common good," the men who drafted the Constitution hoped that the form of the new government would prevent parties from emerging.

But their visions of maintaining unity were in vain. Almost from the start, fundamental conflicts of opinion divided the nation's leaders. As early as 1791, a cohesive political opposition had emerged in response to Secretary of the Treasury Alexander Hamilton's proposed economic program. This opposition took its leadership from James Madison and, less openly, from Secretary of State Thomas Jefferson. Within a few years, the conflict between Hamiltonians (Federalists) and Jeffersonians (Republicans) had actually become party competition and was reinforced by sharp disagreements over American relations with France and England.

By 1800, the two parties were sufficiently distinct and well organized to make the presidential contest between incumbent John Adams and Vice President Thomas Jefferson a test of party strength. At that point, however, the legitimacy of political parties had not been fully accepted.

In retrospect, the "peaceful revolution of 1800"—in which the Federalists turned over control of the government to the victorious Republicans—seems to have established party government in the United States. But historians question whether a party "system" really existed at this time. Forms and behaviors were changing, but antiparty attitudes persisted. Gradually, of course, political parties would gain acceptance as legitimate agents for resolving opposing viewpoints in the democratic republic.

The creation of political parties was a response to the problems that are part of democratic government. How can the will of the majority be determined? Indeed, how—in a large republic—can a majority be forged? What are the roles and rights of a minority, and how can the minority hope to become a majority?

The development of party machinery, especially within the Republican party after 1800, addressed other procedural matters. Who is to lead a party? How are popular views to be communicated to those leaders, and how are the leaders to communicate with their followers?

The selections in this chapter highlight these theoretical and practical questions that were raised—and to some extent answered—by the emergence of American political parties.

Chronology

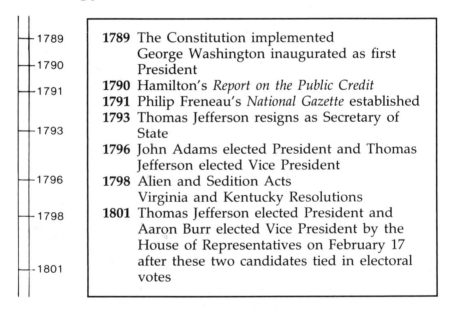

1789	1789 The Constitution implemented
1790	George Washington inaugurated as first President
1791	1790 Hamilton's *Report on the Public Credit*
	1791 Philip Freneau's *National Gazette* established
1793	1793 Thomas Jefferson resigns as Secretary of State
	1796 John Adams elected President and Thomas Jefferson elected Vice President
1796	1798 Alien and Sedition Acts
	Virginia and Kentucky Resolutions
1798	1801 Thomas Jefferson elected President and Aaron Burr elected Vice President by the House of Representatives on February 17 after these two candidates tied in electoral votes
1801	

Documents

7.1   Opposition to the Idea of Party, Richard Hofstadter
      (secondary source)

7.1   Opposition to the Idea of Party

Richard Hofstadter

Although political parties had already emerged in England during the
eighteenth century, they were not envisioned as part of the American republic by those who shaped it. Not only did the Constitution make no
provision for parties, but the leaders who framed the Constitution and
peopled the new government were actively hostile to the idea. Madison, in
fact, used "party" as a synonym for "faction," which he said must be
avoided. This selection from Richard Hofstadter's study of the origins of
parties in America describes the hostility toward the concept of party that
was common among those with influence in the new republic.

Consider:

1. *Whether the rise of political parties was, in fact, inevitable within the
   American constitutional system;*
2. *Whether "loyal opposition" would have been possible without parties;*
3. *Whether parties have a democratic impact on a political system.*

Political discussion in eighteenth-century England and America was
pervaded by a kind of anti-party cant. Jonathan Swift, in his *Thoughts
on Various Subjects*, had said that "Party is the madness of many, for

---

SOURCE: *Richard Hofstadter,* The Idea of a Party System: The Rise of Legitimate Opposition
in the United States, 1780–1840 *(Berkeley: University of California Press, 1970), 2–4, 8–13,
39. © 1969 The Regents of the University of California.*

the gain of the few." This maxim . . . plainly struck a deep resonance in the American mind. Madison and Hamilton, when they discussed parties or factions (for them the terms were usually interchangeable) in *The Federalist*, did so only to arraign their bad effects. In the great debate over the adoption of the Constitution both sides spoke ill of parties. . . . George Washington devoted a large part of his political testament, the Farewell Address, to stern warnings against "the baneful effects of the Spirit of Party." His successor, John Adams, believed that "a division of the republic into two great parties . . . . is to be dreaded as the greatest political evil under our Constitution." . . .

That the anti-party thought and partisan action of the Founding Fathers were at odds with each other is not altogether surprising. What they were trying to resolve—and they did so, after all, with a substantial measure of success—is a fundamental problem of modern democracy. . . . The situation of the Americans in their formative years was unusually complex, and perhaps quite unique. The Founding Fathers had inherited a political philosophy which also denied the usefulness of parties and stressed their dangers. Yet they deeply believed in the necessity of checks on power, and hence in freedom for opposition, and were rapidly driven, in spite of their theories, to develop a party system. . . .

The idea of a legitimate opposition—recognized opposition, organized and free enough in its activities to be able to displace an existing government by peaceful means—is an immensely sophisticated idea, and it was not an idea that the Fathers found fully developed and ready to hand when they began their enterprise in republican constitutionalism in 1788. . . . The Federalists and Republicans did not think of each other as alternating parties in a two-party system. Each side hoped instead to eliminate party conflict by persuading and absorbing the more acceptable and "innocent" members of the other. . . .

There are, of course, many ways of looking at what the first generation under the Constitution accomplished—setting administrative precedents, establishing the national credit, forging a federal union in the teeth of provincial loyalties, winning a national domain, . . . but one of the most important things they did was to come to terms with the idea of opposition and to experiment, despite their theories, with its incarnation in a party system. . . . Their skepticism about the value of parties made it inevitable that their discovery of a party system should be the product of drift and experimentation, that the rather nice system of implicit rules under which the modern two-party duel takes place could be arrived at only after many misunderstandings and some serious missteps. . . .

. . . during the eighteenth century, the root idea we find is that parties are evil. . . .

The very terms, "party" and "faction," which were used by some writers interchangeably, carried invidious overtones, though this is more regularly true of "faction." That word, in fact, seems to have had the meaning of a more sinister version of "party"—party functioning at its worst. . . . in the 1790's the leaders of the emerging Republican party in the United States were sometimes disposed at first to shy away from calling themselves a party. . . . As for faction—that was out of the question: Jefferson indignantly denounced Hamilton in 1792 for "daring to call the Republican party *a faction.*"

Party had . . . come to be conventionally condemned by political writers on three separate but not inconsistent grounds. First, . . . It was a prolific cause of "turbulence" . . . Second, a party or faction was very likely to become the instrument with which some small and narrow special interest could impose its will upon the whole of society. . . .

Finally, the party, with its capacity to arouse malice and hostility and to command loyalty to a political entity much narrower and less legitimate than the "public good" as a whole, was considered to be a force directly counterposed to civic virtue. . . .

A few observers . . . saw that parties could be good because instead of making for aggrandizement of power they offered another possible source of checks and balances in addition to those already built into the constitutional structure. . . . none saw that parties might perform a wide variety of positive functions necessary to representative democracy and unlikely to be performed as well by any other institutions. . . . First, parties had to be created; and then at last they would begin to find a theoretical acceptance.

7.2   Origins of Party: Hamilton's Economic Program

Alexander Hamilton

Though the leaders who assumed control of the new government in 1789 were determined to maintain national unity, dissension arose almost immediately over Secretary of the Treasury Alexander Hamilton's economic program. Hamilton's January 1790 "Report on the Public Credit," excerpted here, produced instant opposition in Congress. By 1792, that opposition, led by Secretary of State Thomas Jefferson and James Madison, was comparing the administration to an illegitimate "faction" and openly criticizing its policies in the press. In less than a decade, divisions had intensified and hardened, producing the first competition between political parties in the new nation.

Consider:

1. *The bases of Hamilton's argument for his program of debt repayment by the national government;*
2. *Why Jefferson and Madison were likely leaders for opposition to the Hamiltonian program;*
3. *Whether the administration should have been willing to compromise on the fundamental points of Hamilton's program for the sake of national unity.*

. . . it is easy to conceive how immensely the expenses of a nation, in a course of time, will be augmented by an unsound state of the public credit. . . .

If the maintenance of public credit . . . be truly so important, the next inquiry which suggests itself is: By what means is it to be effected?

. . . Those who are most commonly creditors of a nation are, generally speaking, enlightened men; . . . when a candid and fair appeal is made to them, they will understand their true interest too well to refuse their concurrence in such modifications of their claims as any real necessity may demand. . . .

To justify and preserve their confidence; to promote the increasing respectability of the American name, to answer the calls of justice; to restore landed property to its due value; to furnish new resources, both to agriculture and commerce; to cement more closely the union of the States, to add to their security against foreign attack; to establish public order on the basis of an upright and liberal policy;—these are the great and invaluable ends to be secured by a proper and adequate provision, at the present period, for the support of public credit. . . .

It is agreed, on all hands, that that part of the debt which has been contracted abroad, and is denominated the foreign debt, ought to be provided for according to the precise terms of the contracts relating to it. The discussions which can arise, therefore, will have reference essentially to . . . that which has been contracted at home. . . .

. . . It involves this question: Whether a discrimination ought not to be made between original holders of the public securities, and present possessors, by purchase? Those who advocate a discrimination are for making a full provision for the securities of the former at their nominal value, but contend that the latter ought to receive no more than the cost to them, and the interest. . . .

The Secretary, after the most mature reflection on the force of this argument, is induced to reject the doctrine it contains. . . .

SOURCE: *Alexander Hamilton, "Report on the Public Credit" (January 14, 1790), in* Alexander Hamilton's Papers on Public Credit, Commerce and Finance, *ed. Samuel McKee, Jr. (New York: The Liberal Arts Press, 1957), 4–5, 7, 10–11, 15–17, 45–46.*

It is inconsistent with justice, because, in the first place, it is a breach of contract—a violation of the rights of a fair purchaser. . . .

. . . there can be no doubt that the rights of assignees and original holders must be considered as equal. . . .

The Secretary, concluding that a discrimination between the different classes of creditors of the United States cannot, with propriety, be made, proceeds to examine whether a difference ought to be permitted to remain between them and another description of public creditors— those of the States individually. The Secretary, after mature reflection on this point, entertains a full conviction that an assumption of the debts of the particular States by the Union, and a like provision for them as for those of the Union, will be a measure of sound policy and substantial justice. . . .

If all the public creditors receive their dues from one source, distributed with an equal hand, their interest will be the same. And, having the same interests, they will unite in the support of the fiscal arrangements of the Government. . . .

Persuaded, as the Secretary is, that the proper funding of the present debt will render it a national blessing, yet he is so far from acceding to the position, in the latitude in which it is sometimes laid down, that "public debts are public benefits". . . that he ardently wishes to see it incorporated as a fundamental maxim in the system of public credit of the United States, that the creation of debt should always be accompanied with the means of extinguishment. . . .

7.3 The French Revolution and American Politics

The American Revolution had served as a stimulus to the French Revolution that began in 1789, and the French Revolution, in turn, had an impact on the developing political life of the United States. At first, Americans seemed almost unanimous in their support of France's revolution for liberty and equality. But as violence in France escalated, the more conservative elements in the United States recoiled, including most of those who backed the Hamiltonian program and came to be called Federalists. The Jeffersonians, on the other hand, not only continued to embrace the revolutionary cause of France, but further alarmed their Federalist foes by adopting the rhetoric of the revolutionaries and forming Democratic-Republican "clubs" that seemed to be egalitarian revolutionary units. The cartoon here, published in New York in 1793, reflects Federalist suspicions of Jefferson and his Republican supporters. Jefferson himself, his head above the crowd, is easily recognizable.

Consider:

1. *What dangers the cartoonist suggests were represented by the "Anti-federal" (Democratic-Republican) clubs;*
2. *The cartoonist's view of Jefferson's character;*
3. *How the elements of the "creed" in the upper left-hand corner compare to republican principles underlying the Constitution.*

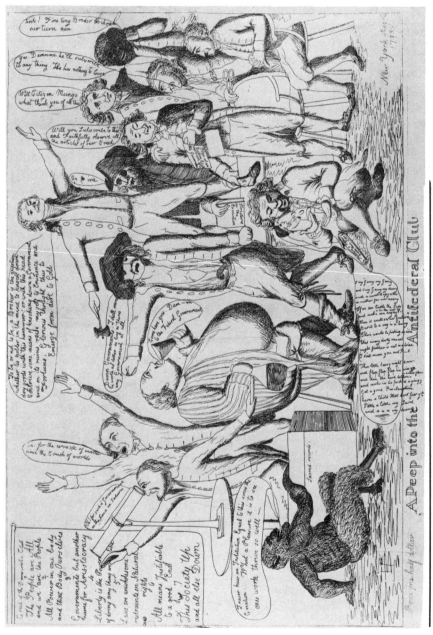

SOURCE: [Anonymous] "A Peep Into the Antifederal Club" (New York, 1793). Library Company of Philadelphia.

7.4   A Warning Against "Party Spirit," 1796

George Washington

Unanimously chosen to be the first President, George Washington was looked upon as a truly national leader, above party or faction. But when conflict over economic and foreign policy erupted early in his administration, Washington clearly sided with Hamilton and his supporters, the "Federalists." Indeed, after Jefferson and Edmund Randolph left the Cabinet, the administration was made up entirely of Federalists. Throughout the years of his presidency, Washington remained hostile to the idea of party. His anxiety about the danger posed by parties in the new republic dominated his "Farewell Address" of September 1796. This selection is taken from that famous address.

Consider:

1. *The validity of the argument that parties may be "indulged" in a monarchy, but not in a republic;*
2. *How Washington's views on party, including its origin and nature, compare to those expressed by Madison in* The Federalist, *No. 10 (Doc. 6.5);*
3. *How Washington, Hamilton, and others in the Federalist administration would have answered charges that they themselves represented a "party."*

United States, September 19, 1796.

Friends, and Fellow-Citizens: The period for a new election of a Citizen, to Administer the Executive government of the United States, being not far distant, and the time actually arrived, when your thoughts must be employed in designating the person, who is to be cloathed with that important trust, it appears to me proper . . . that I should now apprise you of the resolution I have formed, to decline being considered among the number of those, out of whom a choice is to be made. . . .

. . . a solicitude for your welfare, which cannot end but with my life, and the apprehension of danger, natural to that solicitude, urge me on an occasion like the present, to offer to your solemn contemplation, and to recommend to your frequent review, some sentiments; which are the result of much reflection, of no inconsiderable observation. . . .

SOURCE: *George Washington, "Farewell Address" (September 1796), in* The Writings of George Washington, *from the Original Manuscript Sources, 1745–1799, ed. John C. Fitzpatrick (Washington, D.C.: U.S. Government Printing Office, 1940), Vol. 35, 214–15, 218, 223–28.*

In contemplating the causes wch. may disturb our Union, it occurs as matter of serious concern, that any ground should have been furnished for characterizing parties by *Geographical* discriminations: *Northern* and *Southern; Atlantic* and *Western;* whence designing men may endeavour to excite a belief that there is a real difference of local interests and views. One of the expedients of Party to acquire influence, within particular districts, is to misrepresent the opinions and aims of other Districts. You cannot shield yourselves too much against the jealousies and heart burnings which spring from these misrepresentations. . . .

To the efficacy and permanency of Your Union, a Government for the whole is indispensable. . . .

All obstructions to the execution of the Laws, all combinations and Associations, under whatever plausible character, with the real design to direct, control, counteract, or awe the regular deliberation and action of the Constituted authorities are distructive of this fundamental principle and of fatal tendency. They serve to organize faction, to give it an artificial and extraordinary force; to put in the place of the delegated will of the Nation, the will of a party; often a small but artful and enterprizing minority of the Community; and, according to the alternate triumphs of different parties, to make the public administration the Mirror of the ill concerted and incongruous projects of faction, rather than the organ of consistent and wholesome plans digested by common councils and modified by mutual interests. However combinations or Associations of the above description may now and then answer popular ends, they are likely, in the course of time and things, to become potent engines, by which cunning, ambitious and unprincipled men will be enabled to subvert the Power of the People, and to usurp for themselves the reins of Government. . . .

Towards the preservation of your Government and the permanency of your present happy state, it is requisite, not only that you steadily discountenance irregular oppositions to its acknowledged authority, but also that you resist with care the spirit of innovation upon its principles however specious the pretexts. . . .

. . . Let me . . . take a more comprehensive view, and warn you in the most solemn manner against the baneful effects of the Spirit of Party, generally.

This spirit, unfortunately, is inseparable from our nature, having its root in the strongest passions of the human Mind. . . .

The alternate domination of one faction over another, sharpened by the spirit of revenge natural to party dissention, . . . is itself a frightful despotism. . . . The disorders and miseries, which result, gradually incline the minds of men to seek security and repose in the absolute power of an Individual: and sooner or later the chief of some prevailing faction more able or more fortunate than his competitors, turns this disposition to the purposes of his own elevation, on the ruins of Public Liberty. . . .

[Party] serves always to distract the Public Councils and enfeeble the Public administration. . . . It opens the door to foreign influence and corruption, which find a facilitated access to the government itself through the channels of party passions. . . .

. . . in Governments of a Monarchical cast Patriotism may look with endulgence, if not with favour, upon the spirit of party. But in those of the popular character, in Governments purely elective, it is a spirit not to be encouraged. From their natural tendency, it is certain there will always be enough of that spirit for every salutary purpose. . . . A fire not to be quenched; it demands a uniform vigilance to prevent its bursting into a flame, lest instead of warming it should consume. . . .

7.5   Suppression of "Rebellious Spirit"

Nathanael Emmons

President John Adams found himself under constant attack from the Republicans, especially over the issue of American-French relations. To the Federalists, the pro-French sentiments of Jefferson and his supporters seemed subversive. In 1798, the Republican-controlled legislatures of Kentucky and Virginia passed resolutions that laid down a theoretical basis for resisting "wrongful" government. The resolutions raised the specter of rebellion only a decade after the nation's founding. This selection reflects the concerns of New England Federalists that the "seditious and rebellious spirit" might prove fatal to the government if it was not quickly suppressed. The Federalist-sponsored Sedition Act, of course, was an effort to do just that.

Consider:

1. *The ironies in Emmons's arguments, given the history of the young republic;*
2. *How much dissent and/or civil disobedience should be permitted by a democratic government.*

The present appearance of a seditious and rebellious spirit in this happy country is extremely alarming. This spirit has often appeared in the world; and produced the most fatal effects. . . . The last time Jerusalem was besieged, a spirit of sedition proved fatal to the city, and to millions of its deluded inhabitants. The French were happy in their new modelled government, until a spirit of rebellion broke out, and destroyed their monarch, their nobility, their clergy, and their wisest and best citizens. . . . The same spirit has once and again dis-

SOURCE: *Nathanael Emmons, "A Discourse. Delivered on the National Feast" (Wrentham, Mass.,* 1799), in American Political Writing During the Founding Era, 1760–1805, *eds. Charles S. Hyneman and Donald S. Lutz (Indianapolis: Liberty Press, 1983), II, 1037–39.*

turbed the peace of America. . . . Since the establishment of our present general government, some of its enemies, at the Southward, took up arms and violently opposed the collection of duties on distilled liquors. To reduce those sons of sedition to reason and to order, was extremely troublesome and expensive to the public. . . . The present appearance, therefore, is truly alarming. Though but small numbers have yet openly and violently opposed the laws of the land, yet the leaven of rebellion has evidently poisoned the minds of many, in various parts of the Union. It is yet unknown, what will be the effect of either lenient or severe measures towards those, who are now in the hands of public justice. . . . This, however, is certain, that unless a spirit of sedition can be effectually suppressed, and a spirit of subordination effectually established, there can be no peace nor safety to these United States. A very wise and experienced ruler has said, "Rebellion is as the sin of witchcraft." It is not only very contagious, but extremely infatuating. It deprives men of all sober reasoning and reflection. This is demonstrated by the effects, which it has already produced amongst us. Some very honest, and, in other respects, very judicious people have already become deaf and blind. They cannot *see* the increasing light thrown upon the dark designs of France; nor *hear* the voice of the most wise and enlightened statesmen. . . . It will either bring on a general civil war, and reduce us to the dreadful system of liberty and equality; or it will render it absolutely necessary to tighten the reins of government, and lay stronger restraints upon the tongues, the pens, the hands, and the liberties of those, who are now complaining of our free government, and its wise and gentle administration. . . . though the present prospect is, that the prevailing spirit of sedition and rebellion will be eventually suppressed; yet there is ground to fear, that if much time, great exertions, and large sums of money be employed to suppress it, the body of the people will be so irritated, that they will choose to have government strengthened and their liberties abridged, rather than be perpetually exposed to the dire effects of sedition, insurrection, and rebellion. Nothing, therefore, can prevent the horrors of civil war, or the loss of our civil liberties, but the effectual suppression of that seditious spirit, which refuses to be subject to principalities and powers, and to obey magistrates.

7.6 Sectionalism and Party Competition

Grounded initially in differences over the Hamiltonian economic program, the Federalist and Republican parties were also based on sectional interests. Other factors were certainly present as well. But it is clear that in the presidential elections of 1796 and 1800 the Federalists were a New England-based party and the Republicans had their center of support in the South. This map of the results of the 1800 elections provides evidence of the general North-South split underlying the party division, but it shows some deviations from that pattern as well. These deviations are often explained by geographic and/or economic factors.

Consider:

1. *The conclusions you would draw if this were the only evidence available on the results of the election of 1800;*
2. *How well the evidence provided by this map fits with an interpretation that the parties were identified with economic interests.*

ELECTIONS OF 1800

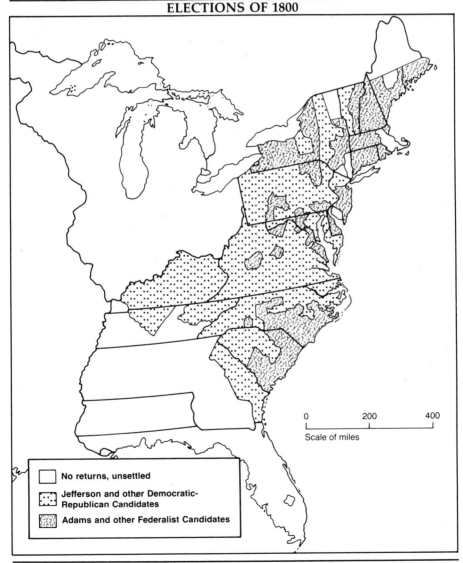

SOURCE: *Charles O. Paullin,* Atlas of the Historical Geography of the United States *(Washington: Carnegie Institute of Washington, 1932), plate 102-D.*

7.7   The Role of the Press in Political Parties

Fisher Ames

Almost immediately after the new national government was established, the press was brought into the political arena. The "official" organ of the administration, John Fenno's *Gazette of the United States*, was soon countered by opposition newspapers subsidized by Jefferson. The Jeffersonians' success in mobilizing public opinion through their press was not lost on the Federalists. In the wake of the Republican victory in 1800, former Congressman Fisher Ames of Massachusetts (1758–1808) wrote to a fellow partisan to point out how useful a broadly-based Federalist press would be in opposing the Jeffersonians. The *New England Palladium*, which Ames founded, served as a model for other Federalist opposition newspapers in the early 1800s.

Consider:

1. The validity of Ames's contention that the public is more receptive to the arguments of those who "find fault" with the government, than to the presentations of the government itself;
2. The advantages and disadvantages of newspapers being connected to political parties.

Dedham, March 19, 1801.

Sir, . . .

Party is an association of honest men for honest purposes, and, when the State falls into bad hands, is the only efficient defence; a champion who never flinches, a watchman who never sleeps. But the federalists are scarcely associated. . . . Is it not, therefore, proper, and indispensably necessary, to be active, in order to prevent the dissolution of the feeble ties by which the federal party is held together? . . .

The newspapers are an overmatch for any government. They will first overawe and then usurp it. This has been done; and the Jacobins owe their triumph to the unceasing use of this engine; not so much to skill in the use of it, as by repetition. . . . We must use, but honestly, and without lying, an engine that wit and good sense would make powerful and safe. . . . The Palladium might be made a great auxiliary to true liberty, and the endangered cause of good order. Its circulation, however, must be greatly increased. Any paper, to be useful at this crisis, must spread ten times as much as any will or can, unless the federal party, by a common concert, join to make it, like the London

SOURCE: *Fisher Ames to Theodore Dwight, March 19, 1801,* in Works of Fisher Ames, *ed. Seth Ames (Boston: Little, Brown and Co., 1854), I, 292–95.*

Gazette, *the* Gazette of the party. Could not your clergy, your legislators, your good men, be impressed with the zeal to diffuse it at once through your State? . . . An active spirit must be roused in every town to check the incessant proselytizing arts of the Jacobins, who will soon or late subvert Connecticut, as surely as other States, unless resisted with a spirit as ardent as their own. . . . We should, I am sanguine enough to believe, throw upon our antagonists the burdens of supporting and vindicating government, and enjoy their late advantages of finding fault, which popular prejudice is ever prone to listen to. We should soon stand on high ground, and be ready to resume the reins of government with advantage. . . .

The success of this design depends on the diffusion of like ideas among all the federalists, and the exertion of the first talents of the party. . . . Mr. Dutton, the editor of the Palladium, has talents, learning, and taste; what is no less essential, he has discretion. It is intended that every clergyman in Massachusetts, New Hampshire, and Vermont shall have a paper one year by a subscription.

I write as much, in confidence, to you as the nature of the subject requires. I am, sir, with great respect, &c.

7.9   The Development of Party Machinery
William Nisbet Chambers

It is interesting to consider whether the rivalry that developed between Federalists and Republicans in the new republic constituted a party "system" in the modern sense of that term. Since competition was not yet regarded as legitimate by most Federalist and Republican leaders, there is good reason to question whether it was a "system." The party organizations tended to be ad hoc, that is, formed for a specific problem or need, and voter mobilization was attempted only sporadically. What is clear, however, is that these first parties—the Republicans in particular—represented an innovative force that left a permanent impression on American politics. This selection, from a book by political scientist William Nisbet Chambers, presents the case that the development of party organization in the first two decades of the nineteenth century marked a transition to "modern" party politics.

Consider:

1. *The extent to which the Republican party machinery described by Chambers was "democratic";*
2. *The compatibility of this new party machinery with the "politics of deference" (see Doc. 4.4);*

3. *The advantages and disadvantages of a government being led by "career" politicians.*

The electoral campaign [of 1800] and preponderant power in succeeding years brought Republican party structure to its ultimate articulation and to expanding organization. The development of organization was highly uneven, rushing ahead in some states and lagging in others. Nonetheless, the Republicans were developing another party innovation which was as epoch-making for politics as Hamilton's program had been for government.

The key elements of early Republican organization became caucus, convention, and committee. The nominating caucus among members of a party in the legislature was regularized and expanded in its functions. Thus by 1804 in New Hampshire, for example, a Republican caucus formed a state committee on elections and "correspondence," with town committees under it. In the South, the caucus was often virtually the only continuing device of coordinated action. . . .

Local conventions marked a more democratic development. The convention, which had also made an early but sporadic appearance, became standard on the county level throughout the Middle Atlantic states. Members or "delegates" were named by local meetings or local committees, although often selection and representation were left loose. The conventions became key agents in making nominations for local and often for Congressional races and in rallying voters. . . .

For the Republicans in the early 1800's, statewide co-ordination depended largely on committees. Proposals were made for state nominating conventions, and new-style New Jersey Republicans soon achieved one. In too many states, however, distance, localism, or inertia still stood in the way. Top leaders, meanwhile, tended to maintain communication face to face, or through correspondence, or in the caucus, and also found their way onto local committees in town or county. The consequence was that state co-ordination tended to fall to informal state cadre groupings or to state committees more or less responsibly established. . . .

In long-hostile New England, Republican structure took on particularly firm lines. . . . a strongly centralized organization emerged in which state committees appointed local committees and held them accountable. The committees appealed to young voters, disseminated propaganda, planned rallies and "celebrations" to gather the faithful, and get out the vote. . . .

Contrasting stages of development characterized neighboring New York and New Jersey. In the mature politics of the Empire State, the

SOURCE: *William Nisbet Chambers,* Political Parties in a New Nation: The American Experience *(New York: Oxford University Press, 1963), 162–65.*

rallying cry of patronage rang out from 1800 on and old George Clinton's young nephew, DeWitt Clinton, became the generalissimo of political jobs. . . . in New Jersey, by contrast, new Republican organization was remarkably open, issue-oriented, and democratic; and as party competition stiffened, suffrage was extended and party action brought new popular participation. . . .

To the South, politics exhibited few developments toward stable modern organization, despite progress in the great domain of Virginia. . . .

Everywhere, indeed, ties grew firmer between Republican party structure and individuals and groups in the public. Yet those who occupied the top party positions remained a comparatively small and compact body of men, and as years passed more and more of them followed the Pennsylvania precept, becoming professional politicians primarily concerned with office and power. Before long, the practical intellectuals who had served as the new nation's first party leaders were virtually replaced by such matter-of-fact non- or even anti-intellectual politicians. . . . not all novitiates of the "new career" found principles, party programs, or intraparty democracy necessary ways of political life. Organization was opening the way to domination by *homo politicus* over the party following. Yet such men did conduct the affairs of party, and thereby sustained parties as potential instruments for popular influence.

CHAPTER QUESTIONS

1. *Did the actions of the nation's leaders in the 1790s demonstrate an implicit acceptance of "parties"?*
2. *What functions did parties serve in the new republic? Did their development represent an increase of democracy?*
3. *Was the competition between Republicans and Federalists a contest over ideas or a contest for power between rival elites, or both?*

Chapter 8

Westward Movement: People and the Land

The history of the American people is in part the story of successive frontiers. Indeed, the myths that have grown up about frontier life have contributed significantly to discussions about the development of an American "national character."

The westward movement and life on the "frontier" were a part of colonial experience from the beginning. Starting from small settlements on the Atlantic coast, the European newcomers pushed slowly but steadily inland. By the mid-eighteenth century, most still lived within a hundred miles of the coast. Still, despite the British attempt in 1763 to block migration west of the Appalachian Mountains, a certain number of hardy souls had already moved beyond that barrier, hundreds of miles from colonial "civilization." Immediately after the Revolution, the new American government addressed itself to the inevitability of this westward movement. With the Northwest Ordinance, passed in 1787, it attempted to provide a framework for the orderly settlement and development of the new lands.

In the period from the Revolution to about 1820, the American frontier consisted of the lands west of the Appalachians as far as the Mississippi River and, on the north, up to the Great Lakes. The geographic and climatic character of these lands had considerable influence on the nature of the settlements and on the activities and problems of those who settled there. But in many ways the experience of westward movement in this period was to be repeated again and again as the frontier moved across the continent. The fundamental questions were the same for successive frontiers. How was national control to be established—over both the tribes of Indians who held the land and the settlers who were moving into it? And how were the newly settled territories to be integrated into American political and economic life? For individual settlers, the questions were even more basic: What was the best place to settle, and how could a living be made in the wilderness?

This chapter focuses on recurrent issues related to westward migration. In treating these issues, the selections shed light on the special nature of frontier settlement in the first decades of the nation's existence. The selections in this chapter also suggest that frontier life may have differed from the myths that have developed about it.

Chronology

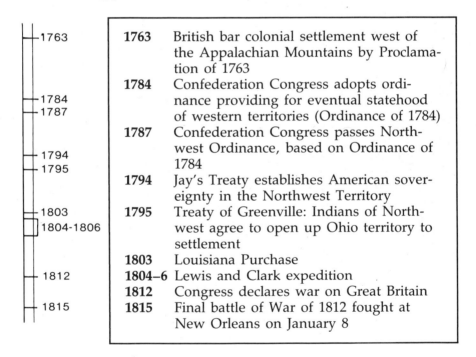

1763	British bar colonial settlement west of the Appalachian Mountains by Proclamation of 1763
1784	Confederation Congress adopts ordinance providing for eventual statehood of western territories (Ordinance of 1784)
1787	Confederation Congress passes Northwest Ordinance, based on Ordinance of 1784
1794	Jay's Treaty establishes American sovereignty in the Northwest Territory
1795	Treaty of Greenville: Indians of Northwest agree to open up Ohio territory to settlement
1803	Louisiana Purchase
1804–6	Lewis and Clark expedition
1812	Congress declares war on Great Britain
1815	Final battle of War of 1812 fought at New Orleans on January 8

Documents

8.1 Myths of the Frontier, Richard A. Bartlett (secondary source)
8.2 "Negotiating" with Native Americans: A 1785 Treaty (primary source)
8.3 Organizing the Frontier: The Northwest Ordinance (primary source)

8.1   Myths of the Frontier
Richard A. Bartlett

The story of the settling of the frontier wilderness has been mythologized as much as the early explorations of this continent. Indeed, there is a good deal of romance in the saga of westward migration. The unknowns were many, the dangers great, and the results dramatic. On the other hand, as historian Richard Bartlett points out in this selection, there is a tendency to exaggerate both the mysteriousness and the "tracklessness" of the American continent. In this selection, he is writing about what was known of the West in 1776. Within three decades, the government-supported explorations of Lewis and Clark and of Zebulon Pike vastly expanded popular knowledge of the great wilderness.

Consider:

1. *The author's purpose in this selection and his success in making his point;*
2. *How knowledge about the "trackless wilderness"—which Jefferson sought in commissioning expeditions into the Louisiana Territory— would have benefited the nation.*

Three myths have hindered the accurate portrayal of the sweep across the continent, and they should be destroyed. They are: (1) the myth of the unknown continent; (2) the myth of the trackless wilderness; (3) the myth of Indian invincibility.

. . . the myth has somehow arisen that our eighteenth-century ancestors knew next to nothing about the North American land mass. They knew that somewhere far, far to the West, so the story goes, the land ended at the "South Sea" (as they called the Pacific), but no one had any inkling of what lay in between. . . . If this ignorance of the continent really existed, then the American achievement in pushing

SOURCE: *Richard A. Bartlett,* The New Country: A Social History of the American Frontier, *1776–1890 (New York: Oxford University Press, 1974), 1, 8–9, 12–13.*

towards the setting sun becomes all the greater, much more romantic, an even bolder venture than it actually was. . . .

This impression is, however, completely inaccurate. In fact, if all the accumulated knowledge of the English, Spanish, French, Dutch, and Russians concerning North America as of 1776 could be gathered, there would be few general geographical facts about the virgin land that were not known by Europeans. . . .

The lobbying activities of land speculators, both British and colonials, and fur traders prevented the home government from ignoring the western country, at least to the Mississippi, for long. . . . There were conflicting claims, some of them "sea to sea," made by the several colonies. Then there was the Indian menace, unsuccessfully dealt with by the Proclamation of 1763. Time and western activity had worked against the British, and their system of control of trade and settlement, based upon the Proclamation Line, collapsed. This was due, however, not to a lack of understanding of the geography so much as a failure to comprehend the forces that were building up pressure for westward advance.

These forces were all set in motion by the actual, permanent inhabitants of the new nation in North America. . . . Before appraising their knowledge of the wilderness, we shall briefly note their condition as of 1776.

There were two and a half million white Americans and possibly three-fourths of a million black slaves in the thirteen states. Although the whites included Scotch-Irish, Germans, French Huguenots, and small representations of Dutch, Irish, and other European nationalities, the English language, English common law, and an English cultural context generally prevailed. Most of these people lived between seaside and fifty miles inland, although there were western extensions south of the Potomac, along the wide coastal plain and then into the upland piedmont, as much as 200 miles into the interior. Some of the easternmost mountain valleys, such as Virginia's Shenandoah, had also been settled. But for the most part the great Appalachian chain, even with its fertile valleys, remained a barrier to western settlement. . . . Beyond the mountains, or on their western fringes, the frontier settlements began. There was usually an actual geographical gap between the settled country and the new country, in some places extending 200 miles east to west, a wild span of mountains, valleys, and thick forests.

In a general way, we may say that Americans knew the main elements of its geography as far west as the "father of waters"—the Mississippi. . . . they knew the Appalachians, and they knew of the prairies of Kentucky, Indiana, and Illinois.

. . . The average man would have known next to nothing of the lands beyond that great river, but educated persons such as Thomas Jefferson certainly possessed some knowledge of the rest of the continent—of Mexico and Texas and the far Pacific. . . .

The Americans knew in a practical way much more than just the geographical elements of the country west to the Mississippi. They were aware that most of the land was thickly forested with deciduous trees . . . that it was teeming with game, and was sparsely populated by Indians. And yet the flora and fauna of this vast region were, after all, no more than a richer, more primitive, and far more extensive version of the deciduous forests of western Europe and the British Isles. . . .

. . . Interspersed through these forested lands were glades and meadows, lakes and streams. A forest in which deer and bison could graze was something less than an impenetrable jungle. . . .

Another false assumption is the myth of the trackless wilderness. Even the densest woods, with the more than 300 different varieties of trees, enormous vines, and thick undergrowth, were traversed by a maze of paths and trails. Most of these were animal-made, of course. . . . Some of these trails were broad as a modern highway, others no wider than necessary for bison to make their way single file along the fringe of the forest. . . .

The perambulations of generations of Indians had also hewn out primitive highways. . . . Whatever the purpose, these trails took the high land, avoided swamps and cane brakes where possible, and, as if attracted by magnetism, forded at the easiest river crossings. They led the pedestrian to his destination with the greatest possible safety.

8.2 "Negotiating" with Native Americans: A 1785 Treaty

In an effort to secure their tribal lands against further colonial expansion, the American Indians who occupied frontier lands actively assisted the British during the American Revolution. The Iroquois Confederacy in New York, the Delaware in Pennsylvania, and the Cherokee in North Carolina and Tennessee, for example, all took part in hostilities against the Americans. Not all of these tribes had been subdued when the Treaty of Paris ended the Revolution in 1783.

The following years saw a succession of treaties—largely the result of American coercion—in which the various tribes agreed to relinquish large areas of land to white control. Many of these agreements quickly fell apart, and the 1790s were marked by extensive warfare between whites and native Americans. The 1785 treaty with the Cherokee, excerpted here, was one of these post-Revolution treaties. Its terms were typical of such agreements, both in substance and in spirit. (The territorial settlement itself is not included in this excerpt.)

Consider:

1. *What the articles of the treaty concerning the punishment of crimes suggest about American attitudes toward the Cherokee;*
2. *What the Cherokees would have gained from signing the treaty and why tribes entered into such agreements with the American government;*
3. *Why it proved so difficult for the Americans to keep their side of these agreements.*

Articles concluded at Hopewell, on the Keowee, between Benjamin Hawkins, Andrew Pickens, Joseph Martin, and Lachlan M'Intosh, Commissioners Plenipotentiary of the United States of America, of the one Part, and the Head-Men and Warriors of all the Cherokees of the other.

The Commissioners Plenipotentiary of the United States, in Congress assembled, give peace to all the Cherokees, and receive them into the favor and protection of the United States of America, on the following conditions:

ARTICLE I.

The Head-Men and Warriors of all the Cherokees shall restore all the prisoners, citizens of the United States, or subjects of their allies, to their entire liberty: They shall also restore all the Negroes, and all other property taken during the late war from the citizens. . . .

ARTICLE II.

The Commissioners of the United States in Congress assembled, shall restore all the prisoners taken from the Indians. . . .

ARTICLE III.

The said Indians for themselves and their respective tribes and towns do acknowledge all the Cherokees to be under the protection of the United States of America, and of no other sovereign whosoever. . . .

ARTICLE V.

If any citizen of the United States, or other person not being an Indian, shall attempt to settle on any of the lands westward or southward of the said boundary which are hereby allotted to the Indians for their hunting grounds, or having already settled and will not remove from the same within six months after the ratification of this treaty, such person shall forfeit the protection of the United States. . . .

ARTICLE VI.

If any Indian or Indians, or person residing among them, or who shall take refuge in their nation, shall commit a robbery, or murder, or other capital crime, on any citizen of the United States, or person under

SOURCE: *Treaty with the Cherokee (November 28, 1785), in* Indian Affairs: Laws and Treaties, *ed. Charles J. Kappler (Washington, D.C.: U.S. Government Printing Office, 1904), II, 8–11.*

their protection, the nation, or the tribe to which such offender or offenders may belong, shall be bound to deliver him or them up to be punished according to the ordinances of the United States. . . .

ARTICLE VII.

If any citizen of the United States, or person under their protection, shall commit a robbery or murder, or other capital crime, on any Indian, such offender or offenders shall be punished in the same manner as if the murder or robbery, or other capital crime, had been committed on a citizen of the United States; and the punishment shall be in presence of some of the Cherokees. . . .

ARTICLE VIII.

It is understood that the punishment of the innocent under the idea of retaliation, is unjust, and shall not be practiced on either side, except where there is a manifest violation of this treaty; and then it shall be preceded first by a demand of justice, and if refused, then by a declaration of hostilities.

ARTICLE IX.

. . . the United States in Congress assembled shall have the sole and exclusive right of regulating the trade with the Indians, and managing all their affairs in such manner as they think proper. . . .

ARTICLE XI.

The said Indians shall give notice to the citizens of the United States, of any designs which they may know or suspect to be formed in any neighboring tribe, or by any person whosoever, against the peace, trade or interest of the United States.

ARTICLE XII.

. . . the Indians . . . shall have the right to send a deputy of their choice, whenever they think fit, to Congress.

ARTICLE XIII.

The hatchet shall be forever buried, and the peace given by the United States, and friendship re-established between the said states on the one part, and all the Cherokees on the other, shall be universal. . . .

8.3 Organizing the Frontier: The Northwest Ordinance

The attempt by the British to bar settlement west of the Appalachians (the Proclamation of 1763) had not stemmed the westward migration of the colonists. By the time the Revolution was over, many Americans already lived in the vast lands that the British ceded in the Treaty of Paris. To bring order to the settlement of these western lands, the Confederation government enacted the Ordinance of 1784, drafted by Thomas Jefferson. That document was the basis for a similar measure, the Northwest Ordinance, passed by the Confederation Congress in 1787. The selection from the Northwest Ordinance included here spells out the steps by which settlers would be able to create new states out of the wilderness. It is significant that the ordinance also banned slavery and involuntary servitude in these western lands.

Consider:

1. *Whether the closely regulated organization of the Northwest prescribed by Congress was consistent with democratic principles;*
2. *Other ways that the government could have dealt with this issue;*
3. *Why it was stipulated that there should be "not less than three nor more than five States" carved out of the territory.*

ORDINANCE OF 1787, JULY 13, 1787.

An Ordinance for the government of the territory of the United States northwest of the river Ohio

. . . Sec. 3. *Be it ordained by the authority aforesaid,* That there shall be appointed, from time to time, by Congress, a governor, whose commission shall continue in force for the term of three years, unless sooner revoked by Congress; he shall reside in the district. . . .

Sec. 5. The governor and judges, or a majority of them, shall adopt and publish in the district such laws of the original States, criminal and civil, as may be necessary, and best suited to the circumstances of the district, and report them to Congress. . . .

Sec. 9. So soon as there shall be five thousand free male inhabitants, of full age, in the district, upon giving proof thereof to the governor, they shall receive authority, with time and place, to elect representatives from their counties or townships, to represent them in the general assembly: *Provided,* That for every five hundred free male inhabitants there shall be one representative, and so on, progressively, with the number of free male inhabitants, shall the right of representation increase, until the number of representatives shall amount to twenty-five; after which the number and proportion of representatives shall be regulated by the legislature. . . . *Provided,* That a freehold in fifty acres of land in the district, having been a citizen of one of the States, and being resident in the district, or the like freehold and two years' residence in the district, shall be necessary to qualify a man as an elector of a representative. . . .

Sec. 11. The general assembly, or legislature, shall consist of the governor, legislative council, and a house of representatives. The leg-

---

SOURCE: Documents Illustrative of the Formation of the Union of the American States *(Washington, D.C.: U.S. Government Printing Office, 1927), 47–51, 53–54.*

islative council shall consist of five members, to continue in office five years, unless sooner removed by Congress; any three of whom to be a quorum; and the members of the council shall be nominated and appointed in the following manner, to wit: As soon as representatives shall be elected the governor shall appoint a time and place for them to meet together, and when met they shall nominate ten persons, resident in the district, and each possessed of a freehold in five hundred acres of land, and return their names to Congress, five of whom Congress shall appoint and commission to serve as aforesaid. . . . And the governor, legislative council, and house of representatives shall have authority to make laws in all cases for the good government of the district, not repugnant to the principles and articles in this ordinance established and declared. . . .

Sec. 12 . . . As soon as a legislature shall be formed in the district, the council and house assembled, in one room, shall have authority, by joint ballot, to elect a delegate to Congress who shall have a seat in Congress, with a right of debating, but not of voting, during this temporary government.

Sec. 13. And for extending the fundamental principles of civil and religious liberty, which form the basis whereon these republics, their laws and constitutions, are erected; to fix and establish those principles as the basis of all laws, constitutions, and governments, which forever hereafter shall be formed in the said territory; to provide, also, for the establishment of States, and permanent government therein, and for their admission to a share in the Federal councils on an equal footing with the original States, at as early periods as may be consistent with the general interest. . . .

There shall be formed in the said territory not less than three nor more than five States; . . . And whenever any of the said States shall have sixty thousand free inhabitants therein, such State shall be admitted by its delegates, into the Congress of the United States, on an equal footing with the original States. . . .

8.4   The Louisiana Purchase: A National Achievement

Boqueto de Woieseri

The land west toward the Mississippi may have seemed almost boundless in 1783 when it was ceded to the Americans, but by the turn of the century, both adventurous pioneers and the national government were interested in the territory beyond that great river. When the financial needs of the French led Emperor Napoleon to offer to sell the vast Louisiana Territory along with the much desired port of New Orleans, President Thomas Jefferson was an eager customer. The Louisiana Purchase of 1803 doubled the territory of the United States and removed the European presence from the interior of the continent. It also revived all the major issues connected with opening up new territories to settlement. Finally, the Louisiana Purchase greatly enhanced national pride. The 1803 painting presented here depicts the bustling port of New Orleans, together with a strongly patriotic message.

Consider:

1. *The patriotic republican symbols shown in this painting;*
2. *The image of New Orleans conveyed by the artist and how it compared to reality.*

8.5   Extending American Dominion to Louisiana
Meriwether Lewis and William Clark

After completing the purchase of Louisiana, President Jefferson dispatched Captains Meriwether Lewis and William Clark to explore the newly acquired territory. Their journey, which took two years to complete (1804–

SOURCE: *Boqueto de Woieseri*, "A View of New Orleans Taken from the Plantation of Marigny, November 1803," *Chicago Historical Society.*

1806), carried them up the Missouri River, across the Rocky Mountains, and on to the Pacific Ocean by way of the Columbia River. The primary purpose of the Lewis and Clark expedition was to chart the Louisiana Territory. Jefferson also commissioned these two explorers to inform the Indian tribes they encountered that the United States now controlled these lands. The language used by Lewis and Clark, as in this message to the Otoes in 1804, reflects the tone Jefferson wanted to set for the relationship between the American government and its new "children." Note here the mixture of appeals based on religion, force, and economic interest.

Consider:

1. *What evidence there is for the contention that Jefferson had ambivalent views toward American Indians, and that his policies as President reflected that ambivalence;*
2. *What the use of the word "children" suggests;*
3. *How the tone of this message compares to that of the 1785 treaty included in this chapter (Doc. 8.2).*

Lewis and Clark to the Oto Indians

[4 August 1804]

To the Petit Voleur, or Wear-ruge-nor, the great Chief of the Ottoes, to the Chiefs and Warriors of the Ottoes, and the Chiefs and Warriors of the Missouri nation residing with the Ottoes. . . .

Children. Commissioned and sent by the great Chief of the Seventeen great nations of America, we have come to inform you . . . that a great council was lately held between this great chief of the Seventeen great nations of America, and your old fathers the french and Spaniards; and that in this great council it was agreed that all the white men of Louisiana, inhabiting the waters of the Missouri and Mississippi should obey the commands of this great chief; . . . your traders . . . are no longer the subjects of France or Spain, but have become the Citizens of the Seventeen great nations of america. . . .

. . . These arrangements being made, your old fathers the french and Spaniards have gone beyond the great lake towards the rising Sun, from whence they never intend returning to visit their former red-children in this quarter. . . .

Children. From what has been said, you will readily perceive, that the great chief of the Seventeen great nations of America, has become

---

SOURCE: *Lewis and Clark to the Oto Indians (August 4, 1804), in* Letters of the Lewis and Clark Expedition, with Related Documents, *2d ed., ed. Donald D. Jackson (Urbana: University of Illinois Press, 1978), I, 203–8.*

your only father; he is the only father; he is the only friend to whom you can now look for protection, or from whom you can ask favours, or receive good councils, and he will take care that you shall have no just cause to regret this change; he will serve you, & not deceive you.

Children. The great chief of the Seventeen great nations of America. . . has sent us out to clear the road, remove every obstruction, and to make it the road of peace between himself and his red children residing there; to enquire into the Nature of their wants, and on our return to inform Him of them, in order that he may make the necessary arrangements for their relief. . . .

Children. Know that this great chief, as powerfull as he is just, and as beneficient as he is wise, always entertaining a sincere and friendly disposition towards the red people of America, has commanded us his war chiefs to undertake this long journey, which we have so far accomplished with great labour & much expence, in order to council with yourselves and his other red-children on the troubled waters, to give you his good advice; to point out to you the road in which you must walk to obtain happiness. He has further commanded us to tell you that when you accept his flag and medal, you accept therewith his hand of friendship, which will never be withdrawn from your nation as long as you continue to follow the councils which he may command his chiefs to give you, and shut your ears to the councils of Bad birds.

. . . you are to live in peace with all the *white men*, for they are his children; neither wage war against the *red men* your neighbours, for they are equally his children and he is bound to protect them. . . .

Children. If you open your ears to the councils of your great father, the great chief of the Seventeen great nations of America, & strictly pursue the advice which he has now given you through us, he will as soon as possible after our return, send a store of goods to the mouth of the river Platte to trade with you for your pelteries and furs; these goods will be furnished you annually in a regular manner, and in such quantities as will be equal to your necessities. . . .

Children. If your great Chief wishes to see your great father and speak with him, he can readily do so. Let your chief engage some trader who may reside with you the ensuing winter, to take him and four of his principal chiefs or warriors with him to St. Louis. . . . The commandant at St. Louis will furnish you with the necessary number of horses, and all other means to make your journey from thence to your great father's town Comfortable and safe. . . .

Children. We hope that the great Spirit will open your ears to our councils, and dispose your minds to their observance. Follow these councils and you will have nothing to fear, because the great Spirit will smile upon your nation. . . .

8.6   Migrating to Ohio in the Early 1800s

Gerald W. McFarland

To some extent, Americans who left the settled areas of the East for the uncertainties of the western frontier shared a common outlook. This was true whether they migrated in the 1760s, the 1800s, or the 1860s. Still, different social, economic, and political conditions in the different periods often produced their own distinct patterns of migration. This document is taken from a history of the transcontinental migrations of four families between the mid-eighteenth and early twentieth centuries. Focusing on the period when the families moved into Ohio, the selection illuminates some important differences between the westward movement of the early 1800s and the movement prior to 1790.

Consider:

1. *How the settlements of the early 1800s might have differed from frontier settlement of earlier decades;*
2. *The benefits and drawbacks of groups of neighbors from the same community moving west together;*
3. *What the lives of frontier women and children in this period might have been like.*

Shortly after Ohio was admitted to the Union in 1803, representatives of three of our families on the move migrated to the new state. . . .

These decisions to go west were at once bold and conservative. It took courage to leave the known for the unknown, to undertake the arduous journey, and to start anew in a wilderness or a semiwilderness. But all three families were fundamentally conservative in their approach to westward migration. None of them went west until the threat of Indian attack had been greatly reduced by diplomacy (Jay's Treaty, 1794) and military victories (Fallen Timbers, Ohio, 1794), until land development companies like the Connecticut Land Company had been organized and had launched campaigns to promote homesteading in the area, and until liberalized government land policies (the Land Act of 1800) and the establishment of federal land offices in Ohio had facilitated settlement there.

. . . In the early decades of the 1800s, tens of thousands of easterners took note of the fact that the Indian threat was on the wane and that plenty of good land was now available in the Buckeye State. The rush to capitalize on these conditions contributed to a dramatic rise in Ohio's population, from 45,365 in 1800 to 230,760 in 1810 and 581,434 in 1820. Moreover, Ohio's swift growth was not unique. Indiana, the next state to the west, had only 24,520 residents in 1810; ten years later the

SOURCE: *Gerald W. McFarland,* A Scattered People: An American Family Moves West, *43–44, 48–51, 62.* © *1985 by Gerald R. McFarland. Reprinted by permission of Pantheon Books, a division of Random House, Inc.*

number had swollen to 147,178 (an increase of 500 percent). The surge in population of western territories led to the admission of state after state in the early nineteenth century: Ohio (1803), Louisiana (1812), Indiana (1816), Mississippi (1817), Illinois (1818), Alabama (1819), and Missouri (1821). Of the present states east of the Mississippi, only Florida, Michigan, and Wisconsin still remained under territorial status in 1820. The trans-Appalachian frontier was well on the way to being settled.

A few heavily traveled roads bore the bulk of the Ohio-bound traffic. The future route of the Erie Canal from Albany to Buffalo, in New York State, was very popular with New Englanders. Other Yankees, however . . . took another well-trodden path, the road through Pennsylvania from Harrisburg to Pittsburgh. Residents of the Upper South frequently used the so-called National Road, which ran from Cumberland, Maryland, to Columbus, Ohio, and points farther west. . . . Virginians . . . who started west from the central Shenandoah Valley region often followed a road that wove its way through a series of west Virginia mountain passes before reaching Point Pleasant, where the migrants crossed the Ohio River into southern Ohio. . . .

Although each group of migrants to the Paint Valley frontier had its own story to tell, the many newcomers had much in common. . . . the great majority of the pioneers were Virginians, and those who were not from Virginia came from neighboring states: Kentucky, the Carolinas, and Pennsylvania. Of course, New Englanders . . . also moved to Ohio in the early 1800s, but they nearly always headed for the state's northern counties. Indeed, so distinct were these North–South migration bands that crossovers from one to the other were rarely found in the Paint Valley prior to 1830.

The adults who migrated to the Paint Valley frontier were mostly young people—either couples . . . or bachelors. . . . The married couples often had small children in tow, "an infant specimen of young America to carry on the knee,". . . The older or grandparent-aged pioneers usually came west for reasons that had to do with their children. . . .

[It was] typical of Ohio's early settlers that they traveled to the frontier in multifamily groups, rather than as individuals or as a single, nuclear family. At an even earlier date, . . . it had not been uncommon for hunters, men with no intention of settling in Ohio, to travel alone or with only a few companions, each bringing a horse, a rifle, and little else. But . . . the great majority of Ohio-bound pioneers in 1805 and afterward, were farmers with plans to clear the land and build homes. To do this they brought teams, wagons, tools, and household items. The difficult task of moving these possessions over miles of wilderness roads prompted them to migrate in groups from which they could draw assistance. . . .

The promise that drew most pioneers to Ohio was land. On this subject migrants divided into two types, settlers and speculators, though the two categories were by no means mutually exclusive. . . .

A land of promise for many, the Ohio frontier was for all a place of hazards and hardships. . . . the danger of Indian warfare was greatly diminished, though it revived, briefly, during the War of 1812. Paint Valley militiamen were mobilized in 1812 in response to fears that Britain's Indian allies, ably led by the great Shawnee chief Tecumseh, might go on a rampage. Few local men actually saw combat, however, and most, like their fathers during the Revolution, served only briefly. . . . Other problems of frontier life, such as the so-called squirrel invasion of 1807, during which hordes of hungry squirrels stripped the settlers' cornfields bare, posed no serious threat to the pioneers' survival, although many families spent the next winter on sparse diets of cabbage and turnips. . . .

A reciprocal relationship existed beween the large and small investors in western lands. Large speculators . . . were in a position akin to that of the owners of an automobile franchise with a large inventory. . . . Although the analogy is not precise—mainly because most western lands were uncleared and therefore not immediately usable, as a new car would be—the comparison holds fairly well. Each party to the transaction received something of value. The wealthy landholders reduced their inventories of Ohio land. The smaller farmers received a reasonably good price for their old farms and the chance to acquire a larger acreage by moving west.

8.7   Patterns of Westward Movement

The first decades after the Revolution saw steady westward migration, especially after more lenient land purchase laws were passed by Congress in 1800 and 1804. Three additional states—Kentucky, Tennessee, and Ohio—had been added to the original thirteen by 1803; by 1820, there were five more—Louisiana, Indiana, Mississippi, Illinois, and Alabama. This westward flow was spurred both by the diminishing of the Indian threat after the War of 1812 and by improvements in the road system (the result of government encouragement of privately owned turnpikes). The two maps that follow provide views of the distribution of the population in 1790 and 1820. They suggest not only which areas were most attractive to settlers, but also which paths were most commonly followed to the West.

Consider:

1. *How westward migratory patterns in the years prior to 1790 compare with patterns in the years between 1790 and 1820;*
2. *What these patterns suggest about the cultural composition of the various areas of settlement in the West;*
3. *Why some areas remained unfilled.*

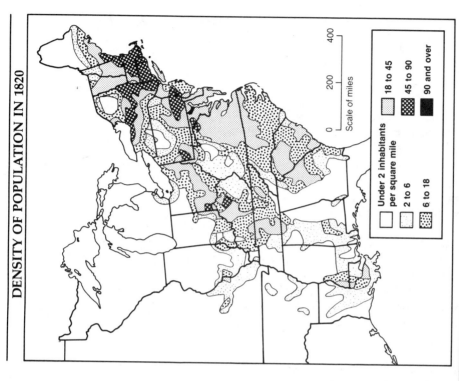

DENSITY OF POPULATION IN 1820

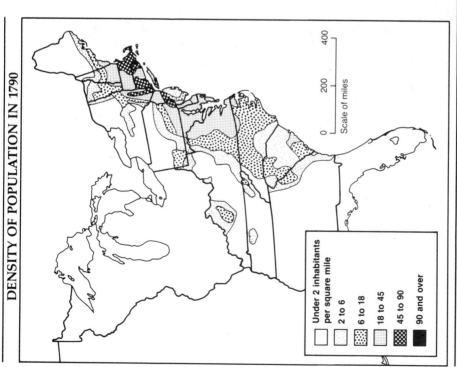

DENSITY OF POPULATION IN 1790

SOURCE: *Charles O. Paullin, Atlas of the Historical Geography of the United States (Washington, D.C.: Carnegie Institute of Washington, 1932), plates 76-B and 76-E.*

8.8   Two Frontiers: Urban and Rural

Richard C. Wade

The image of American frontier life has been fixed by generations of writers and artists, and more recently by movies and television. The scenario consists of rugged pioneers carving their way through the wilderness and then scratching out a living from inhospitable soil, living in log cabins, and only rarely coming into contact with "civilization." Certainly some or all of these descriptions applied to many western settlers, just as every stereotype has some basis in fact. Yet, as Richard Wade and other historians have pointed out, a far different sort of frontier life existed as well. This selection from Wade's book, *The Urban Frontier*, describes life in several bustling frontier cities of the early nineteenth century. Of particular interest is his discussion of such topics as the early onset of suburbanization, the distinctive patterns of work and behavior in these cities, and the sources of population for such communities.

Consider:

1. *Ways in which urban frontier life differed from the stereotype of frontier life;*
2. *Whether urban dwellers in the West would have felt they had more in common with other (rural) westerners or with eastern city residents;*
3. *How politics in the frontier areas might have been affected by the existence of the "urban frontier."*

The towns were the spearheads of the frontier. Planted far in advance of the line of settlement, they held the West for the approaching population. . . .

The first towns in the central portion of the Ohio Valley are younger than those on its eastern and western flanks. Until the American Revolution this area was sealed off from settlement by Indian hostility and British imperial policy. . . .

In a single generation this whole transmontane region was opened to settlement. In the process towns grew up along the waterways and in the heart of fertile farm areas. . . . This growth of urbanism was an important part of the occupation of the West, and it provided the central experience of many settlers who crossed the mountains in search of new homes. . . .

SOURCE: *Richard C. Wade, The Urban Frontier: The Rise of Western Cities, 1780–1830 (Cambridge: Harvard University Press), 1–2, 304–11, 320–21. Copyright © 1959 by the President and Fellows of Harvard College, copyright © 1987 by Richard C. Wade.*

By 1830 the rise of the cities was one of the dominant facts of Western life. . . .

. . . urban growth was so extensive that old municipal boundaries could no longer contain the new settlers, and many spilled over into the suburbs. For instance, Allegheny, Bayardstown, Birmingham, Lawrenceville, Kensington, Hayti, and East Liberty added nearly 10,000 to Pittsburgh's population, bringing the total up to 22,000. . . .

And already urban centers encountered the familiar problems suburbs create. As early as 1813 the Lexington assessor reported difficulty in collecting taxes in the outlots because residents there "alleged no benefit resulted to them from either the Watch, Lamps, fire buckets or fire companies." In other places people on the periphery seemed to be enjoying advantages without paying for them. . . .

. . . Another measure of this process was the growing specialization of activity. The cities offered continually widening opportunities, which attracted mechanics, merchants, and professional men from the East as well as enterprising youths from the countryside. The urban economy rested on occupational diversity, and the larger the town the greater the need for skilled people. Hence those who hoped to develop special talent settled in the cities. . . .

Another and perhaps even more significant mark of increasing urbanization was the growing tendency of residents to work outside their homes. . . . Large numbers now sought employment in factories, mercantile firms, or construction projects. Rising rents forced many to move their families out of the shop into residential districts. . . .

Increasing impersonalization was another result of urban growth. . . . "A next door neighbor is, with them, frequently unknown," a visitor to Pittsburgh observed in 1818, "and months and years pass, without their exchanging with each other the ordinary compliments of friendship and goodwill. . . ."

The appearance of city directories reflected this growing impersonality. These lists of residents by street and occupation became handy guides for individual reference and for business purposes. They also signaled the end of the day when such information was common property. . . . Lexington published a directory as early as 1806, Pittsburgh followed in 1815, Cincinnati in 1819, and St. Louis two years later. . . .

Another mark of the widening inroads of urbanism was the disappearance of grass and foliage. As a result of continuous construction, yards and lots were reduced, grassy areas pared down, and trees destroyed. Despite sporadic protests, the attrition was relentless. Paved landings and warehouses despoiled waterfronts, contiguous building filled empty spaces in business districts, and constant subdividing diminished natural groves in residential sections. . . .

. . . Exact figures are lacking, but the evidence suggests that an extraordinary number of town dwellers in the new country came from other urban communities, and that the large migrations from rural areas did not come until later. These newcomers brought with them some knowledge of city ways which they could draw upon to meet problems in their adopted homes. . . .

The urban origin of Western towndwellers was significant, for it meant that the new cities would be built in the image of older ones. . . . Indeed, the newcomers, their lives disrupted by movement, were anxious to recreate as much as possible of the familiar landscape they had left. Hence it is not surprising that Western towns bore a physical likeness to Eastern ones. Even social institutions were shaped by the same impulse. . . . The urge to imitate . . . sprang from deep needs, giving the urban pioneers both a lifeline to the past and a vision of a grand future.

CHAPTER QUESTIONS

1. *How successful were the early Indian policies of the federal government? Could the government have used other methods in dealing with Indians on the frontier? Has our national consciousness about Indians and their rights changed since the nineteenth century? In what ways?*
2. *How did westward expansion promote strong nationalism in the early republic?*
3. *To what extent, and in what ways, were the realities of the frontier in the period between 1780 and 1820 similar to the myths and stereotypes of frontier life in American history?*

part three

PROBLEMS OF UNION, 1820–1860

Chapter 9

Dimensions of American Nationalism: The Age of Jackson

The War of 1812 finalized American independence from Britain and produced an ardent burst of nationalism in the young republic. The war itself was partly the result of nationalism, pressed on President Madison by "war hawks" who wanted to establish American control in the West and to punish the British for their arrogant interference with the nation's rights on the seas. The three-year war was a military standoff, but it secured for the United States its basic objectives.

There was much evidence of American nationalism in the decades after the war. Expansionist sentiment gained momentum, as the young nation proclaimed its special rights in the Western hemisphere. Both foreign powers and Native American peoples who presented obstacles to national growth were dealt with forcefully. Meanwhile, the American government encouraged bold internal improvement programs, and those improvements, in turn, stimulated the development of an integrated national economy.

This vibrant nationalism was clearly reflected in American politics. Right after the War of 1812, a single, unchallenged "party of national harmony"—as had originally been envisioned by the nation's founders—emerged. By the mid-1820s, however, rivalries—sectional, ideological, and personal—put an end to the possibility of a one-party nation. Around the commanding figures of Andrew Jackson and his rivals—first John Quincy Adams and then Henry Clay—two different national visions took shape. The resulting "second party system" of Democrats and Whigs served to reinforce the bonds of Union while, at the same time, providing an arena for conflict. The emergence of national party conventions and party platforms in the period signaled the nationalization of the party system and ensured its continued existence.

The "Age of Jackson," as the period is called because of the towering influence of the hero-President, was not without disruptions. Traditionally, the era has been characterized as one of confrontation between the forces of "democracy," as personified by the Jacksonians, and elite commercial and financial interests, as represented by the Whigs. Such an interpretation, however, requires much qualification. The more significant divisions at this time were sectional—arising from the divergent economic interests and national visions of the North and the South. Particularly threatening, of course, was the festering issue of slavery. The nullification controversy of the early 1830s provided ominous signs of the divisiveness that lay ahead.

Some major issues remained unresolved. For the most part, these involved questions as old as the republic: What were the proper limits on the powers of government? How were the rights of minorities to be asserted and protected? What, indeed, *were* the rights of minorities? And what course should the nation take now that its viability was firmly established?

This chapter focuses on the varied dimensions of American nationalism in the Age of Jackson, including the ways in which the leaders of the "second party system" articulated and interpreted the national interest. Some of the selections deal with the forces that limited the scope of that nationalism.

Chronology

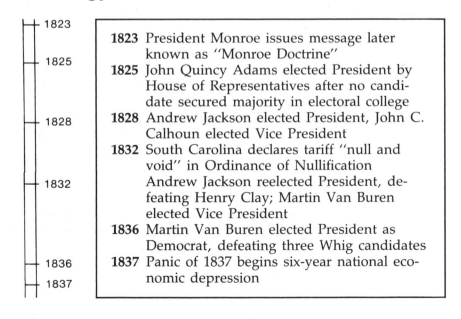

1823	**1823** President Monroe issues message later known as "Monroe Doctrine"
1825	**1825** John Quincy Adams elected President by House of Representatives after no candidate secured majority in electoral college
1828	**1828** Andrew Jackson elected President, John C. Calhoun elected Vice President
1832	**1832** South Carolina declares tariff "null and void" in Ordinance of Nullification
	Andrew Jackson reelected President, defeating Henry Clay; Martin Van Buren elected Vice President
	1836 Martin Van Buren elected President as Democrat, defeating three Whig candidates
1836	**1837** Panic of 1837 begins six-year national economic depression
1837	

Documents

9.1   The National Vision of John Quincy Adams

John Quincy Adams

In December 1825, John Quincy Adams delivered a dramatic message to
Congress. In it, he laid out an aggressive design for national development
that encompassed activities as far-reaching as scientific exploration of the
Northwest, establishment of a national observatory, construction of massive
internal improvements, and cultivation of literature and the arts. Most
troubling to his critics, however, were the phrases near the end of the
message in which he described the vast limits of the national government's
authority. Adams himself viewed the message as a "perilous experiment."
The strong opposition encountered by Adams's policies made it clear that
his vision went too far for most Americans, even in the nationalistic atmosphere of the time.

Consider:

1. *Whether Adams's view that the government should take a firm hand in
the development of science, literature, and the arts is consistent with the
American political tradition;*
2. *The benefits and drawbacks of government involvement in science and
the arts;*
3. *Why Adams's concluding remarks aroused such opposition at the time.*

. . . The great object of the institution of civil government is the improvement of the condition of those who are parties to the social compact, and no government, in whatever form constituted, can accomplish the lawful ends of its institution but in proportion as it improves the condition of those over whom it is established. . . . moral, political, intellectual improvement are duties assigned by the Author of Our Existence to social no less than to individual man. For the fulfillment of those duties governments are invested with power, and to the attainment of the end—the progressive improvement of the condition of the governed—the exercise of delegated powers is a duty as sacred and indispensable as the usurpation of powers not granted is criminal and odious. . . .

In assuming her station among the civilized nations of the earth it would seem that our country had contracted the engagement to contribute her share of mind, of labor, and of expense to the improvement of those parts of knowledge which lie beyond the reach of individual acquisition, and particularly to geographical and astronomical science. . . .

. . . I would suggest the expediency of connecting the equipment of a public ship for the exploration of the whole northwest coast of this continent. . . .

Connected with the establishment of an university, or separate from it, might be undertaken the erection of an astronomical observatory. . . .

The Constitution under which you are assembled is a charter of limited powers. After full and solemn deliberation upon all or any of the objects which . . . I have recommended to your attention should you come to the conclusion that, however desirable in themselves, the enactment of laws for effecting them would transcend the powers committed to you by that venerable instrument which we are all bound to support, let no consideration induce you to assume the exercise of powers not granted to you by the people. But . . . if these powers and others enumerated in the Constitution may be effectually brought into action by laws promoting the improvement of agriculture, commerce, and manufactures, the cultivation and encouragement of the mechanic and of the elegant arts, the advancement of literature, and the progress of the sciences, ornamental and profound, to refrain from exercising them for the benefit of the people themselves would be to hide in the earth the talent committed to our charge—would be treachery to the most sacred of trusts. . . .

. . . were we to slumber in indolence or fold up our arms and proclaim to the world that we are palsied by the will of our constituents, would it not be to cast away the bounties of Providence and doom ourselves to perpetual inferiority? . . .

SOURCE: *John Quincy Adams, Message to Congress (December 6, 1825), in* The State of the Union Messages of the Presidents, 1790–1966, *ed. Fred L. Israel (New York: Chelsea House Publishers, 1967), I, 243–46, 248–49.*

9.2   Jacksonian Nationalism and Its Limits: The Bank Veto

Andrew Jackson

A believer in states' rights in the tradition of Jefferson and Madison, Andrew Jackson nonetheless balanced such beliefs with a fierce national pride. He represented, then, both the expansive patriotic sentiment of the day and the view, most commonly held in the South, that the sphere of activity for the national government ought to be clearly defined. Jackson saw the Bank of the United States as an illegitimate government-inspired monopoly. His position in the clash over renewing the bank's charter was, in a sense, a stand on behalf of "the people" against moneyed interests, and it has frequently been described as such by historians. But it was also an important assertion of the true meaning of the "national interest," entirely consistent with Jackson's strong belief in the sanctity of the Union. His message vetoing the rechartering of the bank is excerpted here.

Consider:

1. *How Jackson's specific objections to the bank reflect a nationalistic viewpoint;*
2. *In what ways Jackson's view of the proper role of the federal government is a limiting one.*

. . . It is not our own citizens only who are to receive the bounty of our Government. More than eight millions of the stock of this bank is held by foreigners. By this act, the American Republic proposes virtually to make them a present of some millions of dollars. . . .

Every monopoly, and all exclusive privileges, are granted at the expense of the public, which ought to receive a fair equivalent. . . .

. . . this act does not permit competition in the purchase of this monopoly. It seems to be predicated on the erroneous idea, that the present stockholders have a prescriptive right, not only to the favor, but to the bounty of Government. It appears that more than a fourth part of the stock is held by foreigners, and the residue is held by a few hundred of our own citizens, chiefly of the richest class. . . .

In another of its bearings this provision is fraught with danger. Of the twenty-five directors of this bank, five are chosen by the Government, and twenty by the citizen stockholders. . . .

Is there danger to our liberty and independence in a bank, that, in its nature, has so little to bind it to our country? The President of the bank has told us that most of the State banks exist by its forbearance.

SOURCE: *Andrew Jackson, Veto Message to Congress (July 10, 1832), U.S. House of Representatives, 22d Cong., 1st sess., Doc. 300, 2, 5–6, 13.*

Should its influence become concentrated, as it may under the operation of such an act as this, in the hands of a self-elected directory, whose interests are identified with those of the foreign stockholder, will there not be cause to tremble for the purity of our elections in peace, and for the independence of our country in war? . . .

Should the stock of the bank principally pass into the hands of the subjects of a foreign country, and we should unfortunately become involved in a war with that country, what would be our condition? Of the course which would be pursued by a bank almost wholly owned by the subjects of a foreign power, and managed by those whose interests, if not affections, would run in the same direction, there can be no doubt. . . .

If we must have a bank with private stockholders, every consideration of sound policy, and every impulse of American feeling, admonishes that it should be *purely American*. Its stockholders should be composed exclusively of our own citizens, who, at least, ought to be friendly to our Government, and willing to support it in times of difficulty and danger. . . .

. . . Equality of talents, of education, or of wealth, cannot be produced by human institutions. . . . every man is equally entitled to protection by law. But when the laws undertake to add to these natural and just advantages, artificial distinctions, to grant titles, gratuities, and exclusive privileges, to make the rich richer, and the potent more powerful, the humble members of society, the farmers, mechanics, and laborers, who have neither the time nor the means of securing like favors to themselves, have a right to complain of the injustice of their Government. . . .

Nor is our Government to be maintained, or our Union preserved, by invasions of the rights and powers of the several States. In thus attempting to make our General Government strong, we make it weak. Its true strength consists in leaving individuals and States, as much as possible, to themselves; in making itself felt, not in its power, but in its beneficence; not in its control, but in its protection; not in binding the States more closely to the centre, but leaving each to move, unobstructed, in its proper orbit.

9.3   Testing the Bonds of Union: Nullification
William W. Freehling

Jackson was involved in a number of confrontations during his presidency, but the one that did the most to reinforce the idea of national union was the nullification crisis of 1830–1832. There the President faced down John C. Calhoun and his South Carolina followers, who insisted on the right of a state to "nullify" a federal law. The immediate cause of the crisis was South Carolina's objection to a strongly protectionist tariff. The specific outcome was that Jackson and the tariff prevailed, with Jackson issuing a forceful proclamation refuting the doctrine of nullification. But, as historian William Freehling argues in the book from which this selection is taken, the issue was not resolved. In addition, though the immediate outcome seemed to be a reinforcement of the bonds of national union, the nullification crisis foreshadowed the much graver division over slavery that would tear apart the Union three decades later.

Consider:

1. *The connection South Carolinians saw between the threat posed by the protective tariff and the threat posed by abolitionists;*
2. *Arguments that might be used to refute the idea that states have a right to nullify federal law;*
3. *Whether the right to nullify federal law is necessary to safeguard minority rights in a democratic republic.*

. . . Put in simple terms, the nullification crusade was produced by two acute problems: protective tariffs and slavery agitation; and to most nullifiers, the separate issues had long since intermeshed in a single pattern of majority tyranny. . . .

. . . leading nullifiers, reflecting the lowcountry's dominant mood, never ceased reiterating that the slavery issue was always in the background and often at the center of their concern. . . .

The nullifiers' decision to fight the abolitionists indirectly by contending against the tariff raises the obvious question, Why didn't South Carolina meet the slavery issue head on? The obvious answer is that in 1832 there was as yet no political abolitionist movement to fight against. Abolitionists were not yet flooding Congress with antislavery petitions, and committees quickly tabled colonization petitions. Carolinians obsessed with what they regarded as signs of a growing antislavery movement could only wage a preventive crusade against the abolitionists by attacking the protectionists' use of broad construction.

Yet leading nullifiers professed other, more revealing, reasons for choosing a contest against the tariff. First, lower tariffs would aid the defense of slavery. Perhaps the most important fact about the rise of the slavery issue and the decline of South Carolina's economy is that they occurred at precisely the same time; the anxiety depression caused heightened the apprehensions about slavery. The sight of planters going into bankruptcy and Carolinians departing for the West increased that sense of southern weakness which helped make the slavery issue so frightening. . . . By gaining a lower tariff, nullifiers could at least hope to end the economic decline. . . . The connection between the protective tariff as an economic threat and the slavery issue as a future

SOURCE: *William W. Freehling,* Prelude to Civil War: The Nullification Controversy in South Carolina, 1816–1836, *255, 257–59, 294. Copyright © 1965, 1966 by William Wilhartz Freehling. Reprinted by permission of Harper & Row, Publishers, Inc.*

danger became most intimate, and explosive, in such a consideration as this. . . .

Nullifiers, then, considered protective tariffs not only an inherently onerous economic burden but also an integral part of a pattern of sectional exploitation which would lead to slave revolts, colonization schemes, and ultimately the abolition of slavery. The nullification impulse was both a result of the severe pecuniary distress which afflicted many Carolinians in the 1820's and an expression of the anxiety surrounding the discussion of slavery in South Carolina in the years immediately before the antislavery crusade became part of the national political scene. Depressed economically, frightened by recurrent slave conspiracies, disturbed by nagging qualms about slavery, threatened by rising worldwide moral condemnation, South Carolinians had every reason to dread an encounter with the abolitionists. To leading Carolina nullifiers, the chance of avoiding the encounter, lowering the tariff, and winning permanent security seemed worth the risk of provoking an American civil war.

9.4 "King Andrew": A Whig View

Whatever views of economic policy or of states' rights may have been reflected in Jackson's actions in the bank and nullification controversies, the supremacy of the Chief Executive was an underlying principle in both responses. By the mid-1830s, the factions opposed to Jackson united in a single political party that took the name "Whig," after the British party of that name that had historically opposed the expansion of royal authority at the expense of Parliament and the people. The cartoon reprinted here, portraying Andrew Jackson as a royal tyrant, captures this essential theme of the Whig opposition. In attacking Jackson in this fashion, of course, the Whigs were charging the leader of the Democratic party with being the opposite of what he claimed to be: the champion of the people against moneyed interests.

Consider:

1. What the cartoon attempts to say about Jackson and how it depicts him as tyrannical;
2. The basis for the Whigs' claim that Jackson's actions were tyrannical;
3. What the names "Democrat" and "Whig," chosen by the parties of this era, suggest about politicians' perceptions of American values.

SOURCE: *Courtesy of the Library of Congress.*

BORN TO COMMAND.

OF VETO MEMORY.

HAD I BEEN CONSULTED.

KING ANDREW THE FIRST.

9.5   Rise of the National Party Convention

James S. Chase

Although the original party "system" had not lasted, by the late 1820s important differences over issues again gave rise to partisan competition. In this new party rivalry, the Democrats (followers of Andrew Jackson) vied for power first with the National Republicans, then briefly with the Anti-Masonic party, and finally with the Whigs, their chief opposition into the mid-1850s.

A major innovation in the years of this "second party system" was the presidential nominating convention, introduced by the Anti-Masonic party in 1831 as a democratic alternative to the congressional nominating caucus. By 1836, the Democrats had instituted a party platform. These important developments reflected the continued nationalization of the American political process. They also gave political parties an institutional momentum that helped ensure the future of a two-party system in the United States. In this selection, historian James Chase discusses some implications of the nominating convention as a political institution.

Consider:

1. *The possibility, as suggested by opponents, that the convention system would undermine democracy;*
2. *Whether conventions did in fact deal with the problem described by Daniel Webster;*
3. *In what ways the institution of nominating conventions and party platforms strengthened the two-party system of the Jacksonian period.*

Most of the objections to the convention were rooted in the fear that it menaced the sovereignty of the people. The Jacksonian era had immense faith in direct democracy. . . . Nominations by conventions, according to resolutions passed at a public meeting in Richmond, "must operate as a restraint upon the free exercise of the elective franchise." . . .

. . . advocates [of the convention system] countered with pragmatic arguments aimed at showing that it made democracy more operative. . . . "Harmony" was a favorite word among the defenders of the nominating conventions. Conventions provided the best guarantee that the men elected would represent the majority of the voters. They would, in addition, protect the "uninformed and ignorant" against "designing demagogues" since consultations among several counties, as opposed to self-nomination, would produce tickets composed of the "wisest and most experienced individuals." At issue was the fundamental question of the relative superiority of an unstructured, pure democracy against the winnowing advantages of representative government.

The organization provided by the convention could be, and often was, used for narrow and selfish ends, but the system at least allowed for popular participation in the choice of candidates. The convention was effective only if it reflected public opinion, only if its nominee won elections. . . . The greatest test for all nominating methods came

SOURCE: *James S. Chase,* Emergence of the Presidential Nominating Convention, 1789–1832 *(Urbana: University of Illinois Press, 1973), 291–95.*

on election day when the voters registered their approval or disapproval of the candidates preselected for their suffrage. The convention owed its ascendancy to its superior ability to meet the theoretical and practical requirements of democratic politics: candidates nominated by conventions, wrapped in the mantle of popular sovereignty and backed by an organization no independent could equal, were likely to be elected. . . .

The greatest contribution of the national convention, though, has been in maintaining the two-party system by providing the means through which groups competing for presidential power can find the common denominators necessary to the formation of only two major parties. The Antimasons and Democrats were particularly aware of the national convention as an agency to locate the candidates most likely to appeal to all the elements within an amorphous political bloc. The Antimasons used the national convention to find a presidential candidate who would compel the National Republicans to unite with them. . . .

The national convention has profoundly shaped the presidency no less than the party structure. In 1824 [Daniel] Webster had predicted that with the passing of the Revolutionary heroes the choice for president would fall "among a greater number, and among those whose merits may not be supposed to be very unequal." . . . Unless strong parties developed Webster feared "the President's Office may get to be thought too much in the gift of Congress."

The national convention has averted this danger by concentrating the electorate behind two candidates, thus keeping the election from Congress and giving the president a base of support independent of the legislative branch. With the emergence of the national convention the parties completed their reproduction of the federal structure of government. Local and state politicians as well as national leaders were given a direct part in making a president. Local interests and voting blocs underrepresented at Washington received a chance to exert their influence, causing local political factions to polarize around presidential candidates. Rather than being dependent on a few great leaders or the members of Congress for his election, the president is indebted to the great cross section of the nation represented in a body whose delegates have been chosen by a process involving every county of every state. The convention brought president making to the notice, if not within the control, of the common man.

9.6   National Economic Crisis: The Panic of 1837

Sectional rivalries were combatted by party leaders, both Whig and Democratic, who stressed the mutuality and interdependence of economic interests throughout the nation. Perhaps the most dramatic evidence of such interdependence was the Panic of 1837. The simultaneous withdrawal of foreign investment capital and the decline in international demand for cotton and other American goods combined with restrictive government currency policies to produce waves of mercantile and banking failures throughout the United States. The Panic of 1837, shown on the map below, developed into a nationwide depression lasting more than five years.

Consider:

1. *What regional or geographic bank and credit connections this map suggests;*
2. *The sectional tensions that would have been heightened by the panic.*

PANIC OF 1837

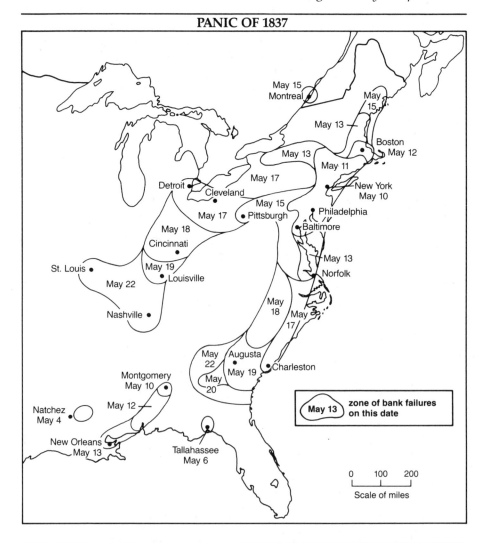

9.7   The "American System"

Daniel W. Howe

Though the Whigs won few national elections, they enjoyed the support of almost as many voters as the Democrats. Perhaps more than most American political parties, they reflected an integrated national vision. Though not as extreme as that of John Quincy Adams (Doc. 9.1), their vision nonetheless went beyond the level of government activism that most Democrats thought proper. As this selection by historian Daniel Howe makes clear, the "American System" promulgated by Whig leader Henry Clay (1777–1852) embodied his party's dominant national vision. But Clay was never elected President, and his "American System" was never enacted.

Consider:

1. *The grounds on which a strong nationalist might oppose Clay's system;*
2. *How voters in various sections of the country might respond to Clay's unified scheme;*
3. *Whether the American System afforded a means to "reconcile the interests of classes," as Clay hoped.*

. . . Henry Clay revealed the mindset of a genuine ideologue. There was nothing diffident about his "moderation." . . . boldness characterized his entire program, to which he gave the immodest name "the American System." Of all major figures in American political history, Clay had the most systematic and multifaceted program. If he had been able to implement it (that is, if he had been as capable a politician as he was an ideologist) he would have changed the course of United States history in the nineteenth century. . . . there would have been much more precedent for government intervention in the economy and for planned response to social problems in general.

The American System was a highly organized articulation of Whig political culture. The leading values of the culture, such as order, harmony, purposefulness, and improvement, found expression in the form of an economic program. Through this System, the future of America would be shaped in accordance with those values. Clifford Geertz has suggested that ideologies appear in new nations to replace

SOURCE: *Daniel W. Howe,* The Political Culture of the American Whigs *(Chicago: The University of Chicago Press, 1979), 137–38. © 1979 by the University of Chicago. All rights reserved.*

their traditional cultures, but the case of the American System was somewhat different. The ideology did not so much replace as summarize and embody much of the cultural inheritance of Whiggery. Even so, the American System reminds one of those bold development programs, sometimes called five-year plans, by which new nations often seek to achieve full independence. The name "American System" distinguished Clay's economic nationalism from the "British system" of laissez-faire. To permit free trade would keep the United States subservient to British economic colonialism, Clay warned.

The American System began to take shape while Clay was still a Jeffersonian Republican. In 1818 he secured passage of a resolution stating the sense of the House of Representatives that Congress possessed constitutional power to finance internal improvements. Having supported the tariff bills of 1816 and 1820, he announced a full-blown doctrine of protection for developing industry and national self-sufficiency in 1824. . . . Before long Clay figured out how to circumvent the scruples of the strict constructionists. He hit upon the device of revenue-sharing, or, as he called it, "distribution" of federal money to the states for specified purposes. This would have the added benefit of forestalling the state bankruptcies and repudiation of bonds that were playing havoc with investors at the time.

A land policy was integrated into Clay's System. Because it kept out some imports, a protective tariff raised less money than a tariff for revenue only. To make up the difference, Clay favored selling the public lands rather than giving them away to settlers. The public lands were a "great resource" for the whole nation, he explained. If they were given away, only the recipients benefited; if they were sold, the proceeds could benefit all the people. Very likely this policy would result in slowing westward migration, but Clay agreed with Henry Carey that population dispersion should be discouraged. Too rapid settlement of the West would outrun the transportation network, draw the work force away from manufacturing, and keep the country at a more primitive economic stage. It would also create more conflicts with the Indians and a higher level of violence generally. The System, which took all these elements into account, was beautifully logical— officious, its enemies thought.

Clay intended his American System to foster national integration and inhibit sectionalism. Economic diversification and good transportation, by creating domestic markets, would encourage commercial bonds of interest. Patriotism, put on a material basis, would enlist the prudence of the businessman in its service. Americans would become "one free, Christian, and commercial people." Meanwhile, the policy of distribution would knit the Union more strongly together by turning the states into eager clients of the federal government instead of its jealous rivals. . . .

The American System was predicated on the basis of a harmony of interests. Whigs conceived such harmony to be providential. . . . Just as the Whig party liked to think of itself as nonpartisan, it also liked to think of itself as transcending locality and section. Certainly it did harmonize the interests of some western and southern agrarians with those of the northeastern business community. The American System also claimed to reconcile the interests of classes, a more questionable proposition.

CHAPTER QUESTIONS

1. *How might it be argued that the party competition of the Jacksonian Age was the first "party system" in the United States? Consider both attitudinal and institutional factors.*
2. *In what ways did Andrew Jackson and his policies mirror and strengthen the forces of American nationalism?*
3. *What were the strengths and liabilities of the Whig party by the 1840s? Why were the Whigs less likely to survive than the Democrats?*

Chapter 10

The Imperatives of Expansion

B y the late 1830s, the confident nationalism of the Jacksonian era, strengthened by popular faith in the inevitability of progress, had led to the attitude that it was a national duty to claim and occupy the continent. Many Americans believed that continental expansion was dictated by geography and ordained by God. Thus, the present boundaries of the continental United States (excluding Alaska) were established in the 1840s. The acquisition of Texas, New Mexico, California, and a portion of Oregon rounded out America's continental empire.

This expansionist drive was the result of a curious combination of forces, some in conflict with others. Many Southerners, fearful of losing their influence in the political arena, viewed expansion as the only way to perpetuate slavery and survive within the nation. Opponents of slavery were equally committed to expansion in order to admit more "free" states.

President James K. Polk believed that America's national interest required the acquisition of California and Oregon. Polk secured both objectives, one through war and the other through negotiation.

America's "Manifest Destiny" legitimized acquisition of new territory, either by diplomacy or by war. A major factor in realizing this expansion was technological advance, both in transportation and communications. The success of the magnetic telegraph, for example, sped up the process of communication. Equally important was the development of a system of railroads that could link various parts of the country. The immediate impact of railroad development, however, was to stimulate expansionist zeal; competing proposals for transcontinental railroads by northern, central, and southern routes all attracted enthusiastic support.

This chapter focuses upon these and other forces advocating expansion in the 1840s and 1850s. The documents address a range of related issues, including the American notion of a "Manifest Destiny," arguments for the perpetuation of slavery, and the perceived necessity of removing Indians who stood in the way.

Chronology

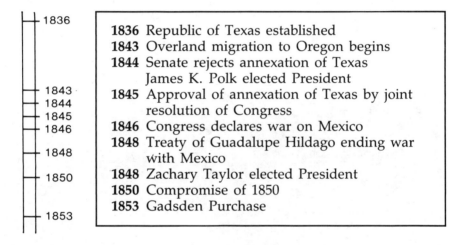

1836	**1836** Republic of Texas established
	1843 Overland migration to Oregon begins
	1844 Senate rejects annexation of Texas
	James K. Polk elected President
1843	**1845** Approval of annexation of Texas by joint
1844	resolution of Congress
1845	**1846** Congress declares war on Mexico
1846	**1848** Treaty of Guadalupe Hildago ending war
1848	with Mexico
1850	**1848** Zachary Taylor elected President
	1850 Compromise of 1850
	1853 Gadsden Purchase
1853	

Documents

10.1 "Manifest Destiny"

John Gast

In 1845, newspaper editor John O'Sullivan used the term "Manifest Destiny" to express the view that the people of the United States had a divine mission to extend their civilization to the Pacific Ocean. Artist John Gast captured the spirit of that belief in the painting "Manifest Destiny," reproduced here. The Goddess of Destiny leads the way west, a schoolbook in her right hand and a telegraph wire in her left.

Consider:

1. *The message Gast is trying to convey in this painting;*
2. *The significance of the sequence of activities shown from right to left;*
3. *Whether you think this portrayal of "Manifest Destiny" had a universal appeal to all Americans.*

SOURCE: *Courtesy of the Library of Congress.*

10.2   "The Destiny of the Race"

Thomas Hart Benton

In the 1840s and 1850s, many Americans believed that the nation's "Manifest Destiny" legitimized expansion, whether it was the annexation of Texas, fixing the Oregon boundary at the 54th parallel, or war with Mexico. One of the more articulate spokesmen for this "Manifest Destiny" was Senator Thomas Hart Benton of Missouri. In this selection, excerpted from a speech Benton delivered on the Senate floor, expansionism is presented as both inevitable and irresistible.

Consider:

1. *The basic assumptions implicit in Benton's argument for America's destiny;*
2. *Arguments that could be raised to rebut Benton's vision of America;*
3. *The usefulness of the concept of "Manifest Destiny" in defining America's role in the world.*

Since the dispersion of man upon earth, I know of no human event, past or present, which promises a greater, a more beneficent change upon earth than the arrival of the van of the Caucasian race (the Celtic-Anglo-Saxon division) upon the border of the sea which washes the shore of eastern Asia. The Mongolian, or Yellow race, is there, four hundred million in number, spreading almost to Europe; a race once the foremost of the human family in the arts of civilization, but torpid and stationary for thousands of years. It is a race far above the Ethiopian, or Black—above the Malay, or Brown (if we must admit five races)—and above the American Indian, or Red; it is a race far above all these, but still, far below the White; and, like all the rest, must receive an impression from the superior race whenever they come in contact. It would seem that the White race alone received the divine command, to subdue and replenish the earth! for it is the only race that has obeyed it—the only one that hunts out new and distant lands, and even a New World, to subdue and replenish. Starting from western Asia, taking Europe for their field, and the Sun for their guide, and leaving the Mongolians behind, they arrived, after many ages, on the shores of the Atlantic, which they lit up with the lights of science and religion, and adorned with the useful and the elegant arts. Three and a half centuries ago, this race, in obedience to the great command, arrived in the New World, and found new lands to subdue and replenish. For a long time, it was confined to the border of the new field (I now

SOURCE: *Thomas Hart Benton,* Congressional Globe, *May 28, 1846.*

mean the Celtic-Anglo-Saxon division); and even fourscore years ago the philosophic Burke was considered a rash man because he said the English colonists would top the Alleghanies, and descend into the valley of the Mississippi, and occupy without parchment if the Crown refused to make grants of land.

What was considered a rash declaration eighty years ago, is old history, in our young country, at this day. Thirty years ago I said the same thing of the Rocky Mountains and the Columbia: it was ridiculed then: it is becoming history to-day. The venerable Mr. Macon has often told me that he remembered a line low down in North Carolina, fixed by a royal governor as a boundary between the whites and the Indians: where is the boundary now? The van of the Caucasian race now top the Rocky Mountains, and spread down to the shores of the Pacific. In a few years a great population will grow up there, luminous with the accumulated lights of European and American civilization. Their presence in such a position cannot be without its influence upon eastern Asia. The sun of civilization must shine across the sea: socially and commercially, the van of the Caucasians, and the rear of the Mongolians, must intermix. They must talk together, and trade together, and marry together. Commerce is a great civilizer—social intercourse as great— and marriage greater. The White and Yellow races can marry together, as well as eat and trade together. Moral and intellectual superiority will do the rest: the White race will take the ascendant, elevating what is susceptible of improvement—wearing out what is not. The Red race has disappeared from the Atlantic coast: the tribes that resisted civilization, met extinction. This is a cause of lamentation with many. For my part, I cannot murmur at what seems to be the effect of divine law. I cannot repine that this Capitol has replaced the wigwam—this Christian people, replaced the savages—white matrons, the red squaws— and that such men as Washington, Franklin, and Jefferson, have taken the place of Powhattan, Opechonecanough, and other red men, howsoever respectable they may have been as savages.

Civilization, or extinction, has been the fate of all people who have found themselves in the track of the advancing Whites, and civilization, always the preference of the Whites, has been pressed as an object, while extinction has followed as a consequence of its resistance. The Black and the Red races have often felt their ameliorating influence. The Yellow race, next to themselves in the scale of mental and moral excellence, and in the beauty of form, once their superiors in the useful and elegant arts, and in learning, and still respectable though stationary; this race cannot fail to receive a new impulse from the approach of the Whites, improved so much since so many ages ago they left the western borders of Asia. The apparition of the van of the Caucasian race, rising upon them in the east after having left them on the west, and after having completed the circumnavigation of the globe, must wake up and reanimate the torpid body of the old Asia. Our position and policy will commend us to their hospitable reception: political considerations will aid the action of social and commercial influences. Pressed upon by the great Powers of Europe—the same that press upon us—they must in our approach see the advent of friends, not of foes—of benefactors, not of invaders. The moral and intellectual superiority of the White race will do the rest: and thus the youngest people, and the newest land, will become the reviver and the regenerator of the oldest.

10.3   Southern Views on Expansionism
William L. Barney

Many Southerners supported expansionism in the 1840s and 1850s for reasons related to maintenance of the South's peculiar institution—slavery. Historian William L. Barney asserts that slavery had persisted in the South largely because of its expansion into new territories. Consequently, he argues in *The Road to Secession: A New Perspective on the Old South*, the book from which this excerpt was taken, that Southerners viewed territorial expansion as a solution to the problems of slavery, rather than as an assertion of the rights of slaveholders. It is in this context that he examines what he calls the "Failure of Expansion."

Consider:

1. *The basic reasons Barney suggests for Southern territorial expansion;*
2. *The arguments that could be raised against Barney's interpretation;*
3. *The long-term implications of the failure of Southern expansionists to achieve their objectives in the 1840s and 1850s.*

THE FAILURE OF EXPANSIONISM

The 1850's witnessed a widening gap between the South's desire to gain more territory and her ability to do so within the Union. The decade opened with the loss of California to the free-soil North. California was the great prize in the lands recently wrested from Mexico. Already noted for its deep ocean ports and its rich valley agriculture, the area became, with the discovery of gold, a mecca for fortune-seeking Americans.

The antislavery forces, with some backing from Southern Whigs, argued that the United States was honor-bound to respect the Mexican

SOURCE: *William L. Barney, The Road to Secession: A New Perspective on the Old South* (New York: Praeger, 1972), 11–12.

decrees that had prohibited slavery in the provinces of California and New Mexico. Southern Democrats reacted scornfully to this position. They stressed that the South had contributed more than her fair share of men and arms to the conquest of these territories and thus had a military, as well as a constitutional, right to carry slaves there. . . .

To arguments that the climate and soil of these territories were unsuitable for slavery, that the institution was debarred by a "decree of Nature," Southerners responded by citing the great profitability of slavery in mining. . . .

The admission of California as a free state was a bitter blow to the South. A small but strategically placed proslavery wing of the California Democracy continued to fight for the introduction of slavery and even succeeded by its control of the judiciary in allowing a limited use of slave labor in the mines until the mid-1850's. But the battle had been lost. . . .

Kansas, although economically less significant than California, represented an even more serious psychological defeat for the South. Badly misjudging the strength and sensitivity of the antislavery movement, many Southerners had deluded themselves into believing that the Kansas-Nebraska Act, by expressly revoking the Missouri Compromise line of 36° 30', would take the issue of territorial slavery out of politics and allow the settlers to decide the question for themselves. . . .

Southern Democrats fought desperately to gain legal recognition of slavery in Kansas. . . .

In March of 1855, David Atchison, a Missouri senator and leader in the struggle to open up Kansas for slavery, offered an early version of the domino theory: "If we win we carry slavery to the Pacific Ocean; if we fail we lose Missouri, Arkansas, and Texas and all the territories; the game must be played boldly. I know that the Union as it exists is in the other scale, but I am willing to take the holyland." . . .

Cuba and Mexico offered unique advantages to Southern expansionists. The former was already a slave society, and the latter seemed ripe for the taking. . . .

The pro-Cuban forces were centered in the Democratic party, and they had some support from the Northern wing of the party, as exemplified by James Buchanan's acquiescence in the Ostend Manifesto of 1854. In this declaration, three American foreign ministers crudely served warning on Spain that the United States meant to have Cuba. . . . "I want Cuba, and I know that sooner or later we must have it. . . . I want Tamaulipas, Potosi, and one or two other Mexican States; and I want them all for the same reason—for the planting or spreading of slavery," announced Albert Gallatin Brown in a speech at Hazlehurst, Mississippi. Cuba was to be the linchpin in a tropical empire founded on outright annexation or on the creation of satellite states. This empire, by giving the South a virtual monopoly over the production of tropical goods, would ensure the perpetuation of slavery. . . .

Despite considerable influence within the Pierce and Buchanan administrations, the Cuban annexationists got nowhere. . . .

For some, Mexico could serve as [the needed] outlet. In a speech before Congress, Representative O. R. Singleton of Mississippi reasoned that, because there was no settled government in Mexico, the United States had every right to intervene to promote order and set up a stable government. . . . "In my opinion we must, and we are compelled to, expand in that direction, and thus perpetuate it [slavery] . . ."

In 1858, William Burwell of Virginia, in urging Senator R. M. T. Hunter of Virginia to exert pressure for a more aggressive Mexican policy, suggested that the acquisition of all Mexico could serve both as a popular issue for the next Presidential election and as a means for the South to re-establish her political equality within the Union. . . . Burwell was confident that Southern whites could easily control the racially mixed population. . . . There was no alternative. "The North has more states and more territory than the South. It has the immigration of Europe to aid it. Your subjugation is as certain as the unrelenting operation of these great causes can render it." Out of self-protection, the South must "seize upon all the territory which produces those great staples of social necessity which the world cannot go without. Do so and you are safe."

10.4   Indian Removal
Alexis de Tocqueville

The Indian Removal Act of 1830 authorized the President to provide eastern Indians with land from the unoccupied public domain in the West in exchange for their land. During the years of Jackson's presidency, about 46,000 Indians exchanged 100 million acres of land east of the Mississippi for $68 million and 32 million acres of land west of the Mississippi. Because the law required voluntary removal, treaty negotiations were conducted with Indian tribes. This was a difficult process involving complex issues. Alexis de Tocqueville, an observant and perceptive Frenchman who traveled in the United States in the 1830s, reviewed many of the problems in his *Democracy in America*, which is excerpted here.

Consider:

1. The basis for de Tocqueville's claim that removal of the Indians "takes place . . . in a regular, . . . legal manner";
2. Whether this description of the removal process suggests any changes in the government's attitude toward Indians since the time of Jefferson's presidency (see Doc. 8.5).

SOURCE: *Alexis de Tocqueville*, Democracy in America, trans. *Henry Reeve* (1862), I, 436, 450–53.

The ejectment of the Indians often takes place at the present day in a regular, and, as it were, a legal manner. When the European population begins to approach the limit of the desert inhabited by a savage tribe, the government of the United States usually sends forward envoys, who assemble the Indians in a large plain, and, having first eaten and drunk with them, address them thus: "What have you to do in the land of your fathers? Before long, you must dig up their bones in order to live. In what respect is the country you inhabit better than another? Are there no woods, marshes, or prairies, except where you dwell? And can you live nowhere but under your own sun? Beyond those mountains which you see at the horizon, beyond the lake which bounds your territory on the west, there lie vast countries where beasts of chase are yet found in great abundance; sell us your lands, then, and go to live happily in those solitudes." After holding this language, they spread before the eyes of the Indians fire-arms, woollen garments, kegs of brandy, glass necklaces, bracelets of tinsel, ear-rings, and looking-glasses. If, when they have beheld all these riches, they still hesitate, it is insinuated that they cannot refuse the required consent, and that the government itself will not long have the power of protecting them in their rights. What are they to do? Half convinced and half compelled, they go to inhabit new deserts, where the importunate whites will not let them remain ten years in peace. In this manner do the Americans obtain, at a very low price, whole provinces, which the richest sovereigns of Europe could not purchase. . . .

. . . The Creeks and Cherokees, oppressed by the several States, have appealed to the central government, which is by no means insensible to their misfortunes, and is sincerely desirous of saving the remnant of the natives, and of maintaining them in the free possession of that territory which the Union has guaranteed to them. But the several States oppose so formidable a resistance to the execution of this design, that the government is obliged to consent to the extirpation of a few barbarous tribes, already half destroyed, in order not to endanger the safety of the American Union.

But the Federal government, which is not able to protect the Indians, would fain mitigate the hardships of their lot; and, with this intention, it has undertaken to transport them into remote regions at the public cost.

Between the 33d and 37th degrees of north latitude, a vast tract of country lies, which has taken the name of Arkansas, from the principal river that waters it. It is bounded on the one side by the confines of Mexico, on the other by the Mississippi. Numberless streams cross it in every direction; the climate is mild, and the soil productive, and it is inhabited only by a few wandering hordes of savages. The government of the Union wishes to transport the broken remnants of the indigenous population of the South to the portion of this country which is nearest to Mexico, and at a great distance from the American settlements. . . .

The Union treats the Indians with less cupidity and violence than the several States, but the two governments are alike deficient in good faith. The States extend what they call the benefits of their laws to the Indians, believing that the tribes will recede rather than submit to them; and the central government, which promises a permanent refuge to these unhappy beings in the West, is well aware of its inability to secure it to them. Thus the tyranny of the States obliges the savages to retire; the Union, by its promises and resources, facilitates their retreat; and these measures tend to precisely the same end.

10.5   A Mandate for Expansion?

Charles G. Sellers

Expansion clearly was an issue in the presidential election of 1844. The Democratic party platform favored the annexation of Texas and reoccupation of Oregon, and its presidential candidate, James K. Polk, strongly endorsed both statements. The party platform of the Whigs and their candidate Henry Clay, on the other hand, opposed the annexation of Texas. Polk's victory, thus, suggested that voters had given a mandate to annex Texas and to push for reoccupation of Oregon. Most political analysts contend, however, that presidential elections seldom provide mandates. In the following selection, historian Charles G. Sellers takes this position with regard to the election of 1844.

Consider:

1. *Whether Sellers overlooks or ignores any evidence that might support the view that annexation was the decisive factor in Polk's victory;*
2. *Whether the election of 1844 was a clear mandate for expansionism;*
3. *What long-term implications expansionism had for national politics.*

There was argument at the time, and there has been since, as to whether the election was a mandate for the annexation of Texas. The New York *Evening Post* claimed that it spoke for many Democrats who had supported Polk in spite of his position on Texas rather than because of it. On the other hand it seems clear that the issue had much to do with the shrinkage of normal Whig strength throughout the South. One prominent southern Whig told Clay after the election that, "For the present the Whig party in the South is dispersed"; while another

SOURCE: *Charles G. Sellers, "Election of 1844," in* History of American Elections, *ed. Arthur M. Schlesinger, Jr., and Fred Israel (New York: Chelsea House, 1971), I, 797–98.*

had no doubt that only the Texas question could have caused the people to elect "a mere *Tom Tit* over the old Eagle." John Quincy Adams was hardly correct in calling the election a "victory of the slavery element"; but those who viewed it in that light were right in sensing a portent of sectional polarization in the returns. A Vermont Whig looked out a window in Washington on the morning after the result was known to see a Democratic victory banner floating over the slave market. "That flag means *Texas*," he exclaimed, "and *Texas* means *civil war*, before we have done with it."

Yet for all the presumed effect of the Texas question in weakening the Whigs throughout the South, it enabled the Democrats to carry, of states they could not have expected otherwise, only Georgia and possibly Indiana, or perhaps also, with the aid of fraudulent voting, Louisiana, having a total of 28 electoral votes; while it may have lost them Ohio with 23.

Even in these states the Texas question and other issues did not determine the bulk of the votes. Probably more voters favored annexation because they were Democrats than voted Democratic because they favored annexation. People voted for the party with which they identified, forming their identifications mainly in terms of the party image's appeal for the social group to which they belonged. Thus the Whigs were nearest the truth when they emphasized the political solidarity of the respectable classes on the one hand and the foreign-born on the other.

Because the social groupings and criteria relevant to party identification—religious, class, ethnic, economic, regional—were so numerous in American society, the parties were coalitions of a variety of social groups with cross-cutting inclinations on the issues. A New York editor illustrated this when he posed the question, "Who elected James K. Polk?" "I," says the free trade man of South Carolina, "I did it; hurrah for free trade!" "No," says the Annexationist of Mississippi, Alabama and Louisiana, "It was I that did it; I went for the enlargement of the territory of slavery." "Not so fast," respond the Annexationists of the North, "It was we who did it—we who went for getting rid of slavery by taking Texas and thus enlarging the bounds of freedom." "No, no"; declare the tariff men of Pennsylvania, "we did it, and did it by shouting for the tariff of 1842". . . . "Don't boast too much," say the Tyler men, "we did it; the post-office and custom house did it; we did it by giving you public offices and public money"; and these are not all who say they did it. The friends of Silas Wright and Mr. Van Buren in New York declare that it was their work. The Irish say they did it—the Germans that they did it; and the Abolitionists of the locofoco creed exult by proclaiming, "We did it."

What is most striking about the election of 1844 is the closeness of the vote throughout the country. Not only did Polk's percentage of the popular vote lead Clay's by a mere 1.4 percentage points, but in fifteen of the twenty-six states the winning party had a lead of less than 8 percentage points. This parity of party strength testified to the skill with which the politicians of both parties had learned to manipulate their parties' images so as to attract enough social groups to bring them toward a majority.

This party parity having been achieved, large blocks of electoral votes turned on handfuls of popular votes, the 113-vote margin in Tennessee being only the most extreme manifestation of a general situation. Under these circumstances Texas, abolition, Nativism, and the tariff had little to do with most of the votes cast, but everything to do with the result of the election. In these marginal but decisive effects the embittered Clay could see only "a most extraordinary combination of adverse circumstances." "If there had been no Native party," he wrote, "or if all its members had been truer to their principles; or if the recent foreigners had not been all united against us; or if the foreign Catholics had not been arrayed on the other side; or if the Abolitionists had been true to their avowed principles; or if there had been no frauds, we should have triumphed."

Actually the candidates had a great deal to do with these effects, and the decisive factors seem to have been: first, Polk's astute handling of the tariff issue, which saved Pennsylvania; second, Clay's contrastingly maladroit handling of the Texas issue, which kept too many antislavery men out of the Whig ranks in New York; and third, the Whigs' too conspicuous sympathy for Nativism, which brought a host of foreign-born voters into the Democratic ranks.

10.6   Vote on Joint Resolution on Annexation of Texas

After Polk's victory in the election of 1844, but before his inauguration, President Tyler proposed that Texas be admitted to the Union under a joint resolution. This would require a simple majority vote in the Senate and the House, rather than the two-thirds majority in the Senate needed to ratify a treaty. Debate over the issue quickly divided along North versus South and antislavery versus proslavery lines. Nevertheless, the resolution passed in the House by a vote of 120 to 98 and in the Senate by a vote of 27 to 25. The distribution of the House vote by Congressional District is shown in the accompanying map. For comparative purposes, a second map shows the House vote on the Kansas-Nebraska Act of 1854, a measure clearly focused on the issue of slavery.

Consider:

1. *Which factor—party lines, regional attachment, or position on slav-ery—determined the distribution of this House vote on Texas;*
2. *The differences between the vote distribution on Texas and the vote on the Kansas-Nebraska Act of 1854;*
3. *How these differences in vote distribution might be explained.*

ANNEXATION OF TEXAS, 1845

yeas   nays
not voting   unsettled

(Votes not shown: New Hampshire, 2 yeas; New York City, 2 yeas)

0   200   400
Scale of miles

SOURCE: *Charles O. Paullin,* Atlas of Historical Geography of the United States *(Washington, D.C.: Carnegie Institute, 1932).*

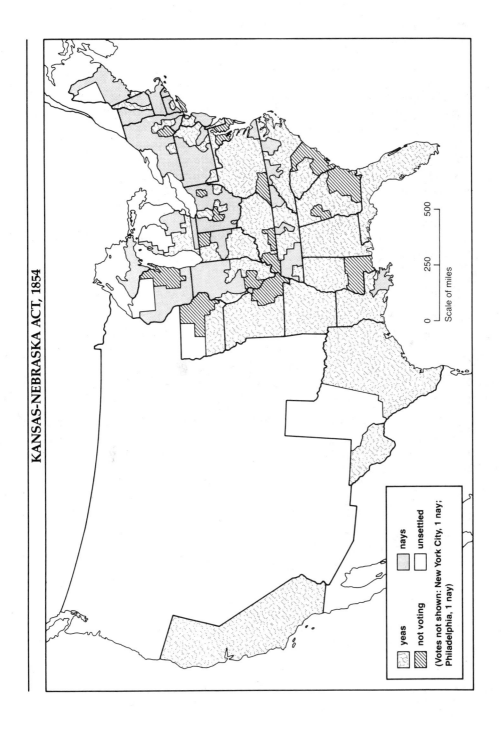

KANSAS-NEBRASKA ACT, 1854

Scale of miles

0   250   500

yeas

not voting

nays

unsettled

(Votes not shown: New York City, 1 nay;
Philadelphia, 1 nay)

10.7 Polk's Reassertion of the Monroe Doctrine

James K. Polk

In the election of 1844, both the Democratic party platform and the party's candidate, James K. Polk, advocated "reoccupation" of Oregon. The crucial issue was where the northern boundary would be drawn. In his first annual message to Congress, Polk rejected the British proposal to set the boundary at the 49th parallel, demanding instead a boundary farther north (54°40'). Building on this assertion of American rights in Oregon, Polk then invoked the Monroe Doctrine to warn European powers (France and England) that the United States would permit no "European interference on the North American continent. . . ." The following selection is excerpted from the text of that message that deals with Texas, Oregon, and the Monroe Doctrine.

Consider:

1. *The tone and intent of this portion of Polk's message;*
2. *Evidence in the message that Polk was an advocate of America's "Manifest Destiny";*
3. *How and why Polk's statement differs from the original Monroe Doctrine.*

This accession to our territory has been a bloodless achievement. No arm of force has been raised to produce the result. . . . In contemplating the grandeur of this event it is not to be forgotten that the result was achieved in despite of the diplomatic interference of European monarchies. . . . We may rejoice that the tranquil and pervading influence of the American principle of self-government was sufficient to defeat the purposes of British and French interference, . . . From this example European Governments may learn how vain diplomatic arts and intrigues must ever prove upon this continent against that system of self-government which seems natural to our soil, and which will ever resist foreign interference. . . .

Oregon is a part of the North American continent, to which, it is confidently affirmed, the title of the United States is the best now in existence. For the grounds on which that title rests I refer you to the correspondence of the late and present Secretary of State with the British plenipotentiary during the negotiation. The British proposition

SOURCE: *James K. Polk, "First Annual Message" (December 2, 1845), in* Compilation of the Messages and Papers of the Presidents, 1789–1897, *ed. J. D. Richardson (1907), IV, 387–88, 397–99.*

of compromise, which would make the Columbia the line south of 49°, with a trifling addition of detached territory to the United States north of that river, and would leave on the British side two-thirds of the whole Oregon Territory, including the free navigation of the Columbia and all the valuable harbors on the Pacific, can never for a moment be entertained by the United States without an abandonment of their just and clear territorial rights, their own self-respect, and the national honor. . . .

The rapid extension of our settlements over our territories heretofore unoccupied, the addition of new States to our Confederacy, the expansion of free principles, and our rising greatness as a nation are attracting the attention of the powers of Europe, and lately the doctrine has been broached in some of them of a "balance of power" on this continent to check our advancement. The United States, sincerely desirous of preserving relations of good understanding with all nations, can not in silence permit any European interference on the North American continent, and should any such interference be attempted will be ready to resist it at any and all hazards.

CHAPTER QUESTIONS

1. *What conditions in the United States facilitated westward expansion between 1820 and 1850? How did this period of expansion differ from that between 1780 and 1820?*
2. *Why was the expansionism of the 1840s and 1850s particularly appealing to Southerners? Were Northerners equally enthusiastic? Why?*

Chapter 11

Reform Ferment: Utopianism, Abolitionism, and Feminism

During the decades from 1820 to 1860, the United States was caught up in a remarkable outburst of fervor for humanitarian reform. Underlying this reformism was a vision of a drastically altered society in which the treatment of individuals would be more equitable, and new institutions and sources of authority would be established. The new social order was to be achieved through immediate action. In some instances, small communities were organized, dedicated to a new, less competitive way of life that nurtured the body as well as the soul.

For some Americans, withdrawal from society seemed ineffectual, in that it meant paying no attention to correcting society's defects. For them, the more appropriate response was to become actively involved in changing society. Horace Mann, for example, almost single-handedly conducted a campaign for greater public support of education. Other activists created organizations that were dedicated to social reform. The aim of these organizations was to awaken the conscience of the public, to mobilize support for reform programs, and to secure enactment of specific legislation. The American Anti-Slavery Society and the American Society for the Promotion of Temperance were two such reform-minded organizations.

Two powerful ideas fueled this reform vision and activity. The first was the idea of progress, which fostered an exuberant optimism that improvement was not only possible but inevitable. Equally important was the belief that individuals should be free to act on their own initiative, free from artificial, unjust, and immoral constraints. The revivalism of the 1820s and 1830s fused these two ideas into a powerful impulse for the reform of society.

This chapter focuses on reform and humanitarian activities in the 1830s and 1840s. The selections reflect both contemporary views and the views of historians about reform in these decades. In reading these selections, it should be kept in mind that the reform movement highlighted a never-ending dilemma of American democracy: how to reconcile individual freedom with the legitimate or perceived needs of society.

Chronology

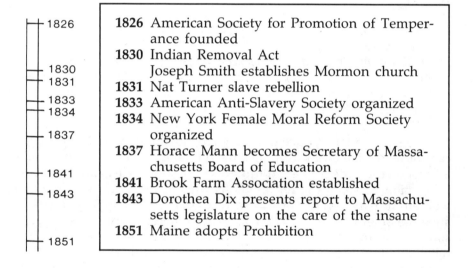

1826	**1826** American Society for Promotion of Temperance founded
	1830 Indian Removal Act
1830	Joseph Smith establishes Mormon church
1831	**1831** Nat Turner slave rebellion
1833	**1833** American Anti-Slavery Society organized
1834	**1834** New York Female Moral Reform Society organized
1837	**1837** Horace Mann becomes Secretary of Massachusetts Board of Education
1841	**1841** Brook Farm Association established
1843	**1843** Dorothea Dix presents report to Massachusetts legislature on the care of the insane
	1851 Maine adopts Prohibition
1851	

Documents

11.1   Why Immediate Emancipation? James Brewer Stewart (secondary source)

11.2   The Seneca Falls Declaration of 1848, Susan B. Anthony, Elizabeth Cady Stanton, and Matilda Joslyn Gage (primary source)

11.3   Newspaper Coverage of the Equal Rights Movement (visual source)

11.4   "Perfectionism," Laurence Veysey (secondary source)

11.5   Demon Rum, Timothy Shay Arthur (primary source)

11.6   The Constitution of the Brook Farm Association (primary source)

11.7   Poverty and Education, Horace Mann (primary source)

11.1   Why Immediate Emancipation?

James Brewer Stewart

In the 1830s, the militant and radical stance of William Lloyd Garrison to end slavery without compensation of slave owners attracted the support of only a small minority, mostly in New England. Historians have offered a variety of explanations for the New England roots of radical abolitionism, including a loss of status, rebellion against parents, and self-doubt among socially conscious young people in New England. In his book *Holy Warriors: The Abolitionists and American Slavery*, excerpted here, historian James Brewer Stewart offers another explanation: that advocates of immediate emancipation were strongly influenced by Protestant revivalism.

Consider:

1. *The basic elements of Stewart's argument, and the validity of the argument;*
2. *What arguments could be developed against Stewart's position;*
3. *Any parallel between this connection of militant abolitionism to Protestant revivalism and similar connections between other religious movements and reform movements in American history.*

The sudden emergence of immediate abolitionism in New England cannot be explained as a predictable offshoot of Yankee revivalism or a legacy from the upper South. Instead, one must emphasize the interaction between the rebellious feelings of these religious men and women and the events of the early 1830's. As the 1830's opened in an atmosphere of crisis, their attentions became intensely fixed on slavery. As in the early 1820's, the nation was again beset by black rebellions and threats of southern secession. Concurrently, events in England and in its sugar islands empire seemed to confirm the necessity of demanding the immediate emancipation of all slaves, everywhere. An unprecedented array of circumstances and jarring events suddenly converged on these anxious young people and launched them upon the lifetime task of abolishing slavery. . . .

In one sense, these sudden espousals of immediate abolition can be understood as a strategic innovation developed because of the manifest failures of gradualism. Slaveholders had certainly shown no sympathy to moderate schemes. In England, too, where immediatism was also gaining followers, the general public had remained unmoved by gradualist proposals. Demands for "immediate, unconditional, uncompensated emancipation" thus appealed to young American idealists—at least the slogan was free of moral qualifications. Indeed, in 1831 the

SOURCE: *James Brewer Stewart,* Holy Warriors: The Abolitionists and American Slavery, *41–49. Copyright © 1976 by James Brewer Stewart. Reprinted by permission of Farrar, Straus and Giroux, Inc.*

British government, responding to immediatist demands, enacted a massive program of gradual, compensated emancipation in the West Indies. But, even more important, by dedicating themselves to immediatism, the young reformers performed acts of self-liberation akin to the experience of conversion.

By freeing themselves from the shackles of gradualism, American abolitionists had finally triumphed over their feelings of selfishness, unworthiness, and alienation. Now they were morally fit to take God's side in the struggle against all the worldliness, license, cruelty, and selfishness that slaveowning had come to embody. Immediatists sensed themselves involved in a cosmic drama, a righteous war to redeem a fallen nation. They now felt ready to make supreme sacrifices and prove their fitness in their new religion of antislavery. . . .

Abolitionists now put their faith entirely in the individual's ability to recognize and redeem himself from sin. No stifling traditions, no restrictive loyalties to institutions, no timorous concern for moderation or self-interest should be allowed to inhibit the free reign of Christian conscience. In its fullest sense, the phrase "immediate emancipation" described a transformed state of mind dominated by God and wholly at war with slavery. . . .

Like many other Americans who took up the burdens of reform, abolitionists envisioned their cause as leading to a society reborn in Christian brotherhood. Emancipation, like temperance, women's rights and communitarianism, became synonymous with the redemption of mankind and the opening of a purer phase of human history. . . .

The challenges which the abolitionists faced as they began their crusade were thus enormous. So was their own capability for disruption, although they were hardly aware of it at first. The ending of slavery whether peacefully or violently would require great changes in American life. Yet, if immediate emancipation provoked fear and violent hostility, it was nevertheless a doctrine appropriate to the age. The evangelical outlook with its rejection of tradition and expedience both embodied and challenged the culture that had created it. In retrospect, moderate approaches to the problem of slavery hardly seemed possible in Jacksonian America.

As a result, immediatist goals were anything but limited. Abolitionists now proposed to transform hundreds of millions of dollars worth of slaves into millions of black citizens by eradicating two centuries of American racism. Nevertheless, they sincerely felt that they promoted a conservative enterprise, and in certain respects this was an understandable (if misleading) self-assessment. Their unqualified attacks on slavery were, as they understood them, simply emulations of well-established evangelical methods. The Temperance Society's assault on liquor and the revivalist's denunciation of unbelief had hardly been characterized by restraint. Besides, immediatists were simply proposing an ideal by which all Christians were to measure themselves. They were not planning bloody revolution. They relied solely on voluntary conversion and rejected violence. As agitators, they defined their task as restoring time-honored American freedoms to an unjustly deprived people. Except for their opposition to racism, they offered no criticism of ordinary Protestant values. Was it anarchy, they wondered, to urge that pure Christian morality replace what they believed was the sexual abandon of the slave quarters? "Are we then fanatics," [William Lloyd] Garrison asked, "because we cry, *Do not rob! Do not murder!?*"

In their own eyes, then, abolitionists were hardly behaving like incendiaries as they opened their crusade. In slaveholding they discovered the ultimate source of the moral collapse which so deeply disturbed them. . . . immediate abolition seemed to hold forth the promise of Christian reconciliation between races, sections, and individuals. All motive for race revolt, all reason for political strife, and all inducement for moral degeneracy would be swept away. Indeed, the alternative of silence only invited the further spread of anarchy in a nation which Garrison described in 1831 as already "full of the blood of innocent men, women and babies—full of adultery and concupiscence—full of blasphemy, darkness and woeful rebellion against God—full of wounds and bruises and putrefying sores.". . .

Nevertheless, the abolitionists launched their crusade on a note of glowing optimism. Armed with moral certitude, they were also completely naïve politically.". . . [Theodore] Weld predicted in 1834 that complete equality for all blacks in the upper South was but two years away, and that "scores of clergymen in the slaveholding states . . . *are really with us.*". . .

All the same, there was wisdom in the naïveté. Without this romantic faith that God would put all things right, abolitionists would have lacked the incentive and creative stamina necessary for sustained assaults against slavery. . . .convinced, and certain of ultimate victory, abolitionists set out to induce each American citizen to repent the sin of slavery.

11.2   The Seneca Falls Declaration of 1848

Susan B. Anthony, Elizabeth Cady Stanton, and Matilda Joslyn Gage

American feminism emerged as an organized movement in the 1830s and 1840s. It was one part of the general reform movement of the period that included separate campaigns to end prostitution, promote temperance, and end slavery. When prominent women of the day became active in the abolition movement, however, they found that they would not be allowed to participate as equals. These women increasingly recognized that their own rights were being denied, and they advocated a feminism that called for full equality between the sexes. In September 1848, nearly three hundred reformers (including forty men) attended the first feminist convention, held at Seneca Falls, New York, and adopted a coherent program for women's equality. That program, which included the demand for suffrage, is reflected in the Seneca Falls Declaration, excerpted below.

Consider:

1. *Why the delegates used the Declaration of Independence as a model to present this statement of women's grievances;*
2. *How this list of grievances compares with those listed in the Declaration of Independence;*
3. *Why the demand for women's suffrage subsequently attracted so much opposition.*

THE SENECA FALLS DECLARATION OF 1848

When, in the course of human events, it becomes necessary for one portion of the family of man to assume among the people of the earth a position different from that which they have hitherto occupied, but one to which the laws of nature and of nature's God entitle them, a decent respect to the opinions of mankind requires that they should declare the causes that impel them to such a course.

We hold these truths to be self-evident: that all men and women are created equal; . . .

The history of mankind is a history of repeated injuries and usurpations on the part of man toward woman, having in direct object the establishment of an absolute tyranny over her. To prove this, let facts be submitted to a candid world.

He has never permitted her to exercise her inalienable right to the elective franchise.

He has compelled her to submit to laws, in the formation of which she had no voice.

He has withheld from her rights which are given to the most ignorant and degraded men—both natives and foreigners.

Having deprived her of this first right of a citizen, the elective franchise, thereby leaving her without representation in the halls of legislation, he has opposed her on all sides.

He has made her, if married, in the eye of the law, civilly dead.

He has taken from her all right in property, even to the wages she earns.

He has made her, morally, an irresponsible being, as she can commit many crimes with impunity, provided they be done in the presence of her husband. In the covenant of marriage, she is compelled to

---

SOURCE: *Susan B. Anthony, Elizabeth Cady Stanton, and Matilda Joslyn Gage, eds.,* History of Woman Suffrage *(1889), I, 75–80.*

promise obedience to her husband, he becoming, to all intents and purposes, her master—the law giving him power to deprive her of her liberty, and to administer chastisement.

He has so framed the laws of divorce, as to what shall be the proper causes, and in case of separation, to whom the guardianship of the children shall be given, as to be wholly regardless of the happiness of women—the law, in all cases, going upon a false supposition of the supremacy of man, and giving all power into his hands.

After depriving her of all rights as a married women, if single, and the owner of property, he has taxed her to support a government which recognizes her only when her property can be made profitable to it.

He has monopolized nearly all the profitable employments, and from those she is permitted to follow, she receives but a scanty remuneration. He closes against her all the avenues to wealth and distinction which he considers most honorable to himself. As a teacher of theology, medicine, or law, she is not known.

He has denied her the facilities for obtaining a thorough education, all colleges being closed against her.

He allows her in Church, as well as State, but a subordinate position, claiming Apostolic authority for her exclusion from the ministry, and, with some exceptions, from any public participation in the affairs of the Church.

He has created a false public sentiment by giving to the world a different code of morals for men and women, by which moral delinquencies which exclude women from society, are not only tolerated, but deemed of little account in man.

He has usurped the prerogative of Jehovah himself, claiming it as his right to assign for her a sphere of action, when that belongs to her conscience and to her God.

He has endeavored, in every way that he could, to destroy her confidence in her own powers, to lessen her self-respect, and to make her willing to lead a dependent and abject life.

Now, in view of this entire disfranchisement of one-half the people of this country, their social and religious degradation—in view of the unjust laws above mentioned, and because women do not feel themselves aggrieved, oppressed, and fraudulently deprived of their most sacred rights, we insist that they have immediate admission to all the rights and privileges which belong to them as citizens of the United States.

In entering upon the great work before us, we anticipate no small amount of misconception, misrepresentation, and ridicule; but we shall use every instrumentality within our power to effect our object. We shall employ agents, circulate tracts, petition the State and National legislatures, and endeavor to enlist the pulpit and the press in our behalf. We hope this Convention will be followed by a series of Conventions embracing every part of the country.

RESOLUTIONS

WHEREAS, The great precept of nature is conceded to be, that "man shall pursue his own true and substantial happiness." Blackstone in his Commentaries remarks, that this law of Nature being coequal with mankind, and dictated by God himself, is of course superior in obligation to any other. It is binding over all the globe, in all countries and at all times, no human laws are of any validity if contrary to this, and such of them as are valid, derive all their force, and all their validity, and all their authority, mediately and immediately, from this original; therefore,

Resolved, That such laws as conflict, in any way, with the true and substantial happiness of woman, are contrary to the great precept of nature and of no validity, for this is "superior in obligation to any other."

Resolved, That all laws which prevent woman from occupying such a station in society as her conscience shall dictate, or which place her in a position inferior to that of man, are contrary to the great precept of nature, and therefore of no force or authority.

Resolved, That woman is man's equal—was intended to be so by the Creator, and the highest good of the race demands that she should be recognized as such.

Resolved, That the women of this country ought to be enlightened in regard to the laws under which they live, that they may no longer publish their degradation by declaring themselves satisfied with their present position, nor their ignorance, by asserting that they have all the rights they want.

Resolved, That inasmuch as man, while claiming for himself intellectual superiority, does accord to woman moral superiority, it is pre-eminently his duty to encourage her to speak and teach, as she has an opportunity, in all religious assemblies.

Resolved, That the same amount of virtue, delicacy, and refinement of behavior that is required of woman in the social state, should also be required of man, and the same transgressions should be visited with equal severity on both man and woman.

Resolved, That the objection of indelicacy and impropriety, which is so often brought against woman when she addresses a public audience, comes with a very ill-grace from those who encourage, by their attendance, her appearance on the stage, in the concert, or in feats of the circus.

Resolved, That woman has too long rested satisfied in the circumscribed limits which corrupt customs and a perverted application of the Scriptures have marked out for her, and that it is time she should move in the enlarged sphere which her great Creator has assigned her.

Resolved, That it is the duty of the women of this country to secure to themselves their sacred right to the elective franchise.

Resolved, That the equality of human rights results necessarily from the fact of the identity of the race in capabilities and responsibilities.

Resolved, therefore, That, being invested by the Creator with the same capabilities, and the same consciousness of responsibility for their exercise, it is demonstrably the right and duty of woman, equally with man, to promote every righteous cause by every righteous means; and especially in regard to the great subjects of morals and religion, it is self-evidently her right to participate with her brother in teaching them, both in private and in public, by writing and by speaking, by any instrumentalities proper to be used, and in any assemblies proper to be held; and this being a self-evident truth growing out of the divinely implanted principles of human nature, any custom or authority adverse to it, whether modern or wearing the hoary sanction of antiquity, is to be regarded as a self-evident falsehood, and at war with mankind.

11.3   Newspaper Coverage of the Equal Rights Movement

According to Elizabeth Cady Stanton, the people (sixty-eight women and thirty-two men) who signed the Seneca Falls Declaration of Principles in 1848 were not prepared for the hostile reaction of the public. With a few exceptions, the nation's newspapers portrayed the equal rights movement with sarcasm and ridicule. This attitude is evident in the 1859 drawing shown here, which conveys an inaccurate impression of the debate over several resolutions. For example, no female speaker denounced men as such; the men who attended did not behave in the manner shown; and the only resolution not adopted unanimously was the call for women's suffrage. In the lower left corner of the picture is a woman dressed in black who represents Amelia Bloomer, but the clothing she is wearing is a gross distortion of the style for women that she promoted in the magazine, *The Lily.*

Consider:

1. *The message the artist is trying to convey;*
2. *The assumptions and views about men and women suggested by the illustration;*
3. *The reasons why the equal rights movement was depicted in this fashion.*

SOURCE: *The Bettmann Archive.*

11.4 "Perfectionism"

Laurence Veysey

The reformers and reform movements of the 1830s and 1840s were certainly a diverse lot, but most of these reformers held a vision of a society in which their humanitarianism and sense of justice prevailed. When translated into social activism, this vision increased the tension between the real and the ideal and often involved a break with the mainstream of American life and society.

In his book *The Perfectionists: Radical Social Thought in the North, 1815–1860,* from which the following excerpt is taken, historian Laurence Veysey compiled and selected writings of seventeen social activists or reformers in the 1830s and 1840s. According to Veysey, they all shared a vision of "perfectionism."

Consider:

1. *What fundamental assumptions about individuals and institutions these reformers made;*
2. *The relationship between the "perfectionist" movements of the 1830s and 1840s and Christianity;*
3. *The connection between utopian movements and other reform activities in the 1830s and 1840s.*

Increasingly historians are attracted to the term "perfectionism" to sum up the spirit of social activism in the years after 1830. Though "ultraism" was a more widely accepted contemporary label, the term "perfection" was indeed then used. . . .

What does "perfectionism" mean? It must first of all be divorced from its twentieth-century connotation of personal finickiness in small details. . . .

In the 1830s the term referred instead to the belief that individuals, groups, or entire nations might make themselves morally blameless through a sudden, conscious act of will. Its original context was religious, in the theology of John Humphrey Noyes and Charles G. Finney, but its easy transference to the secular realm is again shown by the wide use the word received beyond evangelical circles. The assumptions underlying perfectionism were perhaps never stated more clearly than by Adin Ballou:

"Man as a religious being and moral agent acts more or less in three general spheres or departments of effort and responsibility, viz.:— The individual, the social, and the civil or governmental spheres. . . . It follows, therefore, that there are individual duties, virtues, sins; social duties, virtues, sins; and governmental duties, virtues, sins. In each sphere our religious and moral obligations are the same. Right and wrong confront human beings at every step. To be perfect, one must think, say, and do what is right in each and all the spheres of responsibility named."

Though Ballou carefully distinguishes among these several spheres of life, the implication is that private and public morality are ultimately identical; nations are to be judged by the same standards that weigh on the individual. Another implication, repugnant to our own age of relativism, is that in all spheres, right and wrong are total or absolute. There can be, or ought to be, no mixing of the two. Anything that is not morally right is utterly wrong.

Viewed more dynamically, perfectionism is the belief that a state of total righteousness may be achieved all at once—by the individual Christian in the brief experience of conversion or regeneration, and by the whole society in the immediate renunciation of such obvious wrongs as slavery or the consumption of alcohol. It is easier to go the

SOURCE: *Laurence Veysey, "Introduction," in* The Perfectionists: Radical Social Thought in the North, 1815–1860, *ed. Laurence Veysey (New York: John Wiley & Sons, 1973), 10–13.*

whole route toward moral victory in a single swoop, argues Noyes, than to crawl toward it by painfully slow increments. Such a leap can be made thanks to the intensity of the individual's willful desire to bring about the change. It can be seen, then, how closely perfectionism is tied to a supreme optimism about human nature, an optimism first broached during the Enlightenment and seemingly verified by the facts of life on the American continent. . . .

. . . perfectionism may be seen as faith in man's capacity to improve himself drastically, to achieve a qualitatively better pattern of life on earth. The social evils that the radicals of the nineteenth century apprehended often remain those of our own time, as several of the selections below reveal—war, patriotism, racial and sexual discrimination, unequal distribution of wealth, inhumanity toward deprived or unfortunate people. Legal slavery is the great contrary example of an evil that was indeed utterly exterminated. But as regards all such evils, the perfectionist is one who retains an unshakable conviction that sudden movement for the better is possible. It was easier to hold to this faith in the nineteenth century, before the frailty of repeated appeals to man's reason and conscience had become so evident. . . .

Yet the lives of many millions would be incomparably gloomier today if no persons of such pronounced convictions had ever appeared. The logical alternative to perfectionism is the belief that all improvement occurs by accident, a philosophy even more repugnant to most modern people, who do believe that we can will ourselves into better conditions. . . .

What first caused the radical or perfectionist movement to come into being in America at that particular time? It arose independently of the sectional controversy that led to the Civil War, because it gathered steam long before slavery emerged as a burning political issue, and it was internally too diverse and many-faceted to be seen as a response to that single problem . . .

The radical spirit was too sweepingly universalistic for it to make much sense in terms of the national political life . . . it was not closely related to Jacksonianism, nor inseparably linked with the "democratic" tendency of the times. It always bisected the major political parties, or moved far beyond them; . . .

. . . the movement bears the symptoms of a much more persistent tendency in human societies, toward millennialism. Many times and in many places all over the world, small bands of men have seceded from the conventional life that flows around them and announced a new vision that calls for a general social reordering. . . . the utopian movement of the early nineteenth century . . . marks a recurring tendency toward social revitalization. . . .

. . . the tendency to "come out," in a posture of open separation from the larger society, may be crucial, for the erection of a clear boundary between "ourselves" and outsiders is the first step in the creation of a new culture that seeks to replace the old order.

11.5   Demon Rum

Timothy Shay Arthur

The reform movement with the largest following in the 1840s and 1850s was the crusade against liquor. This crusade consisted of two elements, those who favored moderation in drinking (wine and beer) and those who supported total abstinence. The latter became known as prohibitionists because they supported laws to prohibit the manufacture and sale of all alcoholic beverages. Prohibitionists argued that liquor destroyed the home, encouraged crime and violence, and led to the degradation of individuals and society. In 1854, T. S. Arthur published a novel, *Ten Nights in a Bar-Room*, which dramatized prohibitionist arguments. The final chapter in this book, excerpted here, opens with Joe Morgan, the reformed town drunk, playing a leading role in a meeting at the local tavern, the Sickle and Sheaf Bar, where local prohibition was approved.

Consider:

1. *The assumptions Arthur makes about values in American society;*
2. *The validity of Joe Morgan's arguments in favor of prohibition;*
3. *How Arthur deals with the concept of individual rights and private property.*

NIGHT THE TENTH.

The Closing Scene at the "Sickle and Sheaf"

On the day that succeeded the evening of this fearful tragedy, placards were to be seen all over the village, announcing a mass meeting at the "Sickle and Sheaf" that night.

By early twilight, the people commenced assembling. The bar, which had been closed all day, was now thrown open, and lighted; and in this room, where so much of evil had been originated, encouraged, and consummated, a crowd of earnest-looking men were soon gathered. Among them I saw the fine person of Mr. Hargrove. Joe Morgan—or rather Mr. Morgan—was also of the number. The latter I would scarcely have recognised, had not some one near me called him by name. He was well dressed, stood erect, and, though there were many deep lines on his thoughtful countenance, all traces of his former habits were gone. While I was observing him, he arose, and addressing a few words to the assemblage, nominated Mr. Hargrove as chairman of the meeting. To this a unanimous assent was given.

SOURCE: *Timothy Shay Arthur, "Ten Nights in a Bar-Room and What I Saw There," in* Ten Nights in a Bar-Room, *ed. Donald A. Koch (Cambridge, Mass.: Belknap Press, 1964). 235-40.*

On taking the chair, Mr. Hargrove made a brief address, something to this effect.

"Ten years ago," said he, his voice evincing a slight unsteadiness as he began, but growing firmer as he proceeded, "there was not a happier spot in Bolton county than Cedarville. Now, the marks of ruin are every where. Ten years ago, there was a kind-hearted, industrious miller in Cedarville, liked by every one, and as harmless as a little child. Now, his bloated, disfigured body lies in that room. His death was violent, and by the hand of his own son!". . .

"Ten years ago," he went on, "Judge Hammond was accounted the richest man in Cedarville. Yesterday he was carried, a friendless pauper, to the Almshouse; and to-day he is the unmourned occupant of a pauper's grave! Ten years ago, his wife was the proud, hopeful, loving mother of a most promising son. I need not describe what Willy Hammond was. All here knew him well. Ah! what shattered the fine intellect of that noble-minded woman? Why did her heart break? Where is she? Where is Willy Hammond?". . .

"Shall I go on? Shall I call up and pass in review before you, one after another, all the wretched victims who have fallen in Cedarville during the last ten years? Time does not permit. It would take hours for the enumeration! No: I will not throw additional darkness into the picture. Heaven knows it is black enough already! But what is the root of this great evil? Where lies the fearful secret? Who understands the disease? A direful pestilence is in the air—it walketh in darkness, and wasteth at noonday. It is slaying the first-born in our houses, and the cry of anguish is swelling on every gale. Is there no remedy?"

"Yes! yes! There is a remedy!" was the spontaneous answer from many voices. . . .

"And there is but one remedy," said Morgan, as Mr. Hargrove sat down. "The accursed traffic must cease among us. You must cut off the fountain, if you would dry up the stream. If you would save the young, the weak, and the innocent—on you God has laid the solemn duty of their protection—you must cover them from the tempter. Evil is strong, wily, fierce, and active in the pursuit of its ends. The young, the weak, and the innocent can no more resist its assaults, than the lamb can resist the wolf. They are helpless, if you abandon them to the powers of evil. Men and brethren! as one who has himself been wellnigh lost—as one who, daily, feels and trembles at the dangers that beset his path—I do conjure you to stay the fiery stream that is bearing every thing good and beautiful among you to destruction. Fathers! for the sake of your young children, be up now and doing. Think of Willy Hammond, Frank Slade, and a dozen more whose names I could repeat, and hesitate no longer! Let us resolve, this night, that from henceforth, the traffic shall cease in Cedarville. Is there not a large majority of citizens in favour of such a measure? And whose rights or interests can be affected by such a restriction? Who, in fact, has any right to sow disease and death in our community? The liberty, under sufferance, to do so, wrongs the individual who uses it, as well as those who become his victims. Do you want proof of this. Look at Simon Slade, the happy, kind-hearted miller; and at Simon Slade, the tavern-keeper. Was he benefited by the liberty to work harm to his neighbour? No! no! In heaven's name, then, let the traffic cease! To this end, I offer these resolutions:—

"Be it resolved by the inhabitants of Cedarville, That from this day henceforth, no more intoxicating drink shall be sold within the limits of the corporation.

"Resolved, further, That all the liquors in the Sickle and Sheaf be forthwith destroyed, and that a fund be raised to pay the creditors of Simon Slade therefor, should they demand compensation.

"Resolved, That in closing up all other places where liquor is sold, regard shall be had to the right of property . . .

"Resolved, That with the consent of the legal authorities, all the liquor for sale in Cedarville be destroyed; provided the owners thereof be paid its full value out of a fund specially raised for that purpose.". . .

. . . the resolutions passed, and the more ultra-inclined contented themselves with carrying out the second resolution, to destroy forthwith all the liquor to be found on the premises; which was immediately done. After which the people dispersed to their homes, each with a lighter heart, and better hopes for the future of their village.

On the next day, as I entered the stage that was to bear me from Cedarville, I saw a man strike his sharp axe into the worn, faded, and leaning post that had, for so many years, borne aloft the Sickle and Sheaf; and just as the driver gave word to his horses, the false emblem which had invited so many to enter the way of destruction, fell crashing to the earth.

11.6 The Constitution of the Brook Farm Association

One of the more famous communal groups in the 1840s was the Brook Farm Association, whose members hoped to create an environment that fostered the harmonious development of mind, body, and soul. Organized by George Ripley in 1841 and located in a rural area just nine miles from Boston, this experiment in cooperative living reflected the interests of transcendentalists, such as Ralph Waldo Emerson, who sought alternatives to lives and careers spent in the pursuit of wealth. The members of Brook Farm Association agreed to a constitution, excerpted here, that defined the objectives of the association. Brook Farm lasted only six years. Heavily in debt, the association disbanded in 1846 after a fire destroyed one of the main buildings.

Consider:

1. *What this constitution reveals about the values and attitudes of the Brook Farm Association;*
2. *The type of people that were most likely to find life at Brook Farm appealing;*
3. *How democratic the community was.*

CONSTITUTION

In order more effectually to promote the great purposes of human culture; to establish the external relations of life on a basis of wisdom and purity; to apply the principles of justice and love to our social orgnization in accordance with the laws of Divine Providence; to substitute a system of brotherly cöoperation for one of selfish competition; to secure to our children and those who may be entrusted to our care, the benefits of the highest physical, intellectual and moral education, which in the progress of knowledge the resources at our command will permit; to institute an attractive, efficient, and productive system of industry; to prevent the exercise of worldly anxiety, by the competent supply of our necessary wants; to diminish the desire of excessive accumulation, by making the acquisition of individual property subservient to upright and disinterested uses; to guarantee to each other forever the means of physical support, and of spiritual progress; and thus to impact a greater freedom, simplicity, truthfulness, refinement, and moral dignity, to our mode of life;—we the undersigned do unite in a voluntary Association, and adopt and ordain the following articles of agreement, to wit:

ARTICLE I.
NAME AND MEMBERSHIP.

Sec. 1.   The name of this Association shall be "The Brook-Farm Association for Industry and Education." All persons who shall hold one or more shares in its stock, or whose labor and skill shall be considered an equivalent for capital, may be admitted by the vote of two-thirds of the Association, as members thereof.

Sec. 2.   No member of the Association shall ever be subjected to any religious test; nor shall any authority be assumed over individual freedom of opinion by the Association, nor by one member over another;

SOURCE: *Octavius Brooks Frothingham,* Transcendentalism in New England *(New York: G.P. Putnam's Sons, 1876), 159–63.*

nor shall any one be held accountable to the Association, except for such overt acts, or omissions of duty, as violate the principles of justice, purity, and love, on which it is founded; and in such cases the relation of any member may be suspended or discontinued, at the pleasure of the Association. . . .

ARTICLE III.
GUARANTIES.

SEC. I. The Association shall provide such employment for all its members as shall be adapted to their capacities, habits, and tastes; and each member shall select and perform such operations of labor, whether corporal or mental, as shall be deemed best suited to his own endowments and the benefit of the Association.

SEC. 2. The Association guarantees to all its members, their children and family dependents, house-rent, fuel, food, and clothing, and the other necessaries of life, without charge, not exceeding a certain fixed amount to be decided annually by the Association; no charge shall ever be made for support during inability to labor from sickness or old age, or for medical or nursing attendance, except in case of share-holders, who shall be charged therefor, and also for the food and clothing of children, to an amount not exceeding the interest due to them on settlement; but no charge shall be made to any members for education or the use of library and public rooms. . . .

SEC. 4. Children over ten years of age shall be provided with employment in suitable branches of industry. . . .

ARTICLE V.
GOVERNMENT.

SEC. I. The government of the Association shall be vested in a board of Directors, divided into four departments, as follows; 1st, General Direction; 2d, Direction of Education; 3d, Direction of Industry; 4th, Direction of Finance; consisting of three persons each, provided that the same person may be elected member of each Direction.

SEC. 2. The General Direction and Direction of Education shall be chosen annually, by the vote of a majority of the members of the Association. The Direction of Finance shall be chosen annually, by the vote of a majority of the share-holders and members of the Association. The direction of Industry shall consist of the chiefs of the three primary series. . . .

SEC. 6. The department of industry shall be arranged in groups and series, as far as practicable, and shall consist of three primary series; to wit, Agricultural, Mechanical, and Domestic Industry. The chief of each series shall be elected every two months by the members thereof, subject to the approval of the general Direction. The chief of each group shall be chosen weekly by its members.

11.7 Poverty and Education

Horace Mann

Educational reformers in the 1830s and 1840s believed that public elementary schools were the key to the improvement of individuals and to a general upgrading of society. The leader in educational reform and innovation was the state of Massachusetts. Under the leadership of Horace Mann, who served as secretary of the State Board of Education from 1837 to 1850, Massachusetts adopted a public-school program that served as the model for public schools in the United States. One of the reasons for Mann's success was his ability to articulate clearly the necessity for strong public support of public schools. In this selection, taken from his *Twelfth Annual Report*, Mann explains how education can help end poverty.

Consider:

1. *Why Mann was so optimistic about the power of education to end poverty;*
2. *What Mann means by education "enlarging . . . social feelings";*
3. *Whether Mann's definition of the role of public education has any relevance today.*

. . . a State should . . . seek the solution of such problems as these: To what extent can competence displace pauperism? How nearly can we free ourselves from the low-minded and the vicious, not by their expatriation, but by their elevation? To what extent can the resources and powers of Nature be converted into human welfare, the peaceful arts of life be advanced, and the vast treasures of human talent and genius be developed? How much of suffering, in all its forms, can be relieved? or, what is better than relief, how much can be prevented? Cannot the classes of crimes be lessened, and the number of criminals in each class be diminished?

. . . The distance between the two extremes of society is lengthening, instead of being abridged. With every generation, fortunes increase on the one hand, and some new privation is added to poverty on the other. We are verging towards those extremes of opulence and of penury, each of which unhumanizes the human mind. . . .

I suppose it to be the universal sentiment of all those who mingle any ingredient of benevolence with their notions on political economy, that vast and overshadowing private fortunes are among the greatest dangers to which the happiness of the people in a republic can be subjected. Such fortunes would create a feudalism of a new kind. . . .

SOURCE: Horace Mann, *"End Poverty Through Education,"* Twelfth Annual Report, Massachusetts Board of Education *(1848), from Horace Mann,* On The Crisis in Education, *ed. Louis Filler (Yellow Springs, Ohio: Antioch Press, 1965), 121–24.*

Now, surely nothing but universal education can counterwork this tendency to the domination of capital and the servility of labor. . . . if education be equally diffused, it will draw property after it by the strongest of all attractions; for such a thing never did happen, and never can happen, as that an intelligent and practical body of men should be permanently poor. Property and labor in different classes are essentially antagonistic; but property and labor in the same class are essentially fraternal.

Education, then, beyond all other devices of human origin, is the great equalizer of the conditions of men,—the balance-wheel of the social machinery. I do not here mean that it so elevates the moral nature as to make men disdain and abhor and oppression of their fellow-men. This idea pertains to another of its attributes. But I mean that it gives each man the independence and the means by which he can resist the selfishness of other men. It does better than to disarm the poor of their hostility towards the rich: it prevents being poor. Agrarianism is the revenge of poverty against wealth. The wanton destruction of the property of others—the burning of hay-ricks and corn-ricks, the demolition of machinery because it supersedes hand-labor, the sprinkling of vitriol on rich dresses—is only agrarianism run mad. Education prevents both the revenge and the madness. On the other hand, a fellow-feeling for one's class or caste is the common instinct of hearts not wholly sunk in selfish regards for person or for family. The spread of education, by enlarging the cultivated class or caste, will open a wider area over which the social feelings will expand; and, if this education should be universal and complete, it would do more than all things else to obliterate distinctions in society. . . .

. . . But the beneficent power of education would not be exhausted, even though it should peaceably abolish all the miseries that spring from the co-existence, side by side, of enormous wealth and squalid want. It has a higher function. Beyond the power of diffusing old wealth, it has the prerogative of creating new. It is a thousand times more lucrative than fraud, and adds a thousand-fold more to a nation's resources than the most successful conquests. Knaves and robbers can obtain only what was before possessed by others. But education creates or develops new treasures,—treasures not before possessed or dreamed of by any one.

CHAPTER QUESTIONS

1. *How would you explain the fact that reform activity in this period was centered in the Northeast, particularly New England? Consider social, cultural, and economic factors.*
2. *What underlying beliefs and assumptions did reformers and reform programs in the 1830s and 1840s share? How can you explain the radically different programs and approaches of different reformers?*

Chapter 12

The Debate over Slavery

The "second party system" of Democrats and Whigs was threatened from the start by sectional conflict over the slavery question. For a time, both parties continued to enjoy support in the North and the South, as moderates—such as Henry Clay in the Whig party and Stephen A. Douglas in the Democratic—were successful in persuading their party colleagues to accept compromise settlements.

The festering moral and constitutional issues that grew out of the institution of slavery were aggravated by the zealous expansionism of the period. In fact, both pro- and antislavery forces came to treat the question of slavery in the territories as a crucible in which the whole question of the institution might be resolved. And it was during debate over key territorial legislation—in particular, the Compromise of 1850 and the Kansas-Nebraska Act—that the debate over slavery reached its most intense and fully developed stage.

Politicians, of course, mirrored the general public's widely differing viewpoints on slavery in their debates. Those viewpoints were difficult to generalize. Several shades of opinion on race and constitutional questions were woven through both pro- and antislavery arguments, and there was a good deal of confusion and internal contradiction. Occasionally, catalytic events or agents emerged—such as publication of the immensely popular *Uncle Tom's Cabin* or the Supreme Court's controversial ruling in the *Dred Scott* case—that clarified the basic issues and suggested the ultimate impossibility of settling the slavery question through compromise and moderation. For a time, moderates like Clay and Douglas prevailed; but the center could not hold. The Whigs collapsed, to be replaced by the Republicans, a Northern-based, antislavery party. The victory in 1860 of the new party's presidential candidate, Abraham Lincoln, led directly to the final rupture—secession and civil war.

This chapter focuses on several aspects of the debate over slavery, particularly during the critical decade of the 1850s. The selections shed light on contemporary opinions on both sides of the slavery question— on the institution of slavery itself, the constitutional issues it raised, and issues of race. Even the broad array of issues reflected in these documents, however, only begins to suggest the complexity of the problems facing those who tried to resolve the debate over slavery without a civil war.

Chronology

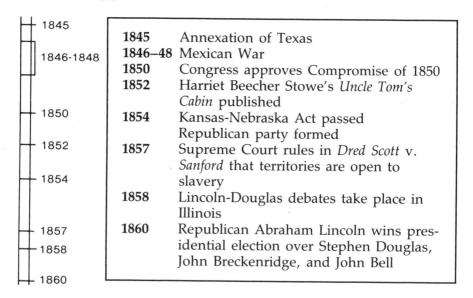

1845	Annexation of Texas
1846–48	Mexican War
1850	Congress approves Compromise of 1850
1852	Harriet Beecher Stowe's *Uncle Tom's Cabin* published
1854	Kansas-Nebraska Act passed Republican party formed
1857	Supreme Court rules in *Dred Scott* v. *Sanford* that territories are open to slavery
1858	Lincoln-Douglas debates take place in Illinois
1860	Republican Abraham Lincoln wins presidential election over Stephen Douglas, John Breckenridge, and John Bell

Timeline markings: 1845, 1846-1848, 1850, 1852, 1854, 1857, 1858, 1860

Documents

12.1 Defense of Slavery As a Benefit to Society, John C. Calhoun (primary source)
12.2 Cruelties of Slavery: The Plight of Slave Women, Jacqueline Jones (secondary source)
12.3 Images of Slavery, C. Giroux, Eyre Crowe (visual sources)
12.4 Changing the Boundaries of Slavery, 1850 and 1854 (maps)
12.5 The Supreme Court Takes the Southern Side, David M. Potter (secondary source)

12.1 Defense of Slavery As a Benefit to Society

John C. Calhoun

Although arguments in defense of slavery varied widely, many Southerners suggested that the institution of slavery was superior to Northern capitalism ("wage slavery") and was an absolute benefit to society. Among the
most forceful and influential proponents of this line of thought was John
C. Calhoun. In the letter excerpted here, written in 1844 while he was
serving as Secretary of State, Calhoun expands on the benefits of slavery.
The immediate issue was Britain's threatened interference in the question
of the legality of slavery in then-independent Texas. But Calhoun's larger
point was that a state had both the right and the responsibility to protect
the existence of slavery for the good of all its citizens.

Consider:

1. *Whether the British had a right to try to abolish slavery outside their
   own borders;*
2. *How abolitionists would have reacted to Calhoun's arguments (see Doc.
   11.1);*
3. *How his arguments relate to the "compact theory" of government.*

So long as Great Britain confined her policy to the abolition of
slavery in her own possessions and colonies, no other country had a
right to complain. . . . But when she goes beyond, and avows it as
her settled policy, and the object of her constant exertions, to abolish
it throughout the world, she makes it the duty of all other countries,
whose safety or prosperity may be endangered by her policy, to adopt
such measures as they may deem necessary for their protection. . . .
. . . The policy she has adopted in reference to the portion of that
race in her dominions may be humane and wise; but it does not follow,
if it prove so with her, that it would be so in reference to the United
States and other countries, whose situation differs from hers. . . . With
us, it is a question to be decided, not by the Federal Government, but

SOURCE: *Secretary of State John C. Calhoun to Richard Pakenham (April 18, 1844), U.S. House of
Representatives, 28th Cong., 1st sess., Doc. 271, 50–53.*

by each member of this Union for itself, according to its own views of its domestic policy, and without any right on the part of the Federal Government to interfere in any manner whatever. . . . A large number of the States has decided that it is neither wise nor humane to change the relation which has existed, from their first settlement, between the two races; while others, where the African is less numerous, have adopted the opposite policy.

It belongs not to the Government to question whether the former have decided wisely or not; . . . if the experience of more than half a century is to decide, it would be neither humane nor wise in them to change their policy. The census and other authentic documents show that, in all instances in which the States have changed the former relation between the two races, the condition of the African, instead of being improved, has become worse. They have been invariably sunk into vice and pauperism . . . while, in all other States which have retained the ancient relation between them, they have improved greatly in every respect—in number, comfort, intelligence, and morals—as the following facts, taken from such sources, will serve to illustrate:

The number of deaf and dumb, blind, idiots, and insane, of the negroes in the States that have changed the ancient relation between the races, is one out of every ninety-six; while in the States adhering to it, it is one out of every six hundred and seventy-two—that is, seven to one in favor of the latter, as compared with the former. . . .

. . . On the other hand, the census and other authentic sources of information establish the fact, that the condition of the African race throughout all the States where the ancient relation between the two has been retained, enjoys a degree of health and comfort which may well compare with that of the laboring population of any country in Christendom; and, it may be added, that in no other condition, or in any other age or country, has the negro race ever attained so high an elevation in morals, intelligence, or civilization.

If such be the wretched condition of the race in their changed relation, where their number is comparatively few, and where so much interest is manifested for their improvement, what would it be in those States where the two races are nearly equal in numbers, and where, in consequence, would necessarily spring up mutual fear, jealousy, and hatred between them? It may, in truth, be assumed as a maxim, that two races differing so greatly, and in so many respects, cannot possibly exist together in the same country, where their numbers are nearly equal, without the one being subjected to the other. Experience has proved that the existing relation, in which the one is subjected to the other in the slaveholding States, is consistent with the peace and safety of both, with great improvement to the inferior; . . . In this view of the subject, it may be asserted, that what is called slavery is in reality a political institution, essential to the peace, safety, and prosperity of those States of the Union in which it exists.

12.2   Cruelties of Slavery: The Plight of Slave Women

Jacqueline Jones

The cruelty suffered by slaves was not limited to physical violence at the hands of slaveholders and overseers, though such violence was certainly widespread. The psychological deprivations caused by the institution of slavery could, over a period of time, be every bit as injurious to blacks as physical punishment. Particularly victimized were slave women, whose plight is described in this excerpt from Jacqueline Jones's study of the history of black women in America.

Consider:

1. *How the situation described by Jones in this selection compares with Calhoun's depiction of the effects of slavery (Doc. 12.1);*
2. *Why family life was so important to black slaves;*
3. *Whether slave women were worse off, as a group, than male slaves.*

. . . A compact, volatile, and somewhat isolated society, the slave-holder's estate represented, in microcosm, a larger drama in which physical force combined with the coercion embedded in the region's political economy to sustain the power of whites over blacks and men over women. . . . As blacks, slave women were exploited for their skills and physical strength in the production of staple crops; as women, they performed a reproductive function vital to individual slaveholders' financial interests and to the inherently expansive system of slavery in general. Yet slave women's unfulfilled dreams for their children helped to inspire resistance against "the ruling race" and its attempts to subordinate the integrity of black family life to its own economic and political interests. . . .

. . . The master took a . . . crudely opportunistic approach toward the labor of slave women, revealing the interaction (and at times conflict) between notions of women *qua* "equal" black workers and women *qua* unequal reproducers; hence a slaveowner just as "naturally" put his bondswomen to work chopping cotton as washing, ironing, or cooking. . . .

However, slave women also worked on behalf of their own families, and herein lies a central irony in the history of their labor. Under slavery, blacks' attempts to sustain their family life amounted to a political act of protest against the callousness of owners, mistresses,

SOURCE: *Jacqueline Jones,* Labor of Love, Labor of Sorrow: Black Women, Work, and the Family from Slavery to the Present, *11–15, 19, 22, 28. Copyright © 1985 by Basic Books, Inc. Reprinted by permission of the publisher.*

and overseers. In defiance of the slaveholders' tendencies to ignore gender differences in making assignments in the fields, the slaves whenever possible adhered to a strict division of labor within their own households and communities. . . . black women's attention to the duties of motherhood deprived whites of full control over them as field laborers, domestic servants, and "brood-sows." . . .

. . . the definition of slave women's work is problematical. If work is any acitvity that leads either directly or indirectly to the production of marketable goods, then slave women did nothing *but* work. Even their efforts to care for themselves and their families helped to maintain the owner's work force and to enhance its overall productivity. . . .

In his efforts to wrench as much field labor as possible from female slaves without injuring their capacity to bear children, the master made "a noble admission of female equality," observed . . . an abolitionist sympathizer, with bitter irony. Slaveholders had little use for sentimental platitudes about the delicacy of the female constitution when it came to grading their "hands" according to physical strength and endurance. . . .

. . . Still, slaveowners faced a real dilemma when it came to making use of the physical strength of women as field workers and at the same time protecting their investment in women as childbearers. These two objectives—one focused on immediate profit returns and the other on long-term economic considerations—at times clashed, as women who spent long hours picking cotton, toiling in the fields with heavy iron hoes, and walking several miles a day sustained damage to their reproductive systems immediately before and after giving birth. At the regional level, a decline in slave fertility and increase in miscarriage rates during the cotton boom years of 1830 to 1860 reveals the heightened demands made upon women. . . .

Work in the soil thus represented the chief lot of all slaves, female and male. . . . Although women predominated as household workers, few devoted their energies full time to this kind of labor; . . . According to [historian] Eugene Genovese, as few as 5 percent of all antebellum adult slaves served in the elite corps of house servants . . .

The allocation of slave women's labor by white men and women was based on three different considerations—the whites' desire to increase staple-crop production, enlarge their work force, and provide for the daily sustenance of their own households. . . . Profit-making was a "rational" basis upon which to set female slaves to work in the fields, but long-term interests related to women's childbearing capacity at times yielded to the demands of the harvest at hand. Owners and overseers alike might easily cross the boundary between chastising black women for work-related offenses and terrorizing them as a means of asserting control over the entire slave labor force. Moreover, the sexual exploitation of a black woman could produce concentric rings of bitterness that engulfed the white mistress, resulting in further (though economically "irrational") abuse of the victim herself.

12.3   Images of Slavery
C. Giroux
Eyre Crowe

Art played an important role in shaping popular perceptions of slavery and plantation life. The vivid imagery of the two paintings reproduced here—one clearly glorifying the plantation and the other portraying the brutalities of black slavery—illustrate the power of visual argument. Not only the specific subjects, but also the style and nature of the artists' respective compositions, convey sharply contrasting messages.

Consider:

1. *The story told by each painting;*
2. *The mood created, in each case, by the artist's style and composition;*
3. *How Eyre Crowe's representation of the slaves leaving the auction at Richmond reinforces and/or expands upon what is said in Document 12.2.*

SOURCE: *C. Giroux, "Cotton Plantation," painted between 1850 and 1865. Courtesy, Museum of Fine Arts, Boston, Karolik Collection of American Paintings, 1815–1865, 47.1144; and Eyre Crowe, "After the Sale: Slaves Going South from Richmond" (1853), oil on canvas, 1957.2, Chicago Historical Society.*

12.4   Changing the Boundaries of Slavery, 1850 and 1854

The Missouri Compromise, the Compromise of 1850, and the Kansas-Nebraska Act all involved the drawing of boundary lines that were designed to resolve the question of where slaveholders could legally take their slave "property" within American territory. Each of these acts was viewed, at least for a time, as a permanent solution. The Missouri Compromise had prohibited slavery north of 36° 30' latitude in the area west of Missouri, which was admitted as a slave state. The two maps reproduced here show how the acts of 1850 and 1854 altered the situation.

Consider:

1. *Whether these maps reveal different underlying principles at work;*
2. *Whether it was realistic for Southerners to hope that slavery would expand westward, given the territories where slavery was allowed after 1854;*
3. *Whether the Missouri Compromise could have served as a permanent solution to the question of slavery in the territories, if the extent of American territory had not changed after 1820.*

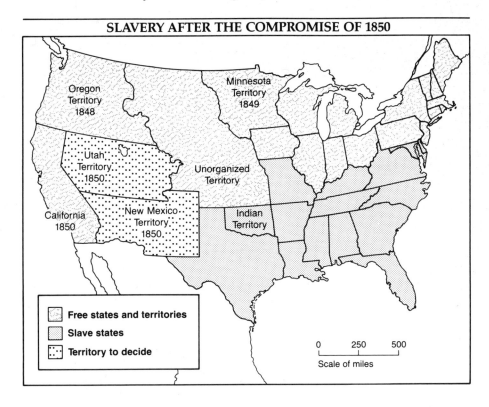

SLAVERY AFTER THE COMPROMISE OF 1850

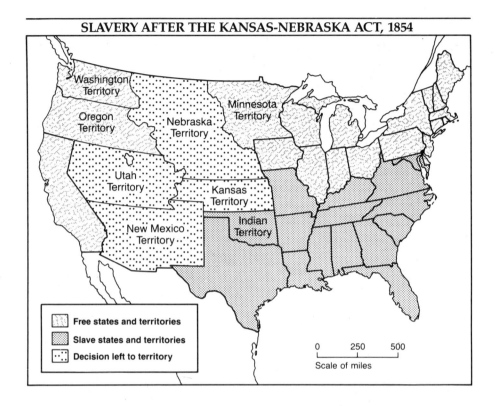

SLAVERY AFTER THE KANSAS-NEBRASKA ACT, 1854

12.5 The Supreme Court Takes the Southern Side

David M. Potter

While moderates in Congress tried to contain the explosive slavery issue through compromises, the Supreme Court struck a blow against their efforts in its controversial ruling in the 1857 case, *Dred Scott* v. *Sanford*. Chief Justice Taney, who spoke for the Court's Southern majority, hoped to resolve the thorny questions related to the expansion of slavery by going well beyond the narrow issue of the case. In a posthumously published book, *The Impending Crisis, 1848–1861*, renowned historian David Potter takes the Court to task for its attempt to accomplish what Congress could not, or would not, do. This excerpt from Potter's book discusses the ways in which the Court failed the American public in rendering its decision.

Consider:

1. *Where Potter's sympathies lie on the issues he is discussing;*
2. *Whether the Supreme Court should have tried to "settle the sectional fight by resolving a question which Congress had avoided";*
3. *Whether the Court should have avoided "strengthening the extremists" in issuing its decision in the* Dred Scott *case.*

Like a good many other measures during these years . . . the Dred Scott decision conspicuously failed to accomplish what was expected of it, either by its advocates or by its opponents. . . . it strangely combined theoretical significance with trivial consequences. Probably no other major judicial decision in history affected the daily lives of as few people as this one. It annulled a law which had in fact been repealed three years previously, and it denied freedom to the slaves in an area where there were no slaves. . . .

Yet, in other respects, it was momentous in its meaning and its indirect results, and by all functional tests, it was a failure for those who supported it and a disaster for the American people. The extent of this failure and disaster can be measured in three ways.

First, it is legitimate to ask what effect the decision had in reducing sectional tensions. Clearly it had none, but instead it placed obstacles in the way of sectional adjustment. In the South, for instance, it encouraged southern rights advocates to believe that their utmost demands were legitimized by constitutional sanction. . . . In the North, on the other hand, it strengthened a conviction that an aggressive slavocracy was conspiring to impose slavery upon the nation, . . . While thus strengthening the extremists, it cut the ground from under the moderates. . . . Second, . . . a question arises as to the realism of the justices in supposing that they could settle the sectional fight by resolving a question which Congress had avoided. . . . It was a ruling which invalidated a measure passed by Congress, and which sought to validate a position that Congress had repeatedly voted against. . . . However admirable may have been the courage of the justices in facing the music, their tactical judgment was wretched.

Finally, the Dred Scott decision was a failure because the justices followed a narrow legalism which led them into the untenable position of pitting the Constitution against basic American values, although the Constitution in fact derives its strength from its embodiment of American values. Concretely, the American people wanted the United States to be a republic of free people and regarded the Constitution as essentially a charter for a free people. The utmost exception which

SOURCE: *David M. Potter,* The Impending Crisis, 1848–1861, *compiled and edited by Don E. Fehrenbacher, 290–93. Copyright © 1976 by The Estate of David M. Potter. Reprinted by permission of Harper & Row, Publishers.*

they would make was to concede the right of local areas (states) to maintain slavery as a local—and, they hoped, temporary—institution. But always they regarded slavery as having only a local sanction, and freedom as having a national sanction. . . . The South, while attempting defensively to ward off attacks on slavery, had adopted a position that went far beyond the defensive. Southern leaders had developed the doctrine that southern citizens with southern property (slaves) could not legally be kept out of the federal territory. The argument was not without legal plausibility, but it fatally reversed the place of slavery and freedom in the American system. It made freedom local—an attribute of those states which abolished slavery, but not of the United States; it made slavery national, in the sense that slavery would be legal in any part of the United States where a state government had not abolished it. Apart from the morality of it, this was a ruinous decision because, in the process of splitting logical hairs, it arrived at a result which converted the charter of freedom into a safeguard of slavery.

12.6   Popular Sovereignty Explained: The Freeport Doctrine

Stephen A. Douglas

In 1858, public attention focused on the campaign in Illinois, where Republican Abraham Lincoln and Democrat Stephen A. Douglas were competing for a seat in the Senate. In a series of seven debates held across the state, Lincoln hammered away at the inconsistencies in the "popular sovereignty" doctrine supported by Douglas. At Freeport, Lincoln extracted from Douglas a statement that was supposed to explain how the people of a territory could exclude slavery in spite of the recent *Dred Scott* ruling. Douglas's "Freeport Doctrine," excerpted here, was artful, but it also opened him up to charges of cynicism and lack of moral concern. In particular, "popular sovereignty" now began to appear to many Northerners as a less useful tool against the expansion of slavery than they had previously thought.

Consider:

1. *The strength of Douglas's argument that the people of a territory could, in effect, evade the Supreme Court's ruling;*
2. *The kinds of voters that would have responded most favorably to Douglas's arguments;*
3. *Why people would have accused Douglas of lacking moral concern about slavery because of his Freeport Doctrine.*

The . . . question propounded to me by Mr. Lincoln is, can the people of a territory in any lawful way against the wishes of any citizen of the United States; exclude slavery from their limits prior to the formation of a state constitution? I answer emphatically, as Mr. Lincoln has heard me answer a hundred times from every stump in Illinois, that in my opinion the people of a territory can, by lawful means, exclude slavery from their limits prior to the formation of a state constitution. . . . It matters not what way the Supreme Court may hereafter decide as to the abstract question whether slavery may or may not go into a territory under the Constitution, the people have the lawful means to introduce it or exclude it as they please, for the reason that slavery cannot exist a day or an hour anywhere, unless it is supported by local police regulations. . . . Those police regulations can only be established by the local legislature, and if the people are opposed to slavery they will elect representatives to that body who will by unfriendly legislation effectually prevent the introduction of it into their midst. If, on the contrary, they are for it, their legislation will favor its extension. Hence, no matter what the decision of the Supreme Court may be on that abstract question, still the right of the people to make a slave territory or a free territory is perfect and complete under the [Kansas-]Nebraska Bill. . . .

The third question which Mr. Lincoln presented is, if the Supreme Court of the United States shall decide that a state of this Union cannot exclude slavery from its own limits will I submit to it? . . . He might as well ask me, suppose Mr. Lincoln should steal a horse would I sanction it; . . . He casts an imputation upon the Supreme Court of the United States by supposing that they would violate the Constitution of the United States. I tell him that such a thing is not possible. . . .

The fourth question of Mr. Lincoln is, are you in favor of acquiring additional territory in disregard as to how such acquisition may effect the Union on the slavery question. This question is very ingeniously and cunningly put.

. . . I answer that whenever it becomes necessary, in our growth and progress to acquire more territory, that I am in favor of it, without reference to the question of slavery, and when we have acquired it, I will leave the people free to do as they please, either to make it slave or free territory, as they prefer. . . . I tell you, increase, and multiply, and expand, is the law of this nation's existence. . . . You cannot limit this great republic by mere boundary lines, saying, "thus far shalt thou go, and no further." . . . With our natural increase, growing with a rapidity unknown in any other part of the globe, with the tide of

SOURCE: Created Equal? The Complete Lincoln-Douglas Debates of 1858, ed. Paul M. Angle (Chicago: University of Chicago Press, 1958), 152, 154–56.

emigration that is fleeing from despotism in the old world to seek a refuge in our own, there is a constant torrent pouring into this country that requires more land, more territory upon which to settle, and just as fast as our interests and our destiny require additional territory in the north, in the south, or on the islands of the ocean, I am for it, and when we acquire it will leave the people . . . free to do as they please on the subject of slavery and every other question.

12.7   The Republican Party and the Race Question

Eric Foner

Some abolitionists believed in absolute equality of the races, but many of those who opposed slavery and its extension to the territories shared, to one degree or another, racist assumptions similar to those held by advocates of slavery. Accordingly, the Republican party, which began as a Northern organization that stood firmly against the spread of slavery, contained a variety of viewpoints on race. In this selection, historian Eric Foner stresses the degree to which Republicans departed from the extreme racist attitudes of their day. He also points out how Lincoln reflected the balance of racial sentiment in the young party.

Consider:

1. *Whether the Republican attitudes described were racist;*
2. *Whether the movement favoring colonization of American blacks in Africa was consistent with the spirit of the Constitution and of the Declaration of Independence.*

. . . Like the Democrats, Republicans often made use of electoral appeals which smacked of racism, and some historians have interpreted this as proof that there existed no fundamental differences between the two parties' racial attitudes. Yet the Republicans did develop a policy which recognized the essential humanity of the Negro, and demanded protection for certain basic rights which the Democrats denied him. Although deeply flawed by an acceptance of many racial stereotypes, and limited by the free labor ideology's assumption that the major responsibility for a person's success or failure rested with

SOURCE: *Eric Foner, Free Soil, Free Labor, Free Men: Ideology of the Republican Party Before the Civil War (New York: Oxford University Press, 1970), 261–62, 280–81, 288, 292–95.*

himself, not society, the Republican stand on race relations went against the prevailing opinion of the 1850's, and proved a distinct political liability in a racist society. . . .

In an age which witnessed the voluntary emigration of millions of Europeans to the United States and the constant flow westward of the American population, the idea that black Americans would wish to seek a better life in other lands did not seem as impractical as it does today. . . . "Colonization," said George Julian, "is one of the great tidal forces of modern civilization." In many ways, therefore, the . . . plan was a logical product of its times, and in its strange mixture of racism and humanitarianism, imperialism and missionary zeal, it reflected many aspects of the Republican ideology as a whole. But in the end, though the colonizationists must be given credit for their awareness of the immense difficulties of achieving racial justice in this country, their proposal was an attempt to escape from the problem, not to solve it.

While racism and colonization were important elements of the Republican attitude toward the Negro, they were by no means the entire story. Many men entered the Republican party with long histories of support for Negro rights, and many of the areas of the North which gave the Republicans their largest majorities had distinguished themselves in the past by their endorsement of Negro suffrage and opposition to Negro exclusion laws. . . .

Even more striking was the large number of Republican leaders who had taken pro-Negro positions earlier in their political careers. . . .

Republicans in Congress had few opportunities to vote on issues of Negro rights in the 1850's but in the instances which did come up, their differences with northern Democrats were clearly demonstrated. . . .

In accordance with their conception of the civil rights of free Negroes, Republicans consistently attacked the policies of the federal government denying the citizenship of the black man. During the 1850's the government generally rejected passport applications from Negroes and denied them the right to benefits under pre-emption laws. Republicans criticized these policies, . . . They also bitterly denounced Chief Justice Taney's opinion in the Dred Scott case that Negroes could not be citizens of the United States, . . . Throughout the North, the Republican press denounced this opinion, and several state conventions of the party in 1857 affirmed free Negro citizenship. . . .

Many Republicans insisted before the Civil War that their party had no position on the questions of race relations and Negro rights, and certainly the differences between easterners and westerners, and men of Whig, Democratic, and Liberty background made it extremely difficult to reach a consensus within the party. . . .

Nevertheless, by the eve of the Civil War there had emerged a distinctive Republican attitude towards the Negro. As on other questions, it was well represented by Abraham Lincoln. . . . Lincoln, coming from Illinois, was well aware of the strength of racial prejudice, and he knew too that "a universal feeling, whether well- or ill-founded, can not be safely disregarded." Like most western Republicans, he opposed Negro suffrage and was an ardent colonizationist, though he insisted that emigration be voluntary. However, he never pandered to racial prejudice, even when confronted with the racist attacks of Douglas. And he consistently affirmed the basic humanity of the Negro and his right to an economic livelihood. . . . Many eastern Republicans would go further than this; many westerners, on the other hand, felt that Lincoln had gone too far; but Lincoln himself articulated a shaky consensus within the party.

CHAPTER QUESTIONS

1. *What were the principal points of view in the 1840s and 1850s on the best way to solve the slavery question?*
2. *How was the issue of minority rights against the "tyranny" of a majority involved in the slavery question? Could both sides use this appeal?*

part four

THE CIVIL WAR AND AFTER, 1860–1877

Chapter 13

The Right of Secession

N o single event or time period in American history has attracted greater interest than the Civil War. Historians have examined the Civil War from a variety of perspectives. Many have focused on the military aspects of the war, while others have studied the long-range effects—how it unleashed or accelerated forces that ultimately replaced existing social, economic, and political patterns.

One question of consuming interest, of course, is the cause of this bloody conflict. The war itself was scarcely over before participants—from both the North and the South—were offering various explanations. Among the explanations that historians have proposed are the institution of slavery, the ineptitude of political leaders, deep-seated differences of culture, and fundamentally conflicting economic systems.

In 1968 historian Richard Hofstadter wrote about a concept he called "comity," a consensus or set of shared values. The American political system, he said, is very fragile because it is held together by this comity, and such a consensus can no longer exist when contending interests do not "have a basic minimum regard for each other. . . ." According to Hofstadter, the coming of the Civil War can be understood as the story of the breakdown of comity in the 1850s; accommodation no longer seemed possible. People in both the North and the South came to believe that their own social and political system must expand in order to survive and to stand up to the evil of the other. Not surprisingly, last-minute compromise efforts failed and President Lincoln's conciliatory gestures to the seceded states were rejected.

This chapter focuses on a very short time period, less than a year, and a single issue—secession. The secession issue is a useful focus because it sheds light on the fundamental nature of the national Union and the political system supporting it. It also brings up again the recurring American dilemma: how to balance the rights of the minority with the wishes of the majority. Most of the documents in this chapter examine secession from the viewpoint of the participants themselves. They emphasize how difficult it is to establish a compromise or centrist position in the absence of a shared consensus.

Chronology

1860	
Nov. 6	**November 6, 1860** Abraham Lincoln elected President
Dec. 20	**December 20, 1860** South Carolina secedes from
Dec. 31	the Union
	December 31, 1860 Crittenden Compromise fails
1861	in the Senate
	February 4, 1861 Confederate constitutional
Feb. 4	convention meets in Mont-
Feb. 9	gomery, Alabama
	February 9, 1861 Jefferson Davis elected pro-
Feb. 25	visional president of the
	Confederacy
Mar. 4	**February 25, 1861** Washington Peace Conven-
	tion fails to resolve the
Apr. 12	secession crisis
	March 4, 1861 Inauguration of Abraham
	Lincoln
	April 12, 1861 Bombardment of Fort Sumter

Documents

13.1   The Irrepressible Conflict?

This cartoon depicts the nation as a classroom where students have become unruly. The teacher, identified as Mistress Columbia, awakens from a nap and calls the class to order. On the left, the side of the North, "Sharps" and "Irrepressible Conflict" represent clergyman Henry Ward Beecher and politician William Henry Seward, respectively. Southerner Hintor R. Helper, whose *Impending Crisis* has been changed to *The Pressent [sic] Conflict,* has been kicked into the North across the Mason-Dixon line that divides the classroom.

Consider:

1. *What message the cartoonist is trying to convey, and what assumptions underlie that message;*
2. *The significance in the cartoon of the two copies of the Constitution— one on Mistress Columbia's desk, the other being studied by one of the Southerners (lower right).*

MISTRESS COLUMBIA, WHO HAS BEEN TAKING A NAP, SUDDENLY WAKES UP AND CALLS HER NOISY SCHOLARS TO ORDER.

SOURCE: Harper's Weekly, *January 17, 1860.*

13.2   Political Party Platforms, 1860

In the presidential election of 1860, the threat of secession by the Southern states was the principal issue. The adoption of party platforms and selection of presidential candidates clearly reflected this. At the Democratic convention, the party split into sectional factions over the question of federal protection of slavery. Northern and western Democrats met again later, adopting a platform supporting popular sovereignty and nominating Stephen A. Douglas for President. Southern Democrats reconvened in Richmond, where they adopted a pro-slavery platform and nominated John C. Breckenridge of Kentucky. In the meantime, the new Republican party met in Chicago, adopting a platform that called for the containment of slavery and nominating Abraham Lincoln. Another newly formed political party, the Constitutional Union, was made up largely of Southerners who hoped to head off secession but could not accept Republican ideals. It nominated John Bell of Tennessee. This selection includes excerpts from the party platforms on which these presidential candidates campaigned.

Consider:

1. *Elements in the excerpted party platforms that might have been the cause of greater hopes and/or fears among Southerners, Northerners, and Westerners;*
2. *To what extent the outcome of the election of 1860 could be considered a national referendum on slavery and disunion.*

DEMOCRATIC PLATFORM OF 1860

. . .

2. Inasmuch as difference of opinion exists in the Democratic party as to the nature and extent of the powers of a Territorial Legislature, and as to the powers and duties of Congress, under the Constitution of the United States, over the institution of slavery within the Territories,

Resolved, That the Democratic party will abide by the decision of the Supreme Court of the United States upon these questions of Constitutional law.

3. *Resolved,* That it is the duty of the United States to afford ample and complete protection to all its citizens, whether at home or abroad, and whether native or foreign born. . . .

6. *Resolved,* That the enactments of the State Legislatures to defeat the faithful execution of the Fugitive Slave Law, are hostile in character, subversive of the Constitution, and revolutionary in their effect.

7. *Resolved,* That it is in accordance with the interpretation of the Cincinnati platform, that during the existence of the Territorial Gov-

SOURCE: National Party Platforms, 1840–1956, *comp. Donald Bruce Johnson (Urbana: University of Illinois Press, 1956), I, 30–33.*

ernments the measure of restriction, whatever it may be, imposed by the Federal Constitution on the power of the Territorial Legislature over the subject of the domestic relations, as the same has been, or shall hereafter be finally determined by the Supreme Court of the United States, should be respected by all good citizens, and enforced with promptness and fidelity by every branch of the general government.

DEMOCRATIC (BRECKENRIDGE FACTION) PLATFORM OF 1860

Resolved, That the platform adopted by the Democratic party at Cincinnati be affirmed, with the following explanatory resolutions:

1. That the Government of a Territory organized by an act of Congress is provisional and temporary, and during its existence all citizens of the United States have an equal right to settle with their property in the Territory, without their rights, either of person or property, being destroyed or impaired by Congressional or Territorial legislation.

2. That it is the duty of the Federal Government, in all its departments, to protect, when necessary, the rights of persons and property in the Territories, and wherever else its constitutional authority extends.

3. That when the settlers in a Territory, having an adequate population, form a State Constitution, the right of sovereignty commences, and being consummated by admission into the Union, they stand on an equal footing with the people of other States, and the State thus organized ought to be admitted into the Federal Union, whether its Constitution prohibits or recognizes the institution of slavery. . . .

REPUBLICAN PLATFORM OF 1860

Resolved, That we, the delegated representatives of the Republican electors of the United States, in Convention assembled, in discharge of the duty we owe to our constituents and our country, unite in the following declarations: . . .

2. That the maintenance of the principles promulgated in the Declaration of Independence and embodied in the Federal Constitution, "That all men are created equal; that they are endowed by their Creator with certain inalienable rights; that among these are life, liberty and the pursuit of happiness; that to secure these rights, governments are instituted among men, deriving their just powers from the consent of the governed," is essential to the preservation of our Republican institutions; and that the Federal Constitution, the Rights of the States, and the Union of the States must and shall be preserved. . . .

7. That the new dogma that the Constitution, of its own force, carries slavery into any or all of the territories of the United States, is a dangerous political heresy, at variance with the explicit provisions of that instrument itself, with contemporaneous exposition, and with legislative and judicial precedent; is revolutionary in its tendency, and subversive of the peace and harmony of the country.

8. That the normal condition of all the territory of the United States is that of freedom: That, as our Republican fathers, when they had abolished slavery in all our national territory, ordained that "no persons should be deprived of life, liberty or property without due process of law," it becomes our duty . . . to maintain this provision of the Constitution against all attempts to violate it; and we deny the authority of Congress, of a territorial legislature, or of any individuals, to give legal existence to slavery in any territory of the United States.

9. That we brand the recent reopening of the African slave trade, under the cover of our national flag . . . as a crime against humanity and a burning shame to our country and age; and we call upon Congress to take prompt and efficient measures for the total and final suppression of that execrable traffic.

10. That in the recent vetoes, by their Federal Governors, of the acts of the legislatures of Kansas and Nebraska, prohibiting slavery in those territories, we find a practical illustration of the boasted Democratic principle of Non-Intervention and Popular Sovereignty, embodied in the Kansas-Nebraska Bill, and a demonstration of the deception and fraud involved therein.

11. That Kansas should, of right, be immediately admitted as a state under the Constitution recently formed and adopted by her people, and accepted by the House of Representatives.

13.3   The Election of 1860

James M. McPherson

The election of 1860 involved four major candidates who presented the voters with clear alternatives on such issues as slavery, the tariff, free land, and the Pacific railroad (see Doc. 13.2). Although winning slightly less than 40 percent of the popular vote, Lincoln carried all the free states but New Jersey and won 180 electoral votes. Douglas came in second in the popular vote with 29.4 percent but received only twelve electoral votes; Breckenridge received 18 percent of the popular vote and seventy-two electoral votes. The following map shows the distribution of popular votes by county in the 1860 election; the table shows the distribution of popular and electoral votes by state. Both are taken from historian James M. McPherson's book, *Ordeal By Fire*.

Consider:

1. *What general areas were carried by each candidate in 1860;*
2. *How the attitudes of Southern voters on the question of secession relate to party preferences in the 1860 election;*
3. *Why Douglas did so poorly in both the North and the South.*

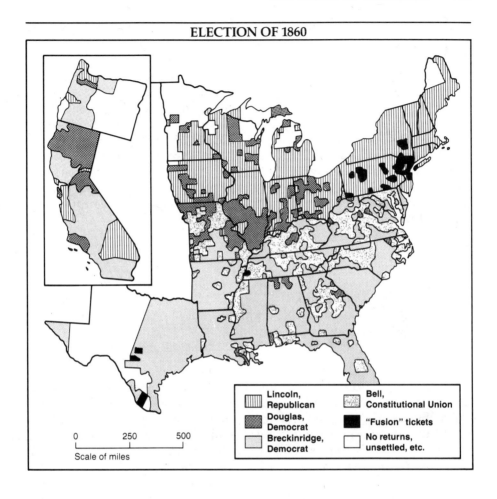

ELECTION OF 1860

Legend:
- Lincoln, Republican
- Douglas, Democrat
- Breckinridge, Democrat
- Bell, Constitutional Union
- "Fusion" tickets
- No returns, unsettled, etc.

0   250   500
Scale of miles

VOTING IN THE 1860 ELECTION

	ALL STATES		FREE STATES (18)		SLAVE STATES (15)	
	Popular Votes	Electoral Votes	Popular Votes	Electoral Votes	Popular Votes	Electoral Votes
Lincoln	1,864,735	180	1,838,347	180	26,388	0
Opposition to Lincoln	2,821,157	123	1,572,637	3	1,248,520	120
Fusion	595,846	—	580,426	—	15,420	—
Douglas	979,425	12	815,857	3	163,568	9
Breckinridge	669,472	72	99,381	0	570,091	72
Bell	576,414	39	76,973	0	499,441	39

SOURCE: *James M. McPherson,* Ordeal By Fire: The Civil War and Reconstruction *(New York: Alfred A. Knopf, Inc., 1982), 124–25. Copyright © 1982 by Alfred A. Knopf, Inc.*

13.4   Justifying Secession

On November 13, 1860, the South Carolina legislature passed a resolution calling for a convention to consider withdrawal from the Union. On December 20, without a single dissenting vote, the delegates to the convention approved an ordinance that ". . . the union now subsisting between South Carolina and other States under the name of the United States of America is hereby dissolved." Four days later the convention offered its explanation and justification for secession in a document entitled "Declaration of the Immediate Causes which induce and justify the Secession of South Carolina from the 'Federal Union'." This selection consists of excerpts from that declaration.

Consider:

1. What arguments are offered in this document to explain South Carolina's secession from the Union;
2. How the arguments in this document compare to the analysis of "social compact" presented in Doc. 6.6;
3. The underlying grievance that South Carolina had with the Union.

. . . the State of South Carolina having resumed her separate and equal place among nations, deems it due to herself, to the remaining United States of America, and to the nations of the world, that she should declare the immediate causes which have led to this act.

In the year 1765, that portion of the British Empire embracing Great Britain undertook to make laws for the Government of that portion composed of the thirteen American Colonies. A struggle for the right of self-government ensued, which resulted, on the 4th of July, 1776, in a Declaration, by the Colonies, "that they are, and of right ought to be, FREE AND INDEPENDENT STATES; and that, as free and independent States, they have full power to levy war, conclude peace, contract alliances, establish commerce, and to do all other acts and things which independent States may of right do."

They further solemnly declared that whenever any "form of government becomes destructive of the ends for which it was established, it is the right of the people to alter or abolish it, and to institute a new government." Deeming the Government of Great Britain to have become destructive of these ends, they declared that the Colonies "are absolved from all allegiance to the British Crown, and that all political connection between then and the State of Great Britain is, and ought to be, totally dissolved."

SOURCE: The Rebellion Record: A Diary of American Events, ed. Frank Moore (New York: G. P. Putnam, 1862), I, 3–4.

Thus were established the two great principles asserted by the Colonies, namely, the right of a State to govern itself; and the right of a people to abolish a Government when it becomes destructive of the ends for which it was instituted. And concurrent with the establishment of these principles, was the fact, that each Colony became and was recognized by the mother country as a FREE, SOVEREIGN AND INDEPENDENT STATE. . . .

. . . We hold that the Government is subject to the two great principles asserted in the Declaration of Independence; and we hold further, that the mode of its formation subjects it to a third fundamental principle, namely, the law of compact. We maintain that in every compact between two or more parties, the obligation is mutual; that the failure of one of the contracting parties to perform a material part of the agreement, entirely releases the obligation of the other; and that, where no arbiter is provided, each party is remitted to his own judgment to determine the fact of failure, with all its consequences.

We affirm that these ends for which the Government was instituted have been defeated, and the Government itself has been destructive of them by the action of the non-slaveholding States. Those States have assumed the right of deciding upon the propriety of our domestic institutions; and have denied the rights of property established in fifteen of the States and recognized by the Constitution; they have denounced as sinful the institution of Slavery; they have permitted the open establishment among them of societies, whose avowed object is to disturb the peace of and eloin [conceal] the property of the citizens of other States. They have encouraged and assisted thousands of our slaves to leave their homes; and those who remain, have been incited by emissaries, books, and pictures, to servile insurrection. . . .

. . . A geographical line has been drawn across the Union, and all the States north of that line have united in the election of a man to the high office of President of the United States whose opinions and purposes are hostile to Slavery. He is to be intrusted with the administration of the common Government, because he has declared that that "Government cannot endure permanently half slave, half free," and that the public mind must rest in the belief that Slavery is in the course of ultimate extinction.

This sectional combination for the subversion of the Constitution has been aided, in some of the States, by elevating to citizenship persons who, by the supreme law of the land, are incapable of becoming citizens; and their votes have been used to inaugurate a new policy, hostile to the South, and destructive of its peace and safety.

On the 4th of March next this part will take possession of the Government. It has announced that the South shall be excluded from the common territory, that the Judicial tribunal shall be made sectional, and that a war must be waged against Slavery until it shall cease throughout the United States.

The guarantees of the Constitution will then no longer exist; the equal rights of the States will be lost. The Slaveholding States will no longer have the power of self-government, or self-protection, and the Federal Government will have become their enemy.

Sectional interest and animosity will deepen the irritation; and all hope of remedy is rendered vain, by the fact that the public opinion at the North has invested a great political error with the sanctions of a more erroneous religious belief.

We, therefore, the people of South Carolina, by our delegates in Convention assembled, appealing to the Supreme Judge of the world for the rectitude of our intentions, have solemnly declared that the Union heretofore existing between this State and the other States of North America is dissolved, and that the State of South Carolina has resumed her position among the nations of the world, as separate and independent state, with full power to levy war, conclude peace, contract alliances, establish commerce, and to do all other acts and things which independent States may of right do.

13.5   Robert E. Lee and Secession
Robert E. Lee

Between November 1860 and March 1861, as the secession of Southern states from the Union became a reality, many Southerners were torn between their loyalty to the Union and their loyalty to their state. This conflict of loyalties is personified in Robert E. Lee, a native Virginian serving as a colonel in the United States Army in Texas. In this excerpt of a letter that Lee wrote to his son, William Henry Fitzhugh ("Rooney") Lee in January, 1861, Lee discusses his view of Virginia's secession from the Union.

Consider:

1. *What Lee meant when he wrote: "The South in my opinion has been aggrieved by acts of the North. . .";*
2. *Why Lee and many other Southerners felt such deep loyalty to a state;*
3. *How Lee's reasons for choosing a side compare to similar decisions made during the Revolutionary War.*

The South in my opinion has been aggrieved by the acts of the North as you say. I feel the aggression, & am willing to take every proper step for redress. It is the principle I contend for, not individual or private benefit. As an American citizen I take great pride in my

SOURCE: *"A Letter of R. E. Lee to his Son 'Rooney',"* January 28, 1861, in Virginia Magazine of History and Biography *69 (1961): 3–6.*

country, her prosperity & institutions & would defend any State if her rights were invaded. But I can anticipate no greater calamity for the country than a dissolution of the Union. It would be an accumulation of all the evils we complain of, & I am willing to sacrifice every thing but honour for its preservation. I hope therefore that all Constitutional means will be exhausted, before there is a resort to force. Secession is nothing but revolution. The framers of our Constitution never exhausted so much labour, wisdom & forbearance in its formation & surrounded it with so many guards & securities, if it was intended to be broken by every member of the confederacy at will. It was intended for peptual [sic] union, so expressed in the preamble, & for the establishment of a government, not a compact, which can only be dissolved by revolution or the consent of all the people in convention assembled. It is idle to talk of secession. Anarchy would have been established & not a government, by Washington, Hamilton, Jefferson, Madison & the other patriots of the Revolution. In 1808 when the New England States resisted Mr Jeffersons Imbargo law & the Hartford Convention assembled secession was termed treason by Virga [Virginia] statesmen. What can it be now? Still a union that can only be maintained by swords & bayonets, & in which strife & civil war are to take the place of brotherly love & kindness, has no charm for me. I shall mourn for my country, & for the welfare & progress of mankind. If the Union is dissolved & the government disrupted, I shall return to my native State & share the miseries of my people & save in her defence will draw my sword on none. Give much love to Charlotte to my dear little son & believe me always your devoted father

RE Lee

P. S. As usual I have been obliged to write mid many interruptions.

13.6 Failure to Compromise: Lincoln and the Crittenden Compromise

Albert D. Kirwan
Allan Nevins

On December 18, 1860, the Senate authorized the creation of a Committee of Thirteen to consider ways to deal with the secession crisis. One member of the committee, John J. Crittenden of Kentucky, had already introduced proposals that many believed could serve as a basis for averting secession. But as one Southern state after another seceded and the date for Lincoln's inauguration drew near, neither Northerners nor Southerners on the committee would agree to the Crittenden Compromise. In refusing to support Crittenden's proposals, Northern Republican senators were following the lead of President-elect Lincoln, who refused to compromise on the extension of slavery. Historians have offered different assessments of Lincoln's inflexibility. Crittenden's biographer, historian Albert D. Kirwan, takes a harsh view of Lincoln's stance, while Allan Nevins expresses the opposite viewpoint in *The Emergence of Lincoln: Prologue to Civil War, 1859–1861*. Excerpts from these two books follow.

Consider:

1. *What assumptions Kirwan and Nevins, respectively, make about the possibility of preventing secession.*
2. *The basic arguments that Kirwan and Nevins use to support their conclusions.*

ALBERT KIRWAN

The committee held its first meeting on Saturday, December 22. The tide of sentiment favoring conciliation was now swelling in influential Republican ranks outside of Congress. . . .

But the long shadow of the President-elect would cast a gloom over the meeting of the committee. . . . Lincoln had already taken an inflexible position against the heart of the Crittenden plan, restoration of the Missouri line. Moreover, he had already informed trusted lieutenants in Washington of his sentiments, and they had passed the word to their colleagues. . . .

When the committee met, therefore, the eight non-Republicans were surprised at the rigidly irreconcilable position taken by their Republican colleagues. . . .

Crittenden had been confident that his plan would receive sympathetic Republican consideration. When Republican members of the committee refused to support him, therefore, he was in despair. The Republicans "refuse to lower their . . . party standard a single hair's breadth, and present their Chicago platform as their ultimatum," he told a group of friends. They seemed convinced, he wrote, that the South was only bluffing and that their best policy was "to stand firm & *do nothing*." . . .

. . . Republicans could not, he [William Seward] said, accept the principle of slavery expansion implied in Crittenden's first resolution. They would not reject all of his proposals, however. Specifically he proposed resolutions guaranteeing slavery in the states where it existed, seeking repeal of the personal liberty laws, and modification of the Fugitive Slave Act. These proposals were insufficient to satisfy Toombs and Davis and were voted down. The committee continued to meet through the week of December 24, but without success. On the last day of the dying year it reported to the Senate its inability to agree on any plan of adjustment.

SOURCE: *Albert D. Kirwan,* John J. Crittenden: The Struggle for the Union *(Lexington: University of Kentucky Press, 1962), 380–83; Allan Nevins,* The Emergence of Lincoln: Prologue to Civil War 1859–1861, *vol. II, 393–95, 403–4. Copyright 1950 Charles Scribner's Sons. Reprinted with the permission of Charles Scribner's Sons, a Division of Macmillan Inc.*

The failure of the Crittenden proposals in the Committee of Thirteen must be charged to its Republican members. Had Seward asked, when he returned to Washington on December 24, for a reconsideration of the vote on Crittenden's proposals, it is highly probable that Collamer and Doolittle would have joined him in voting for them. If so, the proposals would have passed the committee with at least eleven votes. Reported to the Senate by such a majority, they would have been brought to a speedy vote and approval there, probably by a constitutional majority. The House then, with all the pressures of the incoming administration, would probably have been compelled to follow suit. . . .

The refusal of Republicans to accept division of the territories into slave and free-soil sections seems, even in light of the knowledge they possessed, as shortsighted and unstatesmanlike as was the conduct of southern extremists in urging secession because of the refusal. It has long been conceded by all knowing men, North as well as South, that slavery would never prosper there. Popular sovereignty, for all the Republican denunciation of it, actually was working to exclude slavery in the territories as effectively as congressional prohibition could. But Republicans had taken their position on the question long before, some of them decades before, at a time when the eventual triumph of the free-soil element had not yet been demonstrated as it had been everywhere by 1860. The party had been formed to prevent the spread of slavery into the territories at a time when that prospect seemed an imminent probability in Kansas. To concede now that the danger no longer existed . . . would be an admission that popular sovereignty had already achieved the end for which they had waged their battle. In the absence of any program as a substitute, such an admission might result in dissolution of the party. . . .

The stature that Lincoln would gain in the ensuing four years has created a legend about him that all but obscures the fact that at the time of his election, and for some months thereafter, he was a plain country lawyer with a narrowly limited background. He would soon prove that he had great undeveloped capacities for leadership and for sensing the feelings of the great masses of the people. In the winter of 1860–1861, however, he was being led by, rather than leading, his party. . . .

In the ominous public silence that Lincoln maintained from his nomination until his inaugural, he revealed somewhat his failure to understand the temper of the southern people. He apparently thought that the average southerner could distinguish between Lincoln's own philosophy on the slavery question and that of abolitionists like William Lloyd Garrison. When asked to publicize his views, he refused, repeatedly. He also seemed to think that secession was largely talk on the part of a few hotheads, and would be easily put down by an overwhelming Unionist sentiment in the South. The Upper South he believed so steadfast that there was patently no danger of secession there. If there were, the border states would smother the sentiment.

Meantime, he would hold his counsel until March 4, and then in a conciliatory message, he would give such assurances that all fear of him and his party would dissipate. . . .

Believing that secession was only gasconade, Lincoln saw no purpose in stirring up the radicals in his own party by making unnecessary concessions. Many of these radicals, like Lincoln, thought secession a bluff. But many influential Republicans who thought it might result in war were unconcerned if it should. [W.H.] Herndon, returning from a tour of central Illinois, reported that the sentiment everywhere was for a firm stand on the platform regardless of consequences, and Trumbull's correspondence confirms this. It was "the very life blood—the corner stone of the party," wrote one constituent. If the party should surrender on the territorial question, "We are gone hook & line." Another wrote that surrender of the principle of the Chicago platform "would be the annihilation of the party." . . .

Thus it was that Crittenden's proposals were put to death in the Senate Committee of Thirteen in late December. Directly, their failure was due to the opposition of the five Republican members of the committee. Indirectly, the responsibility for their rejection was Lincoln's, who exerted from Springfield the vast influence that was his as President-elect.

ALLAN NEVINS

Lincoln has already made up his mind. . . .

On December 10 he had written Lyman Trumbull, who could tell the next Republican caucus: "Let there be no compromise on the question of extending slavery. If there be, all our labor is lost, and ere long, must be done again. . . . The tug has to come, and better now than at any time hereafter.". . .

This was one of the most fateful decisions of Lincoln's career. The reasons why he made it so quickly and emphatically, without consulting others, require a brief analysis.

"They will have us under again; all our work will have to be redone." By this Lincoln meant a good deal more than the naked words assert. It seems safe to say that he had two important ideas in mind. First, he meant that the whole work of his party in winning the election would have to be redone if the victorious candidate immediately surrendered the central tenet of the party. He could yield on peripheral points—not on the expansion of slavery. And Lincoln believed that the expansion of slavery was implicit in the Crittenden Compromise. . . .

The Republican Party had been born from a great principle—and now it was asked to sacrifice it under threat and menace. If it did so, how could it face honest Northern voters again?

More fundamentally, Lincoln had in mind his statement that "a crisis must be reached and passed," and the country brought to a completely new resolution respecting slavery. He had said explicitly that the nation as a whole must be persuaded to accept the containment of slavery within existing bounds as a prelude to the blest goal of ultimate extinction. His election on the principle of nonextension constituted the crisis; if the South accepted the election, realizing its import, the crisis *would* be passed; the nation could go on to consider slavery from a more constructive point of view. Its psychology on the great question would rapidly alter. But what if the nation backed away from a decision, and refused to accept the only principle on which a permanent solution, in keeping with nineteenth century progress, could be based? What if it turned back to the old policy of drift? . . . Could the United States afford to do so? Could the one leader who had demanded that the country face the crisis now flinch and bid his party recede? To this question, Lincoln said *No.* . . .

Once containment was tacitly accepted by the South, that section must also accept the corollary that slavery was a transitional and not a permanent institution; that the nation must look forward to a time, however distant, when it would be ended; that the country must take some initial step toward gradual abolition, perhaps combined with colonization abroad, and certainly combined with a fair plan of compensation. By arduous labor and heroic sacrifices, beginning in 1846 with the Wilmot Proviso and running through the spasmodic thrust of the Free Soil Party, the organization of the Republicans, their four Congressional campaigns, their two Presidential battles, and a tremendous mobilization of newspapers, orators, and pamphleteers, an Administration had been elected on a platform of containment. It had reached the end of the beginning. And now it was asked to begin all over again! . . .

The psychological and political effects of such an acceptance, however, would in Lincoln's eyes have been disastrous in the extreme. At one blow, all hope of lifting the slavery discussion, so long a futile debate between the positive-evil and positive-good schools and so totally out of key with the aspirations of civilization, to a new, enlightened, and constructive plane, would be ended. For what would be the moral result of accepting the Missouri Compromise extension? Forthwith, the hopes of the slavery extremists would rise anew. They would *toil* to make New Mexico a slave State; they would redouble their filibustering efforts, . . . Instead of changing the climate of opinion, the recent Republican victory would leave it unaltered; instead of seeing a "crisis reached and passed," the country would see the perennial crisis lengthened.

No, the time had come to make a stand. The old American policy of drift, postponement, and politic evasion of fundamental issues would have to be stopped somehow, some day, in some fashion—and the Republican Party was pledged to stop it now. It was committed, in Lincoln's words, to placing the institution of slavery in a position where its ultimate extinction would be generally taken for granted.

13.7   President Lincoln's Inaugural Address, March 4, 1861

Abraham Lincoln

On February 11, 1861, when President-elect Abraham Lincoln began a two-week trip from Springfield, Illinois, to Washington, D.C., eight Southern states had already seceded from the Union. One week later, as Lincoln's train carried him toward Albany, New York, Jefferson Davis assumed the presidency of the Confederate States of America and delivered his inaugural address in Montgomery, Alabama. By the time Lincoln reached Washington, secession had replaced slavery as the single most important issue facing the new administration. In his inaugural address of March 4, excerpted here, President Lincoln tried to reassure the South that there would be no interference with slavery in the states where it already existed and that there would be no invasion of the South. A peaceful solution to the nation's troubles, he said, was his goal. Yet, at the same time, he rejected secession and declared his intention to administer the laws of the United States.

Consider:

1. *Whether any statements in this Inaugural Address suggest that President Lincoln was prepared to be flexible and to accommodate the South;*
2. *What President Lincoln might have said in his address that could have reversed the secession movement.*

Apprehension seems to exist among the people of the Southern States, that by the accession of a Republican Administration, their property, and their peace, and personal security, are to be endangered. There has never been any reasonable cause for such apprehension. Indeed, the most ample evidence to the contrary has all the while existed, and been open to their inspection. It is found in nearly all the published speeches of him who now addresses you. I do but quote from one of those speeches when I declare that "I have no purpose, directly or indirectly, to interfere with the institution of slavery in the States where it exists. I believe I have no lawful right to do so, and I have no inclination to do so." Those who nominated and elected me did so with full knowledge that I had made this, and many similar declarations, and had never recanted them. . . .

I hold, that in contemplation of universal law, and of the Constitution, the Union of these States is perpetual. Perpetuity is implied, if not

SOURCE: *Abraham Lincoln*, The Collected Works of Abraham Lincoln, *ed. Roy P. Basler (New Brunswick, N.J.: Rutgers University Press, 1953), IV, 262–71.*

expressed, in the fundamental law of all national governments. It is safe to assert that no government proper, ever had a provision in its organic law for its own termination. Continue to execute all the express provisions of our national Constitution, and the Union will endure forever—it being impossible to destroy it, except by some action not provided for in the instrument itself.

Again, if the United States be not a government proper, but an association of States in the nature of contract merely, can it, as a contract, be peaceably unmade, by less than all the parties who made it? One party to a contract may violate it—break it, so to speak; but does it not require all to lawfully rescind it? . . .

It follows from these views that no State, upon its own mere motion, can lawfully get out of the Union,—that *resolves* and *ordinances* to that effect are legally void; and that acts of violence, within any State or States, against the authority of the United States, are insurrectionary or revolutionary, according to circumstances.

I therefore consider that, in view of the Constitution and the laws, the Union is unbroken; and, to the extent of my ability, I shall take care, as the Constitution itself expressly enjoins upon me, that the laws of the Union be faithfully executed in all the States. Doing this I deem to be only a simple duty on my part; and I shall perform it, so far as practicable, unless my rightful masters, the American people, shall withhold the requisite means, or, in some authoritative manner, direct the contrary. . . .

In doing this there needs to be no bloodshed or violence; and there shall be none, unless it be forced upon the national authority. The power confided to me, will be used to hold, occupy, and possess the property, and places belonging to the government, and to collect the duties and imposts; but beyond what may be necessary for these objects, there will be no invasion—no using of force against, or among the people anywhere. Where hostility to the United States, in any interior locality, shall be so great and so universal, as to prevent competent resident citizens from holding the Federal offices, there will be no attempt to force obnoxious strangers among the people for that object. While the strict legal right may exist in the government to enforce the exercise of these offices, the attempt to do so would be so irritating, and so nearly impracticable with all, that I deem it better to forego, for the time, the uses of such offices. . . .

Plainly, the central idea of secession, is the essence of anarchy. A majority, held in restraint by constitutional checks, and limitations, and always changing easily, with deliberate changes of popular opinions and sentiments, is the only true sovereign of a free people. Whoever rejects it, does, of necessity, fly to anarchy or to despotism. Unanimity is impossible; the rule of a minority, as a permanent arrangement, is wholly inadmissable; so that, rejecting the majority principle, anarchy, or despotism in some form, is all that is left. . . .

Physically speaking, we cannot separate. We cannot remove our respective sections from each other, nor build an impassable wall between them. A husband and wife may be divorced, and go out of the presence, and beyond the reach of each other; but the different parts of our country cannot do this. They cannot but remain face to face; and intercourse, either amicable or hostile, must continue between them. Is it possible then to make that intercourse more advantageous, or more satisfactory, *after* separation than *before?* Can aliens make treaties easier than friends can make laws? Can treaties be more faithfully enforced between aliens, than laws can among friends? Suppose you go to war, you cannot fight always; and when, after much loss on both sides, and no gain on either, you cease fighting, the identical old questions, as to terms of intercourse, are again upon you. . . .

My countrymen, one and all, think calmly and *well,* upon this whole subject. Nothing valuable can be lost by taking time. . . .

In *your* hands, my dissatisfied fellow countrymen, and not in *mine,* is the momentous issue of civil war. The government will not assail *you.* You can have no conflict, without being yourselves the aggressors. *You* have no oath registered in Heaven to destroy the government, while *I* shall have the most solemn one to "preserve, protect and defend" it.

I am loth to close. We are not enemies, but friends. We must not be enemies. Though passion may have strained, it must not break out bonds of affection. The mystic chords of memory, stretching from every battle-field, and patriot grave, to every living heart and hearthstone, all over this broad land, will yet swell the chorus of the Union, when again touched, as surely they will be, by the better angels of our nature.

CHAPTER QUESTIONS

1. *How did the election of Abraham Lincoln as President reflect a fundamental shift in the balance of political power in the United States?*
2. *Given the conflicting social and political systems of the North and the South, was the Civil War inevitable? Explain.*

Chapter 14

*The Civil War
as Total War:
A View from the North*

When Confederate General Robert E. Lee surrendered to Union General Ulysses S. Grant on April 9, 1865, the four-year long, bloody conflict came to an end. The monetary cost of this war has been put at about $20 billion and the loss of life, due to battle wounds and disease, amounted to more than 600,000 people. The South was defeated and slavery was abolished. The nation would never be the same again.

The Civil War was a turning point in the development of the United States. In the years before the war, industrialization and urbanization were just getting underway in the North; but by the end of the war, they had become major forces that would shape the nation and chart its course for the next fifty years. The Civil War accelerated the development of urbanization and industrialization and released other forces whose implications are still affecting Americans more than a century later. Historian Allan Nevins asserted that the "most far reaching change in the United States was organizational," because the pressures of the gigantic war effort required planning and direction in a hundred new and different ways. Whether this planning and direction involved the deployment of soldiers, weapons, and supplies or the production and delivery of army uniforms, the result was the same—the North was compelled to coordinate and direct various forces within society, and a premium was placed on efficiency.

The increased organization of industry and society were just two aspects of the emergence of modern America. Another new development involved the military side of the war. It was the first war in which the whole nation was involved, with large armies drafted from both the North and the South. Also, it was the first war in which it became a matter of policy to make the civilian population suffer. Finally, it was a war in which unconditional surrender was the only possible end to hostilities. In many respects, then, the Civil War was a modern war—a prelude to the "total war" of the twentieth century.

The focus of this chapter is on the mobilization for total war. The documents deal with such issues as raising, training, and supplying a large army made up mostly of civilians; financing the war; maintaining public support for the war; and the strategy developed by Generals Grant and Sherman for the total defeat of the Confederacy.

Chronology

February 1861	Confederate States of America formed by South Carolina, Mississippi, Florida, Alabama, Georgia, Louisiana, and Texas
March 1861	Morrill Tariff
April 13, 1861	Surrender of Fort Sumter to South Carolina
April–May 1861	Virginia, Arkansas, Tennessee, and North Carolina join Confederacy
May 1862	Homestead Act
July 1862	Pacific Railway Act
September 17, 1862	Battle of Antietam
September 22, 1862	President Lincoln issues Preliminary Emancipation Proclamation
February 1863	National Banking System established
July 1–3, 1863	Battle of Gettysburg
May 1864	Sherman begins march into Georgia
November 1864	Lincoln reelected President

Timeline markings:
1861 — Feb., Mar., Apr. 13, Apr.–May
1862 — May, July, Sep. 17, Sep. 22
1863 — Feb., July 1-3
1864 — May, Nov.

Documents

14.1   Roots of the Modern Industrial State

Louis M. Hacker

In the presidential campaign of 1860, the Republican party had appealed to the interests of Northern industry and agriculture. After the secession of the Southern states, the Republican party controlled Congress and enacted economic legislation that benefited these interests. Generally, the reason for this legislation was the North's war mobilization program. Historians disagree about the meaning of this program and the nature of its economic impact. Following the lead of historians Charles A. and Mary R. Beard, who called the Civil War the "Second American Revolution," historian Louis M. Hacker concluded that the war mobilization program was a turning point in American history. After it, he points out, industrial capitalism dominated political and economic life. Hacker's assessment of the victory of industrial capitalism is given in the excerpt here, taken from his book, *The Triumph of American Capitalism.*

Consider

1. *The main points of Hacker's assessment;*
2. *What counterarguments can be developed against Hacker's view;*
3. *What influence World War II might have had on Hacker's conclusions in* The Triumph of American Capitalism, *published two years after the end of that conflict.*

SOURCE: *Louis M. Hacker,* The Triumph of American Capitalism *(New York: Columbia University Press, 1947), 361–73.*

The war was being won on the floor of Congress in another way as well; for the progress of industrial capitalism was at last being rendered secure. The control of the state apparatus gave the Republican party the opportunity to carry out the economic program—and more— it had promised in its platform of 1860. . . . By the time the war was over Congress had taken a long step forward in placing the services of the state at the command of private enterprise. The devices by which this momentous change was effected must be now set forth.

The Financing of the Civil War. Salmon P. Chase, the Secretary of the Treasury, had two major methods for financing the war and both served excellently the purposes of a booming wartime industry: bond flotations and greenback issues. By an addition of $2,600,000,000 to the debt of the country before the war was over and the printing of $450,000,000 in greenbacks, the nation's credit base was remarkably extended and manufacturing now had its capital fund with which to build up its plant.

The Treasury employed every effort to make its bond offerings palatable. Interest rates were high (5 to 7.3 per cent). After 1863, they were sold at the market rather than at par. The new national banks were virtually compelled to buy. . . .

Protectionism. Morrill of Vermont had fathered a tariff bill during the congressional session of 1859–60, and the House had passed it; but the Senate, still dominated by the Democrats, had refused to act. . . .

Every session of Congress, from 1861 to the middle of 1864, saw new bills, pushing rates upward, introduced and passed. Always the defenses were the same: new revenues were needed to support the war effort; and domestic manufacturers had to be compensated for the heavy excises they were being compelled to pay. But in the Act of June 30, 1864, all pretense was discarded: this was protectionism undisguised and unashamed. Morrill and Stevens rushed the bill through the House in two days; the Senate halved that time. At the end of the Civil War the average rate on dutiable goods stood at about 47 per cent as compared with the 18.8 per cent at its beginning. . . .

A National Banking System. The uncertain conditions attending the outbreak of the war; the fact that the country had not fully recovered from the effects of the depression of 1857–58; the heavy involvement of many mercantile centers in southern financial relations; and the suspension of specie payments first in New York and then officially at the end of the year: all these affected banking seriously. There was a heavy toll of banking failure particularly in the Middle West and in the Border States. Then a sharp inflationary movement set in, as war orders and bonds began to pour from Washington. Bank-note issues multiplied, new banks sprang up, and the old threats once more put in their appearance: an unsound paper currency, inadequately secured, and the absence of reserve mobilizations. Some idea of the expansion of the paper currency may be obtained from the fact that in the Middle Atlantic States alone, in two years, the increase in bank notes was 50 per cent. By 1863, there were 1600 banks of issue with about 12,000 different kinds of notes in circulation. Counterfeiting, too, was general.

The Treasury took two important steps to stabilize banking, having an eye to the future, when the abnormal wartime needs would be over, as well as to its own current requirements. One of the immediate considerations for national banking reform was the creation of financial agencies that would facilitate the absorption of Union bonds; the long-term consideration was the creation of a sound system, under national control, that would help enterprise weather storms like the depressions of 1837–43. . . .

Disposal of the Public Domain. Various interests dictated the passage of the Homestead Act in May, 1862. Undoubtedly, the desire to hold the West in political alliance with the East was paramount. But one must not lose sight of other considerations: homesteads would make possible the quick settlement of the public domain and thus develop the national market for domestic manufactured ware. They would also build up a great home agricultural industry whose surpluses of cereals and meat products could be poured into the world market to right our very unstable international position. . . .

The Homestead Act, which Lincoln signed in May, 1862, gave to heads of families or individuals twenty-one years of age or over, who were citizens or declarants, a quarter section (160 acres) of land. Final title could be entered after a five-year residence and the erection of an improvement. A homesteader was allowed, at any time after his location, to commute his quarter section into a pre-emption and thus buy his farm outright at the regular knockdown price of $1.25 an acre. He could also buy an additional quarter section on the same terms. . . .

Pacific Railways. With southern opposition gone, the Republicans could proceed to the realization of a project so close to the hearts of industrial capitalism: the spanning of the continent by at least one Pacific railway. In July, 1862, two federal corporations were chartered, the Union Pacific which was empowered to build west out of Omaha to the eastern boundary of California, and the Central Pacific which was to build eastward from the Pacific coast for the purpose of effecting a juncture with the Union Pacific. The Republicans were more generous than simply authorizing the laying down of the lines. The rights of way were guaranteed; the Indian titles were extinguished; military protection was promised against marauding bands; and the builders were given free use of timber, earth, and stone from the public lands.

These were only the lesser beneficences. Following the precedent established in the Illinois Central Railroad charter of 1850, the government voted the Pacific railroads huge land grants, to wit, twenty sections (in alternate plots on each side of the right of way) for every mile of track laid down. Nor was this all. The federal government also pledged its credit for the assistance of the builders. Originally taking a first mortgage, then making its claim a junior lien, the government promised to lend the companies $16,000 for every mile built in level country, $32,000 for every mile built in the foothills, and $48,000 for every mile built in the mountains. The Union Pacific was not really begun until 1866; in May, 1869, both lines were finished when a juncture was achieved at Promontory Point, Utah. . . .

Immigration and Labor. The Republican party had promised a federal immigration policy: and this pledge Republican congressmen proceeded to fulfill when in 1864 an Immigration Bureau was set up in Washington. In the same year Congress legalized the entry of contract laborers from Europe and China. For four years the latter law stood on the statute books; but until 1885, nothing was done to bar such laborers from entering. . . .

The American Civil War turned out to be a revolution indeed. But its striking achievement was the triumph of industrial capitalism. The industrial capitalists, through their political spokesmen, the Republicans, had succeeded in capturing the state and using it as an instrument to strengthen their economic position. It was no accident, therefore, that while the war was waged on the field and through Negro emancipation, in Congress' halls the victory was made secure by the passage of tariff, banking, public-land, railroad, and contract-labor legislation.

14.2   The Sweep of Organization
Allan Nevins

America has fought three wars that required total mobilization of the country. One of the ironies of such war efforts, with their enormous cost in human life and resources, is that strong positive forces may be released that continue to shape society after the conflict ends. Such was the case with the Civil War. Historian Allan Nevins, who wrote extensively on the Civil War period, contends that the war not only preserved the Union and eradicated slavery but also forged America into a "well-organized nation." In the excerpt here, taken from Volume III of *The War for the Union*, Nevins summarizes his argument.

Consider:

1. *The strength of Nevins's argument;*
2. *Whether an argument such as Nevins's can be tested by historians;*
3. *What assumptions about post-Civil War America are implicit in Nevins's argument.*

As war contracts multiplied, as expenditures of private philanthropic and patriotic bodies increased, and as the impact of the new National Banking system, the special grant for a transcontinental railroad, the Homestead and Land-Grant laws, and other wartime legislation was felt, a great body of alert young men pressed forward to inaugurate a new era. Thomas A. Scott, made Assistant Secretary of War in his late thirties, discerned during his Western service opportunities for expanding his Pennsylvania rail system; his much younger protégé Andrew Carnegie, who transported the first brigade of troops to Washington and helped organize the military telegraph system, perceived larger opportunities not in railroads, but in the iron industry. John D. Rockefeller, looking for "something big" to undertake, realized during the war that Cleveland might well dominate the fast-growing business of oil-refining. . . . These names would resound down the half-century after Appomattox; and the spirit of these rising men was the spirit of unnumbered others. As the gates of the new era opened, it was an understanding of organization that did most to swing them wide. . . .

The formless, protoplasmic United States of 1861 emerged from the war four years later eagerly groping toward organization, and much more aware of the paths it must take forward. Under the forcing-blast of necessity and opportunity, as well as by government contracts, protective tariffs, and inflation, a thousand businesses doubled or trebled in size. Men's ideas expanded, as government activities swelled to proportions previously incredible, as the national banking system rose, and as the outlines of trunk-line railroads were foreshadowed. Truly national industries, reaching out for regional or continental, as distinguished from local, markets, began to appear—for example in milling, meat packing, and the manufacture of shoes and clothing. Not only capital, but organizing ability was being invested as never before. Half the colonels had learned a great deal in their service about system, celerity, and administrative discipline. . . .

That the Civil War brought a systematic shift in American society from an unorganized society to a well-organized nation is undoubtedly much too strong a statement. But that the Civil War accentuated and acted as a catalyst to already developing local tendencies toward organization, there can be no doubt. As in so many fields of thought and endeavor, the war changed and stimulated the impulse toward organization, and served as a proving ground or experimental phase for numerous tentative expressions of organization. There seems no doubt that this momentum sprang primarily from necessity or pragmatic impulses, rather than from philosophical devotion to organization for its own sake. That such a pragmatic trend would have occurred without wartime demands is unquestionable, but it certainly would have been

SOURCE: *Allan Nevins, The War for the Union, vol. III, 272–73, 328–31. Copyright © 1971 Mary R. Nevins. Reprinted with the permission of Charles Scribner's Sons, a Division of Macmillan Inc.*

different and perhaps slower. The war imposed requirements and opened opportunities. Organization met the demands and grasped many of the opportunities. . . .

Of broad significance in this growth of organization was the instruction Americans had received in the use of credit, along with the new use of the cash system in merchandising practiced by John Wanamaker and others. While the national banking system was being organized, it had joined with the Treasury to sell national government bond issues. Jay Cooke, when the normal market was exhausted, began selling bonds in every street and village. His canvassers sought far and wide for buyers; never before had credit given such a powerful impetus to the industrial revolution and the advance of the machine. A cooperative spirit was hereby engendered that changed the outlook of Americans. While hitherto a nation of "joiners" on strictly local levels, people began to develop a taste for larger voluntary combinations that within a few years ran the gamut from the G.A.R. to the trusts and the Grange.

This effort to organize the energies of the country harmonized with tendencies in its life already partly formed in 1860, and vigorously growing; tendencies necessitated by the natural increase of population and wealth, and given extraordinary impetus by the conflict. Through this effort, as it was carried forward after Gettysburg and Appomattox, ran a vibrant self-confidence, the exuberance of victory, the pride of a service record. . . .

Multitudes of veterans emerged from the hard lessons of war with this self-confidence born of success, and a pride in duty well-done. . . . Tens of thousands of civilians who had built machine-shops, run arms factories, and filled contracts for shovels, canned foods, and blankets, or who had managed recruiting, income-tax collection, or home relief, felt the same thrill of experience, confidence, and pride. The day of small affairs began to pass; visions of great new ventures became common. Improvisation grew into hardheaded planning, individualism was channeled into disciplined action. . . .

Of all the changes effected by the war, this replacement of an amorphous, spineless society by a national life even partially organized for efficient action—organized first to win the war, and then to develop the continent—was perhaps the most striking, and as vital in effect as the unification of the nation and the renascence of all its liberal impulses and commitments by the abolition of slavery. As the first two years of the struggle might be called the improvised war, the last two could be termed the organized war. The transition from one to the other was a transition from the old America to the new, and not in material terms alone, but in psychological terms also. . . . Americans still detested regimentation, but they had learned the power of voluntary combination for definite objects while leaving themselves free in other relations.

14.3 "The Battle Hymn of the Republic"
Julia Ward Howe

Julia Ward Howe wrote the words to "The Battle Hymn of the Republic," one of the most stirring American patriotic anthems, on November 18, 1861. The previous day, Mrs. Howe, an abolitionist, poet, and humanitarian reformer, had watched army maneuvers just outside Washington. On the way back to the city, Mrs. Howe and her friends sang popular army songs, including "John Brown's body lies a-mouldering in the ground . . ." to the tune of "Glory Hallelujah." At a friend's suggestion, Howe decided to write new words for "Glory Hallelujah." The resulting poem was published in the *Atlantic Monthly* under the title of "The Battle Hymn of the Republic," and the sheet music of the song was published several months later. The song soon caught on in the North, and Union soldiers were singing it as they went into battle.

Consider:

1. *What message Mrs. Howe was trying to convey;*
2. *The impact this song would have had on civilians in the North and soldiers in the Union Army, and on civilians and soldiers in the Confederacy;*
3. *What elements in this patriotic anthem give it a timelessness that transcends its original context and continues to move Americans today.*

Mine eyes have seen the glory of the coming of the Lord:
He is trampling out the vintage where the grapes of wrath are stored;
He hath loosed the fateful lightning of His terrible swift sword:
　　　　　His truth is marching on.

I have seen Him in the watch-fires of a hundred circling camps;
They have builded Him an altar in the evening dews and damps;
I can read His righteous sentence by the dim and flaring lamps:
　　　　　His day is marching on.

I have read a fiery gospel writ in burnished rows of steel:
"As ye deal with my contemners, so with you my grace shall deal;
Let the Hero, born of woman, crush the serpent with his heel,
　　　　　Since God is marching on."

He has sounded forth the trumpet that shall never call retreat;
He is sifting out the hearts of men before His judgment-seat:
Oh, be swift, my soul, to answer Him! be jubilant, my feet!
　　　　　Our God is marching on.

SOURCE: *Julia Ward Howe*, in Atlantic Monthly, IX (February 1862).

In the beauty of the lilies Christ was born across the sea,
With a glory in his bosom that transfigures you and me:
As he died to make men holy, let us die to make men free,
                              While God is marching on.

14.4   The Emancipation Proclamation
A. A. Lamb

In the nineteenth century, a number of American artists used patriotic
themes in their work. This practice was no less true during the Civil War,
when President Lincoln was often the major subject. One of the more interesting paintings of the period, "The Emancipation Proclamation," captures the patriotic spirit and mood in the North after President Lincoln's
issuance of the Emancipation Proclamation. In the eyes of many Northerners, the "war to save the Union" had been transformed into a crusade
to rid the nation of slavery. Artist A. A. Lamb's painting of 1863 is reproduced here.

Consider:

1. *The basic message the artist is trying to convey;*
2. *Whether there are any similarities between this painting and patriotic
   art of the early Republic (Doc. 6.4);*
3. *How this painting can be viewed as an allegory, with symbolic figures
   representing real people, ideas, or organizations.*

SOURCE: *National Gallery of Art.*

14.5   The New York City Riots

Adrian Cook

On July 13, 1863, a wave of mob violence erupted in New York City that did not subside for four days. It has been called "New York's Bloodiest Week." Traditionally, historians have attributed the riot to two factors: first, to opposition to the Enrollment Act of 1863, which many people believed turned the Civil War into one to be fought by the poor; second, to the fears of immigrant workers (for the most part Irish) that newly freed slaves would work for low wages and thus present a threat to their jobs. In his 1974 book, *The Armies of the Streets: The New York City Draft Riots of 1863*, historian Adrian Cook challenges this explanation. The New York City antidraft riot, he argues, must be viewed first as part of the social process of the city at this period, when riots were common and political institutions were unstable. Within this social and political context, he presents a profile of the rioters who were arrested. This excerpt from his book summarizes Cook's interpretation.

Consider:

1. *The strength of Cook's argument and the evidence he uses to support it;*
2. *Why Cook's explanation of the riots differs radically from traditional explanations;*
3. *Why the Irish were so violently anti-black.*

. . . Violence was a release, entertainment, a way of expression, and a form of adaptive behavior.

Riot was an integral part of the activities of the slum gangs and the volunteer fire companies, the native forms of association of the poor. The gangs, based on ethnic, communal, or local groups, were characteristically made up of young men between sixteen and thirty. Most of them were employed, and though many were simply unskilled laborers, it was by no means uncommon to find gang members who were skilled artisans or tradesmen. The gangs were not usually criminal, and they did not, as a rule, use guns or knives, preferring instead to rely on bare knuckles and brute strength. Their main concern was fighting other gangs or the police, and a famous gang might be able to turn out over a thousand members, ready for battle. . . .

. . . No one could believe that the police were the impartial enforcers of the law. They behaved more like an army of occupation, and since

SOURCE: *Adrian Cook,* The Armies of the Streets: The New York City Draft Riots of 1863 *(Lexington: The University Press of Kentucky, 1974), 29–30, 44, 196–99, 203–5, 208–9.*

they totally lacked moral authority, they had to use either the threat or reality of force to compel obedience or respect. Their presence in an area increased the probability of an eruption of violence rather than diminishing it. . . .

The occupation of 168 rioters can be determined. Five, perhaps eight, of them could be described as middle-class or professionals of some kind. . . . Forty-seven had occupations that required some skill or training: tailor, carpenter, plumber, blacksmith, boilermaker, stonemason, barber, cabinet maker, shoemaker, rope maker, brass-finisher, bricklayer, glass-cutter, gunsmith. Fifty-seven rioters held jobs calling for no special skills: carman, peddler, barkeeper, cartman, housewife, washerwoman, domestic, street paver, gardener, hostler, milkman. And fifty-six were laborers or factory workers. Out of the eighty-three rioters questioned about their literacy, forty-three could not read or write. This was a mob of the industrial age, with the people at the bottom of the social pyramid predominating.

An overwhelming percentage of the rioters were Irish. Out of 184 whose country of birth can be determined, 117 were born in Ireland, forty in the United States, sixteen in Germany, seven in England, and one each in France, Canada, Denmark, and Switzerland. Most of the American-born were from New York.

. . . The rioters were a fair cross-section of New York's younger male working class.

Most of the roaming bands of rioters who looted stores, wrecked Negroes' homes, invaded brothels, and beat up Republicans were quite small, numbering from twenty to fifty people. . . .

The mobs who met the police and troops in pitched battle were larger, but it does not seem that there were more than three hundred hard-core street fighters gathered in one place at any time during the riots. . . .

The Draft Riots were fundamentally an insurrection of anarchy, an outburst against any kind of governmental control by the people near the bottom of society. The temporary powerlessness of the authorities released a flood of violence and resentment that was usually kept repressed. As the hours went by, the riot itself created a devil-may-care mood of euphoria that led to more rioting. A wild melange of motives drove the mob on. Obviously, there was strong opposition to the draft and to the war. . . .

One extremely strong and persistent motive was deep-rooted hatred of Negroes. Many of those arrested for attacks on Negroes or their houses knew their victims before the riots or lived close to them. The implication is clear that they had long been envious of some Negroes' relative prosperity or resented having to dwell in the same neighborhood. . . .

There was also a certain element of what can only be called sexual vigilantism present in the riots. Several of the Negroes who fell foul of the mobs were married to white women. . . .

The argument, sometimes heard, that the riots were sparked and fueled by white workers' (especially longshoremen's) fears of competition from cheap black labor will not stand up to examination. Only three longshoremen can be identified as rioters, and none of them was involved in attacking Negroes. . . . Nor is there any sign that any other type of worker was worried about the threat of former slaves flooding into the North. Logically, if the mobs had been fearful on this score, they would have sought out and attacked establishments that employed Negroes. But there were no such onslaughts.

In fact, it was the Negroes of New York City who were being undercut by competition from cheap labor. Employers preferred to hire immigrants, especially Germans, who would work long hours for low pay. In the 1850s and 1860s, Negroes were even being forced out of menial positions traditionally assigned to them, such as waiters' and barbers' jobs. . . .

In the early 1870s, riots ceased in New York City. Though immigrants flooded in and poverty, misery, and overcrowding were worse than ever, there were no outbreaks of mass violence. Many reasons can be adduced to explain why this new state of peace came about. A professional fire department replaced the roistering volunteer fire laddies; compulsory education and child labor kept many potential adolescent rioters busy. Industrial expansion and long spells of prosperity meant that, until the 1890s, there were usually few unemployed in New York. The new immigrants of 1870–1914 came from countries where political police were powerful and political activity was repressed. The rise of professional baseball and football provided an alternative to rioting as a form of communal weekend entertainment, and the establishment of working-class amusement centers like Coney Island supplied another safety valve. . . .

All these developments helped in greater or lesser degree to keep the peace in New York City. But the main reason why New York was free of major civil disturbances in the last quarter of the nineteenth century and the first years of the twentieth is that in the mid-1870s Honest John Kelly put together on a permanent basis the machine that Fernando Wood had tried to create and that Boss Tweed had temporarily succeeded in building. Kelly and Croker broke up the ward gangs, which only strengthened the district leaders and made it possible for them to rebel against the Tammany leadership. Under that leadership, the interests of the city's multifarious ethnic groups, the police, and the politicians were harmonized. The result was a corrupt, but peaceful, city, free of the violent conflicts of the mid-nineteenth century. Riots did not resume until the machine faltered and failed to adapt to the needs of a new wave of immigrants.

14.6   Sherman and Total War

William Tecumseh Sherman

The Civil War was an example of a new kind of warfare—total war. During the Civil War, strategies and tactics were introduced that changed the way wars would be conducted in the future. With the full support of General Grant and President Lincoln, General W. T. Sherman developed a "scorch the earth policy" to cut off civilian support of Southern troops as he led his forces toward Atlanta in the summer of 1864. Public statements that he would destroy all property Confederate soldiers could use and would execute as spies any civilians who assisted Confederate troops were part of the psychological warfare directed against Southern civilians. Defeat on the field of battle was no longer sufficient; the civilian population must also experience defeat. The two excerpts presented here are from General Sherman's *Memoirs*. Both deal with his campaign to capture Atlanta and undoubtedly contributed to Sherman's notoriety in the South as barbarous and cruel.

Consider:

1. *The arguments and evidence Sherman uses to support his position;*
2. *Sherman's underlying goal in conducting warfare on the civilian population of the South.*
3. *The logic of Sherman's statement: "I want peace, and believe it can only be reached through union and war, and I will ever conduct war with a view to perfect and early success."*

I gave notice . . . as early as the 4th of September, to General Halleck, in a letter concluding with these words:

If the people raise a howl against my barbarity and cruelty, I will answer that war is war, and not popularity-seeking. If they want peace, they and their relatives must stop the war.

I knew, of course, that such a measure would be strongly criticised, but made up my mind to do it with the absolute certainty of its justness, and that time would sanction its wisdom. I knew that the people of the South would read in this measure two important conclusions: one, that we were in earnest; and the other, if they were sincere in their common and popular clamor "to die in the last ditch," that the opportunity would soon come. . . .

SOURCE: *William Tecumseh Sherman,* Memoirs *(New York: D. Appleton and Company, 1875),* II, 111–12, 125–27.

HEADQUARTERS MILITARY DIVISION OF THE MISSISSIPPI,
IN THE FIELD, ATLANTA, GEORGIA, *September* 12, 1864.

JAMES M. CALHOUN, *Mayor,* E. E. RAWSON *and* S. C. WELLS,
representing City Council of Atlanta.

GENTLEMEN: I have your letter of the 11th, in the nature of a petition to revoke my orders removing all the inhabitants from Atlanta. I have read it carefully, and give full credit to your statements of the distress that will be occasioned, and yet shall not revoke my orders, because they were not designed to meet the humanities of the case, but to prepare for the future struggles in which millions of good people outside of Atlanta have a deep interest. We must have peace, not only at Atlanta, but in all America. To secure this, we must stop the war that now desolates our once happy and favored country. To stop war, we must defeat the rebel armies which are arrayed against the laws and Constitution that all must respect and obey. To defeat those armies, we must prepare the way to reach them in their recesses, provided with the arms and instruments which enable us to accomplish our purpose. . . .

You cannot qualify war in harsher terms than I will. War is cruelty, and you cannot refine it; and those who brought war into our country deserve all the curses and maledictions a people can pour out. I know I had no hand in making this war, and I know I will make more sacrifices to-day than any of you to secure peace. But you cannot have peace and a division of our country. If the United States submits to a division now, it will not stop, but will go on until we reap the fate of Mexico, which is eternal war. The United States does and must assert its authority, wherever it once had power; for, if it relaxes one bit to pressure, it is gone, and I believe that such is the national feeling. This feeling assumes various shapes, but always comes back to that of Union. Once admit the Union, once more acknowledge the authority of the national Government, and, instead of devoting your houses and streets and roads to the dread uses of war, I and this army become at once your protectors and supporters, shielding you from danger, let it come from what quarter it may. . . .

You might as well appeal against the thunder-storm as against these terrible hardships of war. They are inevitable, and the only way the people of Atlanta can hope once more to live in peace and quiet at home, is to stop the war, which can only be done by admitting that it began in error and is perpetuated in pride.

We don't want your negroes, or your horses, or your houses, or your lands, or any thing you have, but we do want and will have a just obedience to the laws of the United States. That we will have, and, if it involves the destruction of your improvements, we cannot help it.

You have heretofore read public sentiment in your newspapers, that live by falsehood and excitement; and the quicker you seek for truth in other quarters, the better. I repeat then that, by the original compact of Government, the United States had certain rights in Georgia, which have never been relinquished and never will be; that the South began war by seizing forts, arsenals, mints, custom-houses, etc., etc., long before Mr. Lincoln was installed, and before the South had one jot or tittle of provocation. I myself have seen in Missouri, Kentucky, Tennessee, and Mississippi, hundreds and thousands of women and children fleeing from your armies and desperadoes, hungry and with bleeding feet. In Memphis, Vicksburg, and Mississippi, we fed thousands upon thousands of the families of rebel soldiers left on our hands, and whom we could not see starve. Now that war comes home to you, you feel very different. You deprecate its horrors, but did not feel them when you sent car-loads of soldiers and ammunition, and moulded shells and shot, to carry war into Kentucky and Tennessee, to desolate the homes of hundreds and thousands of good people who only asked to live in peace at their old homes, and under the Government of their inheritance. But these comparisons are idle. I want peace, and believe it can only be reached through union and war, and I will ever conduct war with a view to perfect and early success.

14.7   Images of Death and Destruction

In his book, *Ordeal by Fire: The Civil War and Reconstruction*, historian James M. McPherson notes that the Battle of Antietam (September 17, 1862) was the bloodiest single day of the war. Some 2,100 Union soldiers and 2,700 Confederate soldiers died on the battlefield, and another 18,000 were wounded, 3,000 of them mortally. Two days after the battle, Alexander Gardner and James Gibson, two photographers who worked for photographer Matthew Brady, took pictures of the Antietam battlefield. When these pictures were exhibited a month later, the *New York Times* carried a story that noted that the pictures "bring home to us the terrible reality and earnestness of war." The real tragedy of war—homes being made desolate and "the light of life in thousands of hearts . . . quenched forever"—must be imagined since "broken hearts cannot be photographed." The picture reproduced here was part of this 1862 exhibit.

Consider:

1. *How you would describe the scene depicted here;*
2. *The impact such graphic images of death and destruction would have on people in the North, who had had no direct experience of the war;*
3. *The role that visual images (photographs and television) play in shaping our perceptions of events today.*

SOURCE: *Library of Congress.*

CHAPTER QUESTIONS

1. *How can it be argued that the Civil War was a turning point in the development of the nation that released new forces in American life? Do you agree?*
2. *What connection do you see between the song "The Battle Hymn of the Republic" and the Emancipation Proclamation?*

Chapter 15

Reconstruction,
1865–1877

When the war ended, the victorious North had two difficult problems to resolve: how to deal with the defeated South and how to protect the interests of former slaves. Among the crucial questions to be decided was the basis on which Confederate states would be reintegrated into the Union: Should the seceded states be required to meet any conditions prior to readmission? Who had the primary responsibility in defining these conditions—the President or Congress? Equally important was the question of how to secure and protect the interests of the former slaves. Although the Emancipation Proclamation ended slavery, the ex-slaves needed assistance of various kinds in order to enjoy the blessings of being free. Over the next decade or so these two issues were at the heart of a stormy conflict, first between Congress and President Johnson and later between the Republican and Democratic parties.

The conflict between President Johnson and Congress resulted in Congress replacing the President's relatively mild "restoration" policy with a more radical "Reconstruction" policy that attempted to rebuild the South socially and politically. The Reconstruction policy included ratification of the Fourteenth and Fifteenth amendments, guaranteeing black Americans "equal protection of the laws" and the right to vote, and passage of a Civil Rights Act. These measures were designed to ensure that the Republican party, which had the support of blacks, would remain dominant in both the North and the South.

However, adoption of the two constitutional amendments and the presence of a military force did not deter the Ku Klux Klan and other similar organizations in the South. These groups terrorized and murdered both blacks and white supporters of Reconstruction in an effort to restore former Confederates to political power. After the election of Ulysses S. Grant as President, the Republican-controlled Congress passed Enforcement Acts that were designed to disband the Ku Klux Klan. By this time, though, white Southerners were gradually regaining political control of their own states and putting white Democrats back in office as state legislators, governors, United States Senators, and Representatives, and Klan activity subsided. After Grant was reelected in 1872 and the Democrats gained control of the House in the election of 1874, the momentum of Reconstruction began to weaken. The contested election of 1876 and the agreements that made Republican Rutherford B. Hayes President confirmed that Reconstruction was finally over. In exchange for Southern Democrats' support of Hayes, Republicans had promised to withdraw the last federal troops from the South, to appoint a Southerner to the cabinet, and to subsidize the construction of a railroad line from Texas to California.

The readings in this chapter focus on an extraordinary period in American political and constitutional history when the Republican party tried to change the social and political structure of the South. That this effort was only partially successful is indicative of the enormous obstacles confronting a change in racial relations. In addition, two selections here focus on the attitudes toward Indians and women in the Reconstruction era. The readings provide some perspective on contemporary problems, as racial and other forms of inequality continue to resist solution today.

Chronology

⊟ Dec. 1865	**December 1865**	Thirteenth Amendment takes effect
⊟ June 1866	**June 1866**	Fourteenth Amendment approved by Congress and sent
⊟ Nov. 1866		to states (ratified July 28, 1868)
⊟ Mar. 1867	**November 1866**	Radical Republicans win a two-thirds majority in both houses of Congress
⊟ May 1868	**March 1867**	Congress passes First Reconstruction Act over President
⊟ Nov. 1868		Johnson's veto
⊟ Feb. 1869	**May 1868**	Johnson impeached by the House

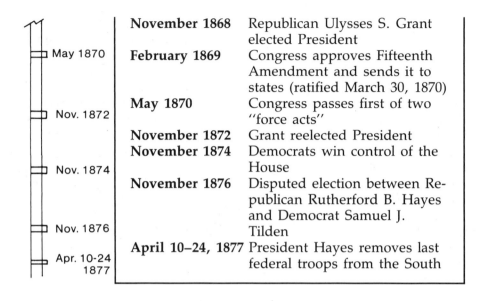

	November 1868	Republican Ulysses S. Grant elected President
May 1870	**February 1869**	Congress approves Fifteenth Amendment and sends it to states (ratified March 30, 1870)
Nov. 1872	**May 1870**	Congress passes first of two "force acts"
	November 1872	Grant reelected President
	November 1874	Democrats win control of the House
Nov. 1874		
	November 1876	Disputed election between Republican Rutherford B. Hayes and Democrat Samuel J. Tilden
Nov. 1876		
Apr. 10-24 1877	**April 10–24, 1877**	President Hayes removes last federal troops from the South

Documents

15.1   President Johnson and Reconstruction
Andrew Johnson

The debate over postwar Reconstruction turned on two issues: whether the Confederate states were to be treated as members of the Union or as nonmembers, and whether the process of Reconstruction was to be under executive or legislative control. Despite vehement opposition from Radical

Republicans in Congress, President Johnson held to the view that the Confederate states were still members of the Union and that Reconstruction should be under the control of the executive branch. He further alienated Republicans in Congress by opposing the Fourteenth Amendment and by vetoing extension of the Freedmen's Bureau and the First Reconstruction Act. Though Congress passed the First Reconstruction Act over his veto, Johnson remained unconvinced. In his Third Annual Message to Congress, Johnson repeated his reasons for taking these actions, including his opposition to black suffrage.

Consider:

1. *The reasons Johnson gives for opposing black suffrage;*
2. *The similarities between the views Johnson and most white Southerners had of blacks;*
3. *How most white Northerners might have reacted to Johnson's views on black suffrage.*

. . . I would be unfaithful to my duty if I did not recommend the repeal of the acts of Congress which place ten of the Southern States under the domination of military masters. . . .

It is manifestly and avowedly the object of these laws to confer upon negroes the privilege of voting and to disfranchise such a number of white citizens as will give the former a clear majority at all elections in the Southern States. . . .

The subjugation of the States to negro domination would be worse than the military despotism under which they are now suffering. . . .

The blacks in the South are entitled to be well and humanely governed, and to have the protection of just laws for all their rights of person and property. If it were practicable at this time to give them a Government exclusively their own, under which they might manage their own affairs in their own way, it would become a grave question whether we ought to do so, or whether common humanity would not require us to save them from themselves. But under the circumstances this is only a speculative point. It is not proposed merely that they shall govern themselves, but that they shall rule the white race, make and adminster State laws, elect Presidents and members of Congress, and shape to a greater or less extent the future destiny of the whole country. Would such a trust and power be safe in such hands?

SOURCE: *Andrew Johnson, "Third Annual Message," December 3, 1867, in* A Compilation of the Messages and Papers of the Presidents, 1789–1897, *ed. James D. Richardson (Washington, D.C.: Government Printing Office, 1897), VI, 564–67.*

. . . if anything can be proved by known facts, if all reasoning upon evidence is not abandoned, it must be acknowledged that in the progress of nations negroes have shown less capacity for government than any other race of people. No independent govenment of any form has ever been successful in their hands. On the contrary, whenever they have been left to their own devices they have shown a constant tendency to relapse into barbarism. In the Southern States, however, Congress has undertaken to confer upon them the privilege of the ballot. Just released from slavery, it may be doubted whether as a class they know more than their ancestors how to organize and regulate civil society. Indeed, it is admitted that the blacks of the South are not only regardless of the rights of property, but so utterly ignorant of public affairs that their voting can consist in nothing more than carrying a ballot to the place where they are directed to deposit it. . . .

I repeat the expression of my willingness to join in any plan within the scope of our constitutional authority which promises to better the condition of the negroes in the South, by encouraging them in industry, enlightening their minds, improving their morals, and giving protection to all their just rights as freedmen. But the transfer of our political inheritance to them would . . . be an abandonment of a duty which we owe alike to the memory of our fathers and the rights of our children.

The plan of putting the Southern States wholly and the General Government partially into the hands of negroes is proposed at a time peculiarly unpropitious. The foundations of society have been broken up by civil war. Industry must be reorganized, justice reestablished, public credit maintained, and order brought out of confusion. To accomplish these ends would require all the wisdom and virtue of the great men who formed our institutions originally. I confidently believe that their descendants will be equal to the arduous task before them, but it is worse than madness to expect that negroes will perform it for us. Certainly we ought not to ask their assistance till we despair of our own competency.

The great difference between the two races in physical, mental, and moral characteristics will prevent an amalgamation or fusion of them together in one homogeneous mass. If the inferior obtains the ascendency over the other, it will govern with reference only to its own interests—for it will recognize no common interest—and create such a tyranny as this continent has never yet witnessed. Already the negroes are influenced by promises of confiscation and plunder. They are taught to regard as an enemy every white man who has any respect for the rights of his own race. If this continues it must become worse and worse, until all order will be subverted, all industry cease, and the fertile fields of the South grow up into a wilderness. Of all the dangers which our nation has yet encountered, none are equal to those which must result from the success of the effort now making to Africanize the half of our country.

15.2   Reconstruction in Indian Territory

M. Thomas Bailey

The Five Civilized Tribes who lived in Indian Territory (present-day Oklahoma)—the Creeks, Seminoles, Cherokees, Choctaws, and Chickasaws—
had joined forces with the Confederacy during the Civil War. As a result,
when the war was over, the Five Civilized Tribes were put through a
unique and tragic Reconstruction process. In his book, *Reconstruction in Indian Territory*, historian M. Thomas Bailey examines this aspect of Recon⸗
struction, concluding that government policies were designed to reduce the
size of tribal holdings and to assert political control over the Indians. The
excerpt printed here is taken from the concluding chapter of Bailey's book.

Consider:

1. *Why ratification of the Thirteenth, Fourteenth, and Fifteenth amendments to the Constitution caused so much turmoil among the Five Civilized Tribes;*
2. *Whether the United States was justified in using postwar Reconstruction to impose a policy of "concentration," that is, confining Indian settlement within certain areas, on Indians in the West.*

. . . Since the Five Civilized Nations had each allied with the Confederacy the problem of reestablishing a working relationship with the
United States had to be encountered.

. . . The relations between the Five Civilized Nations and the United
States were not based on the same constitutional structure as the
relations between the states of the Union and the United States. Since
the political relationship of the Five Civilized Nations with the United
States government was basically international, the accepted method
for working out political relations was through the negotiation of treaties.
Therefore treaties were consummated in order to reestablish political
relations after the Civil War between the Five Civilized Nations and
the United States. . . .

The principal points that came up for settlement were: (1) the
method of adjusting affairs between the loyal and the disloyal Indians,
a problem applying especially to the Cherokees, among whom confiscation laws passed by the National Council had taken effect upon
the property of those who were disloyal; (2) the status of the freedmen

SOURCE: *M. Thomas Bailey, Reconstruction in Indian Territory (New York: Kennekat Press,
1972), 192–95, 201–3. By permission of Associated Faculty Press, Inc., © 1972 by Kennekat
Press.*

in the Nations; (3) compensation for losses of property occasioned by those who remained loyal to the Confederacy; (4) cession of lands by the several tribes to be used for the settlement of Indians from Kansas and elsewhere; and (5) the granting of right of way for railroads to enter Indian Territory from a north-south and an east-west direction. . . .

Reconstruction of the Five Civilized Nations in Indian Territory as viewed by the United States, seemed to offer the opportunity to extract from the Indians more of their land that had been given to them by the earlier treaties and to secure Indian concentration and a consolidated territorial government. These goals had been long sought. Too many tribes occupied land needed by western railroads or coveted by settlers to make acceptance of the status quo advisable in the eyes of the majority of the members of Congress. Congressional investigation revealed that but two areas remained as possible centers for Indian settlement, the public lands to the north of Nebraska and those to the south of Kansas. The administration of President Grant decided that all Indians must be gathered in these locations. This policy guiding the government's effort to confine Indian settlement within these areas was known as concentration. . . .

Reconstruction in Indian Territory for the Indian mixed-blood and the Negro freedmen was to a degree similar to that of the general reconstruction process for the conservative element and the freed Negro of the former Confederate states. . . .

After the war the Choctaws and Chickasaws through their governments attempted to control the economic activity and status of the Negro. Regulations were drawn up similar to the contract, vagrancy and apprenticeship provisions in the postwar Black Codes in most of the states of the South. . . .

The turmoil exhibited over the problem of citizenship of the freedmen in the Cherokee, Choctaw and Chickasaw Nations was similar to the reaction of many conservatives of the South to the ratification of the fourteenth and fifteenth amendments to the Constitution of the United States. . . .

The reconstruction policies which the United States imposed upon the Five Civilized Nations indicated that the reconstruction treaties were not designed primarily to benefit the Indians. They were used instead as a means by which the Federal government could circumvent the old removal treaties and concentrate other tribes in the territory, thus releasing additional land for white settlement in other states as well as Indian Territory. Reconstruction in Indian Territory was a unique, as well as a complicated, disappointing, frustrating and tragic experience for the Indians. The reconstruction policies of the United States exploited the decision of the Five Civilized Nations to ally themselves with the Confederate States. The postwar treatment of loyal Indians in Indian Territory manifested little consideration of certain obvious facts such as the position of the Five Civilized Nations in relation to the border of the Confederate states; the southern sympathy indicated by Indian agents; the holding of investment bonds by southern states; and the abandonment of the area by the United States at the outbreak of the Civil War. The 1866 reconstruction treaties unquestionably provided the United States government with the vehicle by which land and desired political control of Indian Territory could be obtained. The blessings of the Anglo-Saxon laws and practices designed to foster tribal dissolution and ultimate statehood were instituted whether the residing inhabitants desired it or not, because it was "good for them" and for the progress of the western-oriented United States.

15.3   Mississippi Black Code, 1865

The Civil War had scarcely ended before white Southerners were trying to establish a labor system that would give them as much control over blacks as slavery had. Many ex-slaves had left their old plantations and farms to move to towns and cities. Those who remained in the country often refused to work long hours in cotton fields, planting subsistence plots of their own instead. Thus, in 1865–1866, white planters proposed legislation that would give them more social control over former slaves. These "Black Codes," which limited the rights and the mobility of blacks, were enacted in every Southern state. The excerpt printed here is from the Mississippi Black Code, a typical example of this type of legislation. Though these "Black Codes" were eventually overturned, the sentiment underlying them did not disappear.

Consider:

1. Why these "Black Codes" are similar to those issued by the Choctaw and Chickasaw Indian governments (see Doc. 15.2);
2. The racial assumptions and fears underlying this code;
3. Why the penalty for whites who violated the code was more severe than that for blacks.

AN ACT to confer Civil Rights on Freedmen, and for other purposes.

SECTION 1.   *Be it enacted by the Legislature of the State of Mississippi,* That all freedmen, free negroes and mulattoes may sue and be sued, implead and be impleaded in all the courts of law and equity of this State, and may acquire personal property and choses [things] in action, by descent or purchase, and may dispose of the same, in the same

SOURCE: *Laws of the State of Mississippi, 1865 (Jackson, Miss., 1866), 81–88, 90–91.*

manner, and to the same extent that white persons may: Provided that the provisions of this section shall not be so construed as to allow any freedman, free negro or mulatto, to rent or lease any lands or tenements, except in incorporated towns or cities in which places the corporate authorities shall control the same. . . .

SEC. 3.   . . . That it shall not be lawful for any freedman, free negro or mulatto to intermarry with any white person; nor for any white person to intermarry with any freedman, free negro or mulatto; and any person who shall so intermarry shall be deemed guilty of felony, and on conviction thereof, shall be confined in the State Penitentiary for life. . . .

SEC. 5.   Be it further enacted, That every freedman, free negro and mulatto, shall, on the second Monday of January, one thousand eight hundred and sixty-six, and annually thereafter, have a lawful home or employment, and shall have written evidence thereof . . .

SEC. 6.   Be it further enacted, That all contracts for labor made with freedmen, free negroes and mulattoes, for a longer period than one month shall be in writing and in duplicate, attested and read to said freedman, free negro or mulatto, by a beat, city or county officer, or two disinterested white persons of the county in which the labor is to be performed . . . if the laborer shall quit the service of the employer, before expiration of his term of service, without good cause, he shall forfeit his wages for that year, up to the time of quitting. . . .

SEC. 8.   Be it further enacted, That upon affidavit made by the employer of any freedman, free negro or mulatto, or other credible person, . . . that any freedman, free negro or mulatto, legally employed by said employer, has illegally deserted said employment, such justice of the peace or member of the board of police, shall issue his warrant . . . to arrest said deserter and return him or her to said employer. . . .

SEC. 9.   Be it further enacted, That if any person shall persuade or attempt to persuade, entice or cause any freedman, free negro or mulatto, to desert from the legal employment of any person, before the expiration of his or her term of service, or shall knowingly employ any such deserting freedman, free negro or mulatto, or shall knowingly give or sell to any such deserting freedman, free negro or mulatto, any food, rayment or other thing, he or she shall be guilty of a misdemeanor. . . .

AN ACT to be entitled "An act to regulate the relation of Master and Apprentice, as relates to Freedmen, Free Negroes, and Mulattoes.

SECTION 1.   *Be it enacted by the Legislature of the State of Mississippi,* That it shall be the duty of all sheriffs, justices of the peace, and other civil officers of the several counties in this State to report to the probate courts of their respective counties, . . . freedmen, free negroes and mulattoes, under the age of eighteen, within their respective counties, beats or districts, who are orphans, or whose parent or parents have not the means, or who refuse to provide for and support said minors, and thereupon it shall be the duty of said probate court, to order the clerk of said court to apprentice said minors to some competent and suitable person, on such terms as the court may direct, . . .

Sec. 4. Be it further enacted, That if any apprentice shall leave the employment of his or her master or mistress, without his or her consent, said master or mistress may pursue and recapture said apprentice, and bring him or her before any justice of the peace of the county, whose duty it shall be to remand said apprentice to the service of his or her master or mistress . . .

Sec. 2. Be it further enacted, That all freedmen, free negroes and mulattoes in this State, over the age of eighteen years, found on the second Monday in January, 1866, or thereafter, with no lawful employment or business, or found unlawfully assembling themselves together either in the day or night time, and all white persons so assembling with freedmen, free negroes or mulattoes, or usually associating with freedmen, free negroes or mulattoes on terms of equality, or living in adultery or fornication with a freedwoman, free negro or mulatto, shall be deemed vagrants, and on conviction thereof, shall be fined in the sum of not exceeding, in the case of a freedman, free negro or mulatto, fifty dollars, and a white man two hundred dollars, and imprisoned at the discretion of the court, the free negro not exceeding ten days, and the white man not exceeding six months.

15.4   The Ku Klux Klan

In the late 1860s and 1870s, many Southern whites joined secret terrorist societies whose goal was to "redeem" the South from Republicanism and black rule. The most prominent and notorious of these secret societies, the Ku Klux Klan, was particularly active in South Carolina. The intimidation and violence in that state were so great that President Grant suspended the writ of habeas corpus, protecting against imprisonment without charges, in nine counties in an effort to deal with the Klan. A federal grand jury was convened to investigate crimes committed by the Klan. An excerpt from the grand jury's report is reprinted here.

Consider:

1. *The contrast between the Klan's stated purpose and its behavior as described in the grand jury report;*
2. *What the grand jury had in mind with the statement, "for this condition of things . . . many of the leading men of the community were responsible";*
3. *How the government was able to find a grand jury in South Carolina to return such an indictment.*

PRESENTMENT OF THE GRAND JURY.

To the Judges of the United States Circuit Court:

In closing the labors of the present term, the grand jury beg leave to submit the following presentment: During the whole session we have been engaged in investigations of the most grave and extraordinary character—investigations of the crimes committed by the organization known as the Ku-Klux Klan. The evidence elicited has been voluminous, gathered from the victims themselves and their families, as well as those who belong to the Klan and participated in its crimes. The jury has been shocked beyond measure at the developments which have been made in their presence of the number and character of the atrocities committed, producing a state of terror and a sense of utter insecurity among a large portion of the people, especially the colored population. The evidence produced before us has established the following facts.

1. That there has existed since 1868, in many counties of the State, an organization known as the "Ku-Klux Klan," or "Invisible Empire of the South," which embraces in its membership a large proportion of the white population of every profession and class.

2. That this Klan, bound together by an oath, administered to its members at the time of their initiation into the order, of which the following is a copy:

OBLIGATION.

I, (name,) before the immaculate Judge of Heaven and Earth, and upon the Holy Evangelists of Almighty God, do, of my own free will and accord, subscribe to the following sacredly binding obligation:

"1. We are on the side of justice, humanity, and constitutional liberty, as bequeathed to us in its purity by our forefathers.

"2. We oppose and reject the principles of the radical party.

"3. We pledge mutual aid to each other in sickness, distress, and pecuniary embarrassment.

"4. Female friends, widows, and their households, shall ever be special objects of our regard and protection.

"Any member divulging, or causing to be divulged, any of the foregoing obligations, shall meet the fearful penalty and traitor's doom, which is Death! Death! Death!"

That in addition to this oath the Klan has a constitution and by-laws, which provides, among other things, that each member shall furnish himself with a pistol, a Ku-Klux gown, and a signal instrument. That the operations of the Klan were executed in the night, and were invariably directed against members of the republican party by warnings to leave the country, by whippings, and by murder.

SOURCE: *Federal Grand Jury, October 1871, Columbia, South Carolina,* House Reports, *42nd Congress, 2d session (Washington, D.C., 1872), Report No. 22, Pt. 1, 480–89.*

3. That in large portions of the counties of York, Union, and Spartanburgh, to which our attention has been more particularly called in our investigations during part of the time for the last eighteen months, the civil law has been set at defiance, and ceased to afford any protection to the citizens.

4. That the Klan, in carrying out the purposes for which it was organized and armed, inflicted summary vengeance on the colored citizens of these counties, by breaking into their houses at the dead of night, dragging them from their beds, torturing them in the most inhuman manner, and in many instances murdering them; and this, mainly, on account of their political affiliations. Occasionally additional reasons operated, but in no instance was the political feature wanting.

5. That for this condition of things, for all these violations of law and order, and the sacred rights of citizens, many of the leading men of those counties were responsible. It was proven that large numbers of the most prominent citizens were members of the order. Many of this class attended meetings of the Grand Klan. At a meeting of the Grand Klan, held in Spartanburgh County, at which there were representatives from the various dens of Spartanburgh, York, Union, and Chester Counties, in this State, besides a number from North Carolina, a resolution was adopted that no raids should be undertaken, or any one whipped or injured by members of the Klan, without orders from the Grand Klan. The penalty for violating this resolution was one hundred lashes on the bare back for the first offense, and for the second, death. This testimony establishes the nature of the discipline enforced in the order, and also the fact that many of the men who were openly and publicly speaking against the Klan, and pretending to deplore the work of this murderous conspiracy, were influential members of the order, and directing its operations even in detail.

The jury has been appalled as much at the number of outrages as at their character, it appearing that eleven murders and over six hundred whippings have been committed in York County alone. Our investigation in regard to the other counties named has been less full; but it is believed, from the testimony, that an equal or greater number has been committed in Union, and that the number is not greatly less in Spartanburgh and Laurens.

We are of the opinion that the most vigorous prosecution of the parties implicated in these crimes is imperatively demanded; that without this there is great danger that these outrages will be continued, and that there will be no security to our fellow-citizens of African descent.

We would say further, that unless the strong arm of the Government is interposed to punish these crimes committed upon this class of citizens, there is every reason to believe that an organized and determined attempt at retaliation will be made, which can only result in a state of anarchy and bloodshed too horrible to contemplate.

15.5   The Freedmen's Bureau

After his vetoes of the Freedmen's Bureau and the Civil Rights Act were overridden by Congress, President Johnson decided to make the off-year elections in 1866 a referendum on his policies. He appealed to voters to elect members of Congress who backed his policies, and in August he went on an extended speaking tour in the North. In Pennsylvania, Hierston Clymer, a Johnson Democrat, was running for governor. He used the campaign poster reproduced here in his unsuccessful effort to defeat John W. Geary, a Radical Republican.

Consider:

1. *What message this campaign poster conveyed to voters;*
2. *The racial assumptions about both whites and blacks that are reflected in the poster;*
3. *How the poster portrays the Freedmen's Bureau and what this might suggest about the way the government should treat ex-slaves.*

SOURCE: *Courtesy of the Library of Congress.*

15.6   Women's Suffrage
Currier & Ives

When the Fourteenth Amendment was introduced, woman suffragists such as Elizabeth Cady Stanton and Susan B. Anthony were outraged that women were not included in its terms. During the debate on the amendment and in subsequent discussions of women's rights, opponents of women's suffrage argued that the gentler nature of females "disqualifies them for the turmoil and battle of public life." To give women the vote and put them in an adversary position with men would "make every home a hell on earth." Many opponents of women's suffrage viewed it as an attack on the accepted role of women in society. Their opposition to full rights for women often emerged in the form of sharp ridicule. The 1868 lithograph by Currier & Ives, reproduced here, reflects this tactic.

Consider:

1. *The message Currier & Ives are trying to convey;*
2. *The basic attitudes and values about the respective roles of men and women reflected in this lithograph;*
3. *Factors that might account for this kind of response to feminist issues.*

THE AGE OF IRON.

SOURCE: *Museum of the City of New York, Henry T. Peters Collection.*

15.7   The Fifteenth Amendment and Republican Politics

William Gillette

When the Fifteenth Amendment became part of the Constitution on March 30, 1870, blacks celebrated what they believed to be their political salvation. Abolitionists felt their dream had finally been realized. However, states in both the North and the South soon devised a variety of ways to deprive blacks of the vote, including redistricting, changing polling places, and requiring payment of a poll tax. Then in 1875, the Supreme Court ruled that the Fifteenth Amendment did not guarantee the right to vote, only that no citizen could be discriminated against at the polls because of race. Historian William Gillette links the failure of the Fifteenth Amendment to a broader development he calls the "retreat from Reconstruction." In his book *Retreat from Reconstruction*, he argues that the story of the Fifteenth Amendment must be seen from the perspective of the Republican party and Reconstruction politics. In this excerpt, Gillette describes Republican strategy and tactics in securing congressional approval of the amendment and its ratification.

Consider:

1. *Whether enactment of the Fifteenth Amendment (and of the Thirteenth and Fourteenth amendments) represented any fundamental change in the way most white Americans viewed black Americans;*
2. *What changes in American attitudes and institutions would have been necessary for the Fifteenth Amendment to have guaranteed blacks their "political salvation."*

Although the election of 1868 was a Republican victory, it revealed undercurrents of white conservatism and indications of black vulnerability that could endanger Republicanism. It was to be expected that Democratic voters would succumb to the pandering to white prejudice; but the number of reports indicating the disenchantment of white Republican voters with the course of reconstruction was ominous. West Virginia Republicans, their state committee secretary wrote, were "more radical against Rebels than in favor of Negroes." A Californian reported that popular support was stronger for Grant than for the proposed radical reconstruction, which was too extreme for most people: "There are not ten in a hundred of his supporters who favor Negro suffrage." According to a Tennessee Republican, the "future of the Republican

SOURCE: *William Gillette*, Retreat from Reconstruction: A Political History, 1869–1879 *(Baton Rouge: Louisiana State University Press, 1979), 16–23.*

party in the South is by no means secure. Sometimes I feel discouraged when I realize fully the disloyalty, the obstinancy, and the blind folly of the Southern whites; the ignorance, inexperience and the changeableness of the negroes. This element cannot be relied upon, and is going to give us trouble." . . .

Having just narrowly escaped defeat, the Republicans decided it was necessary to augment their strength by enfranchising more blacks, who could be expected to vote Republican en masse. Two years before, Congress had enfranchised Negroes in the South because the Republicans then needed southern black votes to counter southern white votes. Now the Republicans also needed the support of northern and border blacks, especially in closely balanced states. . . .

Although egalitarians had begun the advocacy of Negro enfranchisement, political strategists had made its achievement possible. The institutional needs of the Republican party ultimately proved more important than the burden of prejudice or the sirens of idealism. Republican politicians were frightened by portents of their waning power and, in desperation, were willing to run limited risks and promote political reform in order to maintain power.

Thus, during early 1869 the Republicans in the lame-duck Congress pressed for a constitutional amendment to secure impartial manhood suffrage in every state, therefore avoiding further popular rejection in state referendums. They opted for the usual, but more indirect, method of having Republican state legislatures that were still in session ratify the amendment. Thus they avoided the risk of possible rejection by special conventions.

The amendment finally passed Congress in February, 1869, after a number of compromises. To secure enough moderate votes, the sponsors had to omit a clause that would have outlawed property qualifications and literacy tests. Such a clause was dispensable because the tests would affect more Negroes in the South than in the North, and because the proponents of the amendment were intent primarily upon securing the northern Negro voter for the Republican party. For the same reasons, they omitted any provision for Negro officeholding. A provision for federal authority over voter qualifications was defeated, and so the potential for evasion in the southern and border states was left wide open.

. . . A moderate measure, the amendment had the support of those who understood the limits of party power and who had practical goals in mind; they took into account the possible difficulties of ratification. . . .

The primary objective—the enfranchisement of the blacks in the northern and border states—was clearly understood, stated, and believed by the politicians, the press, and the people. . . . Indeed, most newspapers both in the North and in the South during 1869 and 1870 unequivocally, incontrovertibly, and repeatedly spoke of the Republican objective of ensuring party hegemony by means of the Fifteenth

Amendment. Moreover, congressmen and state legislators, in arguing for passage and ratification, referred again and again to the partisan need for those votes. The southern Negro, already a voter, was not irrelevant—an important secondary purpose of the amendment was to assure the continuance of Negro suffrage in the South by putting it in a virtually unrepealable amendment to the federal Constitution. Still, the anticipated importance of the black electorate in the North and in the borderland was clearly the overriding concern. . . .

. . . Although the struggle over ratification lasted only thirteen months, it was hard going and the outcome was uncertain until the very end. The fight was especially close in the Middle Atlantic states and in Indiana and Ohio, where the parties were competitive and a black electorate had the potential for deciding victory or defeat. In the Democratic border states and on the Pacific Coast, where racial feeling ran high, the Republicans feared that pushing the amendment would lose them votes and so they refrained from working hard in those regions. The amendment had the backing of the Grant administration, with its rich patronage. Those Republican politicians who held or aspired to hold national office added the weight of their influence. As one Ohioan advised, "By hook or by crook you must get the 15th amendment through or we are gone up."

The Fifteenth Amendment became law on March 30, 1870. Republican euphoria followed the hard battle for ratification. Grant, in his message to Congress, wrote that the amendment "completes the greatest civil change and constitutes the most important event that has occurred since the nation came into life." Blacks everywhere celebrated, and their outstanding leader, Frederick Douglass, announced that now they would "breathe a new atmosphere, have a new earth beneath, and a new sky above."

15.8 The End of Reconstruction and the Election of 1876

Between 1869 and 1875, conservative Southerners regained political control from Radical Republicans in eight of the eleven states of the Confederacy. Although the other three Southern state governments were not "redeemed" until after the election of 1876, the end of Reconstruction was evident in the 1874 congressional elections when the Democrats regained control of the House of Representatives. The following map shows when each of the former Confederate states was readmitted to the Union under Congressional Reconstruction. (Tennessee was restored to the Union before Reconstruction began.) It also shows the date when Congressional Reconstruction ended for each state, and how each state voted in the election of 1876.

Consider:
1. *The reasons certain Southern states were not "readmitted" to the Union until 1870;*
2. *The connection between the dates that Congressional Reconstruction ended in specific states and their voting patterns in the presidential election of 1876.*

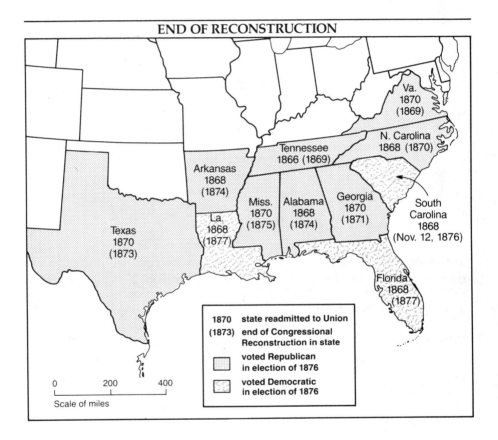

END OF RECONSTRUCTION

Va.
1870
(1869)

N. Carolina
1868 (1870)

Tennessee
1866 (1869)

Arkansas
1868
(1874)

Miss.
1870
(1875)

Alabama
1868
(1874)

Georgia
1870
(1871)

South
Carolina
1868
(Nov. 12, 1876)

La.
1868
(1877)

Texas
1870
(1873)

Florida
1868
(1877)

| 1870 | state readmitted to Union |
| (1873) | end of Congressional Reconstruction in state |

voted Republican in election of 1876

voted Democratic in election of 1876

0   200   400

Scale of miles

CHAPTER QUESTIONS

1. *Were the Radical Republicans attempting to legislate moral and/or social values? Explain.*
2. *What consequences are likely to occur when the President and Congress take inflexible positions on an issue, as was the case in 1867–1868, instead of working out a compromise?*
3. *Were the actions of President Johnson in the conflict over Reconstruction examples of presidential leadership or presidential refusal to compromise? What is the difference between the two?*

Chapter 16

The New South and the New West

Between 1870 and 1900, the whole of the United States was growing, as the population went from 39.8 million to 76.2 million. At the same time, much of the nation shifted from a rural-agrarian economy to an urban-industrial economy. In the South and the West, however, it was a time of new beginnings.

The New West began about two hundred miles west of the Mississippi River and covered a vast area known as "the Great American Desert." This territory, occupied by the Plains Indians, was largely unsettled by whites. The opening of the first transcontinental railroad in 1869 and the development of connecting railroads changed all that, bringing increasing numbers of white settlers into the region.

These settlers faced two great obstacles that earlier settlers in other regions had not encountered: the Plains Indians, who fiercely resisted white settlement on their tribal lands, and an environment that was not suited to traditional agricultural practices. The Plains Indians and white settlers clashed frequently over a period of twenty years, resulting in the direct involvement of United States troops in a series of battles with the Indians.

Conquering the hostile, semiarid environment of "the Great American Desert" was even more difficult, for settlers had to develop new techniques for farming the dry land. By the 1890s these techniques and the introduction of mechanical equipment had helped make the Plains one of the world's most productive wheat areas. Unfortunately, many more farmers failed than succeeded. The great increase in agricultural production resulted in declining prices for farm products, while the cost of manufactured goods (protected by a tariff) and of transportation remained high. By the 1890s, the New West was the scene of an agrarian crusade against all forms of monopoly and oppression.

By contrast, the New South was involved in efforts to recover from a devastating war, transform an impoverished agricultural economy into a modern industrial economy, and work out the status of blacks. Many prominent Southerners believed that progress could be made only if the bitterness and anger of sectional strife and animosity were laid aside and the North and the South cooperated. They also felt that the region must be left alone to work out relationships between whites and their ex-slaves. Although Southern textile, timber, and iron and steel industries prospered during these years, the rise of sharecropping and the crop lien system (in which the farmer pledged his crop in return for money or credit) prevented the development of a diversified system of agriculture. Because so many Southerners, black and white, were poverty-stricken, the New South was also part of the agrarian campaign of the 1890s.

For the blacks in the New South, there was little change during this period. The intimidation and violence of the Reconstruction-era Ku Klux Klan were replaced by a suffocating white paternalism that imposed second-class citizenship on blacks.

The selections in this chapter focus on the New West and New South and the special difficulties encountered by each region. Although they experienced success in many areas, the two regions shared common problems that remained troublesome: establishing a diversified agricultural economy and eliminating injustice for a racial minority.

Chronology

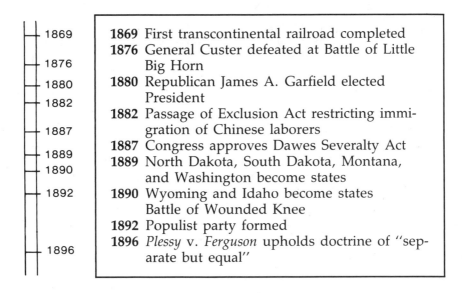

1869	**1869** First transcontinental railroad completed
1876	**1876** General Custer defeated at Battle of Little Big Horn
1880	**1880** Republican James A. Garfield elected President
1882	**1882** Passage of Exclusion Act restricting immigration of Chinese laborers
1887	**1887** Congress approves Dawes Severalty Act
1889	**1889** North Dakota, South Dakota, Montana, and Washington become states
1890	**1890** Wyoming and Idaho become states Battle of Wounded Knee
1892	**1892** Populist party formed
1896	**1896** *Plessy* v. *Ferguson* upholds doctrine of "separate but equal"

Documents

16.1   Chinese Railroad Workers

Sandy Lydon

On May 11, 1869, the tracks of the Central Pacific and Union Pacific railroads met at Promontory Point, Utah, establishing a transcontinental railroad across the United States. The contributions of numerous groups involved in the project were recognized at the festivities. One group not mentioned, however, was the Chinese railroad construction crew of the Central Pacific Railroad. The hard work of these laborers and their willingness to take risks had made it possible for the Central Pacific to meet its schedule. Generally speaking, historians have failed to acknowledge the role of the Chinese in settling the West. One notable exception is historian Sandy Lydon, who explores the contributions of the Chinese in the Monterey Bay region of California in his book, *Chinese Gold* (excerpted here). It is ironic that in the very years the Chinese were making such an important contribution to the development of the West, anti-Chinese sentiment was rising. It culminated in 1882 with the passage of the Chinese Exclusion Act.

Consider:

1. *Why the Chinese comprised the vast majority of railroad construction workers in the Monterey Bay region;*
2. *The different types of work that Chinese and white railroad workers performed;*
3. *Why anti-Chinese sentiment might be so high in an area where their construction skills were so necessary.*

It took one hundred years for the heroic feats of the Chinese who worked on the Transcontinental Railroad to be included in the historical accounts written about the building of the Central Pacific Railroad through and over the Sierra Nevada; the image of Chinese railroad workers hanging over cliffs in baskets as they drilled the blasting holes has finally become part of the history of the American West. When the Central Pacific and Union Pacific Railroads joined in Utah in 1869, the Central Pacific released an estimated five thousand Chinese railroad workers who provided the labor for a decade of railroad building throughout California. In 1870 there were no railroad tracks in the Monterey Bay Region, but by 1880 Chinese railroad builders dug cuts, laid ballast, drilled tunnels, built trestles, laid track, and risked death to build almost one hundred miles of track, bringing Santa Cruz and Monterey counties into the industrial age. . . .

THE MONTEREY AND SALINAS VALLEY RAILROAD

The Monterey and Salinas Valley Railroad was the first of several proposed . . . railroads constructed in central California. . . .

. . . As surveyors moved across the Salinas Valley in April 1874, scrapers, wheelbarrows, and a steam donkey arrived in Monterey by steamer. . . . The first Chinese railroad workers for the project arrived by steamer right behind the steam donkey and wheelbarrows. By May 150 Chinese were cutting the grade between Monterey and the Salinas River. Throughout the next seven months, the M&SVRR tried to supplement its construction crews with white laborers, but few white workers came forward for the arduous work, so the Chinese provided the bulk of the labor on the road's construction. . . .

If nineteenth-century Monterey County owed much to the coming of the railroads, Santa Cruz County owed everything, for railroads constructed during the 1870s tied together the isolated communities along the north coast of Monterey Bay and launched an era of unparalleled development. . . .

. . . Between 1875 and 1880 the Chinese built three separate railroads, laid forty-two miles of track, and drilled 2.6 miles of tunnels to stitch Santa Cruz County together and attach it permanently to the world beyond the Santa Cruz Mountains. The Chinese contributed not only their muscle and sweat, but their lives. At least fifty Chinese were killed in accidents while building those railroads. For every mile of railroad, one Chinese died. . . .

Chinese railroad workers on the Santa Cruz Railroad worked six ten-hour days a week and were paid one dollar a day. Two dollars per week was deducted from their pay for food, while expenses such as clothing and recreation chipped away at the remaining four dollars so that they averaged three dollars per week profit. . . .

SOURCE: *Sandy Lydon,* Chinese Gold: The Chinese in the Monterey Bay Region *(Capitola, Calif.: Capitola Book Company, 1985), 79, 82–85, 87–88, 91, 93–96, 110–11.*

The [South Pacific Coast Railroad] SPCRR route began on the east side of San Francisco Bay (which was not already locked up by the Southern Pacific), came south along the bay to San Jose, then to Los Gatos and over the mountains to Felton. . . . In August 1878 the SPCRR employed seven hundred men, six hundred of whom were Chinese. Chinese did all the grading, tunneling, track-laying, and ballasting, while whites built trestles and supervised the construction. By 1879, when the tunnels were being drilled and track was being laid in the canyons, approximately one thousand Chinese railroad workers laid track in the Santa Cruz Mountains. . . .

. . . The Chinese crews of twenty to thirty men were supervised by a Chinese contractor who took his orders from a white supervisor and acted as paymaster for the Chinese workers. . . . By the end of the project the white contractors praised the Chinese as hard-working, honest, and "possessed of retentive memories." . . . whites found that the Chinese were not docile, however, for when the Chinese railroad workers felt they were being mistreated or abused, they responded quickly and, on occasion, violently. . . .

The Pajaro Valley Consolidated Railroad was the last railroad project in the Monterey Bay Region in which Chinese railroad workers bore the primary responsibility for construction. The restrictions passed on Chinese immigration in the 1880s had done their work, and the aging, diminishing Chinese population in California was replaced by the younger Japanese immigrants. Crucial to the development of the Monterey Bay Region in the nineteenth century, the railroads had a beneficial impact on agriculture, manufacturing, and tourism. Whether shipping lumber out in flat cars or bringing tourists in parlor cars, the trains came through cuts and tunnels and over grades built by the Chinese. The economic successes of the nineteenth century were built on the sweat and blood of Chinese railroad workers.

16.2   Bound for the West: Image and Reality

F.O.C. Darley

Unknown photographer

From the 1860s through the 1880s, hundreds of thousands of people moved west. Some of them traveled by train, others by wagons called prairie schooners that were pulled by horses or oxen. The image of sturdy, virtuous, self-reliant pioneers moving west is a compelling one that is part of the mystique of the American frontier. Artist F.O.C. Darley captured this image in his painting, "Emigrant Crossing the Plains," reproduced here from an engraving by H. B. Hall, Jr. The reality of moving west, however, as shown in the photograph of settlers resting at the end of the day, did not always match the glorified image.

Consider:

1. *The differences between these two views of the westward pioneers;*
2. *Why artists tend to glorify the westward movement and why many Americans, in turn, have accepted this "glorification" as reality.*

SOURCE: *F.O.C. Darley, "Emigrants Crossing the Plains." Courtesy of the Library of Congress; unknown photographer, The Denver Public Library, Western History Department.*

16.3   The Ghost Dance and the Battle at Wounded Knee

James Mooney

On December 29, 1890, a bloody incident at Wounded Knee, South Dakota, put an end to the armed resistance of the Plains Indians. Approximately three hundred Indians, including women and children, were killed there or died later from wounds and exposure; thirty-one white soldiers were killed. At the time, Wounded Knee was called a triumph over treacherous Indians. But some historians and many Indians see Wounded Knee as a massacre of the Indians carried out by soldiers who wanted revenge for the Battle of the Little Big Horn, where General George Custer and his troops were annihilated in 1876. Others view it as an accidental armed confrontation that resulted from white misunderstanding of the actions of believers in the Ghost Dance, an Indian religious revival that was supposed to free Indians from white domination. Perhaps the most reliable account of Wounded Knee comes from James Mooney, an employee of the Bureau of Ethnology at the Smithsonian Institution. In 1890 he began a three-year study of the Ghost-Dance religion and the Sioux uprising. This excerpt is taken from his report, "The Ghost-Dance Religion and the Sioux Outbreak of 1890."

Consider:

1. Mooney's assertion of the peaceful intentions of Big Foot and the United States Army;
2. The role the medicine man, Yellow Bird, may have had in precipitating the conflict;
3. Mooney's explanation of the soldiers' responsibility for the massacre.

On the morning of December 29, 1890, preparations were made to disarm the Indians preparatory to taking them to the agency and thence to the railroad. In obedience to instructions the Indians had pitched their tipis on the open plain a short distance west of the creek and surrounded on all sides by the soldiers. In the center of the camp the Indians had hoisted a white flag as a sign of peace and a guarantee of safety. . . . In front, behind, and on both flanks of the camp were posted the various troops of cavalry, a portion of two troops, together with the Indian scouts, being dismounted and drawn up in front of the Indians at the distance of only a few yards from them. Big Foot himself was ill of pneumonia in his tipi, and Colonel Forsyth, who

SOURCE: *James Mooney, "The Ghost-Dance Rebellion and the Sioux Outbreak of 1890," in* Fourteenth Annual Report of the Bureau of American Ethnology *(Washington, D.C., 1896), 868–70.*

had taken command as senior officer, had provided a tent warmed with a camp stove for his reception.

Shortly after 8 oclock in the morning the warriors were ordered to come out from the tipis and deliver their arms. They came forward and seated themselves on the ground in front of the troops. They were then ordered to go by themselves into their tipis and bring out and surrender their guns. The first twenty went and returned in a short time with only two guns. It seemed evident that they were unwilling to give them up, and after consultation of the officers part of the soldiers were ordered up to within ten yards of the group of warriors, while another detachment of troops was ordered to search the tipis. After a thorough hunt these last returned with about forty rifles, most of which, however, were old and of little value. . . . While the soldiers had been looking for the guns Yellow Bird, a medicine-man, had been walking about among the warriors, blowing on an eagle-bone whistle, and urging them to resistance, telling them that the soldiers would become weak and powerless, and that the bullets would be unavailing against the sacred "ghost shirts," which nearly every one of the Indians wore. As he spoke in the Sioux language, the officers did not at once realize the dangerous drift of his talk, and the climax came too quickly for them to interfere. It is said one of the searchers now attempted to raise the blanket of a warrior. Suddenly Yellow Bird stooped down and threw a handful of dust into the air, when, as if this were the signal, a young Indian, said to have been Black Fox from Cheyenne river, drew a rifle from under his blanket and fired at the soldiers, who instantly replied with a volley directly into the crowd of warriors and so near that their guns were almost touching. . . .

At the first volley the Hotchkiss guns trained on the camp opened fire and sent a storm of shells and bullets among the women and children, who had gathered in front of the tipis to watch the unusual spectacle of military display. The guns poured in 2-pound explosive shells at the rate of nearly fifty per minute, mowing down everything alive. . . . In a few minutes 200 Indian men, women, and children, with 60 soldiers, were lying dead and wounded on the ground, the tipis had been torn down by the shells and some of them were burning above the helpless wounded, and the surviving handful of Indians were flying in wild panic to the shelter of the ravine, pursued by hundreds of maddened soldiers and followed up by a raking fire from the Hotchkiss guns, which had been moved into position to sweep the ravine.

There can be no question that the pursuit was simply a massacre, where fleeing women, with infants in their arms, were shot down after resistance had ceased and when almost every warrior was stretched dead or dying on the ground. . . .

. . . . The butchery was the work of infuriated soldiers whose comrades had just been shot down without cause or warning. In justice to a brave regiment it must be said that a number of the men were new recruits fresh from eastern recruiting stations, who had never before been under fire, were not yet imbued with military discipline, and were probably unable in the confusion to distinguish between men and women by their dress.

After examining all the official papers bearing on the subject in the files of the War Department and the Indian Office, together with the official reports of the Commissioner of Indian Affairs and of the Secretary of War and the several officers engaged; after gathering all that might be obtained from unofficial printed sources and from conversation with survivors and participants in the engagement on both sides, and after going over the battle-ground in company with the interpreter of the scouts engaged, the author arrives at the conclusion that when the sun rose on Wounded Knee on the fatal morning of December 29, 1890, no trouble was anticipated or premeditated by either Indians or troops; that the Indians in good faith desired to surrender and be at peace, and that the officers in the same good faith had made preparations to receive their surrender and escort them quietly to the reservation; that in spite of the pacific intent of Big Foot and his band, the medicine-man, Yellow Bird, at the critical moment urged the warriors to resistance and gave the signal for the attack; that the first shot was fired by an Indian, and that the Indians were responsible for the engagement; that the answering volley and attack by the troops was right and justifiable, but that the wholesale slaughter of women and children was unnecessary and inexcusable.

16.4   The New South
Henry W. Grady

As historian C. Vann Woodward has noted, the phrase "New South" did not identify a place or a time period. Rather, it was a popular slogan, suggesting a faith in the future and a feeling that the South "was at last one with the country." For Henry W. Grady, editor of the newspaper *Atlanta Constitution* and an influential advocate of the "New South," the concept meant laying aside sectional animosities, developing an industrial economy, and leaving Southern whites and blacks to work out their relationship by themselves. Though Grady was not the first to talk about the "New South," his speech to the New England Club of New York on December 21, 1886, made him its chief spokesman. Grady began this address with an emotional description of how the defeated South, without bitterness, had begun the task of rebuilding and recovering from the devastation of war. The excerpt here focuses on the economic situation of the South.

Consider:

1. *Whether Grady's description of the "New South" was based more on appeals to emotion than on statement of fact;*
2. *The status and condition of blacks in the "New South";*
3. *The role of agriculture in the "New South."*

But what is the sum of our work? We have found out that in the summing up the free negro counts more than he did as a slave. We have planted the schoolhouse on the hilltop and made it free to white and black. We have sowed towns and cities in the place of theories, and put business above politics. We have challenged your spinners in Massachusetts and your iron-makers in Pennsylvania. We have learned that the $400,000,000 annually received from our cotton crop will make us rich when the supplies that make it are home-raised. . . . We have learned that one Northern immigrant is worth fifty foreigners and have smoothed the path to Southward . . .

But what of the negro? Have we solved the problem he presents or progressed in honor and equity toward solution? Let the record speak to the point. No section shows a more prosperous laboring population than the negroes of the South, none in fuller sympathy with the employing and land-owning class. He shares our school fund, has the fullest protection of our laws and the friendship of our people. Self-interest, as well as honor, demand that he should have this. Our future, our very existence depend upon our working out this problem in full and exact justice. . . .

To liberty and enfranchisement is as far as law can carry the negro. The rest must be left to conscience and common sense. It must be left to those among whom his lot is cast, with whom he is indissolubly connected, and whose prosperity depends upon their possessing his intelligent sympathy and confidence. . . .

. . . Under the old regime the negroes were slaves to the South; the South was a slave to the system. The old plantation, with its simple police regulations and feudal habit, was the only type possible under slavery. Thus was gathered in the hands of a splendid and chivalric oligarchy the substance that should have been diffused among the people . . .

The old South rested everything on slavery and agriculture, unconscious that these could neither give nor maintain healthy growth. The new South presents a perfect democracy, the oligarchs leading in the popular movement—a social system compact and closely knitted, less splendid on the surface, but stronger at the core—a hundred farms for every plantation, fifty homes for every palace—and a diversified industry that meets the complex needs of this complex age.

SOURCE: *Henry W. Grady,* The New South and Other Addresses, *ed. Edna Henry Lee Turpin (New York: Haskell House Publishers, 1969), 32, 34–38.*

16.5   Sharecropping As a Way of Life

Fred A. Shannon

The 1880 census disclosed that in nine Southern states the average farm size had declined from 347 acres in 1860 to 156 acres in 1880, and that in the same period the number of farms had increased from 449,936 to 1,110,294. These statistics are misleading, however. For planting and harvesting purposes, plantations were subdivided into small plots worked by black and white landless families. Under the definitions used by the Census Bureau, these were considered farms. But such an interpretation failed to acknowledge the persistence of large land holdings or the emergence of the practice of sharecropping. By 1880, one-third of Southern farms were being cultivated by sharecroppers. In this excerpt from his 1945 book, *The Farmer's Last Frontier*, agricultural historian Fred Shannon discusses sharecropping.

Consider:

1. *The idea that while sharecropping might have begun as a substitute system for slavery, it soon included many whites as well as blacks;*
2. *Possible changes in the Southern economy that would have eliminated sharecropping;*
3. *How Henry Grady (Doc. 16.4) and other "New South" spokesmen could reconcile the rise of sharecropping and farm tenancy with their vision of a restored South with thousands of small, independent farmers.*

Since there was no intention on the part of the new reconstruction leaders in Congress (after 1870) to make freedom a reality to the Negro— to equip him with land, implements, necessary livestock, and training in management and self-reliance—it was not difficult for the planters who retained their old estates, and the newcomers who acquired the rest, to devise a new labor system giving the black man no more economic security than he had had in slavery: that is, a bare living. . . .

. . . there was discontent with the inability to maintain or restore the old plantation system of absolute control over the workers. There had to be assurance that the field hands would be present when wanted, and this the wage system did not supply. But more than this was involved. Poor whites, so long as they could refrain, would not work in the fields with Negroes, so they expanded on hitherto unused lands, or else went to town. In the heart of the cotton belt they were never numerous enough, anyway, to substitute for any considerable fraction of the blacks. Immigrants could not be lured into the section, with its servile wage scale. The Negro had to be utilized somehow,

SOURCE: *Fred A. Shannon*, The Farmer's Last Frontier: Agriculture, 1860–1897 *(New York: Holt, Rinehart and Winston, 1945), 83–91.*

and the landlords thought they knew how to get the tasks well done and still keep the worker properly meek and docile. . . . By 1869 the gang-labor system was on the verge of collapse in the Eastern cotton belt, and, as if by common consent, the wage system was dropped, by many of the planters, in favor of share cropping. . . .

. . . It was the outcome of years of experimentation to find what method would produce the most constant supply of submissive labor at the lowest cost. Several devices besides wage payments were tried out from the earliest days of disruption of the slave gangs by invading armies. Frequently, the workers were merely promised their keep, to be charged against them, and a share of the crop at the end of the season, from which their expenses were to be deducted. . . . Another experiment was a modification of serfdom, where the worker got a few acres with a hut, and wood to burn, then worked in the owner's fields four or five days out of the week for the privilege of raising his own food on the plot reserved for him. Occasionally there was to be found the regular form of tenancy; but sooner or later most of the owners adopted the share-cropping system.

Share cropping and tenancy are altogether different things, even to the legal relationships. The tenant has a lease on the land, can generally have some choice in what he grows, and is a free agent in the commercial world. He buys where he wishes to, and at the end of the season or at some other stipulated time pays the landlord the prearranged rental, whether in cash or a share of the produce. The cropper, on the other hand, is hired just before the spring plowing season to grow a crop of cotton or tobacco on a number of acres corresponding to the size of his family. That is, the more prospective pickers there are in the family, the larger the number of acres. The owner gives close supervision to everything that is done, and he wants nothing grown except what he can sell. If the tenant takes time to keep a garden he does so at the neglect of the major interest, and, furthermore, he deprives the owner of the privilege of selling him additional groceries. At the end of the season the whole crop is taken by the landlord, who assesses its value, deducts what the cropper owes from his share, and pays for the remainder, if any. The shares in general are in thirds, one for labor, another for land, and the last for draft animals, implements, seed, fertilizer, and other farming necessities. . . .

THE CROP-LIEN CREDIT SYSTEM

Had the cropper system always been fairly administered and the workers encouraged to do their best—if the tendency toward small landownership had not been positively discouraged—a larger number of the more energetic Negroes could have become possessors of their own soil. . . . But the new practice fell far short of getting the most from the land while building up the soil itself. The main reason for this, aside from the crushing of individual initiative through slaveowner tactics of management, was the credit system that grew up alongside of and merged with the structure of labor control. . . .

. . . But as cropping took the place of slavery, the landlord no longer could mortgage his labor supply for credit, and the uncertainties of crops in the period of transition made necessary some other means of financing the croppers during the season. So the workers, and sometimes the owners as well, turned to the local country storekeepers with whom they were acquainted. . . . it was a safe investment for the storekeeper to advance groceries, seed . . . or other needs to the croppers or independent farmers, in return for a lien on their crops. . . .

Thus there arose the crop-lien system, under which the farmer pledged his crop, to be handled by the merchant when it was harvested. The lien has been officially defined as "a bond for the payment of a specified amount—usually about $100—given to the storekeeper by the farmer, and pledging the growing crop as collateral security. . . .

. . . Loans were for an indeterminate period, but installments had to be paid from each portion of the crops as they were gathered. In South Carolina, which may be considered as typical, "from one-third to three-fifths of the crop" was taken to satisfy these obligations. . . .

Most of the storekeepers, doing nearly all their business on credit, never even set a cash price on many goods, particularly fertilizer and implements. . . . Low prices for cotton, and high costs of all provisions, got the farmer into a perpetual state of indebtedness, so year after year he merely struggled to clean the slate for a new start. Until this could be done, he was wholly at the mercy of the merchant as to what he might buy and how much, what he should grow and the acreage of it, and how he should manage each detail of his work. If the cropper was a Negro, and in the earlier years he usually was, the restrictions were all the more rigorous.

16.6   The "Atlanta Compromise," 1895

Booker T. Washington

In 1895, ex-slave Booker T. Washington, founder and director of Tuskegee Institute in Alabama, was invited to speak at the opening ceremony of the Cotton States and International Exposition in Atlanta, Georgia. Before an audience of Southern whites and blacks—seated in separate sections—and Northern whites, Washington delivered a twenty-minute speech in which he attempted to set forth a conciliatory and practical program for black-white relationships in the South. He suggested that blacks were more interested in equal economic opportunity than in political or social equality. The audience responded enthusiastically, and newspapers across the country hailed him as the spokesman for his race. The speech, excerpted here, has been called the "Atlanta Compromise" because of its conciliatory approach. However, Washington's biographer Louis R. Harlan has noted that the meaning Southern whites attached to Washington's specific words and phrases may not have reflected his own views.

Consider:

1. *Why Southerners and Northern whites responded so positively to Washington's speech;*
2. *The assumptions Washington made about the role whites would play in fulfilling their part of the "bargain";*
3. *The changes in both the South and the North that would have been necessary for Washington to have advocated a partnership of blacks and whites based on equality in all areas.*

One-third of the population of the South is of Negro race. No enterprise seeking the material, civil, or moral welfare of this section can disregard this element of our population and reach the highest success. I but convey to you, Mr. President and Directors, the sentiment of the masses of my race, when I say that in no way have the value and manhood of the American Negro been more fittingly and generously recognized, than by the managers of this magnificent Exposition at every stage of its progress. . . .

A ship lost at sea for many days suddenly sighted a friendly vessel. From the mast of the unfortunate vessel was seen the signal: "Water, water, we die of thirst." The answer from the friendly vessel at once came back, "Cast down your bucket where you are." A second time the signal, "Water, water, send us water," ran up from the distressed vessel and was answered, "Cast down your bucket where you are," and a third and fourth signal for water was answered, "Cast down your bucket where you are." The captain of the distressed vessel, at last heeding the injunction, cast down his bucket and it came up full of fresh, sparkling water from the mouth of the Amazon River. To those of my race who depend on bettering their condition in a foreign land, or who underestimate the importance of cultivating friendly relations with the Southern white man who is their next door neighbor, I would say cast down your bucket where you are, cast it down in making friends, in every manly way, of the people of all races by whom we are surrounded. Cast it down in agriculture, in mechanics, in commerce, in domestic service, and in the professions. And in this connection it is well to bear in mind that, whatever other sins the South may be called upon to bear, when it comes to business pure and simple it is in the South that the negro is given a man's chance in the commercial world; and in nothing is this Exposition more eloquent

SOURCE: *Booker T. Washington,* The Negro and the Atlanta Exposition *(Baltimore, 1896),* 12–15.

than in emphasising this chance. Our greatest danger is that, in the great gap from slavery to freedom, we may overlook the fact that the masses of us are to live by the productions of our hands, and fail to keep in mind that we shall prosper in proportion as we learn to dignify and glorify common labor and put brains and skill into the common occupations of life; shall prosper in proportion as we learn to draw the line between the superficial and the substantial, the ornamental gewgaws of life and the useful. No race can prosper till it learns that there is as much dignity in tilling a field as in writing a poem. It is at the bottom of life we must begin and not the top. Nor should we permit our grievances to overshadow our opportunities.

To those of the white race who look to the incoming of those of foreign birth and strange tongue and habits for the prosperity of the South, were I permitted, I would repeat what I say to my own race, "Cast down your bucket where you are." Cast it down among the 8,000,000 negroes whose habits you know, whose loyalty and love you have tested in days when to have proved treacherous meant the ruin of your firesides. Cast it down among these people who have, without strikes and labor wars, tilled your fields, cleared your forests, builded your railroads and cities, and brought forth treasures from the bowels of the earth and helped make possible this magnificent representation of the progress of the South. Casting down your bucket among my people, helping and encouraging them as you are doing on these grounds, and to education of head, hand, and heart, you will find that they will buy your surplus land, make blossom the waste places in your fields, and run your factories. While doing this you can be sure in the future, as you have been in the past, that you and your families will be surrounded by the most patient, faithful, law-abiding, and unresentful people that the world has seen. . . .

Nearly sixteen millions of hands [of blacks] will aid you pulling the load upwards, or they will pull against you the load downwards. We shall constitute one-third and much more of the ignorance and crime of the South, or one-third its intelligence and progress; we shall contribute one-third to the business and industrial prosperity of the South, or we shall prove a veritable body of death, stagnating, depressing, retarding every effort to advance the body politic. . . .

The wisest among my race understand that the agitation of questions of social equality is the extremest folly, and that progress in the enjoyment of all the privileges that will come to us must be the result of severe and constant struggle, rather than of artificial forcing. No race that has anything to contribute to the markets of the world is long in any degree ostracized. It is important and right that all privileges of the law be ours, but it is vastly more important that we be prepared for the exercise of these privileges. The opportunity to earn a dollar in a factory just now is worth infinitely more than the opportunity to spend a dollar in an opera house.

16.7   Separate but Equal:
Plessy v. *Ferguson,* 1896

In the aftermath of Reconstruction, a series of Supreme Court decisions helped restore "white supremacy" in the South. In 1876, the Court ruled that the Fourteenth Amendment did not protect blacks from discrimination by private individuals. The Court used the same reasoning in an 1883 decision that voided the Civil Rights Act of 1875. Then, in 1896, the Court ruled in *Plessy* v. *Ferguson* that an 1890 Louisiana law that required separate railroad coaches for whites and blacks did not violate the Fourteenth Amendment. With the blessing of the Supreme Court, the doctrine of "separate but equal" became the legal basis for segregation in public facilities in the South. The excerpt here includes portions of the majority opinion written by Justice Henry B. Brown, as well as a section of the dissenting opinion written by Justice John Harlan.

Consider:

1. *The basic assumption about race relations that underlies the majority opinion;*
2. *The validity of the Court's ruling that separation does not stamp "the colored race with a badge of inferiority";*
3. *Justice Harlan's view of race relations and constitutional rights.*

. . . We think the enforced separation of the races, as applied to the internal commerce of the State, neither abridges the privileges or immunities of the colored man, deprives him of his property without due process of law, nor denies him the equal protection of the laws, within the meaning of the Fourteenth Amendment.

We consider the underlying fallacy of the plaintiff's argument to consist in the assumption that the enforced separation of the two races stamps the colored race with a badge of inferiority. If this be so, it is not by reason of anything found in the act, but solely because the colored race chooses to put that construction upon it. The argument necessarily assumes that if, as has been more than once the case, and is not unlikely to be so again, the colored race should become the dominant power in the state legislature, and should enact a law in precisely similar terms, it would thereby relegate the white race to an inferior position. We imagine that the white race, at least, would not acquiesce in this assumption. The argument also assumes that social prejudices may be overcome by legislation, and that equal rights cannot be secured to the negro except by an enforced commingling of the two races. We cannot accept this proposition. . . . Legislation is powerless

SOURCE: *United States Reports: Cases Adjudged in the U.S. Supreme Court at October Term, 1895 (New York, 1899).*

to eradicate racial instincts or to abolish distinctions based upon physical differences, and the attempt to do so can only result in accentuating the difficulties of the present situation. If the civil and political rights of both races be equal one cannot be inferior to the other civilly or politically. If one race be inferior to the other socially, the Constitution of the United States cannot put them upon the same plane. . . .

MR. JUSTICE HARLAN dissenting.
. . . we have before us a state enactment that compels, under penalties, the separation of the two races in railroad passenger coaches, and makes it a crime for a citizen of either race to enter a coach that has been assigned to citizens of the other race. . . .

In respect of civil rights, common to all citizens, the Constitution of the United States does not, I think, permit any public authority to know the race of those entitled to be protected in the employment of such rights. . . .

It was said in argument that the statute of Louisiana does not discriminate against either race, but prescribes a rule applicable alike to white and colored citizens. But this argument does not meet the difficulty. Every one knows that the statute in question had its origin in the purpose, . . . to exclude colored people from coaches occupied by or assigned to white persons. . . .

The white race deems itself to be the dominant race in this country. . . . But in view of the Constitution, in the eye of the law, there is in this country no superior, dominant, ruling class of citizens. There is no caste here. Our Constitution is color-blind, and neither knows nor tolerates classes among citizens. In respect of civil rights, all citizens are equal before the law. . . . It is, therefore, to be regretted that this high tribunal, the final expositor of the fundamental law of the land, has reached the conclusion that it is competent for a State to regulate the enjoyment by citizens of their civil rights solely upon the basis of race.

In my opinion, the judgment this day rendered will, in time, prove to be quite as pernicious as the decision made by this tribunal in the *Dred Scott case*. . . .

The arbitrary separation of citizens, on the basis of race, while they are on a public highway, is a badge of servitude wholly inconsistent with the civil freedom and the equality before the law established by the Constitution. It cannot be justified upon any legal grounds. . . .

CHAPTER QUESTIONS

1. *Compare the economic difficulties of farmers in the "New South" and those in the "New West" between 1865 and 1900.*
2. *In what respects did the majority opinion in* Plessy v. Ferguson *reflect the racial attitudes of most whites in both the North and the South?*

part five

INDUSTRIALIZATION AND MODERNIZATION, 1877–1920

Chapter 17

Industrialization and Reorganization of the American Economy, 1875–1900

Between 1875 and 1900, factories, shops, and offices replaced the farm as the primary workplace for most Americans. This shift was accompanied by a profound change in the structure of American life resulting from the impact of industrialization and the reorganization of business on a very large scale.

These major changes in the economy were facilitated by technological innovations, such as the development of techniques for the mass production of steel, the growth of a national transportation network, the introduction of electricity, and the use of telephones for rapid communication. Large-scale industrialization resulted in the mass production of both producers' goods, such as factory equipment, and consumer goods, such as clothing. Since an economy based on mass production required centralized control and standardization, new techniques of modern business administration also appeared at this time.

Following some of the managerial techniques used by American railroads, large companies moved toward an organizational structure that integrated all the activities associated with a product. A "vertically" integrated business controlled other businesses on which the company depended for its principal product or service. Vertically integrated companies had a central office with a number of departments, each with responsibility for a specific area of activity. Big business became the rule, rather than the exception, and by 1900 the hundred largest companies controlled about one-third of the nation's industrial activity. Congressional efforts to place some controls on big business were set back by key decisions of the Supreme Court in this period.

Another requirement for a modern industrial economy—the concentration of a large labor force—was met by American cities, especially those in the Northeast. By the end of the century, foreign immigrants and farmers' sons and daughters were flooding cities and providing the necessary work force. At the same time, the development of urban transportation systems permitted a labor force that lived in areas around a city to travel to and from work cheaply.

The general trend toward large-scale organization and centralization did not necessarily apply to workers. Creation of the American Federation of Labor (1886) marked the beginning of labor's organizational efforts. By the end of the century, however, the A. F. of L. was only marginally successful, primarily because of resistance from powerful companies. Furthermore, a series of Supreme Court decisions and several disastrous strikes made the task of organized labor even more difficult.

Paralleling the conflict between big business and organized labor was a conflict between the rising self-consciousness of working women and traditional values of a society in which work outside the home was not highly regarded. Thousands of women tried to reconcile their individual aspirations with society's expectations of them.

The selections in this chapter focus on physical aspects of economic growth and organization, factors encouraging or hindering that economic development, and the growing awareness that the new economic order was changing traditional American values.

Chronology

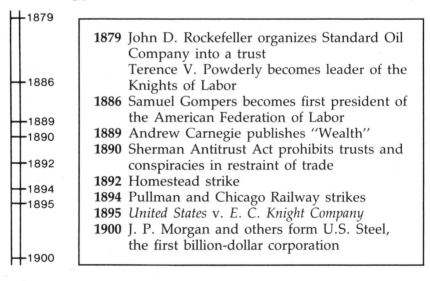

-1879

-1886

-1889
-1890

-1892

-1894
-1895

-1900

1879 John D. Rockefeller organizes Standard Oil Company into a trust
Terence V. Powderly becomes leader of the Knights of Labor
1886 Samuel Gompers becomes first president of the American Federation of Labor
1889 Andrew Carnegie publishes "Wealth"
1890 Sherman Antitrust Act prohibits trusts and conspiracies in restraint of trade
1892 Homestead strike
1894 Pullman and Chicago Railway strikes
1895 *United States* v. *E. C. Knight Company*
1900 J. P. Morgan and others form U.S. Steel, the first billion-dollar corporation

Documents

17.1   The Beginnings of "Big Business" in American Industry

Alfred D. Chandler

Between 1865 and 1900, a revolutionary transformation of American business occurred. Stimulated largely by technological innovation, especially mechanization and the use of electricity, American industry was able to produce producers' goods (such as machinery and locomotives) and consumer goods (such as shoes and canned foods) on an enormous scale. By the end of the nineteenth century, the nation was about to become a mass-production economy. Such changes obviously required a reordering and restructuring of the way business was managed. In an influential article entitled "The Beginnings of 'Big Business' in American Industry," excerpted here, economic historian Alfred D. Chandler summarized the results of his study of the widespread institutional changes.

Consider:

1. *How American railroads made it possible for American industrial development to take place;*
2. *The basic characteristics of a "vertically integrated" industry;*
3. *The implications for politics of a highly organized industrial society.*

Between the depression of the 1870's and the beginning of the twentieth century, American industry underwent a significant transformation. In the 1870's, the major industries serviced an agrarian economy. Except

SOURCE: *Alfred D. Chandler, "The Beginnings of 'Big Business' in American Industry,"* Business History Review 32 *(Spring 1959): 4–8, 14–17. Reprinted by permission of the* Business History Review. *Copyright © 1959 by the President and Fellows of Harvard College.*

for a few companies equipping the rapidly expanding railroad network, the leading industrial firms processed agricultural products and provided farmers with food and clothing. These firms tended to be small, and bought their raw materials and sold their finished goods locally. Where they manufactured for a market more than a few miles away from the factory, they bought and sold through commissioned agents who handled the business of several other similar firms.

By the beginning of the twentieth century, many more companies were making producers' goods, to be used in industry rather than on the farm or by the ultimate consumer. Most of the major industries had become dominated by a few large enterprises. These great industrial corporations no longer purchased and sold through agents, but had their own nation-wide buying and marketing organizations. Many, primarily those in the extractive industries, had come to control their own raw materials. In other words, the business economy had become industrial. Major industries were dominated by a few firms that had become great, vertically integrated, centralized enterprises. . . .

These basic changes came only after the railroads had created a national market. The railroad network, in turn, had grown swiftly primarily because of the near desperate requirements for efficient transportation created by the movement of population westward after 1815. Except for the Atlantic seaboard between Boston and Washington, the construction of the American railroads was stimulated almost wholly by the demand for better transportation to move crops, to bring farmers supplies, and to open up new territories to commercial agriculture.

By greatly expanding the scope of the agrarian economy, the railroads quickened the growth of the older commercial centers, such as New York, Philadelphia, Cincinnati, Cleveland, and St. Louis, and helped create new cities like Chicago, Indianapolis, Atlanta, Kansas City, Dallas, and the Twin Cities. This rapid urban expansion intensified the demand for the products of the older consumer goods industries—particularly those which processed the crops of the farmer and planter into food, stimulants, and clothing.

At the same time, railroad construction developed the first large market in this country for producers' goods. . . . More than this, the railroads, with their huge capital outlay, their fixed operating costs, the large size of their labor and management force, and the technical complexity of their operations, pioneered in the new ways of oligopolistic competition and large-scale, professionalized, bureaucratized management.

The new nation-wide market created by the construction of the railroad network became an increasingly urban one. From 1850 on, if not before, urban areas were growing more rapidly than rural ones. In the four decades from 1840 to 1880 the proportion of urban population rose from 11 per cent to 28 per cent of the total population, or about 4 per cent a decade. In the two decades from 1880 to 1900 it grew from 28 per cent to 40 per cent or an increase of 6 per cent a decade. . . .

The industries first to become dominated by great business enterprises were those making consumer goods, the majority of which were processed from products grown on the farm and sold in the urban markets. Consolidation and centralization in the consumers' goods industries were well under way by 1893. . . .

The story of the changes and the possible reasons behind them can be more clearly understood by examining briefly the experience of a few innovating firms. . . . Gustavus F. Swift, an Easterner, came relatively late to the Chicago meat-packing business. Possibly because he was from Massachusetts, he appreciated the potential market for fresh western meat in the eastern cities. For after the Civil War, Boston, New York, Philadelphia, and other cities were rapidly outrunning their local meat supply. At the same time, great herds of cattle were gathering on the western plains. Swift saw the possibilities of connecting the new market with the new source of supply by the use of the refrigerated railroad car. In 1878, shortly after his first experimental shipment of refrigerated meat, he formed a partnership with his younger brother, Edwin, to market fresh western meat in the eastern cities.

For the next decade, Swift struggled hard to carry out his plans, the essence of which was the creation, during the 1880's, of the nationwide distributing and marketing organization built around a network of branch houses. Each "house" had its storage plant and its own marketing organization. The latter included outlets in major towns and cities, often managed by Swift's own salaried representatives. In marketing the product, Swift had to break down, through advertising and other means, the prejudices against eating meat killed more than a thousand miles away and many weeks earlier. At the same time he had to combat boycotts of local butchers and the concerted efforts of the National Butchers' Protective Association to prevent the sale of his meat in the urban markets.

To make effective use of the branch house network, the company soon began to market products other than beef. The "full line" soon came to include lamb, mutton, pork, and, some time later, poultry, eggs, and dairy products. The growing distributing organization soon demanded an increase in supply. So between 1888 and 1892, the Swifts set up meat-packing establishments in Kansas City, Omaha, and St. Louis, and, after the depression of the 1890's, three more in St. Joseph, St. Paul, and Ft. Worth. At the same time, the company systematized the buying of its cattle and other products at the stockyards. In the 1890's, too, Swift began a concerted effort to make more profitable use of by-products.

Before the end of the 1890's, then, Swift had effectively fashioned a great, vertically integrated organization. The major departments— marketing, processing, purchasing, and accounting—were all tightly controlled from the central office in Chicago. . . .

. . . The great modern corporation, carrying on the major industrial processes, namely, purchasing, and often production of materials and parts, manufacturing, marketing, and finance—all within the same organizational structure—had its beginnings in the 1880's. By 1900 they had become the basic business unit in American industry.

Each of these major processes became managed by a corporate department, and all were coordinated and supervised from a central office. The creation of nation-wide distributing and selling organizations was the initial step in the growth of many large consumer goods companies.

The consolidation of plants under a single manufacturing department usually accompanied or followed the formation of a national marketing organization. The creation of such a manufacturing department normally meant the concentration of production in fewer and larger plants, and such consolidation probably lowered unit costs and increased output per worker. The creation of such a department in turn led to the setting up of central traffic, purchasing, and often engineering organizations. Large-scale buying, more rational routing of raw materials and finished products, more systematic plant lay-out, and plant location in relation to materials and markets probably lowered costs still further. . . .

The coming of the large vertically integrated, centralized, functionally departmentalized industrial organization altered the internal and external situations in which and about which business decisions were made. Information about markets, supplies, and operating performance as well as suggestions for action often had to come up through the several levels of the departmental hierarchies, while decisions and suggestions based on this data had to be transmitted down the same ladder for implementation. . . .

Costs, rather than interfirm competition, began to determine prices. With better information on costs, supplies, and market conditions, the companies were able to determine price quite accurately on the basis of the desired return on investment. . . . To increase their share of the market and to improve their profit position, the large corporations therefore concerned themselves less with price and concentrated more on obtaining new customers by advertising, brand names, and product differentiations; on cutting costs through further improvement and integration of the manufacturing, marketing, and buying processes; and on developing more diversified lines of products.

17.2 Industrialism and the Rise of Urban America

Zane L. Miller

Urbanization and industrial development seemed to go hand in hand in the nineteenth century. Just as industrialization stimulated urban growth, urban growth contributed to the nation's economic expansion, especially in the areas of steel production, electrification, and urban transportation. As cities expanded, both upward and outward, a range of technological problems had to be overcome. The human aspect of this growth involved dramatic population shifts, new residential patterns, and new developments in business. These developments were generally repeated in city after city throughout the country. In his book, *The Urbanization of America*, excerpted here, urban historian Zane L. Miller examines the emergence of metropolitan America.

Consider:

1. *The economic connections that Miller makes between industrialization and urbanization, especially concerning producers' goods;*
2. *The implications of the fact that American cities, especially those in the Northeast, served as "safety valves" for excess populations from American farms and European countries;*
3. *The technological innovations that led to new patterns of land use— location of factories, downtown business districts, and residential areas.*

. . . Between 1880 and 1910, American cities and the national economic and political structures assumed the shape they would retain for nearly fifty years. Throughout the period, rural-urban migration and foreign immigration persisted, and the proportion of the nation's total population that ranked as urban continued to rise. Equally important, technological innovations in mass rapid transit provided the means by which the gradual mid-nineteenth-century expansion of the territorial limits of cities gave way to urban sprawl. These developments established the environment in which the nation's economic structure shifted from a commercial to an industrial orientation. The rapid physical and population growth of cities created vast new markets for manufactured goods, and the entrepreneurial response to these demands carried the economy from the mixed commercial, manufacturing, and agrarian phase characterized by diversity in the scale and managerial structure of business organizations into the industrial phase dominated by large, mass-production corporations. . . .

The magnitude of both the physical and population aspects of urban growth was impressive. . . . By 1900 the walking city, covering five to eight square miles, had been replaced by distended metropolises spreading over twenty, fifty, and more square miles. In 1880, 28.2 percent of the American people lived in cities. A decade later the figure stood at 35.1, at the turn of the century it reached 39.7. . . .

SOURCE: Zane L. Miller, *The Urbanization of Modern America: A Brief History,* 63–66, 68, 72–73, 75–77, 79–80. Copyright © 1973 by Harcourt Brace Jovanovich, Inc. *Reprinted by permission of the publisher.*

The geographic expansion of cities and the consequent extension of services into the newly settled edges created a sudden and spiraling demand for producers' goods. The expansion of lighting, heating, power, transportation, water, sewerage, telegraph, and telephone facilities in the new cities absorbed ever growing quantities of electric lighting apparatus, copper wire, streetcars, iron, steel, and lead pipe. In addition, the rising volume of residential, office, and factory construction in and about cities created enlarged markets for power, construction machinery, and explosives as well as for metals, and the continued rapid increase of the urban population established vast outlets for a host of new consumer goods, including the sewing machine, typewriter, bicycle, and eventually, the automobile. Firms manufacturing these goods provided yet another avenue of growth for the "heavy" or "basic" producers' goods industries.

The impact of these new demands for both producers' and consumers' goods completed the shift in the economy from a city-organized agricultural and commercial base to an urban-industrial base. . . .

. . . the emergence of an industrial corporate society had surprisingly little effect on the relationship among the nation's economic regions or on regional differentials in rates of urbanization. Although the big businesses sold their goods in a national market, the jobs created by the increased productive capacity of the producers' and consumers' goods industries were not spread evenly among cities in every region of the country. They concentrated, instead, in the [Northeast] urban-industrial heartland, where the corporations had ready access to raw materials and large pools of skilled and semiskilled workers and managerial talent. . . .

Throughout the period from 1880 to 1910, most of the new urban population came not from natural increase, but from the internal and international movement of people. Though the rural population did not decline in absolute terms, the continued improvement of agricultural techniques reduced the demand for farm laborers to such an extent that the high fertility and low death rates in uncongested rural areas produced an "excess" farm population, which was attracted to the cities by the economic opportunities created by the growth of mass production industries. . . .

Immigrants were also engaged in a quest for broader opportunities, and they made up another important component of the new urban population. In the two generations after 1880 the decennial census counted more new arrivals per decade than ever. Between 1900 and 1909 alone some 8.2 million people landed on American shores, and the total for the forty-year span from 1880 to 1920, when the great era of foreign immigration closed, came to almost 23.5 million, while the average number of arrivals per decade amounted to about 6 million individuals. The bulk of the newcomers settled in cities. . . .

Whatever the composition of its population, the post-1880 city possessed a distinctive interior structure. After 1880, improvement in transport and communications technologies, as well as a spate of construction innovations, such as the elevator, accelerated the mid-nineteenth century expansion and the development of central business districts. . . .

While downtown in the mid-nineteenth-century walking city had been dominated by warehouses, small workshops, and embryo financial districts, the technological changes at the turn of the century and the increased purchasing power of a large segment of the urban population rearranged land use patterns and concentrated a wide range of economic activities at the core of the new cities. . . .

Shopping comprised the chief new function of downtown. Before 1870, most general retailing had been unspecialized and widely dispersed throughout the city. The organization of department stores, which, because of the large scale of their operations, could offer a variety of goods at low prices, completed the creation of a separate and extensive centrally located retail district. The big new emporiums hovered around focal points in the street railway system. . . . [These] stores derived much of their business from the growing numbers of commuters who came daily to the central business district to work. . . .

The new city also displayed a distinctive residential structure, one which precisely reversed the social geography of the walking city. Although the pattern in detail varied from place to place, the residential configuration of major cities divided generally into three broad sections, based primarily on income. The new modes of intracity transportation, especially the electric trolly and, after 1910, the automobile, cab, and bus, played a critical role in producing this tripartite division. The improved speed and power of these new transportation facilities snapped the bonds of convenience that had held the wealthy to sites near the focus of their social, economic, and political activities in the center of town. . . .

Electric rapid transit also provided middle-income groups with increased residential latitude, and they, like the rich, pushed away from the center.

The poor in the new city lacked the freedom of residential choice of the other two groups. Consequently, the lower classes were left behind in districts that in the mid-nineteenth century had been slums. As the city's total population rose and shifted outward, the poor moved into the abandoned houses of the wealthy and former dwelling sites of the middle-income groups near the expanding central business district. In the late nineteenth century these shifts of population distribution produced the familiar pattern of the modern metropolis. The rich claimed the periphery, the poor and the newcomers the "inner" city, and the middle classes the region between the slums and suburbs.

17.3   Urban Mass Transportation

As noted in the previous selection (Doc. 17.2), urban transportation, especially the development of the electric streetcar or trolley, was a critical factor in the growth and development of American cities between 1880 and 1900. When the electric streetcar was introduced in Boston in the 1880s, it profoundly altered the urban landscape of that city. The map reproduced here is taken from the book by Samuel Bass Warner, Jr., *Streetcar Suburbs: The Process of Growth in Boston, 1870–1900.*

Consider:

1. *The ways in which electric streetcars affected urban life and development;*
2. *Whether the map supports the points made in Document 17.2;*
3. *The political and social implications of public transportation systems that permitted upper- and middle-class residents to work downtown and live in the suburbs.*

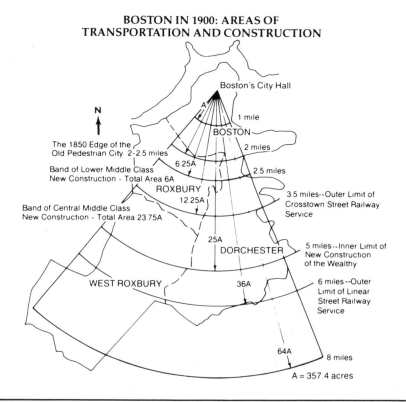

**BOSTON IN 1900: AREAS OF
TRANSPORTATION AND CONSTRUCTION**

SOURCE: *Sam B. Warner, Jr.,* Streetcar Suburbs: The Process of Growth in Boston, 1870–1900 *(Cambridge, Mass.: Harvard University Press, 1962), 63, 171. Excerpted by permission.*

17.4   Working-Class Women

Sarah Eisenstein

Accompanying the changing organizational structure of American businesses (see Doc. 17.1) was another change, equally profound and far more subtle—the increase of women in the work force. The number of women employed in manufacturing and mechanical industries, for example, jumped from 364,097 in 1870 to 1,380,469 in 1900. During the same period, the number of women employed in the transportation and communication industries increased from 1,050 to 42,181, and in clerical jobs the number climbed from 1,910 to 187,053. Sociologists and historians have been very interested in the way working women of this time viewed themselves. In the excerpt reprinted from her book *Give Us Bread but Give Us Roses*, historian Sarah Eisenstein discusses the contradictory strains in the emerging self-consciousness of these working women.

Consider:

1. Why Sarah Eisenstein distinguishes among moral, biological, and social conceptions of "woman";
2. The validity of Eisenstein's argument that the work experience helped develop a self-awareness in working-class women;
3. Whether it was beneficial for immigrant women to enter the work force.

. . . The institutional relationships which define the common role of women in industrial society—i.e., those which characterized the development of the nuclear family in the context of industrialization and urbanization—tend to militate against recognition by women of their shared situation. They are not, through their roles in the family, involved in interactions with other women which would tend to encourage recognition of a common position as women in social terms. Rather, those roles structure a situation which is privatized and personal, and which tends to generate a conception of the category 'woman' in moral, biological or 'natural,' rather than social, terms.

. . . For women from working-class families in this period, work in factory or store was their first collective experience in a situation where the social position they shared as women could emerge. This

SOURCE: *Sarah Eisenstein*, Give Us Bread but Give Us Roses: Working Women's Consciousness in the United States, 1890 to the First World War *(Boston: Routledge & Kegan Paul, 1983), 39, 42–43, 50–53.*

is not to imply that working-class women were isolated from each other as long as they remained in family roles. On the contrary, most descriptions of traditional working-class communities emphasize the degree to which their social networks are sex-segregated, the connections among women within and across generations, and their importance as sources of support, community integration, and the continuity of tradition. But these networks are primarily extensions of family relationships and thus part of a context which people are used to seeing as personal and natural. The identification of working-class women with one another in the context of those relations was a major source of support in daily life. It often served, when women did go to work, as a source of reinforcement of work-based solidarity. But the experience in itself did not provide the basis for identification with other women as members of a social group. . . .

. . . For working-class women at the turn of the century, work outside the home was probably a necessary condition for overcoming the consequences of that situation and laying the basis for their 'self-discovery' as a social group. . . .

. . . The women who entered the labor force in increasingly large numbers were predominantly of working-class background. They entered, in the majority of cases, occupations in industry and in the lower ranks of the newly developing white-collar fields.

The vast majority of women who entered the labor force during this period did so in industrial occupations, and although the entry of smaller numbers of women into professional work and the emerging white-collar occupations tended to capture the popular imagination, it was industrial work which was the more representative experience of employed women. Although significant numbers of middle-class women entered professional careers, their decision to work was most often a matter of choice. That decision often reflected an initial awareness of the ideological conflicts involved and even some eagerness to confront them. Women from working-class families who worked did so primarily because they found it necessary in order to support themselves and/or their families. . . .

. . . Working women tended to be overwhelmingly, although not exclusively, young and unmarried. They tended to work for a relatively brief portion of their lives. A majority were immigrants or the daughters of immigrants, and they tended to live and work in large or middle-sized industrial cities in the North-east and Mid-west. Each of these factors helped to structure their experience in particular ways, and to influence the manner in which they understood it.

Most women who worked at this time did so in the period between leaving school, at a relatively early age, and marriage. They did not expect to work after marriage, such being the fate only of women unfortunate enough to be widowed, deserted, married to drunkards, etc. Thus working outside the home, however important its immediate impact, was essentially a temporary phase in most women's lives. This was extremely important in structuring the ways in which women negotiated the tension between the fact of their working and the emphasis placed by the ideas of the period on women's commitment to home and family. . . .

The fact that many working women were of immigrant background was also important in structuring their experience of work. It meant that the dislocation and adjustment attendant on that situation were often experienced coextensively with the changes in orientation involved in going to work. For example, the shifts in a working girl's relation to her family was often bound up with the changing patterns of immigrants' relationship to their children. Indeed, going to work was sometimes an important influence, along with school, in the 'Americanization' of immigrant women, particularly the younger among them. It was often in the shop that young immigrant women learned American patterns of speech, dress, amusement, social relationship—and there also, consequently, that certain conflicts with more traditional parents were generated. The fact that many working women belonged to immigrant communities in large industrial centers like New York, Pittsburgh, and Chicago, also meant that they went to work out of a background in which a majority of the women in their age group did likewise. That is, although working women comprised only a relatively small proportion of the female population nationally, many working women, particularly those from immigrant groups, came out of immediate milieux in which as many as 60 per cent of the women in their age group worked and expected to work for a period in their lives. . . .

. . . various ethnic groups placed different emphases on various aspects of traditional expectations about women and these affected their participation in work outside the home—Italians tended to circumscribe the activity of women most closely, and until rather late in our period, Italian women were more likely to work at home manufacture than in factories; Scandinavian women tended to prefer the more traditional setting of domestic service to factory or sales work; native-born women seem to have assigned more weight to questions of propriety and respectability in choosing work. In addition to the direct impact of cultural differences, considerations growing out of the differing situations of various groups also affected the work experience of women. The order of arrival of different immigrant groups, their geographic locations, and the intersection of these with the development of particular industries tended to structure the kinds of work which women did— for example, East European Jewish women working in garment trades in New York and Chicago; Poles and other Slavs in Chicago stockyards; Irish women in more skilled trades like bookbinding.

17.5   *United States* v. *E. C. Knight Company,* 1895

The Sherman Antitrust Act became law in 1890. It prohibited any contract, trust, or conspiracy that resulted in a restraint of trade or commerce. Four years later, Attorney General Richard Olney brought suit against the American Sugar Refining Company and four Philadelphia sugar refining companies, charging that the merger of these companies had created a monopoly. The Supreme Court ruled against the government in 1895, nullifying for all practical purposes government regulation of trusts and monopolies. The case takes its title from the name of one of the defendant sugar refining companies. Chief Justice Melville Fuller wrote the majority opinion of the Court, excerpted here.

Consider:

1. *How the opinion distinguishes between commerce and manufacture, and how the Court used this distinction;*
2. *The impact this view of restraint of commerce could have when applied to union organizations;*
3. *The economic and political assumptions underlying Judge Fuller's opinion.*

The fundamental question is, whether conceding that the existence of a monopoly in manufacture is established by the evidence, that monopoly can be directly suppressed under the act of Congress in the mode attempted by this bill. . . .

The argument is that the power to control the manufacture of refined sugar is a monopoly over a necessary of life, to the enjoyment of which by a large part of the population of the United States interstate commerce is indispensable, and that, therefore, the general government in the exercise of the power to regulate commerce may repress such monopoly directly and set aside the instruments which have created it. . . . Commerce succeeds to manufacture, and is not a part of it. The power to regulate commerce is the power to prescribe the rule by which commerce shall be governed, and is a power independent of the power to suppress monopoly. . . .

. . . Congress did not attempt [in the Sherman Antitrust Act] to assert the power to deal with monopoly directly as such; or to limit and restrict the rights of corporations created by the States or the citizens of the States in the acquisition, control, or disposition of property; or to regulate or prescribe the price or prices at which such property or the products thereof should be sold; or to make criminal the acts

SOURCE: *United States Reports,* Cases Adjudged in the Supreme Court at October Term, 1894, *Vol. 156 (New York: Banks & Brothers, 1895), 11–12, 16–17.*

of persons in the acquisition and control of property which the States of their residence or creation sanctioned or permitted. . . . what the law struck at was combinations, contracts, and conspiracies to monopolize trade and commerce among the several States or with foreign nations; but the contracts and acts of the defendants related exclusively to the acquisition of the Philadelphia refineries and the business of sugar refining in Pennsylvania, and bore no direct relation to commerce between the States or with foreign nations. The object was manifestly private gain in the manufacture of the commodity, but not through the control of interstate or foreign commerce. There was nothing . . . to indicate any intention to put a restraint upon trade of commerce, and . . . the act of Congress only authorized the Circuit Courts to proceed by way of preventing and restraining violations of the act in respect of contracts, combinations, or conspiracies in restraint of interstate or international trade or commerce.

17.6   The Best Fields for Philanthropy

Andrew Carnegie

A 1892 survey indicated that there were 4,047 millionaires in the United States and that most of them had amassed their wealth through industry, trade, and railroads. These captains of industry equated democracy with capitalism: liberty meant freedom to acquire and use property; equality meant equal opportunity for economic gain; and progress was defined as economic change and the accumulation of capital. Andrew Carnegie, one of these captains of industry, believed that wealth involved a stewardship that required the rich to use their wealth for the good of the community. In June of 1889, Carnegie published an essay on wealth in the *North American Review* that was reprinted in England under the title, "The Gospel of Wealth." In December 1889 he published a second essay, "The Best Fields for Philanthropy," in which he expanded on the ideas in the earlier essay. The excerpt here is from this second essay.

Consider:

1. *Carnegie's justification for the accumulation of wealth;*
2. *The assumptions underlying Carnegie's assertion that the "gospel of wealth" would resolve problems of poverty and wealth;*
3. *The validity of Carnegie's equation of the "gospel of wealth" with the teachings of Christ.*

. . . it may be advantageous to restate the positions taken in the former paper, ["Wealth"] for the benefit of those who may not have read it, or who cannot conveniently refer to it. It was assumed that the present laws of competition, accumulation, and distribution are the best obtainable conditions; that through these the race receives its most valuable fruits; and, therefore, that they should be accepted and upheld. Under these it was held that great wealth must inevitably flow into the hands of the few exceptional managers of men. The question then arose, What should these do with their surplus wealth? and the "Gospel of Wealth" contended that surplus wealth should be considered as a sacred trust, to be administered during the lives of its owners, by them as trustees, for the best good of the community in which and from which it had been acquired.

It was pointed out that there were but three modes of disposing of surplus wealth, and two of these were held to be improper. First, it was held that to leave great fortunes to children did not prove true affection for them or interest in their genuine good, regarded either as individuals or as members of the state; . . .

The second mode open to men is to hoard their surplus wealth during life, and leave it at death for public uses. It was pointed out that in many cases these bequests become merely monuments of the testators' folly; that the amount of real good done by posthumous gifts was ridiculously disproportionate to the sums thus left. . . .

The aim of the first article was thus to lead up to the conclusion that there is but one right mode of using enormous fortunes—namely, that the possessors from time to time during their own lives should so administer them as to promote the permanent good of the communities from which they have been gathered. . . .

The purpose of this article is to present some of the best methods of performing this duty of administering surplus wealth for the good of the people. . . .

First—Standing apart by itself there is the founding of a university by men enormously rich, such men as must necessarily be few in any country. Perhaps the greatest sum ever given by an individual for any purpose is the gift of Senator Stanford, who undertakes to establish upon the Pacific coast, where he amassed his enormous fortune, a complete university, which is said to involve the expenditure of ten millions of dollars, and upon which he may be expected to bestow twenty millions of his surplus. . . .

Second—The result of my own study of the question, What is the best gift which can be given to a community? is that a free library occupies the first place, providing the community will accept and maintain it as a public institution, as much a part of the city property as its public schools, and, indeed, an adjunct to these. . . .

SOURCE: *Andrew Carnegie, "The Best Fields for Philanthropy,"* The North American Review 149 (December 1899): 684–85, 687–89, 692, 694–98.

Many free libraries have been established in our country, but none that I know of with such wisdom as the Pratt Library, of Baltimore. Mr. Pratt presented to the city of Baltimore one million dollars, requiring it to pay 5 per cent. per annum, amounting to fifty thousand dollars per year, which is to be devoted to the maintenance and development of the library and its branches. . . .

This is the finest picture I have ever seen of any of the millionaire class. As here depicted, Mr. Pratt is the ideal disciple of the "Gospel of Wealth." We need have no fear that the mass of toilers will fail to recognize in such as he their best leaders and their most invaluable allies; for the problem of poverty and wealth, of employer and employed, will be practically solved whenever the time of the few is given, and their wealth is administered during their lives, for the best good of that portion of the community which has not been burdened by the responsibilities which attend the possession of wealth. We shall have no antagonism between classes when that day comes, for the high and the low, the rich and the poor, shall then indeed be brothers. . . .

Third—We have another most important department in which great sums can be worthily used,—the founding or extension of hospitals, medical colleges, laboratories, and other institutions connected with the alleviation of human suffering, and especially with the prevention rather than the cure of human ills. . . .

Fourth—In the very front rank of benefactions public parks should be placed, always provided that the community undertakes to maintain, beautify, and preserve inviolate the parks given to it. No more useful or more beautiful monument can be left by any man than a park for the city in which he was born or in which he has long lived, nor can the community pay a more graceful tribute to the citizen who presents it than to give his name to the gift. . . .

Fifth—We have another good use for surplus wealth, in providing for our cities halls suitable for meetings of all kinds, especially for concerts of elevating music. . . .

The "Gospel of Wealth" but echoes Christ's words. It calls upon the millionaire to sell all that he hath and give it in the highest and best form to the poor, by administering his estate himself for the good of his fellows, before he is called upon to lie down and rest upon the bosom of Mother Earth. So doing, he will approach his end no longer the ignoble hoarder of useless millions, poor, very poor indeed, in money, but rich, very rich, twenty times a millionaire still, in the affection, gratitude, and admiration of his fellow-men, and—sweeter far—soothed and sustained by the still small voice within, which, whispering, tells him that, because he has lived, perhaps one small part of the great world has been bettered just a little. This much is sure: against such riches as these no bar will be found at the Gates of Paradise.

17.7   Workers and the Church

Richard T. Ely

The social gospel movement in the late nineteenth century represented an effort to apply Christianity to problems arising from the industrialization and urbanization of the United States. These included such problems as the unequal distribution of wealth and the worsening living conditions of the urban poor. One of the most influential proponents of this "social Christianity" was Richard T. Ely, an economist on the faculty of the University of Wisconsin at Madison. In 1889, Ely delivered a lay sermon in which he expounded the social side of the church's mission and called attention to the "alienation of wage-workers from the church." Later he expanded the sermon into an essay, excerpted here, that was published in a book entitled *Social Aspects of Christianity*.

Consider:

1. *The role Ely believed appropriate for churches to undertake in behalf of workers;*
2. *The implications for political and social reform of Ely's call to "go back to Christ and learn of him";*
3. *The role of Christianity in promoting social reform.*

There are those who deny that wage-workers are alienated from the church, and I have carefully considered their arguments; but after years of observation and reflection I have been forced to the conclusion that there is a clear alienation of thinking wage-workers from the church which, on the whole, is growing. . . .

One reason why wage-workers do not love the church is not peculiar. The wickedness of men's hearts leads them to resist the gospel. Workingmen are like others in this respect, although certain temptations, as pride, and arrogance, and absorption by concerns of this world, are not so powerful in their case. We must remember that Christ said it was hard for a rich man to enter the kingdom of heaven, and never alluded to any special difficulties in the way of the poor as a class. We are also told that time was when the common people heard Christ gladly. These, however, are general considerations. What is now desired is to know the peculiar cause which alienates wage-workers as a class

---

SOURCE: *Richard T. Ely, "Social Aspects of Christianity," in* The Social Gospel in America, 1870–1920, *ed. Robert T. Handy (New York: Oxford University Press, 1966), 204–7, 209.*

of industry society from the church, and this may be stated in a single sentence.

The leaders of the church, the representative men and women in the church, profess to love the working classes, but as a matter of fact, they do not love them, and this wide divergence between profession and practice is keenly felt. I here state a grave charge, but who among my readers will deny it? . . .

First, these church leaders are so far away from the toiling masses that they fail to understand their desires, and the motives of their action. I meet few clergymen who, even when they want to be friendly, can give an intelligent statement of the side of labor in any of its many controversies with capital. They rarely converse with leaders of the workingmen, and perhaps more rarely read any labor paper. If they loved the masses, they would instinctively draw near enough to know their aims and motives. Christ moved among the masses and understood them, and today the poorest laborer and the most obstinate trades unionist, yes, even the despised walking delegate, will feel a strange attraction for that wonderful Being who spoke words which go straight to the heart. . . .

Second, the failure to rebuke wickedness in high places is noticed. When you go into a church on Fifth Avenue in New York, rarely, if ever, do you hear the corrupt methods by which the masses have been robbed, and prominent people made millionaires, described and denounced with righteous indignation. When not a workingman is present, the wicked labor agitators are lashed with fury. Why this? Is there any danger that a wealthy congregation in one of our cities will be carried away by the pleadings of the agitator? None at all. Those who sit in the pews have a sufficient appreciation of the wickedness of Knights of Labor and socialists. If the aim were to draw men together, those who minister to congregations made up of employers would so put the case of their employees that it could be understood, and would say everything favorable which could be said in their behalf. . . .

Third, the negative attitude of the church with respect to every proposed reform discourages, disgusts, and even angers, workingmen. The religious press is concerned with the "errors of socialism," "the errors of Henry George," and, in short, the errors of any one who proposes anything positive. . . .

Workingmen—I am talking all the time about the thinking work-ingmen—instinctively feel that if the church were animated by love, she would be more anxious to discover truths than errors in the plans of those who are working for the elevation of the masses.

Nothing so disheartens one as the failure of Christians to engage in positive work for the masses. One would at least suppose that such a question as freedom from toil on Sunday would concern the clergy. Yet is does not seem to. Scarcely a question is more alive today among all labor organizations than compulsory Sunday work. All over the country, when laboring men meet, they pass resolutions on this subject, and appeal to the public to help them to secure one day in seven for rest. Yet the pulpit is silent. . . .

. . . I trust that it [this essay] may start useful trains of thought in my readers, and arouse more than one conscience to a keener sense of duty. It is not pleasant to write a paper like this, but I believe it is time some one should speak plainly. Some say the condition of the church is hopeless. This I do not believe.

There is in the church a conscience which can be pricked, and it is probably as sensitive today as it has been in centuries gone by. There is a power back of the church, in her divine Master, which makes for righteousness, and which urges her on to a higher life. What is needed is to go back to Christ and learn of him.

CHAPTER QUESTIONS

1. *Discuss the managerial and technological innovations that were essential to the rise of big business between 1875 and 1900.*
2. *How did Andrew Carnegie and Richard T. Ely relate their Christian beliefs to the values represented by the emerging economic order of big business?*

Chapter 18

A Nation of Immigrants

From the time the first white settlers arrived at Jamestown, there was a constant flow of immigrants to America. The trans-Atlantic migration increased sharply in the 1840s and 1850s, however, largely because of unsettled political and economic conditions in Europe. In 1850, the annual number of immigrants arriving in this country passed 300,000 for the first time; between 1880 and 1910, immigration figures of half a million or more a year were not uncommon. More than ever, America seemed to be a nation of immigrants, and the period was dominated by the "immigrant problem."

In the years around the turn of the century, the ethnic composition of the arriving immigrants changed. Many Americans—including the "Old Immigrants" from Ireland, Germany, and Scandinavia—viewed this "New Immigration" with alarm, believing that these people from Southern and Eastern Europe posed a serious threat to national life. Religious, racial, and economic arguments were all employed to justify restrictions on the growing tide of immigrants. In 1903 and again in 1917, advocates of restrictionist legislation won important victories in Congress. By 1917, however, World War I had already seriously disrupted the mass emigration from Europe. Further restrictionist legislation in the 1920s would complete this trend, curtailing the steady immigration of the foreign-born that had given the United States its uniquely multinational character.

The dramatic increase in the number of immigrants entering the nation in the late nineteenth century had important effects on political and social institutions. In the cities, where so many of the "New Immigrants" settled, overcrowded tenement houses sprang up in certain districts, and new political structures flourished—in particular, "boss" rule. Meanwhile, as the "New Immigrants" poured into the nation by the thousands, earlier immigrants—many of whom lived in small towns and on farms—continued to try to adapt to American culture, sometimes using the newer arrivals as scapegoats in order to prove their own "Americanness."

The "New Immigration" and reactions to it raised important questions about the openness of American society, especially in relation to those who differed from the dominant Anglo-Saxon population. Issues concerning the separation of church and state, equality of opportunity, and the role of government in dealing with the disadvantaged all surfaced with troubling frequency. Most fundamentally, it seemed doubtful whether the nation that had been acclaimed as a "melting pot" for immigrants of all varieties would continue to foster such peaceful intermixture of peoples.

The selections in this chapter are intended to illustrate the varied nature and quality of the immigrant experience in the United States in the decades between 1880 and 1920. They also deal with the institutional and social effects of the massive immigration of foreign peoples during those years.

Chronology

1877	Railway strikes and riots
1878	"Dumbbell" tenement house designed
1882	Chinese Exclusion Act bans Chinese immigration
1885	Josiah Strong's *Our Country* published
1886	Haymarket bombing
	American Protective Association formed
1889	Hull House established by Jane Addams
1894	Immigration Restriction League formed
1901	New York Tenement Reform Law
	President McKinley assassinated by Leon Czolgosz
1903	Immigration Act of 1903 permits deportation of illegal immigrants
1914	Beginning of World War I, ending mass immigration from Europe to the United States
1917	Literacy Test for aliens enacted
1919–20	Red Scare

Documents

18.1   Sources of Immigration, 1880–1919

The years between 1880 and 1920 witnessed both a dramatic increase in the number of immigrants arriving in the United States and a shift in their ethnic composition. The so-called "New Immigration" of this period brought problems relating to racial and ethnic differences to the forefront. The pie graphs that follow show how the sources of immigration to the United States shifted during this period. The areas exhibiting the greatest relative increases were the major sources of the "New Immigration."

Consider:

1. *What generalizations might be made about the changing nature of immigration in this period;*
2. *What features characterized the "New Immigration."*

**DECENNIAL IMMIGRATION TO
THE UNITED STATES, 1880-1919**

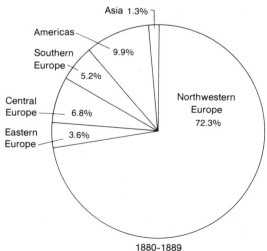

1880-1889

DECENNIAL IMMIGRATION TO THE UNITED STATES, 1880-1919

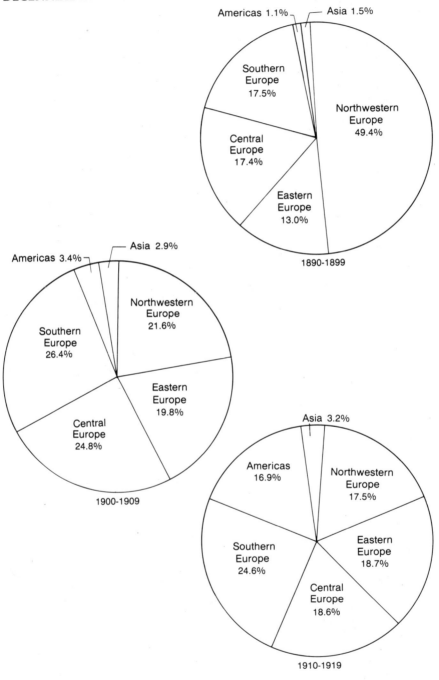

SOURCE: *Niles Carpenter, "Immigrants and Their Children,"* U.S. Bureau of the Census Monograph, *no. 7 (Washington, D.C.: Government Printing Office, 1927), 324–25.*

18.2 Anglo-Saxon Supremacy

Josiah Strong

Social Darwinism took Charles Darwin's theory of the survival of the fittest and applied it to society. It supported the concept of the natural supremacy of Anglo-Saxons—who had provided the majority of the early immigrants to America—over other ethnic groups. In turn, Anglo-Saxon supremacist sentiments inspired a campaign against non-Anglo-Saxon newcomers. In 1885, Congregationalist clergyman Josiah Strong wrote a best-selling manifesto for Anglo-Saxon exclusionism, entitled *Our Country*. The excerpt here, taken from Strong's book, presents some of the major arguments against continuing the kind—and extent—of immigration that had characterized the last years of the nineteenth century.

Consider:

1. *What Strong believed to be the greatest threats posed by the "New Immigration";*
2. *What similarities there are between Strong's argument and John C. Calhoun's argument regarding black slaves (Doc. 12.1);*
3. *What "special interests" Strong was appealing to with his arguments.*

The Tenth Census gave our total foreign-born population as 6,679,943; but we must not forget their children of the first generation, who, as we shall see, present a more serious problem than their parents, the immigrants. This class numbered in 1880, 8,276,053, making a total population of nearly 15,000,000 which was foreign by birth or parentage. . . .

So immense a foreign element must have a profound influence on our national life and character. . . .

. . . Our population of foreign extraction is sadly conspicuous in our criminal records. This element constituted in 1870 twenty per cent of the population of New England, and furnished seventy-five per cent of the crime. That is, it was twelve times as much disposed to crime as the native stock. The hoodlums and roughs of our cities are, most of them, American-born of foreign parentage. . . .

Moreover, immigration not only furnishes the greater portion of our criminals, it is also seriously affecting the morals of the native population. It is disease and not health which is contagious. Most foreigners bring with them continental ideas of the Sabbath, and the

SOURCE: *Josiah Strong,* Our Country: Its Possible Future and Its Present Crisis *(New York: Baker and Taylor, 1885, 1891), 54–55, 57–60.*

result is sadly manifest in all our cities, where it is being transformed from a holy day into a holiday. But by far the most effective instrumentality for debauching popular morals is the liquor traffic, and this is chiefly carried on by foreigners. . . .

We can only glance at the political aspects of immigration. As we have already seen, it is immigration which has fed fat the liquor power; and there is a liquor vote. Immigration furnishes most of the victims of Mormonism; and there is a Mormon vote. Immigration is the strength of the Catholic church; and there is a Catholic vote. Immigration is the mother and nurse of American socialism; and there is to be a socialist vote. Immigration tends strongly to the cities, and gives to them their political complexion. And there is no more serious menace to our civilization than our rabble-ruled cities. . . .

We have seen that immigration is detrimental to popular morals. It has a like influence upon popular intelligence, for the percentage of illiteracy among the foreign-born population is thirty-eight per cent greater than among the native-born whites. Thus immigration complicates our moral and political problems by swelling our dangerous classes. . . .

. . . Our safety demands the assimilation of these strange populations, and the process of assimilation will become slower and more difficult as the proportion of foreigners increases.

18.3 Tenement Living

Immigrants who settled in large cities were likely to make their homes in tenements—overcrowded, multistory buildings situated on small lots and divided into many apartments. In 1878, a contest sponsored by an architectural trade journal produced the "dumbbell" tenement. Initially considered a significant improvement in housing, the new design was hailed for combining safety concerns and convenience for tenants with profitability for owners. The tenement's distinctive "dumbbell" shape accommodated an air shaft between each pair of buildings; windows were found only at the front and rear of each building. The supposed advantages of the "dumbbell" design proved to be illusory. In fact, the shortcomings were so obvious that, in 1901, the New York legislature outlawed the construction of any more such buildings. The diagram reproduced here illustrates the main features of the "dumbbell" design.

Consider:

1. *Why the "dumbbell" design would have been greeted as a great architectural advance;*
2. *The major drawbacks and/or health hazards, aside from overcrowding and lack of privacy, of the "dumbbell" design.*

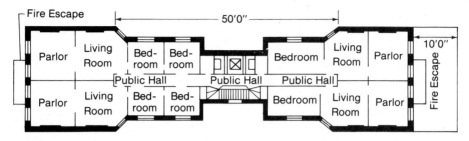

DUMBBELL TENEMENT

18.4 "Practical Politics" for Urban Immigrants: The Machine at Work

William L. Riordon

One of the major forces in the lives of immigrants who settled in American cities was the political "machine." The machine was run by bosses, often recent immigrants themselves, who traded favors for votes. These bosses not only dispensed jobs and material benefits to local residents, but also— often by methods that shocked "good government" reformers—managed to deliver necessary city services with unprecedented efficiency. In 1905, William Riordon, a New York reporter, conducted lengthy interviews with George Washington Plunkitt, one of the bosses of the notorious Tammany Hall machine. In this excerpt from Riordon's book, Plunkitt explains what fueled the urban political machine and how it worked for the benefit of all concerned.

Consider:

1. *The special appeal Plunkitt's values and methods might have had to recent immigrants;*
2. *Whether the machine was really beneficial to immigrants;*
3. *How Plunkitt's approach compares with the way a political leader should function in a representative government.*

There's only one way to hold a district: you must study human nature and act accordin'. . . .

To learn real human nature you have to go among the people, see them and be seen. I know every man, woman, and child in the Fifteenth District, except them that's been born this summer—and I know some

SOURCE: *William L. Riordon,* Plunkitt of Tammany Hall, *1905 (New York: E. P. Dutton, 1963), 25–28, 33, 35–36. All rights reserved. Reprinted by permission of the publisher, E. P. Dutton, a division of NAL Penguin Inc.*

of them, too. I know what they like and what they don't like, what they are strong at and what they are weak in, and I reach them by approachin' at the right side.

For instance, here's how I gather in the young men. I hear of a young feller that's proud of his voice, thinks that he can sing fine. I ask him to come around to Washington Hall and join our Glee Club. He comes and sings, and he's a follower of Plunkitt for life. Another young feller gains a reputation as a baseball player in a vacant lot. I bring him into our baseball club. That fixes him. You'll find him workin' for my ticket at the polls next election day. Then there's the feller that likes rowin' on the river, the young feller that makes a name as a waltzer on his block, the young feller that's handy with his dukes— I rope them all in by givin' them opportunities to show themselves off. I don't trouble them with political arguments. I just study human nature and act accordin'. . . .

As to the older voters, I reach them, too. No, I don't send them campaign literature. That's rot. People can get all the political stuff they want to read—and a good deal more, too—in the papers. Who reads speeches, nowadays, anyhow? It's bad enough to listen to them. You ain't goin' to gain any votes by stuffin' the letter boxes with campaign documents. . . .

What tells in holdin' your grip on your district is to go right down among the poor families and help them in the different ways they need help. I've got a regular system for this. If there's a fire in Ninth, Tenth, or Eleventh Avenue, for example, any hour of the day or night, I'm usually there with some of my election district captains as soon as the fire engines. If a family is burned out I don't ask whether they are Republicans or Democrats, and I don't refer them to the Charity Organization Society, which would investigate their case in a month or two and decide they were worthy of help about the time they are dead from starvation. I just get quarters for them, buy clothes for them if their clothes were burned up, and fix them up till they get things runnin' again. It's philanthropy, but it's politics, too—mighty good politics. Who can tell how many votes one of these fires bring me? The poor are the most grateful people in the world, and, let me tell you, they have more friends in their neighborhoods than the rich have in theirs. . . .

Another thing, I can always get a job for a deservin' man. I make it a point to keep on the track of jobs, and it seldom happens that I don't have a few up my sleeve ready for use. I know every big employer in the district and in the whole city, for that matter, and they ain't in the habit of sayin' no to me when I ask them for a job. . . .

There's no crime so mean as ingratitude in politics. . . .

The politicians who make a lastin' success in politics are the men who are always loyal to their friends, even up to the gate of State prison, if necessary; men who keep their promises and never lie. . . .

The question has been asked: Is a politician ever justified in goin' back on his district leader? I answer: "No; as long as the leader hustles around and gets all the jobs possible for his constituents." When the voters elect a man leader, they make a sort of a contract with him. They say, although it ain't written out: "We've put you here to look out for our interests. You want to see that this district gets all the jobs that's comin' to it. Be faithful to us, and we'll be faithful to you."

18.5   The Other Immigrant Experience: Rural Immigrants in the Midwest

Jon Gjerde

The "New Immigration" and the urban immigrant experience were the dominant patterns in the decades between 1880 and 1920. But significant numbers of immigrants continued to arrive from Northern and Western Europe (see Doc. 18.1), and for millions of these people and their children, home was not a city tenement but a farmhouse in the Midwest. This selection is taken from Jon Gjerde's innovative study of the mass migration of residents from a community in southern Norway to Wisconsin and Minnesota. It describes how this rural group of "older" immigrants adapted and became more "American" in the late nineteenth century. Gjerde's study suggests that there were sharp differences between the lives of these rural immigrants and the lives of "New Immigrants" in the cities.

Consider:

1. *The most significant changes in the cultural patterns of the Norwegian immigrants;*
2. *Whether it was easier for immigrants living in rural areas or those living in urban areas to retain a sense of ethnic community in America;*
3. *Why these Norwegian immigrants seemed to adapt more easily than the "New Immigrants" to American social patterns.*

Immigrants from Balestrand experienced a similar . . . transition. Moving from an area with extremely high rates of illegitimacy . . . [these] immigrants lived in settlements that by the turn of the century rarely saw either illegitimate or prenuptially conceived births. . . .

SOURCE: *Jon Gjerde,* From Peasants to Farmers: The Migration from Balestrand, Norway, to the Upper Middle West *(New York: Cambridge University Press, 1985), 202, 204–5, 277–31. Copyright © Cambridge University Press. Reprinted with permission.*

Traditional marriage customs operating in the new American environment worked to lower age at marriage and increase the proportion of people ever married. Since marriages continued to be based on livelihoods, the availability of land and work in the American settlements permitted younger ages at first marriage. . . .

American Balestranders were wed about four years younger than their friends and relatives who remained in Norway.

That age at marriage dropped more precipitously for women than for men was partly due to a scarcity of marriageable women in the pioneer settlements. . . .

Greater availability of livelihoods led not only to lowered marriage ages but to lessened lifelong bachelorhood and spinsterhood as well. . . .

. . . Women increasingly maintained domestic roles, . . . but their behavior simultaneously remained traditional and underwent great modification. On the one hand, their domestic inclination in a sense insulated them from American life. Women's duties kept them closely tied to the farm and the Norwegian social group, so that they were less likely to learn English than men. . . .

. . . Accordingly, English loan words were more prevalent in spheres of activity dominated by men. . . .

Women's activities in the home, on the other hand, reflected a transition to a more "modern" behavior in both work and leisure. Upon arriving in America, Norwegians were quick to notice conduct among native women. . . .

Similarly, the juxtaposition of tradition and change set the church in a position at once of conservatism and of progressivism in the community. The church remained the keeper of the tradition, the keeper of the faith. Services using the Norwegian language and the Lutheran liturgy were obvious links to a European past. Even small changes in church ceremonies could meet with stiff resistance. . . .

Yet the keeper of the tradition could also facilitate change. The pastor and the congregation used a powerful peer pressure to work against night courting and the use of alcohol through public confession before the congregation. . . .

. . . changed conditions induced changes in the Norwegian settlements. As internal migration continued, the nuclear family took on greater significance. Likewise, farm organization and operations magnified the importance of labor within the nuclear family while it encouraged shifts in work responsibilities. Women took on increasing domestic tasks of child raising and housekeeping, and men steadily assumed greater responsibilities in farm production. . . .

. . . Traditional conduct during courtship gave way to a new propriety, alcoholism apparently declined, and opportunities for greater leisure even permitted piano or melodeon playing. Such changes in behavior and attitude . . . diffused throughout the immigrant settlements and set them radically apart from the peasant Balestrand they had left. . . .

18.6   The Literacy Test:
An "Un-American" Restriction
of Immigration?
Woodrow Wilson

A device favored by many advocates of immigration restriction in the late nineteenth and twentieth centuries was the literacy test. The test would be given to all immigrant adults in their own language; those who failed would not be admitted to the United States. Bills to establish a literacy test were enacted by Congress in 1897, 1913, and 1915, only to be vetoed by Presidents Grover Cleveland, William Howard Taft, and Woodrow Wilson. Finally, in 1917, a second veto by Wilson was overridden by Congress, and the literacy test became law. Supporters of this and other laws designed to restrict immigration frequently used economic arguments, but the image of immigrants as habitual criminals and paupers also helped passage of restrictive laws. By contrast, Woodrow Wilson's 1915 veto message, included here, drew on values long considered basic to American life.

Consider:

1. *What Wilson means by his comment about the effect such restrictive policies would have had on the United States earlier in its history;*
2. *Wilson's suggestion that the nation had a virtual obligation to keep its "doors open to all who were not unfitted by reason of disease or incapacity for self-support or . . . were likely to [be] a menace to . . . peace and order . . .";*
3. *What are valid criteria for deciding who should be admitted to the United States.*

TO THE HOUSE OF REPRESENTATIVES: It is with unaffected regret that I find myself constrained by clear conviction to return this bill (H.R. 6060, "An act to regulate the immigration of aliens to and the residence of aliens in the United States") without my signature. . . .

Restrictions like these, adopted earlier in our history as a Nation, would very materially have altered the course and cooled the humane ardors of our politics. The right of political asylum has brought to this country many a man of noble character and elevated purpose who was marked as an outlaw in his own less fortunate land, and who has yet become an ornament to our citizenship and to our public

SOURCE: *Woodrow Wilson, Message to the House of Representatives, January 28, 1915.*

councils. The children and the compatriots of these illustrious Americans must stand amazed to see the representatives of their Nation now resolved, in the fullness of our national strength and at the maturity of our great institutions, to risk turning such men back from our shores without test of quality or purpose. It is difficult for me to believe that the full effect of this feature of the bill was realized when it was framed and adopted, and it is impossible for me to assent to it in the form in which it is here cast.

The literacy test and the tests and restrictions which accompany it constitute an even more radical change in the policy of the Nation. Hitherto we have generously kept our doors open to all who were not unfitted by reason of disease or incapacity for self-support or such personal records and antecedents as were likely to make them a menace to our peace and order or to the wholesome and essential relationships of life. In this bill it is proposed to turn away from tests of character and of quality and impose tests which exclude and restrict; for the new tests here embodied are not tests of quality or of character or of personal fitness, but tests of opportunity. Those who come seeking opportunity are not to be admitted unless they have already had one of the chief of the opportunities they seek, the opportunity of education. The object of such provisions is restriction, not selection.

. . . Does this bill rest upon the conscious and universal assent and desire of the American people? I doubt it. It is because I doubt it that I make bold to dissent from it. I am willing to abide by the verdict, but not until it has been rendered. Let the platforms of parties speak out upon this policy and the people pronounce their wish. The matter is too fundamental to be settled otherwise.

18.7 Below the Immigrant: The Black Urban Experience

Olivier Zunz

In a sense, the "New Immigration" represented the introduction of new ethnic groups that would replace older immigrant groups at the bottom of the American social and economic pyramid. However, these new groups—though they were targets of discrimination and persecution—did not remain on the bottom for long in most Northern cities. In the early twentieth century and especially during World War I, thousands of Southern blacks who migrated north in search of jobs in industry took their place on the lowest rungs of society. Demographic historian Olivier Zunz's excellent study, *The Changing Face of Equality,* examines the experiences and changing circumstances of diverse ethnic groups in Detroit in the period 1880–1920. The excerpts that follow describe the arrival and special handicaps of the blacks who came to that city.

Consider:

1. Why, *according to Zunz, the experience of Southern black migrants to Detroit was so different from that of white migrants;*
2. *The role of the "cross-class" communities of Detroit;*
3. *What seemed to be required for blacks to improve their social and economic position in Detroit and other cities.*

. . . the Black community had none of the means of white immigrant communities to incorporate newcomers into its ranks. The tragedy of Blacks in Detroit is that . . . they had the almost opposite experience to that of white ethnic groups.

. . . Instead of working for poor Blacks, "the physicians, dentists and attorneys had mostly white practices, and the managers and clerks worked for white businesses or were in government service." Members of this very small Black elite were often congregants in white churches, and some belonged to the exclusive Republican Michigan Club. This small group of integrationist Blacks lived separated from the vast majority of nonelite Blacks. In contrast, white ethnic groups had developed independent neighborhoods and supported communitywide institutions . . . in part through the cross-class nature of their communities. . . .

While immigrant families adopted family strategies of income pooling between the heads of households and teenaged children—strategies which helped Germans, Poles, and other workers to support their institutions and to survive difficult times, most Black families in late nineteenth-century Detroit had no teenaged children to send to work and could not develop similar strategies. The majority of Black nuclear families were either childless couples or single parents with children, rather than complete families. . . .

. . . [one] pervasive social problem [was] the basic inability of most Blacks to expand their community to make room for newcomers. In sharp contrast to their idealized view of the past, the majority of the Blacks in Detroit before the World War I migration were already living in such dismal conditions that they had no means to establish a strong chain migration process to receive newcomers. It was only because the Black community was so small—and posed no threat of growing—that the dismal conditions in which most Blacks had lived had gone relatively unnoticed; and the existence of a tiny elite integrated into the white institutional and residential environment served to mask the true lot of the Black community. It is no surprise, then, that when full-scale industrialization brought many single Black workers from the South, the tremendous pressure of numbers simply overwhelmed an already vulnerable community. Southerners came to work. They found

SOURCE: *Olivier Zunz,* The Changing Face of Inequality: Urbanization, Industrial Development, and Immigrants in Detroit, 1880–1920 *(Chicago: University of Chicago Press, 1982), 378–80, 387, 393, 398.*

work, but for the most part they failed to become more than a floating labor force . . .

The contrasts between the structure of the Black ghetto and that of all other concentrations of recent Detroit immigrant groups are startling. If we . . . follow the 1920 census takers into areas of Polish, Hungarian, Russian-Jewish, and Italian concentrations, we find a very large proportion of homeowners, and a flourishing nuclear family life— the two missing components of life in the ghetto. . . .

Decidedly, the Blacks were a unique case in Detroit, as they were in other cities. The brutal facts of segregation—racial violence combined with demographic pressure—greatly handicapped Black newcomers. In all other immigrant communities, family and economic autonomy were intimately related: a high birth rate within the nuclear family was the key to income pooling, which provided a degree of economic security, including the possibility of buying a home. Segregation, however, made home ownership impossible for most Blacks, and the practice of income pooling with boarders only helped to pay the exorbitant rents. In turn, Blacks in the ghetto remained childless, partly because of poor health and sterility caused by tuberculosis, partly because of high infant mortality. . . .

. . . when we analyze the process of ghetto-making from the late nineteenth century to the early 1920s, not only do we see the intense segregation Blacks suffered from all corners of the white community, but we also see that, compared with white ethnic groups, Blacks lived history in reverse. When ethnic neighborhoods were flourishing cross-class communities providing opportunities to their members, Blacks were atomized and dispersed. With the formation of the large industrial working class, cross-class ethnic neighborhoods were transformed into primarily working-class ethnic areas, abandoned by upwardly mobile people dispersed throughout the metropolitan area. It was at the very time when occupational bonds began to replace ethnic bonds in the white community that Blacks were drawn into an ever growing ghetto . . . With white ethnic groups more and more segmented along class lines in the many sections of the metropolis, the growth of the Black ghetto was a dramatic anachronism.

CHAPTER QUESTIONS

1. *In what ways did events of the period 1880–1920 reinforce the image of the United States as a "melting pot" for different races and ethnic groups? In what ways did events seem to contradict that image?*
2. *Did reactions to the "New Immigration" reflect new attitudes and currents of thought in American society? Explain.*

Chapter 19

Establishing a New Order

Periods of reformist fervor have occurred at fairly regular intervals in American history, separated from one another by about a generation. Such bursts of reform occurred in the 1830s and 1840s (Chapter 11) and again during the first years of Reconstruction (Chapter 15). Yet another era of reform began in the 1890s, encompassing a broad range of ideas for improving American society. Some of the reformers of this period, such as the Nationalist followers of novelist Edward Bellamy, were utopians whose ideas had little practical impact. Others, such as the Populists and Socialists, represented—and attracted—Americans with economic grievances that they felt could be corrected only by major changes in the political and social structure. There were also reform movements with longer histories—for example, those favoring prohibition and women's suffrage—that took on new force and eventually achieved their goals by capitalizing on the widespread sentiment for change at this time.

This era of reform extending from the 1890s through World War I is known as the "progressive era." The term "progressivism" is not easy to define, since it covers a wide range of reform movements concerned with such issues as cleaning up city politics, breaking the power of corporate monopolies, and democratizing the political process. All these reform movements were active at the same time and often succeeded by appealing to the same groups of people. What elements do these varied movements—and those of settlement-house workers, woman suffragists, and prohibitionists—have in common? How are they related to one another?

This chapter addresses some of the most fundamental issues in American history. How does a democracy deal with the problem of economic inequality? What limits are there on the role government plays in "adjusting" economic and social relationships? Reformers of the progressive era could not resolve these basic questions. But they did perhaps help create a new order—one that ensured that life in twentieth-century America would be very different from what had gone before, though it was still based on republicanism and capitalism.

The selections in this chapter are intended to illustrate both the diversity and coherence of the progressive era. Collectively, the documents examine the economic and social context in which reformers operated—and on which they capitalized. They also deal with the arguments and tactics used by supporters and opponents of reform.

Chronology

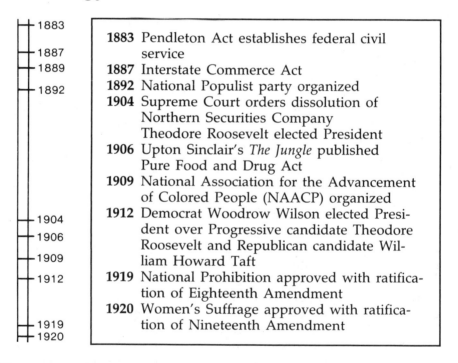

1883	
1887	**1883** Pendleton Act establishes federal civil service
1889	**1887** Interstate Commerce Act
1892	**1889**
	1892 National Populist party organized
	1904 Supreme Court orders dissolution of Northern Securities Company
	Theodore Roosevelt elected President
	1906 Upton Sinclair's *The Jungle* published
	Pure Food and Drug Act
	1909 National Association for the Advancement of Colored People (NAACP) organized
1904	**1912** Democrat Woodrow Wilson elected President over Progressive candidate Theodore Roosevelt and Republican candidate William Howard Taft
1906	
1909	
1912	
	1919 National Prohibition approved with ratification of Eighteenth Amendment
1919	**1920** Women's Suffrage approved with ratification of Nineteenth Amendment
1920	

Documents

19.1 The Populist Vision

The growth of labor violence in the 1870s, 1880s, and 1890s was one indication of dissatisfaction with the emerging industrial order. The most serious challenge to the system, however, came from angry farmers in the South and Midwest. The People's, or Populist, party, which emerged first as an outgrowth of the Farmers' Alliances at the state level, set forth a series of proposals that addressed the grievances of farmers and aimed at remaking the capitalist order. The party's first national platform (1892), excerpted here, brought together a number of proposals that had been developed by Populists in various states. The Populists gained important victories at the state level in 1890, but on the national level the party failed to mount an effective challenge to the two major parties in either 1892 or 1896.

Consider:

1. *Whether the Populist party was essentially a forward-looking or backward-looking movement;*
2. *The kinds of problems the Populists would have faced in trying to build a coalition at the national level;*
3. *Which, if any, part of the Populist platform represented a radical departure from traditional American policies and/or ideals.*

We have witnessed for more than a quarter of a century the struggles of the two great political parties for power and plunder, while grievous wrongs have been inflicted upon the suffering people. We charge that the controlling influence dominating both these parties have permitted the existing dreadful conditions to develop without serious effort to prevent or restrain them. Neither do they now promise us any substantial

SOURCE: *Platform of the People's (Populist) Party, 1892, in* National Party Platforms, 1840–1956, *comp. Kirk H. Porter and Donald B. Johnson (Urbana, Ill.: University of Illinois Press, 1956), 90–91.*

reform. They have agreed together to ignore, in the coming campaign, every issue but one. They propose to drown the outcries of a plundered people with the uproar of a sham battle over the tariff, so that capitalists, corporations, national banks, rings, trusts, watered stock, the demonetization of silver and the oppressions of the usurers may all be lost sight of. They propose to sacrifice our homes, lives, and children on the altar of mammon; to destroy the multitude in order to secure corruption funds from the millionaires. . . .

We declare that this Republic can only endure as a free government while built upon the love of the whole people for each other and for the nation; that it cannot be pinned together by bayonets; that the civil war is over and that every passion and resentment which grew out of it must die with it, and that we must be in fact, as we are in name, one united brotherhood of freemen.

Our country finds itself confronted by conditions for which there is no precedent in the history of the world; our annual agricultural productions amount to billions of dollars in value, which must, within a few weeks or months be exchanged for billions of dollars' worth of commodities consumed in their production; the existing currency supply is wholly inadequate to make this exchange; the results are falling prices, the formation of combines and rings, the impoverishment of the producing class. We pledge ourselves that, if given power, we will labor to correct these evils by wise and reasonable legislation, in accordance with the terms of our platform.

We believe that the power of government—in other words, of the people—should be expanded (as in the case of the postal service) as rapidly and as far as the good sense of an intelligent people and the teachings of experience shall justify, to the end that oppression, injustice and poverty, shall eventually cease in the land. . . .

We declare, therefore,

First—That the union of the labor forces of the United States this day consummated shall be permanent and perpetual; may its spirit enter into all hearts for the salvation of the Republic and the uplifting of mankind.

Second—Wealth belongs to him who creates it, and every dollar taken from industry without an equivalent is robbery. "If any will not work, neither shall he eat." The interests of rural and civic labor are the same; their enemies are identical.

Third—We believe that the time has come when the railroad corporations will either own the people or the people must own the railroads, and should the government enter upon the work of owning and managing all railroads, we should favor an amendment to the Constitution by which all persons engaged in the government service shall be placed under a civil service regulation of the most rigid character, so as to prevent the increase of the power of the national administration by the use of such additional government employees.

Finance—We demand a national currency, safe, sound, and flexible, issued by the general government only, a full legal tender for all debts, public and private, and that without the use of banking corporations, a just, equitable and efficient means of distribution direct to the people, at a tax not to exceed 2 per cent per annum, to be provided as set forth by the sub-treasury plan of the Farmers' Alliance, or a better system; also by payments in discharge of its obligations for public improvements.

1. We demand free and unlimited coinage of silver and gold at the present legal ratio of 16 to 1.

2. We demand that the amount of circulating medium be speedily increased to not less than $50 per capita.

3. We demand a graduated income tax.

4. We believe that the money of the country should be kept as much as possible in the hands of the people, and hence we demand that all State and national revenues shall be limited to the necessary expenses of the government, economically and honestly administered.

5. We demand that postal savings banks be established by the government for the safe deposit of the earnings of the people and to facilitate exchange.

Transportation—Transportation being a means of exchange and a public necessity, the government should own and operate the railroads in the interest of the people. The telegraph and telephone, like the post office system, being a necessity for the transmission of news, should be owned and operated by the government in the interest of the people.

Land—The land, including all the natural sources of wealth, is the heritage of the people, and should not be monopolized for speculative purposes, and alien ownership of land should be prohibited. All land now held by railroads and other corporations in excess of their actual needs, and all lands now owned by aliens, should be reclaimed by the government and held for actual settlers only.

19.2   An Industrial Utopia: *Looking Backward*
Edward Bellamy

One of the more radical visions of society in the late nineteenth century can be found in Edward Bellamy's popular book, *Looking Backward, 2000–1887*, which appeared in 1888. Actually a blueprint for industrial socialism, Bellamy's description of what the nation could, or should, be like in the year 2000 spawned a utopian movement that was called "Nationalism." The name came from the nationalization of industry, a principal ingredient of Bellamy's fictional society. In the early 1890s, the movement claimed a few thousand adherents, largely from the educated upper classes. Bellamy, who was sharply critical of the competitive nature of capitalism, envisioned a harmonious society without class conflict. The hero of this novel, Julian West, awakens in the year 2000 after a sleep of more than a hundred years to find America transformed. In this excerpt, West's conversation with his host, Dr. Leete, focuses on one important aspect of the new society—the condition of labor.

Consider:

1. *How the values underlying Bellamy's utopia compare with those on which Sir Thomas More based his* Utopia *in the sixteenth century (Doc. 2.1);*
2. *How Populists would have responded to Bellamy's ideas about "The Great Trust" (see Doc. 19.1);*
3. *What arguments can be offered to counter Bellamy's view of the way labor could be "tamed" within the industrial system.*

At my feet lay a great city. Miles of broad streets, shaded by trees and lined with fine buildings, for the most part not in continuous blocks but set in larger or smaller inclosures, stretched in every direction. Every quarter contained large open squares filled with trees, among which statues glistened and fountains flashed in the late afternoon sun. Public buildings of a colossal size and an architectural grandeur unparalleled in my day raised their stately piles on every side. Surely I had never seen this city nor one comparable to it before. Raising my eyes at last towards the horizon, I looked westward. That blue ribbon winding away to the sunset, was it not the sinuous Charles? I looked east; Boston harbor stretched before me within its headlands, not one of its green islets missing.

I knew then that I had been told the truth concerning the prodigious thing which had befallen me. . . .

. . . After Dr. Leete had responded to numerous questions on my part, as to the ancient landmarks I missed and the new ones which had replaced them, he asked me what point of the contrast between the new and the old city struck me most forcibly. . . .

"In general," I said, "what impresses me most about the city is the material prosperity on the part of the people which its magnificence implies." . . .

. . . "What should you name as the most prominent feature of the labor troubles of your day?" [he asked]

"Why, the strikes, of course," I replied.

SOURCE: *Edward Bellamy,* Looking Backward: 2000–1887 *(Cambridge, Mass.: The Belknap Press of Harvard University Press, 1967), 115, 117, 124, 126–27, 130–31.*

"Exactly; but what made the strikes so formidable?"

"The great labor organizations."

"And what was the motive of these great organizations?"

"The workmen claimed they had to organize to get their rights from the big corporations," I replied.

"That is just it," said Dr. Leete; "the organization of labor and the strikes were an effect, merely, of the concentration of capital in greater masses than had ever been known before. Before this concentration began, while as yet commerce and industry were conducted by innumerable petty concerns with small capital, instead of a small number of great concerns with vast capital, the individual workman was relatively important and independent in his relations to the employer. . . . But when the era of small concerns with small capital was succeeded by that of the great aggregations of capital, all this was changed. The individual laborer, who had been relatively important to the small employer, was reduced to insignificance and powerlessness over against the great corporation, while at the same time the way upward to the grade of employer was closed to him. Self-defense drove him to union with his fellows. . . .

". . . To restore the former order of things, even if possible, would have involved returning to the day of stage-coaches. Oppressive and intolerable as was the régime of the great consolidations of capital, even its victims, while they cursed it, were forced to admit the prodigious increase of efficiency which had been imparted to the national industries, the vast economies effected by concentration of management and unity or organization, and to confess that since the new system had taken the place of the old the wealth of the world had increased at a rate before undreamed of. To be sure this vast increase had gone chiefly to make the rich richer, increasing the gap between them and the poor; but the fact remained that, as a means merely of producing wealth, capital had been proved efficient in proportion to its consolidation. . . .

"Early in the last century the evolution was completed by the final consolidation of the entire capital of the nation. The industry and commerce of the country, ceasing to be conducted by a set of irresponsible corporations and syndicates of private persons at their caprice and for their profit, were intrusted to a single syndicate representing the people, to be conducted in the common interest for the common profit. The nation, that is to say, organized as the one great business corporation in which all other corporations were absorbed; . . . The epoch of trusts had ended in The Great Trust. . . . At last, . . . the obvious fact was perceived that no business is so essentially the public business as the industry and commerce on which the people's livelihood depends, and that to entrust it to private persons to be managed for private profit is a folly similar in kind, though vastly greater in magnitude, to that of surrendering the functions of political government to kings and nobles to be conducted for their personal glorification." . . .

"But you have not yet told me how you have settled the labor problem. It is the problem of capital which we have been discussing," I said. . . .

"The moment the nation assumed the responsibilities of capital those difficulties vanished," replied Dr. Leete. "The national organization of labor under one direction was the complete solution of what was, in your day and under your system, justly regarded as the insoluble labor problem. When the nation became the sole employer, all the citizens, by virtue of their citizenship, became employees, to be distributed according to the needs of industry."

"That is," I suggested, "you have simply applied the principle of universal military service, as it was understood in our day, to the labor question."

"Yes," said Dr. Leete, "that was something which followed as a matter of course as soon as the nation had become the sole capitalist. The people were already accustomed to the idea that the obligation of every citizen, not physically disabled, to contribute his military services to the defense of the nation was equal and absolute. That it was equally the duty of every citizen to contribute his quota of industrial or intellectual services to the maintenance of the nation was equally evident. . . .

19.3 The Changing Economic Order: Shifts in the Work Force

The emergence of a new order in the United States can be shown in many ways—for example, in the nature of the intellectual and political discourse; by shifts in public and private values; or by changes in the patterns of daily life. One set of changes that clearly reflects the evolution of society between 1880 and 1920 concerned the work force. The figures presented here on the distribution of employed workers in the United States between 1880 and 1920 give some indication of the nature of economic growth in this period. These changes played a major role in the dislocations experienced by some Americans during these years (see Doc. 19.1).

Consider:

1. *What generalizations can be made, based on these figures, about social and economic change in the United States between 1880 and 1920;*
2. *What are the most significant trends in employment;*
3. *The long-range conclusions Americans might have drawn about the nation's economic life from this information.*

DISTRIBUTION OF EMPLOYED WORKERS: 1880–1920 (IN THOUSANDS)

Year	Total	Agri-culture	Forestry, fisheries, and mining	Manufac-turing and con-struction	Trans-portation and other public utilities	Trade, finance, and real estate	Education and other profes-sional service	Domestic and personal service	Govern-ment and not classified
1920	41,610	11,120	1,510	13,050	4,190	4,860	2,250	3,330	1,300
1910	36,730	11,340	1,300	10,530	3,190	3,890	1,670	3,670	1,140
1900	29,070	10,710	970	8,000	2,100	2,760	1,150	2,710	670
1890	23,740	9,990	660	6,190	1,530	1,990	860	2,160	360
1880	17,390	8,610	405	4,000	860	1,220	520	1,440	335

SOURCE: Historical Statistics of the United States: Colonial Times to 1970 (Washington, D.C.: Government Printing Office, 1975), I, 138.

19.4   Varieties of Progressivism: T. R. and Wilson

John Milton Cooper, Jr.

"Progressivism" encompassed a variety of reform interests and mentalities, as well as separate movements at the local, state, and national levels. The diversity of progressivism was reflected in the three-cornered presidential election of 1912 in which Theodore Roosevelt and Woodrow Wilson presented competing "progressive" visions: the New Nationalism of Roosevelt versus the New Freedom of Wilson. Many historians of the progressive era have attempted to explain the differences between these two views. One of the best recent analyses comes from political historian John Milton Cooper, Jr. In his book *The Warrior and the Priest*, excerpted here, Cooper compares the personalities, beliefs, and styles of leadership of these two towering figures of the early twentieth century.

Consider:

1. *What, according to Cooper, were the most important differences between the views of Roosevelt and Wilson;*
2. *Which of the two had the more "democratic" view of leadership;*
3. *Whether the label "progressive" fits Roosevelt or Wilson better.*

. . . According to the great majority of analysts at the time and later, Roosevelt and Wilson did not differ greatly on the major issues. . . . Both Roosevelt and Wilson strained to accentuate their differences and thereby, albeit often unwittingly, misrepresented each other. . . .

The distortions by both candidates arose from the heat of the campaign but also in part from the two men's agreement on many specific issues. Roosevelt and Wilson had to play up their differences because on matters of immediate concern, their real differences were few. . . .

The similarities and agreements between Roosevelt's and Wilson's positions did not mean, however, that no important differences separated them. . . . the outlines of their divergence showed up on the two issues they discussed most in 1912—the trusts and leadership. . . .

. . . Roosevelt implicitly accepted three propositions: that the biggest corporations had for the most part achieved their stature through efficient competition, that large corporations were here to stay, and that present economic conditions represented progress. But for him those were not the most important concerns. . . . He believed that the main economic task of government lay in protecting the victims and clients of large-scale enterprise through greatly strengthened regulation and supervision. . . .

Wilson disagreed on all [these] points. In his distinction between big business and the trusts and in his insistence on restoring competition, he implicitly accepted three opposite economic propositions: that comparatively few of the biggest corporations had achieved their stature through efficient competition, that those corporations were not necessarily here to stay, and that present conditions did not always represent progress over the past. . . . Far from believing in laissez-faire, Wilson maintained that government must intervene actively and continuously in the economy because "unregulated competition" had resulted in the growth of the trusts and the stifling of competition. The other consideration he stressed was the entry of new competitors into the market. Contrary to their public images, Wilson held much more dynamic economic views than Roosevelt. He believed that the main task of reform was to revitalize the economy through governmental actions to open the market to fresh entrants. . . .

. . . The leadership issue boiled down to inspiration versus education. With his prophetic, evangelical approach Roosevelt sought, in the root sense of the word, to inspire. He wanted to breathe into people a resolve to be better than they were, to instill in them devotion to larger goals and greater effort. With his "schoolmaster" approach to leadership, Wilson similarly sought, in the root sense, to educate. He wished to draw out of people recognition of their own best interests, to let them enlighten their ordinary pursuits. The issue between them over the purposes of government came down to one of paternalism versus representation. . . .

To an extent, Roosevelt and Wilson stood as twentieth-century analogues to Hamilton and Jefferson. . . . Unlike Hamilton and Jefferson,

SOURCE: *John Milton Cooper, Jr., The Warrior and the Priest: Woodrow Wilson and Theodore Roosevelt (Cambridge, Mass.: The Belknap Press of Harvard University Press, 1983), 208–209, 211–14, 217–20. Excerpted by permission.*

they did not differ over governmental power and centralization, despite Roosevelt's assertions to the contrary. Nor did they laud either manufacturing or agriculture as morally or socially superior to the other. . . . But Roosevelt and Wilson did differ fundamentally over the same matters—their conceptions of human nature and the role of self-interest in society—that they believed had separated Hamilton and Jefferson.

. . . Roosevelt remained, by his lights, self-consciously Hamiltonian and anti-Jeffersonian in his views. For all his buoyancy and his spirits, Roosevelt was not an optimistic man, and his politics were not based upon an optimistic view of people. He regarded individuals' selfish, private interests as not only barriers to the attainment of public good but also sources of antisocial passion and potential civil conflict. . . .

During the 1912 campaign Wilson came closer than at any other time in his political career to becoming an exponent of what he saw as Jeffersonian views. . . . Wilson's politics were based upon an optimistic view of people. He regarded individuals' selfish interests as not only inescapable facts of life but as instruments that must be used to improve society. . . .

Wilson was more realistic than Roosevelt in recognizing that a better society could come only by serving the interests of a majority. He did not entirely renounce service to particular interest groups. He claimed that aid to industrial workers and farmers would help such large and vital segments of society that everyone's interests would be served. Wilson did not yet embrace the proposition that government should foster the interests of less-advantaged groups or regions, but he had gone a long way toward the "broker state," which became the central political concept in support of governmental aid to social welfare and regulation of private economic activity in twentieth-century America. . . . Wilson had no answer to Roosevelt's questions about how to promote national unity, except to work through coalitions of interests. His performance at that task played a big part in shaping not only his presidency and the fortunes of his party but also the main course of twentieth-century domestic American politics.

19.5   Reform as Social Control: Prohibition and the Progressive Movement

Norman H. Clark

Though it had gone through two earlier waves of popularity in the nineteenth century, the prohibition movement achieved ultimate success during the progressive era in the form of the Eighteenth Amendment to the Constitution. A number of historians have noted that prohibitionism had much in common with reform movements that were explicitly "progressive." One historian who makes this point is Norman Clark, whose study of the prohibition movement is excerpted here. Clark discusses the importance of progressive methods and themes in the later stages of the prohibition movement and examines how American participation in World War I provided the impetus needed for the movement's final success.

Consider:

1. *How prohibitionists relied on motives and arguments that were typical of the progressive era;*
2. *The connection, according to Clark, between the progressive mentality and American attitudes concerning participation in the war;*
3. *Whether national prohibition could have been achieved without the impetus of World War I.*

. . . the emergence in the twentieth century of a new generation of reformers who were determined to use bureaucratic techniques to impose their pietist values upon what they saw as a chaotically pluralistic society—determined, in the interest of social discipline, to deny their fellow citizens access to any alcoholic drinks, and grimly determined, it seemed, to abolish alcohol as well as the saloon—suggests a triumph of fanaticism inconsistent with the liberal and humane temper which since the beginning had guided most temperance activities. The conversion of the Anti-Saloon League into an antidrink pressure group further suggests that real radicals had captured one of the most powerful political machines ever fashioned in American life.

But the problem here is that by 1916 in the United States, antidrink sentiment was no longer a clearly radical persuasion; it rose as much from liberal and humane considerations as it did from any other. Just as today it is difficult to understand the debauchery of the old-time saloon, so is it difficult to understand the climate of national opinion in which antidrink proposals could receive such general and solid support. . . .

The essential insight . . . is that the vast disorder of American life surely justified keen moral anxieties. Thus the "search for order" was quite naturally directed toward the official and national validation of values which could sustain the family as the vital social institution.

SOURCE: *Norman H. Clark,* Deliver Us From Evil: An Interpretation of American Prohibition, *120–21, 124, 127–29. Copyright © 1976 by W. W. Norton & Company, Inc. Reprinted by permission.*

The configuration of individual responsibilities implied by these values—duty, restraint, self-discipline—were, in an open society, often violently at odds with any tolerance for personal indulgences or moral pluralisms. . . .

. . . another essential insight lies in the impressive body of scientific evidence which by 1916 supported the case for total abstinence. There were, for example, the fairly recent discoveries that alcohol does not warm the body, that it is a depressant rather than a stimulant, and that it depresses the higher mental functions as well as muscular control. Such findings had been the topics of articles in middle-class magazines for a decade. . . .

. . . Moreover, investigators in the new social sciences supplied a mass of statistics to show relationships between alcohol and crime, prostitution, and poverty. . . .

. . . The course toward war led through intensified fears of disorder, through realities of sacrifice, and through urgent demands for a strong and healthy nation. Like most wars, it made people extraordinarily sensitive to their common interests, and it brought common—or dominant—values into sharp focus. The effort also sanctified bureaucratic and impersonal efficiencies to the point where almost total social control was possible. And it seemed even necessary to those who believed there could be no victories for boozy nations. . . .

In February, when Congress granted the President authority to arm merchant ships, it also passed laws banning the sale of intoxicating beverages in Alaska and in Washington, D.C. In March, as people read of the Zimmermann Note and came to feel that war was surely imminent, Congress amended the Post Office Appropriations Bill to forbid interstate shipments of alcoholic beverages, "except for scientific, sacramental or medicinal puposes," into any state which, like Oklahoma, forbade "the manufacture or sale therein of intoxicating liquors," whether or not these states still allowed importations for personal use. . . .

Having thus embraced the crusade for national and international purity, Congress on May 18 forbade the sale of intoxicating drinks to men in uniform. . . . Under the slogan "Shall the many have food, or the few have drink?" Congress forbade, with the Lever Food and Fuel Control Act, the use of foodstuffs for distilling liquor. This shut down the stills; the saloons would soon die of the hard thirst. And the drys, in their progress, had not overlooked the deadly linkage between brewers and German influences in the nation; they made them well known and notorious. On December 8, a presidential proclamation forbade brewers to brew at an alcoholic content of more than 2.75 percent, and beer was thus converted into the kind of pale temperance beverage which had been admired by Thomas Jefferson. The President also severely limited the amount of grains that would thereafter be available for legal brewing. The country had thus gone nearly dry during the first eight months of wartime sacrifice. Then, on December

22, 1917, with majorities well in excess of the two-thirds requirement, Congress submitted to the states the 18th Amendment. . . .

. . . By January 1919, ratification was complete, and 80 percent of the members of forty-six state legislatures were recorded in approval.

19.6   Women's Suffrage and the Working Class
National American Woman Suffrage Association
Harper's

Although the movement for women's suffrage was much older than progressivism, the suffragists of the progressive era linked their campaign with other crusades of the time. The suffragists came mostly from the same middle-class background as the other reformers, and they faced the same challenge: how to win support for their cause from the working class. Posters such as the one reproduced on page 323, "What Will Save the Home?" were used to appeal to working-class women. Yet, as suggested by the 1914 cartoon from *Harper's* magazine, these women did not respond enthusiastically.

Consider:

1. *What elements in the poster identify it as an appeal to working-class women;*
2. *What the cartoon suggests about the attitude of working-class women toward the suffrage campaign;*
3. *Whether these illustrations reflect traditional conceptions of women's roles in society.*

VISITOR: *"But surely you believe that women should vote?"*
"Oh, I s'pose it's all right if ye haven't nothin' better to do."

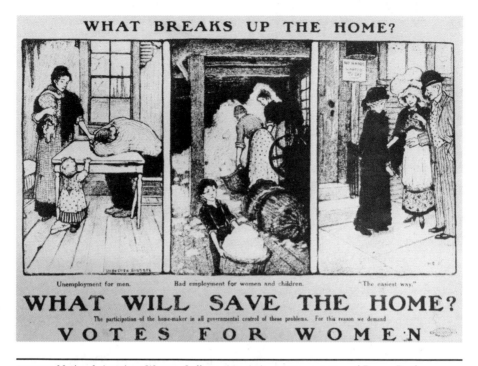

SOURCE: *National American Woman Suffrage Association poster, courtesy of Brown Brothers; cartoon from* Harper's Magazine. *Copyright © 1914 by* Harper's Magazine. *All rights reserved. Reprinted from the January issue by special permission.*

CHAPTER QUESTIONS

1. *Based on the documents in this chapter, would you say that reformers of this period had a strong commitment to democracy? Explain your answer.*
2. *Which reform movements met with the greatest degree of success in this period? Which failed? Explain why.*
3. *Would you describe progressivism as a forward-looking, or modern, force in American life? Explain.*

Chapter 20

Becoming a World Power

The last decades of the nineteenth century witnessed a great increase in American involvement overseas. There were many reasons for this new outward thrust. One was the nation's rapid industrial growth, which created a need for both sources of raw materials and markets for finished products. This commercial expansion led to a demand for the buildup of American naval forces and overseas naval bases to protect American trade abroad. These developments provided a strong impetus for the United States to expand its role in world affairs.

Equally important as commercial and strategic arguments for expansion were two other factors: a revitalized American nationalism and an intense missionary zeal. The resurgent nationalism that followed the Civil War and Reconstruction led the American government to insist that it be taken seriously in international affairs, especially in the Western Hemisphere. Meanwhile, the nation's historic sense of Manifest Destiny seemed to compel expansion beyond continental frontiers to territories across the Pacific. Then there was the "white man's burden"—the commitment of Christian missionaries to bring religion to far-off lands as well as a strong patriotic urge to civilize and democratize "backward" people. Taken up by poets, journalists, and politicians, the idea of "white man's burden" led the United States to join in the imperialistic scramble that consumed the European powers. In 1898, the brief and successful Spanish-American War confirmed these imperialistic sentiments. Even so, some Americans raised their voices in protest against this new expansionist thrust in national policy.

Theodore Roosevelt contributed significantly to the emergence of the United States as a world power in the twentieth century. His Corollary to the Monroe Doctrine proclaimed the nation's dominance in the Western Hemisphere, and his successful mediation of the Russo-Japanese war symbolized the nation's assumption of its rightful place among the world powers. Roosevelt also started construction of the Panama Canal, an undertaking that provided dramatic evidence of America's new international role.

The most important force in the nation's transition to a world power, however, was World War I. After maintaining neutrality for the first three years of the war, President Woodrow Wilson asked for a declaration of war against the Central Powers in April 1917, and almost immediately moved to take leadership of the Allied cause. His "Fourteen Points" in early 1918 amounted to the imposition of American values of self-determination and open diplomacy on all participants in the war.

By 1920, the United States had clearly joined the ranks of the world's most powerful nations. It remained, of course, for the country to adjust to the unfamiliar role of world creditor and international power. That adjustment would take another two decades—and another World War.

The selections in this chapter illustrate the forces that led to greater American involvement overseas; they also deal with the objections that were raised to that involvement. Reflected in the documents is a certain consistency in values and motives. These have served as a guiding force throughout American history.

Chronology

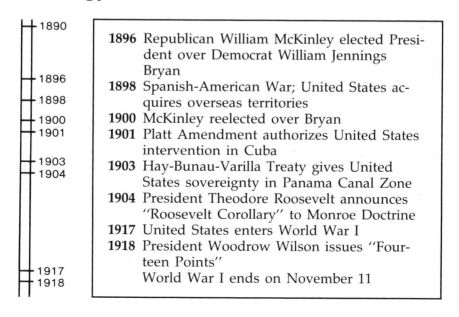

1890
1896
1898
1900
1901
1903
1904
1917
1918

1896 Republican William McKinley elected President over Democrat William Jennings Bryan

1898 Spanish-American War; United States acquires overseas territories

1900 McKinley reelected over Bryan

1901 Platt Amendment authorizes United States intervention in Cuba

1903 Hay-Bunau-Varilla Treaty gives United States sovereignty in Panama Canal Zone

1904 President Theodore Roosevelt announces "Roosevelt Corollary" to Monroe Doctrine

1917 United States enters World War I

1918 President Woodrow Wilson issues "Fourteen Points"

World War I ends on November 11

Documents

20.1 Strategic Reasons for American Expansion: The "Big Navy" Argument

Alfred Thayer Mahan

In the late nineteenth century, a buildup of the American navy was urged by those who supported an activist foreign policy, as well as by those who supported commercial expansion. The most effective propagandist for "big navy" interests was Captain Alfred Thayer Mahan, a naval officer, and his book *The Influence of Sea Power upon History, 1660–1783*, published in 1890, helped popularize the cause. Mahan discussed the connection between commercial expansion and the need for overseas naval bases. In this excerpt, Mahan presents the "defensive" reasons for a strong navy and suggests a need to acquire far-flung naval bases. Widely cited by politicians who favored American expansion and imperialism, Mahan's arguments influenced leaders in other nations as well and played a major role in stimulating the worldwide buildup of naval forces preceding World War I.

Consider:

1. *Why Mahan advocated a United States naval buildup in spite of its great cost;*
2. *How Mahan believed popular support for a strong United States navy could be generated;*
3. *Why Mahan favored a strategy of securing overseas naval bases.*

To turn now . . . to the general question of the influence of government upon the sea career of its people, it is seen that that influence
can work in two distinct but closely related ways.

First, in peace: The government by its policy can favor the natural
growth of a people's industries and its tendencies to seek adventure
and gain by way of the sea; or it can try to develop such industries
and such sea-going bent, when they do not naturally exist; or, on the
other hand, the government may by mistaken action check and fetter
the progress which the people left to themselves would make. In any
one of these ways the influence of the government will be felt, making
or marring the sea power of the country in the matter of peaceful
commerce; upon which alone, it cannot be too often insisted, a thoroughly strong navy can be based.

Secondly, for war: The influence of the government will be felt in
its most legitimate manner in maintaining an armed navy, of a size
commensurate with the growth of its shipping and the importance of
the interests connected with it. . . . Undoubtedly under this second
head of warlike preparation must come the maintenance of suitable
naval stations, in those distant parts of the world to which the armed
shipping must follow the peaceful vessels of commerce. The protection
of such stations must depend either upon direct military force, as do
Gibraltar and Malta, or upon a surrounding friendly population, such
as the American colonists once were to England, . . .

Colonies attached to the mother-country afford, therefore, the surest
means of supporting abroad the sea power of a country. . . .

Such colonies the United States has not and is not likely to have.
. . . Having . . . no foreign establishments, either colonial or military,
the ships of war of the United States, in war, will be like land birds,
unable to fly far from their own shores. To provide resting-places for
them, where they can coal and repair, would be one of the first duties
of a government proposing to itself the development of the power of
the nation at sea. . . .

The question is eminently one in which the influence of the government should make itself felt, to build up for the nation a navy
which, if not capable of reaching distant countries, shall at least be
able to keep clear the chief approaches to its own. The eyes of the
country have for a quarter of a century been turned from the sea; . . .
it may safely be said that it is essential to the welfare of the whole
country that the conditions of trade and commerce should remain, as
far as possible, unaffected by an external war. In order to do this, the
enemy must be kept not only out of our ports, but far away from our
coasts.

Can this navy be had without restoring the merchant shipping? It

SOURCE: *Alfred Thayer Mahan,* The Influence of Sea Power upon History, 1660–1783 *(New
York: Sagamore Press, Inc., 1957), 71–72, 75–76.*

is doubtful. History has proved that such a purely military sea power can be built up by a despot, as was done by Louis XIV.; . . . But in a representative government any military expenditure must have a strongly represented interest behind it, convinced of its necessity. Such an interest in sea power does not exist, cannot exist here without action by the government. How such a merchant shipping should be built up, whether by subsidies or by free trade, by constant administration of tonics or by free movement in the open air, is not a military but an economical question. Even had the United States a great national shipping, it may be doubted whether a sufficient navy would follow; the distance which separates her from other great powers, in one way a protection, is also a snare. The motive, if any there be, which will give the United States a navy, is probably now quickening in the Central American Isthmus. Let us hope it will not come to the birth too late.

20.2 American Foreign Trade, 1880–1920

Arguments in support of a "big navy" were usually related to the need to protect the growing overseas trade interests of the United States. The years between 1880 and 1920 did see an expansion of American commerce abroad. But as the following graphs show, both exports and imports increased slowly until 1910. Then, with the end of World War I, the nation's economic involvement abroad took a dramatic upward turn.

Consider:

1. *What these figures reveal about general trends in the international commerce of the United States between 1880 and 1920;*
2. *What developments might have accounted for these trends;*
3. *The impact the growth in America's international trade may have had on its foreign policy interests.*

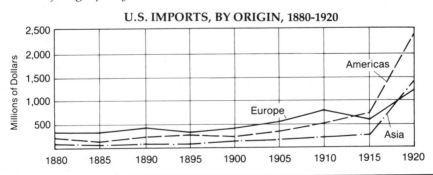

SOURCE: Historical Statistics of the United States: Colonial Times to 1970, *pt. 2 (Washington, D.C.: Government Printing Office, 1975).*

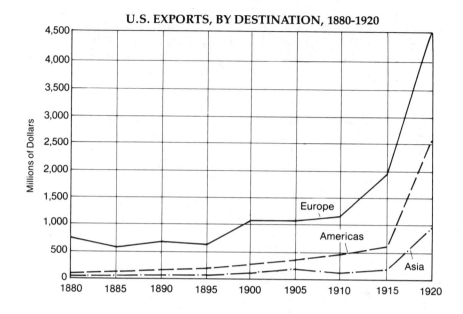

U.S. EXPORTS, BY DESTINATION, 1880-1920

(y-axis: Millions of Dollars, 0 to 4,500; x-axis: 1880 to 1920)

Labeled lines: Europe, Americas, Asia

20.3   The White Man's Burden

David Healy

American expansionism abroad was fostered by two interrelated currents of thought that gained considerable strength in the late nineteenth century: the racist doctrine of Anglo-Saxon supremacy and the impulse to carry Christianity and Western democracry to the "backward," dark-skinned peoples of other lands. Such attitudes, frequently expressed by religious and political leaders, were not necessarily in conflict with economic benefits for the United States, but economic advantage was not the primary objective. In this selection, diplomatic historian David Healy discusses some of the elements of "the white man's burden" argument.

Consider:

1. *How the ideas discussed in this document compare with American attitudes toward the "New Immigration" of the same period (Chapter 18);*
2. *The ways in which the United States' assumption of "the white man's burden" helped serve the nation's commercial expansion overseas.*

. . . Many of the expansionist leaders . . . believed deeply in the righteousness of their actions . . . It was comforting to conclude that the nation was doing God's work as well as its own. . . .

SOURCE: *David Healy,* U.S. Expansionism: The Imperialist Urge in the 1890s *(Madison: University of Wisconsin Press, 1970), 127–30, 134–35.*

In an often-used phrase, Assistant Secretary of State David J. Hill described American expansion as "the extension of civilization." . . .

William McKinley, too, reiterated his belief that the nation acted from duty as well as interest. In the autumn of 1898 he toured the Midwest and South, both judging and molding public opinion on expansion, and everywhere he touched upon the subject of mission. He told an Iowa audience that "wherever our flag floats . . . , it is always for the sake of humanity and the advancement of civilization." Chicagoans learned that "duty determines destiny." In Indiana, the President appealed to his listeners to "help the oppressed people who have by the war been brought within the sphere of our influence," and in Ohio he spoke of "the trust which civilization puts upon us." . . .

The concept of a world divided between civilized and barbarous peoples had never been stronger, and it was accompanied by a conviction that the time was at hand when the advanced nations must begin the final assault on barbarism. . . .

. . . The United States could help to bring backward peoples forward, and thus alleviate the barbarian threat. Interest and altruism ran together, he [Mahan] wrote . . . , but duty must be in the forefront: "if the ideas get inverted, and the nation sees in its new responsibilities, first of all, markets and profits, with incidental resultant benefit to the natives, it will go wrong." The primary aim must be to "regenerate" the "stagnant societies." . . .

There were certain "focal points" observable in history, Josiah Strong had asserted in *Our Country*, and he believed that the close of the nineteenth century would bring one of them, second in importance only to the birth of Christ. The coming generation would shape the destinies of mankind for centuries. The pace of events was speeding to a crisis, in which tewnty years of the new century might "outmeasure a millenium of older time." . . .

Conquest was even more moral, of course, if its object was to conquer souls for God, and to much of the Protestant religious press in America, it appeared that the Spanish War would ultimately serve just that purpose. The churches had been slow to obey God's command to preach the gospel to the heathen, said the *Congregationalist* in the summer of 1898: "And now our Father is taking matters into his own hands, and is forcing the nation to pay its hundreds of millions and to give up its tens of thousands of sons to spread the gospel. For this war is to be God's means of hastening the time when all shall know him." The *Christian Herald* found that "it is in no sense man's war at all . . . . The God of Battles called us to arms . . . ."

. . . it is not surprising that missionaries, even more than other apostles of western civilization, took for granted the superiority of western values over indigenous ones. To the missionaries, they were superior precisely because they were Christian; Christianity was the essential condition for creating any truly advanced society, anywhere. Western, Christian civilization had therefore not only the right but the duty to attack the very foundations of the non-Christian societies. . . .

20.4   Arguments Against American Imperialism

The American Anti-Imperialist League

The expansion of United States involvement overseas—particularly the American attempt to control the Philippines after the Spanish-American War—aroused strong opposition at home. One result was the formation of the formidable Anti-Imperialist League in 1899. During the presidential campaign of 1900, the League adopted a platform, reprinted here, that it hoped would turn the election into a referendum on the expansionist policies of President McKinley and the Republicans.

Consider:

1. *Whether American efforts to establish control over the Philippines was inconsistent with the principles of the Declaration of Independence and the Constitution;*
2. *Whether, in urging Americans not to support government policies in the Philippines, the League was advocating a form of dissent that is unacceptable in a democracy.*

We hold that the policy known as imperialism is hostile to liberty and tends toward militarism, an evil from which it has been our glory to be free. We regret that it has become necessary in the land of Washington and Lincoln ro reaffirm that all men, of whatever race or color, are entitled to life, liberty and the pursuit of happiness. We maintain that governments derive their just powers from the consent of the governed. We insist that the subjugation of any people is "criminal aggression" . . .

We earnestly condemn the policy of the present National Administration in the Philippines. It seeks to extinguish the spirit of 1776 in those islands. We deplore the sacrifice of our soldiers and sailors, whose bravery deserves admiration even in an unjust war. We denounce the slaughter of the Filipinos as a needless horror. We protest against the extension of American sovereignty by Spanish methods. . . .

The United States have always protested against the doctrine of international law which permits the subjugation of the weak by the strong. A self-governing state cannot accept sovereignty over an unwilling people. The United States cannot act upon the ancient heresy that might makes right.

. . . Much as we abhor the war of "criminal aggression" in the Philippines, greatly as we regret that the blood of the Filipinos is on American hands, we more deeply resent the betrayal of American institutions at'home. . . .

SOURCE: *Platform of the American Anti-Imperialist League, October 17, 1899, in* Speeches, Correspondence and Political Papers of Carl Schurz, *ed. Frederic Bancroft (New York: G. P. Putnam's Sons, 1913), VI, 77–79.*

Whether the ruthless slaughter of the Filipinos shall end next month or next year is but an incident in a contest that must go on until the Declaration of Independence and the Constitution of the United States are rescued from the hands of their betrayers. Those who dispute about standards of value while the foundation of the Republic is undermined will be listened to as little as those who would wrangle about the small economies of the household while the house is on fire. The training of a great people for a century, the aspiration for liberty of a vast immigration are forces that will hurl aside those who in the delirium of conquest seek to destroy the character of our institutions.

We deny that the obligation of all citizens to support their Government in times of grave National peril applies to the present situation. If an Administration may with impunity ignore the issues upon which it was chosen, deliberately create a condition of war anywhere on the face of the globe, debauch the civil service for spoils to promote the adventure, organize a truth-suppressing censorship and demand of all citizens . . . their unanimous support while it chooses to continue the fighting, representative government itself is imperiled. . . .

We hold, with Abraham Lincoln, that "no man is good enough to govern another man without that other's consent. When the white man governs himself, that is self-government, but when he governs himself and also governs another man, that is more than self-government—that is despotism." "Our reliance is in the love of liberty which God has planted in us. Our defense is in the spirit which prizes liberty as the heritage of all men in all lands. Those who deny freedom to others deserve it not for themselves, and under a just God cannot long retain it."

20.5   Black Americans View American Expansion
Willard Gatewood

Like whites, blacks had mixed feelings about the expansion of American influence in territories such as Cuba and the Philippines. The fact that these overseas territories were populated by dark-skinned peoples, however, tended to produce particular responses among American blacks. At first, as historian Willard Gatewood explains in the following excerpt, most blacks saw some possible benefits in expansionist activities. Within a few years, though, black opinion seemed to swing in the opposite direction.

Consider:

1. *The changes in perception that led blacks to reverse their opinion on the issue of overseas expansion;*
2. *Why emigration did not appeal to many American blacks in this period;*

3. *The relationship between the attitudes of blacks toward "inferior aliens" and conditions they themselves faced in the United States (see also Doc. 18.7).*

Although black Americans displayed no more consistency or unanimity of opinion regarding imperialism than other citizens, the context within which they viewed the issue was substantially different. Theirs was the perspective of a colored minority in a white-dominated society— a minority whose emergence from the "forge and fire of American slavery" had been followed by a generation of frustrated hopes and thwarted aspirations. The last decade of the nineteenth century in particular witnessed a dramatic increase in racial repression and legal discrimination. By the end of the decade, as an epidemic of negrophobia threatened to trap black citizens in a new form of slavery, a sense of mounting crisis pervaded the black community. Whether one of endorsement or opposition, Negro Americans' initial response to overseas expansion was prompted largely by their view of its effect upon the future of the race in the United States.

At one extreme were those blacks who from the outset maintained an anti-expansionist position principally on the grounds that a crusade abroad would divert attention from the racial crisis at home, thereby allowing what was left of the heritage of Reconstruction to be obliterated altogether. At the other were the champions of imperialism, a group made up primarily of black Republican officeholders, who argued that by participating in the acquisition of an empire Negroes would reap a rich and varied harvest, especially in terms of respect and recognition from the dominant element in American society. According to their rationale, contact with the colored peoples and colored cultures outside the United States would have a beneficent effect upon the racial attitudes of white citizens.

. . . Although the black citizen considered participation in the military struggle for empire a civic duty and hoped that a display of patriotism would dissipate anti-Negro prejudice, he was suspicious of the humanitarian rhetoric employed by white imperialists and persisted in the belief that charity ought to begin at home.

. . . Keenly aware of the tendency to equate criticism of the expansionist policy with disloyalty, he was hesitant, at least initially, to jeopardize his precarious position by embracing the anti-imperialist cause. As a Negro, he recognized the similarity between his predicament in the United States and that of the colored peoples in Cuba, Puerto Rico, Hawaii, and the Philippines. Like them, he longed for liberty and freedom from white oppression. . . .

In the case of Cuba, Negro Americans encountered few ideological difficulties; military intervention there promised not only to relieve the

SOURCE: *Willard B. Gatewood, Jr.*, Black Americans and the White Man's Burden, 1898– 1903 *(Urbana: University of Illinois Press, 1975)*, 320–24.

island of Spanish rule but also to assure its independence. That many of the islanders were of African descent made it easy for Negroes in the United States to identify with the cause of Cuba Libre. . . . Indeed, the role of Afro-Cubans in the struggle for freedom lent credence to [the] idea that Cuba would become another black republic in the Caribbean. . . .

By 1899, even before the Senate approved the treaty ending the war with Spain, black Americans had begun to alter their views regarding the outward thrust of the United States. . . . the war seemed to have multiplied the black citizens' grievances. In the South, where the presence of black soldiers aroused fear and resentment among whites, the reward for the Negro's demonstration of patriotism and valor was a tightening of racial lines. . . . And with the disbandment of the volunteer army after the Spanish-American War, one state after another eliminated the remaining Negro units from its militia. More ominous was the effect which the much-heralded sectional reunion accomplished by the war was likely to have upon race relations. Black spokesmen agreed that the dissipation of sectionalism actually meant northern acquiescence in the "southern solution" to the Negro Problem. . . .

Against this background of frustrated hopes, the black man's original reservations about overseas expansion reemerged in 1899 in the form of forthright opposition to the war in the Philippines. . . . the black community in general established an affinity of complexion with the Filipinos and tended to take a sympathetic view of [Emilio] Aguinaldo's resistance to American rule. . . .

The acquisition of insular possessions inhabited by darker races spawned a variety of emigration schemes, all of which promised Negro Americans an escape from their yoke of prejudice and oppression. Cuba and the Philippines, in particular, were described as places where racial distinctions were virtually nonexistent and where wealth could be acquired by any enterprising black man with a little capital and a willingness to work. Individual Negroes did emigrate to the islands, and a few prospered. But there was never the large-scale exodus advocated by emigrationists. . . . Convinced that color prejudice had accompanied the American flag to Cuba, the Philippines, and other islands, Negroes preferred to fight their battles in the familiar environment of their birth rather than to confront the same enemy among alien civilizations thousands of miles away.

By the time the United States declared the Filipino insurrection at an end, black Americans were thoroughly disenchanted with the expansionist policy and less inclined to identify with the peoples of the insular possessions. Rather than viewing the islanders as colored cousins, they came to look upon them as inferior aliens—a shift explained largely by the growing feeling that the nation was less concerned with the welfare of its black citizens than with that of the peoples in the colonies. . . . By 1903 Negro Americans might still sympathize with Filipino aspirations for independence and freedom, but they were convinced that the first obligation of the American government was to its own colored minority. The nation's saving hand was needed in taking up the black man's burden at home, rather than in looking across the seas for more "little brown brothers."

20.6   Theodore Roosevelt as World Policeman

Louis Dalrymple

Once in the White House, Theodore Roosevelt fulfilled his swashbuckling image as the rough-riding hero of San Juan Hill. He reasserted American prerogatives in the Western Hemisphere and greatly increased the nation's involvement in international affairs. Roosevelt's activity in the world arena ranged from mediating a settlement of the Russo-Japanese War in 1905 (for which he received the Nobel Peace Prize), to engaging in talks with several European powers over the fate of Morocco, and to intervening militarily in the affairs of Latin American nations. To critics and admirers alike, Roosevelt's policies made him appear to be a world policeman. This is suggested by the 1905 cartoon by Louis Dalrymple reprinted on p. 336.

Consider:

1. What elements of Roosevelt's approach to international diplomacy the cartoon reflects;
2. The significance of the depictions of individual nations to the right and left of Roosevelt in the cartoon;
3. The cartoonist's own attitude toward Roosevelt.

SOURCE: Louis Dalrymple, "The World Constable," Judge, 48 (January 14, 1905).

THE WORLD'CONSTABLE.

20.7 American Intervention in World War I
Ross Gregory

The reasons for American entry into World War I have been much debated. Historians have variously emphasized economic reasons (including pressure from powerful American economic interests), the momentum produced by the "non-neutral" policies followed by the Wilson administration, and that vague but important concept, "national honor." In this excerpt from his 1971 book on United States intervention in the war, historian Ross Gregory weaves these three strands of argument together, suggesting that they reinforced one another and led inevitably to Wilson's decision to call for a declaration of war.

Consider:

1. *How Gregory's statements about American economic interests compare with the data shown in Document 20.2;*

2. *The implications of the American view that Germany was an "evil world force";*

3. *Whether Wilson had any options in April 1917 besides going to war against Germany.*

. . . Wilson asked Congress to declare war in 1917 because he felt Germany had driven him to it. He could find no way, short of an unthinkable abandonment of rights and interests, to avoid intervention. He briefly had tried armed neutrality, and as he said in the war message, that tactic had not done the job. Germany was making war on the United States, and Wilson had no reasonable alternative to a declaration of hostilities. Hence submarine warfare must bear the immediate responsibility for provoking the decision for war. It nonetheless is not enough to say that the United States went to war simply because of the submarines. . . .

Any account of American intervention would go amiss without some reference to the pro-Ally nature of American neutrality. American money and supplies allowed the Allies to sustain the war effort. While Wilson did not act openly partial to the Allies, he did promote American economic enterprise and declined to interfere—indeed showed no signs of dismay—when the enterprise developed in ways that were beneficial to Britain and France. . . . he could not bring himself to limit the provisioning of Britain and France; and it was this traffic that brought on submarine warfare. Without American assistance to the Allies, Germany would have had no reason to adopt policy injurious to the interests of the United States.

. . . While pro-Ally feeling was tempered by a popular desire to stay out of the conflict and by the president's wish to remain fair and formally neutral, it was sufficiently strong to discourage any policy that would weaken the Allied war effort. . . . Wilson frequently complained about Britain's intolerable course; he sent notes of protest and threatened to do more. . . . Yet he did nothing to halt Britain's restrictions on trade with continental Europe . . . Wilson declined to press the British because he feared that such action would increase Germany's chances of winning and lead to drastic economic repercussions in the United States.

. . . A prewar suspicion of German militarism and autocratic government, and accounts, during the war, of "uncivilized" German warfare influenced Wilson and a majority of the American people to believe

SOURCE: *Ross Gregory, The Origins of American Intervention in the First World War, 130–36. Reprinted by permission of W. W. Norton & Company, Inc. Copyright © 1971 by W. W. Norton & Company, Inc.*

that the United States faced an evil world force, that in going to war with Germany the nation would be striking a blow for liberty and democracy. . . .

The most important influence on the fate of the United States 1914–17 was the nation's world position. National need and interests were such that it was nearly impossible to avoid the problems which led the nation into war. Even if the administration had maintained a rigidly neutral position and forced Britain to respect all maritime rights of the United States, it is doubtful that the result would have been different. . . . Germany used submarines not because of the need to obtain American supplies, but from a desire to prevent the Allies from getting them.

The course that would have guaranteed peace for the United States was unacceptable to the American people and the Wilson administration. Only by severing all its European ties could the nation obtain such a guarantee. In 1914 that act would have placed serious strain on an economy that already showed signs of instability; by 1916 it would have been economically disastrous. At any time it would have been of doubtful political feasibility, even if one were to premise American popular disinterest in who won the war. . . .

. . . Wilson argued that yielding one concession on the seas ultimately would lead to pressure to abandon all rights. The pragmatic behavior of belligerents, especially the Germans, makes that assessment seem fair. . . . It also is worth noting that Germany, when it reopened submarine warfare in 1917, was interested not merely in sinking munitions ships, but wanted to prevent all products going to Britain and was especially anxious to halt shipments of food. . . .

. . . What had started as efforts to promote prosperity and neutral rights developed into questions of national honor and prestige. Wilson faced not merely the possibility of abandoning economic rights but the humiliating prospect of allowing the Germans to force him to it. The more hazardous it became to exercise American rights, the more difficult it was to yield them. . . .

It is tempting to conclude that inasmuch as the United States was destined to enter the conflict, it might as well have accepted that fact and reacted accordingly. Presumably this response would have involved an earlier declaration of war, certainly a large and rapid rearmament program. . . . However wise that policy might have been, it did not fit conditions of the period of neutrality. Wilson opposed entering the war earlier, and had he thought differently, popular and congressional support were highly questionable. People did not know in 1914 that commercial relations would lead them into the World War; most of them believed during the entire period that they could have trade and peace at the same time. The body of the United States was going one way during the period of neutrality, its heart and mind another. . . .

CHAPTER QUESTIONS

1. *In what ways did American foreign policy interests and objectives change in the decades between 1880 and World War I? What remained consistent about American foreign policy?*

2. *How did both supporters of United States expansion and anti-imperialists argue their cases on the basis of traditional American political and cultural values? Whose arguments seem more persuasive?*

part six

PROSPERITY, DEPRESSION, AND WAR, 1920–1945

Chapter 21

Cultural Tensions in the New Era: The 1920s

The 1920s, customarily viewed as a period of conservative reaction after the war, were in reality dynamic, tension-filled years. It was a time when the forces of tradition and modernism collided violently, and diverse groups of Americans asserted their identities and frequently came into conflict with one another. The Republicans, who were in power throughout the 1920s, called it the "New Era."

Various trends that began during World War I extended into the 1920s. In politics, bureaucratic government continued to grow; in society at large, movements such as Prohibition and women's suffrage reflected the tensions and conflicts that had emerged during the war. Even the ratification in 1919 and 1920 of constitutional amendments that made alcoholic beverages illegal and gave women the vote did not put an end to social conflict over these issues.

Other forces unleashed or intensified by the war also played themselves out during the 1920s. Antiforeign and antiradical sentiment took on increased momentum in this period, as seen in the activities of a revived Ku Klux Klan and the passage of two successive immigration restriction acts. On the other hand, the decade also saw the emergence of a "new Negro," emboldened by the experiences of military service abroad and new economic opportunities at home during the war. The artistic and literary Harlem Renaissance was one outgrowth of this new black assertiveness. Garveyism—a social and political movement that attempted to instill a sense of racial pride in blacks—was another.

Religion, too, was marked by conflict in the 1920s. The celebrated trial of Tennessee biology teacher John Scopes in 1925 emphasized the deep divisions between Christian Fundamentalists and religious "modernists." At the same time, the political rise of Al Smith, the first Roman Catholic to run as a majority-party candidate for the presidency, aggravated Protestant-Catholic tensions. The candidacy of Smith, from New York City's Lower East Side, also contributed to the rift between rural and urban Americans, brought on in part by the economic distress of the nation's farm population.

In view of the deep flaws and tensions that characterized American life in the 1920s, the "New Era" of progress and prosperity proclaimed by the nation's Republican leadership seems to have been built on illusion. Even without the economic cataclysm of the Great Crash in October 1929, American society was headed for disruptive—even explosive—times.

The documents in this chapter illustrate the sources and nature of the cultural tensions of the 1920s. Collectively, they raise significant questions about the degree to which the United States had become a unified, integrated society, as well as about the social price of "progress" and "modernization."

Chronology

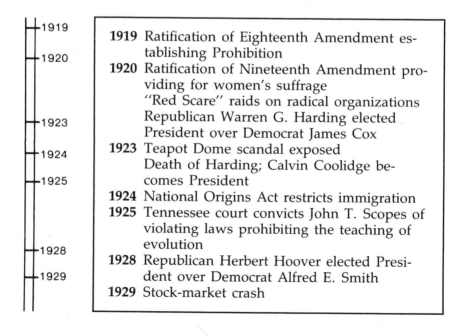

1919	Ratification of Eighteenth Amendment establishing Prohibition
1920	Ratification of Nineteenth Amendment providing for women's suffrage
	"Red Scare" raids on radical organizations
	Republican Warren G. Harding elected President over Democrat James Cox
1923	Teapot Dome scandal exposed
	Death of Harding; Calvin Coolidge becomes President
1924	National Origins Act restricts immigration
1925	Tennessee court convicts John T. Scopes of violating laws prohibiting the teaching of evolution
1928	Republican Herbert Hoover elected President over Democrat Alfred E. Smith
1929	Stock-market crash

Documents

21.1   The Troubled Countryside:
Problems Amidst Plenty

The 1920s witnessed the reemergence in rural America of a strong antagonism toward cities and toward modern developments in general. This revival of rural-urban conflict was primarily social and political in nature,
but—as had been the case in the late nineteenth century—the resentment
of the farmers was intensified by their economic distress in a prosperous
time. The graph and cartoon reproduced here provide two perspectives on
the plight of farmers during the decade. The graph depicts the changing
value of farmers' holdings, as well as the degree of farmers' indebtedness.
Both the graph and the cartoon are taken from a 1927 study of farm problems, *Rural Life at the Crossroads*, by Macy Campbell, a professor of rural
education at Iowa State Teachers College. The cartoon, by J. N. Darling
("Ding"), originally appeared in the *Des Moines Register*.

Consider:

1. *The probable causes for the situation reflected in the graph;*
2. *How the farmer's indebtedness shown in the graph is illustrated in the
cartoon;*
3. *What the cartoon suggests about government response to the needs of
farmers in the 1920s.*

SOURCE: *Macy Campbell,* Rural Life at the Crossroads *(Boston: Ginn and Company, 1927),*
4, 7.

MORTGAGED FARMS IN THE UNITED STATES
IN 1910, 1920, AND 1925

Value of mortgaged farms in 1910

Farmers' equity   72.7%   Debt   27.3%

Inflated values of mortgaged farms in 1920

Farmers' equity 70.9%   Debt 29.1%

Estimated values of mortgaged farms in 1925

Farmers' equity 60%   Debt 40%

WHY NOT TRY SOME OF THE HOME REMEDIES?

Ding, in the *Des Moines Register*

21.2 The Revived Ku Klux Klan

Hiram W. Evans

The most striking example of the pervasive intolerance and resurgent nativism of the 1920s was the revived Ku Klux Klan. Founded in 1915, the "new" Klan was patterned on the white supremacist organization that had terrorized blacks in the South during Reconstruction. It used terrorism and violence less than its predecessor, but the new Klan's list of grievances extended well beyond opposition to blacks. At its height in the mid-1920s, the Klan exercised considerable political influence in several Southern and Midwestern states and its membership was estimated at five million. This excerpt, taken from a 1926 article by Klan "Imperial Wizard" Hiram Wesley Evans, summarizes the Klan's complaints about modern American society and mentions some of its proposals for dealing with those problems.

Consider:

1. *The reasons for the Klan's hostility toward "aliens" and Catholics;*
2. *Whether the revived Klan could be described as "anti-black";*
3. *The kinds of whites to whom the Klan was most likely to appeal.*

. . . The Nordic American today is a stranger in large parts of the land his fathers gave him. . . .

. . . the plain people realize . . . that merely stopping the alien flood does not restore Americanism, nor even secure us against final utter defeat. America must also defend herself against the enemy within, or we shall be corrupted and conquered by those to whom we have already given shelter.

The first danger is that we shall be overwhelmed . . . by the aliens' "mere force of breeding." With the present birthrate, the Nordic stock will have become a hopeless minority within fifty years . . . Unless some means is found of making the Nordic feel safe in having children, we are already doomed.

An equal danger is from disunity, so strikingly shown during the war and from a reorganization of thought and purpose. . . .

One more point about the present attitude of the old stock American: he has revived and increased his long-standing distrust of the Roman Catholic Church. It is for this that the native Americans, and the Klan as their leader, are most often denounced as intolerant and prejudiced. This is not because we oppose the Catholic more than we do the alien, but because our enemies recognize that patriotism and race loyalty

SOURCE: Hiram Wesley Evans, "The Klan's Fight for Americanism," North American Review 223 (March 1926): 39, 43–47, 51, 53–54, 60.

cannot safely be denounced, while our own tradition of religious freedom gives them an opening here, if they can sufficiently confuse the issue. . . .

The real indictment against the Roman Church is that it is, fundamentally and irredeemably, in its leadership, in politics, in thought, and largely in membership, actually and actively alien, un-American and usually anti-American. . . .

We Americans see many evidences of Catholic alienism. We believe that its official position and its dogma, its theocratic autocracy and its claim to full authority in temporal as well as spiritual matters, all make it impossible for it as a church, or for its members if they obey it, to cooperate in a free democracy in which Church and State have been separated. . . .

Another difficulty is that the Catholic Church here constantly represents, speaks for and cares for the interests of a large body of alien peoples. Most immigration of recent years, so unassimilable and fundamentally un-American, has been Catholic. The Catholics of American stock have been submerged and almost lost; the aliens and their interests dictate all policies of the Roman Church which are not dictated by Rome itself.

Also, the Roman Church seems to take pains to prevent the assimilation of these people. Its parochial schools, its foreign born priests, the obtacles it places in the way of marriage with Protestants unless the children are bound in advance to Romanism, its persistent use of the foreign languages in church and school, its habit of grouping aliens together and thus creating insoluble alien masses—all these things strongly impede Americanization. . . .

Finally, there is the undeniable fact that the Roman Church takes an active part in American politics. . . .

. . . The white race must be supreme, not only in America but in the world. This is equally undebatable, except on the ground that the races might live together, each with full regard for the rights and interests of others, and that those rights and interests would never conflict. . . . The world has been so made that each race must fight for its life, must conquer, accept slavery or die. The Klansman believes that the whites will not become slaves, and he does not intend to die before his time.

Moreover, the future of progress and civilization depends on the continual supremacy of the white race. The forward movement of the world for centuries has come entirely from it. Other races each had its chance and either failed or stuck fast, while white civilization shows no sign of having reached its limit. . . .

The Negro, the Klan considers a special duty and problem of the white American. He is among us through no wish of his; we owe it to him and to ourselves to give him full protection and opportunity. But his limitations are evident; we will not permit him to gain sufficient power to control our civilization. Neither will we delude him with promises of social equality which we know can never be realized. The

Klan looks forward to the day when the Negro problem will have been solved on some much saner basis than miscegenation and when every State will enforce laws making any sex relations between a white and a colored person a crime. . . .

21.3   The Results of Immigration Restriction

A number of forces converged after World War I and intensified pressures for immigration restriction. In 1921, Congress enacted a new immigration law that introduced quotas on national origin. This law was amended by the National Origins Act of 1924, which limited immigration from outside the Western Hemisphere to just over 150,000 and continued to set quotas for immigration by national origin. Under the new law, the annual quota of each nation was based on the percentage of people of that nationality living in the United States in 1890. (The 1921 law had used 1910 as the base year for computing quotas.) The table that follows presents data on immigration to the United States from various nations during the 1920s.

Consider:

1. *What the data reveal about changes in the ethnic composition of immigrants during the 1920s (see Doc. 18.1);*
2. *How these changes were related to the selection of 1890, rather than 1910, as the base year for national-origin quotas;*
3. *The impact on immigration of other events in the period, such as the end of World War I and the Great Depression.*

IMMIGRATION TO THE UNITED STATES, 1920–1930

Year	All countries	Great Britain	Ireland	Germany	Poland	U.S.S.R. and Baltic States	Italy	Asia	Americas
1930	241,700	31,015	23,445	26,569	9,231	2,772	22,327	4,535	88,104
1929	279,678	21,327	19,921	46,751	9,002	2,450	18,008	3,758	116,177
1928	307,255	19,958	25,268	45,778	8,755	2,652	17,728	3,380	144,281
1927	335,175	23,669	28,545	48,513	9,211	2,933	17,297	3,669	161,872
1926	304,488	25,528	24,897	50,421	7,126	3,323	8,253	3,413	144,393
1925	294,314	27,172	26,650	46,068	5,341	3,121	6,203	3,578	141,496
1924	706,896	59,490	17,111	75,091	28,806	20,918	56,246	22,065	318,855
1923	522,919	45,759	15,740	48,277	26,538	21,151	46,674	13,705	199,972
1922	309,556	25,153	10,579	17,931	28,635	19,910	40,319	14,263	77,448
1921	805,228	51,142	28,435	6,803	95,089	10,193	222,260	25,034	124,118
1920	430,001	38,471	9,591	1,001	4,813	1,751	95,145	17,505	162,666

SOURCE: Historical Statistics of the United States: Colonial Times to 1970 *(Washington, D.C.: Government Printing Office, 1975), I, 105, 107.*

21.4   Marcus Garvey and Black Nationalism

For black Americans, the 1920s were a time of sharp contrasts. Persecution at the hands of the Ku Klux Klan was widespread, the number of lynchings remained shockingly high, and white politicians paid no attention to issues of racial discrimination. On the other hand, the decade also saw the development of a strong racial pride, particularly among the growing numbers of blacks who lived in northern cities. One result of this new attitude was the "Harlem Renaissance" in literature and the arts. Another, more vivid expression was a phenomenon called Garveyism, named for its leader, Jamaican-born Marcus Garvey. Garvey founded the Universal Negro Improvement Association (UNIA) and the Black Star Line, a black-owned shipping company, to appeal to and stimulate black pride. The 1922 photograph reproduced here shows Garvey in the regalia he commonly wore in public; the two posters show how the Black Star Line was advertised to blacks.

Consider:

1. *How the type of clothing worn by Garvey in the photograph would have evoked racial pride among blacks;*
2. *The characteristics of blacks who would have been attracted to Garveyism;*
3. *The kinds of appeals to blacks that are made in the Black Star Line posters.*

SOURCE: *The Bettmann Archive/UPI Photo*

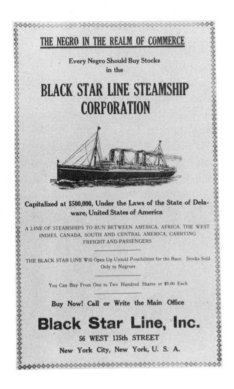

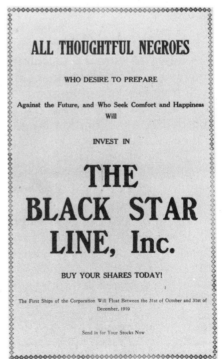

SOURCE: *Courtesy New York State Archives, State Education Department, Albany, N.Y.*

21.5   The Controversy Over Evolution
Ronald L. Numbers

One of the most colorful and dramatic clashes of the 1920s was the "monkey trial" held in Dayton, Tennessee, in 1925. In this case, high school science teacher John Scopes was charged with violating Tennessee's Butler Law, which prohibited teaching evolution in public schools. The Butler Law reflected the Christian Fundamentalist view that the idea of evolution was antithetical to Christianity. The selection that follows, from a 1982 article by historian of science Ronald Numbers, examines the motives and tactics of the Fundamentalists, as represented by William Jennings Bryan. Numbers points out that the attack on evolution was not necessarily based on hostility to modern science.

Consider:

1. *Why Fundamentalists such as Bryan were concerned about evolutionist teachings;*
2. *How the antievolution crusade compared with the prohibition movement in motives and tactics (see Doc. 19.5);*
3. *Who "won" the Scopes case.*

Early in 1922 William Jennings Bryan . . . heard of an effort in Kentucky to ban the teaching of evolution in public schools. "The movement will sweep the country," he predicted hopefully, "and we will drive Darwinism from our schools". . . . His prophecy proved overly optimistic, but before the end of the decade more than 20 state legislatures did debate antievolution laws, and at least five—Oklahoma, Florida, Tennessee, Mississippi, and Arkansas—passed restrictive legislation. . . .

The development of Bryan's own attitudes toward evolution closely paralleled that of the fundamentalist movement. Since early in the century he had occasionally alluded to the silliness of believing in monkey ancestors and to the ethical dangers of thinking that might makes right, but until the outbreak of World War I he saw little reason to quarrel with those who disagreed. The war, however, exposed the darkest side of human nature and shattered his illusions about the future of Christian society. Obviously something had gone awry, and Bryan soon traced the source of the trouble to the paralyzing influence of Darwinism on the conscience. By substituting the law of the jungle

SOURCE: *Ronald L. Numbers, "Creationism in 20th-Century America,"* Science 218 (5 November 1982): 538–41. Copyright 1982 by the AAAS.

for the teaching of Christ, it threatened the principles he valued most: democracy and Christianity. . . .

. . . he also became aware, to his great distress, of unsettling effects the theory of evolution was having on America's own young people. From frequent visits to college campuses and from talks with parents, pastors, and Sunday School teachers, he learned about an epidemic of unbelief that was sweeping the country. Upon investigating the cause, reported his wife, "he became convinced that the teaching of Evolution as a fact instead of a theory caused the students to lose faith in the Bible, first, in the story of creation, and later in other doctrines, which underlie the Christian religion." . . .

Armed with this information about the cause of the world's and the nation's moral decay, Bryan launched a nationwide crusade against the offending doctrine. Throughout his political career Bryan had placed his faith in the common people, and he resented the attempt of a few thousand scientists "to establish an oligarchy over the forty million American Christians" and to dictate what should be taught in the schools. . . . Confident that nine-tenths of the Christian citizens agreed with him . . . he decided to appeal directly to them, as he had done successfully in fighting the liquor interests. "Commit your case to the people," he advised creationists. "Forget, if need be, the high-brows both in the political and college world, and carry this cause to the people. They are the final and efficiently corrective power."

Leadership of the antievolution movement came not from the organized churches of America but from individuals like Bryan and interdenominational organizations such as the World's Christian Fundamentals Association, a predominantly premillennialist body founded in 1919. . . . The early 20th century witnessed the unprecedented expansion of public education (enrollment in public high schools nearly doubled between 1920 and 1930), and fundamentalists . . . wanted to make sure that students attending these institutions would not lose their faith. Thus they resolved to drive every evolutionist from the public school payroll. . . .

In 1922 [Minneapolis Baptist pastor] William Bell Riley outlined the reasons why fundamentalists opposed the teaching of evolution: "The first and most important reason for its elimination," he explained, "is in the unquestioned fact that evolution is not a science; it is a hypothesis only, a speculation." . . .

In the spring of 1925 John Thomas Scopes, a high school teacher in the small town of Dayton, Tennessee, confessed to having violated the state's recently passed law banning the teaching of human evolution in public schools. His subsequent trial focused international attention on the antievolution crusade and brought William Jennings Bryan to Dayton to assist the prosecution. In anticipation of arguments on the scientific merits of evolution, Bryan sought out the best scientific minds in the creationist camp to serve as expert witnesses. The response to his inquiries could only have disappointed the aging crusader. . . .

. . . Eventually [Defense Attorney Clarence] Darrow forced Bryan to concede that the world was indeed far more than 6000 years old and that the 6 days of creation had probably been longer than 24 hours each. . . .

Although the court in Dayton found Scopes guilty as charged, creationists had little cause for rejoicing. The press had not treated them kindly, and the taxing ordeal no doubt contributed to Bryan's death a few days after the trial ended. Nevertheless, the antievolutionists continued their crusade, winning victories in Mississippi in 1926 and in Arkansas 2 years later. By the end of the decade, however, their legislative campaign had lost its steam. The presidential election of 1928, pitting a Protestant against a Catholic, offered fundamentalists a new diversion, and the onset of the depression in 1929 further diverted their energies.

But contrary to appearances, the creationists were simply changing tactics, not giving up. Instead of lobbying state legislatures, they shifted their attack to local communities, where they engaged in "the emasculation of textbooks, the 'purging' of libraries, and above all the continued hounding of teachers." Their new approach attracted less attention but paid off handsomely, as school boards, textbook publishers, and teachers in both urban and rural areas, North and South, bowed to their pressure. Darwinism virtually disappeared from high school texts, and as late as 1941 one-third of American teachers feared being identified as evolutionists.

21.6 Religion and Politics: A Catholic Runs for President

Alfred E. Smith

The election campaign of 1928 saw another clash over religious principles, with implications as far-reaching as the Scopes Trial. Democrat Al Smith, the son of Irish immigrants, was the first Roman Catholic to be nominated for the presidency. Smith's Catholicism raised for many voters, especially Protestants, the question of separation of church and state. The year before his nomination, Smith tried to confront public fears about his religion directly in an open letter in *The Atlantic Monthly*. In his letter he replied to charges that loyalty to the Catholic church and loyalty to the Constitution were incompatible. The results of the 1928 election indicated that Smith was not successful in disspelling public doubts about having a Catholic in the White House.

Consider:

1. *Whether Smith adequately answers Marshall's charges;*
2. *Why, in spite of Smith's assurances, thousands of non-Catholic Democrats refused to support his candidacy;*
3. *Whether a candidate's religion ought to be a factor in the voter's choice.*

CHARLES C. MARSHALL, ESQ.

DEAR SIR:

In your open letter to me in the April *Atlantic Monthly* you 'impute' to American Catholics views which, if held by them, would leave open to question the loyalty and devotion to this country and its Constitution of more than twenty million American Catholic citizens. I am grateful to you for defining this issue in the open and for your courteous expression of the satisfaction it will bring to my fellow citizens for me to give 'a disclaimer of the convictions' thus imputed. Without mental reservation I can and do make that disclaimer. These convictions are held neither by me nor by any other American Catholic, as far as I know. . . .

I should be a poor American and a poor Catholic alike if I injected religious discussion into a political campaign. Therefore I would ask you to accept this answer from me not as a candidate for any public office but as an American citizen, honored with high elective office, meeting a challenge to his patriotism and his intellectual integrity. . . .

Taking your letter as a whole and reducing it to commonplace English, you imply that there is conflict between religious loyalty to the Catholic faith and patriotic loyalty to the United States. Everything that has actually happened to me during my long public career leads me to know that no such thing as that is true. . . . If there were conflict, I, of all men, could not have escaped it, because I have not been a silent man, but a battler for social and political reform. These battles would in their very nature disclose this conflict if there were any. . . .

. . . you quote from the *Catholic Encyclopedia* that my Church 'regards dogmatic intolerance, not alone as her incontestable right, but as her sacred duty.' And you say that these words show that Catholics are taught to be politically, socially, and intellectually intolerant of all other people. If you had read the whole of that article in the *Catholic Encyclopedia*, you would know that the real meaning of these words is that for Catholics alone the Church recognizes no deviation from complete acceptance of its dogma. . . . The very same article in another chapter dealing with toleration toward non-Catholics contains these

SOURCE: *Alfred E. Smith, "Catholic and Patriot: Governor Smith Replies,"* Atlantic Monthly 139 *(May 1927): 721–26, 728. Reprinted with permission.*

words: 'The intolerant man is avoided as much as possible by every high-minded person. . . . The man who is tolerant in every emergency is alone lovable.' . . .

Similar criticism can be made of many of your quotations. But, beyond this, by what right do you ask me to assume responsibility for every statement that may be made in any encyclical letter? . . . these encyclicals are not articles of our faith. . . . You have no more right to ask me to defend as part of my faith every statement coming from a prelate than I should have to ask you to accept as an article of your religious faith every statement of an Episcopal bishop, or of your political faith every statement of a President of the United States. . . .

Your first proposition is that Catholics believe that other religions should, in the United States, be tolerated only as a matter of favor and that there should be an established church. You may find some dream of an ideal of a Catholic State, having no relation whatever to actuality, somewhere described. But, voicing the best Catholic thought on this subject, Dr. John A. Ryan, Professor of Moral Theology at the Catholic University of America, writes . . . ;

' . . . "When several religions have firmly established themselves and taken root in the same territory, nothing else remains for the State than to exercise tolerance towards them all, or, as conditions exist to-day, to make complete religious liberty for individual and religious bodies a principle of government."

That is good Americanism and good Catholicism. . . .

. . . I stand squarely in support of the provisions of the Constitution which guarantee religious freedom and equality.

I come now to the speculation with which theorists have played for generations as to the respective functions of Church and State. You claim that the Roman Catholic Church holds that, if conflict arises, the Church must prevail over the State. You write as though there were some Catholic authority or tribunal to decide with respect to such conflict. Of course there is no such thing. . . .

What is this conflict about which you talk? It may exist in some lands which do not guarantee religious freedom. But in the wildest dreams of your imagination you cannot conjure up a possible conflict between religous principle and political duty in the United States, except on the unthinkable hypothesis that some law were to be passed which violated the common morality of all God-fearing men. And if you can conjure up such a conflict, how would a Protestant resolve it? Obviously by the dictates of his conscience. That is exactly what a Catholic would do. . . .

. . . Archbishop Ireland thus puts the Church's attitude toward the State:—

'To the Catholic obedience to law is a religious obligation, binding in God's name the conscience of the citizen. . . . Both Americanism and Catholicism bow to the sway of personal conscience.' . . .

I summarize my creed as an American Catholic. I believe in the worship of God according to the faith and practice of the Roman Catholic Church. I recognize no power in the institutions of my Church to interfere with the operations of the Constitution of the United States or the enforcement of the law of the land. I believe in absolute freedom of conscience for all men and in equality of all churches, all sects, and all beliefs before the law as a matter of right and not as a matter of favor. I believe in the absolute separation of Church and State and in the strict enforcement of the provisions of the Constitution that Congress shall make no law respecting an establishment of religion or prohibiting the free exercise thereof. I believe that no tribunal of any church has any power to make any decree of any force in the law of the land, other than to establish the status of its own communicants within its own church. I believe in the support of the public school as one of the corner stones of American liberty. I believe in the right of every parent to choose whether his child shall be educated in the public school or in a religious school supported by those of his own faith. I believe in the principle of noninterference by this country in the internal affairs of other nations and that we should stand steadfastly against any such interference by whomsoever it may be urged. And I believe in the common brotherhood of man under the common fatherhood of God.

21.7   The Impact of Prohibition

David Kyvig

Ratification of the Eighteenth Amendment in 1919 appeared to reflect a national consensus for Prohibition. The decade that followed, however, was marked by a continuous challenge to the new law. Disrespect for this law was most evident in the rise of organized crime, which took over the supply and distribution of alcoholic beverages in many of the nation's largest cities. While the "noble experiment" of Prohibition significantly reduced drinking, as historian David Kyvig notes in this selection from his book *Repealing National Prohibition*, the pervasive image of lawlessness tended to overshadow the amendment's constructive effects and contributed to its eventual repeal in 1933.

Consider:

1. *Whether Prohibition represented an unacceptable infringement on the rights of a minority (see Doc. 6.6);*
2. *Why the pervasive image of lawlessness undermined public support for Prohibition;*
3. *Whether the media acted responsibly in devoting so much coverage to violations of Prohibition.*

Most Americans obeyed the national prohibition law. Many, at least a third to two-fifths of the adult population if Gallup poll surveys in the 1930s are any indication, had not used alcohol previously and simply continued to abstain. Others ceased to drink beer, wine, or spirits when to do so became illegal. The precise degree of compliance with the law is difficult to determine because violation levels cannot be accurately measured. . . .

Any evidence to the contrary notwithstanding, national prohibition rapidly acquired an image, not as a law which significantly reduced the use of alcoholic beverages, but rather as a law that was widely flouted. . . . In part this commonly held impression stemmed from the substantial amount of drinking which actually did continue. Even given a 60 percent drop in total national alcohol consumption, a considerable amount of imbibing still took place. Yet the image also derived in part from the unusually visible character of those prohibition violations which did occur.

Drinking by its very nature attracted more notice than many other forms of law-breaking. It was, in the first place, generally a social, or group, activity. Moreover, most drinking took place . . . in urban areas where practically any activity was more likely to be witnessed. Bootleggers had to advertise their availability, albeit carefully, in order to attract customers. The fact that the upper classes were doing much of the imbibing further heightened its visibility. . . .

The behavior of those who sought to profit by meeting the demand for alcoholic beverages created an indelible image of rampant lawlessness. National prohibition provided a potentially very profitable opportunity for persons willing to take certain risks. "Prohibition is a business," maintained the best known and most successful bootlegger of all, Al Capone of Chicago. "All I do is supply a public demand." Obtaining a supply of a commodity, transporting it to a marketplace, and selling it for an appropriate price were commonplace commercial activities; carrying out these functions in the face of government opposition and without the protections of facilities, goods, and transactions normally provided by government made bootlegging an unusual business. . . . participants in the prohibition-era liquor business had to develop their own techniques for dealing with competition and the pressures of the marketplace. The bootlegging wars and gangland killings, so vividly reported in the nation's press, represented, on one level, a response to a business problem. . . .

The nation's press drew a vivid picture of a disregarded law. Newspapers constantly carried reports of police raids on stills and speakeasies.

SOURCE: *David E. Kyvig*, Repealing National Prohibition *(Chicago: University of Chicago Press, 1979), 23–27, 31–32, 35.*

Such stories, along with reports of the many gangland killings in New York, Chicago, and elsewhere, of course represented legitimate news, but their impact far outweighed the statistical evidence of reduced drinking nationwide. . . .

Congress steadily increased enforcement appropriations but never enough to accomplish the goal. In 1927 prohibition agents were finally placed under civil service, and in 1930 the Prohibition Bureau was at last transferred to the Justice Department. As useful as these congressional steps may have been, they came long after the enforcement effort had acquired a dismal reputation and doubts as to whether prohibition could possibly be effective had become deeply ingrained. . . .

While in reality national prohibition sharply reduced the consumption of alcohol in the United States, the law fell considerably short of expectations. It neither eliminated drinking nor produced a sense that such a goal was within reach. So long as the purchaser of liquor, the supposed victim of a prohibition violation, participated in the illegal act rather than complained about it, the normal law enforcement process simply did not function. As a result, policing agencies bore a much heavier burden. The various images of lawbreaking, from contacts with the local bootlegger to Hollywood films to overloaded court dockets, generated a widespread belief that violations were taking place with unacceptable frequency. Furthermore, attempts at enforcing the law created an impression that government, unable to cope with lawbreakers by using traditional policing methods, was assuming new powers in order to accomplish its task. The picture of national prohibition which emerged over the course of the 1920s disenchanted many Americans and moved some to an active effort to bring an end to the dry law.

CHAPTER QUESTIONS

1. *What were the major sources of the social and cultural tensions that characterized American society in the 1920s?*
2. *Did traditionalists generally seem to prevail in their opposition to "modernist" forces and developments in the 1920s? Explain.*
3. *To what extent did American politics reflect the social and cultural conflicts of the decade?*

Chapter 22

Depression and New Deal

T he era of the Great Depression and the New Deal probably had a greater impact on American society than any other period except that of the Civil War. On the one hand, the economic catastrophe that followed the stock market crash of October 1929 wiped out illusions of ever-increasing economic growth and inevitable social progress. On the other, the government programs that made up the New Deal dramatically changed the role of the federal government in American life.

When Franklin D. Roosevelt came to the White House in 1933, the American people looked to him for creative solutions to the massive unemployment and decreased production that were plaguing the nation. FDR's "New Deal" could have taken any number of different directions and still met with public acceptance. In the end, most historians agree, although Roosevelt's programs resulted in a significant expansion of the role of the government, they stopped far short of political revolution. Nevertheless, Roosevelt and his programs were under almost constant attack from both the political Left and the political Right.

If the New Deal did not effect a political revolution, neither did it bring about total economic recovery. Measures of American economic performance in the 1930s show an erratic pattern of recovery with periodic downturns until the nation became involved in defense production in 1940 and 1941.

While aiming to help millions of Americans escape from poverty and regain regular employment, the New Deal paid only limited attention to women and minorities, especially blacks. These groups had been regarded as marginal in the labor force before the Depression, and they continued to meet with discrimination in the economic marketplace under the New Deal. Blacks did, however, find enough about the New Deal that was attractive to switch in massive numbers from the Republican to the Democratic party.

The selections in this chapter deal with the impact of the Great Depression on American society, the nature of FDR's New Deal, and the reactions of various people and groups to New Deal programs. Collectively, the documents touch on such important issues as the changing role of the federal government and the limits on political discussion in a period that seemed to invite imaginative social and political experimentation.

Chronology

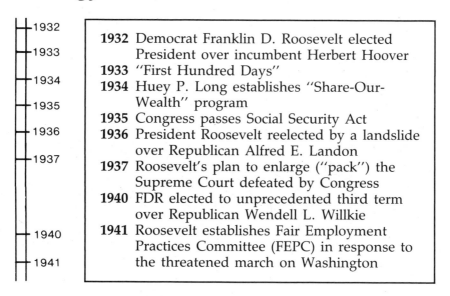

1932	Democrat Franklin D. Roosevelt elected President over incumbent Herbert Hoover
1933	"First Hundred Days"
1934	Huey P. Long establishes "Share-Our-Wealth" program
1935	Congress passes Social Security Act
1936	President Roosevelt reelected by a landslide over Republican Alfred E. Landon
1937	Roosevelt's plan to enlarge ("pack") the Supreme Court defeated by Congress
1940	FDR elected to unprecedented third term over Republican Wendell L. Willkie
1941	Roosevelt establishes Fair Employment Practices Committee (FEPC) in response to the threatened march on Washington

Documents

22.1   Launching the New Deal, Franklin D. Roosevelt (primary source)

22.2   Radicalism on the Left, Huey P. Long (primary source)

22.3   The Depression and the New Deal: Measures of Recovery (graphs)

22.4   Documenting Poverty in the Depression, Dorothea Lange (visual source)

22.5   Women's Roles in the Depression, Lois Scharf (secondary source)

22.6   The New Deal and Blacks' Frustrations, Manning Marable (secondary source)

22.1 Launching the New Deal

Franklin D. Roosevelt

In 1932, the Great Depression worsened and the American people turned away from Republican President Herbert Hoover, electing Democrat Franklin D. Roosevelt by a landslide. Although FDR had been an activist governor in New York, his campaign for the White House conveyed a mixed message about the course he would take if elected. When accepting his party's nomination, Roosevelt spoke of a "New Deal," and during the campaign he frequently referred to bold social and economic programs that he might follow as President. Yet, at the same time, he sharply criticized Hoover for excessive federal spending. There was great interest, therefore, in Roosevelt's inaugural address of March 4, 1933, for an indication of the directions the "New Deal" would take. This speech, one of Roosevelt's most inspirational, is excerpted here.

Consider:

1. *What Roosevelt understood to be his "mandate" from the results of the 1932 election;*
2. *Why many voters were reassured by Roosevelt's speech;*
3. *Why Roosevelt's opponents might have been uneasy about the nation's future under his leadership.*

. . . This great Nation will endure as it has endured, will revive and will prosper. So, first of all, let me assert my firm belief that the only thing we have to fear is fear itself—nameless, unreasoning, unjustified terror which paralyzes needed efforts to convert retreat into advance. In every dark hour of our national life a leadership of frankness and vigor has met with that understanding and support of the people themselves which is essential to victory. I am convinced that you will again give that support to leadership in these critical days.

In such a spirit on my part and on yours we face our common difficulties. They concern, thank God, only material things. Values have shrunken to fantastic levels; taxes have risen; our ability to pay has fallen; government of all kinds is faced by serious curtailment of income; the means of exchange are frozen in the currents of trade; the withered leaves of industrial enterprise lie on every side; farmers find no markets for their produce; the savings of many years in thousands of families are gone.

More important, a host of unemployed citizens face the grim problem

---

SOURCE: *Inaugural Address of March 4, 1933,* The Public Papers and Addresses of Franklin D. Roosevelt *(New York: Random House, 1938), II, 11–13, 15–16.*

of existence, and an equally great number toil with little return. Only a foolish optimist can deny the dark realities of the moment.

Yet our distress comes from no failure of substance. . . . Nature still offers her bounty and human efforts have multiplied it. Plenty is at our doorstep, but a generous use of it languishes in the very sight of the supply. Primarily this is because rulers of the exchange of mankind's goods have failed through their own stubbornness and their own incompetence, . . . Practices of the unscrupulous money changers stand indicted in the court of public opinion, rejected by the hearts and minds of men. . . .

The money changers have fled from their high seats in the temple of our civilization. We may now restore that temple to the ancient truths. The measure of the restoration lies in the extent to which we apply social values more noble than mere monetary profit. . . .

Restoration calls, however, not for changes in ethics alone. This Nation asks for action, and action now.

Our greatest primary task is to put people to work. This is no unsolvable problem if we face it wisely and courageously. It can be accomplished in part by direct recruiting by the Government itself, treating the task as we would treat the emergency of a war, but at the same time, through this employment, accomplishing greatly needed projects to stimulate and reorganize the use of our natural resources.

Hand in hand with this we must frankly recognize the overbalance of population in our industrial centers and, by engaging on a national scale in a redistribution, endeavor to provide a better use of the land for those best fitted for the land. The task can be helped by definite efforts to raise the values of agricultural products and with this the power to purchase the output of our cities. . . .

Finally, in our progress toward a resumption of work we require two safeguards against a return of the evils of the old order: there must be a strict supervision of all banking and credits and investments, so that there will be an end to speculation with other people's money; and there must be provision for an adequate but sound currency.

These are the lines of attack. I shall presently urge upon a new Congress . . . detailed measures for their fulfillment . . .

It is to be hoped that the normal balance of Executive and legislative authority may be wholly adequate to meet the unprecedented task before us. But it may be that an unprecedented demand and need for undelayed action may call for temporary departure from that normal balance of public procedure.

I am prepared under my constitutional duty to recommend the measures that a stricken Nation in the midst of a stricken world may require. These measures, or such other measures as the Congress may build out of its experience and wisdom, I shall seek, within my constitutional authority, to bring to speedy adoption.

But in the event that the Congress shall fail to take one of these two courses, and in the event that the national emergency is still critical, I shall not evade the clear course of duty that will then confront me. I shall ask the Congress for the one remaining instrument to meet the crisis—broad Executive power to wage a war against the emergency, as great as the power that would be given to me if we were in fact invaded by a foreign foe. . . .

. . . The people of the United States have not failed. In their need they have registered a mandate that they want direct, vigorous action. They have asked for discipline and direction under leadership. They have made me the present instrument of their wishes. In the spirit of the gift I take it.

22.2   Radicalism on the Left
Huey P. Long

Though Roosevelt's election in 1932 carried no clear mandate, certainly some who backed him hoped he would preside over a radical reform of American political and economic institutions. One such supporter was Louisiana Senator Huey Long, a charismatic personality who dominated Louisiana politics and had nominated FDR at the 1932 convention. By 1935, however, Long had broken with the New Deal. His "Share-Our-Wealth" crusade, attacking Roosevelt from the egalitarian Left, gained enormous popular support and—to Roosevelt at least—made him seem a potentially dangerous challenger in the 1936 presidential race. The threat ended with Long's assassination in Baton Rouge in 1935. The excerpt that follows outlines Long's "Share-Our-Wealth" program.

Consider:

1. *Whether Long's criticisms of Roosevelt's program were fair;*
2. *The assumptions that lay behind Long's program;*
3. *Whether the "Share-Our-Wealth" program was consistent with the government's constitutional powers.*

Ladies and gentlemen, there is a verse which says that the
"Saddest words of tongue or pen
Are these: 'It might have been.' "
I must tell you good people of our beloved United States that the

SOURCE: Congressional Record, *Seventy-Fourth Congress, 1st Session (January 14, 1935), vol. 79, part 1, 410–11.*

saddest words I have to say are:

"I told you so!"

. . . How I wish tonight that I might say to you that all my fears and beliefs of last year proved untrue! But here are the facts—

1. We have 1,000,000 more men out of work now than 1 year ago.

2. We have had to put 5,000,000 more families on the dole than we had there a year ago.

3. The newspapers report from the Government statistics that this past year we had an increase in the money made by the big men, but a decrease in the money made by the people of average and small means. In other words, still "the rich getting richer and the poor getting poorer."

4. The United States Government's Federal Deposit Insurance Corporation reports that it has investigated to see who owns the money in the banks, and they wind up by showing that two-thirds of 1 percent of the people own 67 percent of all the money in the banks, . . .

I begged, I pleaded, and did everything else under the sun for over 2 years to try to get Mr. Roosevelt to keep his word that he gave to us; I hoped against hope that sooner or later he would see the light and come back to his promises on which he was made President. . . .

All the time we have pointed to the rising cloud of debt, the increases in unemployment, the gradual slipping away of what money the middle man and the poor man have into the hands of the big masters, all the time we have prayed and shouted, begged and pleaded, and now we hear the message once again from Roosevelt that he cannot touch the big fortunes. . . .

. . . We ran Mr. Roosevelt for the Presidency of the United States because he promised to us by word of mouth and in writing:

1. That the size of the big man's fortune would be reduced so as to give the masses at the bottom enough to wipe out all poverty; and

2. That the hours of labor would be so reduced that all would share in the work to be done and in consuming the abundance mankind produced.

Hundreds of words were used by Mr. Roosevelt to make these promises to the people, but they were made over and over again. He reiterated these pledges even after he took his oath as President. Summed up, what these promises meant was: "Share our wealth." . . .

So therefore I call upon the men and women of America to immediately join in our work and movement to share our wealth.

There are thousands of share-our-wealth societies organized in the United States now. . . .

We have nothing more for which we should ask the Lord. He has allowed this land to have too much of everything that humanity needs.

So in this land of God's abundance we propose laws, viz:

1. The fortunes of the multimillionaires and billionaires shall be reduced so that no one person shall own more than a few million

dollars to the person. We would do this by a capital levy tax. . . . we would not levy any capital levy tax on the first million one owned. But on the second million a man owns we would tax that 1 per cent, so that every year the man owned the second million dollars he would be taxed $10,000. On the third million we would impose a tax of 2 percent. On the fourth million we would impose a tax of 4 percent. On the fifth million we would impose a tax of 8 percent. On the sixth million we would impose a tax of 16 percent. On the seventh million we would impose a tax of 32 percent. On the eighth million we would impose a tax of 64 percent; and on all over the eighth million we would impose a tax of 100 percent. . . .

2. We propose to limit the amount any one man can earn in 1 year or inherit to $1,000,000 to the person.

3. Now, by limiting the size of the fortunes and incomes of the big men we will throw into the Government Treasury the money and property from which we will care for the millions of people who have nothing, and with this money we will provide a home and the comforts of home, with such common conveniences as radio and automobile, for every family in America, free of debt.

4. We guarantee food and clothing and employment for everyone who should work by shortening the hours of labor to 30 hours per week, maybe less, and to 11 months per year, maybe less. We would have the hours shortened just so much as would give work to everybody to produce enough for everybody; and if we were to get them down to where they were too short, then we would lengthen them again. As long as all the people working can produce enough of automobiles, radios, homes, schools, and theaters for everyone to have that kind of comfort and convenience, then let us all have work to do and have that much of heaven on earth.

5. We would provide education at the expense of the States and the United States for every child, not only through grammar school and high school but through to a college and vocational education. . . . Yes; we would have to build thousands of more colleges and employ a hundred thousand more teachers; but we have materials, men, and women who are ready and available for the work. Why have the right to a college education depend upon whether the father or mother is so well to do as to send a boy or girl to college? We would give every child the right to education and a living at birth.

6. We would give a pension to all persons above 60 years of age in an amount sufficient to support them in comfortable circumstances, excepting those who earn $1,000 per year or who are worth $10,000.

7. Until we could straighten things out—and we can straighten things out in 2 months under our program—we would grant a moratorium on all debts which people owe that they cannot pay.

And now you have our program, none too big, none too little, but every man a king. . . .

Our plan would injure no one. It would not stop us from having millionaires—it would increase them tenfold, because so many more people could make a million dollars if they had the chance our plan gives them. Our plan would not break up big concerns. The only difference would be that maybe 10,000 people would own a concern instead of 10 people owning it.

22.3   The Depression and the New Deal: Measures of Recovery

Despite fluctuations and periods of seeming recovery, the Great Depression lasted until the nation entered World War II. The graphs that follow illustrate the course of the Depression, using various statistical "yardsticks."

Consider:

1. *The basic patterns in recovery and decline that are reflected in the graphs;*
2. *Why the patterns are similar for the three different sets of figures shown in the graphs;*
3. *The degree to which various New Deal measures affected economic recovery.*

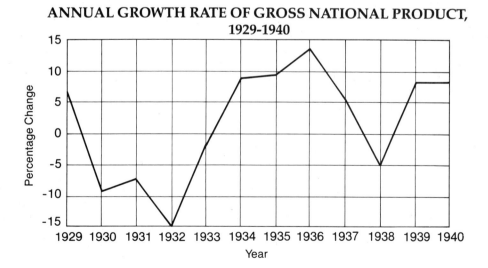

ANNUAL GROWTH RATE OF GROSS NATIONAL PRODUCT, 1929-1940

SOURCE: Historical Statistics of the United States: Colonial Times to 1970, *part 1 (Washington, D.C.: Government Printing Office, 1975).*

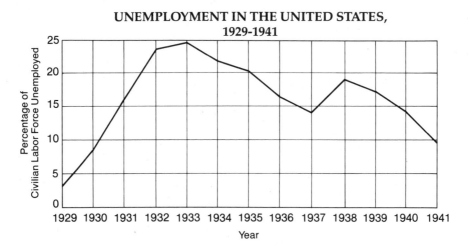

UNEMPLOYMENT IN THE UNITED STATES, 1929-1941

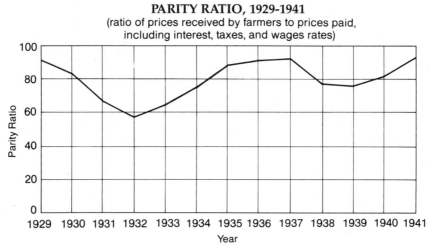

PARITY RATIO, 1929-1941
(ratio of prices received by farmers to prices paid,
including interest, taxes, and wages rates)

22.4 Documenting Poverty in the Depression
Dorothea Lange

As in the progressive era, some of the most important contributions to the
cause of reform during the Depression were made by writers, artists, and
photographers, who portrayed the suffering of the poor in graphic and
dramatic ways. Especially powerful was the work of the Photography Unit
of the Farm Security Administration (FSA), whose job was to document rural life in America. Headed by Roy Stryker, and including such noted photographers as Dorothea Lange and Walker Evans, the FSA Photography
Unit produced moving portraits that inspired sympathy and respect for the
rural poor. The FSA documentary photograph reproduced here, depicting a
migrant mother with her children, is the work of Dorothea Lange.

Consider:

1. *What this FSA photograph says about the rural poor;*
2. *Whether the purpose of the documentary photography of the FSA seems to have been informational or propagandistic, or both;*
3. *The value of dramatic "documentation" of social conditions to the cause of reformers.*

SOURCE: *Dorothea Lange photo, Magnum.*

22.5   Women's Roles in the Depression
Lois Scharf

The experience of women in the Depression years, like that of men, was dramatically affected by economic forces. Whether women should work or not was no longer a theoretical question in families where the male "breadwinners" had lost their jobs. On the other hand, the fact that so many men were unemployed often intensified male resistance to women—especially wives and mothers—entering the work force. Moreover, the persistence of traditional attitudes about gender roles made life very hard for women who did work outside the home. As described in the following excerpt from Lois Scharf's 1980 book, *To Work and To Wed*, women were caught in a social dilemma as they sought to support themselves and their families in this era of scarcity.

Consider:

1. Why widespread economic hardship reinforced traditional "cultural assumptions concerning the proper sexual division of labor";
2. The impact of the Depression on feminists and their supporters;
3. The impact of the Depression on family stability.

. . . The contracted economy of the 1930s mandated that many women seek gainful employment while the competition for limited jobs reinforced cultural assumptions concerning the proper sexual division of labor within family and society. At the same time women were caught in this dilemma, the nature of family life, needs, and values were altering, further complicating choices and attitudes regarding employment by wife and mother. . . .

Male hostility to married women workers crossed class lines; men were conscious that status within the family was closely linked to earning capacity. This situation even prevailed in working-class families, where inadequate or unstable income often required financial supplements by wives. Industrial employment had been irregular long before the 1930s, and brief periods of wage earning by married women were not uncommon. The Depression forced a continuation of established practices. But family members tried to preserve the semblance of patriarchal organization during crises, for wives as well as husbands accepted conventional familial patterns. The employment of married women was justifed in terms of absolute economic necessity or as the

SOURCE: *Lois Scharf*, To Work and To Wed: Female Employment, Feminism, and the Great Depression *(Westport, Conn.: Greenwood Press, Inc., 1980), 139–44, 155–56, 158. Copyright © 1980 by Lois Scharf. Reprinted with permission of author and publisher.*

result of circumstances, such as ill health, which were beyond anyone's control. The temporary nature of the wife's job was constantly emphasized. . . .

Yet, instances were frequent in which no attempt to rationalize the necessity of a wife's employment succeeded. The degree to which many men internalized their roles as breadwinners and endured loss of self-respect when unemployment undermined their ability to support their families was dramatic. The psychological impact of enforced idleness was often as emotionally debilitating as the loss of income was economically disruptive. One jobless working-class husband insisted that "the women's place is in the home. I would rather starve than let my wife work." . . .

Even the possibility of sizable increments in family income did not sway many men. Gallup asked married men their opinion of their wives' obtaining employment, and approximately 80 percent indicated their disapproval. . . .

In middle-class families caught in the economic maelstrom of the 1930s "the effort to meet the situation included the employment of the mother not previously employed," but as in the case of working-class families, the temporary and emergency nature of her efforts was stressed. Those families with some financial reserves fell back on savings or reduced expenditures before resorting to the employment of wives. . . .

The facts that working wives sought to perpetuate the male-dominated household and that most men and women alike opposed working wives were related to anxiety over family stability and social order. When pollsters asked opponents of married women workers to explain their attitudes, two-thirds indicated that they adhered to traditional modes of sexual division of labor. They believed either that working wives usurped jobs that rightfully belonged to male breadwinners or that "women's place is in the home." . . .

Most Americans could not envision social order, generally, and family stability, specifically, in any context other than one that included the rigid demarcation of sexual spheres. Testimonial and advice literature reiterated the imperatives of the female role as supportive wife and nurturing mother. The virtues of adhering to idealized roles were explicit in the written testimonials of admitted ex-feminists who renounced their jobs and subsequently enjoyed the thrills of homemaking and child rearing. All of the training and effort expended in pursuit of careers, they insisted, could better be spent at home. . . .

In spite of arguments to the contrary, household chores remained time consuming, and married working women found themselves with two jobs. The benefits of the highly vaunted labor-saving devices, which supposedly eased homemaking functions and, for feminists, necessitated out-of-home activities for married women, were more apparent than real. While students of census data attributed the growing numbers of working wives to the spread of household conveniences such as washing machines and vacuum cleaners, social commentators overlooked the higher, more demanding standards of homemaking that accompanied the growing availability of electrical appliances. The washing machine often replaced the hired laundress, added a function to homemaking, and resulted in higher standards of cleanliness as well. . . .

Within the context of these cross-currents, contradictions, and complexities, the proportion of married women workers continued to grow. More young women married and remained at work at least until the birth of their first child, while older women entered the labor force in direct response to Depression-induced deprivation or changing patterns of consumer demand. During the decade, women encountered fewer professional opportunities and found more menial jobs in those supposedly desirable white-collar areas where they also encountered the greatest incidence of discrimination. At the same time, uncertainty existed over work roles; domestic and child-rearing functions were occasionally eased by family members or by hired assistance, but seldom was the issue of primary responsibility raised.

The possibility of debate over these questions, first raised during the 1920s, was stifled. In a decade during which economic recovery and social stability monopolized public attention, and intellectuals toyed with economic but not social revolution, feminism retreated. Monitoring women's economic gains outside the home and social obligations within it ceased. Defenders of the position of working wives clung to the status quo and envisioned their employment in terms that emphasized the familial context within which most married women themselves perceived their work. . . .

22.6   The New Deal and Blacks' Frustrations
Manning Marable

An important part of the "Roosevelt revolution" in American politics was the mass conversion of black voters from the Republican to the Democratic party. This shift clearly indicated that blacks viewed the New Deal favorably, in spite of the racial discrimination—and even racial violence—that persisted through the 1930s. Yet, if the New Deal failed to address civil-rights issues, it did help create an environment in which blacks could organize and express their frustrations to political officials. In the selection that follows, Manning Marable, a leading black Marxist scholar, describes the continuing inequities faced by the black "underclass" during the Depression and discusses the rising assertiveness among blacks that culminated in the March on Washington movement in 1941.

Consider:

1. *The ways in which the author's Marxist viewpoint is revealed in this selection;*
2. *How the goals and methods of the National Negro Congress differed from those of the NAACP and other earlier black organizations;*
3. *Why black voters strongly supported Roosevelt and the New Deal despite his apparent lack of commitment to black civil-rights issues.*

The context of the democratic movement against US racial segregation in the 1930s and 1940s was largely determined by four factors: the election of Franklin D. Roosevelt as president in 1932, and the subsequent shift in the Afro-Americans' electoral allegiance from the Republican to the Democratic party; the unprecedented crisis in the domestic and world capitalist economies, the Great Depression; the rise of fascism and the outbreak of the Second World war; and domestically, the rise of militant trade unionism and the emergence of the CIO. By previous standards, Roosevelt was the most liberal chief executive in American history in regard to the civil rights of national minorities. The number of Black Federal employees was increased from fifty thousand in 1933 to two hundred thousand by 1946. Roosevelt had selected a small group of prominent middle-class Blacks, including lawyers Robert C. Weaver and William H. Hastie, journalist Robert L. Vann and educator Mary McLeod Bethune, to hold administrative posts. However, government agencies in the 'New Deal' administration of Roosevelt were organized on strictly segregated lines. Youth who worked in the Civilian Conservation Corps camps were segregated by race; provisions in the Public Works Administration were often denied to Black rural farmers through fraud and outright corruption. Key elements of New Deal reform legislation simply extended the colour line. One blatant example was the passage of the National Labour Relations Act in 1935, which gave American workers the right to vote for unions and banned gross anti-union activities by capital. Blacks demanded that a clause outlawing racial discrimination by unions should be added to the act. But white AFL leaders 'let it be known that, if the antidiscrimination clause were incorporated into the proposed bill, the federation would prefer to see the entire measure defeated.' Roosevelt sided with white labour, and the antidiscrimination clause was defeated. . . .

To complicate matters there was a growing collaboration between capital, white political leaders and the leadership of the fragile Black middle class—Black newspaper editors, clergy, entrepreneurs, civil leaders—which often presented a serious obstacle to the building of

SOURCE: *Manning Marable,* Black American Politics: From the Washington Marches to Jesse Jackson *(London: Verso, 1985), 79–87.*

desegregation movements. . . . When the Brotherhood of Sleeping-Car Porters attempted to mobilize Black workers, most Black publishers rallied behind the interest of capital. . . . Several years later, during the initial formation of the CIO, many influential Blacks charged that the organization was being financed by 'Moscow Gold', and declared that Afro-Americans should be at best neutral towards unionization. . . . In reaction to the accommodationism of the traditional Black leadership, Black workers and radical intellectuals organized by [A. Philip] Randolph founded the National Negro Congress (NNC). At its initial session on 14 February 1936, the NNC had attracted the support of 585 Black and integrated groups with a combined Black membership of 1.2 million. The focus of the organization, which operated essentially as both a Black united front and a more progressive alternative to the NAACP, was, in Randolph's words, to 'seek to broaden and intensify the movement to draw Negro workers into labour organizations and break down the colour bar in the trade unions that now have it.' The unity between such diverse factions as Black liberal Republicans and Black Marxist-Leninists, however, was all too brief. . . . Randolph, Black intellectual Ralph Bunche and other more moderate Blacks resigned from the NNC as the Communist Party's influence inside the front became dominant. . . .

By 1940, the situation of Black labour was still critical. Over a quarter of the Black force was jobless, despite the plethora of public programmes. Increasingly, Blacks' grievances focused on defence-related industries. . . . In September 1940, a group of middle-class Black leaders met with Roosevelt personally in an effort to obtain concessions, but came away empty-handed. Even NAACP leader Walter White, no paragon of Black militancy, was deeply angered by an unproductive meeting with Roosevelt in November 1940. In White's words, "Bitterness [was growing] at an alarming rate throughout the country."

. . . Black workers were involved in the mid to late 1930s in a series of bloody union-organizing efforts, especially in heavy industry. Throughout the Depression, common poverty and hunger brought a new militancy to Black and white unemployed workers alike. Across the country, . . . thousands of relief and unemployment marches and public demonstrations erupted spontaneously . . . Most of these demonstrations had few visible 'leaders', lacked prior coordination, and tended to focus their energies on symbols of bourgeois democratic authority, such as a city hall or state assembly building. In a number of instances, these mass mobilizations secured some basic material concessions, yet they did not overturn the hegemony of capital. . . .

. . . With the decline of the NNC and the failure of the NAACP to initiate any mass mobilizations similar to those of labour, Randolph and the leaders of Brotherhood proposed their own solution to the problem of racial hiring policies in defence plants: a national march on Washington DC, which would be staged on 1 July 1941. Randolph's challenge to the Roosevelt Administration departed sharply from the legalistic and non-confrontational tactics of White's NAACP. . . . Randolph issued the march's ambitious demands: an executive order forbidding government contracts to be awarded to any firm that practised racial discrimination in hiring; an executive order abolishing segregation in the armed forces; an executive order abolishing racial discrimination in government defence training courses; an executive order requiring the US Employment Service to supply workers without regard to race; an executive order abolishing Jim Crow in every department of the Federal government; and a formal request from Roosevelt to the Congress to pass legislation forbidding any benefits of the National Labour Relations Act to be given to unions denying membership to Blacks. The demands represented something qualitatively new in Black desegregationist strategy: the active pursuit of executive intervention to overturn the major pillars of Jim Crow. . . .

. . . From the beginning, Randolph decided that the mobilization should include only Blacks. Some Black leftists, civil rights leaders and white liberals criticized Randolph in this regard, reminding him of his bitter opposition to the Black nationalist efforts of Marcus Garvey two decades before. How could the Black trade unionist fight for integration while mobilizing Blacks separately? . . . Randoph's uncompromising response evoked even greater support among thousands of Black trade unionists and the unemployed, many of whom had been members of the UNIA or sympathetic to militant Black nationalism. By April 1941, the Negro March on Washington Movement had fifty thousand members who had each paid one dollar or more toward the campaign. . . . By late spring, the Roosevelt Administration had clearly begun to panic. The spectre of an estimated fifty thousand Black workers surrounding the White House grounds at a time when Nazi Germany was winning its war against Britain caused considerable anxiety. . . . Finally, on 24 June, a compromise was reached. For Randoph's cancelling the march, the President agreed to sign Executive Order 8802 which would outlaw racist hiring policies inside war production plants. . . .

. . . Many Blacks once again bitterly accused Randolph of political opportunism, citing the unfulfilled list of demands that Roosevelt had refused to grant. Jim Crow would have received a devastating blow had the original set of militant reforms been enacted. . . . Always an astute politician, Roosevelt turned the compromise into a publicity *coup*. Civil rights historian Herbert Garfinkel observed that the white 'press hailed the Executive Order as further demonstration of America's love of democracy, but continued to ignore the role of the "march" in applying pressure on the administration. . . . Southern segregationists comprehended that the Executive Order was a necessary accommodation to ensure Blacks' loyalty in the war that loomed ahead; and on balance, the compromise left the larger national commitment to white supremacy unchallenged. . . .

Conversely, the Negro March on Washington Movement of 1941 set into motion a variety of protest currents which would be manifested fifteen years later in the 'Second Reconstruction'. . . .

Randolph's abortive march was only one factor in the desegregation efforts of the early 1940s. Without question, however, the campaign for racial justice and the public policy trend against Jim Crow would not have assumed such a decisive character had the mobilization not taken place. . . .

CHAPTER QUESTIONS

1. *Which view of the New Deal seems to you more justified—that it went too far or that it did not go far enough?*
2. *In what ways did the New Deal serve the interests of "marginal" members of the work force, such as women and blacks?*
3. *Was the New Deal consistent with an "American reform tradition"? Why or why not?*

Chapter 23

*America's Emergence
as a World Leader
1921–1945*

On April 29, 1945, representatives of fifty nations met in San Francisco to adopt a United Nations Charter and create a permanent United Nations organization. Largely the product of Franklin D. Roosevelt's vision and wartime leadership, the new organization was to keep peace through conciliation and, when necessary, through collective military action. The crucial role the United States played in 1945 in bringing the UN into being stands in sharp contrast to America's rejection of the League of Nations in 1920. This contrast, however, should not obscure a continuity that helps explain the emergence of America as a world leader.

Although few participants acknowledged it at the time, America did not withdraw from involvement in international affairs in the 1920s. During that time, the architects of American foreign policy recognized that the prosperity of the United States depended on an economic policy that supported a world economy, and the nation participated in European efforts to stabilize the world economy. There was a dramatic increase in American involvement in international economic affairs in the period between the wars, but the United States remained resistant to collective security as the way to avoid war.

In the 1930s, President Roosevelt recognized that American public opinion and key members of Congress were not ready for collective security arrangements; but Roosevelt believed he could educate the American people to accept a greater role in international affairs. No doubt he was less optimistic after he saw how much opposition there was to his "Quarantine Speech." The United States finally joined the struggle to achieve peace through military power after Japan's atta ᵔk on Pearl Harbor.

Even before the United States entered World War II, Roosevelt had voiced America's hopes for the world in his "Four Freedoms" speech and also in the Atlantic Charter, issued jointly with England. Once the United States had entered the war, the President offered as a postwar goal the Wilsonian dream of an end to spheres of influence and balance of power politics. On January 1, 1942, after twenty-six nations signed a joint declaration of the Atlantic Charter, Roosevelt pronounced it a "declaration by United Nations," hoping it would become the basis for a postwar system for peace. In private, however, he conceded it was unlikely that spheres of influence and balance-of-power politics could be entirely eliminated. The emphasis Roosevelt and his successor, Harry Truman, placed on winning the war and establishing the United Nations sometimes led to decisions that critics regard as moral failures. Roosevelt probably would have responded that we live in an imperfect world in which there are imperfect solutions.

The readings in this chapter cover a period of twenty-five years, 1921–1945. Although American foreign policy seemed to move from one extreme to the other during these years, it was in reality consistent and continuous. The readings themselves reveal the gradual emergence of American leadership in world affairs.

Chronology

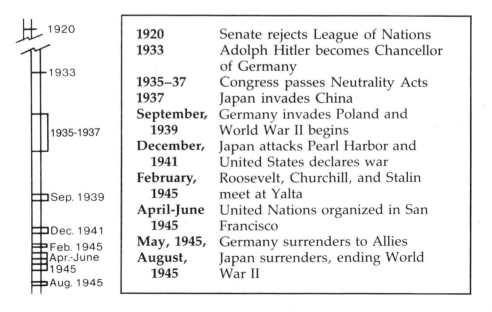

1920	Senate rejects League of Nations
1933	Adolph Hitler becomes Chancellor of Germany
1935–37	Congress passes Neutrality Acts
1937	Japan invades China
September, 1939	Germany invades Poland and World War II begins
December, 1941	Japan attacks Pearl Harbor and United States declares war
February, 1945	Roosevelt, Churchill, and Stalin meet at Yalta
April-June 1945	United Nations organized in San Francisco
May, 1945,	Germany surrenders to Allies
August, 1945	Japan surrenders, ending World War II

Documents

23.1   American Foreign Policy During the 1920s

Warren I. Cohen

Until recently, most historians regarded American foreign policy during the 1920s as an "isolationist" interlude between the internationalism of Woodrow Wilson and of Franklin Roosevelt. The first significant challenge to this view appeared in 1954 with William Appleman Williams's incisive article, "The Legend of Isolationism in the 1920s." Over the last decade or so, a number of historians specializing in American foreign policy have portrayed the 1920s as a dynamic period in which the United States was deeply involved in international matters. In his 1987 book, *Empire Without Tears*, from which this excerpt is taken, historian Warren Cohen argues that the American "empire" was greatly extended during the 1920s and that this expansion required the United States "to be profoundly engaged in international matters."

Consider:

1. Why Cohen called his book Empire Without Tears *and what that title implies about American foreign policy during the 1920s;*

2. *Which foreign policy debates and events during the 1920s support Cohen's argument;*

3. *The relation between "collective security" concerns in the 1920s and contemporary debate over American foreign policy.*

SOURCE: *Warren I. Cohen,* Empire Without Tears: America's Foreign Relations, 1921–1933 *(New York: Alfred A. Knopf, 1987), xii, 8–9, 13, 16–17.*

Prior to 1917, . . . few Americans were aware of the impact of the world on their country or their country's role in the world. The world war shattered popular complacency and engaged mass attention. From 1914, certainly from 1917 to 1919, . . . The government of the United States became more deeply occupied with international affairs than likely or even possible in time of peace. The American military establishment grew enormously, and its power was projected overseas. American financial power grew enormously as the United States was transformed from debtor to creditor nation and as the financial center of the world passed from London to New York. . . .

In Washington, the United States Senate failed to muster the two-thirds vote necessary to ratify the Treaty of Versailles and bring the United States into the League—although majority support was available even in the Senate. Rejection of the Treaty of Versailles and lack of membership in the League had little impact, however, on American involvement in world affairs in the decade that followed. In the 1920s the United States was more profoundly engaged in international matters than in any peacetime era in its history. The empire was maintained, with minor modifications in the Caribbean and China. Military power, as is usual in the absence of war or serious threat, declined—but never to prewar levels. Financial power, on the other hand, grew at nearly geometric rates, and the dollar, if not the flag, could be found wherever the sun might shine at any given moment.

. . . In the 1920s, military power was allowed to atrophy. There would be few American boys fighting for the empire: it would be an empire without tears. (I use "empire" throughout to encompass two very different manifestations of American wealth and power. First, I use the term in the traditional sense of territories controlled, directly or indirectly, by the government of the United States . . . Second, I use "empire" in the less than universally accepted sense of "informal empire," to include cases in which the principal instruments for the control of other peoples or their resources are private, generally economic, and profit-motivated, in which the role of the U.S. government is secondary or nonexistent. Those who are its objects rarely distinguish between the exercise of official and private American power.) . . .

. . . The struggle over ratification of the Treaty of Versailles had focused much of the historic tension between executive and legislative branches on foreign policy issues. Participation in the war and in the peacemaking bred a group of experts on world affairs who formed the foreign policy "establishment." Harding's cabinet contained at least two men, Hughes and Hoover, who had spoken for their party on foreign affairs issues in the past and perceived a leadership role for the United States. For all Harding and his constituency's longing to return to "normalcy," there could be no retreat from the rest of the world for the generation of the twenties. The search for order, so pronounced in the Progressive era, had become a search for world order. . . .

In this setting, there emerged what the historian Richard Leopold has called the "interwar compromise." The central question for the 1920s was how to stay out of war, preferably while increasing the benefits Americans enjoyed from expanding involvement in world affairs. A minority, strongly represented by the Council on Foreign Relations and the League of Nations Association, argued that the United States could not avoid being drawn into a second world war. Once such a war started, American participation was inevitable. The only way to keep the United States out of war was to cooperate with other nations for the preservation of peace, most obviously through membership in the League or . . . cooperation with Britain and France.

Most people with views on American foreign policy in the 1920s had a simpler solution: The United States could stay out of future wars as an act of will. It had intervened voluntarily in 1917—next time it would not, even if all of Europe and Asia were at war. [Senator William E.] Borah, representative of much of this thinking, was convinced that the key to peace for America was to avoid obligations or commitments that might lead to war. He and many of those who shared his outlook were unwilling to surrender the overseas interests of the United States, but insisted on looking after those interests independently. They favored a course another historian, Joan Hoff Wilson, has labeled "independent internationalism." When foreign policy was an issue in the 1920s, there were few advocates of an American retreat from world affairs. Rather, the debate was between a minority that advocated collective security and a majority that rejected collective security as the best means to preserve the American empire without war.

In the 1920s the United States attempted to pursue an independent policy, compromising frequently to cooperate with other nations for specific purposes. The policies of the era were epitomized by agreements with other nations on an ad hoc basis, to solve specific problems. Commitments, except to consult, were carefully avoided, as were provisions for enforcement, for sanctions if the agreements were violated. A generation aware of the tendency of post-1945 America toward overcommitment might see the policy of the 1920s as timid, but what is really striking is the increased participation of the United States in major developments around the world, compared with the role the nation played prior to 1917.

23.2   Roosevelt and the Aftermath of the Quarantine Speech

John McV. Haight, Jr.

On October 5, 1937, in Chicago, Illinois, President Franklin D. Roosevelt delivered a major foreign-policy address designed to counteract a growing isolationist trend in the country. In a key passage, the President said that an "epidemic of lawlessness" was spreading throughout the world and that a quarantine of aggressors was necessary to protect the rest of the world community. The conventional view is that the speech was a "trial balloon" and that after isolationists pounced on the "quarantine" idea as a back door to the kind of collective security envisioned in the League of Nations, the President quickly dropped the idea. In a valuable and insightful article, "Roosevelt and the Aftermath of the Quarantine Speech," historian John McV. Haight, Jr., concludes that the "Quarantine Speech" was not an aberration, nor did the President immediately back off from the ideas contained in the speech. Rather, the speech was part of a strategy designed to make the world community so hostile to aggression that no nation would dare initiate it. The excerpt printed here summarizes Haight's argument.

Consider:

1. *The evidence Haight presents to support his argument;*
2. *Whether President Roosevelt acted as a statesman in deciding to drop the quarantine issue until there was strong public support for his position;*
3. *How a nation's foreign policy is affected when it must be guided by public opinion.*

The opinion that Roosevelt backed down immediately after his Chicago speech in the face of public opposition has been widely accepted. At first glance this conclusion rests upon good evidence. . . .

There is, however, stronger evidence that Roosevelt neither considered the public reaction to this speech as overwhelmingly negative nor did he retreat immediately from his newly voiced foreign policy. . . .

Roosevelt recognized the storm raised by the isolationists and one of his reasons for speaking softly in public appears to have been his desire to prevent additional fuel from being added to the isolationist fires. But, instead of retreating, he apparently hoped that ultimately his opponents' campaign would die down before disturbing the American public too deeply. His private letters do indeed reflect a hopefulness for the future. In two written October 16 he remarked he was "fighting against a public psychology which comes very close to saying 'peace at any price,' " and he added that he looked forward to "a growing response to the ideal that when a few nations fail to maintain fundamental

SOURCE: *John McV. Haight, Jr., "Roosevelt and the Aftermath of the Quarantine Speech,"* The Review of Politics, *24 (April 1962): 233–35, 237, 243–46, 252–55, 258–59.*

rules of conduct, the most practical and peaceful thing to do in the long run is to 'quarantine' them."

. . . the President recognized in the meeting of the Nine Powers not only the opportunity to awaken world opinion but the opportunity of applying against a specific aggressor nation the collective procedures which he had publicly defined as a quarantine. . . .

In his effort to stir Americans and the rest of mankind Roosevelt seized two further opportunities to make a universal appeal to support law and order. Both were presented to him immediately after the Chicago speech . . . One, of course, was the plan Sumner Welles proposed on October 6 and the other was the conference of the signers of the Nine Power Treaty. . . .

The Welles Plan has long been identified as a move by the President and his Under Secretary of State to "rally a still vocal public opinion in Europe." To do so these two men planned to assemble at the White House on Armistice Day all the ambassadors present in Washington and to issue at that dramatic time a call for an international meeting. Its purpose would be to delineate the basic rules for international conduct, thereby making the lawlessness of the aggressors easier to define and to condemn. This meeting was planned to arouse public opinion on a world scale . . .

The President primarily desired that the Far Eastern troubles should be solved by negotiation. "The purpose of the conference," he stated on October 12, "will be to seek by agreement a solution to the present situation in China." . . .

Though obviously he could not say so in public, Roosevelt did not rest all his plans upon Japan's willingness to settle its differences with China by negotiation rather than by arms. . . .

. . . If Roosevelt did intend to have the United States join with the other Conference nations to take positive action against Japan, how did he propose to circumnavigate two serious obstacles, Japanese retaliation and the American Neutrality Act?

. . . Roosevelt . . . believed "it was most probable that Japan would come to terms and not attempt any retaliation, which would be futile, if she were convinced we meant business." Here was the key to the President's thinking. If the peace-loving nations of the world could be persuaded to "mean business," Japan would never dare retaliate. . . .

As to the American Neutrality Act, how could the President persuade his countrymen to renounce isolation and convince the aggressors "we mean business?" Roosevelt . . . believed he had found a way. . . . a policy known as collective neutrality . . . Roosevelt believed Japan could be persuaded to seek a peaceful solution, if the nations meeting at Brussels would agree to a collective neutrality and apply against Japan the pressures which the American nations agreed to apply in the New World. As the Congress of the United States had already approved such steps against an American aggressor, Roosevelt apparently hoped that joint action with the Nine Powers could also be fitted within his nation's Neutrality Act.

A review of [American delegate] Norman Davis' actions at the Nine Power Conference provides the culminating evidence that President Roosevelt did hope to implement his quarantine speech in the Far East by a concerted action with the other peace-loving nations. . . .

Initially Davis emphasized the necessity of persuading Japan to accept a mediated peace. . . .

By November 10, following an adjournment of the Conference for a long week end, the delegates of the three major powers, France, Britain and the United States, met twice to discuss future steps. The prospects of the conference looked bleak, for Japan's refusal of mediation had not prompted world opinion to revulsion. . . .

It was during the second meeting on November 10 that . . . Davis [learned] that the President still regarded a Japanese attack upon Indo-China, Hong Kong, or the Dutch East Indies as an attack upon the Philippines . . .

If Davis stirred a new optimism amongst the other delegates to the Nine Power Conference about American support of a concerted effort against Japan, they were to be fully disillusioned when Secretary [of State] Hull's reply arrived by cable two days later. "None of the measures envisaged should be proposed by the United States." . . . Only after it became apparent the President would not override his Secretary of State did Davis admit defeat and cable back to Hull "I bow before your judgment."

After the high point of the talks on November 10, . . . the Nine Power Conference disintegrated into a fiasco. . . .

. . . Why finally did President Roosevelt back down? Why did he fail to support Davis in his efforts to follow a constructive policy at Brussels? There appear to be several explanations for the President's failure: the hesitancy of Cordell Hull, the weight of Congressional opposition, the economic recession then plaguing the United States, the failure of American opinion to swing behind a quarantine of Japan, and finally the efforts of some of the Nine Power nations to push the United States out in front. . . .

The quarantine speech had been heralded as a revolution in American foreign policy. It had raised the expectations for those throughout the world who feared the appetite of the aggressor nations. Roosevelt fully recognized the position of leadership he had assumed at Chicago and was prepared to associate his country with other neutrals in applying pressure against Japan. He was no idealist speaking idly and irresponsibly but rather a realist with a broad plan for positive action. . . . Without a strong public affirmation he could not break the grip which the isolationists held upon Congress. . . .

23.3   America and the War in Europe

Charles A. Lindbergh

In 1941, Colonel Charles A. Lindbergh, a national hero since his solo flight across the Atlantic in 1927, became a member of an isolationist group called the America First Committee. Lindbergh had just spent three years in England and had visited Germany, where he reviewed the German Air Force. Lindbergh felt that, on purely military grounds, he could speak with considerable authority about American involvement in the European war. In the radio speech excerpted here, Lindbergh explained why the United States should stay out of the war and called for widespread public support of the America First Committee.

Consider:

1. *What Lindbergh meant by an "independent American destiny" and how intervention undermined this;*
2. *The basic assumption Lindbergh made about America's security from foreign attack.*

I know I will be severely criticized by the interventionists in America when I say we should not enter a war unless we have a reasonable chance of winning. That, they will claim, is far too materialistic a standpoint. They will advance again the same arguments that were used to persuade France to declare war against Germany in 1939. But I do not believe that our American ideals, and our way of life, will gain through an unsuccessful war. And I know that the United States is not prepared to wage war in Europe successfully at this time. . . .

. . . We have only a one-ocean Navy. Our Army is still untrained and inadequately equipped for foreign war. Our air force is deplorably lacking in modern fighting planes because most of them have already been sent to Europe. . . .

. . . There is a policy open to this nation that will lead to success— a policy that leaves us free to follow our own way of life, and to

SOURCE: *Speech of Charles A. Lindbergh in New York City, April 23, 1941. Copyright © 1941 by The New York Times Company. Reprinted by permission.*

develop our own civilization. It is not a new and untried idea. It was advocated by Washington. It was incorporated in the Monroe Doctrine. . . .

It is based upon the belief that the security of a nation lies in the strength and character of its own people. It recommends the maintenance of armed forces sufficient to defend this hemisphere from attack by any combination of foreign powers. It demands faith in an independent American destiny. This is the policy of the America First Committee today. It is a policy not of isolation, but of independence; not of defeat, but of courage. It is a policy that led this nation to success during the most trying years of our history, and it is a policy that will lead us to success again. . . .

The United States is better situated from a military standpoint than any other nation in the world. Even in our present condition of unpreparedness no foreign power is in a position to invade us today. If we concentrate on our own defenses and build the strength that this nation should maintain, no foreign army will ever attempt to land on American shores. . . .

23.4   German and Japanese Aggression, 1935–1941

Between 1935 and 1941, many national boundaries in Europe and Asia were redrawn as Germany and Japan expanded their territorial holdings and influence. Despite President Roosevelt's efforts—in his "Quarantine Speech" and his support for Britain in 1940—American public opinion still opposed any intervention requiring the use of American military power. The two maps reproduced here show the expansion of German and Japanese territories and influence. The situation troubled many Americans—but not to the point of supporting intervention.

Consider:

1. *How the territorial expansion of Germany and Japan threatened American vital interests;*
2. *How "interventionists" could use these two maps to support American intervention as a means of preventing further expansion.*

GERMAN AND ITALIAN EXPANSION, 1935-1940

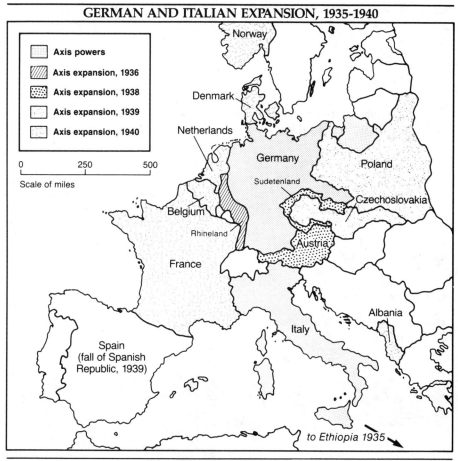

Axis powers
Axis expansion, 1936
Axis expansion, 1938
Axis expansion, 1939
Axis expansion, 1940

0   250   500
Scale of miles

Norway
Denmark
Netherlands
Germany
Poland
Sudetenland
Czechoslovakia
Belgium
Rhineland
Austria
France
Albania
Italy
Spain
(fall of Spanish
Republic, 1939)
to Ethiopia 1935

JAPANESE EXPANSION, 1937-1941

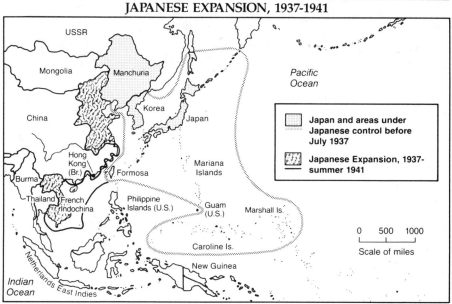

USSR
Mongolia   Manchuria
Pacific
Ocean
China   Korea
Japan
Hong
Kong
(Br.)   Formosa
Burma
Thailand French
Indochina
Philippine
Islands (U.S.)
Mariana
Islands
Guam
(U.S.)   Marshall Is.
Caroline Is.
New Guinea
Indian
Ocean   Netherlands East Indies

Japan and areas under
Japanese control before
July 1937

Japanese Expansion, 1937-
summer 1941

0   500   1000
Scale of miles

23.5   "To Fight for Freedom"

Norman Rockwell

On January 6, 1941, President Roosevelt delivered his State of the Union Address, known as the "Four Freedoms Speech." In it, the President declared America an arsenal for democracy that would support people everywhere "who are resisting aggression." The end result, he said, would be a victory for democratic principles and a "future world founded upon four essential human freedoms—freedom of speech, freedom of religion, freedom from want, and freedom from fear." The popular American artist Norman Rockwell, best known for his depiction of life in small-town USA, decided to illustrate the Four Freedoms in simple, everyday scenes that everyone could understand. Rockwell's versions of the Four Freedoms, reproduced here, were reprinted and distributed by the Office of War Information and became known around the world.

Consider:

1. *The image of America these posters conveyed to overseas audiences;*
2. *The ethnic or racial implications of the posters.*

Freedom of Worship

Freedom from Want

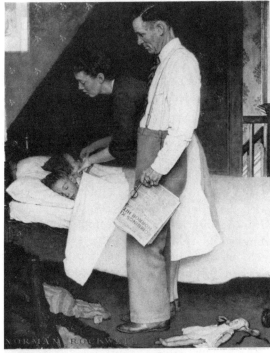

Freedom from Fear

Freedom of Speech

23.6   America and the Holocaust

David S. Wyman

In 1933, Adolph Hitler launched a program to "cleanse" Germany of Jewish influence through the forced emigration of Jews. In 1936, this program was extended to countries occupied by Germany. Hitler announced in January 1939 that European Jews would be liquidated if war came, and three years later, Germany adopted a "Final Solution" policy of massive annihilation of Jews, using modern industrial methods. Concentration camps were established where millions of Jews were sent to their death in gas chambers, after being subjected to torture and other atrocities. It was not until after the war ended that the public, especially in America, became aware of the death and horror inflicted in these camps. During the war, however, the Roosevelt administration did have reliable evidence of what was happening. Roosevelt's failure to deal with the issue of mass extermination of Jews has been attributed to his unwillingness to permit any distraction from the main task of defeating Germany. In his recent book, *The Abandonment of the Jews*, from which this excerpt is taken, historian David S. Wyman challenges this explanation, concluding that a more accurate description of why the Roosevelt administration did so little was "the absence of a strong desire to rescue Jews."

Consider:

1. *Why the United States State Department was unwilling to admit more Jewish refugees;*
2. *Whether the course of action suggested by Wyman would have been realistic;*
3. *Whether an American President has a moral responsibility to speak out and take action against nations that engage in "crimes against humanity."*

What could the American government have achieved if it had really committed itself to rescue? The possibilities were narrowed by the Nazis' determination to wipe out the Jews. War conditions themselves also made rescue difficult. And by mid-1942, when clear news of the systematic murder reached the West, two million Jews had already been massacred and the killing was going forward at a rapid rate. Most likely, it would not have been possible to rescue millions. But without impeding the war effort, additional tens of thousands—probably hundreds of thousands—could have been saved. What follows is a selection of twelve programs that could have been tried. All of them, and others, were proposed during the Holocaust.

(1) Most important, the War Refugee Board should have been established in 1942. And it should have received adequate government funding and much broader powers.

(2) The U.S. government, working through neutral governments or the Vatican, could have pressed Germany to release the Jews. If nothing else, this would have demonstrated to the Nazis—and to the world—that America was committed to saving the European Jews. . . .

(3) The United States could have applied constant pressure on Axis satellites to release their Jews. By spring 1943, the State Department knew that some satellites, convinced that the war was lost, were seeking favorable peace terms. Stern threats of punishment for mistreating Jews or allowing their deportation, coupled with indications that permitting them to leave for safety would earn Allied goodwill, could have opened the way to the rescue of large numbers from Rumania, Bulgaria, Hungary, and perhaps Slovakia. . . .

(4) Success in setting off an exodus of Jews would have posed the problem of where they could go. Strong pressure needed to be applied to neutral countries near the Axis (Spain, Portugal, Turkey, Switzerland, and Sweden) to take Jews in. . . .

(5) Locating enough outside havens, places beyond continental Europe where refugees could safely await postwar resettlement, would have presented difficulties. . . . But an American government deeply

SOURCE: *David S. Wyman,* The Abandonment of the Jews: America and the Holocaust, *1941–1945 (New York: Pantheon Books, 1985), 331–34, 336–37, 339.*

concerned about the Jews and willing to share the burden could have used its prestige and power to open doors. . . .

(6) Shipping was needed to transfer Jews from neutral countries to outside havens. Abundant evidence . . . proves that it could have been provided without interfering with the war effort. . . .

(7) A campaign to stimulate and assist escapes would have led to a sizable outflow of Jews. Once the neutral nations had agreed to open their borders, that information could have been publicized throughout Europe by radio, airdropped leaflets, and underground communications channels. . . .

(8) Much larger sums of money should have been transferred to Europe. After the WRB [War Refugee Board] was formed, the earlier, tiny trickle of funds from the United States was increased. But the amounts were still inadequate. . . .

(9) Much more effort should have gone into finding ways to send in food and medical supplies. The American government should have approached the problem far sooner than it did. And it should have put heavy pressure on the International Red Cross and British blockade authorities on this issue.

(10) Drawing on its great prestige and influence, the United States could have applied much more pressure than it did on neutral governments, the Vatican, and the International Red Cross to induce them to take earlier and more vigorous action. . . .

(11) Some military assistance was possible. The Air Force could have eliminated the Auschwitz killing installations. Some bombing of deportation railroads was feasible. The military could have aided in other ways without impeding the war effort. . . .

(12) Much more publicity about the extermination of the Jews should have been disseminated through Europe. Allied radio could have beamed the information for weeks at a time, on all possible wavelengths. . . .

. . . In November 1943, [Assistant Secretary of State] Breckinridge Long told the House Foreign Affairs Committee that lack of transportation was the reason the State Department was issuing so few visas. . . . In reality, ample shipping existed. Neutral vessels crossed the Atlantic throughout the war. Three Portuguese liners, with a combined capacity of 2,000 passengers, sailed regularly between Lisbon and U.S. ports. Each ship made the trip about every six weeks. Most of the time, because of the tight American visa policy, they carried only small fractions of their potential loads. . . .

. . . [Another] well-worn excuse for rejecting rescue proposals was the claim that they would detract from the military effort and thus prolong the war. This argument, entirely valid with regard to projects that actually would have hurt the war effort, was used almost automatically to justify inaction. Virtually none of the rescue proposals involved enough infringement on the war effort to lengthen the conflict at all or to increase the number of casualties, military or civilian. . . .

It was not a lack of workable plans that stood in the way of saving many thousands more European Jews. Nor was it insufficient shipping, the threat of infiltration by subversive agents, or the possibility that rescue projects would hamper the war effort. The real obstacle was the absence of a strong desire to rescue Jews.

23.7   Truman's Decision to Drop the Atomic Bomb

Harry S. Truman

In late July 1945, President Truman went to Potsdam, near Berlin, for a meeting with Winston Churchill and Josef Stalin. While the President and his entourage were on the way back to the United States, an atomic bomb was dropped on Hiroshima, Japan. Two days later a second bomb was dropped on Nagasaki. On August 15, 1945, the Japanese surrendered. Many Americans have questioned the wisdom and morality of using the atomic bomb. In recent years, some historians have suggested that the real reason for dropping the atomic bomb was to show the Soviet Union that the United States had a trump card in any postwar dispute. In his memoirs, from which this excerpt is taken, President Truman offers his own explanation of his decision to use the atomic bomb.

Consider:

1. *Whether President Truman attached too much importance to the high cost of a conventional land invasion of Japan;*
2. *Whether the President erred in viewing the atomic bomb strictly as a military weapon;*
3. *Whether public opinion today would support a similar Presidential decision to use atomic weapons.*

The historic message of the first explosion of an atomic bomb was flashed to me in a message from Secretary of War Stimson on the morning of July 16. The most secret and the most daring enterprise of the war had succeeded. We were now in possession of a weapon

---

SOURCE: *Harry S. Truman,* Memoirs: Year of Decision *vol. I (Doubleday & Co., Inc. Publishers, 1955), 415–17, 419–21. Used by permission of Margaret Truman Daniel.*

that would not only revolutionize war but could alter the course of history and civilization. . . .

The Army plan envisaged an amphibious landing in the fall of 1945 on the island of Kyushu, the southernmost of the Japanese home islands. . . . The first landing would then be followed approximately four months later by a second great invasion, which would be carried out by our Eighth and Tenth Armies, followed by the First Army transferred from Europe, all of which would go ashore in the Kanto plains area near Tokyo. In all, it had been estimated that it would require until the late fall of 1946 to bring Japan to her knees.

This was a formidable conception, and all of us realized fully that the fighting would be fierce and the losses heavy. . . .

There was, of course, always the possibility that the Japanese might choose to surrender sooner. Our air and fleet units had begun to inflict heavy damage on industrial and urban sites in Japan proper. . . .

Acting Secretary of State [Joseph] Grew had spoken to me in late May about issuing a proclamation that would urge the Japanese to surrender but would assure them that we would permit the Emperor to remain as head of the state. . . . I told him that I had already given thought to his matter myself and that it seemed to me a sound idea. . . .

It was my decision then that the proclamation to Japan should be issued from the forthcoming conference at Potsdam. . . . By that time, . . . we might know more about two matters of significance for our future effort: the participation of the Soviet Union and the atomic bomb. We knew that the bomb would receive its first test in mid-July. If the test of the bomb was successful, I wanted to afford Japan a clear chance to end the fighting before we made use of this newly gained power. If the test should fail, then it would be even more important to us to bring about a surrender before we had to make a physical conquest of Japan. General Marshall told me that it might cost half a million American lives to force the enemy's surrender on his home grounds. . . .

My own knowledge of these developments had come about only after I became President, when Secretary Stimson had given me the full story. He had told me at that time that the project was nearing completion and that a bomb could be expected within another four months. It was at his suggestion, too, that I had then set up a committee of top men and had asked them to study with great care the implications the new weapon might have for us. . . .

It was their [the committee's] recommendation that the bomb be used against the enemy as soon as it could be done. They recommended further that it should be used without specific warning and against a target that would clearly show its devastating strength. I had realized, of course, that an atomic bomb explosion would inflict damage and casualties beyond imagination. . . .

The final decision of where and when to use the atomic bomb was up to me. Let there be no mistake about it. I regarded the bomb as a military weapon and never had any doubt that it should be used. The top military advisers to the President recommended its use, and when I talked to Churchill he unhesitatingly told me that he favored the use of the atomic bomb if it might aid to end the war.

In deciding to use this bomb I wanted to make sure that it would be used as a weapon of war in the manner prescribed by the laws of war. That meant that I wanted it dropped on a military target. I had told Stimson that the bomb should be dropped as nearly as possibly upon a war production center of prime military importance.

Stimson's staff had prepared a list of cities in Japan that might serve as targets. Kyoto, though favored by General Arnold as a center of military activity, was eliminated when Secretary Stimson pointed out that it was a cultural and religious shrine of the Japanese.

Four cities were finally recommended as targets: Hiroshima, Kokura, Niigata, and Nagasaki. They were listed in that order as targets for the first attack. The order of selection was in accordance with the military importance of these cities, but allowance would be given for weather conditions at the time of the bombing. Before the selected targets were approved as proper for military purposes, I personally went over them in detail with Stimson, Marshall, and Arnold, and we discussed the matter of timing and the final choice of the first target.

. . . In order to get preparations under way, the War Department was given orders [that] the first bomb would be dropped as soon after August 3 as weather would permit. . . .

With this order the wheels were set in motion for the first use of an atomic weapon against a military target. I had made the decision. I also instructed Stimson that the order would stand unless I notified him that the Japanese reply to our ultimatum was acceptable. . . .

On July 28 Radio Tokyo announced that the Japanese government would continue to fight. There was no formal reply to the joint ultimatum of the United States, the United Kingdom, and China. There was no alternative now. The bomb was scheduled to be dropped after August 3 unless Japan surrendered before that day.

On August 6, the fourth day of the journey home from Potsdam, came the historic news that shook the world. . . .

CHAPTER QUESTIONS

1. *Identify and explain the continuous elements in American foreign policy between the years 1921–1932 and 1933–1941.*
2. *Critics have charged that President Roosevelt's failure to rescue European Jews from the German Holocaust and President Truman's decision to drop the atomic bomb on Japan were both failures in moral leadership. Do you feel these charges are justified? Explain.*

Chapter 24

Homefront: The Experience of Total War

The Japanese attack on Pearl Harbor propelled the United States into total war for the first time since the Civil War. Although no battles were fought on American soil, the nation's military and industrial mobilization efforts affected the lives of nearly all Americans. Social and economic changes occurred rapidly at home and had far-reaching consequences. In some instances, trends that started during the Depression and New Deal were reinforced—as, for example, the expanding size and scope of the federal government, the widespread mobility of the population, and the extensive participation of women in the work force. In other instances, the war produced new developments. These included the beginning of a successful attack on racial segregation, the rise of organized labor as an important political force, and the emergence of a close relationship between industry and government—especially for defense purposes—that would outlast the war.

After Pearl Harbor, most Americans supported the nation's entry into the war wholeheartedly. This unity did not, however, dispel racial antagonisms, and in some cases civil liberties were curtailed. The most drastic example of such abridgment of rights was the forced relocation of over 100,000 Japanese-Americans from their homes on the West Coast—an action that was approved by the Supreme Court.

Many other people relocated voluntarily during the war, responding to job opportunities in areas where defense plants were located. These massive population movements disrupted many traditional social patterns, and aggravated racial and ethnic tensions.

Full-scale industrial mobilization also created special opportunities for minority and women workers, people who had been the "last hired, first fired" during the Depression. Though social attitudes failed to keep pace with economic realities, minority groups' civil rights and women's rights received substantial boosts from wartime developments.

Fighting against Nazi racial supremacy, the United States could not continue to condone racial discrimination at home (though the relocation of Japanese-Americans represented a major blot on this awakening civil-rights consciousness). Because the government depended on popular commitment for fighting the war, it had to ensure that all Americans felt they were important participants in the mobilization effort. The "democratizing" of the tax burden was one result of this policy.

The selections in this chapter deal with these important aspects of American participation in World War II. They describe and illuminate economic, social, and political developments that redefined relationships among American citizens and between organizations and individuals and the government. These changing relationships, in turn, were to lead to a distinctively different society in postwar America.

Chronology

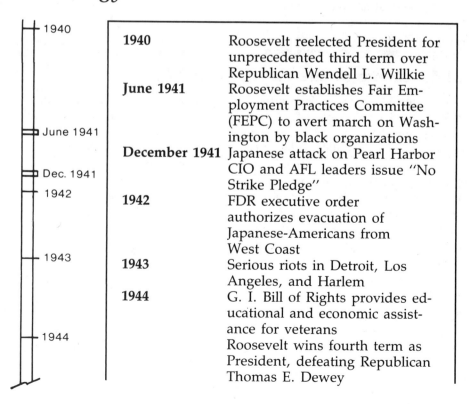

1940	Roosevelt reelected President for unprecedented third term over Republican Wendell L. Willkie
June 1941	Roosevelt establishes Fair Employment Practices Committee (FEPC) to avert march on Washington by black organizations
December 1941	Japanese attack on Pearl Harbor CIO and AFL leaders issue "No Strike Pledge"
1942	FDR executive order authorizes evacuation of Japanese-Americans from West Coast
1943	Serious riots in Detroit, Los Angeles, and Harlem
1944	G. I. Bill of Rights provides educational and economic assistance for veterans Roosevelt wins fourth term as President, defeating Republican Thomas E. Dewey

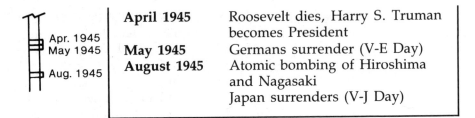

April 1945	Roosevelt dies, Harry S. Truman becomes President
May 1945	Germans surrender (V-E Day)
August 1945	Atomic bombing of Hiroshima and Nagasaki Japan surrenders (V-J Day)

Apr. 1945
May 1945
Aug. 1945

Documents

24.1   Image of the Republic at War

The United States was drawn into World War II by an attack on its military forces. Unlike World War I, there was little need for the government to persuade the public of the need to fight. Total war, however, required total mobilization—military, industrial, and even social—and this massive national effort called for extraordinary public commitment. To sustain this commitment and enthusiasm, President Roosevelt established the Office of War Information, which channeled war news and propaganda to newspapers, magazines, and radio broadcasting stations (see Doc. 23.5). At least as important in stimulating patriotism, however, were the many posters produced by the government during the war. One such poster is reproduced here.

Consider:

1. *The symbols that are employed in the poster to call up patriotic, democratic, and militaristic responses;*
2. *How the symbols in this poster compare to early "images of the Republic" (see Doc. 6.9).*

SOURCE: *Library of Congress.*

24.2   Labor Debates the "No Strike Pledge"
Michigan CIO Council

As defense production boosted the American economy in 1940 and 1941, organized labor became militant, attempting through numerous strikes to increase wages that workers considered to be insufficient. Therefore, the "no strike pledge" of the Congress of Industrial Organizations (CIO) and American Federation of Labor (AFL), issued shortly after the attack on Pearl Harbor, was controversial among rank-and-file union members. Worker opposition to the pledge increased with unpopular rulings by the newly established National War Labor Board. At its annual meeting in the summer of 1943, the Michigan CIO Council debated and eventually passed a resolution calling for repeal of the pledge. This excerpt from the proceedings of that meeting includes arguments for and against the resolution.

Consider:

1. *What the strongest arguments were on each side of the question;*
2. *Whether the leaders of the CIO and AFL acted in the best interests of union members in making such a pledge;*
3. *What options dissatisfied workers had during the war, after their leaders had promised no work stoppages.*

DELEGATE RUTH BIGGIN . . . Mr. Chairman, I think this resolution is an insult to Phil Murray, to President Roosevelt and to all the win-the-war forces and labor organization itself and to all labor people who are interested in winning the war. . . .

I think this resolution should be defeated. I came here in the interest of extending the CIO program and policy for winning the war. . . .

DELEGATE REYNOLDS: . . . Mr. Chairman, I rise to support the resolution. I believe that we of labor should stay on the side of labor. The reactionary forces are trying to have us vote down this resolution which takes away the right of labor to get its rightful gains and the only way to get those gains, and there isn't any use of kidding ourselves, is by striking. I don't believe we should strike these plants unless we absolutely have to. You can take the Chrysler workers. Chrysler workers are underpaid. We have our contract. We have been trying to get a contract or some six or seven months out of the War Labor Board and what do we get. We get just a plain run around! When we had a three-day stoppage, the War Labor Board promised us that they would get the Chrysler contract out of the red tape that it is meshed down in Washington inside of two weeks. Here it is going into another five or six weeks and we still have not a contract. . . . When we had that three day stoppage we wanted them to upgrade people, people with seniority, people that have a right to be upgraded. The company goes out on the street hiring, hiring for the good jobs and leaving the people with seniority on those lower priced jobs. . . .

The corporation that I work for knows only one language and that is the language of strike, and there isn't any one in this convention that can say they can deal with the Chrysler Corporation on any other terms. The only language they understand is the language of strike, and I say, let's give it to them. . . .

DELEGATE PAUL WEBER . . . : Brother President, I am speaking against the resolution. . . .

I would like . . . to make this point,—that when you strike in a war industry, you do not damage the management. Unfortunately,

SOURCE: Proceedings of the Sixth Annual Convention of the Michigan CIO Council, *June 28–July 1, 1943 (Detroit, Mich.), 137–39, 142.*

that is true. . . . The company has a contract with the government for X number of guns and they don't care whether you make those guns in six weeks or eight weeks. The only one hurt is the future of the labor movement and the capacity of the armed forces that defend us all. . . .

DELEGATE LUCAS: . . . Sometime ago labor made a very noble gesture. That was a matter of giving a no-strike pledge. Arguments to the contrary notwithstanding, there were certain commitments that were made to labor at that particular time. Does anyone in this hall question that these commitments have not been lived up to by the administration? I don't think that we can honestly say that the administration has done the things that [it] stated would be done at the time of giving the no-strike pledge.

. . . I have become convinced that the giving of the no-strike pledge was the biggest mistake that labor has ever made. (Applause and boos) . . .

24.3   Democratizing the Tax Structure
Mark H. Leff

Tax policy played an important role in the government's approach to conducting the war. Higher taxes could be used to raise needed revenues and, at the same time, to check the threat of inflation caused by too much money flowing into the economy. One key tax measure of the war years was the Revenue Act of 1942. This dramatically increased the tax rolls to include most wage-earning Americans, while raising corporate taxes and the excess profits tax. Historian Mark Leff discusses a second tax measure, the Current Tax Payment Act of 1943, in this excerpt from his study of New Deal tax policies. Leff argues that Roosevelt's wartime policies had symbolic and political as well as economic implications, and that they helped keep the spirit of the New Deal alive.

Consider:

1. *Whether taxation is an effective device for creating a sense of shared sacrifice—and thus, national unity—in wartime;*
2. *Whether Congress acted appropriately in shielding middle-class Americans from tax increases as high as those on the wealthy;*
3. *The factors, besides commitment to the war effort, that may have shaped FDR's wartime tax policies.*

. . . In World War II, the personal income tax ceased to be an indicator of affluence and became a mere token of citizenship. In 1943, the Current Tax Payment Act introduced the now-familiar withholding system in which estimated tax was deducted from paychecks (before World War II, tax bills only came due in quarterly installments in the year after the income was earned – an unsustainable system once the tax applied to most Americans, for it demanded too much of both the Internal Revenue Service and popular patterns of savings and accounting). No more than 5 percent of the population had been covered by taxable income-tax returns in any year in the 1930s; in World War II, the ranks of income-tax payers swelled to 74 percent. No longer was the income tax reliant on the $50,000+ brackets for most of its revenue; in fact, by the end of the war, these opulent Americans, though several times as numerous as in the Depression, accounted for only 13 percent of income-tax collections. Treasury Secretary Morgenthau observed that "for the first time in our history, the income tax is becoming a people's tax."

. . . Many recognized that the wartime hike in taxes on the upper brackets "would not yield great revenue" because of already-high rates and because "the total of income in these brackets is not a large percentage of the national income." To cap strong wartime inflationary pressures, the income tax needed to rein in mass purchasing power and to significantly narrow the budget deficit, and that required a revamped income tax. . . . Lower tax exemptions and higher tax rates were also sanctified by the ethos of universal wartime participation and sacrifice, in which it became an asset "that the greatest possible number of persons may contribute directly to the costs of the defense program." Wartime economic advances facilitated this process, for it was far easier to raise taxes when paychecks, even after tax deductions, were substantially higher than those before the war. . . .

As in the New Deal, however, the financial and economic context of taxation affords an incomplete understanding of its role. Though the relatively affluent middle brackets faced vastly increased tax bills over those of the New Deal years (a family with two children, for example, owed less than $50 tax on a $5,000 salary in the late 1930s, but theoretically could pay more than $700 by 1943), the tax hammer did not come down as hard as it might have on this group. . . . Congressmen, of course, still sought to defend the middle class from excessive tax increases. This group, after all, made up "the most articulate part of the voting public," and congressmen were quick to assert that this "good solid element of society upon which we have to depend"

SOURCE: *Mark H. Leff, The Limits of Symbolic Reform: The New Deal and Taxation, 1933– 1939, 287–91. Copyright © 1984, Cambridge University Press. Reprinted with permission.*

deserved protection as "the backbone of the country." Though demands to tax the rich had slackened (particularly with the refurbished wartime reputation of industrialists), the . . . 1930s tendency to focus on taxing "them" (the surplus incomes of the specially privileged) carried over into the World War II conceptualization of income taxes. Thus, middle brackets were shielded from higher burdens by being included in the category of the presumptively overburdened common man.

Taxation also continued to play an important symbolic function. President Roosevelt was acutely aware that "a fair distribution of the war burden," or at least the semblance of it, was "necessary for national unity" at a time when the government needed to "impose sacrifices on all of us." . . . Not to "cut the superfluities of the few" would "have a shattering effect on morale," for wage earners' sacrifice seemed contingent on the assurance that "their bosses are making at least faintly equivalent sacrifices." . . .

FDR was a past master at the use of taxation to convey the image of the hour. He explained at one point that he would prefer "to see a tax which would tax all income above $100,000 at the rate of 99½%." This even shocked his budget director, but the president's joking comeback was a revealing one: "Why not? None of us is ever going to make $100,000 a year. How many people report on that much income?" . . . In 1942 and again in 1943, he proposed that all income above $25,000 ($50,000 for families) be taxed away, saying that "all excess income should go to win the war." Inequities, he warned, "seriously affect the morale of soldiers and sailors, farmers and workers, imperiling efforts to stabilize wages and prices, and thereby impairing the effective prosecution of the war." When this income limit got nowhere in Congress, FDR acted on his own, handing down an executive order limiting after-tax salaries to $25,000 plus certain allowances, only to have his action indignantly repealed by Congress.

Surely more than posturing was involved here. Franklin Roosevelt sincerely disapproved of efforts to shift the wartime tax burden away from the rich; he played a critical role in blocking congressional efforts to substitute a regressive federal sales tax for income-tax increases. He also became increasingly disillusioned with what he saw as forces of petty selfishness in the midst of a far nobler world crusade, a bitterness that emerged most prominently in 1944 when he vetoed a loophole-ridden tax bill as "not for the needy, but for the greedy." . . . taxes and other countermeasures against wartime profiteering were an integral part of the administration's antiinflation program, not simply to collect revenue, but also to legitimize the sacrifices that war necessitated and to take the edge off the grievances that war engendered.

Thus, even in war, which required a vast expansion and renovation of the tax system, the symbolic role of New Deal tax policy was prominent.

24.4   Japanese-American Relocation: Civil Rights Abridged
U.S. House Select Committee Hearings

The surprise attack on Pearl Harbor intensified long-held prejudices and fears in the United States of the "yellow peril." In February 1942, President Roosevelt yielded to strong pressure, largely from politicians and the press on the West Coast, and issued an executive order that enabled the army to relocate more than 110,000 *Issei* (foreign-born Japanese noncitizens) and *Nisei* (United States-born Japanese-American citizens) to government-run processing centers and eventually to ten internment camps. The War Relocation Authority that was in charge of the camps allowed 35,000 of these detainees to leave for new jobs elsewhere in the country and about 8,000 (mostly *Nisei*) to go to Japan. The remaining Japanese-Americans were kept in the camps until January 1945.

In these excerpts from hearings held by a select House committee right after Roosevelt's executive order, California Attorney General Earl Warren (later Chief Justice of the Supreme Court) and Louis Goldblatt of the California State Industrial Union Council (affiliated with the CIO) present some of the arguments for and against relocation.

Consider:

1. *The persuasiveness of Warren's reasoning on the nature of the Japanese-American threat;*
2. *How the attitudes expressed by Warren compare to fears of alien subversion during World War I;*
3. *Why the CIO spoke out against the sweeping nature of Japanese-American relocation.*

Attorney General WARREN. . . . For some time I have been of the opinion that the solution of our alien enemy problem with all its ramifications, which include the descendants of aliens, is not only a Federal problem but is a military problem. We believe that all of the decisions in that regard must be made by the military command that is charged with the security of this area. I am convinced that the fifth-column activities of our enemy call for the participation of people who are in fact American citizens, and that if we are to deal realistically with the problem we must realize that we will be obliged in time of stress to deal with subversive elements of our own citizenry.

SOURCE: *U.S. House of Representatives,* Hearings Before the Select Committee Investigating National Defense Migration, *Seventy-Seventh Congress, 2d Session (February 21 and 23, 1942),* *11010–12, 11014–15, 11017, 11179–80, 11185.*

. . . the civil authorities cannot take protective measures against people of that character. . . .

. . . We believe that any delay in the adoption of the necessary protective measures is to invite disaster. It means that we, too, will have in California a Pearl Harbor incident. . . .

Unfortunately, . . . many of our people and some of our authorities and, I am afraid, many of our people in other parts of the country are of the opinion that because we have had no sabotage and no fifth column activities in this State since the beginning of the war, that means that none have been planned for us. But I take the view that that is the most ominous sign in our whole situation. It convinces me more than perhaps any other factor that the sabotage that we are to get, the fifth column activities that we are to get, are timed just like Pearl Harbor was timed. . . .

I believe that we are just being lulled into a false sense of security and that the only reason we haven't had disaster in California is because it has been timed for a different date. . . .

I want to say that the consensus of opinion among the law-enforcement officers of this State is that there is more potential danger among the group of Japanese who are born in this country than from the alien Japanese who were born in Japan. That might seem an anomaly to some people, but the fact is that, in the first place, there are twice as many of them. There are 33,000 aliens and there are 66,000 born in this country.

In the second place, most of the Japanese who were born in Japan are over 55 years of age. There has been practically no migration to this country since 1924. But in some instances the children of those people have been sent to Japan for their education, either in whole or in part, and while they are over there they are indoctrinated with the idea of Japanese imperialism. They receive their religious instruction which ties up their religion with their Emperor, and they come back here imbued with the ideas and the policies of Imperial Japan. . . .

. . . We believe that when we are dealing with the Caucasian race we have methods that will test the loyalty of them, and we believe that we can, in dealing with the Germans and the Italians, arrive at some fairly sound conclusions because of our knowledge of the way they live in the community and have lived for many years. But when we deal with the Japanese we are in an entirely different field and we cannot form any opinion that we believe to be sound. Their method of living, their language, make for this difficulty. . . .

It seems strange to us that airplane manufacturing plants should be entirely surrounded by Japanese land occupancies. It seems to us that it is more than circumstance that after certain Government air bases were established Japanese undertook farming operations in close proximity to them. You can hardly grow a jackrabbit in some of the places where they presume to be carrying on farming operations close to an Army bombing base. . . .

MR. GOLDBLATT. . . . We naturally go along and concur with all the recommendations that the Government deems necessary to safeguard this territory. We feel, however, that a good deal of this problem has gotten out of hand, . . . inasmuch as both the local and State authorities, instead of becoming bastions of defense, of democracy and justice, joined the wolf pack when the cry came out "Let's get the yellow menace." As a matter of fact, we believe the present situation is a great victory for the yellow press and for the fifth column that is operating in this country, which is attempting to convert this war from a war against the Axis Powers into a war against the "yellow peril." . . .

What we are concerned with, Mr. Chairman is this: That if this is to become the index of our dealings with the alien problem—in other words, that if we are not to deal only with aliens but also with the descendants of aliens—then there is no limit to this problem and the program, and this vitally affects our unions. . . . I am positive the military authorities know that neither Hitler nor Mussolini will hesitate a moment to sacrifice any Germans or Italians in this country if that will suit their purpose in an all-out war.

So that we can expect, I think, that if this campaign of isolating the Japanese is successful the next step will be for several incidents to occur which involves Germans or Italians; then the whole of the wolf pack will scream to the moon again and this time it will be "Evacuate all Italians, evacuate all Germans." The principle will have been set; the pattern will have been cut as it has been by the Hearst press, by the rabid, hysterical elements. . . .

We believe the efforts of the Federal Government should not be based on making distinctions by race, nationality, or citizenship. We favor a campaign that will detect sabotage no matter what its source and from which there will be no immunity by virtue of wealth, political connections, or position in society.

24.5 Race Relations during the War

Carey McWilliams

To a nation at war against Nazi ideals of racial supremacy, persistent problems of race relations at home were embarrassing. Moreover, the large-scale industrial and military mobilization required by the war effort made discrimination against blacks and other minorities impractical. These factors, together with the rising self-consciousness and assertiveness of racial minorities (see Doc. 22.6), helped produce an environment in which advances in civil rights were possible. However, the road to better race relations was bumpy, for the economic and demographic developments of the war also stimulated new interracial tensions. The following excerpt from a 1946 essay by civil-rights authority Carey McWilliams discusses race relations during World War II.

Consider:

1. *How wartime mobilization increased interracial tensions;*
2. *Why, in World War II, "the wartime prejudices of the majority tended to be directed at our own racial minorities rather than, as in World War I, against enemy aliens";*
3. *Whether the developments McWilliams describes justify the optimism of his concluding observation.*

Outwardly "the race question" has passed through three clearly defined phases since the war began: a period of mounting tension and friction (from the outset of the defense program to January 1, 1943); a period of overt hostility and aggression (through 1943); and a period in which the democratic forces of the nation mobilized to meet the menace so clearly apparent in the shocking events of 1943 (from midsummer, 1943, to date).

To fight a total war successfully on a global scale, America quickly realized that all available sources of manpower, including the racial minorities, must be utilized—in the services, in the defense industries, in all phases of the war effort. The attempt to make full utilization of the racial minorities, however, ran counter to long-established usages and customs. Since it involved the grafting of emergency wartime requirements upon a peacetime structure of race relations, the effort was naturally productive of considerable friction, particularly in the crowded defense areas, where sharp issues arose over housing, employment, and transportation. By rapidly shifting populations from rural to urban areas, the war heightened existing tensions and created new tension areas. . . .

. . . On February 28, 1942, a savage riot occurred at the Sojourner Truth Housing project in Detroit, in which prospective Negro tenants were attacked with clubs, knives, rifles, and shotguns, resulting in many injuries and over 104 arrests. When 14 Negro families were finally moved into the project in May, 2,000 National Guardsmen were on duty to give them protection. Two of the men arrested for fomenting this riot—which was a dress rehearsal for the Detroit riots of 1943— were members of an organization which had been disseminating pro-Axis propaganda. . . .

SOURCE: *Carey McWilliams, "What We Did About Racial Minorities," in* While You Were Gone: A Report on Wartime Life in the United States, *ed. Jack Goodman (New York: Simon and Schuster, 1946), 89–97. Copyright © 1946, 1973 by Simon and Schuster, Inc.*

Also during this period enemy agents sought to foment racial discord by direct instigation. . . . The evidence would indicate, however, that these activities were not particularly successful. Even the limited effectiveness of such enemy-inspired activity was largely due to the fact that the war had momentarily created a situation which could be exploited to advantage.

Where the enemy did make effective use of racial discord in America was in their world-wide propaganda. Every racial "incident" was immediately seized upon for propaganda purposes. Not only did such incidents serve to discredit America, but they tended to support the Japanese propaganda thesis that this was a racial war. . . .

In the United States important changes began to take place, as the war progressed, in the attitude of the minorities toward each other and toward the majority; in the attitude of the majority toward the minorities; and in the conception which the minorites entertained of their own predicament. A noticeable ferment began to develop in the minority groups, in particular the Negro minority. . . .

Strangely enough, the wartime prejudices of the majority tended to be directed at our own racial minorities rather than, as in World War I, against enemy aliens and naturalized citizens of German descent. . . .

Realizing that the dynamics of the war were releasing new forces which were profoundly disturbing the racial *status quo* in America, the traditionally biased section of the white majority became increasingly provocative. Demagogues, in and out of Congress, began to indulge in rabid anti-Negro speeches which not only infuriated the Negro minority but shocked large sections of the white majority. . . .

Also during 1941 and 1942 a noticeable ferment began to develop among middle-class white elements on the racial question. . . . As the American people became more deeply involved in the war, the inconsistency between our traditional ideals and our racial practices became increasingly embarrassing and progressively indefensible. . . .

Thus, as the war developed, a triangle of forces began to form in America: better organized than ever before, the racial minorities were struggling to fight free from all restrictions of caste and color; one section of the majority, responding to the challenging issues of the war, began to rally to the defense of the minorities; while a minority of the majority redoubled its efforts in defense of the prewar racial *status quo.*

The dangers implicit in these mounting tensions were clearly apparent. . . .

The explosions came in 1943. They began with the so-called "zoot-suit" riot in Los Angeles early in June (although there had been some violence in connection with a "hate" strike in the shipyards at Mobile, Alabama, on May 29). Then came the Detroit race riot of June 20–21, the worst race riot which America had experienced in twenty-five years, followed by subsequent disturbances in Beaumont and Harlem. . . . The rapid succession of these violent and destructive riots, coming as they did in the midst of the greatest war in which America has participated, profoundly shocked the American people. . . .

Out of this . . . activity came a host of conferences, institutes, programs, and studies, constituting in the aggregate an enormous amount of energy and effort. Much of this activity was sporadic and unintegrated and will doubtless lapse now that the war is over. But it was this activity which accounts for the fact that few racial disturbances were recorded in 1944 . . . or 1945. Interest in racial minorities, moreover, has continued to increase.

. . . Forced to deal with the realities of the problem, if only on an emergency wartime basis, the American people have begun to see through some of the myths and fallacies which have long enshrouded their thinking about racial issues.

24.6   Women and Wartime Mobilization

Susan M. Hartmann

The war not only opened up employment opportunities for women, it virtually forced them to enter the work force. As a result, several million female workers took jobs for the first time, often in defense industries where hours were long and wages relatively high. These working women had special problems. As in the past, they encountered discrimination in unions; and those who were mothers with husbands away at war had to worry about maintaining a home, obtaining enough food and other necessities, and caring for their children—at the end of their long working days. In this selection from her book *The Home Front and Beyond*, historian Susan Hartmann points out that social attitudes toward women in the work force changed only gradually—and partially—during the war. Still, most historians agree that these years marked a turning point. Though attitudes about working women were slow to change, the economic opportunities open to them expanded significantly during and after the war.

Consider:

1. *How attitudes toward working women during the Depression (see Doc. 22.5) compare with attitudes during World War II;*
2. *The impact on family life of wartime employment patterns;*
3. *The overall impact of the war years on the status of American women.*

The material deprivation, the economic discrimination and the psychological discouragement experienced by women during the Depression made the Second World War all the more important in improving their lives and status. Because the nation mobilized for war required the active support of every member, the media continuously made women aware of their importance, not alone as mothers, wives and homemakers, but also as workers, citizens, and even as soldiers. As their value in extrafamilial roles increased in the public consciousness, women also benefited from real opportunities to earn income, to enter new employment fields, and to perform in a wide variety of areas that had hitherto been reserved for men.

Although the popular ideology that women's primary role was in the home survived the war both in public discourse and in the beliefs of most women, the military crisis did create an ideological climate supportive of women's movement into the public realm. In the first place, the public depiction of the war as a struggle for freedom and democracy provided symbols for women to enlist in their own cause. Moreover, where the Depression had encouraged public criticism of women workers, the labor shortage of the war years necessitated appeals by government and employers for women to take jobs. The need for female labor lent a new legitimacy to the woman worker and made government, employers, and labor unions more willing to consider the needs of women. Finally, wartime propaganda enhanced the importance of women as citizens and assigned them significant public responsibilities. . . .

Women's employment grew in every occupational field but that of domestic service. Their most spectacular gains, however, were in factory work, particularly in those industries producing defense materials where their numbers mushroomed by 460 percent. . . .

Women enjoyed higher incomes in the war economy as their wages in industry increased both absolutely and in relation to men's. Female gains were highest in war manufacturing, where they worked in formerly male jobs, but their earnings also rose in industries where women were traditionally concentrated, as well as in office work and in service industries. The general labor shortage elevated women's earnings, but of greatest importance were the opportunities for women to work in jobs where rates were historically higher. In addition, women, though not to the same extent as men, worked longer hours during the war, and government and union equal pay policies, while never systematically applied, helped to raise women's income. . . .

Public awareness of women's real and potential contributions to national goals was manifested in legislative action which chipped away at some of the legal and civil disabilities suffered by women. Four

SOURCE: *Susan M. Hartmann*, The Home Front and Beyond: American Women in the 1940s *(Boston: Twayne Publishers, 1982), 20–23, 26–27. Copyright © 1982. Reprinted with the permission of G. K. Hall and Co., Boston.*

state legislatures enacted equal pay laws during the war, and several others removed their bans against women jurors. In direct contrast to attitudes and practices during the Depression, a number of states passed laws protecting married women from discrimination in employment. In addition, for the first time Congress seriously considered an equal pay bill and an equal rights amendment to the Constitution. . . .

Less apparent at the time were the limitations placed upon women's aspirations by the very agencies that were encouraging women to assume larger functions outside the home. The nation desperately needed the services of women during the war, but it was equally resolutely attached to the traditional sexual order. Indeed, as war brought social dislocation of an inordinate degree, the institution of the family with wife and mother at its core took on even more significance. Americans adjusted to women's new prominence in the public realm because that position was defined in terms which denied the erosion of cherished social norms.

The public discourse on women's new wartime roles established three conditions which set limits on social change. The first was that women were replacing men in the world outside the home only "for the duration." . . . The second condition was that women would retain their "femininity" even as they performed masculine duties. Photographs of women war workers emphasized glamour, and advertising copy assured readers that beneath the overalls and grease stains there remained a true woman, feminine in appearance and behavior. Finally, the media emphasized the eternal feminine motivations behind women's willingness to step out of customary roles. Patriotic motives were not ignored; but also highlighted was women's determination to serve their families albeit in novel ways. In the public image, women took war jobs to bring their men home more quickly and to help make the world a more secure place for their children. . . .

That many of the crisis-induced changes in women's lives were reversed by the end of the 1940s does not cancel out the importance of World War II in altering sex roles. The contradiction between women's behavior and deeply entrenched social beliefs had never been greater, and the resolution of that disharmony failed to return women to the status quo ante bellum. Although those conventional standards survived . . . women's behavior in the public realm had undergone considerable change and would continue to develop in altered patterns.

24.7   The Returning Hero: Contrasting Images
Norman Rockwell

The way soldiers returning from a war are viewed provides a good indication of the public's attitude toward that war. American artist Norman Rockwell (see Doc. 23.5), whose cover illustrations for the popular *Saturday*

Evening Post consistently reflected "mainstream" American values, captured two very different images of the "returning hero" in the *Post* covers reproduced here. The first appeared in February 1919, the second in May 1945.

Consider:

1. *The attitudes toward military life the two illustrations suggest;*
2. *What might account for these differences in outlook after the two wars.*

SOURCE: *Copyright © 1919 by the Curtis Publishing Company. Reprinted by permission of the Estate of Norman Rockwell.*

SOURCE: *Copyright © 1945 by the Curtis Publishing Company. Reprinted by permission of the Estate of Norman Rockwell.*

CHAPTER QUESTIONS

1. *Explain how the experience of World War II represented a "democratizing" influence on American life.*
2. *Discuss the major effects of the war on American economic life.*
3. *Compare the way the government handled issues related to civil rights and civil liberties during World War I and World War II.*

part seven

part seven THE FRUSTRATIONS OF POWER, SINCE 1945

Chapter 25

The Cold War, 1949–1963

The unity of the wartime Allies began to fall apart in the postwar years as Russia and the United States emerged as superpowers with conflicting interests. Convinced that the Soviet Union would not adhere to agreements made during war, the Truman administration tried to contain Russian expansion without resorting to armed conflict. At first, containment consisted of rebuilding the economy and defenses of Europe. President Truman soon came to the conclusion, however, that a long-term strategic policy was needed, and his concern resulted in a National Security Council policy paper, NSC-68, that served as a blueprint for American foreign policy for the next two decades.

The first test of NSC-68 came in June 1950 when North Korea invaded South Korea, and the United States joined the United Nations in providing air, naval, and ground support to South Korea. Though it began as a "police action," American involvement increased sharply after China intervened in the Korean War in November. For more than two years, a series of see-saw battles were fought with no clear-cut victor. When the war turned into a stalemate, American public opinion called for withdrawal of American troops.

In the late 1940s and early 1950s, conservative elements at home were concerned about Communist subversive activities in the United States. Between 1950 and 1954, Republican Senator Joseph R. McCarthy of Wisconsin turned the investigation and exposure of Communist activities into a personal crusade that came to be known as "McCarthyism."

Dwight D. Eisenhower, elected President in 1952, succeeded in ending the Korean War and soon revised America's containment policy.

His "New Look" defense policy emphasized the development and use of high-technology weaponry: strategic bombers and nuclear missiles were to respond in "massive retaliation" against any Soviet infringement of America's national interests. During the Eisenhower years, these national interests expanded, through a series of mutual security agreements, to cover most of the globe. In the same period, the United States attempted to stop Communist aggression worldwide by a variety of covert actions.

The election of John F. Kennedy in 1960 marked another shift in America's national-defense policy and a change in the Cold War as well. Like Eisenhower, President Kennedy endorsed the policy of resisting Communism with military force wherever America's vital interests were at stake; but Kennedy replaced the "New Look" with a policy of "flexible response" and limited war.

In the 1960s, Southeast Asia became the first major battleground for this policy. Kennedy accepted without question the strategic importance of South Vietnam in the fight against Communism. Rejecting the view that the Vietnamese conflict was a civil war, the President escalated the American presence there. By November 1963, at the time of his death, 16,000 American troops were in South Vietnam.

The selections in this chapter deal with a number of critical issues of the Cold War during the period from 1949 to 1963. These include the connection between public opinion and foreign policy, the use of covert activities against the Communist threat, the rise of a military-industrial complex, and the beginning of the war in Vietnam.

Chronology

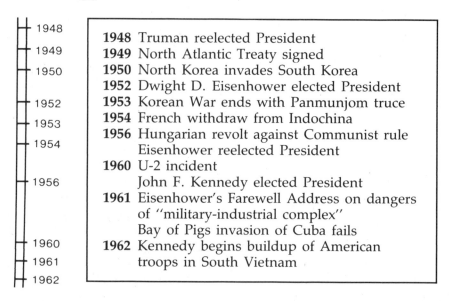

1948	**1948** Truman reelected President
1949	**1949** North Atlantic Treaty signed
1950	**1950** North Korea invades South Korea
	1952 Dwight D. Eisenhower elected President
1952	**1953** Korean War ends with Panmunjom truce
1953	**1954** French withdraw from Indochina
1954	**1956** Hungarian revolt against Communist rule
	Eisenhower reelected President
	1960 U-2 incident
1956	John F. Kennedy elected President
	1961 Eisenhower's Farewell Address on dangers
	of "military-industrial complex"
	Bay of Pigs invasion of Cuba fails
1960	**1962** Kennedy begins buildup of American
1961	troops in South Vietnam
1962	

Documents

25.1   American Commitment to Cold War: National Security Council Document 68

Department of State

After the fall of the nationalist Chinese government and Russia's explosion of an atomic bomb in 1949, President Truman called for a reevaluation of American foreign policy. On January 31, 1950, the President directed the Secretary of State and the Secretary of Defense to reexamine American national security objectives and strategic plans. In April 1950, a report called NSC-68 was submitted to President Truman. His approval of the document committed the United States to a policy of protecting the Free World from Soviet domination or subversion. The underlying themes of this report were that American-Soviet conflict was global in scope and military in nature and that budget considerations should not limit the actions of the United States. This excerpt from the report discusses Soviet aims and recommends eleven specific tasks for the United States.

Consider:

1. *How NSC-68 influenced America's responses to Communist North Korea's invasion of South Korea in June 1950 and to Communist expansion in Southeast Asia in the 1960s;*

2. *The implications of NSC-68 for military spending by the United States and its allies;*

3. *The implications of the call for "covert actions" in NSC-68.*

It is quite clear from Soviet theory and practice that the Kremlin seeks to bring the free world under its dominion by the methods of the cold war. The preferred technique is to subvert by infiltration and intimidation. Every institution of our society is an instrument which it is sought to stultify and turn against our purposes. Those that touch most closely our material and moral strength are obviously the prime targets, labor unions, civic enterprises, schools, churches, and all media for influencing opinion. The effort is not so much to make them serve obvious Soviet ends as to prevent them from serving our ends, and thus to make them sources of confusion in our economy, our culture and our body politic. . . .

At the same time the Soviet Union is seeking to create overwhelming military force, in order to back up infiltration with intimidation. In the only terms in which it understands strength, it is seeking to demonstrate to the free world that force and the will to use it are on the side of the Kremlin, that those who lack it are decadent and doomed. . . .

. . . The frustration of the Kremlin design requires the free world to develop a successfully functioning political and economic system and a vigorous political offensive against the Soviet Union. These, in turn, require an adequate military shield under which they can develop. It is necessary to have the military power to deter, if possible, Soviet expansion, and to defeat, if necessary, aggressive Soviet or Soviet-directed actions of a limited or total character. . . .

A program for rapidly building up strength and improving political and economic conditions will place heavy demands on our courage and intelligence; it will be costly; it will be dangerous. But half-measures will be more costly and more dangerous, for they will be inadequate to prevent and may actually invite war. Budgetary considerations will need to be subordinated to the stark fact that our very independence as a nation may be at stake.

A comprehensive and decisive program to win the peace and frustrate the Kremlin design should be so designed that it can be sustained for as long as necessary to achieve our national objectives. It would probably involve:

(1) The development of an adequate political and economic framework for the achievement of our long-range objectives.

(2) A substantial increase in expenditures for military purposes. . . .

(3) A substantial increase in military assistance programs, designed to foster cooperative efforts, which will adequately and efficiently meet the requirements of our allies. . . .

(4) Some increase in economic assistance programs and recognition of the need to continue these programs until their purposes have been accomplished.

SOURCE: *Department of State*, Foreign Relations of the United States, 1950 *(Washington, D.C.: Government Printing Office, 1977), II, 263–264, 282, 285.*

(5) A concerted attack on the problem of the United States balance of payments, along the lines already approved by the President.

(6) Development of programs designed to build and maintain confidence among other peoples in our strength and resolution, and to wage overt psychological warfare calculated to encourage mass defections from Soviet allegiance and to frustrate the Kremlin design in other ways.

(7) Intensification of affimative and timely measures and operations by covert means in the fields of economic warfare and political and psychological warfare with a view to fomenting and supporting unrest and revolt in selected strategic satellite countries.

(8) Development of internal security and civilian defense programs.

(9) Improvement and intensification of intelligence activities.

(10) Reduction of Federal expenditures for purposes other than defense and foreign assistance, if necessary by the deferment of certain desirable programs.

(11) Increased taxes.

25.2   American Public Opinion and the Korean War, 1950–1952

The Gallup Poll

Since World War II, public opinion polls have played a significant role in influencing government policy on both domestic and foreign issues. Based upon scientific sampling techniques, public opinion polls such as the Gallup Poll and the Roper Poll provide reliable information about Americans' views on a wide variety of topics. Between August 1950 and July 1952, the Gallup Poll asked a representative sample of Americans a series of questions about the Korean War. The responses to these questions are excerpted here.

Consider:

1. *What these responses reveal about attitudes toward American involvement in the Korean War;*
2. *Which events in the war may have influenced responses in the polls of October 13, 1950, and January 22, 1951;*
3. *How much public opinion polls should influence the conduct of American foreign policy.*

OCTOBER 4, 1950
KOREAN WAR SURVEY

Survey #460–TPS   Question #9

In view of the developments since we entered the fighting in Korea, do you think the United States made a mistake in deciding to defend Korea, or not?

Mistake 20%
Not a mistake.. 65
No opinion 15

OCTOBER 13, 1950
KOREAN WAR SURVEY

Survey #461–K   Question #8c

What do you, yourself, think—should the fighting stop when we have succeeded in pushing the North Koreans back over the line from where they started— or do you think we should continue the fight in their own territory until they have surrendered?

Stop fighting... 27%
Continue fighting 64
No opinion   9

JANUARY 22, 1951
KOREAN WAR SURVEY

Survey #469–K   Question #6

Now that Communist China has entered the fighting in Korea with forces far outnumbering the United Nations troops there, which one of these two courses would you, yourself, prefer that we follow: Pull our troops out of Korea as fast as possible, or keep our troops there to fight these larger forces?

Pull out 66%
Stay there 25
No opinion   9

Survey #469–K   Question #3

In view of developments since we entered the fighting in Korea, do you think the United States made a mistake in deciding to defend South Korea, or not?

Yes 49%
No 38
No opinion 13

SOURCE: *George Gallup*, The Gallup Poll: Public Opinion, 1935–1971 *(New York: Random House, 1972), II, 942–43, 960–61, 972–73, 1052.*

MARCH 28, 1951
KOREAN WAR SURVEY

Survey #472–K   Question #8

If Communist China and the North Koreans agree to stop fighting in Korea, would you approve or disapprove of letting Korea be divided at the 38th parallel —the northern part to be run by the Chinese and North Korean Communists and the southern part by the South Koreans and the United Nations?

Approve.. 43%
Disapprove 36
No opinion 21

Survey #471–K   Question #4

Do you think the United States made a mistake in going into the war in Korea, or not?

By Education
College

Mistake 43%
Not a mistake.. 50
No opinion 7

High School

Mistake 50%
Not a mistake.. 41
No opinion 9

Grade School

Mistake 52%
Not a mistake.. 35
No opinion 13

APRIL 2, 1951
KOREAN WAR SURVEY

Survey #487–K   Question #4a

Do you think the United States made a mistake in going into the war in Korea, or not?

Yes 51%
No.. 35
No opinion 14

Survey #487–K   Question #4b

*Suppose that a truce settlement is reached in Korea. As matters stand today,
which side—ours or the enemy's—do you think will have won the bigger
victory?*

Our side. 30%
Enemy 33
Neither. 23
No opinion 14

25.3   The Origins of "McCarthyism"
Robert Griffith

Between 1950 and 1954, Republican Senator Joseph R. McCarthy of Wisconsin rose to national prominence by denouncing alleged Communist subversion and Communist sympathizers, particularly in the government.
Many historians have used the term "McCarthyism" to mean suspicion
about the loyalty of anyone who voiced unpopular, liberal, or controversial
views. McCarthyism, they argue, was an anti-liberal movement, a resurgence of a current in American history that tried to impose ideological
conformity on an ideologically and culturally pluralistic society. Historian
Robert Griffith has challenged this view. In his essay "American Politics
and the Origins of 'McCarthyism'," excerpted here, Griffith argues that
McCarthyism was not a mass movement launched by McCarthy but rather
a "product of the political system and its leaders."

Consider:

1. *Whether Griffith's evidence supports his evaluation of McCarthy and
   McCarthyism;*
2. *Whether Griffith's view of McCarthyism helps explain American politics
   in the 1950s;*
3. *Whether conditions similar to McCarthyism occurred in any other period
   in American history.*

. . . what is all too often overlooked is the congruence between
popular attitudes toward Communism and the attitudes of influential

public figures. Many prominent Republicans, for example, were constantly accusing the Roosevelt and Truman Administrations of selling out to Communism at home and abroad. . . . In denouncing Communism, then, Joe McCarthy . . . was adopting a political issue already sanctioned by much of the nation's political leadership.

The commonly accepted portrait of McCarthyism as a mass movement and McCarthy as a charismatic leader is, thus, badly overdrawn. People were less concerned about the threat of Communism and less favorably inclined toward McCarthy than is generally thought. Support for McCarthy, moreover, was closely identified with partisan Republicanism. . . .

But if McCarthyism is not to be understood primarily in terms of popular passion, then how do we explain the contentious and tumultuous politics of the mid-twentieth century? . . . it was primarily a product of the political system and its leaders. The latter did not simply respond to popular protest, but rather helped to generate the very sense of concern and urgency that came to dominate the decade. . . .

. . . Foremost among such politicans were those Republican and Democratic conservatives who had championed the anti-Communist issues since the thirties and who had maintained all along that Democratic liberalism was leading the country down the road to Communism. After 1945, however, this anti-reformist impulse was joined with the new foreign policy and internal security issues bred by the cold war. Congressional conservatives now charged that the Roosevelt and Truman Administrations were "soft" on Communism abroad and tolerant of subversion and disloyalty at home; and beginning in 1945 they launched a series of investigations into Communist activities designed in part to embarrass the government. . . .

The Communist issue was injected into the 1946 elections and was apparently a factor in the Republican triumph, especially among urban Catholics. In 1947–48 the Truman Administration responded to these pressures by justifying its foreign policies with a crusading anti-Communist rhetoric, by instituting a federal loyalty-security program, by prosecuting Communist party leaders under the Smith Act, and in general by stressing its own firm anti-Communist credentials. Indeed, by 1948 the Administration had succeeded, if only temporarily, in using the Communist issue to its own advantage against both the Progressives and the Republicans. . . .

SOURCE: *Robert Griffith, "American Politics and the Origins of 'McCarthyism',"* in The Specter: Original Essays on the Cold War and the Origins of McCarthyism, *ed. Robert Griffith and Athan Theoharis (New York: New Viewpoints, 1974), 4–5, 13–17.*

The rise of anti-Communism as an issue in national politics was accompanied by the growth of a derivative anti-Communist politics at the state and local levels. . . .

. . . state legislatures responded almost slavishly to the force of federal law and precedent and to the anxieties aroused by national leaders. . . .

Thus state and local anti-Communist legislation, though widespread, is best understood as a reflection, not a cause, of national priorities. Unlike populism, the impact of which was felt first at the local and state level and only later at the national level, the politics of anti-Communism originated at the national level and then spread to the states.

By 1950, then, political leaders had succeeded, through the manipulation of popular myths and stereotypes, in creating a mood conducive to demagogues such as Joseph R. McCarthy. The Wisconsin senator's crude attacks on American policy and policymakers resonated through the political system not because of their uniqueness, but because of their typicality. To call this political impulse "McCarthyism," however, is to exaggerate the senator's importance and to misunderstand the politics that he came to symbolize. McCarthy was the product of anti-Communist politics, not its progenitor. Had he never made that speech in Wheeling, West Virginia, had his name never become a household word, what people came to call "McCarthyism" would nevertheless have characterized American politics at the mid-century.

25.4 Restraining Communism: United States Security Agreements, 1947–1959

During the presidential campaign of 1952, Dwight Eisenhower charged that Truman's "containment policy" was too accepting of coexistence with Communism and suggested the need to liberate "captive peoples." Once in office, however, President Eisenhower found a policy of "liberation" difficult to implement and returned to an aggressive containment policy. Under Eisenhower and his Secretary of State, John Foster Dulles, the United States tried to halt the advance of Communism by setting up NATO-like mutual security alliances with nations bordering Communist countries. They believed that these mutual security pacts would discourage Soviet aggression, since initiating a local war could result in "massive retaliation." The map reproduced here identifies countries with which the United States made mutual security agreements between 1947 and 1959.

Consider:

1. *The assumptions about Soviet aggression this map suggests;*
2. *How these mutual security alliances reinforced the idea of the United States as "world policeman";*
3. *Whether such mutual security alliances were in the best interests of the United States.*

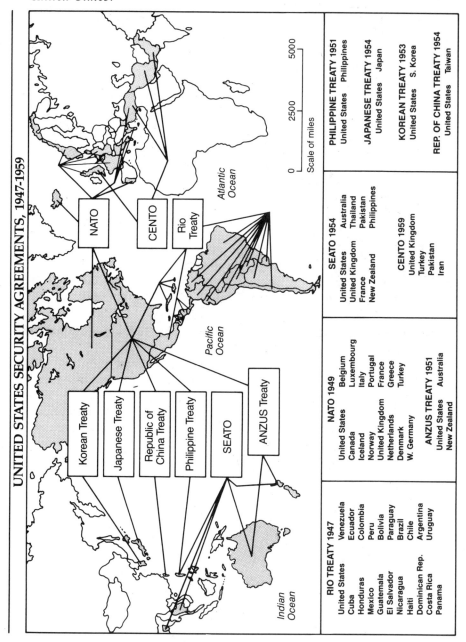

UNITED STATES SECURITY AGREEMENTS, 1947–1959

NATO

CENTO

Rio Treaty

Korean Treaty

Japanese Treaty

Republic of China Treaty

Philippine Treaty

SEATO

ANZUS Treaty

Atlantic Ocean

Pacific Ocean

Indian Ocean

Scale of miles

0   2500   5000

PHILIPPINE TREATY 1951
United States   Philippines

JAPANESE TREATY 1954
United States   Japan

KOREAN TREATY 1953
United States   S. Korea

REP. OF CHINA TREATY 1954
United States   Taiwan

SEATO 1954
United States   Australia
United Kingdom   Thailand
France   Pakistan
New Zealand   Philippines

CENTO 1959
United Kingdom
Turkey
Pakistan
Iran

NATO 1949
United States   Belgium
Canada   Luxembourg
Iceland   Italy
Norway   Portugal
United Kingdom   France
Netherlands   Greece
Denmark   Turkey
W. Germany

ANZUS TREATY 1951
United States   Australia
New Zealand

RIO TREATY 1947
United States   Venezuela
Cuba   Ecuador
Honduras   Colombia
Mexico   Peru
Guatemala   Bolivia
El Salvador   Paraguay
Nicaragua   Brazil
Haiti   Chile
Dominican Rep.   Argentina
Costa Rica   Uruguay
Panama

25.5   Eisenhower and the U-2

Stephen E. Ambrose

Under President Eisenhower, America's national defense policy called for a reduction in conventional armed forces and the buildup of nuclear deterrence capability. This "New Look" defense policy included the development and stockpiling of atomic and hydrogen bombs that would be launched in "massive retaliation" if the United States were attacked. The President explained that this nuclear shield was designed as a defensive measure, that it would not threaten the Soviet Union, and that it would cost less than conventional military forces. A key element in this policy was accurate and timely intelligence about military activities in the Soviet Union, to be obtained by high-flying U-2 planes. Historian Stephen Ambrose contends, in his book *Ike's Spies*, that Eisenhower personally authorized many of the U-2 flights and used the information to confirm that the Soviet Union was not building up either conventional or nuclear forces. In the excerpt that follows, Ambrose reviews the benefits of the U-2 flights.

Consider:

1. *The long-term implications for national defense of relying on high technology for information about trouble spots in the world;*
2. *Whether President Eisenhower should have gone "public" with U-2 information during the "bomber gap" and "missile gap" discussion.*

By the beginning of 1957, the U-2 program was securely in place, including flights over the Soviet Union. . . .

. . . this information gave the President an accurate picture of what was going on and thus allowed him to make his policy decisions on the basis of facts, not guesses.

Ike made immediate practical use of the results of other U-2 flights. As one example, in September 1958 the Chinese were making the most dreadful threats against Formosa. . . .

U-2 flights revealed that there was no Chinese buildup for an invasion. Armed with that intelligence, Ike went on national television to report, "There is not going to be any appeasement, and . . . there is not going to be any war." The "crisis" disappeared.

The U-2s paid off in the long-range strategic sense, as well as for short-term tactical decisions. In fact, the U-2 photographs undoubtedly saved the American taxpayer more money than any other government initiative of the 1950s, because those photographs gave Ike the essential information he had to have to hold to his New Look in defense policy.

SOURCE: *Steven E. Ambrose*, Ike's Spies: Eisenhower and the Espionage Establishment, 274–77. *Copyright © 1980 by Stephen E. Ambrose. Reprinted by permission of Doubleday & Company, Inc.*

As President, Eisenhower was responsible first and foremost for the defense of his country. . . . As a statesman, however, he had long ago concluded that the greatest threat was that the Russians would frighten the United States into an arms race that would lead to unmanageable inflation and ultimate bankruptcy. He believed that America's greatest strength lay in her economic productivity, not in bombs and missiles. He believed further that a sound economy depended on a balanced federal budget, which he thought was the key to stopping inflation. To balance the budget, he had to cut back on defense spending. . . .

. . . [Eisenhower] argued that to deter the Russians what one had to do was be in a position to drop one or two bombs on Moscow. No Russian gain anywhere would be worth the loss of Moscow. The United States did not need thousands of bombers and missiles to make the threat believable. . . .

Under those circumstances, the United States did not have to go into an all-out, fabulously expensive program of producing atomic bombs and ICBMs to deliver them. . . .

Eisenhower's Democratic critics, led by three Senate hawks, John F. Kennedy, Lyndon B. Johnson, and Hubert H. Humphrey, assailed him. They charged that he was allowing his Neanderthal fiscal views to endanger the national security. By 1958 they were claiming that a "bomber gap" existed; in 1959 it became a "missile gap." . . .

Ike knew that the "gaps" were all nonsense. He knew because of the U-2 flights. They revealed, in 1957 and 1958 and 1959, that the Rusians had by no means gone into a crash program of building either missiles or bombers. They proved that the United States, even with its modest bomber fleet and relatively small ICBM fleet . . . had a clear lead over the Soviets, a lead of about two to one. . . .

In addition, . . . the flights showed what the Russians were *not* doing. If Khrushchev had been building bombers and rockets at maximum capacity, the "bomber gap" and the "missile gap" might have become reality. But photographic intelligence showed conclusively that the Soviets were building at a rate considerably short of capacity, and there was nothing . . . to indicate that they intended to speed up. . . .

25.6   The Military-Industrial Complex

Dwight D. Eisenhower

During both the Truman and Eisenhower presidencies, American foreign policy was designed to maintain an equilibrium with the Soviet Union in economic, diplomatic, technological, and military power. As a result of the high cost of maintaining such a policy, defense spending increased from 37 percent of the total budget in 1947 to 48 percent in 1960. During World

War II, the development of the atomic bomb had been made possible by massive spending on government contracts with universities. This connection between the government and universities continued to grow after the war, and whole industries arose around the business of national defense.

It is ironic that in his last official address to the American people, President Eisenhower, a five-star general and advocate of strong defense, warned that the power and influence of the "military-industrial complex" presented a danger to democratic processes. His "Farewell Radio and Television Address to the American People," delivered on January 17, 1961, is excerpted here.

Consider:

1. Whether events in the 1970s and 1980s have borne out President Eisenhower's warning to the American people;
2. How to ensure that the "military-industrial complex" does not endanger American liberties and the democratic process.

A vital element in keeping the peace is our military establishment. Our arms must be mighty, ready for instant action, so that no potential aggressor may be tempted to risk his own destruction.

Our military organization today bears little relation to that known by any of my predecessors in peacetime, or indeed by the fighting men of World War II or Korea.

Until the latest of our world conflicts, the United States had no armaments industry. American makers of plowshares could, with time and as required, make swords as well. But now we can no longer risk emergency improvisation of national defense; we have been compelled to create a permanent armaments industry of vast proportions. Added to this, three and a half million men and women are directly engaged in the defense establishment. We annually spend on military security more than the net income of all United States corporations.

This conjunction of an immense military establishment and a large arms industry is new in the American experience. The total influence— economic, political, even spiritual—is felt in every city, every State house, every office of the Federal government. We recognize the imperative need for this development. Yet we must not fail to comprehend its grave implications. Our toil, resources and livelihood are all involved; so is the very structure of our society.

In the councils of government, we must guard against the acquisition of unwarranted influence, whether sought or unsought, by the military-industrial complex. The potential for the disastrous rise of misplaced power exists and will persist.

We must never let the weight of this combination endanger our liberties or democratic processes. We should take nothing for granted.

SOURCE: *Dwight D. Eisenhower, "Farewell Radio and Television Address to the American People, January 17, 1961," in Eisenhower,* Public Papers of the President of the United States, *1960–61 (Washington, D.C.: Government Printing Office, 1961), 1037–39.*

Only an alert and knowledgeable citizenry can compel the proper meshing of the huge industrial and military machinery of defense with our peaceful methods and goals, so that security and liberty may prosper together.

Akin to, and largely responsible for the sweeping changes in our industrial-military posture, has been the technological revolution . . .

In this revolution, research has become central; it also becomes more formalized, complex, and costly. A steadily increasing share is conducted for, by, or at the direction of, the Federal government.

Today, the solitary inventor, tinkering in his shop, has been overshadowed by task forces of scientists in laboratories and testing fields. In the same fashion, the free university, historically the fountainhead of free ideas and scientific discovery, has experienced a revolution in the conduct of research. Partly because of the huge costs involved, a government contract becomes virtually a substitute for intellectual curiosity. . . .

The prospect of domination of the nation's scholars by Federal employment, project allocations, and the power of money is ever present—and is gravely to be regarded.

Yet, in holding scientific research and discovery in respect, as we should, we must also be alert to the equal and opposite danger that public policy could itself become the captive of a scientific-technological elite.

It is the task of statesmanship to mold, to balance, and to integrate these and other forces, new and old, within the principles of our democratic system . . .

25.7   Globalization of the Monroe Doctrine

Richard Yardley

Historically, the United States has adhered to the Monroe Doctrine, a set of principles defining American national interests that were set down by President James Monroe in 1823. Monroe declared that the United States' would "consider any attempt on their [the countries of Europe] part to extend their system to any portion of this hemisphere as dangerous to our peace and safety. . . . Our policy in regard to Europe is, not to interfere in the internal concerns of any of its powers; to consider the government de facto as the legitimate government."

The Monroe Doctrine did not seem particularly relevant in the years following World War II. But in the early 1960s, Russian support for Fidel Castro and the accompanying buildup in Cuba of Soviet missiles, arms, and technicians seemed to be a clear violation of the Monroe Doctrine. In October 1962, as public debate over the Soviet presence in Cuba intensified, cartoonist Richard Yardley presented another side of the question. In the cartoon reproduced here Yardley implied that American anti-Communist activities around the world might also be viewed as violations of the Monroe Doctrine.

Consider:

1. *Whether the nation's Cold War policy to contain Communism outside the Western Hemisphere was consistent with the Monroe Doctrine;*
2. *Whether the presence of offensive missiles and other high-technology weapons in Cuba really made any difference in the modern world;*
3. *Whether it is realistic for United States foreign policy in the twentieth century to be guided by principles developed in the nineteenth century.*

A Doctrine Discuss'd

SOURCE: *Richard Yardley,* The Sun *(Baltimore), October 17, 1962.*

CHAPTER QUESTIONS

1. *How did American foreign policy interests and goals change between 1949 and 1963?*
2. *Compare the rise of McCarthyism in the 1950s with the Red Scare in the 1920s.*
3. *How successful were United States responses to the Soviet Union in the 1950s? Were there alternatives to these responses?*

Chapter 26

Affluence and Its Problems

World War II dramatically altered American society, bringing a return to prosperity and an optimistic spirit that took progress for granted. After an uneven period right after the war, when industry was reconverted to peacetime production, the economy took off and grew steadily into the 1960s. Technological advances spawned by war had a major impact on the postwar era, as massive "research and development" efforts by industry and universities produced breakthroughs at incredible speed.

The federal government was involved in these postwar developments to an unprecedented degree. The experiences of the Depression and World War II had made it clear that government spending played a key role in stimulating the nation's economy. Even if this spending led to an ever-increasing national debt after the war, at least the Gross National Product was also growing. And even though American industry was becoming more and more dependent on government spending for defense, it was also turning out consumer goods in record-breaking quantities.

Consumerism, in fact, became a prominent part of postwar American life. The widespread availability of consumer credit for home mortgages, automobiles, and less essential goods fostered a national spending spree. Some of this spending was used to support larger families, as the nation's population increased by nearly 15 percent in the 1940s and by almost 20 percent in the 1950s. In a literal sense, this postwar "baby boom" transformed the United States into "the land of the young."

Prosperity, larger families, the need for new housing and—on a less positive note—interracial tensions all contributed to the postwar movement of Americans to the suburbs. Within a few years of the war's end, mass-produced suburban housing tracts ringed most major cities. These burgeoning suburbs, inhabited almost exclusively by whites, signaled a widening of the gap between whites and nonwhites at a time when the courts were beginning to take stands that supported the civil rights of minorities. The Supreme Court's 1954 decision in *Brown* v. *Board of Education,* which banned segregation in the public schools, was a sign of social change to come.

The documents in this chapter illustrate the forces of growth, stability, and change that shaped the years following World War II. Taken together, they help explain why this period, characterized by apparent public complacency and political equilibrium, can be viewed as a dynamic time that laid the groundwork for the tremendous social change of the 1960s and 1970s.

Chronology

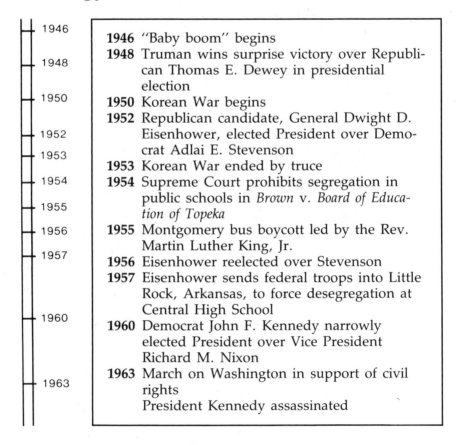

1946	**1946** "Baby boom" begins
1948	**1948** Truman wins surprise victory over Republican Thomas E. Dewey in presidential election
1950	**1950** Korean War begins
1952	**1952** Republican candidate, General Dwight D. Eisenhower, elected President over Democrat Adlai E. Stevenson
1953	**1953** Korean War ended by truce
1954	**1954** Supreme Court prohibits segregation in public schools in *Brown* v. *Board of Education of Topeka*
1955	**1955** Montgomery bus boycott led by the Rev. Martin Luther King, Jr.
1956	**1956** Eisenhower reelected over Stevenson
1957	**1957** Eisenhower sends federal troops into Little Rock, Arkansas, to force desegregation at Central High School
1960	**1960** Democrat John F. Kennedy narrowly elected President over Vice President Richard M. Nixon
1963	**1963** March on Washington in support of civil rights President Kennedy assassinated

Documents

26.1   Postwar Prosperity and Government Spending

The two decades following World War II were characterized by consistent growth and relative stability in the national economy. Both the national wealth and government spending, especially for national defense, expanded steadily during this period. The nation's military involvement in Korea (1950–1953), however, had much less impact on the economy than either World War II or the later conflict in Vietnam. The graphs that follow illustrate the trends in production of wealth, federal spending, and the national debt for the twenty years after the war.

Consider:

1. *Whether wartime spending levels, as shown by the figures for 1945, had any permanent impact on the American economy;*
2. *How the trend in defense spending can be explained.*

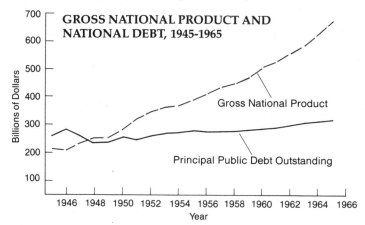

GROSS NATIONAL PRODUCT AND NATIONAL DEBT, 1945-1965

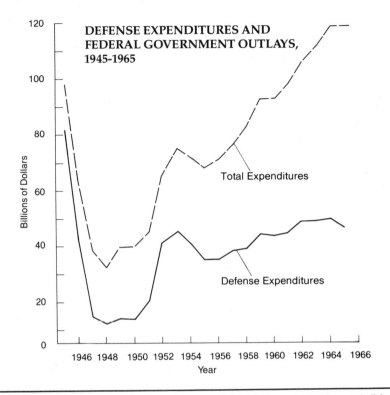

SOURCE: Historical Statistics of the United States: Colonial Times to 1970, part 2 (Washington, D.C.: Government Printing Office, 1975).

26.2   Frustration of Truman's Fair Deal

Fred L. Packer
John Baer

When President Truman declared in his 1949 State of the Union message that "every individual has a right to expect from our Government a fair deal," he gave his domestic reform program a name. The Fair Deal was actually a reworking of a twenty-one-point agenda Truman had announced in 1945. With its proposals for national health insurance, expanded agricultural price supports, federal aid to education, and civil rights, the Fair Deal encountered opposition from all sides. The two cartoons reproduced here suggest the difficulties Truman had with Congress over these proposals.

Consider:

1. *What type of opposition to the Fair Deal each cartoon portrays;*
2. *Why cartoonist Fred Packer depicts Truman as a woman.*

SOURCE: *James N. Giglio and Greg G. Thielen, eds.,* Truman in Cartoon and Caricature *(Ames: Iowa State University Press, 1984), 71, 77. Courtesy of The University of Iowa Libraries, Iowa City, Iowa.*

26.3   Desegregation and the Southern Reaction

Brown v. *Board of Education of Topeka*
"Southern Manifesto"

In May 1954, the Supreme Court issued a landmark ruling in *Brown* v. *Board of Education of Topeka*, reversing the "separate but equal" doctrine of *Plessy* v. *Ferguson* (1896) that had permitted legal segregation in public schools. One year later, the Court delivered an implementation decision calling for desegregation with "all deliberate speed." Southern opposition to the Court's actions took many forms, including the revival of states' rights arguments and the use of "massive resistance." In March 1956, nineteen Southern Senators and seventy-seven Southern Congressmen outlined their concerns in a declaration that is known as the "Southern Manifesto." Excerpts from the 1954 Court decision and the "Southern Manifesto" follow.

Consider:

1. *Whether the Court's 1954 opinion took into account the majority opinion in Plessy v. Ferguson (see Doc. 16.7);*
2. *Whether the Southern legislators were justified in claiming that the Court was "undertaking to legislate, in derogation of the authority of Congress, and to encroach upon the reserved rights of the States and the people";*
3. *The constitutional implications of the "Southern Manifesto."*

BROWN ET AL. *v.* BOARD OF EDUCATION OF TOPEKA ET AL.

Decided May 17, 1954

The plaintiffs contend that segregated public schools are not "equal" and cannot be made "equal," and that hence they are deprived of the equal protection of the laws. . . .

In approaching this problem, we cannot turn the clock back to 1868 when the Amendment was adopted, or even to 1896 when *Plessy* v. *Ferguson* was written. We must consider public education in the light of its full development and its present place in American life throughout the Nation. . . .

Today, education is perhaps the most important function of state and local governments. . . . Today it is a principal instrument in awak-

SOURCE: Brown *v.* Board of Education of Topeka, 347 *U.S.* 488, 492–95; "Southern Manifesto," in Congressional Record, *Eighty-Fourth Congress, 2d Session, vol. 102, part 4, 4460.*

ening the child to cultural values, in preparing him for later professional training, and in helping him to adjust normally to his environment. . . .

We come then to the question presented: Does segregation of children in public schools solely on the basis of race, even though the physical facilities and other "tangible" factors may be equal, deprive the children of the minority group of equal educational opportunities? We believe that it does.

. . . To separate them from others of similar age and qualifications solely because of their race generates a feeling of inferiority as to their status in the community that may affect their hearts and minds in a way unlikely ever to be undone.

We conclude that in the field of public education the doctrine of "separate but equal" has no place. Separate educational facilities are inherently unequal. Therefore, we hold that the plaintiffs and others similarly situated for whom the actions have been brought are, by reason of the segregation complained of, deprived of the equal protection of the laws guaranteed by the Fourteenth Amendment. This disposition makes unnecessary any discussion whether such segregation also violates the Due Process Clause of the Fourteenth Amendment. . . .

"SOUTHERN MANIFESTO"

The unwarranted decision of the Supreme Court in the public school cases is now bearing the fruit always produced when men substitute naked power for established law. . . .

We regard the decision of the Supreme Court in the school cases as a clear abuse of judicial power. It climaxes a trend in the Federal Judiciary undertaking to legislate, in derogation of the authority of Congress, and to encroach upon the reserved rights of the States and the people.

The original Constitution does not mention education. Neither does the 14th amendment nor any other amendment. The debates preceding the submission of the 14th amendment clearly show that there was no intent that it should affect the system of education maintained by the States. . . .

In the case of *Plessy* v. *Ferguson* in 1896 the Supreme Court expressly declared that under the 14th amendment no person was denied any of his rights if the States provided separate but equal public facilities. This decision has been followed in many other cases. It is notable that the Supreme Court, speaking through Chief Justice Taft, a former President of the United States, unanimously declared in 1927 in *Lum* v. *Rice* that the "separate but equal" principle is "within the discretion of the State in regulating its public schools and does not conflict with the 14th amendment." . . .

Though there has been no constitutional amendment or act of Congress changing this established legal principle almost a century old, the Supreme Court of the United States, with no legal basis for such action, undertook to exercise their naked judicial power and substituted their personal political and social ideas for the established law of the land.

This unwarranted exercise of power by the Court, contrary to the Constitution, is creating chaos and confusion in the States principally affected. . . .

Without regard to the consent of the governed, outside agitators are threatening immediate and revolutionary changes in our public-school systems. If done, this is certain to destroy the system of public education in some of the States. . . .

We decry the Supreme Court's encroachments on rights reserved to the States and to the people, contrary to established law, and to the Constitution.

We commend the motives of those States which have declared the intention to resist forced integration by any lawful means.

We appeal to the States and people who are not directly affected by these decisions to consider the constitutional principles involved against the time when they too, on issues vital to them, may be the victims of judicial encroachment.

Even though we constitute a minority in the present Congress, we have full faith that a majority of the American people believe in the dual system of government which has enabled us to achieve our greatness and will in time demand that the reserved rights of the States and of the people be made secure against judicial usurpation.

We pledge ourselves to use all lawful means to bring about a reversal of this decision which is contrary to the Constitution and to prevent the use of force in its implementation.

In this trying period, as we all seek to right this wrong, we appeal to our people not to be provoked by the agitators and troublemakers invading our States and to scrupulously refrain from disorder and lawless acts.

26.4   Problems of Suburbia

David Riesman

The trend toward suburbanization in the United States had started in the 1880s with the arrival of streetcars, but it accelerated sharply in the years after World War II. In many ways, the new homogeneous communities, full of upwardly mobile young families, seemed to typify the vigor and optimism of the postwar period. But there were negative aspects of suburbanization as well. In the 1940s and 1950s, many writers criticized the impact of suburbs on the people who lived in them and on American society in general. The selection that follows is from a work by sociologist David Riesman, called "The Suburban Dislocation."

Consider:

1. *Whether Riesman uses stereotypes in discussing the problems of people who lived in suburban communities;*
2. *The problems Riesman sees for American society as a whole as a result of postwar suburbanization;*
3. *Whether Riesman's predictions about life in the cities have been borne out.*

In the days of Lincoln Steffens and later, people emphasized the "shame of the cities," and in the Twenties major novelists emphasized the constraints of small-town and occasionally of small-suburban life. Today, the comparable worry . . . is conformity: writers point to the uniformity of the ranch style, the everpresent television antennae, the lamp in the picture-window (which usually provides a view of the nearly treeless street, the cars, and someone else's picture-window). Observers have been struck by a kind of massification of men in Levittown and other housing developments such as was once postulated for the endless residential blocks of the cities created by the industrial revolution. . . .

. . . The city today, for many, spells crime, dirt, and race tensions, more than it does culture and opportunity. While some people still escape from the small town to the city, still more are escaping from the city to the suburbs. . . .

. . . I have not stressed here the vicious circle of urban decay and Negro and poor-white in-migration which, for many middle-income families, contribute an additional push from the city quite apart from the direct appeal of suburban domesticity. . . .

Although upper-class and upper-middle-class people have lived in the suburbs of our great cities since the 1880's or earlier, the cities before World War II still retained their hegemony: they engrossed commercial, industrial, and cultural power. The city represented the division and specialization not only of labor but of attitude and opinion. . . . The city, that is, provided a "critical mass" which made possible new combinations—criminal and fantastic ones as well as stimulating and productive ones. Today, however, with the continual loss to the suburbs of the elite and the enterprising, the cities remain huge enough for juveniles to form delinquent subcultures; but will our cities be able to continue to support cultural and educational activities at a level appropriate to our abundant economy? . . .

Where the husband goes off with the car to work (and often, in the vicious circle created by the car, there is no other way for him to travel), the wife is frequently either privatized at home or must herself,

SOURCE: *David Riesman, "The Suburban Dislocation," in David Riesman,* Abundance or What? *and Other Essays (Doubleday, 1964). Reprinted by permission of the author.*

to escape isolation, take a job which will help support her own car, as well as the baby-sitter.

The children themselves, in fact, before they get access to a car, are captives of their suburb, save for those families where the housewives surrender continuity in their own lives to chauffeur their children to lessons, doctors, and other services which could be reached via public transport in the city. In the suburban public schools, the young are captives, too, dependent on whatever art and science and general liveliness their particular school happens to have. . . .

. . . the suburban kaffee-klatsch is proverbial in which the women sit around and discuss their children—the main "surrogates" they have in common. Their husbands, working downtown or in a nearby plant, have some opportunity to meet people on an occupational basis who are of different backgrounds, different ages, and different life-chances than they themselves; but the wives, falling into or forced into a neighborly gregariousness, tend to see others of similar age, setting, and TV exposure. . . . cross-sex friendships are ruled out by lack of sophistication in such relations and by the lack of privacy. And the husbands, if not the tired businessmen of legend, are less eager than some of their wives to drive long distances at night for out-of-suburb contacts, . . . In this situation, many women of college education feel trapped, aware of falling behind their own ideals and their husbands' in breadth of view and nourishing experience. The various leisure-time activities they undertake do not seem to fill this void. . . .

Indeed, for millions of suburbanites, their post-War experience has been prosperous and open far beyond their Depression-born expectations. For them, the suburbs have been one vast supermarket, abundantly and conveniently stocked with approved yet often variegated choices. . . . Life on credit has worked out well for many such homeowners, allowing them to have their children young, and in circumstances far better than those in which they themselves grew up. . . . such first-generation suburbanites [have] found the taste of abundance pleasant and, for the younger ones with wages rising faster than prices, not notably problematic. But what will occur when the urban qualities have been dissipated, while the suburban ones elude all but the rich?

26.5   Eisenhower and the Postwar Political Balance

Alonzo L. Hamby

The years between 1945 and 1960 represented a distinctive period in American politics. Presidents Harry Truman and Dwight Eisenhower both reflected the traditional values of a generation that had come to maturity early in the century. Though they differed in their political views, neither one sought basic changes in the status quo. For more than half of this period, one party controlled Congress while the other held the White House; the electorate seemed to want the two major parties to serve as checks on one another. As the following selection by political historian Alonzo Hamby suggests, Eisenhower's leadership was especially well suited to the times.

Consider:

1. *Why Eisenhower was able to win two landslide victories while his party remained in the minority for most of his presidency;*
2. *Whether the qualities Hamby ascribes to Eisenhower are generally desirable in American presidents;*
3. *Whether the two-party system benefited from this period of "equilibrium" without strong interparty differences.*

Dwight D. Eisenhower was the last of the twentieth-century American presidents to be nurtured in the Victorian climate of opinion that had produced Roosevelt and Truman. He was also the only twentieth-century president, other than Theodore Roosevelt, to have experienced public celebration as a military hero, and he possessed a more tangible democratic touch than any of his predecessors save Truman. These attributes coalesced to make his administration an oasis of placidity between eras of extraordinary turbulence in American politics. Eisenhower's espousal of the values of a cherished past provided Americans with a sense of continuity in a troubled, changing time. His status as a hero blended with his image as a democrat to secure him a combination of reverence and trust that made him all but invulnerable to political sniping. . . .

Eisenhower's presidential objectives have been well summarized by the titles of two historical works on his administration: Charles C. Alexander's *Holding the Line* and Gary W. Reichard's *The Reaffirmation of Republicanism.* He and the people around him wanted to preserve the essence of traditional Republicanism and at the same time make it palatable to mid-twentieth-century America. They wanted to impart a fresh tone to old values, produce policies that would somehow reconcile the needs of the present with the outlook of the past, and eventually develop the new personalities that would carry their effort into the future. They hoped to use his administration as the springboard for a viable new conservative tradition that would assimilate much of the accomplishment of the New Deal–Fair Deal tradition while drawing a line against its extension. . . .

Eisenhower's handicaps as president are obvious. His political experience was severely limited, and he had little working knowledge

SOURCE: *Alonzo L. Hamby,* Liberalism and Its Challengers: FDR to Reagan *(New York: Oxford University Press, 1985), 94, 118–19, 122–23, 125, 136–38.*

of the civilian Washington bureaucracy. What he eventually gained in experience may have been more than countered by the deterioration of his health through a heart attack, a stroke, and a major abdominal operation; there can be little question that he had lost substantial vigor and capacity for work by the end of his second term. Moreover, his well-established distaste for detail no doubt served him less well in the White House than it had in the military. . . .

However much he rejected vigorous Roosevelt-Truman–style leadership in some areas, Eisenhower never doubted that the presidency was a post that called for vigorous moral leadership. By preachment and deed, he sought to bring America back to the values of his youth—pietistic religion and self-help. . . .

The corporate tone of the Eisenhower administration was never in doubt. The president surrounded himself with successful financiers, corporate lawyers, and high-level business executives; those of his advisers who did not fit those categories usually possessed the values of the people who did. . . .

Much like executives who had learned to live with labor unions and government regulations even while grumbling about them, the president and those around him resignedly adapted themselves to the social-political structure of a new America. They reflected the values of both the managerial subclass and much of the broader middle class by working hard to govern efficiently, control costs, and thereby contain inflation. . . .

Eisenhower's moderation had a powerful appeal to a nation ready for a period of peace and tranquility after years of domestic change and bitterness. But it also was a style of leadership incapable almost by definition of dealing with extreme situations that required something more than bland, moderate treatment. . . .

Any evaluation of Eisenhower's presidency must be equivocal. . . . He was a moderate conservative who accepted American society as it existed while encouraging the nurture of traditional values. This led him to give scant attention to important new currents, such as the black revolution, but it also gave the nation and the Republican party time to digest most of the New and Fair Deals and make them part of the national consensus. . . .

. . . Eisenhower offered Americans not tangible help but rather a sense of reassurance emanating from the qualities he embodied. Most visible among them were the qualities of the hero—strength, authority, command, identification with the aspirations and triumphs of the nation itself. Less visible but probably more fundamental were the qualities of the managerial conservative as this type had evolved halfway through this century—organization, adaptation, cooperation—coexisting uneasily with a nostalgia for a simpler, more individualistic past. They were qualities that in the aggregate made Eisenhower a father figure to a nation that wanted a breathing spell from the relentless pace of twentieth-century change.

26.6   Feminism in Postwar America
Leila J. Rupp and Verta Taylor

Though women had made some gains during World War II, the postwar period, with its emphases on political stability and traditional values, was not conducive to a renewal of the feminist movement. Some critics contended that life in suburbia confined and limited women in significant new ways (see Doc. 26.4). This "confinement" was the subject of *The Feminist Mystique*, a 1963 book by Betty Friedan that has been widely credited with reawakening the feminist movement. Yet, as historian Leila Rupp and sociologist Verta Taylor suggest in their recent book, *Survival in the Doldrums* (1987), the dynamic women's movement of the 1960s and 1970s owed much to an undercurrent of feminism that continued during the postwar years. The following excerpt from their book discusses the specific aims and the lasting impact of the postwar feminists.

Consider:

1. *Why, though it was endorsed by both major parties in the 1940s and 1950s, an ERA (Equal Rights Amendment) could not be passed by Congress at that time;*
2. *Why postwar feminists had difficulty attracting young women to their cause;*
3. *The legacy of postwar feminism.*

The Equal Rights Amendment was the foremost, as well as the most controversial, feminist issue in the 1940s and the 1950s. Drafted by Alice Paul immediately after the suffrage victory in 1920, it had won little support until after World War II. . . . At stake was the fate of protective legislation, for which most women's organizations had battled long and hard in the late nineteenth and early twentieth centuries. The anti-ERA forces believed that the Woman's Party and other pro-ERA organizations consisted of wealthy women and professional women . . . who cared not a whit for the well-being of working women who desperately needed the protection of social legislation to allow them to compete in the labor market. Pro-ERA groups, on the other hand, believed that protective legislation in fact discriminated against women, and that only through complete legal equality would women ever advance in American society. . . .

. . . Those opposed to the ERA emphasized the differences in the biological and social functions of men and women, which in their eyes made the concept of equality something that could not be achieved by the ERA. . . .

SOURCE: *Leila J. Rupp and Verta Taylor,* Survival in the Doldrums: The American Women's Rights Movement, 1945 to the 1960s *(New York: Oxford University Press, 1987), 59–60, 64, 68, 79, 82–84, 190.*

The ERA remained the foremost feminist issue in the post–1945 period, even though it could not pass Congress. The 1940s and 1950s saw more and more women's organizations begin to change from opposition to support, thus laying the groundwork for the women's movement's solid support of the ERA in the 1960s and 1970s. . . .

Both supporters and opponents of the ERA worked on a second feminist issue, the struggle to win for women policy-making roles in American society. Staunch ERA advocates tended to see this as a second priority item. . . . But to many women, the fight for policy-making jobs seemed a practical approach to fighting for women's rights. They believed that women would bring special qualities to top posts that would change the course of American politics and that . . . recognition of individual women would benefit all women. . . .

All of the women's organizations in the movement supported women for high-level positions in government, but some . . . distrusted those who put this issue first. . . . The suspicion that some female activists worked only to advance their own careers was voiced. . . . It is not hard to see why such charges would be made against those who worked to attain high-level positions for women, especially because the very women who promoted this tactic often received appointments. . . .

It is clear that women's organizations in the post–1945 period never managed to establish any lasting and well-functioning coalition. Nevertheless, the various organizations active on women's rights were linked by overlapping membership, cooperation, competition, and coalition-building. . . .

. . . Women's rights advocates for the most part recognized that the majority of women knew nothing about their activity and had no interest in their cause. Sometimes they used the metaphor of women sleeping through the decades to describe their apathy. . . .

. . . The majority of American women remained indifferent to, or uninformed about, women's rights until the resurgence of the movement in the mid–1960s. . . .

The women's rights movement in the post–1945 period did not always reach the wider public with its program, but probably the best measure of its influence was the establishment of the President's Commission on the Status of Women in 1961. That the activity of pro-ERA feminists instigated the creation of such a body and entered into its deliberations is clear. . . . Kennedy might never have agreed to lend the prestige of the presidency to such an undertaking without the persistent efforts of ERA supporters. The Commission, sparked by women's rights activity, ultimately served as a stimulus for the growth of a new and more broad-based cycle of the women's movement.

The effects of feminist activism in this period for the next phase of the women's movement were at least as important as the consequences it had in its own time. . . . it is useful to think of this cycle as providing crucial resources that molded the strategies and possibilities for action in subsequent years. . . .

26.7   A Strategy for the Civil Rights Revolution

Martin Luther King, Jr.

Beginning with the Montgomery, Alabama, bus boycott in 1955, black Americans took a strong activist approach in pressing the government for expanded guarantees of their civil rights. The Reverend Martin Luther King, Jr., who led the boycott, emerged as the leading spokesman of the civil-rights movement, and he remained in the forefront until his assassination in 1968. King's main contribution was to introduce the strategy of nonviolent resistance, based on the teachings of India's Mohandas Gandhi. In his "Letter from Birmingham City Jail" (1963), excerpted here, King explains why nonviolent resistance is necessary.

Consider:

1. *Why King believes nonviolent resistance to be the best course of action for blacks;*
2. *How King's distinction between just and unjust laws compares with Timothy Stone's description of "just laws" (Doc. 6.3) and the position taken by white Southerners in the "Southern Manifesto" (Doc. 26.3).*

My dear Fellow Clergymen,

While confined here in the Birmingham city jail, I came across your recent statement calling our present activities "unwise and untimely." Seldom, if ever, do I pause to answer criticism of my work and ideas. . . . But since I feel that you are men of genuine good will and your criticisms are sincerely set forth, I would like to answer your statement. . . .

You may well ask, "Why direct action? Why sit-ins, marches, etc.? Isn't negotiation a better path?" You are exactly right in your call for negotiation. Indeed, this is the purpose of direct action. Nonviolent direct action seeks to create such a crisis and establish such creative tensions that a community that has constantly refused to negotiate is forced to confront the issue. . . . there is a type of constructive nonviolent tension that is necessary for growth. Just as Socrates felt that it was necessary to create a tension in the mind so that individuals could rise from the bondage of myths and half-truths to the unfettered realm of creative analysis and objective appraisal, we must see the need of

SOURCE: "Letter from Birmingham Jail, April 16, 1963," *in A Testament of Hope: The Essential Writings of Martin Luther King, Jr., ed. James M. Washington, 289, 291–94. Copyright © 1986 by Coretta Scott King, Executrix of the Estate of Martin Luther King, Jr. Reprinted by permission of Harper & Row, Publishers, Inc.*

having nonviolent gadflies to create the kind of tension in society that will help men to rise from the dark depths of prejudice and racism to the majestic heights of understanding and brotherhood. . . .

We know through painful experience that freedom is never voluntarily given by the oppressor; it must be demanded by the oppressed. Frankly, I have never yet engaged in a direct action movement that was "well-timed," according to the timetable of those who have not suffered unduly from the disease of segregation. . . .

You express a great deal of anxiety over our willingness to break laws. This is certainly a legitimate concern. . . . The answer is found in the fact that there are two types of laws: there are *just* and there are *unjust* laws. I would agree with Saint Augustine that "An unjust law is no law at all."

. . . A just law is a man-made code that squares with the moral law or the law of God. An unjust law is a code that is out of harmony with the moral law. . . . Any law that uplifts human personality is just. Any law that degrades human personality is unjust. All segregation statutes are unjust because segregation distorts the soul and damages the personality. . . .

. . . One who breaks an unjust law must do it *openly, lovingly* (not hatefully as the white mothers did in New Orleans when they were seen on television screaming, "nigger, nigger, nigger"), and with a willingness to accept the penalty. I submit that an individual who breaks a law that conscience tells him is unjust, and willingly accepts the penalty by staying in jail to arouse the conscience of the community over its injustice, is in reality expressing the very highest respect for law.

CHAPTER QUESTIONS

1. *In what ways did the postwar years reflect a resurgence of traditional values? An assertion of new values?*
2. *Compare the role of the federal government before World War II with its role in the postwar period.*
3. *To what degree were the dominant social forces of the postwar period reflected in American politics? Explain.*

Chapter 27

The Vietnam War and Political Crisis

One of the most turbulent periods in American history began in 1963 when Lyndon Baines Johnson succeeded to the presidency after the assassination of John F. Kennedy. It ended in 1974 with Richard Nixon's forced resignation as President. These years witnessed profound changes in American political, social, and economic institutions as the experience of the Vietnam War and its attendant constitutional and social crises dominated the nation's life.

The nation's experience in the Vietnam War led to a growing awareness that the Cold War could not be "won," even by fighting limited "hot" wars. Vietnam also caused many Americans to reconsider the policy of subordinating the nation's domestic concerns to its responsibility as the leader of the Free World (see Doc. 25.1). Virulent opposition to the war also drove from office Lyndon Johnson, a powerful President who had been elected by a landslide only four years earlier. These challenges to political authority were mirrored in other areas, as blacks, Indians, and women became increasingly militant in their demand for justice and equality.

The violence in Vietnam was amplified by television coverage and spilled over onto American soil, where antiwar protests, civil-rights demonstrations, and urban riots disrupted the nation. Fearful of these challenges to its authority, government at all levels mounted surveillance of thousands of private citizens who participated in protests and demonstrations against the war.

Perhaps the most significant new issue that emerged during the Vietnam era involved the power to wage war: how that power is exercised and in whom it is vested. The disclosure that President Nixon had carried out secret war activities in Cambodia, Laos, and North Vietnam without consulting with Congress heightened public concern about presidential authority to conduct war. In less than a decade, Congress moved from virtually unanimous support for the Gulf of Tonkin Resolution to repeal of that resolution and then to the overriding of President Nixon's veto of the War Powers Act, a measure designed to curtail presidential war-making power.

A dramatic series of events that came to be known as Watergate fused many of these developments into a single crisis. Brought on by Nixon's resolve to neutralize political enemies he considered a threat to his policies, the Watergate crisis that began in June 1972 ended three years later by destroying the President himself. The relatively smooth transition from the Nixon presidency to that of Gerald Ford suggested to many observers that the nation's institutions had weathered the storm and a new course could be charted. Other observers, however, felt far less certain. The wounds and scars of the "Vietnam Decade" would not heal quickly nor be forgotten.

The documents in this chapter come largely from participants in the events and activities of the Vietnam decade. Although fragmentary, these accounts written from different perspectives shed considerable light on the period. Only with the passage of time, however, will it be possible to understand the real significance of the events they describe.

Chronology

1963	**1963**	President Kennedy assassinated in Dallas, Texas
1964	**1964**	Congress approves a comprehensive Civil Rights Act
1965		Gulf of Tonkin Resolution authorizes U.S. military actions in Vietnam
		Lyndon Johnson elected President over Barry Goldwater
	1965	Watts riots in Los Angeles
	1968	President Johnson withdraws from presidential race
		Martin Luther King assassinated in Memphis, Tennessee
1968		Richard Nixon narrowly elected President over Hubert Humphrey

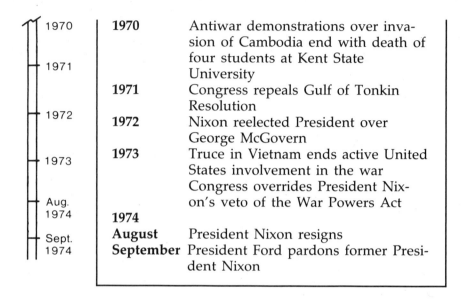

1970	**1970**	Antiwar demonstrations over invasion of Cambodia end with death of four students at Kent State University
1971	**1971**	Congress repeals Gulf of Tonkin Resolution
1972	**1972**	Nixon reelected President over George McGovern
1973	**1973**	Truce in Vietnam ends active United States involvement in the war Congress overrides President Nixon's veto of the War Powers Act
Aug. 1974	**1974**	
Sept. 1974	**August**	President Nixon resigns
	September	President Ford pardons former President Nixon

Documents

27.1   Challenge and Response: The Gulf of Tonkin

Lyndon Baines Johnson

President Lyndon Johnson inherited from the Kennedy administration a substantial American commitment to protect South Vietnam from Communist aggression. This commitment increased sharply in August 1964 after

North Vietnamese torpedo boats attacked American destroyers in the Gulf of Tonkin. In retaliation, Johnson ordered an air attack on North Vietnam and requested congressional support for his actions. Congress quickly (and virtually unanimously) passed a resolution authorizing the President to take the "necessary measures" to protect American forces and "prevent further aggression" in Southeast Asia. Though there were few such charges at the time, Johnson's critics argue that the American destroyers provoked the torpedo attacks and that the resolution itself was a blank check to escalate the conflict. In this excerpt from his memoirs, *Vantage Point*, Johnson offers his view of these events.

Consider:

1. *Whether President Johnson and his advisers responded prudently to the first torpedo-boat attacks;*
2. *Why President Johnson called the congressional resolution the "Southeast Asia Resolution" rather than the "Gulf of Tonkin Resolution";*
3. *The reliability of a former President's memoirs in evaluating his actions in office.*

In August 1964 an unexpected crisis developed, one that threatened for a time to change the nature of the war in Vietnam. During the early hours of Sunday morning, August 2, a high-priority message came in reporting that North Vietnamese torpedo boats had attacked the destroyer USS *Maddox* in the Gulf of Tonkin. . . .

Though we had decided to treat the first North Vietnamese strike against our destroyer as a possible error, we drafted a stiff note to the Hanoi regime. We said that our ships had always operated freely on the high seas, and added: "They will continue to do so." We advised the North Vietnamese to be "under no misapprehension as to the grave consequences which would inevitably result from any further unprovoked offensive military action against United States forces.". . .

Two days later the North Vietnamese struck again at our destroyers, . . . we received messages from the destroyer *Maddox* that its radar and that of the USS *C. Turner Joy* had spotted vessels they believed to be hostile. The enemy ships appeared to be preparing an ambush. The *Maddox* and *C. Turner Joy* had changed course to avoid contact, but they then sent word that the enemy vessels were closing in at high speed. Within an hour the destroyers advised that they were being attacked by torpedoes and were firing on the enemy PT boats. . . .

Action reports continued to arrive from our destroyers, and from

SOURCE: *Lyndon Baines Johnson,* The Vantage Point: Perspectives of the Presidency, 1963–1969, *112–18. Copyright © 1971 by HEC Public Affairs Foundation. Reprinted by permission of Henry Holt Inc.*

the Pacific Command. A few were ambiguous. One from the destroyer *Maddox* questioned whether the many reports of enemy torpedo firings were all valid.

I instructed [Secretary of Defense] McNamara to investigate these reports and obtain clarification. . . . We wanted to be absolutely certain that our ships had actually been attacked before we retaliated.

Admiral Sharp called McNamara to report that after checking all the reports and evidence, he had no doubt whatsoever that an attack had taken place. McNamara and his associates reached the same firm conclusion. Detailed studies made after the incident confirmed this judgment. . . .

I was determined, from the time I became President, to seek the fullest support of Congress for any major action that I took, whether in foreign affairs or in the domestic field. . . . Concerning Vietnam, I repeatedly told Secretaries Rusk and McNamara that I never wanted to receive any recommendation for actions we might have to take unless it was accompanied by a proposal for assuring the backing of Congress. . . .

. . . We could not be sure how Hanoi would react to our reprisal strike. . . . I wanted us to be ready for the worst. Part of being ready, to me, was having the advance support of Congress for anything that might prove to be necessary. . . .

My first major decision on Vietnam had been to reaffirm President Kennedy's policies. This was my second major decision: to order retaliation against the Tonkin Gulf attacks and to seek a congressional resolution in support of our Southeast Asia policy. . . .

. . . [Secretary of State Dean] Rusk brought me a draft of the Southeast Asia Resolution (often miscalled the "Gulf of Tonkin Resolution"), which he and George Ball, in consultation with the congressional leaders of both parties, had worked out. . . . I approved it and prepared a written message to the Congress to accompany it. In that message I made it clear that I was asking the support of the Congress not merely to reply to attacks on our own forces, or simply to carry out our obligations in South Vietnam, but to be in a position to do what had to be done to fulfill our responsibilities in all of Southeast Asia.

The resolution as finally approved gave congressional support for the President to "take all necessary measures to repel any armed attack against the forces of the United States and to prevent further aggression." The resolution also stated that the United States was "prepared, as the President determines, to take all necessary steps, including the use of armed force, to assist any member or protocol state of the Southeast Asia Collective Defense Treaty requesting assistance in defense of its freedom."

The resolution reaffirmed our obligations under SEATO and asserted that the maintenance of peace and security in Southeast Asia was vital to our own national interests and to world peace.

27.2   A Soldier's Experience in Vietnam

Specialist 5 Harold "Light Bulb" Bryant

Most of the reports and memoirs by participants in the war in Vietnam
have been written by white officers and white civilians. Yet in the early
years of the war 14.5 percent of army troops were black. Little was known
about these black soldiers—other than that they suffered heavy casualties—until Wallace Terry's *Bloods: An Oral History of the Vietnam War by
Black Veterans* appeared in 1984. The recollections of Specialist 5 Harold
"Light Bulb" Bryant of East St. Louis, Illinois, a combat engineer with the
1st Cavalry Division in Vietnam, are included in the book. Here Bryant describes his experiences in Vietnam and his first visit to the Vietnam Veterans Memorial in Washington, D.C.

Consider:

1. *The wartime experiences that influenced Bryant's outlook on the war in
   Vietnam;*
2. *Why American authorities used exaggerated body counts to measure success of the war;*
3. *The implications of Bryant's asking "what happened" after coming home
   from Vietnam.*

I enlisted in the Army to stay out of the Marines. I had went to
college for a semester at Southern Illinois University at Edwardsville.
But the expenses had gotten too much for my family, so I went and
got me a job at McDonnell Aircraft as a sheet-metal assembler. About
eight months later, two guys I went to high school with got drafted
by the Marines. So I joined the Army so I could get a choice.

It was August of '65. I was twenty. . . .

I did my basic and my AIT at Fort Leonardwood, Missouri. "Lost
in the Woods," yeah. Trained for combat engineer to build bridges,
mountain roads. But we didn't build too many bridges. Cleared a lot
of LZs [landing zones]. Did a lot of demolition work. . . .

When I came to Vietnam, I thought we were helping another country
to develop a nation. About three or four months later I found out that
wasn't the case. In high school and in the papers I had been hearing

SOURCE: *Wallace Terry,* Bloods: An Oral History of the Vietnam War by Black Veterans
(New York: Random House, 1984), 20–23, 30–32.

about Indochina, but I couldn't find Indochina on the map. I didn't know anything about the country, about the people. Those kinds of things I had to learn on myself while I was there.

We had a Vietnamese interpreter attached to us. I would always be asking him questions. He had told me this war in Vietnam had been going on for hundreds of years. Before the Americans, they had been fighting for hundreds of years against the Chinese aggressors. I thought we had got into the beginning of a war. But I found out that we were just in another phase of their civil wars.

And we weren't gaining any ground. We would fight for a hill all day, spend two days or two nights there, and then abandon the hill. Then maybe two, three months later, we would have to come back and retake the same piece of territory. . . .

And they had a habit of exaggerating a body count. If we killed 7, by the time it would get back to base camp, it would have gotten to 28. Then by the time it got down to Westmoreland's office in Saigon, it done went up to 54. And by the time it left from Saigon going to Washington, it had went up to about 125. To prove we were really out there doing our jobs, doing, really, more than what we were doing.

I remember a place called the Ashau Valley. The 7th went in there and got cut up real bad. They had underestimated the enemy's power. So they sent in the 9th, and we cleared the Ashau Valley out. All we was doing was making contact, letting the gunships know where they were, and then we would draw back. We had 25 gunships circling around, and jet strikes coming in to drop napalm. We did that all day, and the next day we didn't receive any other fire.

Stars and Stripes said we had a body count of 260 something. But I don't think it was true. . . .

When I came to Washington to see the Vietnam Veterans Memorial, I looked through the book and there were about 15 guys from my hometown who were killed. And six of them I knew.

But I looked up the memorial for James Plummer first.

Plummer was a black guy from Cincinnatti. We were the same age. Twenty. We were at Camp Alpha together. That's where they assign you when you first come to 'Nam. . . .

He was my best friend.

One day we were at the airfield at the LZ. Plummer was out of the truck, over by the ammo dump. And the ammo dump received a mortar round. It blew him up.

It freaked me out. I mean that here I saw him, and five minutes later he's instantaneously dead. . . .

. . . I've talked to chaplains, talked to preachers about Vietnam. And no one could give me a satisfactory explanation of what happened overseas.

. . . I keep looking for the explanation.

I can't find it. I can't find it.

27.3   America's Failure in Vietnam: Lessons Learned

George C. Herring

In April of 1975 the last American military personnel in South Vietnam were evacuated from Saigon only hours before the city fell to the North Vietnamese. Thus ended America's longest and most unpopular war, in which more than 58,000 Americans died and billions of dollars were spent in a futile effort to support South Vietnam. In the ensuing years there has been a vigorous, sometimes bitter, debate over American involvement in South Vietnam. In his book, *America's Longest War: The United States and Vietnam, 1950–1975*, historian George C. Herring reviews the history of this tragic period. In the concluding chapter, excerpted here, he summarizes the conflicting views over United States involvement in Vietnam and offers his own assessment of the lessons learned there.

Consider:

1. *The implications of the failure in Vietnam for American foreign policy in the 1980s;*
2. *The accuracy of Herring's assessment that United States intervention was based on a misjudgment of the nature of the struggle between North Vietnam and South Vietnam;*
3. *The conditions under which the American people might support direct American military intervention abroad.*

The lessons drawn are as divergent as the arguments advanced. Those who feel that the United States lost because it did not act decisively conclude that if the nation becomes involved in war again, it must employ its military power with a view to winning quickly before public support erodes. Those who feel that the basic problem was the formulation rather than the execution of strategy insist that military and civilian leaders must think strategically, that they must examine more carefully the nature of the war and formulate more precisely the ways in which American power can best be used to attain clearly defined objectives.

Such lessons depend on the values and belief systems of those who pronounce them, of course, and those who opposed the war have reached quite different conclusions. To some former doves, the fundamental lesson is never to get involved in a land war in Asia; to others, it is to avoid intervention in international trouble spots unless

SOURCE: *George C. Herring,* America's Longest War: The United States and Vietnam, 1950–1975, *2d ed. (New York: Alfred A. Knopf, 1986), 277–81.*

the nation's vital interests are clearly at stake. Some commentators warn that policymakers must be wary of the sort of simplistic reasoning that produced the domino theory and the Munich analogy. Others point to the weaknesses of South Vietnam and admonish that "even a superpower can't save allies who are unable or unwilling to save themselves." For still others, the key lessons are that American power has distinct limits and that in order to be effective, American foreign policy must be true to the nation's historic ideals. . . .

The fundamental weakness of many of the lessons learned thus far is that they assume the continued necessity and practicability of the containment policy, at least in modified form, thereby evading or ignoring altogether the central questions raised by the war. The United States intervened in Vietnam to block the apparent march of a Soviet-directed Communism across Asia, enlarged its commitment to halt a presumably expansionist Communist China, and eventually made Vietnam a test of its determination to uphold world order. By wrongly attributing the Vietnamese conflict to external sources, the United States drastically misjudged its internal dynamics. By intervening in what was essentially a local struggle, it placed itself at the mercy of local forces, a weak client, and a determined adversary. It elevated into a major international conflict what might have remained a localized struggle. By raising the stakes into a test of its own credibility, it perilously narrowed its options. A policy so flawed in its premises cannot help but fail, and in this case the results were disastrous. . . .

. . . The development of significant military capabilities by the Soviet Union and China made it extremely risky for the United States to use its military power in Vietnam on a scale necessary to achieve the desired results. Conditions in Vietnam itself and the constraints imposed by domestic opinion made it impossible to reach these goals with limited means. Vietnam makes clear that the United States cannot uphold its own concept of world order in the face of a stubborn and resolute, although much weaker, foe. The war did not bring about the decline of American power, as some have suggested, but was rather symptomatic of the limits of national power in an age of international diversity and nuclear weaponry. . . .

. . . To carry the "Never Again" syndrome to its logical conclusion and turn away from an ungrateful and hostile world could be calamitous. To regard Vietnam as an aberration, a unique experience from which nothing can be learned, would invite further frustration. To adapt to the new era, the United States must recognize its vulnerability, accept the limits to its power, and accommodate itself to many situations it does not like. Americans must understand that they will not be able to dictate solutions to world problems or to achieve all of their goals. Like it or not, Vietnam marked the end of an era in world history and of American foreign policy, an era marked by constructive achievements but blemished by ultimate, although not irreparable, failure.

27.4 Demonstrations and Protest Against the War

Although public opinion polls in 1965 supported escalation of the Vietnam War, an antiwar movement that began on university campuses grew rapidly. In 1967, antiwar demonstrations occurred in several major cities, with more than 200,000 demonstrators marching on the Pentagon in Washington. Supporters of the war held their own marches and demonstrations, sometimes attempting to break up antiwar demonstrations. Demonstrations for and against the war are shown in the two photographs that follow.

Consider:

1. *What conclusions can be drawn from the two pictures concerning anti-war and prowar demonstrators;*
2. *How the two demonstrations pictured here might have affected Americans who were "uncommitted" on the war;*
3. *How antiwar and prowar demonstrations might have influenced government decisions about continued involvement in Vietnam.*

SOURCE: *Antiwar demonstration in San Francisco, Mau Copland, Black Star; hard-hats' demonstration, Burt Glinn, Magnum.*

27.5   The War Powers Act: A President's View

Richard M. Nixon

In the early 1970s, as public and congressional opposition to the war increased, President Nixon ordered secret bombings of Cambodia and Laos, bombed targets near Hanoi, and mined Haiphong Harbor. Reasserting its initiative, Congress began to look for secret foreign commitments President Nixon might have made, to scrutinize presidential foreign policy initiatives, and to cut foreign aid appropriations. In 1973, a War Powers Bill, designed to limit presidential power to commit American troops abroad, became law over President Nixon's veto. The bill required the President to inform Congress within forty-eight hours of any deployment of American military forces abroad and to withdraw them within sixty days unless Congress authorized an extension. In his veto message, excerpted here, Nixon argued that the bill usurped his constitutional powers and undercut the ability of the United States to "act as an effective influence for peace."

Consider:

1. *The major points on which Nixon differed with Congress;*
2. *How disclosures of the Watergate scandal might have related to passage of the War Powers Act;*
3. *Whether the War Powers Act has served to limit the activities of subsequent Presidents.*

I hereby return without my approval House Joint Resolution 542—the War Powers Resolution. While I am in accord with the desire of the Congress to assert its proper role in the conduct of our foreign affairs, the restrictions which this resolution would impose upon the authority of the President are both unconstitutional and dangerous to the best interests of our Nation. . . .

The Founding Fathers understood the impossibility of foreseeing every contingency that might arise in this complex area. They acknowledged the need for flexibility in responding to changing circumstances. They recognized that foreign policy decisions must be made through close cooperation between the two branches and not through rigidly codified procedures. . . .

House Joint Resolution 542 would attempt to take away, by a mere legislative act, authorities which the President has properly exercised under the Constitution for almost 200 years. One of its provisions would automatically cut off certain authorities after sixty days unless the Congress extended them. Another would allow the Congress to eliminate certain authorities merely by the passage of a concurrent resolution—an action which does not normally have the force of law, since it denies the President his constitutional role in approving legislation. . . .

While all the specific consequences of House Joint Resolution 542 cannot yet be predicted, it is clear that it would undercut the ability of the United States to act as an effective influence for peace. For example, the provision automatically cutting off certain authorities after 60 days unless they are extended by the Congress could work to prolong or intensify a crisis. Until the Congress suspended the deadline, there would be at least a chance of United States withdrawal and an adversary would be tempted therefore to postpone serious negotiations until the 60 days were up. Only after the Congress acted would there be a strong incentive for an adversary to negotiate. In addition, the very existence of a deadline could lead to an escalation of hostilities in order to achieve certain objectives before the 60 days expired.

SOURCE: *Richard M. Nixon, "Veto of the War Powers Resolution. October 24, 1973,"* Public Papers of the Presidents of the United States: Richard Nixon, 1973 *(Washington, D.C.: Government Printing Office, 1975), 893–95.*

The measure would jeopardize our role as a force for peace in other ways as well. It would, for example, strike from the President's hand a wide range of important peace-keeping tools by eliminating his ability to exercise quiet diplomacy backed by subtle shifts in our military deployments. . . .

I am particularly disturbed by the fact that certain of the President's constitutional powers as Commander in Chief of the Armed Forces would terminate automatically under this resolution 60 days after they were invoked. No overt Congressional action would be required to cut off these powers—they would disappear automatically unless the Congress extended them. In effect, the Congress is here attempting to increase its policymaking role through a provision which requires it to take absolutely no action at all.

In my view, the proper way for the Congress to make known its will on such foreign policy questions is through a positive action, with full debate on the merits of the issue and with each member taking the responsibility of casting a yes or no vote after considering those merits. The authorization and appropriations process represents one of the ways in which such influence can be exercised.

27.6 Black Power

Stokely Carmichael and Charles V. Hamilton

In the mid-1960s, militant young blacks began attacking the white power structure, claiming that the legal equality achieved under the Civil Rights Act of 1964 did not address the basic social and psychological problems of blacks in America. Stokely Carmichael, one of these militants, called for black unity in confronting white America and talked about "black power." The phrase *black power* carried different meanings for different blacks, and it led to the formation of such diverse groups as the Black Panthers (originally a self-help organization whose varied tactics sometimes included taking up arms) and Jesse Jackson's Operation PUSH (People United to Save Humanity). In 1968, Carmichael and sociologist Charles V. Hamilton published *Black Power: The Politics of Liberation in America*, in which they analyze the political, economic, and cultural impotence of blacks in America. In the excerpt reprinted here, Carmichael and Hamilton discuss why blacks in America have so little power.

Consider:

1. *The validity of Carmichael's and Hamilton's argument that blacks in America are exploited by white colonization;*
2. *Why Carmichael and Hamilton were hostile to the "Negro Establishment";*
3. *Whether taking up arms would help "the black community to redefine itself, set forth new values and goals and organize around them."*

The black community perceives the "white power structure" in very concrete terms. The man in the ghetto sees his white landlord come only to collect exorbitant rents and fail to make necessary repairs, while both know that the white-dominated city building inspection department will wink at violations or impose only slight fines. The man in the ghetto sees the white policeman on the corner brutally manhandle a black drunkard in a doorway, and at the same time accept a pay-off from one of the agents of the white-controlled rackets. He sees the streets in the ghetto lined with uncollected garbage, and he knows that the powers which could send trucks in to collect that garbage are white. When they don't, he knows the reason: the low political esteem in which the black community is held. . . . He is faced with a "white power structure" as monolithic as Europe's colonial offices have been to African and Asian colonies.

. . . the white power structure rules the black community through local blacks who are responsive to the white leaders, the downtown, white machine, not to the black populace. These black politicians do not exercise effective power. They cannot be relied upon to make forceful demands in behalf of their black constituents, and they become no more than puppets. They put loyalty to a political party before loyalty to their constituents and thus nullify any bargaining power the black community might develop. Colonial politics causes the subject to muffle his voice while participating in the councils of the white power structure. The black man forfeits his opportunity to speak forcefully and clearly for his race, and he justifies this in terms of expediency. Thus, when one talks of a "Negro Establishment" in most places in this country, one is talking of an Establishment resting on a white power base; of hand-picked blacks whom that base projects as showpieces out front. These black "leaders" are, then, only as powerful as their white kingmakers will permit them to be. This is no less true of the North than the South. . . .

. . . There has developed in this country an entire class of "captive leaders" in the black communities. These are black people with certain technical and administrative skills who could provide useful leadership

SOURCE: *Stokely Carmichael and Charles V. Hamilton,* Black Power: The Politics of Liberation in America *(London: Jonathan Cape, 1967), 9–11, 13, 30–32.*

roles in the black communities but do not because they have become beholden to the white power structure. These are black school teachers, county agents, junior executives in management positions with companies, etc. . . .

. . . American society indicates avenues of escape from the ghetto for those individuals who adapt to the "mainstream." This adaptation means to disassociate oneself from the black race, its culture, community and heritage, and become immersed (dispersed is another term) in the white world. What actually happens, as Professor E. Franklin Frazier pointed out in his book, *Black Bourgeoisie*, is that the black person ceases to identify himself with black people yet is obviously unable to assimilate with whites. He becomes a "marginal man," living on the fringes of both societies in a world largely of "make-believe." This black person is urged to adopt American middle-class standards and values.

. . . "adaptation" operated to deprive the black community of its potential skills and brain power. All too frequently, these "integrated" people are used to blunt the true feelings and goals of the black masses. They are picked as "Negro leaders," and the white power structure proceeds to talk to and deal only with them. Needless to say, no fruitful, meaningful dialogue can take place under such circumstances. Those hand-picked "leaders" have no viable constituency for which they can speak and act. . . .

The time is long overdue for the black community to redefine itself, set forth new values, and goals, and organize around them.

27.7   The End of Watergate: Pardoning Nixon

Gerald R. Ford

On August 9, 1974, after the House Judiciary Committee had approved articles of impeachment against him, Richard Nixon became the first President to resign from office. There were also indications that a grand jury would indict him for obstruction of justice. Although a public opinion poll revealed that 56 percent of those questioned believed Nixon should be brought to trial, many thoughtful Americans believed it would not be advisable. One alternative was for President Ford to issue an executive pardon and avoid the spectacle of a former President standing trial and perhaps being sent to jail. On September 9, 1974, Ford issued such a pardon, which is reprinted here. Also included here is an excerpt from Ford's autobiography in which he explains his reasons for granting Nixon's pardon.

Consider:

1. *Why it was thought that the pardon cost Ford many votes in the election of 1976;*
2. *Whether Richard Nixon's acceptance of the pardon constituted an admission of guilt.*

THE PRESIDENTIAL PARDON

. . . The hearings of the [Judiciary] Committee and its deliberations, which received wide national publicity over television, radio, and in printed media, resulted in votes adverse to Richard Nixon on recommended Articles of Impeachment.

As a result of certain acts or omissions occurring before his resignation from the Office of President, Richard Nixon has become liable to possible indictment and trial for offenses against the United States. Whether or not he shall be so prosecuted depends on findings of the appropriate grand jury and on the discretion of the authorized prosecutor. Should an indictment ensue, the accused shall then be entitled to a fair trial by an impartial jury, as guaranteed to every individual by the Constitution.

It is believed that a trial of Richard Nixon, if it became necessary, could not fairly begin until a year or more has elapsed. In the meantime, the tranquility to which this nation has been restored by the events of recent weeks could be irreparably lost by the prospects of bringing to trial a former President of the United States. The prospects of such trial will cause prolonged and divisive debate over the propriety of exposing to further punishment and degradation a man who has already paid the unprecedented penalty of relinquishing the highest elective office of the United States.

Now, THEREFORE, I, GERALD R. FORD, President of the United States, pursuant to the pardon power conferred upon me by Article II, Section 2, of the Constitution, have granted and by these presents do grant a full, free, and absolute pardon unto Richard Nixon for all offenses against the United States which he, Richard Nixon, has committed or may have committed or taken part in during the period from January 20, 1969 through August 9, 1974. . . .

PRESIDENT FORD'S EXPLANATION

I agonized over the idea of a pardon, and eventually several key conclusions solidified in my mind. First of all, I simply was not convinced

SOURCE: *"Proclamation 4311, Granting Pardon to Richard Nixon. September 8, 1974."* Public Papers of the Presidents of the United States: Gerald R. Ford, 1974 *(Washington, D.C.: Government Printing Office, 1974), 104. Gerald R. Ford,* A Time to Heal: The Autobiography of Gerald R. Ford, *160–61. Copyright © 1979 by Gerald R. Ford. Reprinted by permission of Harper & Row, Publishers, Inc.*

that the country wanted to see an ex-President behind bars. We are not a vengeful people; forgiveness is one of the roots of the American tradition. And Nixon, in my opinion, had already suffered enormously. His resignation was an implicit admission of guilt, and he would have to carry forever the burden of his disgrace. But I wasn't motivated primarily by sympathy for his plight or by concern over the state of his health. It was the state of the *country's* health at home and around the world that worried me. . . .

. . . I was very sure of what would happen if I let the charges against Nixon run their legal course. Months were sure to elapse between an indictment and trial. The entire process would no doubt require years: a minimum of two, a maximum of six. And Nixon would not spend time quietly in San Clemente. He would be fighting for his freedom, taking his cause to the people, and his constant struggle would have dominated the news. The story would overshadow everything else. No other issue could compete with the drama of a former President trying to stay out of jail. It would be virtually impossible for me to direct public attention to anything else. Passions on both sides would be aroused. A period of such prolonged vituperation and recrimination would be disastrous for the nation. America needed recovery, not revenge. The hate had to be drained and the healing begun.

CHAPTER QUESTIONS

1. *Why did the war in Vietnam lose the support of the American people?*
2. *In drawing up a balance sheet on the 1960s and early 1970s, what were the positive developments and negative developments?*
3. *Did the Watergate episode and Richard Nixon's resignation from office seriously "wound the presidency" as an institution? Explain.*

Chapter 28

*Challenges of
A Changing World*

The 1970s and 1980s represented a new stage of American history. Not only did the United States experience significant demographic shifts, but the nation's economic life and its relations with the rest of the world underwent important modifications as well. The magnitude of these changes and public reactions to political changes that began in the early 1960s produced a sharp political reaction in the 1980s—the Reagan Revolution—the legacy of which was still not entirely clear when the decade ended.

Demographic trends in the 1970s and 1980s changed the face of America. With the baby boom over, and the average life expectancy of Americans rising steadily, the population was rapidly growing older. This "graying" of America promised to have significant social, economic, and political effects. So, too, did the relatively high birth and immigration rates for nonwhites compared to whites, which shifted the racial composition of American society.

Perhaps the most dramatic transformation of the era occurred in the nation's economic life. Few doubted that America's unchallenged domination of the world economy had ended. The international oil price increases of the 1970s, for example, caused a full-scale energy crisis that reinforced the United States' dependence on foreign oil. In addition, in the early 1970s the nation began to import more goods than it exported—creating a negative trade balance, a problem that was to linger throughout the 1980s. The triumph of supply-side economics during the Reagan administration—that is, reducing taxes on the wealthiest Americans in order to produce economic expansion—proved popular in the short run, but—unaccompanied by promised reductions in federal spending—led to an ever-expanding budget deficit.

Despite the Reagan Revolution, which many commentators saw as a reversal of post-World War II political coalitions, some significant continuities characterized American politics during the 1970s and 1980s. For example, notwithstanding occasional setbacks, the nation continued to move steadily toward legal equality for all its citizens without regard to race, creed, or sex. Moreover, politics itself became more representative of the nation's diverse elements, as the numbers of women, African Americans, and Hispanics holding important offices increased. Innovations such as busing to achieve interracial balance in schools and affirmative action programs to equalize employment opportunities may have raised new problems, but they also helped solve old ones. Even the seemingly more "revolutionary" aspects of political life in the period, such as the rise of the New Right, in some ways paralleled the earlier political participation of longer established religious groups.

The most distressing area of continuity in the period was the continuing Cold War. Aside from some hopeful interludes, the United States and the Soviet Union remained locked in an arms race that kept the threat of a nuclear war alive. More disturbing was that many other nations raced to develop nuclear weapons, further pushing the world toward nuclear holocaust.

The selections in this chapter are intended to illuminate some of the major changes and challenges faced by American society in these two critical decades.

Chronology

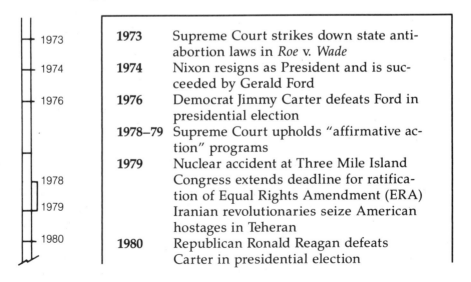

1973	1973	Supreme Court strikes down state anti-abortion laws in *Roe* v. *Wade*
1974	1974	Nixon resigns as President and is succeeded by Gerald Ford
1976	1976	Democrat Jimmy Carter defeats Ford in presidential election
	1978–79	Supreme Court upholds "affirmative action" programs
1978	1979	Nuclear accident at Three Mile Island Congress extends deadline for ratification of Equal Rights Amendment (ERA) Iranian revolutionaries seize American hostages in Teheran
1979		
1980	1980	Republican Ronald Reagan defeats Carter in presidential election

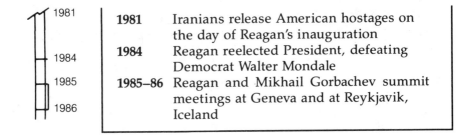

1981	**1981**	Iranians release American hostages on the day of Reagan's inauguration
1984	**1984**	Reagan reelected President, defeating Democrat Walter Mondale
1985	**1985–86**	Reagan and Mikhail Gorbachev summit meetings at Geneva and at Reykjavik, Iceland
1986		

Documents

28.1   Presidential Leadership and Public Confidence

Jimmy Carter   Ronald Reagan

The widespread disillusionment brought on by the Vietnam War and Watergate was not easily disspelled. Certainly, President Jimmy Carter was unable to restore confidence in the political system. In fairness, it should be noted that Carter faced a host of very difficult problems; but his introspective, low-key style also worked against him. Ronald Reagan had much greater success with the public. Again, style was a significant factor. Strong-willed, genial, and optimistic, Reagan managed to revive the electorate's faith in the system and in the presidency, even though major problems remained unresolved. The selections that follow, taken from a 1979 speech to the nation by President Carter and from President Reagan's speech accepting his party's renomination in 1984, illustrate the contrast of styles and approaches of these two leaders.

Consider:

1. ·Whether Carter's speech is an example of effective moral exhortation by a President (compare to Doc. 22.1);
2. In what ways the tone and substance of the two speeches differ;
3. The degree to which presidents can affect the public mood through their individual personalities and approaches.

JIMMY CARTER, July 15, 1979

. . . as I was preparing to speak, I began to ask myself the same question that I now know has been troubling many of you. Why have we not been able to get together as a nation to resolve our serious energy problem?

It's clear that the true problems of our Nation are much deeper—deeper than gasoline lines or energy shortages, deeper even than inflation or recession. . . .

The threat is nearly invisible in ordinary ways. It is a crisis of confidence. It is a crisis that strikes at the very heart and soul and spirit of our national will. . . .

The erosion of our confidence in the future is threatening to destroy the social and the political fabric of America. . . .

In a nation that was proud of hard work, strong families, close-knit communities, and our faith in God, too many of us now tend to worship self-indulgence and consumption. . . .

As you know, there is a growing disrespect for government and for churches and for schools, the news media, and other institutions. . . .

What you see too often in Washington and elsewhere around the country is a system of government that seems incapable of action. . . .

We are at a turning point in our history. There are two paths to choose. One is a path I've warned about tonight, the path that leads to fragmentation and self-interest. . . .

All the traditions of our past, all the lessons of our heritage, all the promises of our future point to another path, the path of common purpose and the restoration of American values. . . .

I do not promise you that this struggle for freedom will be easy. I do not promise a quick way out of our Nation's problems, when the truth is that the only way out is an all-out effort. . . .

. . . Let us commit ourselves together to a rebirth of the American spirit. Working together with our common faith we cannot fail.

RONALD REAGAN, August 23, 1984

The choices this year are not just between two different personalities or between two political parties. They're between two different visions

---

SOURCES: Public Papers of the Presidents of the United States: Jimmy Carter, 1979, Book II (Washington, D.C.: Government Printing Office, 1980), 1235, 1237–38, 1240–41; Weekly Compilation of Presidential Documents, September 3, 1984 (Washington, D.C.: Government Printing Office, 1984), 20: 1167, 1169, 1172–73.

of the future, two fundamentally different ways of governing—their government of pessimism, fear and limits, or ours of hope, confidence, and growth. . . .

In 1980 the people decided with us that the economic crisis was not caused by the fact that they lived too well. Government lived too well. . . .

Our government was also in serious trouble abroad. . . .

But worst of all, Americans were losing the confidence and optimism about the future that has made us unique in the world. . . .

We can all be proud that pessimism is ended. America is coming back and is more confident than ever about the future. Tonight, we thank the citizens of the United States whose faith and unwillingness to give up on themselves or this country saved us all. . . .

Isn't our choice really not one of left or right, but of up or down? Down through the welfare state to statism, to more and more government largesse accompanied always by more government authority, less individual liberty and, ultimately, totalitarianism . . . The alternative is the dream conceived by our Founding Fathers, up to the ultimate in individual freedom consistent with an orderly society. . . .

We came together in a national crusade to make America great again, and to make a new beginning. Well, now it's all coming together. With our beloved nation at peace, we're in the midst of a springtime of hope for America. Greatness lies ahead of us.

28.2   Politics and Moral Issues: The Moral Majority
Jerry Falwell

The rise of a New Right in American politics—a broad-based movement against many of the social and political products of liberal activism— helped Ronald Reagan win the presidency in 1980. The New Right consisted of such diverse elements as direct-mail public relations organizations, traditional conservative political organizations, and political action groups dedicated to furthering specific causes. The foundation of the New Right, however, was legions of fundamentalist Protestants who entered the political arena at the urging of popular television evangelists such as Jerry Falwell, Pat Robertson, and others. In 1979 Falwell founded a powerful new organization to further the New Right's "social agenda": Moral Majority, Inc. The political activities of Falwell and other fundamentalist religious leaders, through Moral Majority and other organizations, drew heavy fire from those who opposed its aims. In a brief essay that appeared in *Newsweek* in 1981, excerpted below, Falwell defended the legitimacy of church leaders like himself taking part in politics.

SOURCE: *Jerry Falwell, "The Maligned Moral Majority," Newsweek (September 21, 1991): 17.*

Consider:

1. *Whether Falwell's interpretation of how the Framers of the Constitution viewed the relationship of church and state is reasonable, and how such a view might affect minority rights;*
2. *How Falwell's arguments compare to those of Martin Luther King, Jr., in his "Letter from Birmingham City Jail" (Doc. 26.7).*

When liberals first began attacking the Moral Majority, they said we had no right to speak out. When it was pointed out that the liberal agenda was well represented in the 1960s and '70s in the government, in the streets and in liberal churches, the liberals conceded that while we had the right to speak, it was wrong for us to try to "impose" our moral viewpoint on everyone else.

Of course, there was nothing wrong, so far as liberals were concerned, with "imposing" their own views, whether those views had to do with civil rights, the Vietnam War, busing, the eradication of voluntary school prayer or the extermination of unborn babies through abortion. Liberals could impose their views because liberals were right! . . .

The Moral Majority has touched a sensitive nerve in the American people. Many Americans are sick and tired of the way their government has been run. They are tired of being told that their values and beliefs don't matter and that only those values held by government bureaucrats and liberal preachers are worthy of adoption in the area of public policy. Our people are the previously inactive, turned-off voters who believed that who wins an election doesn't matter. . . .

The Founding Fathers, contrary to what our liberal friends believe, wanted to preserve and encourage the church, not to restrict it or its influence. For them, the separation of church and state was a check on the *government*, not the church. The First Amendment prohibits the government from establishing a church (as had been done in England). It does not prohibit the churches from doing anything, except collecting taxes. Any person who suggests that separation of church and state requires more than this—that it requires churches to remain silent on "political issues" or preachers to be neutral on candidates or religious organizations to pursue only "spiritual goals"—is simply grinding his own ax rather than reading the law. . . .

Let's remember that all law is the imposition of someone's morality to the exclusion of someone else's morality. We have laws against murder, rape, incest, cannibalism and stealing. No doubt, there are murderers, rapists, practitioners of incest, cannibals and thieves who are upset that their "rights" have been denied. But in order to provide for the common defense and promote the general welfare, it was deemed necessary to pass such laws. . . .

The grossest immorality has been perpetrated not by those who carried it out, but by those who remained silent and did nothing. We may not always be right, but we will never stand accused of doing nothing.

28.3   Energy Crisis and Environmental Issues
Martin V. Melosi

In the 1970s, the nation faced a new set of problems related to energy and the environment. The steep increases in oil prices in 1973–1974 made Americans suddenly realize how dependent the United States had become on other nations for its energy needs. A full-scale national debate on the energy needs of the future ensued, but the issue was complicated by the fact that Americans had become very sensitive to the dangers of abusing their environment. In the excerpt that follows, historian Martin Melosi discusses the interplay of the energy and environmental issues in the 1970s and 1980s, and points out basic questions that the nation needed to confront as it chose among alternative "energy futures."

Consider:

1. *The "fundamental questions of values, lifestyle, and the future aspirations of the nation" involved in the energy issue;*
2. *The degree of success achieved by environmentalists on energy-related issues in the 1970s;*
3. *Why the Three Mile Island accident did not result in a full-scale reevaluation of the use of nuclear energy for peaceful purposes.*

Scarcity replaced abundance as a major focus during the 1970s. . . . Concern over energy scarcity clashed with concern over ecological, or environmental scarcity. A sense of the finite quantities of energy sources (or access to them) came face to face with a sense of the finite nature of a habitable physical environment. . . .

. . . A change in energy consumption habits, capital outlays for pollution control devices, and an emphasis on "soft" energy paths might help preserve the environment, but it might also threaten economic growth. Encased in these seemingly tangible issues were fundamental questions of values, lifestyle, and the future aspirations of the nation. . . .

. . . Exploring for oil in undeveloped regions, land or sea, set off debates over economic productivity versus preservation. . . .

The major battle over oil production during the 1970s was fought on the land not on the sea. It was a conflict over the Alaska pipeline. . . .

Environmentalists fought hard against the pipeline, largely for the sake of wilderness preservation in one of the few remaining frontiers of the United States. The 1973 oil embargo undermined their case, and, in that year, Congress passed the Trans-Alaska Pipeline Authorization Act. . . .

. . . The first oil began to flow three years later. . . .

SOURCE: *Martin V. Melosi*, Coping With Abundance: Energy and Environmental in Industrial America *(Philadelphia: Temple University Press, 1985), 295-96, 299-302, 304, 310-12, 332.*

COAL, STRIP MINING, AND ELECTRICAL POWER

The energy crisis stimulated interest in America's most abundant energy resource—coal. The environmental implications of coal mining and coal burning, however, detracted from its rise as a panacea to the nation's energy woes. For reasons of economy and efficiency, surface mining (or strip mining) of coal had become the preferred method in several areas of the country—and also invited the greatest criticism from environmentalists. . . .

The Federal Strip Mining Control Act of 1977 was the culmination of efforts to curtail the greatest abuses. . . .

The new law was not as strict as many environmentalists wanted. Small operators were exempted for about three years, and it allowed strip mining on several terrains as well as national forests and prime agricultural lands. In addition, it provided that surface owners must consent before mining was allowed on federal land. An incomplete victory, the passage of the Federal Strip Mining Control Act was another example of linking national environmental goals to energy production. . . .

NUCLEAR POWER

. . . To advocates, nuclear power had a spotless record; reactors incorporated the latest technology and were constructed under rigorous supervision. Opponents questioned these claims, arguing that accidents had occurred in the past but were covered up, and they were likely to happen in the future if the technology proliferated. . . .

. . . [In 1979] the accident at Three Mile Island brought into sharp focus the conflict between the need for alternative energy supplies and the environmental cost of that quest. . . .

The accident occurred on March 28, . . . At 4:00 A.M., a pump on the main water-feed system malfunctioned. Within two seconds, the flow of water to cool the reactor stopped, and the plant safety system automatically shut down the steam turbine and electric generator. A relief valve popped open to reduce the pressure in the reactor and stayed in that position. Unfortunately, an indicator on the control panel led the crew to believe that the valve was shut. Instead, it drained water from the reactor for more than two hours. Believing that the reactor was adequately supplied with cooling water, the operators shut off the emergency cooling pump. The loss of cooling water caused the fuel to overheat and brought the core dangerously close to a meltdown. The top of the core became uncovered, hydrogen was generated, and an explosion in the containment building occurred. (Not until a day later did the operators learn about the explosion.)

By about 7:30 A.M., the station manager declared a general emergency. . . .

. . . Rampant rumors of large-scale evacuation led Governor Richard Thornburgh to recommend that pregnant women and preschool children leave the area within a five-mile radius of the plant. Independently of the governor's announcement, many people had already left their homes. Chaos did not break out, but citizens were confused, scared, and uncertain. . . .

. . . Public reaction ranged from relief to indignation. . . .

Yet the accident at Three Mile Island seemed to have little effect on the strongest proponents and opponents of nuclear power. Even an event as dramatic as the accident of Three Mile Island could do little more than to leave nuclear power in limbo. . . .

ALTERNATIVE ENERGY FUTURES

. . . Americans have taken a short-term view of their energy needs. In part, this response is the result of the many competing interests in American society, but it is also the result of the nation's rich natural wealth and its ability to acquire the resources of others. . . . Energy is not simply a commodity to produce wealth or heat, light, and power—it is an expression of the culture in terms of how we choose to exploit it, produce it, and use it. . . .

28.4 Sunbelt, Frostbelt, and Rustbelt

For most of the nation's history, the basic pattern of population movement has been westward and into urban centers. After World War II, the urban trend accelerated with a massive move to the suburbs, and the westward trend changed somewhat with the greatest population increases occurring in the "Sunbelt"—the Far West and South. In the 1970s, the Sunbelt continued to grow, while population plummeted in the states of the Midwest and Northeast—sometimes called the "Frostbelt" or "Rustbelt." Although the downward population trend in many of these northern states has turned around somewhat in the 1980s, the general movement to the Sunbelt is still a major demographic force in American life. The map on page 472 shows the amount by which the population of the Northeast, Midwest, South, and West changed through migration in the years 1970–1985.

Consider:

1. *The political implications of the demographic trends shown on this map;*
2. *What factors might have accelerated the movement of Americans to the Sunbelt states after 1970.*

REGIONAL MIGRATION IN THE UNITED STATES, 1970-1985

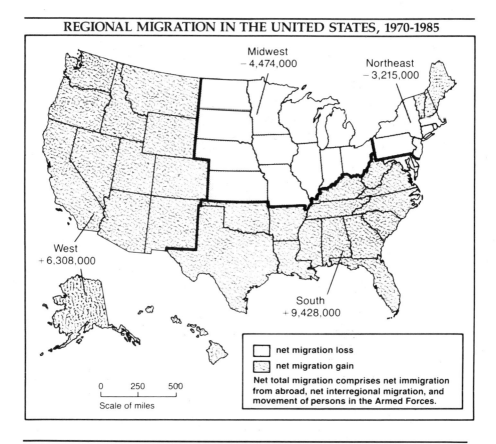

Midwest
– 4,474,000

Northeast
– 3,215,000

West
+ 6,308,000

South
+ 9,428,000

☐ net migration loss
▧ net migration gain

Net total migration comprises net immigration from abroad, net interregional migration, and movement of persons in the Armed Forces.

0   250   500
Scale of miles

SOURCE: *U.S. Bureau of the Census*, Statistical Abstract of the United States: 1987 *(Washington, D.C.; Government Printing Office, 1986), 24.*

28.5 Implementing Equality: Affirmative Action
U.S. Commission on Civil Rights

The persistent economic problems of the 1970s and early 1980s had a significant impact on the campaigns for minority civil rights and women's rights. Although racial minorities and women could still point to serious inequities and discrimination in the mid-1970s, a body of law protecting their basic social, political, and economic rights had been enacted. This progress, however, had come largely in areas where advancement did not threaten the rights of the majority. Such was not the case with "affirmative action," a policy designed to increase the representation of minorities and women in the work force. By the late 1970s, affirmative action came under fierce attack by those who saw it as "reverse discrimination." Shrinking economic opportunities, with more people competing for fewer jobs, intensified these attacks. In 1981, a report by the United States Civil Rights Commission, excerpted here, attempted to explain the rationale for "affirmative action."

Consider:

1. *The ways in which the commission answers the charge that "affirmative action" amounts to "reverse discrimination";*
2. *How the concept of "affirmative action" relates to the concept of minority rights as discussed in Doc. 6.6, and to the concept of "just laws" as treated in Docs. 6.3 and 26.7;*
3. *Whether affirmative action is an adequate substitute for the proposed Equal Rights Amendment (ERA).*

. . . When discrimination is widespread and entrenched, it becomes a self-regenerating process capable of converting what appear to be neutral acts into further discrimination. . . . These activities, separately and together, routinely confer privileges and advantages upon the dominant group, while imposing penalties and disadvantages upon minorities and women.

When these processes are at work, antidiscrimination remedies that insist on "color blindness" or "gender neutrality" are insufficient. . . . In such circumstances, the only effective remedy is affirmative action, . . .

By affirmative action, the Commission means active efforts that take race, sex, and national origin into account for the purpose of remedying discrimination. . . .

Arguments against affirmative action have come from the top ranks of academia and the most powerful sectors of our economy. They are supported by a large segment of the American public. Some of these critics have a long history of commitment to civil rights progress. . . . Their arguments are diverse. They range from vigorous assertions that all race-conscious remedial measures are no different from the racism they seek to remedy to positions that draw the line only at rigid quotas imposed without judicial findings of discrimination. . . . In general, those opposed to affirmative action portray it as violating the rights of individual white men in order to remedy group disadvantages of women and certain "preferred" minorities. . . .

. . . Few fair-minded persons argue with the objective of increasing the participation of minorities and women in those areas from which they historically have been excluded. Heated controversy occurs, however, over particular methods employed in affirmative action plans to achieve this common objective. . . .

. . . There is widespread acceptance of such measures as undertaking recruiting efforts, establishing special training programs, and reviewing selection procedures. On the other hand, firing whites or men to hire minorities or women, and choosing unqualified people simply to increase participation by minorities and women, are universally condemned practices. . . .

SOURCE: *Affirmative Action in the 1980s: Dismantling the Process of Discrimination—A Statement of the United States Commission on Civil Rights (Washington, D.C.: U.S. Commission on Civil Rights, 1981), 2–3, 5, 33, 35–36, 38–39.*

What distinguishes . . . "preferential treatment" attributable to affirmative action plans from quotas used in the past is the fact that the lessened opportunities for white males are incidental, temporary, and not generated by prejudice against those who are excluded. The purpose of affirmative action plans is to eliminate, not perpetuate, practices stemming from ideas of racial, gender, and ethnic inferiority or superiority. . . .

Although affirmative action plans may adversely affect particular white men as *individuals*, they do not unfairly burden white men *as a group*. . . . Affirmative action plans reduce the share of white men as a group to what it would roughly be had there been no discrimination against minorities and women. In this sense, an affirmative action plan simply removes the unfair advantages that white males as a class enjoy due to past discrimination. . . .

Affirmative action plans, regardless of how well they are implemented, are viewed by some as perpetuating the belief of minority and female inferiority. . . . According to its critics, affirmative action casts doubt on the legitimacy of the achievements of women and minorities by implying that these accomplishments were not earned by hard work and on the basis of merit.

These alleged "stigmas," however, do not result from the concept of affirmative action itself. They predate the concept. . . .

Race, sex, and national origin statistics in affirmative action plans do not mean . . . that certain "protected groups" are entitled to have their members represented in every area of society in a ratio proportional to their presence in society. . . . We reject the allegation that numerical aspects of affirmative action plans inevitably must work as a system of group entitlement that ignores individual abilities in order to apportion resources and opportunities like pieces of pie.

28.6 Reaganomics: Economic Policies and Results In The Eighties

Reaganomics, a term coined by the media in the 1980s to describe the economic policies embraced by the Reagan administration, was mostly a synonym for supply-side economics, the fundamental principle of which was reducing taxes on the wealthiest Americans to encourage investment and produce economic expansion. To implement this principle, Reagan secured from Congress two major tax reductions, in 1981 and 1986. Meanwhile, federal spending on defense increased, while certain domestic programs were cut. The results were mixed; indeed, one's view of whether or not Reaganomics was a success tended to depend on one's politics. Presented here are two documents reflecting a critical perspective on the Reagan policies: a cartoon by John Trever of the *Albuquerque Journal* and a chart from the best-selling book *America: What Went Wrong?*, published in 1992 by two

Pulitzer Prize-winning reporters of the *Philadelphia Inquirer.* Also included are some statistical measures of economic performance in the 1980s.

Consider:

1. *What types of criticisms of Reaganomics are reflected by the cartoon and the chart;*
2. *How both critics and defenders of Reagan administration economic policies could cite statistical evidence from the table presented here to defend their points of view.*

GNP AND FEDERAL DEBT 1980–1989

Year	GNP (in Billions of Dollars)	Federal Debt (in Millions of Dollars)	Debt as Percentage of GNP
1980	2,670.6	908,503	34.0
1981	2,986.4	994,298	33.3
1982	3,139.1	1,136,798	36.2
1983	3,321.9	1,371,164	41.3
1984	3,687.7	1,564,110	42.4
1985	3,952.4	1,816,974	46.0
1986	4,180.9	2,120,082	50.7
1987	4,430.2	2,345,578	52.9
1988	4,792.2	2,600,753	54.3
1989	5,151.3	2,866,188	55.6

"...AND THIS IS OUR WORKING MODEL...."

SOURCE: *Fred Barnes, ed.* A Cartoon History of the Reagan Years *(Washington, DC: Regnery Gateway, 1988), p. 45.*

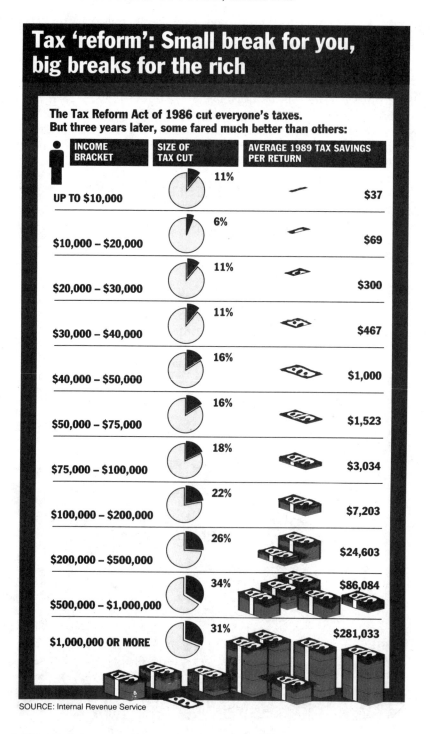

Tax 'reform': Small break for you, big breaks for the rich

The Tax Reform Act of 1986 cut everyone's taxes. But three years later, some fared much better than others:

INCOME BRACKET	SIZE OF TAX CUT	AVERAGE 1989 TAX SAVINGS PER RETURN
UP TO $10,000	11%	$37
$10,000 – $20,000	6%	$69
$20,000 – $30,000	11%	$300
$30,000 – $40,000	11%	$467
$40,000 – $50,000	16%	$1,000
$50,000 – $75,000	16%	$1,523
$75,000 – $100,000	18%	$3,034
$100,000 – $200,000	22%	$7,203
$200,000 – $500,000	26%	$24,603
$500,000 – $1,000,000	34%	$86,084
$1,000,000 OR MORE	31%	$281,033

SOURCE: Internal Revenue Service

SOURCE: *Donald L. Barlett and James B. Steele, America: What Went Wrong?* (Kansas City: Andrews and McMeel, 1992), p. 6.

28.7   The Cold War in the 1980s

Michael Mandelbaum and Strobe Talbott

In many respects, American foreign policy concerns in the 1970s and 1980s were notably different from those of the early years of the Cold War. New dilemmas arose from changing patterns in world trade, the growing assertiveness of developing nations, complex intraregional conflicts, and the danger of nuclear proliferation. Yet, other important aspects of world politics remained unchanged. Perhaps the most striking continuity concerned the Cold War between the United States and the Soviet Union. Reviving the pattern established by Presidents Eisenhower, Kennedy, and Nixon before him, Ronald Reagan chose to conduct relations with the Soviets by blending hard-line anti-Communist rhetoric and a strong defense posture with forays into personal diplomacy with his Soviet counterpart, Mikhail Gorbachev. The following excerpt from a work by two experts in United States-Soviet relations, Michael Mandelbaum and Strobe Talbott, discusses Reagan's interactions with Gorbachev at the 1986 Reykjavik, Iceland, summit.

Consider:

1. *Whether the common concerns of Reagan and Gorbachev might have been beneficial in reaching agreements in summit negotiations;*
2. *Why both Reagan and Gorbachev chose to "break the rules" of summit conference procedures at Reykjavik;*
3. *The purpose and value of summit meetings between the leaders of the United States and the Soviet Union.*

Ronald Wilson Reagan. . . . and Mikhail Sergeyevitch Gorbachev. . . . met face-to-face twice in less than a year. At both meetings—in Geneva in November 1985, and in Reykjavik in October 1986—the two leaders were reenacting a ritual that had come to have a central place in the political affairs of the planet. . . .

Both Reagan and Gorbachev had put their political skills to good use in consolidating power. For all the differences between the two positions, the American presidency and the office of General Secretary of the Communist Party of the Soviet Union have some institutional features in common. . . . The authority of the incumbent depends in large part on his personal skill at balancing the interests and demands of various constituencies and keeping rivals and opponents at bay. . . .

Neither was beyond challenge. Both faced political difficulties. . . .

In July and August [1986] the President and the General Secretary exchanged letters and dispatched delegations of arms-control experts to each other's capitals. Momentum seemed to be building toward a

SOURCE: *Michael Mandelbaum and Strobe Talbott,* Reagan and Gorbachev *(New York: Vintage Books, 1987), 3–4, 9, 160–62, 175, 182–83.*

summit in Washington at the end of the year. Then an American journalist was arrested in Moscow. Suddenly the mood soured, and the momentum slowed. But in the midst of what turned out to be a minor crisis, Reagan and Gorbachev made clear first to each other and then to the world that they were determined to proceed with the business between them. They agreed to hold a meeting that turned out to be one of the most extraordinary encounters in the history of the relations between their countries. . . .

The two-day meeting in Reykjavik, Iceland, on October 11–12, 1986, broke with virtually all the precedents of U.S.-Soviet relations. There were scarcely any preparations. . . . the agenda turned out to be much broader and the issues discussed far more consequential than even those the Americans had envisioned for the anticipated summit itself. . . .

In violation of all the conventional wisdom about sound negotiating tactics and prudent diplomacy, Reagan and Gorbachev engaged each other on the biggest, most difficult issue dividing them—how to structure and limit their huge stockpiles of nuclear weapons—and proceeded to improvise. Working groups of experts with no clear instructions toiled through the night to hammer out compromises on matters that years of negotiation had failed to resolve. . . .

They failed at the last minute to overcome the principal obstacle to a treaty that might have significantly reduced levels of offensive weaponry on both sides. They could not resolve the question of how, if at all, to constrain SDI [Strategic Defense Initiative]. . . .

During their long and tiring sessions in Iceland, Reagan and Gorbachev had apparently been caught up in a make-or-break atmosphere. At the end they had engaged in a bout of feverish one-upmanship, with each trying to outdo the other in demonstrating his devotion to the dream of a nuclear-free world. . . .

The first half of the 1980s, and the policies that both sides pursued in that period, . . . showed that neither was likely to gain a decisive advantage over the other. By agreeing in principle to meet on a regular basis and to seek diplomatic accommodation on some of the issues that divided them, the two leaders were implicitly acknowledging the limits of their ability to get their way unilaterally. For both men, this was a lesson that took some time to learn.

CHAPTER QUESTIONS

1. *Were any of the problems that the United States faced in the 1970s and 1980s truly "new"? Explain.*
2. *In what ways and to what degree were political events in the 1980s a reaction to politics in the 1960s and 1970s?*
3. *How did economic realities affect public attitudes about social problems and issues in the 1970s and 1980s?*

Chapter 29

Entering the Global Era

The collapse and breakup of the Soviet Union and the communist regimes of eastern Europe in the early 1990s completely changed the world as Americans had known it for nearly half a century. United States leaders, caught off guard by the speed of events, searched for policies that would create a new post-Cold War world order. A particularly difficult question was how the United States should respond to the desperate economic circumstances of the republics of the former Soviet Union. At the same time, bitter ethnic warfare tore apart some former Soviet states and the small republics that had arisen out of the communist state of Yugoslavia. Now that the United States was alone as the world's superpower, with no enemy against which to define itself on the international stage, it was not clear how—or to what degree—these murderous conflicts and the resultant political instability related to American national interest. The United States joined an international effort to help restore peace to these trouble-spots, but as the twenty-first century dawned, stability had not yet been achieved.

Another significant phenomenon in world politics during the 1990s was the emergence of new regional economic compacts. Most prominent of the new regional groupings was the European Union (EU), which ended trade barriers among the nations of western Europe and introduced a new common currency, the Euro. In the Western Hemisphere, the North American Free Trade Agreement (NAFTA) reduced barriers to commerce between the United States and its neighbors, Canada and Mexico. As the Clinton administration leaned more toward free trade, many Americans openly questioned such policies. Yet, the creation of the World Trade Organization (WTO) in 1995 signaled Americans' growing acceptance of global markets.

Other global matters began to supplant more traditional foreign policy issues as a new global economy evolved. Concerns about the environment, which had first surfaced in a significant way in the 1970s, moved to center stage. This revived concern led to the convening of a United Nations "Earth Summit" in 1992, and later in the decade to strident protests against the WTO for its allegedly short-sighted pro-industrial policies that threatened fragile ecosystems around the globe. The natural environment seemed to be under increasing threat, too, from scientific and technological advances at the end of the century, particularly breakthroughs in the area of genetic engineering.

Although fear of nuclear war between the superpowers had ended after the Cold War, threats to world peace remained. The United States felt vulnerable to terrorist attacks that could be neither anticipated nor averted. Whereas it was once possible to imagine "winning" the Cold War with superior nuclear power, there seemed to be no way to "win" against the perpetrators of terrorist attacks that were often rooted in religious fundamentalism rather than political or military objectives.

Chronology

1989	U.S. and Soviet Union sign the Intermediate Nuclear Forces (INF) Treaty, removing 2,500 missiles from Europe
	Berlin Wall torn down; Germany reunified in next year
1990-91	U.S. troops victorious over Iraq in Persian Gulf War
1991	Collapse of the Soviet Union
1992	First "Earth Summit" (Rio de Janeiro)
1993	Creation of European Union (EU)
	President Clinton agrees to provide economic and technical assistance to the Russian Federation to help in transition to democracy
1993	U.S. ratifies North American Free Trade Agreement (NAFTA)
1994	World Trade Organization established
1995	U.S. forces sent into Bosnia as part of United Nations peacekeeping force
1998	Terrorist attack on American embassies in Kenya and Tanzania
	NATO expanded to include former Communist Bloc nations Hungary, Poland, and the Czech Republic
2000	Terrorist attack on U.S.S. *Cole*

Documents

29.1   The Monroe Doctrine Transformed: The North American Free Trade Agreement

Robert Gilpin

One of the most significant forces in the new global politics was economic regionalism—the phenomenon whereby neighboring nations put aside long-standing political and cultural rivalries to advance common economic interests. The first and perhaps most significant such effort was the creation of the European Union (EU) in 1993. In response to the European regional compact, the United States, Canada, and Mexico entered into their own regional pact in late 1993, the North American Free Trade Agreement (NAFTA). This excerpt discusses the complex forces and motives that underlay the new North American regional compact, as well as some of the political implications in the United States.

Consider:

1. *How American motives and interest in entering into the North American Free Trade Agreement compared to attitudes that underlay assertions of American "rights" as reflected in the Monroe Doctrine (Document 10.7);*
2. *The ways in which issues raised in connection with American participation in NAFTA may have affected public opinion concerning immigration;*
3. *How economic regionalism would be likely to affect international cooperation in such venues as the United Nations and the World Court.*

The 1994 creation of the North American Free Trade Agreement (NAFTA), comprising the United States, Canada, and Mexico, was another manifestation of the U.S. move away from multilateralism to a multitrack foreign economic policy. The United States supported NAFTA at least initially, to increase its bargaining leverage vis-à-vis the European Union; later, North American regionalism became an end in itself. NAFTA also entailed a reversal of Canada's and Mexico's historic policies of maintaining distance from their giant (and not always congenial) neighbor. Although these radical changes grew from economic roots, political factors were important in the decisions of all three countries.

. . . Although some critics have argued that the North American Free Trade Agreement (NAFTA) originated in an American effort to dominate and economically conquer its neighbors, it was Mexico that initiated the negotiations that produced NAFTA. For economic and political reasons of their own, the United States and Canada responded favorably to the Mexican initiative. The negotiations, begun in 1991 and completed by a treaty signed in 1993, constituted a historic development. . . .

Led by American-trained economists and technocrats, Mexico in the 1980s had undertaken an ambitious program of economic and political reforms. . . . Joining NAFTA, Mexican leaders believed, would "lock in" their liberalization reforms and convince foreign investors that the Mexican government would not backtrack on its commitments to deregulate and to open the Mexican economy to trade and foreign investment. . . .

The American decision to participate in the NAFTA negotiations was strongly influenced by political motives, including the need to resolve the issue of illegal Mexican immigration into the United States. Stated crudely, the United States was motivated by a very simple calculus: it had to accept either an ever-increasing flow of illegal Mexican immigrants or a greater number of manufactured goods from Mexico. . . . Many believed that, in addition, a stable and prosperous Mexico would become a better partner in the battle against drugs. . . .

. . . NAFTA generated an intense and bitter debate both in Mexico and the United States. Although this debate focused on the terms of the Agreement itself, there were powerful reactions in both countries to market liberalization and to economic globalization in general. Mexicans opposed to NAFTA objected to the dangers of unbridled capitalism and the increased likelihood that American imperialism would threaten Mexican independence. American opponents, led by Ross Perot, feared that the agreement would inevitably lead to the "Mexicanization" of the American standard of living. In this battle, Perot was joined by a surprising coalition between organized labor and environmental organizations, both of which were concerned about the consequences of integrating one of the most economically

SOURCE: *Robert Gilpin,* The Challenge of Global Capitalism: The World Economy in the 21st Century *(Princeton: Princeton University Press, 2000), 239-244.*

advanced and democratic countries in the world with a low-wage, underdeveloped, and, in their opinion, nondemocratic country. . . .

The Clinton Administration initially vacillated in its responses to these hostile criticisms of the Treaty, but eventually supported the Treaty and claimed that the Agreement would create hundreds of thousands of new jobs for Americans. The Agreement, said one Administration spokesperson, would create "jobs, jobs, jobs." The Administration attempted to mollify critics by forcing Mexico to accept two side-accords to the Treaty that dealt with labor standards and environmental protection, but attacks on NAFTA continued. Persistent opposition from American labor, environmentalists, and others has been due not only to lax enforcement of the side agreements on labor and environmental standards, but also to concerns about the larger issue of economic globalization and its allegedly negative consequences for jobs, wages, and the environment. NAFTA's opponents believe that globalization works to the disadvantage of American workers because it increases importing of products and exporting of jobs.

29.2   Dilemmas of the Lone "Superpower"

Kirk Anderson
Henry H. Shelton

By 2000, the United States stood as the lone global "superpower." The purpose of "collective security" agreements between America and its allies became less clear without a strong enemy to defend against. Many former Warsaw Pact countries began negotiating for membership in the European Union; some joined an expanding North American Treaty Organization (NATO). At the same time, deep and bitter ethnic hostilities erupted into violence in the former Yugoslavia, as well as in parts of the former Soviet Union. The respective roles of NATO and the United Nations were not clear in these international crises. America was forced to reexamine the way it defined its "national interest." The cartoon on page 484 symbolically contrasts the roles of the United Nations and NATO, while the remarks of General Henry Shelton that follow reflect an American military leader's perspective on the uses of military might in this new world.

Consider:

1. *What differences the cartoon suggests concerning the roles of the United Nations and NATO, respectively;*
2. *How American "responsibilities" in the world as of the year 2000 compared with the situation during the early Cold War (See Document 25.4);*
3. *The most reasonable guidelines for defining American "national interest" in the world as the twenty-first century began.*

UN   NATO

SOURCE: *Kirk Anderson,* St. Paul Pioneer Press, *1999*

The use of force is the most important decision that our Nation can make. And, of course, it is and it must be a civilian decision. A decision that is based, hopefully, on sound military advice, but one that is ultimately made by our political leaders on behalf of the American people.

In making decisions of such consequence, I think we would do well to remember that there is no template, no cookie cutter solution that can be applied to all situations. It's naive to think that we can develop hard-and-fast rules to handle the myriad of contingencies and crises—both great and small—which confront America at the end of the 20th Century, and that I think we face as we enter into this next century in just a few short weeks. However, each case has its own context and it must be weighed based on its own merit. And this doesn't mean that we have to deal with contingencies ad hoc. There are clear parameters that should inform our decisions about managing crises. . . .

. . . intervention, unless it is linked to a discernable national interest, is not sustainable.

And by "interest" I mean basically three broad categories: vital national interests, important national interests, and humanitarian and other types of interests. . . .

It is the employment. . . of our troops and the use of force in support of humanitarian and other interests that engender the most debate. The use of

SOURCE: Vital Speeches of the Day, *January 15, 2000. "The Military: An Instrument of Statecraft, Force, Diplomacy and National Security" by Henry H. Shelton, General, Chairman of the Joint Chiefs of Staff (City News Publishing Co., Mt. Pleasant SC, 29465) 66:194-196.*

military forces in this arena focuses on their capabilities and resources and less on their combat power.

While the military is not generally the best tool to solve humanitarian crises, under certain circumstances the appropriate use of our Armed Forces can bring about a solution to the problem at hand. For example, if the scale of the catastrophe dwarfs the ability of international relief agencies to respond, such as we saw happen in Rwanda, then the military can be used and be used in a very efficient and effective manner. . . .

Such efforts, I believe, should first of all be limited in duration. Secondly, they should have a clearly defined end state, should entail minimal risk to our troops, and should be designed to give the affected country the opportunity to restore its own basic services. And, at the same time, they should not jeopardize our ability to respond to direct threats to our national security in other regions of the world. . . .

. . . in any intervention that we face, anytime we want to use our forces abroad, we're going to face some opposition at home. This is not only the nature of American democracy, but it is the heart and soul of our very system. Therefore, to gauge whether we should or shouldn't intervene, we must examine whether our involvement advances our interests—be they vital, important, or humanitarian. Does it advance the interests of the American people? In the final analysis, if we decide in the affirmative, then we must remain very clear in the purpose that we have going in, and very resolute in our action. . . .

The challenge, of course, in deploying our military forces to perform military tasks on the front end of a contingency operation is rather straightforward. We train and prepare for exactly those types of operations. But the tougher task, the real tough piece on most of the missions that we are asked to perform, and have been for the last several years, comes in addressing the civil and political tasks that lie at the heart of many conflicts and normally come about at the latter stage of the operation. . . .

In a troubled world, what we see today are many worthy causes that cry out for military intervention. And "the better angels of our nature," to use President Lincoln's phrase, will often prompt us to want to get involved very quickly to help. Sometimes providing help is exactly what we should do. And it is also prudent to consider that unintended consequences may accompany well-intentioned impulses to use our strength for the good of the international community.

The military is a very powerful hammer. But not every problem that we face as a Nation is a nail.

We may find that sorting out the good guys from the bad is not as easy as it seems.

We also may find that getting in is much easier than getting out.

These, then, are the issues we need to confront when we make the decision—based on our understanding of the particular mission—to commit our military forces. And that is as it should be because, when we use our military forces, we in essence lay our prestige, our word, our leadership, and the lives of our young Americans on the line.

29.3   Conserving The Environment: Global Climate Change

George Bush

During the 1980s there was growing international concern about possible global climate changes. Many people feared that deforestation and unwise land use were releasing so much carbon dioxide (CO_2) in the atmosphere that changes in weather patterns would result. In order to address these issues a United Nations Conference on Environment and Development (UNCED), known as the Earth Summit, was held June 3-14, 1992, in Rio de Janeiro, Brazil. More than 150 nations reviewed a wide range of environmental and development issues, resulting in an international action plan—called Agenda 21—intended to carry well into the twenty-first century. The United States opposed specific targets and timetables for reducing CO_2 emissions, as well as a biodiversity agreement that would undermine U.S. biotechnology businesses. Many environmentalists criticized the U.S. positions. Before his departure for the Earth Summit, President George Bush offered his assessment of American environmental policy. The following is an excerpt from his remarks.

Consider:

1. *The implications of President Bush's policy of balancing environmental concerns with concern for economic growth;*
2. *The extent to which the U.S. position on issues at the Earth Summit Conference helped promote a global solution to environmental problems;*
3. *Why environmentalists were so critical of the U.S. position announced by the President.*

Well, today I travel to Rio de Janeiro to join over 100 heads of state at the United Nations Conference on Environment and Development. Informally, the Rio meeting has been called the Earth Summit. But I want to focus for just a minute on the official name. It think it's critical that we take both those words, environment and development, equally seriously, and we do.

On the environment, America's record is second to none. No other nation has done more, more rapidly to clean up the water, the air, or preserve public land. No other nation has done more to advance the state of technology that promises cleaner growth. . . . No other nation has put in place stricter standards to curb pollution in the future. . . .

But let me say up front: I am determined to protect the environment, and I'm also determined to protect the American taxpayer. The day of the open checkbook is over. I will go to Rio with a series of sound proposals designed to foster both environmental protection and economic growth. I'll sign a cli-

SOURCE: *Weekly Compilation of Presidential Documents (Washington: Office of Federal Registers, National Archives and Records Administration, 1992), Vol 28 (June 24, 1992): 1035–1036.*

mate convention that calls for sound action, like increased energy efficiency and cleaner air. I'll offer technology cooperation because I believe American technology can help clean up the world's environment. I'll propose to share U.S. science, the most advanced in the world, to increase understanding of these complex issues. . . .

I go to Rio with a firm conviction: Environmental protection and a growing economy are inseparable. No matter what some people may want to pretend, they are inseparable. It is counterproductive to promote one at the expense of the other.

For the past half-century, the United States has been a great machine of global economic growth, and it's going to stay that way. Every American knows what that means for us. What many may not know is that the world also has a stake in a strong American economy. Right now, one-half of the developing countries' exports of manufactured goods to all industrialized nations are sold, yes, in the United States of America. A weak economy in this country would harm workers in other nations and cut their exports to a trickle. Nations struggling to meet the most elemental needs of their people can spare little to protect the environment.

Many governments and many individuals from the U.S. and other nations have pressed us to sign a treaty on what's called biodiversity. I don't expect that pressure to let up when I reach Rio. The treaty's intent is noble, to ensure protection of natural habitat for the world's plant and animal life. The U.S. has better protection for species and habitat than any nation on Earth. No one disagrees with the goals of the treaty. But the truth is, it contains provisions that have nothing to do with biodiversity.

Take just one example: The private sector is proving it can help generate solutions to our environmental problems. The treaty includes provisions that discourage technological innovations, treat them as common property though they are developed at great cost by private companies and American workers. We know what will happen. Remove incentives, and we'll see fewer of the technological advances that help us protect our planet. . . .

I cannot speak for actions that other nations may take. But this I promise: I will stand up for American interests and the interests of a cleaner environment. . . .

I believe deeply in protecting our common environment, and I will proudly present in Rio the U.S. record that is second to none anywhere in the world.

29.4 Resistance to American Technology: The Conflict Over Genetically Improved Foods

Robert Paarlberg

Throughout the twentieth century, American technology and industry were the wonder of the world. But while many admired and imitated American achievement, others resented it. This resentment on the part of other nations some-times produced outright hostility to the products of United States technology. Such was the case with genetically improved foods, which American producers began to aggressively market in the mid-1990s. Foreign consumers were reluctant to buy American-grown products that were the result of genetic modification. It was sometimes difficult to ascertain whether such resistance stemmed more from concern about the side effects of the technology or simply from cultural pride. This excerpt assesses the nature and extent of the resistance to genetically modified crops, as well as its impact on producers and consumers.

Consider:

1. *The possible impact of conflicts over genetically modified commodities on the World Trade Organization and regional trading partnerships such as NAFTA (see Doc. 29.1);*
2. *Whether national governments should take a more active role in the shaping of new technologies.*

Powerful new technologies often provoke strong resistance. . . . today's backlash against the commercial use of recombinant DNA technology for food production should not be surprising. Consumer and environmental groups, mostly in Europe, depict genetically modified (GM) food crops, produced mostly in the United States, as dangerous to human health and the environment. These critics want tight labeling for GM foods, limits on international trade in GM crops, and perhaps even a moratorium on any further commercial development of this new technology—all to prevent risks that are still mostly hypothetical.

The international debate over GM crops pits a cautious, consumer-driven Europe against aggressive American industry. Yet the real stakeholders in this debate are poor farmers and poorly fed consumers in Asia, Africa, and Latin America. These are the regions most in need of new transgenic crop technologies, given their difficult farming conditions and rapidly growing populations. . . .

The genetic modification of plants and animals through domestication and controlled breeding has gone on with little debate for roughly 10,000 years. But since 1973, genetic modification has also been possible through the transfer of isolated genes into the DNA of another organism. This type of genetic engineering—also known as genetic transformation, transgenesis, or simply GM—is a more powerful and more precise method of modifying life.

. . . the large corporate investments needed to develop commercial applications for transgenic crops did not begin until 1980, when the U.S. Supreme Court extended patent protection to new types of plants and plant parts, including seeds, tissue cultures, and genes. . . .

SOURCE: *Robert Paarlberg, "The Global Food Fight,"* Foreign Affairs 79, no. 3 (May/June 2000): 24-32, 37-38.

Enthusiasm for GM crops among American farmers is not hard to understand, given the decreased need for chemical sprays and tillage. Most U.S. farmers growing "Roundup Ready" soybeans need to spray only once, cutting chemical costs by 10-40 percent. Transgenic cotton often requires no spraying at all (compared to the 4-6 sprayings previously needed), reducing production costs by $60-$120 per acre. . . .

. . . Yet within the European Union the new technology has not taken hold. As of 1999, only a few farms in Spain, France, and Portugal were planting transgenic crops.

European farmers have stayed away from transgenic crops largely because European consumers have become frightened of eating them. Consumers in Europe are now leading a backlash against GM crops—even though no safety risks linked to any GM crops on the market have ever been documented in Europe or anywhere else. . . .

. . . expert reassurances are discounted by European consumers, distrustful since the 1996 "mad cow disease" scare. That crisis undermined consumer trust in expert opinion after U.K. public health officials gave consumers what proved to be a false assurance that there was no danger in eating beef from diseased animals. Although mad cow disease had nothing to do with the genetic modification of food, it generated new consumer anxieties about food safety at precisely the moment in 1996 when U.S.-grown GM soybeans were first being cleared for import into the EU. . . .

. . . To avoid consumer boycotts and lawsuits brought by activist groups, a growing number of food companies, retail stores, and fast-food chains (including both Burger King and McDonald's) in Europe pledged in 1999 not to use GM ingredients—at least where it could be avoided.

This backlash began to spread in 1999 to food-importing nations outside of Europe. . . .

. . . U.S. officials have opposed the mandatory labeling of GM products. But the U.S. farm sector is so heavily export-oriented (U.S. farmers export more than 25 percent of the corn, soybean, and cotton they produce, and more than 50 percent of wheat and rice) that foreign pressure is prompting an informal movement in the other direction. . . .

Credible labeling of all food produced from GM commodities would be an expensive proposition for U.S. farms, agribusinesses, and consumers. It would require complete physical segregation of GM and non-GM food along every step of production, from the farm gate to the grocery shelf. U.S. officials estimate that this could increase costs by 10–30 percent.

In the meantime, the European and Asian backlash against U.S.-grown GM crops could generate sharp conflicts in several international settings, including the World Trade Organization (WTO) and the Convention on Biological Diversity (CBD). . . .

. . . conflicts between the United States and Europe over GM crops may continue to escalate in the months and years ahead. Yet the most important stakeholders in the fight over GM foods have not been heard. It is among poor farmers and poor consumers in developing countries that the potential gains from this new technology are most significant. . . .

. . . modern transgenic technology carries special promise for the tropics: it can engineer plants and animals with highly specific pest and disease resistances. . . .

Genetic technology could also improve nutrition. If the 250 million malnourished Asians who currently subsist on rice were able to grow and consume rice genetically modified to contain Vitamin A and iron, cases of Vitamin A deficiency (which currently kills 2 million a year and blinds hundreds of thousands of children) would fall, as would the incidence of anemia (one of the main killers of women of childbearing age). . . .

Critics of the GM revolution fear that the environment might be hurt if engineered crops are released into rural tropical settings where wild relatives of food plants can often be found. If an engineered herbicide-resistance trait breeds into a weedy wild relative, the result might be a hard-to-manage "superweed." Or widespread planting of Bt crops [crops engineered to contain Bt, a pest-killing toxin] might trigger an evolving population of "superbugs" resistant to the toxin. Legitimate biosafety concerns such as these have so far been addressed in rich countries on a case-by-case basis, through field testing under closely monitored conditions; the means for such testing and monitoring are still largely missing in the developing world. . . .

Tragically, the leading players in this global GM food fight—U.S.-based industry advocates on the one hand and European consumers and environmentalists on the other—simply do not reliably represent the interests of farmers or consumers in poor countries. With government leadership and investment missing, the public interest has been poorly served. When national governments, foreign donors, and international institutions pull back from making investments of their own in shaping a potentially valuable new technology, the subsequent public debate naturally deteriorates into a grudge match between aggressive corporations and their most confrontational NGO adversaries. This confrontation then frightens the public sector, deepening the paralysis.

29.5   The United States and the "New Terrorism"

Mark Juergensmeyer

One of the novel aspects of international relations in the late 1990s was the rise of a "new terrorism"—a pervasive threat to national security characterized by seemingly random attacks on non-military entities and private citizens as expressions of religious fundamentalism. Two dramatic instances of such terrorism were the bombing of New York's World Trade Center in 1993 and the attack on the U.S.S. *Cole* in 2000. Americans could not help but be increasingly concerned about such unpredictable attacks. Fighting the Cold War had been costly and difficult, but at least that challenge was definable—and, therefore, potentially winnable. The threat the "new terrorism" posed was different in that no one knew exactly who the enemy was. Without a clear-cut enemy, no one knew how the United States should respond. This excerpt discusses the sources and effects of the "new terrorism" and raises important questions about the best ways for the United States to respond.

Consider:

1. *How the sources and motives of the "new terrorism" differed from the threat to American security posed by the Soviet Union during the Cold War (Document 25.1);*
2. *Whether the President's responsibility to respond to terrorist attacks is different in the case of terrorism within the United States as compared to terrorism elsewhere in the world.*

The adjectives that we use to describe acts of the new terrorism—symbolic, dramatic, theatrical—suggest the idea of viewing them not as tactics but as performance violence. In using the term "performance" I knowingly invoke the idea of theater. This analogy is apt not only because terrorist acts are dramatic but also because they are conducted with an awareness of particular settings, appropriate timings, and the various audiences for the events. By discussing terrorism as performance I am not suggesting that such acts are undertaken lightly or capriciously. Rather, like religious ritual or street theater, they are dramas designed to have an impact on the several audiences they affect. Witnesses to the violence, even at a distance, through the news media, therefore are part of the incident itself. . . .

How can we respond to such acts of terrorism—acts that are not only tactics in political strategies but performances of violence that symbolize a cosmic war? One temptation is to respond in kind, as the United States government did when Muslim activists—allegedly under the guidance of Osama bin Laden—bombed the American embassies in Kenya and Tanzania in 1998. But the acts of retaliation seemed to stray far from their marks. The cruise missiles launched by the United States military fell on a pharmaceutical plant in Sudan and a hillside in Afghanistan without achieving any obvious strategic objective. No significant damage was done to bin Laden's organization, nor did he or any other activist appear to be intimidated as a result of the missile attack.

A quid pro quo for terrorism usually fails, if for no other reason than few governments have been willing to sink to the same savage levels and adopt the same means of gutter combat that groups involved in terrorist acts have been willing to undertake. Moreover, governments have usually been aware that terrorists observe their responses to acts of terrorism. Any response, even in the form of retaliatory strikes, enhances the perpetrators' credibility.

Another, quite different response to terrorist acts is to do nothing violent in response. After the World Trade Center bombing, for instance, the United

SOURCE: Mark Juergensmeyer, "Understanding the New Terrorism," Current History 99, no. 636 (April 2000): 160, 162–163.

States government made no retaliatory raids on the perpetrators' bases of operations. . . .

A complete hands-off approach is also problematic: it might or might not quell violence. Moreover, terrorist acts are real threats to public safety, and no government can afford the perception by its citizens that it is too weak to respond when public order is under assault. . . .

Such assaults on public authority are unnerving because they come at a sensitive time. The last decade of the twentieth century and the first years of the twenty-first are a moment of transition on a global scale. With the fall of the Soviet Union and the end of the Cold War in 1990 came the removal of a secure bipolar view of the world. In its wake appeared a rush of new expressions of local control. At the same time, local cultural identities are being threatened by new forces of globalization that have economic, technological, and cultural dimensions. People throughout the world are increasingly being linked to a vast global economic structure and subjected to images that invariably express the most superficial and secular aspects of popular culture in the West. New alliances are emerging in Asia, the Middle East, and Europe. As the twenty-first century dawns, it is not yet clear whether the new world order will consist of transnational entities, regional alliances, or nation-states—and if the latter, whether they will be modeled on the secular image of nations built on social contracts or on the religious ideal of states based on culture.

CHAPTER QUESTIONS

1. *To what degree are the international problems confronting the United States today different from those that confronted the nation during the Cold War?*
2. *What challenges does the United States face when it intervenes with military force in conflicts between other countries?*
3. *What are the likely impacts of the tendency for nations to group together into regional economic compacts.*

Chapter 30

Social and Political Dilemmas at the Turn of the Century

In contrast to the dramatic changes in world politics and America's responses to them, the nation's major domestic dilemmas at the end of the twentieth century centered on issues of longstanding concern. Some reflected recurrent debates in American society—such as the role of the Supreme Court and immigration. Others had emerged in the 1970s and 1980s and dealt with guaranteeing adequate health care and economic security for an aging population.

The Supreme Court by the end of the century had gradually retreated from its activist decisions of the 1960s and 1970s. Many scholars were surprised when the Court agreed to hear two appeals in the disputed presidential election of 2000. The Court had traditionally left the interpretation of state election laws to the states, and had steered itself away from involvement in political issues. In its controversial decision in *Bush* v. *Gore*, the Court abruptly ended Gore's contest of the Florida election, effectively giving the presidency to George W. Bush.

Sharp political differences also arose between right and left in the 1990s over how to deal with rising numbers of immigrants who had entered the country illegally. In some ways, the dispute over this issue mirrored the debate of nearly a century earlier, when many had considered "new immigration" to be a threat to the nation's social fabric. The absence of a defined policy was the price that the nation paid for the deadlock (or "gridlock," as some called it) that characterized American politics after the Reagan presidency.

Health care and financial security for an aging citizenry were other unresolved issues. Even though the Great Society of the 1960s had extended the New Deal's safety net for older Americans, access to health care had remained a critical problem in the United States. As in European countries, the financial resources of the U.S. Social Security system were being stretched by an aging population.

Although the two major parties struggled with (and campaigned on) these critical issues, they failed to resolve them. Intense partisan bickering developed between the Republican-controlled Congress and the White House, contributing to a rising tide of public disgust with politics and politicians. Voters began to believe that powerful special interest groups controlled politicians in both parties through their massive campaign contributions. To bypass politicians, voter initiatives at the state level became popular, but special interest campaigns came to dominate these initiatives, as well. Significant political reform was clearly needed as the new century dawned. Whether—and when—such reform would occur was uncertain.

Chronology

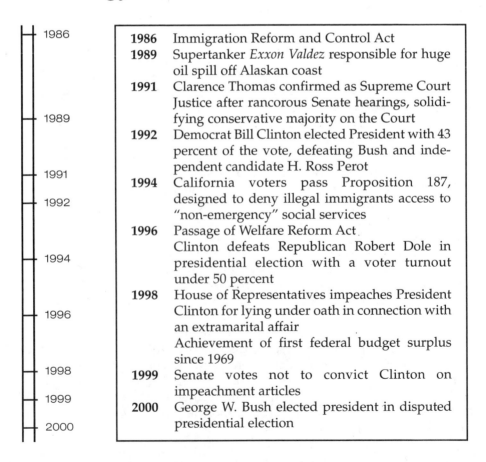

1986	Immigration Reform and Control Act
1989	Supertanker *Exxon Valdez* responsible for huge oil spill off Alaskan coast
1991	Clarence Thomas confirmed as Supreme Court Justice after rancorous Senate hearings, solidifying conservative majority on the Court
1992	Democrat Bill Clinton elected President with 43 percent of the vote, defeating Bush and independent candidate H. Ross Perot
1994	California voters pass Proposition 187, designed to deny illegal immigrants access to "non-emergency" social services
1996	Passage of Welfare Reform Act. Clinton defeats Republican Robert Dole in presidential election with a voter turnout under 50 percent
1998	House of Representatives impeaches President Clinton for lying under oath in connection with an extramarital affair Achievement of first federal budget surplus since 1969
1999	Senate votes not to convict Clinton on impeachment articles
2000	George W. Bush elected president in disputed presidential election

Documents

30.1   The Role of the Supreme Court in Resolving Political Controversy

Bush v. *Gore* (2000)

The outcome of the 2000 presidential election turned on which candidate won Florida's 25 electoral votes. On election night, with Florida's vote undetermined, Al Gore had captured 267 electors, and George W. Bush had won 246. The vote in Florida was so close that a recount was required by law to determine who would win the state's electors, and thereby the presidency. Disputes over several thousand ballots not counted by machine led Gore to ask state courts to order hand recounts in certain counties. The U.S. Supreme Court twice heard appeals from Bush, who was trying to stop the recounts. The second case, *Bush* v. *Gore* (2000), centered on whether the Florida Supreme Court could order hand recounts of thousands of punch card ballots without setting a specific standard for determining the "intent of the voter." In a complicated decision, seven justices ruled that the lack of uniform standards violated the Fourteenth Amendment guarantee of equal protection of the laws. However, four of the justices issued blistering dissents, arguing that the Court broke with judicial precedent in agreeing to hear the case. The excerpt from the Court's ruling defends the decision to take the case. The dissenting opinions of Justices Breyer and Stevens that follow show a fractured Court struggling to define its role in political controversies.

Consider:

1. *The way in which the Court justified its decisions in this case. How does its reasoning compare with the Court's handling of* Brown v. Board of Education of Topeka *(Doc 26.3) in 1954;*
2. *How the decision by the Court to overturn the Florida Supreme Court's ruling would have been seen as "a surrender to political pressure";*
3. *What is the purpose of dissenting Supreme Court opinions?*

Per Curiam

The right to vote is protected in more than the initial allocation of the franchise. Equal protection applies as well to the manner of its exercise. Having once granted the right to vote on equal terms, the State may not, by later arbitrary and disparate treatment, value one person's vote over that of another. . . .

. . . Respondents say that the very purpose of vindicating the right to vote justifies the recount procedures now at issue. The question before us, however, is whether the recount procedures the Florida Supreme Court has adopted are consistent with its obligation to avoid arbitrary and disparate treatment of the members of its electorate. . . .

The question before the Court is not whether local entities, in the exercise of their expertise, may develop different systems for implementing elections. Instead, we are presented with a situation where a state court with the power to assure uniformity has ordered a statewide recount with minimal procedural safeguards. When a court orders a statewide remedy, there must be at least some assurance that the rudimentary requirements of equal treatment and fundamental fairness are satisfied.

*   *   *

None are more conscious of the vital limits on judicial authority than are the members of this Court, and none stand more in admiration of the Constitution's design to leave the selection of the President to the people, through their legislatures, and to the political sphere. When contending parties invoke the process of the courts, however, it becomes our unsought responsibility to resolve the federal and constitutional issues the judicial system has been forced to confront.

Breyer, J., dissenting

The Court was wrong to take this case. It was wrong to grant a stay. It should now vacate that stay and permit the Florida Supreme Court to decide whether the recount should resume. . . .

The decision by both the Constitution's Framers and the 1886 Congress to minimize the Court's role in resolving close federal presidential elections is as wise as it is clear. However awkward or difficult it may be for Congress to resolve difficult electoral disputes, Congress, being a political body, expresses the people's will far more accurately than does an unelected Court. And the people's will is what elections are about. Moreover, Congress was fully aware of the danger that would arise should it ask judges, unarmed with appropriate legal standards, to resolve a hotly contested presidential election contest. . . .

At the same time, as I have said, the Court is not acting to vindicate a fundamental constitutional principle, such as the need to protect a basic human liberty. No other strong reason to act is present. Congressional statutes tend to obviate the need. And, above all, in this highly politicized matter, the appearance of a split decision runs the risk of undermining the public's confidence in the Court itself. That confidence is a public treasure. It has been

SOURCE: *Bush* v. *Gore* 531 U.S. ___(2000)

built slowly over many years, some of which were marked by a Civil War and the tragedy of segregation. It is a vitally necessary ingredient of any suc-' cessful effort to protect basic liberty and, indeed, the rule of law itself. We run no risk of returning to the days when a President (responding to this Court's efforts to protect the Cherokee Indians) might have said, "John Marshall has made his decision; now let him enforce it!" But we do risk a self-inflicted wound—a wound that may harm not just the Court, but the Nation.

I fear that in order to bring this agonizingly long election process to a definitive conclusion, we have not adequately attended to that necessary "check upon our own exercise of power," "our own sense of self-restraint." *United States* v. *Butler*, 297 U.S. 1, 79 (1936) (Stone, J., dissenting). Justice Brandeis once said of the Court, "The most important thing we do is not doing." What it does today, the Court should have left undone. I would repair the damage done as best we now can, by permitting the Florida recount to continue under uniform standards.

Stevens, J., dissenting

What must underlie petitioner's entire federal assault on the Florida election procedures is an unstated lack of confidence in the impartiality and capacity of the state judges who would make the critical decisions if the vote count were to proceed. Otherwise, their position is wholly without merit. The endorsement of that position by the majority of this Court can only lend credence to the most cynical appraisal of the work of judges throughout the land. It is confidence in the men and women who administer the judicial system that is the true backbone of the rule of law. Time will one day heal the wound to that confidence that will be inflicted by today's decision. One thing, however, is certain. Although we may never know with complete certainty the identity of the winner of the year's presidential election, the identity of the loser is perfectly clear. It is the Nation's confidence in the judge as an impartial guardian of the law.

30.2   Changing Views on Immigration
James Goldsborough

In the 1980s and 1990s, immigration again became a major issue in the United States. The last decade of the twentieth century saw the highest level of legal immigration in United States history, and—like the so-called "new immigration" a century earlier—a dramatic shift in its composition. Ever greater numbers of newcomers arrived from Asia, Central America, and Caribbean nations. As in the earlier period of new immigration, there was also a resurgence of strong nativist impulses, perhaps best symbolized by the action of California voters in approving the anti-immigrant Proposition 187 in 1994. Just as further curbs on immigration appeared imminent, dramatic and sustained economic growth in the late 1990s created a nationwide need for workers, improving the prospects for greater liberalization of immigration laws. The excerpt that follows argues that the newly optimistic outlook produced by economic "good times" was essentially irrational.

Consider:

1. *How domestic economic conditions might affect the attitudes of different groups of Americans—for example, workers, business leaders, politicians—concerning legal immigration;*
2. *How problems created by large numbers of illegal aliens residing in the U.S. affect public attitudes toward legal immigration;*
3. *What "unreasonable solutions" might be proposed to resolve the problems identified by the author.*

The immigration debate in America has recently switched direction by about 175 degrees. Only five years ago, the U.S. Commission on Immigration Reform (the so-called Jordan Commission) proposed to cut legal immigration by at least a third and eliminate illegal immigration through new workplace enforcement measures. The commission's recommendations were based both on critiques of the 1986 and 1990 immigration reform laws and on a growing sentiment that as America entered the twenty-first century immigration should be reduced from its record levels. This sentiment was reflected in annual Gallup polls, votes on measures such as California's Proposition 187, and studies showing new immigrants doing less well today than in previous times. It was also shown in increasing hostility toward new arrivals in immigrant-heavy states such as California, Arizona, and Florida—hostility that showed signs of spreading to other parts of the country.

Yet only five years later, immigration into the United States is at its highest absolute levels in history: more than 1.1 million annually, some 400,000 higher than the previous high-water mark of around 700,000 annually during the 1900-1920 "Great Migration" (though as a percentage of population, today's rate of immigration, 0.4 percent, is actually lower than that at the turn of the century, 0.7 percent). Despite these high numbers, Congress' interest has faded. Immigration policy today is driven by businesses that need more workers—skilled and unskilled, legal and illegal. Somehow, the process has gotten out of control. . . .

The Jordan Commission was established in 1990 to reexamine U.S. immigration policy. Should immigration remain at historically high levels? The rationale for adding 700,000 immigrants annually during the first two decades of the past century was clear, but what was the rationale for adding 1.1 million immigrants annually in the 1990s and beyond?

Led by the late Representative Barbara Jordan (D-Tex.), who had earned a reputation for lucidity and probity in the House, the commission undertook the most exhaustive examination of immigration ever carried out in this or probably any country. . . . Its mandate was to examine both legal and illegal immigration, and it found that the two were inseparable. . . .

SOURCE: *James Goldsborough, "Out of Control Immigration,"* Foreign Affairs 79, no. 5 (Sept/Oct 2000): 89, 96–101.

Congress began work on comprehensive immigration reform in 1995. The Jordan Commission's proposals, moderate and backed by the president, seemed likely to pass. In essence, they specified that legal immigration (including refugees) would be cut by a third, to 550,000 annually, to bring immigration back into line with historical levels; skills-based immigration targeting the nation's economic needs would be reemphasized by phasing out preferences for members of extended families (i.e., brothers and sisters); and illegal immigration would be eliminated through a computer-registry system that would verify legal job status. On the third point, virtually all immigration experts agree that if illegal immigrants are not allowed to work, they will not come. There is no evidence that people come to America to go on welfare, as proponents of California Proposition 187 maintained. Illegal immigrants are not eligible for the most common forms of welfare—food stamps, Temporary Aid to Needy Families (TAN), and Supplemental Security Income (though their children may be). . . .

The fruit of six years of work, the Jordan Commission's recommendations came to naught. The bill to reduce legal immigration was scuttled; the computer-registry proposal enabling employers to verify the status of workers was killed, gutting the bill on illegal immigration. . . .

So what? With America at full employment, why not bring in immigrants one way or another to keep prices and wages down? How much more would strawberries cost if they were picked by unionized American farm workers? (according to some economists, such as Wallace Huffman and Alan McCunn of Iowa State University, not much more.) America has always been an immigrant nation, so why quibble over the difference between a half-million and a million more people per year? Doesn't the country need more workers to pay taxes to support an aging population? And why should it matter whether they are legal or illegal, since illegal immigrants are eventually legalized anyway?

Here is the nub of the issue: the effect of high levels of immigration on America today. In 2000, exactly one century after America opened its doors to all European comers to settle the West and realize its "manifest destiny," immigration is at record levels—despite the fact that the West no longer needs immigrants and has a serious water shortage. During debate over the Jordan proposals in 1996, California's Feinstein warned of a population and cultural "Armageddon" for her state, where one-third of all immigrants settle. . . .

One of the paradoxes of America's failed immigration policy is the phenomenon known as "citizen children," the American children of illegal immigrants. These children, like any poor American child, are eligible for TANF. The United States, nearly alone among developed nations, grants citizenship to all children born within its borders, regardless of their parents' status. According to the Los Angeles County Welfare Department, of the 620,000 children in Los Angeles receiving food stamps and TANF, between 120,000 and 150,000 were born to parents in America illegally. An estimated half-million such children live in the United States today. For the INS, citizen children create a difficult situation: illegal immigrants can be deported (even if they rarely are), but what of their American Children?

. . . [I]t is time to recognize the hazards of unreasonable and uncontrolled immigration. Instead of being a source of strength, upwardly spiraling immigration has begun to create imbalances in education, income distribution, employment levels, and welfare demands. It is creating tensions between immigrants and natives, between immigrant and nonimmigrant states, and among state, local, and federal governments. This shows up in English-only laws and initiatives, suits brought by several states against the federal government to recover social charges related to immigrants, and disputes among federal, state, and local law-enforcement agencies about how to apprehend, process, detain, and repatriate illegal immigrants. . . .

. . . If Congress and the next president do not come up with reasonable solutions along the lines proposed by the Jordan Commission, the field will be clear for unreasonable solutions.

30.3   Who Decides? The Health Care Controversy

Steve Greenberg

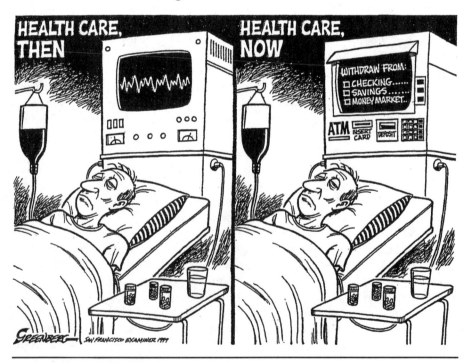

SOURCE: *Steve Greenberg,* San Francisco Examiner, *1999*

By the early 1990s, access to health care had become a major social and political issue. As an advanced industrial nation, the United States offered some of the best medical care in the world. However, in contrast to more socialized developed economies, the benefits of this care were unavailable to millions of Americans who could not afford it or whose employers did not offer health insurance benefits. Moreover, many of those who did enjoy health benefits found themselves enrolled in Health Maintenance Organizations (HMOs) where they could not choose their own physician. As HMOs proliferated in the 1990s, medical decisions seemed to many to be delegated to administrators and insurance industry workers, rather than to physicians. This cartoon reflects a critical perspective on the changes in health care in the 1990s.

Consider:

1. *What the cartoon suggests about changes in the way health care was provided to Americans "then," as opposed to how it is provided "now";*
2. *How the desire for government-backed health care related to the "freedoms" that are guaranteed by the U.S. Constitution (see Doc. 23.5).*

30.4   The Baby-Boomers Grow Old: Implications of an Aging Society

Peter G. Peterson

Since the end of World War II, the baby boom generation has been a major factor in American society, In the 1950s, a teen-age consumer culture appeared. In the late 1960s, campus rebellions sparked nationwide debate about the Vietnam War. Beginning in the early nineties, as the first wave of the baby boom generation began to approach senior citizen status, Americans began to worry about the viability of Social Security. Although estimates varied, most observers agreed that, without major changes, Social Security could become bankrupt by the second or third decade of the twenty-first century. The swelling numbers of older voters, who tended to have higher political participation rates than any other age group, made this issue critical in national elections. As much as any other phenomenon, this rising "senior power" threatened to transform the American political terrain at the turn of the century.

Consider:

1. *How the shift in "voter demographics" shown in the first graphic might affect American elections and public policy;*
2. *How younger Americans would be affected if the "official retirement" age were to change as depicted in the second graphic;*
3. *What types of solutions political leaders might offer to avert the situation depicted in the third graphic.*

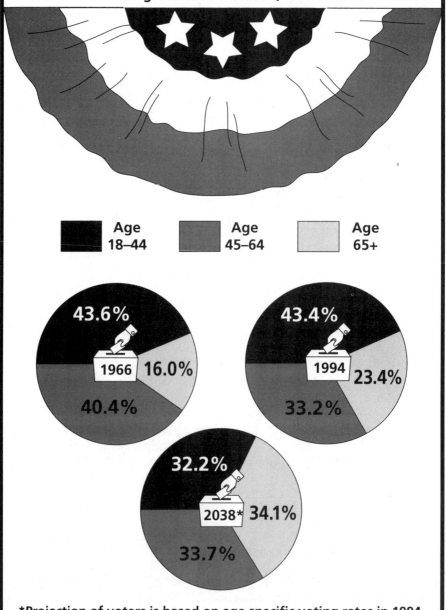

The balance of electoral power will continue to shift toward the elderly.

Voters in U.S. congressional elections, as a % of all voters.

Age 18–44   Age 45–64   Age 65+

43.6%
1966   16.0%
40.4%

43.4%
1994   23.4%
33.2%

32.2%
2038*   34.1%
33.7%

*Projection of voters is based on age specific voting rates in 1994.

Sources: Bureau of the Census, author's calculations

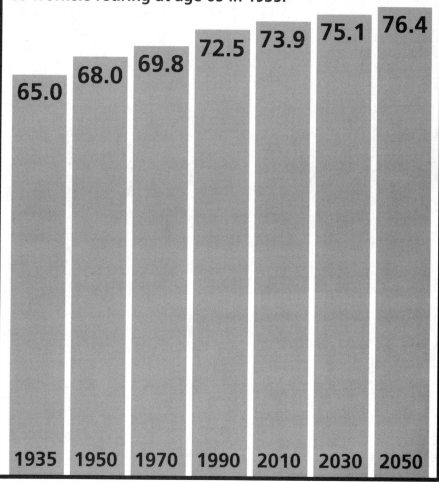

To keep pace with growing life spans, the official retirement age in the U.S. would have to rise well beyond age 70.

Retirement age at which U.S. workers would spend the same number of years in retirement as workers retiring at age 65 in 1935.

1935	1950	1970	1990	2010	2030	2050
65.0	68.0	69.8	72.5	73.9	75.1	76.4

Sources: SSA; author's calculations

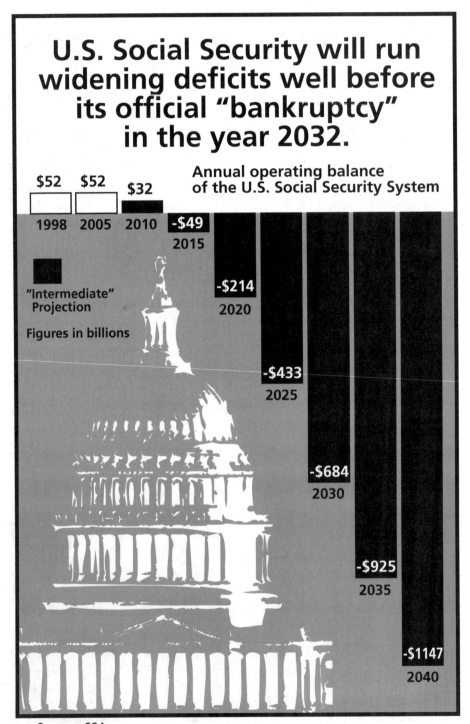

U.S. Social Security will run widening deficits well before its official "bankruptcy" in the year 2032.

Annual operating balance of the U.S. Social Security System

$52 $52 $32

1998   2005   2010

-$49
2015

"Intermediate" Projection

Figures in billions

-$214
2020

-$433
2025

-$684
2030

-$925
2035

-$1147
2040

Source: SSA

30.5   The Republic Subverted? The Impact of Voter Initiatives

David S. Broder

In the Progressive Era of the early twentieth century, one of the "citizen-based" reforms that swept state after state was the voter initiative, which allowed voters to propose and vote on legislation in state and local elections. By the end of the twentieth century—fueled by voter disaffection with the major parties and "politics as usual" in Washington—voter initiative had become a prominent tool of public policy in several states, especially in California and other western states. Because voters' attention to the nuances of policy-making was limited and the access of interest groups to mass advertising was almost unlimited, some observers of American politics came to question the "democracy" of voter initiatives. This excerpt points out some of the dangers inherent in an extensive reliance on such "democratic" policy-making in a republic.

Consider:

1. *How the voter initiative concept related to the principles of republicanism espoused by James Madison in Federalist, No. 10 (Doc. 6.5);*
2. *What popular attitudes about American government and politics were reflected in the trend toward the use of voter initiatives;*
3. *What effects the rise of voter initiatives would be likely to have on the provision of social services by state and federal governments.*

At the start of a new century—and millennium—a new form of government is spreading in the United States. It is alien to the spirit of the Constitution and its careful system of checks and balances. Though derived from a reform favored by Populists and Progressives as a cure for special-interest influence, this method of lawmaking has become the favored tool of millionaires and interest groups that use their wealth to achieve their own policy goals—a lucrative business for a new set of political entrepreneurs.

Exploiting the public's disdain for politics and distrust of politicians, it is now the most uncontrolled and unexamined arena of power politics. It has given the United States something that seems unthinkable—not a government of laws but laws without government. The initiative process, an import now just over one hundred years old, threatens to challenge or even subvert the American system of government in the next few decades. . . .

. . . even as the system of government invented by the founders—a system based on the separation of powers and a complex matrix of procedures designed to require the creation of consensus before the enactment of laws—has proved its worth in crisis after crisis, public impatience with "the

SOURCE: *David S. Broder,* Democracy Derailed: Initiative Campaigns and the Power of Money *(New York: Harcourt, 2000), 1–3, 7–8, 45–46, 163, 199, 208–209, 217.*

system" has grown. Some argue that the science of public-opinion sampling and the speed of electronic communications make the political arrangements of the eighteenth-century constitution as out-of-date as the one-horse shay. With journalism focused on the foibles in the private lives of political leaders, disdain for those in government has mounted with each new scandal. Political campaigns have become demolition derbies, in which even the winners emerge with ruined reputations. The trust between governors and governed, on which representative democracy depends, has been badly depleted. Polls consistently show an alarmingly small percentage of Americans believe the government in Washington will do what is right all—or even most—of the time. With the end of the Cold War, that distrust of Washington has brought about a significant shift in political power. . . . And states have become the innovators in vital areas of domestic policy, from welfare to education to growth policies. . . .

The initiative game has become a big—and very lucrative—business for those who collect petition signatures and run the ballot campaigns. And it also has produced great controversy, with some praising it as the purest form of democracy and others taking the view expressed in the headline on a 1998 *San Francisco Chronicle* series, marking the twentieth anniversary of Prop. 13: DEMOCRACY GONE AWRY. . . .

California's Proposition 13 deserves much of the credit or blame for the renewed popularity of initiatives. What propelled the voter rebellion was clear. In the housing boom of the late 1970s, property values soared and local communities, reaping a property tax bonanza, were slow to reduce property tax rates. Many longtime residents, especially retirees, feared they would be taxed out of their homes. Adding to the frustration was the fact that the legislature in Sacramento, watching the budget surplus rise to $6 billion, fell into a partisan dog-fight and failed to pass any state tax relief.

Howard Jarvis and Paul Gann offered a simple, sweeping remedy of immense appeal: No community could tax property at more than 1 percent of its assessed value. It rolled back all assessments to the 1975 level—wiping out three years of housing market inflation—and further decreed that whatever future inflation might be, property assessments could not increase by more than 2 percent a year. Instead of the biennial reappraisals most cities did, Prop. 13 decreed that property would be reassessed only when sold. It barred any new taxes based on property values; said any new taxes levied locally would have to be approved by two thirds of the voters; and for any new or higher levies imposed at the state level, it would require a two-thirds majority in the legislature.

The rhetoric of the campaign was as much antipolitician as it was antitax. The legislature and the governor became the whipping boys. . . .

The effect of the vote was to reduce property-tax revenue in fiscal 1979 by two thirds, slashing the annual revenue of local governments by more than $6 billion. Surprisingly, surveys at the time indicated that the voters who approved Prop. 13 were not trying to shrink government. One poll showed a 38 percent plurality believed that services could continue at the same level, even if revenues were cut by two fifths, simply by eliminating waste and inefficiency. . . . Even those voters who told pollsters that they favored higher spending by government on schools, health, and other programs supported Prop. 13. They must have been shocked by the cutbacks that occurred. . . .

Money does not always prevail in initiative fights, but it is almost always a major—even dominant—factor. Like so much else in American politics, the costs of these ballot battles have escalated enormously in the past decade. To a large extent, it is only those individuals and interest groups with access to big dollars who can play in the arena the Populists and Progressives created in order to balance the scales against the big-bucks operators.

Just as in presidential campaigns, the first test for any contender is the ability to raise the needed money. In the autumn of 1997 more than two hundred petitions were circulating for initiatives the sponsors hoped to place on the ballot the following year. The vast majority of them did not make it. Some lacked the necessary support. But the hurdle that eliminated most of them was the ready cash needed to hire the people who wage initiative campaigns. . . .

. . . The question is whether the initiative process as it actually operates today serves the public interest or subverts it. . . .

In every state where polling numbers are available, the initiative process is enormously popular with the voters. In mid-1999, Rasmussen Research surveyed a five-hundred-person sample of Washington state voters and found the initiative favored by 84 percent, while only 8 percent wanted it eliminated. The Field Institute did a comprehensive survey in California in 1997, and those results reflect broader currents of opinion. By a margin of 74 percent to 7 percent, voters said ballot propositions were a good thing, not a bad thing. That was down slightly from a similar question in 1979—the year after Prop. 13 was approved—when the margin of approval was 83 percent to 4 percent. But it is still an overwhelming endorsement. A follow-up question found that 59 percent of those surveyed said the initiatives "reflect the concerns of organized special-interest groups" and only 19 percent said they reflect the concerns of the average voter. Only two out of five said they know what interest groups are supporting or opposing initiatives most or all of the time. More than three quarters of the voters favored spending limits on initiative campaigns, and nearly as many would require sponsors to submit initiatives to the secretary of state for review and comment on their clarity and conformity to present law, before the signature gathering begins. But they overwhelmingly opposed letting the legislature amend initiatives after they have been passed. A survey taken in the same year by another firm, Charlton Research, found that 51 percent of California voters cited initiatives as the main reason for voting in 1996, compared to 36 percent who said the presidential contest was the principal motivator. . . .

When it comes to evaluating the initiative process, I believe there are two different sets of criteria to apply. The first asks: Are there particular causes, ideologies, or interests that are advanced or impeded by this process? The second set of issues goes to the structure of our system of government. Is the increasing use of the initiative a boon or a curse for the American democracy? . . .

CHAPTER QUESTIONS

1. *Discuss the possible effects of demographic trends on American politics in the 1990s and early years of the twenty-first century.*
2. *To what degree are the most serious problems faced by Americans today susceptible to government solutions?*
3. *At century's end, what political reforms of the twentieth century seemed to have the most lasting impact on American life?*